LISTEN THIRD BRIEF EDITION

LISTEN

THIRD BRIEF EDITION

JOSEPH KERMAN

University of California, Berkeley

with

VIVIAN KERMAN

WORTH PUBLISHERS

Value-Pak bundled items with corresponding ISBN numbers:

1-57259-127-7
Kerman: L I S T E N, Third Brief Edition (Softcover)
with Set of Three Cassettes

1-57259-128-5
Kerman: L I S T E N, Third Brief Edition (Softcover)
with Set of Three Compact Discs

1-57259-129-3
Kerman: L I S T E N, Third Brief Edition (Softcover)
with Set of Six Cassettes

1-57259-130-7
Kerman: L I S T E N, Third Brief Edition (Softcover)
with Set of Six Compact Discs

1-57259-131-5
Kerman: L I S T E N, Third Brief Edition (Hardcover)
with Set of Three Cassettes

1-57259-132-3
Kerman: L I S T E N, Third Brief Edition (Hardcover)
with Set of Three Compact Discs

1-57259-133-1
Kerman: L I S T E N, Third Brief Edition (Hardcover)
with Set of Six Cassettes

1-57259-134-X
Kerman: L I S T E N, Third Brief Edition (Hardcover)
with Set of Six Compact Discs

L I S T E N   Third Brief Edition

Library of Congress Card Catalog No. 95-061215
ISBN: 1-57259-059-9 (Hardcover Edition)
ISBN: 1-57259-058-0 (Softcover Edition)
ISBN: 1-57259-642-2 (Revised Edition)
Printing: 3 4 - 99 98 97

Development editor: Richard Wallis
Design: Malcolm Grear Designers
Art director: George Touloumes
Project editor: Elizabeth Geller
Production supervisor: Lou Capaldo
Layout: Heriberto Lugo
Picture editor: Elaine Bernstein
Line art: Demetrios Zangos
Composition: Monotype Composition Company, Inc.
Music typesetting: A-R Editions, Inc.
Printing and binding: R. R. Donnelley & Sons Company

Cover: Josef Albers, *Violinschlüssel G-6*, 1935
Gouache, 36.5 × 20.5
Josef Albers Museum, Bottrop
Photo: The Josef Albers Foundation

Worth Publishers
33 Irving Place
New York, NY 10003

Preface

This new edition of LISTEN incorporates substantial revisions. First, LISTEN: THIRD BRIEF EDITION is a simpler and shorter book than the second brief edition. It has fewer pages, more streamlined discussions, and fewer long words (one can nearly always find strong, simple words that are just as good as complex ones). With clear, direct exposition as our goal, we overhauled three of the five units, beginning with Unit I, *Fundamentals*. This unit has been improved by reordering certain of its topics, and also by supplementing them by recorded examples drawn from the various recording sets accompanying LISTEN.

Other units have also been reorganized, and the sequence of material is now tighter and more logical. In Unit III, the discussion of Classical music begins by focusing on the symphony; all the Classical forms are taught by way of a single symphony. In Unit V, late twentieth-century music has a chapter for itself, and so does jazz and music influenced by jazz (Gershwin, Bernstein): this is our new last chapter, Chapter 24 "American Music: Jazz." In the never-ending search for the most effective teaching pieces, we have replaced about 15% of the musical selections.

There are other new features of various kinds; more about these in a moment. First, for those unacquainted with the LISTEN texts, we should explain that their emphasis has always been on music, rather than on theory, history, or listening techniques in the abstract. As far as possible, theoretical and historical materials are introduced not for their own sake, or for the sake of "memorization," but to help convey the aesthetic qualities of actual pieces to which students *listen*. We also attempt to place music in its cultural context—at least partly for practical reasons. People who find careful listening difficult or abstract can often listen more intensely and fruitfully when the music is analyzed in relation to history, painting, literature, and ideas.

To assist in this learning process, the main discussions of Baroque, Classical, Romantic, and twentieth-century music are preceded by "Prelude" chapters summarizing the culture of the times, especially as this involves music. The extensive color illustrations and captions in these chapters (and others) are a LISTEN specialty. The "Prelude" chapters also include concise accounts of the musical style of the era, so that they furnish background of two kinds—cultural and stylistic—for listening to the specific pieces of music discussed in the chapters that follow.

Coverage, that perpetual problem for teachers, is also a major problem for textbook writers. How much emphasis should be placed on music of the so-called common-practice period, and how much on "early music" and music of the twentieth century? We believe that this text will work for instructors who feel a special sense of commitment to any one of these broad areas. Our main emphasis is indeed on the standard repertory—once again, on practical grounds: only so much can be accomplished in a short time, and we are convinced that students learn more from the presentation of a limited amount of material in some depth than from overambitious surveys. A strong argument can be made that beginning courses in music should introduce students to the good music they are most likely to hear.

So we want to stress that Unit II, *Early Music: An Overview,* is **strictly optional** in the book's sequence. Since some courses will omit Unit II altogether, nothing in the book depends on having studied it. Those who start with Unit III, *The Eighteenth Century,* will not have to skip back for explanations of continuo texture, recitative, fugue, and so on. On the other hand, for those who wish to include selections of early music without teaching the entire unit, the fairly modest amount of prose in Unit II should prove manageable as a general orientation for the music chosen.

There are many pedagogical highlights in LISTEN: THIRD BRIEF EDITION:

❧ Rather than starting directly with the elements of music, the book opens with an "Overture"—an immediate listening experience to engage students at the very beginning of the course. The Overture to *The Bartered Bride* by Bedřich Smetana is traced through simply, with an emphasis on direct impressions rather than on terminology (though en route we unobtrusively slip in some basic technical terms, which are explained more fully in Chapters 2 through 5).

Instructors often like to work out a special presentation in the first week to break the ice and interest students in the subject matter (and keep them from wandering off in the direction of other courses). Chapter 1 of LISTEN offers a specific suggestion for such an ice-breaker.

❧ As fundamental concepts are introduced in Unit I—dynamics, syncopation, melody, mode, form, and more—students are guided through recorded examples illustrating them, drawn from the various recording sets accompanying LISTEN.

❧ Between the short chapters in Unit I, there are optional "interludes" covering "Musical Notation" and "Musical Instruments." You can assign these interludes whole or in part, or omit them without loss of continuity. We use musical notation in this book; we do not rely on it.

❧ Brief biographies of all the main composers are included close to where their music is discussed. The revised format of this edition sets the biographies and composer portraits off clearly from the main text, with easy-to-read lists of chief works provided for study purposes or reference.

❧ Tabular guides to listening, with timings geared to recordings issued with the text, are now a fixture in music instruction. Our Listening Charts have always been superior in format, and in this edition their design has been further refined. And there are more of them—40% more. In addition, timings are now given for recorded selections that do not require full-scale, annotated Listening Charts, i.e., pieces with text and short compositions. Thus nearly every piece on the six-CD and six-cassette sets have timings in the text making it easy for students to follow.

⁊ All of the 75 compositions discussed in the text appear on the accompanying six-CD and six-cassette recording sets. Much effort has been spent to find the very best possible recordings—performances that we think are likely to interest, excite, and captivate the listener. Many students will keep listening to these recordings long after the course is over.

Three-CD and three-cassette sets are also available, for instructors who do not have time to cover as much of the book or who prefer students to have access to a less expensive listening package. These smaller recording sets contain 33 selections, including all seven of the selections from Chapter 24, "American Music: Jazz"; 23 of the selections have Listening Charts.

To make maximum use of disk space (over 99%), certain selections in the CD sets have been placed out of order, that is, not in the sequence of their treatment in the book. Logos in the text margins tell the listener *which number* CD or cassette to select (this is the numeral inside the circle or box) and then *which track or band* to play (the numeral below it).

For selections with multiple CD tracks, CD-track reference boxes to the left of the Listening Chart show where each new track begins; the green track numbers refer to the six-CD set and the black numbers refer to the three-CD set.

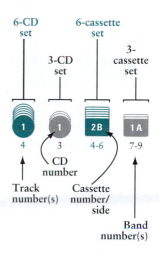

⁊ Previous editions of LISTEN covered only one complete multi-movement work, Beethoven's Fifth Symphony. Responding to many suggestions, we have added several more to the text and to the six-CD/cassette sets: a Corelli trio sonata (Op. 3 No. 1) and a Vivaldi concerto (Op. 4 No. 12), Haydn's Symphony No. 88, and Music for Strings, Percussion, and Celesta by Bartók. Not everyone will want to use all the movements—indeed, not all of the Bartók movements are included in the three-CD/cassette sets, and none of the Corelli—but the option is offered for instructors who want to teach entire pieces rather than the single movements that are usually made available.

⁊ Features carried over from earlier editions include timeline charts showing the life spans of composers and other important historical figures, and the indispensable Glossary. A new feature in LISTEN: THIRD BRIEF EDITION is the inclusion of short marginal quotes from musicians and others, drawn from letters, diaries, treatises, and the like. Each of them, we think, throws at least a thin shaft of extra light on the text, making it more personal and vivid.

The supplements for this text include:

⁊ The **Instructor's Resource Manual** (by Mark Harbold) offers Chapter Outlines, Important Terms, Teaching Objectives, and Lecture Suggestions for each chapter, and Class Discussion Ideas, Lecture-Demonstration Ideas, and Listening Ideas that go beyond the textbook chapters. A Multimedia Resources section gives many suggestions for video and software enhancements, additional Listening Charts, and much more.

⁊ The **Test Bank** (by Julie Brye) has 1274 multiple-choice and 529 essay questions. It serves as a data-base for a Computerized Test-Generation System, available in DOS, Windows, and Macintosh versions, that makes it easy to produce tailor-made exams on your IBM compatible or Macintosh computer.

This edition of LISTEN also has its own site on the worldwide web, which you can visit at http://www.worthpublishers.com/listen.

We are extremely grateful to the many battle-scarred music appreciation instructors who agreed to review draft chapters of the book and give us the benefit of their advice for this revision. Some (whose names are marked by asterisks in the list following) even took the time to meet with us in focus groups. Their responses ranged from brisk red-pencilings to detailed arguments about matters of pedagogical and historical principle, and there wasn't one from which we did not derive something to improve the text. In addition to many users of our previous editions who over the years have given us suggestions, we wish to thank:

Hugh Albee, *Palm Beach Community College*

Janet Averett, *San Jose State University*

*Jeanne Marie Belfy, *Boise State University*

*Mark Benson, *Bucks County College*

Tharald Borgir, *Oregon State University*

Roger L. Briscoe, *Raritan Valley Community College*

Andrew D. Brown, *Central Missouri State University*

Steve Brown, *University of Northern Iowa*

Julie Brye, *University of Kansas*

*Richard Burke, *Hunter College*

William K. Burns, *Seton Hall University*

John Clark, *Santa Barbara City College*

*Vicki Curry, *University of Utah*

Nancy L. Davis, *Lorain County Community College*

Mark DeBellis, *Columbia University*

David DeBolt, *Kent State University*

Craig De Wilde, *University of California at Santa Barbara*

David P. Doerksen, *University of Oregon*

David M. Edris, *Peru State College*

G. Daniel Fairchild, *University of Wisconsin, Platteville*

*David Feller, *Weber State University*

Stephen G. Gates, *University of Arkansas*

William B. George, *San Jose State University*

Richard H. von Grabow, *Iowa State University*

Sharon Davis Gratto, *Gettysburg College*

David Grayson, *University of Minnesota, Minneapolis*

Richard D. Green, *Northwestern University*

Mark Harbold, *Elmhurst College*

*Steven Johnson, *Brigham Young University*

Phyllis Juszczyk, *St. Francis College*

Ronald J. Klimko, *University of Idaho*

*Steven Kreinberg, *Temple University*

Leo Kreter, *California State University, Fullerton*

Robert C. Mann, *Stephen F. Austin State University*

Bruce Mayhall, *University of Nevada, Reno*

B. G. McCloud, *Appalachian State University*

Earl B. Miller, *University of Tennessee at Chattanooga*

Dale E. Monson, *Penn State University, University Park*

Raymond D. Moore, *University of Georgia*

Arthur Motycka, *University of Rhode Island*

R. C. Nelson, *Lock Haven University of Pennsylvania*

Jo-Ann Reif, *Penn State University, Scranton*

Patricia Root, *Washington State University*

William R. Rudolph, *Burlington County College*

*Bryce Rytting, *Brigham Young University*

K. Robert Schwarz, *Brooklyn College*

Terence S. Small, *University of Florida*

*Edgar J. Thompson, *University of Utah*

Jane B. Weidensal, *Manhattan School of Music*

Robert L. Weiss, *Southern Illinois University at Carbondale*

William T. Whitener, *University of Alaska, Anchorage*

Steven Winick, *Georgia State University*

Thomas Wright, *Florida State University*

Thanks also to Jan Robinson for specific editorial assistance. Tom Laskey of Sony Special Products was efficient and patient beyond the call of duty.

However imperfectly, writing about music should evoke the quality of an art—music; therefore we have always felt it should be read from pages that are artistic, too. One of the many satisfactions of our long association with Worth Publishers has been working with the distinguished designers Malcolm Grear Associates. Once again, Pat Appleton has made this book beautiful in itself, and also functionally beautiful: the two-color press works wonders to clarify diagrams, music examples, and listening charts, and the design allows these to be integrated vividly into the text. To George Touloumes, the miracle man who has implemented this design, and to our support system at Worth—project editor Liz Geller, picture editor Elaine Bernstein, our admirable new development editor Richard Wallis, and the astonishingly resourceful and tenacious, the indispensable Tom Gay—warm thanks.

JOSEPH KERMAN
VIVIAN KERMAN

Berkeley, California
June 1995

In response to requests from users, the Listening Charts in the third printing of LISTEN: THIRD BRIEF EDITION have been enhanced. As well as timings to the right of the vertical rule, giving the total time elapsed from the beginning of the selection, we have added timings to the left of the rule, giving the time *since the last new CD track*. Students with CD timers will find it easy to follow the charts with these left-hand timings, whereas those with cassettes should follow the timings to the right of the rule.

About the Author

JOSEPH KERMAN is a professor of music at the University of California at Berkeley. Kerman is known as a particularly stimulating and influential writer on music; among his more recent books are **Beethoven** (with Alan Tyson) in the New Grove Series (Norton), **Contemplating Music** (Harvard), a new, 1988 edition of his classic **Opera as Drama** (University of California Press), and **Write All These Down** (California). He was a founding editor of the journal *19th Century Music*. Also well known are Kerman's articles in nonmusic publications such as *The New York Review of Books* and *Critical Inquiry*. He has been awarded numerous prizes and fellowships; in 1997 he was appointed Charles Eliot Norton Professor of Poetry at Harvard University.

Kerman has been teaching in college since he was nineteen. His "music major" assignments have ranged from ear training and opera coaching to seminars in musicology. He inherited a lasting commitment to nonmajor instruction from a legendary "Music I" course at Princeton, in which he participated as a young teacher. At Berkeley, he pioneered such courses. His other textbooks include **Listen, Third Edition** (Worth), **A History of Art and Music** (with H.W. Janson, Abrams), and **Mozart: Concerto in C, K. 503.**

Contents in Brief

Contents

Fundamentals

Unit I, the introductory unit in this book, covers music fundamentals and their standard terminology. In Chapter 1 we are introduced at once to a piece of music, the Overture to The Bartered Bride *by the Czech composer Bedřich Smetana. Chapter 2 presents the basic concepts of sound and time—pitch, dynamics, tone color, and duration—and Chapter 3 explains how time is organized into rhythm and meter, and how pitch is deployed in scales. Then Chapter 4 deals with melody, harmony, and other combinations of the basic elements that have already been treated. Chapter 5 carries the discussion one stage further, to a consideration of musical form and style. Our "Interludes" treat musical instruments and musical notation.*

Listening

The basic activity that leads to the love of music and to its understanding—to what is sometimes called "music appreciation"—is listening to particular pieces of music again and again. Such, as least, is the premise of this book. Its pages are filled mostly with discussions of musical compositions—symphonies, concertos, operas, and the like—that people have found more and more rewarding as they have listened to them repeatedly. These discussions are meant to introduce you to the contents of these works and their aesthetic qualities: what goes on in the music, and how it affects us.

The kind of hands-on knowledge of music that is necessary for a music professional—for a composer or a performer—is of no special use to you as a nonprofessional listener. But an acquaintance with musical concepts and musical terms can *be useful, by helping you grasp more clearly what you already hear in music. Analyzing things, pinpointing things, even simply using the right names for things all make us more actively aware of them. Sometimes, too, this process of analysis, pinpointing, and naming can actually assist listening. We become more alert, as it were, to aspects of music when they have been pointed out. And sharper awareness contributes to greater appreciation of music, and of the other arts as well.*

Since our emphasis is on music, that is where we start—with an actual listening experience, our "overture" to this book. This will exemplify in a general way some of the concepts to be introduced in the following chapters, and make understanding the terminology of music, when we come to explain it, seem less abstract and mysterious, more immediate and alive.

CHAPTER 1

Overture

L isten, then, to the Overture to *The Bartered Bride,* a comic opera by Bedřich Smetana (1824–1884). Smetana is not as well-known a name as some of his nineteenth-century contemporaries, such as Chopin, Wagner, Brahms, and others, whom we will be studying in Unit IV of this book. In his native Bohemia, however, later called Czechoslovakia and now the Czech Republic, Smetana is revered because he insisted on endowing his music with a distinctively Czech flavor—and this at a time when Bohemians were struggling for independence from the Austrian Empire. Several of Smetana's pieces, including this overture, have an unshakable place in today's concert repertory. For a word about *The Bartered Bride,* see page 6.

You may prefer to skip the indented, colored paragraphs in the following discussion and leave them until later, at a second listening. They give the standard terminology for effects and features mentioned in the main text, terms that will be explained in later chapters. The idea is not to learn these terms at the present stage, but simply to get some impression about their use in the context of an actual piece of music, Smetana's Overture to *The Bartered Bride.*

If you want to understand music better, you can do nothing more important than listen to it. Nothing can possibly take the place of listening to music. Everything I say in this book is about an experience that you can only get outside this book.

From what is still one of the best books on "music appreciation," *What to Listen for in Music* by composer Aaron Copland (see page 335), 1939

Opening Outburst Overtures are relatively short orchestral pieces played before the beginnings of operas, ballets, musicals, and (occasionally) stage plays. Nearly all of them start with something bright and forceful, to quiet the audience down and put them in the mood for the show that is about to begin. Smetana has fulfilled this necessary if modest task brilliantly. The music he provides at this point is a regular outburst, a blast, a noisy wake-up call: loud, irregular, insistent, and irresistible.

> One of the basic properties of sound is its volume, its loudness or softness, referred to as *dynamics* in music terminology. The Italian word *forte* (fórteh) is used for "loud," *piano* for "soft" (abbreviated *f* and *p*). After the opening outburst, Smetana writes *subito p* on his score, calling for a sudden change in dynamics from loud to soft.

Build-up The outburst feels like the preparation for something exciting; yet what it leads into is a long, fast passage played softly by violins, which seem to rustle or rush, expectantly and a bit nervously. Suddenly another group of violins breaks in with music that we recognize: the ending portion of the outburst (slightly shortened). Then they too start rustling.

The Bartered Bride: Mařenka looks on as Kecal, the village marriage-broker, delivers his pitch to her mother.

This happens twice more, as shown in the diagram below (the four *f*'s stand for four loud spurts—like machine-gun spurts—of loud music; *p* stands for the rustling):

f f f f p –

　　　　f f f f p –

　　　　　　　f f f f p – – – – – – – – – – – – – – – – – – –

　　　　　　　　　　f f f f p – – – – – –

> This is a good passage for help in recognizing the sound of the violin and other violin-like instruments, members of the violin **family:** entering first are the **violins,** next the larger and lower **cellos,** next the even lower **double basses.** Orchestras have two violin groups, the **first violins** and the **second violins.**
>
> The ending portion of the outburst, which has already been heard five times and will be heard many more, is the main **theme** of the overture. A theme is a section of music that is heard throughout a composition and that contributes significantly to its sense.

Two, three, four simultaneous rustling strands—the tension is getting to be unbearable! Extra instruments come in. The music grows louder and louder.

> *Crescendo* (creshéndo) is the term for gradually increasing dynamics, *diminuendo* the term for decreasing dynamics. Compare with **subito f** and **subito p** (see page 10).

Polka　At last the whole orchestra explodes into a loud, enthusiastic Czech dance, a polka—which is cut off almost at once by more rustling. Notice a new two-note rhythmic figure that energizes the rustling from below.

> The two-note figure sounds doubly energetic because the stringed instruments are being plucked with a finger, not bowed; the term for this is *pizzicato* (pitzicáhto). The percussive, dynamic quality produced by pizzicato is well known from double-bass playing in jazz.

The polka fragment is repeated, softly now, as though the composer were trying again . . . then repeated again, extended somewhat . . . we get the feeling that Smetana is struggling to construct an entire dance out of that fragment, before our very ears. He moves a short bit of the dance through several levels, using the new two-note figure as a lever or propeller.

> A fragment of music that is repeated several times at different levels, higher and higher or lower and lower, is called a **sequence**. The sequence here has four levels.

Finally he gives us the entire polka: a joyous, noisy item. Its varied, lively rhythms give way to fast even notes, which seem to be preparing for a stop. But it takes a return of the opening outburst to make the music *really* stop.

> An ending or a stop in music is called a **cadence**; the stoppage can be total, partial, or tentative-sounding. Cadences are an extremely important feature of music, because of the (often) subtle way in which they punctuate music's constant flow.

Closing Outburst   Listening to the outburst for the second time, and to the theme part in particular, you may be struck by the way its four spurts of music focus on the same note, more and more insistently (this note is the TAK in the rhythmic shorthand in the margin). You may even find it rather comical, like someone impatiently shaking a clogged-up salt shaker.

Four spurts:
> ta-ki TAK *(wait)*
> ta-ki ta-ki TAK *(wait)*
> ta-ki ta-ki-ta-ki TAK
> ta-ki ta-ki-ta-ki-
> -ta-ki-ta-ki-**TAK**

It also gives a very strong sense of finality; no wonder this music works so well as a cadence. Smetana has ingeniously concocted a theme that sounds like an opener in one context and like a termination in another. It is an achievement we can appreciate and perhaps enjoy, the way we enjoy a pun.

New, Slower Melody   The quiet rustling that follows the closing outburst fades almost at once, turning into a regular and distinctly slower ticking.

Above this quiet ticking, a relatively long melody emerges, unlike anything that has been heard in the overture so far: slower, with smoother rhythms and richer, more emotional harmonies. Even at first hearing, we perceive this melody in three segments. The first two are played by wind instruments and start the same way, the third starts differently and more richly, in the strings.

> The term for quality of sound is **tone color**, or **timbre**. These wind instruments are **oboes**, recognizable by their clear, concentrated tone color.
> Segments of a melody are called **phrases**; something in the music makes one phrase sound separate from the next. Smetana's melody can be diagrammed **a a′ b**, where **a′** denotes a varied version of **a**, and **b** is a contrasting phrase.

Interruption: Return to the Opening Outburst   The melody does *not* reach a cadence; it has hardly had a chance to work its way into our memory before it is cut off by a drum—as the outburst crashes in again. Notice that in its position after the melody (and after three hard drum strokes), this passage sounds less like a cadence, and more like a new beginning and a new lead-in. What it leads into is the by-now familiar rustling.

New Build-up   So we might expect another build-up, such as happened after the very first outburst. What we now hear differs in (at least) three ways from the first build-up:

1.   the theme comes many more times, more closely spaced than before

2. the theme is focused on many different notes, played by a whole array of different instruments

Another good passage for help in recognizing instrument sounds: in order, the theme is played by **violas** (a viola is a slightly larger violin), a **clarinet, flutes** (wind instruments), oboes, violins plus one oboe, and then oboes again.

3. Wind instruments are now added to the strings, as the rustling grows louder, clearer, and more interesting. It is heard not only simultaneously with the theme, but also on a par with it, competing for the listener's attention. It sounds less like rustling than rattling, arguing.

Texture is a term used for the "weave" of music, for the blending together of various elements heard at the same time. The new build-up passage is said to have a polyphonic texture, or to be in **polyphony**, meaning that many melodies are playing at once.

The polka is **homophonic**, because all the instruments playing it are coordinated or synchronized. On the other hand, whenever the theme comes in the outburst, it is **monophonic**—just the one musical line, without any accompaniment. The Greek prefixes *poly-, homo-,* and *mono-* mean "many" (*polygamy*), "same" (*homogenize*), and "single" (*monopoly*).

And after a while, Smetana really mixes things up, combining fragments of various elements—the theme, the rustling material, even of the polka—to complete the build-up and the crescendo. This leads as before to the polka.

Polka   This time, however, there is a difference: by now everyone has heard this polka, and it would be boring to hear it being built up bit by bit a second time. So the entire dance is played right away. Wind instruments, including the trumpet, play a brisk new rhythmic figure back of the polka, derived from the main theme: *ta-ki ta-ki-ta-ki TAK* (see margin).

ta-ki TAK *(wait)*
ta-ki ta-ki TAK *(wait)*
ta-ki ta-ki-ta-ki TAK
ta-ki ta-ki-ta-ki-
-ta-ki-ta-ki-**TAK**

While listening to the polka for the second time, try beating time to the music, in *duple meter*: ONE *two,* ONE *two* . . .. This is easy enough to do at the end, less easy at the beginning, where the *fourth* and *fifth* notes of the polka refuse to fall out on the strong ONE beats. But of course it is just these notes—called **syncopated** notes—that give this polka its special verve. Best known, perhaps, from jazz, syncopation occurs in nearly all music.

Closing Outburst   The polka ends as it did before, with its cadence hammered home by the closing outburst.

At this point you are probably aware of having heard the same series *Opening Outburst—Build-up—Polka—Closing Outburst* twice, albeit with significant differences the second time. This is an experience of musical **form**, the "shape" of music in time. There is usually a sense of satisfaction in coming back, after new material (here, that middle slower melody), to something we remember from before.

Distant Echoes   The polka ends as it did before—but with a surprise. The theme gets a new destination: instead of all four spurts ending on the same note, the final one goes to a new, very strange note. Smetana lets the strangeness sink in, by stopping the music dead for the first time, and then by extending the note (actually, two quiet notes are present here).

What is altogether unexpected (and indescribable) is the mood: nostalgic, delicate, half-sensuous, as though this earthy overture has been jolted into a magical dream world. The music glides through several new, mysterious-sounding regions, all of them echoing with distant polka recollections.

The strange "regions" through which we are guided by Smetana's shifting chords are **keys;** the process of changing keys, called **modulation,** is a major compositional resource. Another passage in the overture that features modulation is the *New (second) Build-up* passage, with the theme focused on different notes. Each note modulates to a new key.

At the end of this passage, do you notice that the music sounds even more dreamlike because it is slowed down, just a little? The speed of music is called its **tempo.** **Ritardando** is the term for slowing down the tempo; **accelerando** (acheleráhndo) means speeding up (accelerating).

Final Rush   The dream (if that is what it is) is shattered by a drum roll and a fast crescendo. The polka appears for a moment, with new harmonies. And we hear yet another outburst, ending with rocking motion which seems to say "we really *have* to stop!"—though not before the woodwinds try to throw a final block, using the opening portion of the outburst (not the end).

Eventful as this final segment of the overture may be, it feels like a single mad rush to the finish line. A fragment of music that repeats many times at the same level (like the sixfold rocking motion here) is called an **ostinato,** "obstinate" in Italian.

Smetana's **The Bartered Bride**   The show that is introduced by this cheerful overture is a light-hearted affair, half-way between an opera and what we would now call a musical. Originally there was spoken dialogue between the musical numbers. *The Bartered Bride* acquired its status as a model for Czech national music for three rather simple reasons: it is written to Czech words (not German or Italian, the usual languages for opera at that time); its score is full of Czech tunes and dances and rhythms; and it tells a rose-tinted story of Czech peasant life. Young lovers Mařenka and Jeník have to contend with a characteristic "folk" figure, the marriage broker Kecal, who tries to pair Mařenka off with Vašek, the wealthy village half-wit. But Vašek runs off with a circus, and *The Bartered Bride* comes to the mandatory happy ending.

All the themes of the overture turn up again during the opera, at the end of the first act. And the interesting main theme—with its four spurts focusing on a single note, each longer than the last—seems to derive from a special feature in the opera itself. As though being dim and shy were not enough, poor Vašek is also given a stutter; the music he sings on stage depicts the stutterer's frustration when he can't get through a sentence, and his relief when he finally succeeds. So does the overture theme: "it's an *in–,* it's an inter*es–,* it's an interesting *ov–,* it's an interesting overture to *hear."*

ta-ki TAK *(wait)*
ta-ki ta-ki TAK *(wait)*
ta-ki ta-ki-ta-ki TAK
ta-ki ta-ki-ta-ki-
-ta-ki-ta-ki **TAK**

Listening Charts

So hear it one more time, in order to become familiar with the Listening Charts that form an integral feature of this book. Follow the first of these charts on page 7. Note that it is not necessary to read music to use these charts. Even people who think they are tone deaf (there's no such condition) can follow the music with the help of the timings at the left side, cued to the performance of the piece on the CD/Cassette set accompanying *Listen.* For the benefit of those who are able to read music, the charts in subsequent chapters include brief notations of the main themes, directly across from the timing indication and the reference.

LISTENING CHART 1

1-5   1-5   1   1

Smetana, Overture to *The Bartered Bride*

6 min. 23 sec.

	0:00	**Opening Outburst and**	*f*	Loud (*f*) "wake-up" passage played by the full orchestra,
1	0:11	**Build-up**	*subito p*	followed by rushing, rustling strings, interrupted
1				several times by a "spurting" effect (tak-i-TAK . . .)

The interruptions are played by **stringed instruments**. Tak-i-TAK is a **motive**, a short rhythmic figure used many times and developed during the composition.

Tension builds

The **dynamics** are changing from soft (*piano*) to loud (*forte*); the term for increasing dynamics is *crescendo*. On this chart, dynamics are noted systematically for each segment of music.

	1:18	**Polka**	*f*	Fragment of a Polka
2			*p*	A similar fragment comes several more times, more quietly
2				
0:24	1:42			Another shorter fragment is played four times at different levels

A passage played at several different levels is called a **sequence**.

0:37	1:55		*f*	**At last the Polka appears extended to its full length**
				Continuations lead to a big cadence
0:58	2:16	**Closing Outburst**	*f*	As at the beginning—but now the music sounds cadential

Cadence is the term for a stopping place in music.

| **3** | 2:30 | **Slowdown:** | | |
| 3 | 2:34 | **New, Slower Melody** | *p* | A new melody is begun by a wind instrument—an oboe |

The melody falls into segments, called **phrases**.

4	2:59	**Interruption: Return to**		Fast timpani strokes, leading to the outburst as at the
4		**the Opening Outburst;**	*f*	beginning (though it starts with wind instruments only). The
		New Build-up	*p*	rushing string figure follows, with different interruptions by
				the theme—closer together, new instruments, different levels

In order, we hear the theme in the violas, clarinet, flutes, and other instruments. The texture is **polyphonic** (many melodies sounding at once).

0:42	3:41			Smetana mixes it up—bits of the outburst, the Polka, and new material
1:01	4:00	**Polka**	*ff*	**Polka in its extended form,** louder than ever; trumpets play
				New continuations, with rhythmic figure ta-ki ta-ki ta-ki TAK
1:47	4:47	**Closing Outburst**	*ff*	

We've now twice heard the series *Opening Outburst—Build-up—Polka—Closing Outburst,* though with interesting differences. This is an experience of musical **form**.

| **5** | 4:57 | **Stop: Distant Echoes** | *pp* | Quiet Polka fragments come at mysterious different levels |
| 5 | | | | |

The different levels are different **keys**. Changing keys is called **modulation**.

0:25	5:22	**Final Rush**		A timpani roll, rushing strings, crescendo
0:48	5:44		*ff*	Another Polka fragment, with some new harmonies
1:03	6:00			One (not quite) final appearance of the outburst
				Final cadence

CHAPTER 2

Music, Sound, and Time

M usic is the art of sound in time. We start with an outline of the basic properties of sound as it is produced, each of which corresponds to an effect that we experience when sound is heard. The scientific terms for sound all have their analogues in the terminology of music.

1 Sound Vibrations

As everyone who has taken a course in elementary physics knows, sound is produced by vibrations that occur when objects are struck, stroked, or otherwise agitated. The vibrations are transmitted through the air, or some other medium, and picked up by our ears.

For the production of sound in general, almost anything will do—the single rusted hinge on a creaky door as well as the vast air masses of a thunderstorm. For the production of musical sounds, the usual objects are taut strings and membranes, columns of air enclosed in pipes of various kinds, and silicon chips. The point is that these produce relatively simple vibrations, which translate into clearly focused or, as we say, "musical" sounds. Often the membranes are alive: they are called vocal cords.

Sound-producing vibrations are very fast; the range of audible sound extends from around 20 to 20,000 cycles (that is, our vocal cords warble that many times every second). The vibrations are also very small. Look inside a piano while it is being played: you will not detect any movement in the

It has always seemed to me more important for the listener to be sensitive to the musical tone than to know the number of vibrations that produce the tone. . . . What the composer desires above all is to encourage you to become as completely conscious and wideawake a listener as possible.

Aaron Copland, *What to Listen For in Music*

Natural resonators: *left,* gourds in a pair of Mexican maracas; *right,* a tortoise shell in the ancient Greek lyre, a small harplike instrument.

8

lengthy strings, except possibly for some blurring of the very biggest ones. To be heard, sound vibrations often need to be *amplified*, either electronically or with the aid of something physical that echoes or resonates along with the vibrating body. In a piano, this is the big wooden soundboard.

Pitch (Frequency)

The scientific term for the rate of sound vibration is **frequency**. Frequency is measured in cycles (per second). On the level of perception, our ears respond differently to sounds of high and low frequencies, and to very fine gradations in between. Indeed, people speak about "high" and "low" sounds quite unselfconsciously, as though they knew that the latter actually have a low frequency—relatively few cycles—and the former a high frequency.

The musical term for this quality of sound, which is recognized so instinctively, is **pitch.** Noises, with their complex, unfocused vibrations, do not have pitch. And the totality of musical sounds, as distinct from noises, serves as a kind of quarry from which musicians of every age and every culture carve the exact building blocks they want for their music. They never (or virtually never) make use of the total range of pitches—which we experience when we hear the sliding scale of a siren, starting low and going higher and higher until it is out of earshot. Instead a limited number of fixed pitches is selected from this sound continuum. These pitches are calibrated scientifically (orchestras tune to a pitch with a frequency of 440 cycles), given letter names (that pitch is labeled A), and collected in *scales*. Scales are discussed in Chapter 3.

The experience of pitch is gained very early; babies only a few hours old respond to human voices, and they soon distinguish between high and low ones. They seem to prefer higher pitches, naturally—those in their mothers' pitch range. At the other end of life, it is the highest frequencies that older people find they are losing. The range of pitches that strike us as "normal," those spoken or sung by most men and women, is shown to the right. (If you are not familiar with the notation for pitch, consult pages 22–23.)

NORMAL
VOICE RANGES
as in a chorus

Soprano Contralto

Tenor Bass

2 Dynamics (Amplitude)

In scientific terminology, *amplitude* is the level of strength of sound vibrations—more precisely, the amount of energy they contain and convey. As anyone who has been near a big guitar amplifier knows, very small string vibrations can be amplified up until the energy in the air that is transmitting them rattles the eardrums. Amplitude is measured in *decibels*.

In musical terminology, the level of sound is called its **dynamics.** Musicians make use of very subtle dynamic gradations from very soft to very loud, but they have never worked out a calibrated scale of dynamics, as they have for pitch. The terms used are only approximate. They are usually in Italian, because all European music looked to Italy when this terminology first came into use.

The main categories are simply loud and soft, *forte* (pronounced fórteh) and *piano*, which may be qualified by expanding to "very loud" or "very soft" and by adding the Italian word for "medium," *mezzo* (medzo):

pianissimo	piano	mezzo piano	mezzo forte	forte	fortissimo
pp	***p***	***mp***	***mf***	***f***	***ff***
very soft	soft	medium soft	medium loud	loud	very loud

Other terms are **più** (pyōō) **forte** and *meno forte,* "more loud" and "less loud." Changes in dynamics can be sudden *(subito),* or they can be gradual—a soft passage swells into a loud one, or a powerful blare fades into quietness. Below are the terms for changing dynamics and their notational signs (sometimes called "hairpins"):

crescendo (**cresc.**)

_____

gradually getting louder

decrescendo (**decresc.**), or *diminuendo* (**dim.**)

_____

gradually getting softer

LISTEN

1-2   1-2   1   1

In Unit I of this book, we will illustrate the concepts introduced with short selections from the CD/Cassette set. We can skip pitch—the difference between high and low pitch is heard so instinctively that it requires no illustration—and start with dynamics. Again, everyone can tell loud from soft, but it may be well to show how many different gradations can exist in an actual piece of music.

Turn back to Listening Chart 1 for Smetana's Overture to *The Bartered Bride,* on page 7. Play the sections labeled **Opening Outburst and Build-up** and **Polka,** the first minute and a half of cassette 1 or track 1 of CD 1 (either set). The dynamics you hear are:

0:00	opening outburst, full orchestra	*fortissimo*
0:11	sudden change to quiet rustling sounds (produced by violins)	*subito piano*
0:24	three appearances of a short, gruff bit of music, (a *theme*), spaced out from one another	each is *forte*
1:14	the music gradually gets louder	*crescendo*
1:17	culminating in a rowdy dance, the polka	*fortissimo,* again
1:22	but the rustling soon returns (etc.)	*mezzo forte*

3 Tone Color: Overtones

At whatever pitch, and whether loud or soft, musical sounds differ in their general *quality,* depending on the instruments or voices that produce them. **Tone color**, or **timbre**, is the term for this quality.

The scientific explanation of tone color is more complex (and more amazing) than the explanations of pitch and dynamics. Guitar strings and other sound-producing bodies vibrate not only along their total length, but also simultaneously in half-lengths, quarters, eighths, and so on. The diagrams below attempt to illustrate this. The amplitudes of these fractional vibrations, called **partials** by scientists, **overtones** by musicians, are much lower than the

STRING VIBRATIONS

FULL-LENGTH:

¼ cycle   ¾ cycle
      ½ cycle

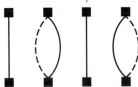

HALF-LENGTH:

¼ cycle   ¾ cycle
      ½ cycle

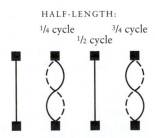

BOTH SIMULTANEOUSLY:

¼ cycle   ¾ cycle
      ½ cycle

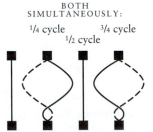

amplitude of the main vibration. Indeed, overtones are not heard as new pitches, but as part of the string's basic or fundamental pitch. It is the amount and proportion of overtones in a sound that gives it its characteristic tone color. A flute has few overtones. Luciano Pavarotti has many.

Musicians make no attempt to tally or describe tone colors; about the best one can do is apply imprecise adjectives such as *bright, warm, ringing, hollow,* or *brassy.* Yet tone color is surely the most easily recognized of all musical elements. Even people who cannot identify instruments by name can distinguish between the smooth, rich sound of violins, the bright sound of trumpets, and the thump of drums.

LISTEN

For illustration of a few different instrumental tone colors (just a very few of those available in a symphony orchestra), turn back again to the Listening Chart 1 on page 7. Play the sections labeled **Interruption: Return to the Opening Outburst** and **New Build-up**—CD 1 track 4, or three minutes after the start of Cassette 1 band 1. This passage goes like the wind, with the tone color changing every five seconds or so. The same gruff theme is played by different instruments, each with its characteristic tone color.

2:59	three drum strokes and an outburst	timpani, then massed woodwind instruments
3:04	(part 2 of the outburst is the *theme*)	massed string instruments, timpani
3:08	quiet rustling	violins (about twenty, playing together)
3:11	theme (consists of four spurts of music)	violas (about ten)
3:16	theme again	clarinet
3:21	theme, third time	flutes (two)
3:26	theme, fourth time	oboe (and bassoon below—hard to hear!)
3:40	by now, so many instruments are playing that tone colors are hard to distinguish	

Musical instruments are the subject of Interlude B, directly following Chapter 4. The variety of devices invented for the different tone colors that people have desired for their music, in all societies, is quite extraordinary.

The most distinctive tone color of all, however, belongs to the first, most beautiful, and most universal of all the sources of music—the human voice.

4 Duration

Sound exists in time, and any sound we hear has its **duration**—the length of time we hear it in minutes, seconds, or microseconds. Though duration is not an actual property of sound, like frequency, amplitude, and other of sound's attributes that are taught in physics courses, it is obviously of central importance for music, which is the art of sounds in time. The broad term for the time aspect of music is **rhythm.**

The primacy of rhythm in the experience of music is practically an act of faith in our culture. However, there is some music in which rhythm counts for less than, say, tone color; such a piece will be studied in Chapter 23, the chorus *Lux aeterna* by the contemporary composer György Ligeti. Think also of New Age music. But rhythm is the driving force in the vast majority of music both popular and classical, music of all ages and all cultures, and rhythm is where we will begin our discussion of the elements of music, in Chapter 3.

"The first, most beautiful, and most universal of all sources of music": Cecilia Bartoli, a leading young opera singer of the 1990s.

Time and Pitch

W e start this chapter by discussing *rhythm*, the way composers organize musical time by the use of durations of various magnitudes. We then go on to the organization of pitch into *scales* and *intervals*.

Music has four essential elements: rhythm, melody, harmony, and tone color. These four ingredients are the composer's materials. He works with them in the same way that any other artisan works with his materials.

Aaron Copland, *What to Listen For in Music*

1 Rhythm

As we have seen, the term **rhythm** in its broadest sense refers to the time aspect of music. In a more specific sense, *a rhythm* refers to the actual arrangement of durations—long and short notes—in a particular melody or some other musical passage. Of course, the term is also used in other contexts, about golfers, quarterbacks, poems, and even paintings. But no sport and no other art handles rhythm with such precision and refinement as does music.

The term *rhythmic* is often used to describe music that features simple patterns (such as ONE *two* ONE *two*) repeating over and over again, but that is not really right (think about rhythm in golf). Such patterns should be described as *metrical,* or strongly metrical, not rhythmic. See the section "Rhythm and Meter" below.

Beat

The basic unit for measuring time in music is the **beat.** When listening to a marching band, to take a clear example, we surely sense a regular recurrence of short durational units. These units serve as a steady, vigorous background for more complicated durational patterns that we discern at the same time. We can't help beating time to the music, waving a hand or tapping a foot, following the motion of the drum major's baton and of the big-drum players' drumsticks. The simple durational pattern that is being signaled by waving, tapping, or thumping is the music's beat.

Accent

Beats provide the basic unit of measurement for time; if ordinary clock time is measured in seconds, musical time is measured in beats. There is, however, an all-important difference between a clock ticking and a drum beating time.

Mechanically produced ticks all sound exactly the same, but it is virtually impossible to beat time without making some beats more emphatic than others. This is called giving certain beats an **accent.**

And accents are really what enable us to beat time, since the natural way to do this is to alternate accented ("strong") and unaccented ("weak") beats in patterns such as ONE *two,* ONE *two,* ONE *two,* . . . or ONE *two three,* ONE *two three,* ONE *two three.* . . . To beat time, then, is not only to measure time but also to organize it, at least into these two- and three-beat patterns. That is why a drum is a musical instrument and a clock is not.

Accents are not always indicated in musical notation, since in many types of music they are simply taken for granted. When composers want a particularly strong accent—something out of the ordinary—they put the sign > above or below a note. Thus a pattern of alternating very strong and weak beats is indicated as shown to the right. An even stronger accent is indicated by the mark *sfz* or *sf,* short for *sforzando,* the Italian word for "forced."

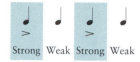

Strong Weak Strong Weak

The beat: there are times when the drummers in a band do little more than bang it out.

Meter

Any recurring pattern of strong and weak beats, such as we have already referred to and illustrated above, is called a **meter.** Meter is a strong/weak pattern repeated again and again. Each occurrence of this repeated pattern, consisting of a principal strong beat and one or more weaker beats, is called a **measure,** or **bar.** In musical notation, measures are indicated by vertical lines called **bar lines.** The meter indicated schematically in the margin above is notated as shown to the right.

There are two basic kinds of meter, called **simple meters:** duple meter and triple meter, plus a third, **compound meter,** which involves a subdivision of one of the simple meters.

Bar line   Bar line

❦   In duple meter the beats are grouped in twos (ONE *two*, ONE *two*). Duple meter is instantly familiar from marches—such as "Yankee Doodle," below—which tend always to use it in deference to the human anatomy (LEFT *right*, LEFT *right*).

Duple meter   Triple meter

❦   In triple meter the beats are grouped in threes (ONE *two three*, ONE *two three*). As it happens, our national songs "America" and "The Star-Spangled Banner" are both in triple meter. "America" starts on a strong ONE beat of the triple meter; "The Star-Spangled Banner" starts on a weak *three* beat.

❦   Not infrequently, there is a clearly marked subdivision of the main beats into threes, resulting in *compound meters* with six or nine beats:

ONE			two					
ONE	two	three	*four*	five	six			

ONE			two			*three*		
ONE	two	three	*four*	five	six	*seven*	eight	nine

Compound meters can be treated as subtypes of duple and triple meter. In the round "Row, row, row your boat," while the first voice is moving at a fast six-beat clip at the words "Merrily, merrily," the second voice comes in pounding out the basic duple meter, "Row, *row,* row":

first voice:

Row,	row,	row your	boat	gently	down the	stream,		Merrily,	merrily,	merrily,	merrily
1 2 3	4 5 6	1 2 3	4 5 6	1 2 3	4 5 6	1 2 3	4 5 6	1 2 3	4 5 6	1 2 3	4 5 6
ONE	*two*	ONE	*two*	ONE	*two*	ONE	*two*	ONE	*two*	ONE	*two*

second voice:

		Row,	row,	row . . .
		ONE	*two*	ONE	*two*

❦   Meters with five beats, seven beats, and so on have never been used widely in Western music, though composers have often experimented with them, especially in the twentieth century. It was an unusual tour de force for Tchaikovsky to have provided his popular Sixth Symphony with a very convincing waltzlike movement in *quintuple* meter (five beats to a bar).

Tchaikovsky, Symphony No. 6

Rhythm and Meter

We have already seen that, in the most general sense, *rhythm* refers to the whole time aspect of music and, more specifically, that *a rhythm* refers to the particular arrangements of long and short notes in a musical passage. In most Western music, duple or triple *meter* serves as the regular background against which we perceive music's actual rhythms.

As the rhythm now coincides with the meter, then cuts across it independently, then even contradicts it, all kinds of variety, tension, and excitement can result. Meter is background; rhythm is foreground.

Musical notation has developed a conventional system of signs (see pages 21–22) to indicate relative durations; combining various signs is the way of indicating rhythms. Following are examples of well-known tunes in duple and triple meters. Notice from the shading (even better, sing the tunes to yourself and *hear*) how the rhythm sometimes corresponds with the meter and sometimes departs from it. The shading indicates passages of rhythm-meter correspondence:

The most exciting rhythms seem unexpected and complex, the most beautiful melodies simple and inevitable.

Poet W. H. Auden, 1962

The above diagrams should not be taken to imply that meter is always emphasized behind music's rhythms. Often the meter is not explicitly beaten out at all. It does not need to be, for the listener can almost always sense it under the surface. People will even imagine they hear a duple or triple meter behind the steady dripping of a faucet or the ticking of a clock.

Naturally, meter is strongly stressed in music designed to stimulate regular body movements, such as marches, dances, and much popular music. In former times, the associations between strongly metrical music and sex went largely unreported, but that was before the uninhibited gesturing of rock stars and the explicit imagery of MTV.

At the other extreme, there is *nonmetrical* music. The meandering, nonmetrical rhythms of Gregorian chant contribute to the cool, unworldly, and spiritual quality that devotees of this music cherish.

Rhythm might be described as, to the world of sound, what light is to the world of sight. It shapes and gives new meaning.

Dame Edith Sitwell, poet and critic, 1965

Syncopation

One way of obtaining interesting, striking effects in music is to displace the accents in a foreground *rhythm* away from their normal position on the beats of the background *meter*. This is called **syncopation.** In duple meter, accents can be displaced so they go *one* TWO, *one* TWO instead of ONE *two,* ONE *two;* or the syncopation can occur in between beats ONE and *two,* as in this Christmas ballad:

Ru**dolf** __ the red - nosed rein - deer _____
ONE   *two*   ONE   *two*   ONE   *two*   ONE   *two*

If you know the George M. Cohan classic "Give my regards to Broadway," you know that it starts with the same syncopation as in "Rudolf," and has another syncopation in its second line:

Give **my** __ re -gards to   Broad - - -   way,   Re- member me to   **Herald** ____   Square
ONE   *two*   ONE   *two*   ONE   *two*   ONE   *two*   ONE   *two*   ONE   *two*   ONE

Syncopation gives the polka in *The Bartered Bride* Overture its sparkle.

The consistent use of syncopation is the hallmark of all African-American-derived popular music, from jazz to world beat. See Chapter 24.

Polka

ONE *two* ONE *two*   ONE *two*

Tempo

Our discussion so far has referred to the *relative* duration of sounds—all beats are equal; some notes are twice as long as others, and so on—but nothing has been said yet about their *absolute* duration in fractions of a second. **Tempo** accounts for this. It is the term for the speed of music. In metrical music, the tempo is the rate at which the basic, regular beats of the meter follow one another.

Tempo can be expressed quantitatively by such indications as ♩ = 60, meaning 60 quarter-note beats per minute. These indications are called **metronome marks,** after the metronome, a mechanical or electrical device that ticks out beats at any desired tempo.

When composers give directions for tempo, however, they usually prefer general terms. Rather than freezing the music's speed by means of a metronome mark, they prefer to leave some latitude for different performers, different acoustical conditions in concert halls, and so on. Like the indications for dynamics, the conventional terms for tempo are Italian:

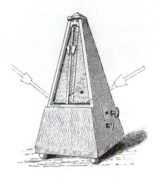

An early metronome owned by Beethoven, who was a friend of the inventor, Johannes Maelzel. A clock-work mechanism made the bar swing back and forth, ticking, at a rate determined by the movable weight.

COMMON TEMPO INDICATIONS

adagio: slow
andante: on the slow side, but not too slow
moderato: moderate tempo
allegretto: on the fast side, but not too fast
allegro: fast
presto: very fast

LESS COMMON TEMPO INDICATIONS

largo, lento, grave: slow, very slow
larghetto: somewhat faster than *largo*
andantino: somewhat faster than *andante*
vivace, vivo: lively
molto allegro: faster than *allegro*
prestissimo: very fast indeed

In their original meaning, many of these Italian words refer not to speed itself but rather to a mood, action, or quality that can be associated with tempo only in a general way. Thus, *vivace* is close to our "vivacious," and *andante,* derived from the common Italian word for "go," might be translated as "going along steadily."

Other terms indicate irregularities of tempo and tempo changes:

accelerando (acheleráhndo) (accel.)   gradually getting faster
ritardando (rit.) or *rallentando (rall.)*   gradually getting slower
più lento, più allegro   slower, faster
⌢ (fermata symbol)   a hold of indefinite length on a certain note
      or rest, which in effect suspends the tempo
a tempo   back to the main tempo

The most important terms to remember are those listed under "common tempo indications" above. When they appear at the top of a symphony movement or the like, they usually constitute its only heading. People refer to the "Andante" of Beethoven's Fifth Symphony, meaning a certain movement of the symphony (the second), which is played at an *andante* tempo.

LISTEN

3   2   3A   1B
5-11 19-25 2   7

For illustrations of the rhythmic terms discussed here, turn first to Mozart's Piano Concerto in G, the last movement—named (after its tempo) the **Allegretto.**

0:00   The **beats** in this melody are **accented** lightly but incisively. Beat time in a moderate (Allegretto) duple meter: ONE *two,* ONE *two.* (There are usually two notes per beat.) After about 10 to 30 seconds skip ahead to track 9 or 22.

3:13   The **tempo** has not changed, but many of the notes are now **syncopated.** Notice, too, that the beats are not as heavily **accented** as before.

3:27   The piano comes in—and is syncopated on another, faster level. If you can manage to beat a double-time ONE *two,* ONE *two* here, you will find that the piano is syncopating dizzily against this faster unit. Anything the orchestra can do, the piano can do better.

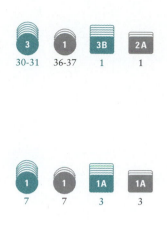

Now turn to the famous third movement (**Allegro**) of Beethoven's Fifth Symphony.

0:00 A mysterious quiet theme is played by the cellos. It is in a fairly fast **triple meter,** starting on the weak *three* beat (this may be hard to hear).

0:03 The cellos are answered by wind instruments, and the **tempo** slows (*ritardando*). One can no longer beat time, for the **meter** stops too: Beethoven has marked a **fermata.**

0:08 The cello music returns, up to speed again (Beethoven marks *a tempo*).

0:14 Another answer by wind instruments, another *ritardando,* another fermata.

0:20 *A tempo,* and French horns announce a very clear **triple meter.**

Once past its initial hesitations, this music is highly *metrical.* For a *non-metrical* excursion into Gregorian chant, play "In paradisum" (p. 57).

2 Pitch

Music, as we noted in Chapter 2, generally does not make use of the total continuous range of sounds that exists in nature. Instead, it draws on only a limited number of fixed pitches. These pitches can be assembled in a collection called a <u>scale</u>. In effect, a scale is the pool of pitches available for the making of music.

Which exact pitches make up a scale differ from culture to culture. Twelve basic pitches have been fixed for most of the music we know. Five were once used in Japan, as many as twenty-four have been used in Arab countries, and Western Europe originally used seven.

Intervals (I): The Octave

The difference, or distance, between any two pitches is called an **interval.** Of the many different intervals used in music, one has a special character that makes it particularly important.

This is the **octave.** If a series of successive pitches is sounded, one after another—say, running up the white keys on the piano—there comes a point at which the pitch seems in some sense to "duplicate" an earlier pitch, but at a higher level. This new pitch does not sound identical to the old one, but somehow the two sounds are very similar. They blend extremely well; they almost seem to melt into each other.

What causes the phenomenon of octaves? Recall from Chapter 2 that when strings vibrate to produce sound they vibrate in partials, that is, not only along their full length but also in halves and other fractions (page 10). A vibrating string that is twice as short as another will *reinforce* the latter's strongest partial. This reinforcement causes the duplication effect of octaves.

As strings go, so go vocal cords: when men and women sing together, they automatically sing in octaves, duplicating each other's singing an octave or two apart. If you ask them, they will say they are singing "the same tune"— not many will think of adding "at different octave levels."

As a result of the phenomenon of octaves, the full continuous range of pitches that exists in nature (and that is covered, for example, by a siren starting low and going up higher and higher) falls into a series of "duplicating" segments. About ten of these octave segments are audible. Two or three octaves is a normal range for most voices and instruments; a large pipe organ covers all ten; a piano covers about seven. Two octaves are shown in the piano diagram on page 18.

The Diatonic Scale

The set of seven pitches originally used in Western music is called the **diatonic scale.** Dating from ancient Greek times, it is still in use today. When the first of the seven pitches is repeated at a higher duplicating pitch, the total is eight—hence the name *octave,* meaning "eight span."

Anyone who knows the series *do re mi fa sol la ti do* is at home with the diatonic scale. You can count out the octave for yourself starting with the first *do* as *one* and ending with the second *do* as *eight.* The set of white keys on the piano (or other) keyboard constitutes this scale. Shown below is a keyboard and diatonic scale notes running through two octaves.

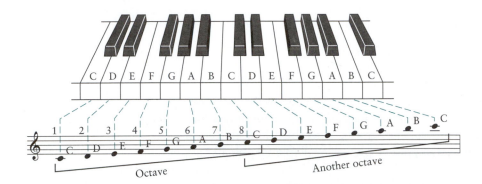

Choral singing, the route by which millions of people come to know and love music

The Chromatic Scale

The diatonic scale was the basic scale of Western music; at a later period, five more pitches were added between certain of the seven members of the diatonic scale, making a total of twelve. This is the **chromatic scale**, represented by the complete set of white and black keys on a keyboard.

The earliest European keyboards had only the seven white keys in each octave, since all music used only the seven-note diatonic scale, as shown above. The fact that the black keys occupy a secondary position physically on today's keyboards—they are thinner, and set back—reminds us that these pitches were originally regarded as secondary insertions within the diatonic scale. Black keys were introduced for the extra pitches.

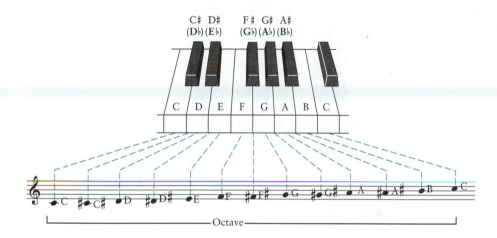

These extra pitches caused a problem for musical notation. The pitches of the diatonic scale are indicated on the lines and spaces of the staff; there are no positions in between, so symbols such as those shown to the right were introduced. B♭ stands for B **flat**, the pitch inserted between A and B; C♯ stands for C **sharp**, the pitch between C and D, and so on.

Intervals (II): Half Steps and Whole Steps

As previously noted, the difference, or distance, between any two pitches is called the interval between them. Look at the chromatic scale in the diagram above, where the C-to-C octave interval is marked with a bracket. Besides the octave, eleven other kinds of interval exist between C and the other notes of the scale.

For our present purposes, only two additional interval types need be specified:

❧ The smallest interval is the **half step**, or semitone, which is the distance between any two successive notes of the chromatic scale. ("Step" is a name for small intervals.) On a keyboard, a half step is the interval between the closest adjacent notes. The distance from E to F is a half step; so is the distance from F to F sharp (F♯), G to A flat (A♭) and so on.

As the smallest interval in regular use, the half-step is also the smallest that most people can "hear" easily and identify. Many tunes, such as "The Battle Hymn of the Republic," end with two half-steps, one half-step going down and then the same one going up again ("His truth is *march-ing on*").

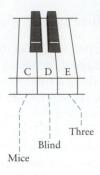

¶   The **whole step,** or whole tone, is equivalent to two half steps: D to E, E to
F♯, F♯ to G♯, and so on. "Three Blind Mice" starts with two whole steps, going
down.

The chromatic scale consists exclusively of half steps. Therefore, this scale
can be described as "symmetrical," in the sense that one can start on any of its
pitches and sing up or down the scale by half steps with exactly the same effect
as if one started anywhere else. The diatonic scale is *not* symmetrical in this
sense. It includes both half steps and whole steps. Between B and C and between E and F, the interval is a half step, but between the other pairs of adjacent notes the interval is twice as big—a whole step.

Music is made out of these scales, and the diatonic and chromatic scales
differ in the intervals between their constituent pitches; hence the importance
of intervals. In the diagram below, the two scales are lined up in order to show
the differences in their interval structure.

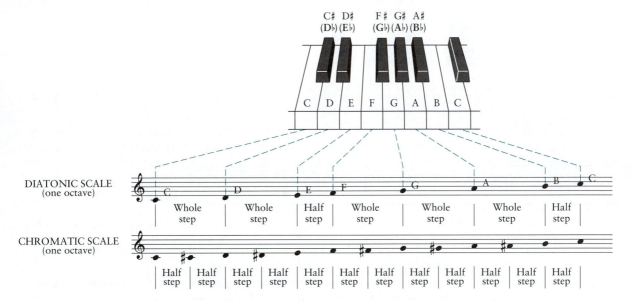

Scales and Instruments

Until fairly recently, Western music used the twelve pitches of the chromatic
scale, duplicated through all the octaves, and in principle no other pitches.
Features of many instruments are designed to produce these particular pitches
exactly: frets on guitars, carefully measured holes in flutes, and the tuned sets
of strings of harps and pianos.

Other instruments, such as the violin and the slide trombone, have a more
continuous range of pitches available to them (as does a police siren or the
human voice). In mastering these instruments, one of the first tasks is learning
to pick out exactly the right pitches. This is called *playing in tune*; singing in
tune is a matter of constant concern for vocalists, too.

It is true that many instrumentalists and all singers regularly perform certain notes slightly out of tune for important and legitimate artistic effects.
"Blue" notes in jazz are an example. However, these "off" pitches are only
small, temporary deviations from the main pitches of the scale—the same
twelve pitches that, on instruments such as the piano, are absolutely fixed.

INTERLUDE A: **Musical Notation**

It is *not* necessary to read music to understand it or love it, obviously, and it is not necessary to read music in order to learn from this book. It will help, however, if you learn to follow music from music examples in an approximate way. The following brief survey of musical notation can be used for study or reference.

As we have seen in our discussion of musical elements, *time* and *pitch* can be specified (and therefore notated) much more exactly than *dynamics* or *tone color.* Think of pitch and time as the coordinates of a graph on which music is going to be plotted. The resulting pitch/time grid is quite close to actual musical notation:

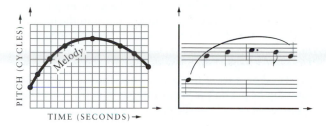

Notes and Rests

The longest note in common use is the *whole note:* ○
A half note (♩) lasts for half the time of a whole note, a quarter note (♩) lasts for a quarter of the time, an eighth note (♪) for an eighth, a sixteenth (♬) for a sixteenth, and so on.

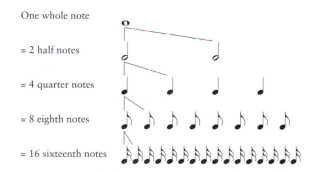

One whole note
= 2 half notes
= 4 quarter notes
= 8 eighth notes
= 16 sixteenth notes

When the shorter notes come in groups, they can also be notated as shown below. The "flags"—they look more like pennants—at the sides of the note "stems" have been "starched" up into horizontal "beams," for easier reading:

Rests To make rhythms, composers use not only sounds but also short silences called *rests* (because the players rest—or at least catch their breath). The diagram below shows the relation between rests, which are equivalent in duration to their corresponding notes. (Compare the whole- and half-note rests: a slug beneath or atop one of the lines of the staff.)

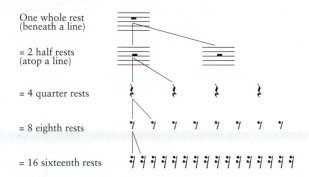

One whole rest (beneath a line)
= 2 half rests (atop a line)
= 4 quarter rests
= 8 eighth rests
= 16 sixteenth rests

The shorter rests have their own sort of flags. As with notes, more flags can be added to rests, with each flag cutting the time value in half. Thus, three flags on a rest (𝄽) make it a thirty-second rest.

Rhythmic Notation

Beyond the notation of basic notes and rests, a number of other conventions are necessary to indicate the combining of notes and rests into actual rhythms.

Dotted Notes and Dotted Rhythms A dot placed after a note or rest lengthens its duration by 50 percent. Thus a dotted half note lasts as long as a half note plus a quarter note: ♩. = ♩ + ♩ And a dotted quarter-note rest equals an eighth plus a quarter: 𝄽. = 𝄽 + 𝄾 Even simple tunes, such as "America," make use of the dot convention.

A dotted rhythm is one consisting of dotted (long) notes alternating with short ones:

Ties Two notes of the same pitch can be connected by means of a curved line called a *tie.* This means they are played continuously, as though they were one note of the combined duration. Any number of notes of the same pitch can be tied together, so that this notational device can serve to indicate a pitch of very long duration.

Ties

The same sort of curved line is also used to connect notes that are *not* of the same pitch. In this case it means that they are to be played smoothly (*legato*). These curved lines are called *slurs*.

Slurs: legato

To indicate that notes are to be played in a detached fashion (*staccato*), dots are placed above or below them.

Staccato dots

Triplets Three notes bracketed together and marked with a 3 (♩ ♩ ♩) are called a *triplet*. This indicates that the three notes take exactly the same time that would normally be taken by two. A quarter-note triplet has the same duration as two ordinary quarters notes: ♩ ♩ ♩ = ♩ ♩.

The convention is occasionally extended to groups of five notes, seven notes, etc. For an example, see page 241.

Meter: Measures and Bar Lines A *measure* (or *bar*) is the basic time unit chosen for a piece of music, corresponding to the meter of the piece (see page 13). Measures are marked in musical notation by vertical *bar lines*. Each measure covers the same time span. In the following example, the time span covered by each measure is one whole note, equivalent to two half notes (measure 1), or four quarter notes (measure 2), or eight eighth notes (measures 3, 4).

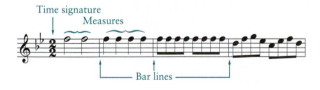

Time signature
Measures
Bar lines

Time Signatures In the example above, the meter is indicated by means of a *time signature*. Time signatures are printed on the staffs at the beginning of all pieces of music; they are not repeated on later staffs.

In spite of appearances, time signatures are not fractions. The top digit shows *how many beats* are in each measure and the bottom digit shows *what kind of note* represents a beat. If the bottom digit is 2, the beat is represented by a half note: if 4, by a quarter note, and so on.

In our example, the 2 at the top indicates there are two beats in each measure (duple meter), and the 2 at the bottom indicates that the beats are half-note beats. This time signature is often indicated by the sign ¢.

Pitch Notation

The letter names A B C D E F G are assigned to the original seven pitches of the diatonic scale. Then the letters are used over and over again for pitches in the duplicating octaves. Octaves are distinguished by numbers (c^1, c^2) or prime marks (A′, A″); so-called "middle C" (c^1) is the comfortable note that virtually any man, woman, or child can sing and that can be played by the great majority of instruments. On a keyboard, middle C sits in the middle, right under the maker's name—Casio, Yamaha, Steinway.

The Staff: Ledger Lines For the notation of pitch, notes are placed on a set of five parallel lines called a *staff*. The notes can be put on the lines of the staff, in the spaces between them, or right at the top or bottom of the staff:

Notice that above and below the regular five lines of the staff, short extra lines can be added to accommodate a few higher and lower notes. These are called *ledger lines*.

Clefs Nothing has been said so far about which pitch each position on the staff represents. To clue us in to precise pitches, signs called *clefs* (French for "key" or "clue") are placed at the beginning of each staff. Clefs calibrate the staff: that is, they connect one of the five lines of the staff to a specific pitch.

Thus in the treble clef or G clef (𝄞), the spiral in the middle of the antique capital G curves around line 2, counting up from the bottom of the staff. Line 2, then, is the line for the pitch G—the first G above middle C. In the bass clef or F clef (𝄢), the two dots straddle the fourth line up. The pitch F goes on this line—the first F below middle C.

Adjacent lines and spaces on the staff have adjacent letter names, so we can place all the other pitches on the staff in relation to the fixed points marked by the clefs:

G

F

D E F G A B C D E F G   F G A B C D E F G A B

There are other clefs, but these two are the most common. Used in conjunction, they accommodate the maximum span of pitches without overlapping. The treble and bass clef staffs fit together as shown in Figure 1 below.

The notation of six A's, covering five octaves, requires two staffs and seven ledger lines; see Figure 2.

Sharps and Flats; Naturals The pitches produced by the black keys on the piano are not given letter names of their own. (This is a consequence of the way they arose in history; see page 19.) Nor do they get their own individual lines or spaces on the staffs. The pitch in between A and B is called A sharp (or A♯, using the conventional sign for a sharp), meaning "higher than A." It can also be called B flat (B♭), meaning "lower than B." In musical notation, the signs ♯ and ♭ are placed on the staff just *before* the note that is to be sharped or flatted.

Which of these two terms is used depends partly on convenience, partly on convention, and partly on theoretical considerations that do not concern us here. In the example below, the third note, A♯, sounds just like the B♭ later in the measure, but for technical reasons the composer (Béla Bartók) notated it differently.

The original pitches of the diatonic scale, played on the white keys of the piano, are called "natural." If it is necessary to cancel a sharp or a flat within a measure and to indicate that the natural note should be played instead, the natural sign is placed before a note (♮♩) or after a letter (A♮) to show this. The following example shows A sharp and G sharp being canceled by natural signs:

Key Signatures In musical notation, it is a convention that a sharp or flat placed before a note will also affect any later appearance of that same note *in the same measure*—but not in the next measure.

Provision is also made for specifying that certain sharps or flats are to be applied throughout an entire piece, in every measure, and in every octave. Such sharps and flats appear on the staffs at the very beginning of the piece, even prior to the time signature, and at the beginning of each staff thereafter. They constitute the *key signature:*

is equivalent to:

Scores

Music for a melody instrument such as a violin or a trumpet is written on one staff; keyboard instruments require two—one staff for the right hand, another staff for the left hand. Music for two or more voices or instruments, choirs, bands, and orchestras is written in scores. In scores, each instrument and voice that has its own independent music gets one staff. Simultaneously sounding notes and measure lines are aligned vertically. In general, high-sounding instruments go on top, the low ones on the bottom.

Shown on page 24 is a page from Mozart's "Jupiter" Symphony, with arrows pointing to the various details of notation that have been explained above.

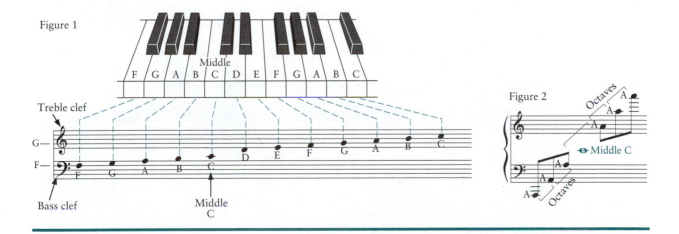

Figure 1

Figure 2

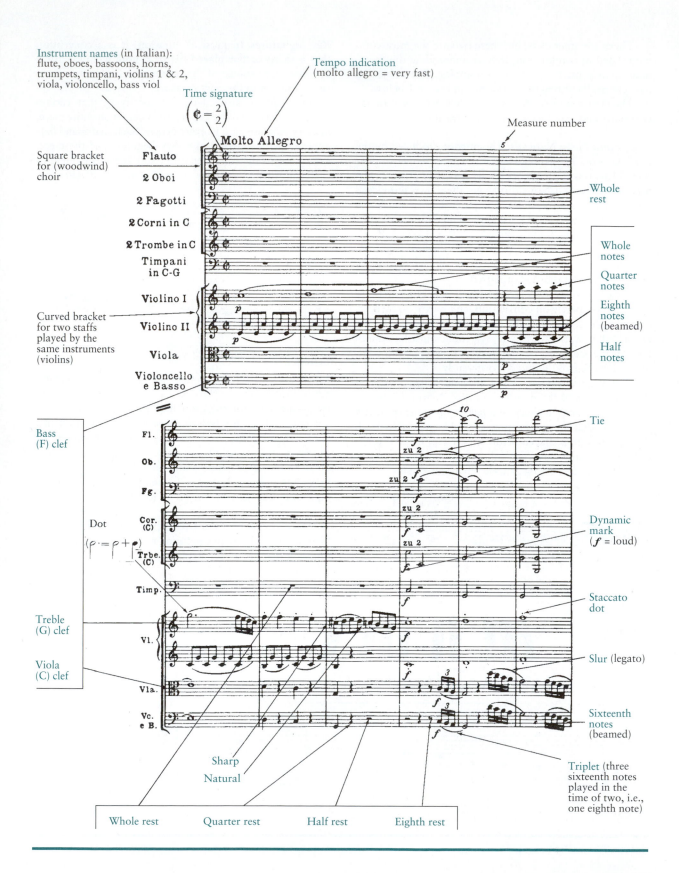

CHAPTER **4**

The Structures of Music

I n this chapter we take up musical concepts that combine the basic elements discussed in Chapters 2 and 3. Listening to an actual piece of music, we do not experience its rhythm, pitch, tone color and dynamics in isolation from one another. Indeed, rhythms, pitches, and the rest are seldom experienced one at a time. Rather, music consists of simple and complex "structures" built from these elements.

1 Melody

Think for a moment, if you can, of pitch and time as the two coordinates of a graph on which music is going to be plotted. A series of single pitches played in a certain rhythm will appear as dots, high or low, on the pitch/time grid, and the dots can be connected by a line (see the marginal diagram). Such a series of pitches is called a **melody**, and indeed musicians commonly speak of "melodic line" (or simply "line") in this connection.

Just as an actual line in a painting or a drawing can possess character —can strike the viewer as forceful, graceful, or tentative—so can a melodic line. A melody in which each note is higher than the last can seem to soar; a low note can feel like a setback; a long series of repeated notes on the same pitch can seem to wait ominously. The listener develops a real interest in how the line of a satisfactory melody is going to come out.

In such a melody, the succession of notes seems to hold together in a meaningful, interesting way—interesting, and also emotional. Of all music's structures, melody is the one that moves people the most, that seems to evoke human sentiment most directly. Familiar melodies "register" simple qualities of feeling instantly and strongly. These qualities vary widely: romantic in "Yesterday," martial in "Dixie," mournful in "St. Louis Blues," extroverted and cheerful in "Happy Birthday to You."

Tunes

The most familiar type of melody is a **tune**—a simple, easily singable, catchy melody such as a folksong or a dance. In this book the word *tune* will be reserved for this use. A tune is a special kind of melody. *Melody* is a term that includes tunes, but also much else.

Always remember that in listening to a piece of music you must hang on to the melodic line. It may disappear momentarily, withdrawn by the composer, in order to make its presence more powerfully felt when it reappears. But reappear it surely will . . .

Aaron Copland, *What to Listen For in Music*

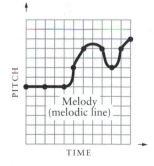

Melody (melodic line)

PITCH

TIME

LISTEN

How "singable" is the tune in the last movement of Mozart's Piano Concerto in G? How many times do you need to hear it before you can sing it back, not necessarily note for note, but so that it is recognizable? It counts as "catchy" if you like singing it. (For the notation for this tune, see page 188).

0:00   The tune starts with an upward passage.

0:06   This is "balanced" by a downward passage with exactly the same rhythm.

0:12   These two short passages are repeated.

0:24   Now Mozart writes an even shorter, fanfare-like passage, contrasting with what we have just heard, which he repeats immediately with some little changes . . .

0:30   . . . then returns to something similar (not identical) to the downward passage.

0:35   There is another repetition, and we feel the tune has definitely come to its end.

For an example of more complex melody, less singable and lacking the obvious repetitions and balances that characterize tunes, turn to Duke Ellington's *Conga Brava*. Like many jazz numbers, this starts with a tune (played by a trombone) that we could analyze in the same way we analyze Mozart. However, other instruments interrupt with quite different melodic fragments, and when a long saxophone solo begins, after 0:58, what we hear is certainly melody, but it is melody of very elaborate kind, not a tune.

"The Star-Spangled Banner," which everyone knows, can be used to illustrate the general characteristics of tunes. See the box on page 27.

Motives and Themes

Tunes are relatively short; longer pieces may have tunes embedded in them, but they also contain other musical material. Two terms are frequently encountered in connection with melody in longer pieces of music.

The first is **motive** (sometimes seen in its French form, *motif*). A motive is a distinctive fragment of melody, distinctive enough so that it will be easily recognized when it returns again and again within a long composition. Motives are shorter than tunes, shorter even than phrases of tunes; they can be as short as two notes. Probably the most famous motive in all music is the four-note *da da da DA* motive in Beethoven's Fifth Symphony.

da da da DA

The second term, **theme**, is the most general term for the basic subject matter of longer pieces of music. *Theme* is another name for "topic": the themes or topics of a political speech are the main points that the politician announces, repeats, develops, and hammers home. The composer of a symphony or a fugue treats musical themes in much the same way.

Since the term theme refers to the *function*, not the *nature*, of musical material, in principle almost anything can serve as a theme. A melody can perform this function, or a phrase, a motive, even a distinctive tone color. It depends on the kind of music. The theme of the last movement of Mozart's Concerto in G is the entire tune we have just heard. The theme of Smetana's Overture to *The Bartered Bride* is a phrase, consisting of a short motive plus three expansions of it. Many of the themes of Richard Wagner's operas are closely identified with a particular tone color and instrument (the trombone, in the excerpt discussed on page 265).

ta ki TAK

ta ki ta ki TAK

ta ki ta ki ta ki TAK

ta ki . . .   TAK

2   Harmony

A single melodic "line" in time is enough to qualify as music: sometimes, indeed, as great music. The man singing in his shower and the woman singing to her baby are producing melody, and that is all, to everyone's full satisfaction.

Characteristics of Tunes

The best way to grasp the characteristics of tunes is not by listening but by *singing* one that you know, either out loud or "in your head."

❧ *Division into Phrases* Tunes fall naturally into smaller sections, called **phrases.** This is, in fact, true of all melodies, but with tunes the division into phrases is particularly clear and sharp.

In tunes with words (that is, songs), the musical phrases typically coincide with the poetic lines. Most lines in a song lyric end with a rhyming word and a punctuation mark. These features clarify the musical phrase divisions:

And the rockets' red *glare* [comma]
The bombs bursting in *air*

Singing a song, one has to breathe—and one tends to breathe at the end of phrases. You may not need to breathe after phrase 1 of our national anthem, but you had better not wait any longer than phrase 2:

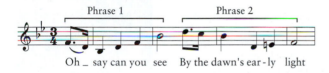

❧ *Balance between Phrases* In many tunes, all the phrases are 2, 4, or 8 measures long. (The *measure* or bar is the basic time unit of music; see page 13). Blues tunes, for example, usually consist of three four-measure phrases; hence the term *twelve-bar blues.*

Almost all the phrases of "The Star-Spangled Banner" are two measures long. But one phrase broadens out to four measures, with a fine effect: "Oh say, does that star-spangled banner yet wave." One doesn't want to breathe in the middle of this long phrase.

Other phrase lengths—three measures, five, and others—can certainly occur in a tune and make for welcome contrast. For a good tune, the main requirement is that we sense a balance between the phrases, in terms of phrase lengths and in other terms, too, so that taken together the phrases add up to a well-proportioned whole.

❧ *Parallelism and Contrast* Balance between phrases can be strenghtened by means of *parallelism.* For example, phrases can be exactly parallel except for the words ("Oh, say can you see," "Whose broad stripes and bright stars"). Others have the same rhythm but different pitches ("Oh say can you see," "By the dawn's early light").

Sometimes phrases have the same general *pattern of pitches,* but one phrase is slightly higher or lower than the other ("And the rockets' red glare," "The bombs bursting in air"). **Sequence** is the technical term for this device. Such duplication of a phrase at two or more different pitch levels occurs frequently in music, and is a hallmark of certain musical styles.

Composers also take care to make certain phrases *contrast* with their neighbors—one phrase short, another long, or one phrase low, another high (perhaps even *too* high, at "O'er the land of the *free*"). A tune with some parallel and some contrasting phrases will seem to have logic, or coherence, and yet will avoid monotony.

❧ *Climax and Cadence* A good tune has *form.* It has a clear, purposeful beginning, a feeling of action in the middle, and a firm sense of winding down and concluding at the end.

Most tunes have a distinct high point, or *climax,* which their earlier portions seem to be heading toward. A melodic climax is always an emotional climax; feelings rise as voices soar. The climax of our national anthem highlights what was felt to be the one crucial word in it—"free."

Then the later part of the tune relaxes from this climax, until it reaches a solid stopping place at the end. Emotionally, this is a point of relaxation and satisfaction. In a less definite way, the music also stops—or, if it does not fully stop, at least seems to pause—at earlier points in the tune. The term for these stopping or pausing places is **cadence.**

Composers can write cadences with all possible shades of finality. "And the home of the brave" is a very final-sounding cadence; "That our flag was still there" has an interim feeling. The art of making cadences is one of the most subtle and basic processes in musical composition.

The same was true of the early Christian Church, whose music, Gregorian chant, consisted of over two thousand subtly differentiated melodies, sung without instruments or any kind of "harmonizing."

Today, however—and this is the outcome of a long and complicated historical development—it seems very natural to us to hear melodies together with other sounds, which we call "accompaniments." A folk singer singing and playing a guitar is performing a song and its accompaniment. As we sing hymn tunes in church, the organist plays the accompaniment.

A highly imaginative picture of Francis Scott Key composing "The Star-Spangled Banner." In fact, Key wrote only the words; later, his new poem—with its fine rousing climax on "land of the *free*"—was adapted to an older melody.

Folksinger Jean Ritchie singing and playing the Appalachian dulcimer— melody and harmony

The folk singer uses a number of standard groupings of simultaneous pitches, or **chords,** that practice has shown are sure to work well in combination. Imaginative players will also discover non-standard chords and unexpected successions of chords in order to enrich their accompaniments. The song is said to be **harmonized;** the continuous matrix of changing chords provides a sort of constantly shifting sound-background for the song.

Any melody can be harmonized in many different ways using different chords, and the overall effect of the music depends to a great extent on the nature of these chords, or the **harmony** in general. We can instinctively sense the difference in harmony between Mozart and Philip Glass or between New Orleans jazz and rock. However, the differences are almost impossible to characterize except in technical language, and we shall not make the attempt in this book.

Consonance and Dissonance

A pair of terms used in discussions of harmony is **consonance** and **dissonance,** meaning (roughly speaking) chords that sound at rest and those that sound tense, respectively. *Discord* is another term for dissonance. These qualities depend on the kind of intervals (see pages 17–20) that are sounding simultaneously to make up these chords. Octaves are the most consonant of intervals, whereas half steps are among the most dissonant.

In everyday language, "discord" implies something unpleasant; discordant human relationships are to be avoided. But music does not avoid dissonance in its technical meaning, for a little discord supplies the subtle tensions that are essential to make music flow along. A dissonant chord leaves the listener with a feeling of expectation; it requires a consonant chord following it to complete the gesture, and to make the music come to a point of stability. The dissonance is said to be **resolved.** Without dissonance, music would be like food without salt or spices.

Medicine, to produce health, must know disease; music, to produce harmony, must know discord.

Plutarch, A.D. c. 46–120

Cadences—the ends of pieces of music—are almost always helped by the use of dissonance. Movement from tension (dissonance) to rest (consonance) contributes centrally to a sense of finality and satisfaction.

3 Texture

<u>Texture</u> is the term used to refer to the blend of the various sounds and melodic lines occurring simultaneously in music. The word is adopted from textiles, where it refers to the weave of the various threads—loose or tight, even or mixed. A cloth such as tweed, for instance, leaves the different threads clearly visible. In fine silk or percale, the weave is so tight and smooth that the constituent threads are almost impossible to detect.

Thinking again of the pitch/time graph on page 25, we can see that it is possible to plot more than one pitch for every time slot. Melody exists in the "horizontal" dimension, texture in the "vertical" dimension. For the moment, we leave the lower dots (below the melody) unconnected.

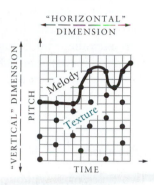

Monophony

This is the term for the simplest texture, a single unaccompanied melody: Gregorian chant, singing in the shower, "Row, Row, Row Your Boat."

Row, row, row your boat gent-ly down the stream _

Simple as this texture is, some very beautiful and sophisticated **monophonic** music has been composed, just as artists have done wonderful things with line drawings: see page 308.

Homophony

When there is only one melody of real interest and it is combined with other sounds, the texture is called **homophonic**. A harmonized melody is an example of homophonic texture: for example, one person singing the tune of "Row, Row, Row Your Boat" while playing chords on a guitar:

Row,   row,   row your boat gent-ly down the stream

We might indicate a chord on the pitch/time graph by a vertical box enclosing the dots. The sum of these boxes represents the harmony. Homophony can be thought of as a tight, smooth texture, like silk among the textiles.

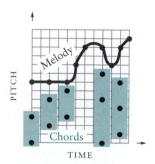

Polyphony

When two or more melodies are played or sung simultaneously, the texture is described as **polyphonic**. In polyphony, the melodies are felt to be independent and of approximately equal interest. The whole is more than the sum of the parts, however: the way the melodies play off against one another makes for the possibility of greater richness and interest than if they were played singly. In the textile analogy, polyphony would be compared to a rough texture where the strands are all visible, such as tweed.

It is also important to recognize that polyphonic music automatically has harmony. For at every moment in time, on every beat, the multiple horizontal melodies create vertical chords; those chords make harmony.

Another term frequently applied to polyphonic texture is *contrapuntal,* which comes from the word **counterpoint,** the technique of writing two or more melodies that fit together. Strictly speaking, polyphony refers to the texture and counterpoint refers to the technique of producing that texture—one *studies* counterpoint to *produce* polyphony—but in practice the two terms are used interchangeably.

Imitation

Two types of polyphony, or counterpoint, should be distinguished: *imitative polyphony* and *non-imitative polyphony.* **Imitative polyphony** results when the various lines sounding together use the same or fairly similar melodies, with one coming in shortly after another. The simplest example of imitative polyphony is a round, such as "Row, Row, Row Your Boat" or "Frère Jacques"; the richest kind is a fugue (see Chapter 9).

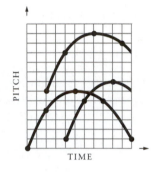

When you and your friends (or classmates) sing a round, with the same tune coming at staggered time intervals, the result is imitative polyphony:

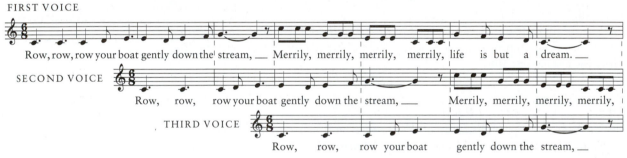

Non-imitative polyphony occurs when the melodies are essentially different from one another. An example that many will know is the typical texture of a New Orleans jazz band, with the trumpet playing the main tune flanked top and bottom by the clarinet and the trombone playing exhilarating melodies of their own. Here is a made-up example of non-imitative counterpoint, with a new melody added to the tune of "Row, Row, Row Your Boat":

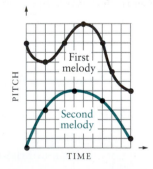

This imaginative portrayal of imitative counterpoint is like our first pitch/time graph on page 30, at least in principle. Paul Klee (1879–1940) entitled this painting "Fugue in Red"; a fugue is the supreme example of imitative texture, as we shall see.

LISTEN

A short section from the Overture to *The Bartered Bride* provides clear examples of several textures. Start track 4 (from three minutes after the start of band 1):

2:59   The "outburst" on this occasion has no accompaniment; this is **monophony**, a single unaccompanied melody (played, however, by numerous instruments).

3:12   The theme, many times repeated, and the rustling sounds come thick and fast, running into one another and overlapping. This is **imitative polyphony.**

3:33   When the polka arrives, we have a loud tune with accompaniment—**homophony.**

For an example of **non-imitative polyphony,** play the third movement of Johann Sebastian Bach's Cantata No. 4, "Christ lag in Todesbanden." A simple tune is sung, one phrase at a time, by a tenor, while faster, different music is played by violins.

Or play the climactic section in the last movement of Berlioz's *Fantastic* Symphony (after eight minutes). Berlioz combines a slow-moving theme in the brass with a fast-moving theme in the rest of the orchestra, both very loud. (You can hear the faster theme in imitative polyphony, without the slower one, on CD track 5.)

4   Tonality and Modality

Tonality and modality are aspects of harmony, and as such they could logically have been taken up at an earlier point in this chapter. We have left them for last because more than the other basic structures of music, these require careful explanation.

Tonality

We start with a basic fact about melodies and tunes: melodies nearly always give a sense of focusing around a single "home" pitch that feels more important than do all the other members of the scale. Often this is *do* in the *do re mi fa so la ti do* scale. This pitch feels fundamental, and on it the melody seems to come to rest most naturally. The other notes in the melody all sound close or remote, dissonant or consonant, in reference to the fundamental note, and some of them may actually seem to "lean" or "lead" toward it.

This homing instinct that we sense in melodies can be referred to in the most general terms as the feeling of **tonality**. The music in question is described as **tonal**. The "home" pitch *(do)* is called the *tonic pitch*, or simply the **tonic.**

The easy way to identify the tonic is to sing the whole melody through, because the last note is almost invariably *it*. Thus "The Star-Spangled Banner" ends on its tonic, *do*, and it also includes the tonic in two different octaves as its first two accented notes ("Oh, *say* can you *see*"). An entire piece of music, as well as just a short melody, can give this feeling of focusing on a home pitch and wanting to end there.

The difficulty of describing the facts of tonality is not the difficulty of describing red to the color-blind. It is the difficulty of describing red to anybody; you can only point to red things and hope that other people see them as you do. It is even more like trying to describe the taste of a peach. . . .

Sir Donald Tovey, pianist, conductor, and educator, 1935

Modality: Major and Minor

Turn back to page 18 and the diagram of the diatonic scale, the basic scale of Western music. We have been speaking of melodies in the *do re mi fa so la ti do* segment of this scale with *do* as their tonic. But there is another important class of melodies built around *la* as tonic. The term for these different ways of centering or organizing the diatonic scale is **modality;** the different "home" pitches are said to determine different **modes** of music.

We will get to the actual listening experience of the modes in a moment. Music with the *do* orientation is in the **major mode.** Music with the *la* orientation is in the **minor mode.**

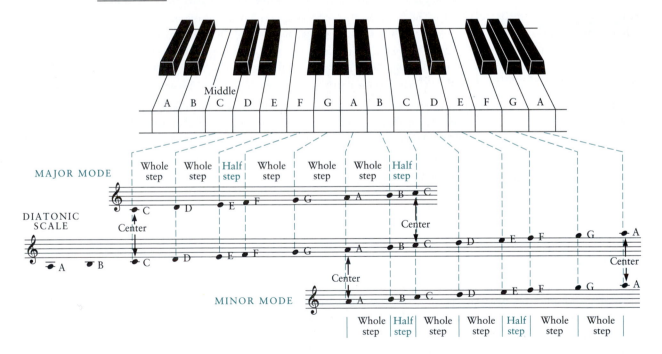

Keys

Mode and key are concepts that are often confused. Let us see if we can clarify them.

We have just seen how the two modes, the major with its "tonic" or home note on C and the minor on A, are derived from the diatonic scale (and this was the way it happened in history). At the piano, if you try to play a scale starting with any other note of the diatonic scale—D, E, F, or B—you will find that in each case, if you stick to the white notes, the arrangement of invervals is different from that of either the major or the minor mode. The scales you play will sound wrong.

If you use all the twelve notes of the *chromatic* scale, however—the black notes as well as the white—you can construct both the major and the minor modes starting from any note at all. Whichever note you choose as tonic, starting from there you can pick out the correct sequence of half steps and whole steps. (This is because the chromatic scale is "symmetrical"—it includes all possible half steps, and therefore all possible whole steps.) If C is the starting point, the major mode comes out all on the white notes; if the same mode is started from D, two black notes are required; and so on.

Thanks to the chromatic scale, then, many positions are possible for the major and minor modes. These different positions are called **keys**. If the major mode is positioned on C, the music is said to be in the key of C major, or just "in C"; positioned on D, the key is D major. Likewise we have the keys of C minor, D minor, and—since there are twelve pitches in the chromatic scale—a grand total of twenty-four different major and minor keys.

This already hints at an important resource available to composers: the possibility of changing (or moving) from one key to another. Changing keys in the course of a composition is called **modulation.**

Hearing the Major and Minor Modes

On paper, it is easiest to show the difference between major and minor if we compare a major and minor key that has the same tonic: C major and C minor. We therefore modulate from the A-minor scale shown in the previous diagram to C minor:

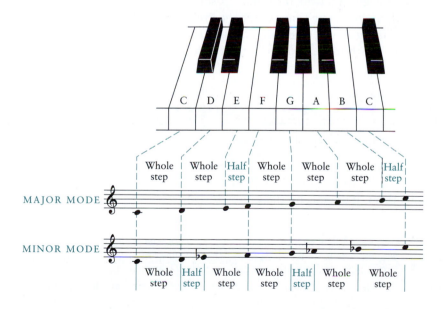

The difference between the modes is easy enough to see: three of the scale degrees are lower in the minor (hence the term "minor"), and as a result, the arrangement of intervals is not the same as you sing up the scale.

Actually *hearing* the difference is another matter; this comes easily to some listeners, less easily to others. As a result of the three lower scale degrees, music in the minor mode tends to sound more subdued, more clouded than

Music is the latest of the arts to have developed; her beginnings were the simple moods of joy and sorrow (major and minor). . . . We have learned to express the more delicate nuances of feeling by penetrating more deeply into the mysteries of harmony.

Composer Robert Schumann, 1833

Is it fair to represent the major and minor modes by comedy and tragedy masks? Yes, but only in a very general sense—there are many exceptions.

music in the major. It is often said that major sounds cheerful and minor sounds sad, and this is true enough in a general way; but there are many exceptions, and in any case people can have different ideas about what constitutes "sadness" and "cheerfulness" in music.

To learn to distinguish the major and minor modes requires comparative listening. Listen especially for the third scale degree up from the tonic. "Joshua Fit the Battle of Jericho," "Summertime," and "We Three Kings of Orient Are" are all in the minor mode. Singing them through, we come to recognize the characteristic minor-mode sound involving the third scale degree at the final cadence.

Compare this with the third note up from the tonic at the end of major-mode songs such as "Happy Birthday to You," "Row, Row, Row Your Boat," "The Star-Spangled Banner," and many others. It sounds brighter, more positive.

And here is the whole of "Row, Row, Row Your Boat" one more time—but this time in an altered version, with the mode switched from major to minor. Can you sing it?

Hearing Keys and Modulation

The major and minor modes can be said to differ from one another "intrinsically," for in each mode the pitches form their own special set of intervals and interval relationships. As we have seen, C major and C minor, while sharing the same central or tonic note, each has its own arrangement of half- and whole-step intervals. Different keys, however, merely entail the same set of intervals moved to a new position within the pitch continuum. This is a significant difference, but not an "intrinsic" one. First base is different from second base, but only because the same sort of bag, intrinsically, has been put in a significant new place.

As for actually *hearing* keys—that is, recognizing the different keys and the modulations between them—for some listeners this presents an even greater problem than hearing modality, though to others it comes more easily. The latter are the fortunate ones born with perfect pitch, the innate faculty of identifying pitches the way most people can identify colors. However, this is not the great boon of nature it is sometimes believed to be. The important thing is not to be able to identify keys in themselves, but rather to be able to tell when keys change. For modulating or changing the key of music changes its mood or the way it feels; generations of composers have used this resource for some of their most powerful effects, as we shall see. And we can hear *changes* of tonality in large compositions, that is, changes of the tonic or "home" note, whether or not we were born with perfect pitch.

Indeed, we hear such changes instinctively in shorter compositions. If you know "The Twelve Days of Christmas," you will remember the modulation at the words "Five gold rings." (Try singing this cumulative carol all the way through leaving out the fifth gift with its modulation—the result is utter monotony). In another Christmas carol, "Deck the Halls," modulation causes an agreeable little lift at the end of the third line, "Don we now our gay apparel, *Fa-la la, la-la la, la la la.*"

Modulation is used for its emotional effect at tied baseball and basketball games, when the organist plays a little musical figure over and over, higher and higher, louder and louder. This is a brute-force modulation, and it is supposed to get you *excited*.

LISTEN

To hear the difference between the **major** and **minor modes**, listen to excerpts from the second movement of Beethoven's Fifth Symphony:

0:00   This theme is in the **major mode**. After half a minute switch to the next track:

6:42   The same theme is played, now with the mode changed to **minor.** The orchestration also changes.

Another good example of major/minor difference—at least, good for those who know the round "Frère Jacques"—is provided by Gustav Mahler's First Symphony. Remind yourself of the round by singing it: "Frère Jacques, Frère Jacques, Dormez vous, Dormez vous. . . ." Then play the symphony's second movement:

0:00   Mahler has written a strange, slow **minor-mode** version of the round. Note the difference in the third scale-degree on the syllables *"Jacques* and *"Dormez."*

For changes of **key (modulation)**, play track 4 of *The Bartered Bride* Overture:

3:11   After the opening outburst, the short theme modulates through six keys in about twenty seconds.

INTERLUDE B: **Musical Instruments**

Different voices and different instruments produce different tone colors, or timbres. Over the course of history and over the entire world, an enormous number of devices have been invented for making music, and the range of tone colors they can produce is almost endless.

This interlude will discuss and illustrate the instruments of Western music that make up the orchestra, and a few others.

Instruments of the Orchestra

Musical instruments can be categorized into four groups: *stringed instruments* or *strings, woodwinds, brass,* and *percussion.* Musical sound, as we know, is caused by rapid vibrations. Each of the four groups of instruments produces sound vibrations in its own distinct way.

Stringed Instruments These are instruments that have their sound produced by taut strings. The strings are always attached to a "sound box," a hollow box containing a body of air that resonates (that is, vibrates along with the strings) to amplify the string sound.

The strings themselves can be played with a bow, as with the violin and other orchestral strings; the *bow* is strung tightly with horsehair, which is coated with rosin so that the bow grips the strings. Or else the strings can be plucked or strummed, as on the guitar or the banjo, using the fingers or a small pick.

Strings can be plucked on bowed instruments, too, for special effects. This is called **pizzicato.**

The Violin and Its Family The **violin** is often called the most beautiful instrument used in Western music. Also one of the most versatile of instruments, its large range covers alto and soprano registers and many much higher pitches. As a solo instrument, it can play incisively or delicately, and it excels in both brilliant and songlike music. Violinists also play chords by bowing two or more of the four strings at once, or nearly so.

The violin is an excellent ensemble instrument; and it blends especially well with other violins. An orchestra violin section, made up of ten or more instruments playing together, can produce a strong, yet sensitive, flexible tone. Hence the orchestra has traditionally relied on strings as a solid foundation for its composite sound.

Like most other instruments, violins come in *families,* that is, in several sizes with different pitch ranges. Very young children learn the violin on miniature instruments that fit their small hands. Standard-sized members of the violin family are basic to the orchestra.

⅋ The *viola* is the tenor-range instrument, larger than a violin by several inches. It has a throaty quality in its lowest range, from middle C down an octave, yet it fits especially smoothly into accompaniment textures. The viola's highest register is powerful and intense.

Violin

⅋ The **cello,** short for *violoncello,* is the bass of the violin family. This large instrument is played between the legs. Unlike the viola, the cello has a rich, gorgeous sound in its low register. It is a favorite solo instrument, as well as an indispensable member of the orchestra.

Viola and cello

Cello

Harp

Bass Viol Also called **string bass, double bass,** or just **bass,** this deep instrument is used to back up the violin family in the orchestra. (However, in various details of construction the bass viol differs from members of the violin family; the bass viol actually belongs to another, older stringed instrument family, the *viols.*)

Played with a bow, the bass viol provides a splendid deep support for orchestral sound. The bass viol is often (in jazz, nearly always) plucked to give an especially vibrant kind of accent and to emphasize the meter.

Harp Harps are plucked stringed instruments with one string for each pitch available. The modern orchestral harp is a large instrument with forty-seven strings covering a range of six and a half octaves. A pedal mechanism allows the playing of chromatic (black-key) as well as diatonic (white-key) pitches.

In most orchestral music, the swishing, watery quality of the harp is treated as a striking occasional effect rather than as a regular thing.

Woodwind Instruments As the name indicates, woodwind instruments were formerly made of wood and some still are; but today certain woodwinds are made of metal. Sound in these instruments is created by setting up vibrations in the column of air in a tube.

Of the main woodwind instruments, *flutes, clarinets,* and *oboes* have approximately the same range; all three are used in the orchestra because each has a quite distinct tone quality, and composers can obtain a variety of effects from them. It is not hard to learn to recognize and appreciate the different sounds of these woodwinds.

The Flute and Its Family The **flute** is a long cylinder, held horizontally; the player sets the air vibrating by blowing through a side hole. The flute is the most agile of the woodwind instruments and also the gentlest. It nonetheless stands out clearly in the orchestra when played in its high register.

ᛉ The **piccolo,** the small, highest member of the flute family, adds special sparkle to band and orchestral music.

ᛉ The **alto flute** and **bass flute**—larger flutes—are less frequently employed.

ᛉ The **recorder,** a different variety of flute, is blown not at the side of the tube but through a mouthpiece at the end. Used in older orchestral music, the recorder was superseded by the horizontal, or "transverse," flute because the latter was more powerful and flexible.

Recorders have made a spectacular comeback for modern performances of old music using reconstructed

Flute

Clarinet

period instruments. The instrument is also popular (in various family sizes) among musical amateurs today. It is easy to learn and fun to play.

Clarinet   The **clarinet** is a slightly conical tube made, usually, of ebony. The air column is not made to vibrate directly by blowing into the tube, as with the flute. The way the player gets sound is by blowing on a reed—a small piece of cane fixed at one end—in much the same way as we can blow on a blade of grass held taut between the fingers. The vibrating reed activates the vibration of the air in the clarinet itself.

Compared to the flute, clarinet sound is richer and more flexible, more like the human voice. The clarinet is capable of warm, mellow tones and quite strident, shrill ones; it has an especially intriguing quality in its low register, below middle C.

The small **E-flat clarinet** and the large **bass clarinet** are family members with a place in the modern orchestra. The tube of the bass clarinet is so long that it has to be bent back, like a thin black saxophone.

Oboe   The **oboe** also uses a reed, like the clarinet, but it is a double reed—two reeds lashed together so that the air must be forced between them. This kind of reed gives the oboe its clearly focused, crisply clean, and sometimes plaintive sound.

The **English horn** is a larger, lower oboe, descending into the viola range. (Scores often give the French equivalent, *cor anglais;* in either language, the name is wildly deceptive, since the instrument is not a horn but an oboe, and it has nothing to do with England.)

Bassoon   The **bassoon** is a low (cello-range) instrument with a double reed and other characteristics similar to the oboe's. It looks somewhat bizarre: the long tube is bent double, and the reed has to be linked to the instrument by a long, narrow pipe. Of all the double-reed woodwinds, the bassoon is the most varied in expression, ranging from the mournful to the comical.

The **contrabassoon** or **double bassoon** is a very large member of the bassoon family, in the bass viol range.

Saxophone   The saxophone is the outstanding case in the history of music of the successful invention of a new instrument family. Its inventor, the Belgian instrument maker Adolphe Sax, also developed saxhorns and other instruments. First used around 1840 in military bands, the saxophone (or "sax") is sometimes included in the modern orchestra, but it really came into its own in jazz.

Oboe

Alto Saxophone

Bassoon (with a clarinet in the background)

Saxophones are close to clarinets in the way they produce sound. Both use single reeds. Since the saxophone tube is wider and made of brass, its tone is even mellower than that of the clarinet, yet at the same time more forceful. The long saxophone tube has a characteristic bent shape and a flaring "bell," as its opening is called.

Most common are the **alto saxophone** and the **tenor saxophone**. But the big family also includes *bass, baritone, soprano,* and even *contrabass* (very low) and *sopranino* (very high) members.

Brass Instruments The brass instruments are the loudest of all the wind instruments because of the unusual way their sound is produced. The player blows into a small cup-shaped mouthpiece of metal, and this makes the player's lips vibrate. The lip vibration activates vibration of the air in the brass tube.

All brass instruments have long tubes, and almost always these are coiled in one way or another—something that is easy to do with the soft metal they are made from.

Trumpet The **trumpet,** highest of the main brass instruments, has a bright, strong, piercing tone that provides the ultimate excitement in band and orchestral music alike. Pitch is controlled by three pistons or valves that connect auxiliary tubes with the main tube or disconnect them, so as to lengthen or shorten the vibrating air column.

French Horn The **French horn** has a lower, mellower, "thicker" tone than the trumpet. It is capable of mysterious, romantic sounds when played softly; played loudly, it can sound like a trombone. Chords played by several French horns in harmony have a rich, sumptuous tone.

Trombone The **tenor trombone** and the **bass trombone** are also pitched lower than the trumpet. The pitch is controlled by a sliding mechanism (thus the term "slide trombone"), rather than a valve or piston, as in the trumpet and French horn.

   Less bright and martial in tone than the trumpet, the trombone can produce a surprising variety of sounds, ranging from an almost vocal quality in its high register to a hard, powerful blare in the low register.

Tuba The **bass tuba** is typically used as a foundation for the trombone group in an orchestra. It is less flexible than other brass instruments. And like most other deep bass instruments, it is not favored for solo work.

Other Brass Instruments All the brass instruments described so far are staples of both the orchestra and the band. Many other brass instruments (and even whole families of instruments) have been invented for band use and have then sometimes found their way into the orchestra.

French horn

   Among these are the *cornet* and the *flügelhorn,* which resemble the trumpet, the *euphonium, baritone horn,* and *saxhorn,* which are somewhere between the French horn and the tuba, and the *sousaphone,* a handsome type of bass tuba named after the great American bandmaster and march composer, John Philip Sousa.

   Finally there is the *bugle.* This simple trumpetlike instrument is very limited in the pitches it can play because it has no piston or valve mechanism. Buglers play "Taps" and military fanfares and not much else.

   The way buglers get different pitches is by "overblowing," that is, by blowing harder into the mouthpiece so as to get strong partials (see page 10). Overblowing is, indeed, an important resource of trumpets and many other brass instruments.

The trombones with their horizontal slides, and the sousaphones with their dramatic bells, make a striking navy band picture

Percussion Instruments Instruments in this category produce sound by being struck (or sometimes rattled, as with the South American maraca). Some percussion instruments, such as drums and gongs, have no fixed pitch, just a striking tone color. Other percussion instruments, such as the vibraphone, have a whole series of wooden or metal elements tuned to regular scales.

Timpani The **timpani** (or *kettledrums*) are large hemispherical drums that can be tuned precisely to certain low pitches. They are used in groups of two or more. As with most drums, players can obtain different sounds by using different kinds of drumsticks, tapping at different places on the drumhead, and so on.

Timpani are tuned by tightening the drumhead by means of screws set around the rim. During a concert, one can often see the timpani player, when there are rests in the music, leaning over the drums, tapping them quietly to hear whether the tuning is just right. Also available is a pedal mechanism to retune the timpani instantaneously.

Since they are tuned to precise pitches, timpani are the most widely used percussion instruments in the orchestra. They have the effect of "cementing" loud sounds when the whole orchestra plays.

Glockenspiel, Xylophone, Marimba, Vibraphone, Celesta, Tubular Bells These are all "scale" instruments, consisting of whole sets of metal or wooden bars or plates played with sticks or hammers. While they add unforget-

table special sound effects to many compositions, they are not usually heard consistently throughout a piece, as the timpani are. They differ in their materials:

⁍ The *glockenspiel* has small steel bars. It is a high instrument with a bright, penetrating sound.

⁍ The *xylophone* has hardwood plates or slats. It plays as high as the glockenspiel but also lower, and it has a drier, sharper tone.

⁍ The *marimba,* an instrument of African and South American origins, is a xylophone with tubular resonators under each wooden slat, making the tone much more mellow.

⁍ And the *vibraphone* has metal plates, like a glockenspiel with a large range, and is furnished with a controllable electric resonating device. This gives the "vibes" a flexible, funky quality unlike that of any other instrument.

⁍ Like the glockenspiel, the *celesta* has steel bars, but its sound is more delicate and silvery. This instrument, unlike the others in this section, is not played directly by a percussionist wielding hammers or sticks. The hammers are activated from a keyboard; a celesta looks like a miniature piano.

⁍ *Tubular bells* or *chimes* are hanging tubes that are struck with a big mallet. They sound like church bells.

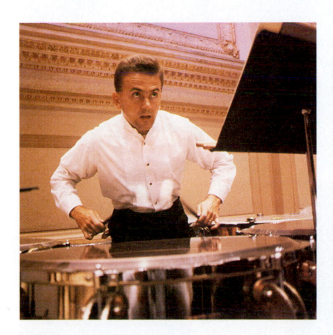

Timpani

Cymbals

Unpitched Percussion Instruments In the category of percussion instruments without a fixed pitch, the following are the most frequently found in the orchestra:

¶ The *triangle*—a simple metal triangle—gives out a bright tinkle when struck.

¶ *Cymbals* are concave metal plates, from a few inches to several feet in diameter. In orchestral music, pairs of large cymbals are clapped together to support forceful moments in the music with a grand clashing sound.

¶ The *tam-tam* is a large unpitched gong with a low, often sinister quality.

¶ The *snare drum, tenor drum,* and *bass drum* are among the unpitched drums used in the orchestra.

The Orchestra The orchestra has changed over the centuries just as greatly as orchestral music has. Bach's orchestra in the early 1700s was about a fifth of the size of the orchestra required by ambitious composers today. (See pages 111, 158, and 225 for charts showing the make-up of the orchestra at various historical periods.)

So today's symphony orchestra is a fluid group. Eighty musicians or more will be on the regular roster, but some of them sit out some of the pieces on almost every program. And freelancers have to be engaged for many special compositions in which composers have imaginatively expanded the orchestra for their own expressive purposes. A typical large orchestra today includes:

¶ *Strings:* about thirty to thirty-six violinists, twelve violists, ten to twelve cellists, and eight double basses.

¶ *Woodwinds:* two flutes and a piccolo, two clarinets and a bass clarinet, two oboes and an English horn, two bassoons and a contrabassoon.

¶ *Brass:* at least two trumpets, four French horns, two trombones, and one tuba.

¶ *Percussion:* one to four players, who between them manage the timpani and all the other percussion instruments, moving from one to the other. For unlike the violins, for example, the percussion instruments seldom have to be played continuously throughout a piece. If a composition uses a great deal of percussion—and many modern compositions do—more players will be needed.

ORCHESTRAL SEATING PLAN

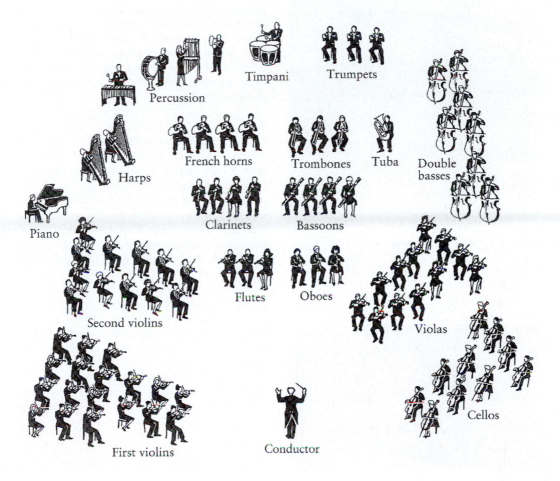

There are several seating plans for orchestras; which is chosen depends on at least two factors. The conductor judges which arrangement makes the best sound in the particular hall. And some conductors feel they can control the orchestra better with one arrangement, some with another. One such seating plan is shown above.

Keyboard and Plucked Stringed Instruments Though most orchestras today include a pianist, the piano is a relatively new addition to the symphony orchestra. In earlier times, the orchestra regularly included another keyboard instrument, the harpsichord.

The great advantage of keyboard instruments, of course, is that they can play chords and full harmony as well as melodies. One can play a whole piece on a keyboard instrument without requiring any other musicians

at all. Consequently the solo music that has been written for piano, harpsichord, and organ is much more extensive than (accompanied) solo music for other instruments—more extensive, and ultimately more important.

Piano The tuned strings of a **piano** are struck by felt-covered hammers, activated from a keyboard. Much technological ingenuity has been devoted to the activating mechanism, or *action*.

The hammers must strike the string and then fall back at once, while a felt damper simultaneously touches the string to stop the sound crisply. All this must be done so fast that the pianist can play repeated notes as fast as the hand can move. Also, all possible shades of loudness and softness must lie ready under the player's fingers. This dynamic capability is what gave the piano its name: "piano" is short for *pianoforte*, meaning "soft-loud."

In the nineteenth century, the piano became *the* solo instrument. The list of great virtuoso pianists who were also major composers extends from Frédérick Chopin to Sergei Rachmaninoff. At the same time, every middle-class household had a piano. Obligatory piano lessons served (and still serve) for millions of young people as either an unwelcome chore or a magical introduction to the world of music.

Harpsichord   The **harpsichord** is an ancient keyboard instrument that has enjoyed a healthy revival in recent years for the playing of Baroque music, in particular.

Like the piano, the harpsichord has a set of tuned strings activated from a keyboard. The action is much simpler, however—instead of hammers striking the strings, little quills pluck them. This means, first, that the tone is brittle and pingy. Second, it means that the player cannot vary dynamics; a string plucked, in this way, always sounds the same.

Harpsichord makers had to compensate for this limitation in dynamics by adding one or two extra full sets of strings, controlled by an extra keyboard. One keyboard would be soft, the other loud. A mechanism allowed the keyboards to be coupled together for the loudest sound of all.

In spite of its brittle tone and its lack of flexibility in dynamics, the harpsichord can be a wonderfully expressive instrument. Good harpsichord playing requires, first and foremost, great rhythmic subtlety.

Clavichord   Another ancient keyboard instrument, the **clavichord,** was strictly for private use. Small and relatively inexpensive, its strings (only one set) are struck by simple metal levers. The clavichord has a very sensitive but also very quiet sound—it cannot be heard across a large room, let alone a concert hall.

Organ   The pipe organ has a great many sets of tuned pipes through which a complex wind system blows air, again activated from a keyboard. The pipes have different tone colors; a large organ is capable of an almost orchestral variety of sound. Most organs have, in fact, more than one keyboard to control different sets of the pipes. There is also a pedal board—a short, big keyboard on the floor, played with the feet—to control the lowest pipes.

Each set of tuned pipes is called a *stop;* a moderate-sized organ has forty to fifty stops, but much bigger ones exist. (The biggest organ on record, at Atlantic City, has

A fantastically ornamented Victorian square piano

An elaborately painted eighteenth-century harpsichord

A five-manual organ. The round knobs are *stops* (or *stop knobs*); the player pulls them out to change the sets of pipes that sound.

Banjo

1477 stops, for a total of 33,112 pipes.) Called "the king of instruments," the pipe organ is certainly the largest of them. Organs need their size and power in order to provide enough sound to fill the large spaces of churches and cathedrals on a suitably grand scale.

Electronic Keyboard Instruments For many today, "keyboard" or "organ" means an electronic instrument. The synthesizers of today can simulate the sound of organs, pianos, and harpsichords. Today's electronic pianos look like acoustic ones and sound quite like them, though the "feel" is different. They cost a great deal less.

Modern concert music, from the 1960s on, has made occasional use of electronic keyboards. On the whole, however, synthesizers have been used more to compose concert music than to play it.

Plucked Stringed Instruments Plucked stringed instruments figure much less in art music of the West than in Asian countries such as India and Japan. One exception is the orchestral harp, mentioned on page 37. The acoustic **guitar,** the **mandolin,** and the **banjo** are used very widely in Western popular music, only occasionally in orchestras.

However, a now-obsolete plucked instrument, the **lute,** was of major importance in earlier times. One of the most beautiful-looking of instruments, the lute sounds rather like a gentle guitar. It differs in its rounded sound box, and in the way its pegboard is set nearly perpendicular to the neck. Large members of the lute family were the **theorbo** and the **archlute.**

Like keyboard instruments, plucked stringed instruments have been revolutionized by electronic technology. The **electric guitars** of rock music have not (not yet?) found their way into concert music.

Lute

The Waverly Ensemble, a well-known early-music performing group. Fifty years ago, the instruments in this picture would have been regarded as obsolete—rendered obsolete by the development of all the symphonic and other instruments discussed above. But today many ancient instruments are restored or reconstructed in order to present early music from ca. 1200 to 1750 using the sounds of its own time.

This picture shows a small pipe organ, called a *portative;* a bowed *vielle,* forerunner of the violin; a *cittern,* like a flat-backed lute; and a harp. Instruments half visible on the wall include tuned hand bells; a *vihuela,* the major Spanish plucked string instrument (right of center; see also page 54); and an English *orpharion* (far right).

CHAPTER 5

Musical Form and Musical Style

F *orm* is a general word with a long list of dictionary definitions. As applied to the arts, **form** is an important concept that refers to the shape, arrangement, relationship, or organization of the various elements. In poetry, for example, the elements of form are words, phrases, meters, rhymes, and stanzas; in painting, they are lines, colors, shapes, and space.

1 Form in Music

In music, the elements of form and organization are those we have already discussed: rhythm, pitch and melody, dynamics, tone color, and texture. A musical work, whether a simple song or a symphony, is formed or organized by means of repetitions of some of these elements, and by contrasts among them. The repetitions may be strict or free (that is, exact or with some variation). The contrasts may be of many different kinds—the possibilities are virtually limitless—conveying many different kinds of feeling.

Over the centuries, composers of Western music have learned to create longer and more impressive pieces in this way: symphonies, operas, string quartets, and more. Each piece is a specific sound experience in a definite time span, with a beginning, middle, and end, and often with subtle routes between. Everyone knows that music can make a nice effect for a minute or two. But how does music extend itself—and hold the listener's interest—for ten minutes, or half an hour, or three whole hours?

This is one of the main functions of musical form. Form is the relationship that connects those beginnings, middles, and ends.

Form and Feeling

Form in art also has a good deal to do with its emotional quality; it is a mistake to consider form as a merely structural or intellectual matter. Think of the little (or big) emotional "click" we get at the end of a limerick, or a sonnet, where the accumulated meanings of the words are summed up with the final rhyme. This is an effect to which form—limerick form or sonnet form—

Keep two things in mind, then. Remember the general outlines of the [outer form], and remember that the content of the composer's thought forces him to use that formal mold in a particular and personal way—in a way that belongs only to the particular piece that he is writing.

Aaron Copland, *What to Listen For in Music*

Music: That one of the fine arts which is concerned with the combination of sounds with a view to beauty of form and the expression of emotion.

—*Oxford English Dictionary,* 1961

contributes. Similarly, when at the end of a symphony a previously heard melody comes back, with new orchestration and new harmonies, the special feeling this gives us emerges from a flood of memory; we remember the melody from before, in its earlier version. That effect, too, is created by musical form.

How easy is it, actually, to perceive form in music and to experience the feelings associated with form? Easy enough with a short tune, such as "The Star-Spangled Banner," as our analysis on page 27 has shown. And the various phrases of this tune, with their repetitions, parallel features, contrasts, and climax provide a microcosm of musical form in longer pieces. For a large-scale composition like a symphony is something like a greatly expanded tune, and its form is experienced in basically the same way.

To be sure, a symphony requires more from the listener—more time and more attention—than a tune does. Aware of the potential problem here, composers scale their musical effects accordingly. The larger the piece, the more strongly the composer is likely to help the memory along by emphasizing the repetitions and contrasts that determine the musical form.

Form and Forms

Like the word *rhythm* (see page 12), the word *form* has its general meaning and also a more specific one. "Form" in general refers to the organization of elements in a musical work, but "*a* form" refers to one of many standardized formal patterns that composers have used over the centuries.

Form in painting: a madonna by Raphael Sanzio (1483–1520), built out of two cunningly nested triangles. To balance the boys at the left, the Virgin faces slightly to the right, her extended foot "echoing" their bare flesh. On a larger scale, the activity at the left is matched by a steeper landscape.

Forms in this sense are sometimes called "outer" forms; the ones treated later in this book are listed in the margin at right. The fixed elements in outer forms provide a welcome source of orientation for listeners, but they are always general enough to allow composers endless possibilities on the detailed level. The quality and feeling of works in the same outer form can therefore vary greatly. Or, to put it another way, any work adhering to a common "outer form" can also have an individual "inner form" of its own.

One of the simplest and most familiar outer forms is **A B A** or **a b a** form (small letters tend to be used for shorter pieces of music). This begins with the presentation of a section of music (**A**) followed by another section (**B**) that contrasts with the first, and then the first one returns (**A**). If **A** returns with significant modification, a prime mark is added: **A′**.

But this tells us only so much. With any particular work, what about the inner form: is **B** in a different mode? A different key? Does it present material that contrasts in rhythm, texture, or tone color—or does it work its contrast by ringing changes on the original material, on **A**? The returns in **A B A′** form, too, can convey very different feelings. One return can sound exciting, another tricky, while yet another provides a sense of relief.

So identifying "outer forms"—getting the letters right—is just a preliminary step in musical appreciation. The real point about great music is the way composers refine, modify, and personalize outer forms for their own expressive purposes.

LISTEN

"The Star-Spangled Banner" is in **a a b** form. "Oh, say can you see . . . twilight's last gleaming" is **a**, "Whose broad stripes . . . gallantly streaming" is the second **a**, and the rest of the anthem is **b**.

The Furiant, a dance from Smetana's *The Bartered Bride,* is in **A B A B′** form, where **B** is a quiet contrasting section and **B′** a shorter version of it that gets louder and faster for a bang-up ending. There is also a tiny introduction and a *transition* section.

0:00   introduction

0:04   **A:** loud, jagged rhythms

0:27   **B:** makes a contrast: quiet, smooth waltz rhythm

1:06   transition: music whose only function is to lead expectantly to the next **A**

1:23   **A**

1:34   **B′:** shorter, gets louder. (Fragments of **A** are also heard.)

With careful listening, you will note that on a lower level, the first **A** consists of shorter phrases, **a b a** with **b a** repeated. The second **A** contains just **a b a**.

For a longer example, listen to the third movement of Beethoven's Fifth Symphony.

0:00   **A:** Listen on a longer time scale, passing by the motives to experience larger spans of music. This section includes two very different themes. See page 213.

1:47   **B:** Like Smetana, Beethoven makes his second element contrast radically with the first. Virtually all musical elements are different here, except for the meter.

3:14   **A′:** Another radical contrast, as the motives and melodies of **A** are played very quietly, with different tone colors and dynamics, produced by different orchestration: pizzicato (plucked) strings, bassoon, and oboe instead of bowed strings and loud French horns. (At 4:26 the movement is over, and a transition begins to the next movement.)

The central, contrasting unit of this building seems almost to flow into the unit at the right. The musical analogy would be to an interesting **A B A′** form, in which **A** comes back after **B** in an expanded version (**A′**), and that version includes some new rhythm or instrument that we first heard during **B**.

Musical Genres

One often hears symphonies, sonatas, madrigals, and operas referred to as "forms" of music. But this is loose terminology, best avoided in the interests of clarity, because symphonies and other works can be composed in completely different forms ("outer forms")—that is, their internal orders or organizations can be of quite different kinds. Thus, the last movement of Joseph Haydn's Symphony No. 88 is in rondo form, whereas the last movement of Hector Berlioz's *Fantastic* Symphony follows no standard form whatsoever.

The best term for these general categories of music is *genre* (jáhn-ruh), borrowed from French. A genre can be defined by its text (a madrigal has Italian words), or by its function (a Mass is written for a service), or by the performing forces (a quartet is for four singers or instrumentalists). The main genres treated in this book are listed in the margin.

2 Musical Style

Style, like *form,* is another of those broad, general words—general but very necessary. The style of a tennis player is the particular way he or she reaches up for the serve, swings, follows through on the forehand, hits the ball deep or short, and so on. A life-style means the whole combination of things one does and doesn't do: the food one eats, the way one dresses and talks, one's habits of thought and feeling.

The style of a work of art, similarly, is the combination of qualities that make it distinctive. One composer's style may favor jagged rhythms, simple harmonies, and tunes to the exclusion of other types of melody. Another composer may reveal a highly refined preference for certain kinds of tone color; still another may concentrate on a particular form. The type of emotional expression a composer cultivates is also an important determinant of musical style.

Even *where* people listen to music reflects their life-style. This open-air brass concert is at Van Cortlandt Manor in New York.

One can speak of the life-style of a generation as well as the life-style of a particular person. Similarly, a distinction can be made between the style of a particular composer and the style of a historical period. For example, to a large extent George Frideric Handel's manner of writing falls within the parameters of the Baroque style of his day. But some features of Handel's style are unique, and perhaps it is those features that embody his musical genius.

Musical Style and Life-Style

In any historical period or place, the musical style must bear some relation to the life-style in general; this seems self-evident. Perhaps the point is clearest of all with popular music, where distinct (and distinctly different) worlds are evoked by rock, rap, and country music, to say nothing of earlier styles such as 1950s rhythm and blues rock or 1930s swing.

Older styles of music, too, relate to total cultural situations, though how this works in detail is not fully understood. We can, however, at least suggest some of these musical-cultural relationships for music of the various historical periods. For each period, we will sketch certain aspects of the culture, history, and life-style of the time. We will then briefly outline the musical style and, wherever possible, suggest correlations. Then the musical style will be examined in more detail through individual composers and individual pieces of their music.

These individual pieces are our principal concern, of course—not history, or culture, or concepts of musical style in the abstract. Learning the basic concepts of music is useful only insofar as it focuses and sharpens the process of listening to actual music. This book is called *Listen,* and it rests on the belief that the love of music depends first and foremost on careful listening to particular pieces. We experience this music for its own sake; we are not primarily interested in whether it is a "good example" of some musical style, form, or genre, or whether it is "typical" of some historical period. But we *are* interested in what history and style may be able to tell us that illuminates music. The general can reflect upon the particular; and in this indirect way, history too can help us to *listen.*

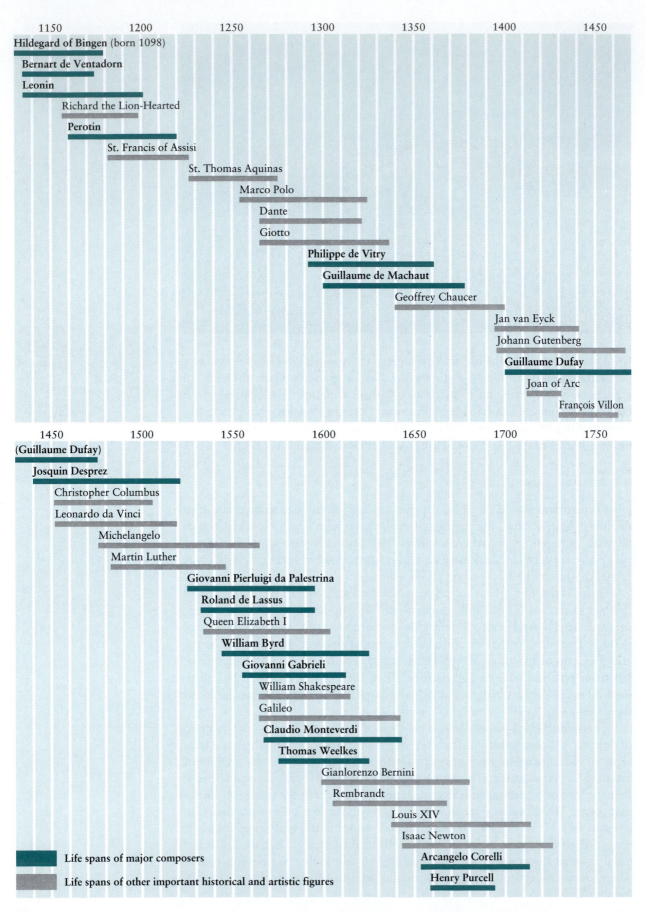

1150   1200   1250   1300   1350   1400   1450

Hildegard of Bingen (born 1098)

Bernart de Ventadorn

Leonin

Richard the Lion-Hearted

Perotin

St. Francis of Assisi

St. Thomas Aquinas

Marco Polo

Dante

Giotto

Philippe de Vitry

Guillaume de Machaut

Geoffrey Chaucer

Jan van Eyck

Johann Gutenberg

Guillaume Dufay

Joan of Arc

François Villon

1450   1500   1550   1600   1650   1700   1750

(Guillaume Dufay)

Josquin Desprez

Christopher Columbus

Leonardo da Vinci

Michelangelo

Martin Luther

Giovanni Pierluigi da Palestrina

Roland de Lassus

Queen Elizabeth I

William Byrd

Giovanni Gabrieli

William Shakespeare

Galileo

Claudio Monteverdi

Thomas Weelkes

Gianlorenzo Bernini

Rembrandt

Louis XIV

Isaac Newton

Arcangelo Corelli

Henry Purcell

■ Life spans of major composers

■ Life spans of other important historical and artistic figures

52

Early Music: An Overview

Western art music extends from the great repertory of Gregorian chant, assembled around the year A.D. *600, to electronic compositions that were programmed yesterday and today. One does not have to be a specialist to have some feeling for the sheer scope, variety, and almost bewildering richness of all this music. Some of it was developed to uphold Christianity through centuries of barbarism, some to glorify great monarchs such as Queen Elizabeth I of England or Louis XIV of France. Some of it is being produced in today's recording studios for the enjoyment of connoisseur listeners. The field ranges from music attributed to the shadowy figures Leonin and Perotin in the twelfth century, through compositions by familiar masters such as Bach and Beethoven, to work in progress by Pierre Boulez, a former conductor of the New York Philharmonic who now runs a state-of-the-art laboratory for sound research in Paris. All of this is music that has fascinated, moved, and inspired humanity.*

Certainly there is too much here to "cover" in a single semester or quarter course—too much, that is, if one is going to do more than skim the music, picking up a few frantic facts and figures about it without really listening. It cannot be said often enough that listening to particular pieces again and again is the basic activity that leads to the love of music and to its understanding. A galloping survey does justice to none of the world's significant music. In acknowledgment of this fact, the essential coverage of this book begins in Unit III with the music of Bach and Handel, who are the first composers with a long-standing place in the "standard repertory" of concert music. This term refers to a large but not limitless body of music from which concert artists and conductors usually draw their programs.

As an optional introduction to all of this, Unit II presents a brief overview of music before the eighteenth-century. So-called "early music" was forgotten for centuries, and is still seldom performed at standard concerts. But in today's music world, less attuned to concerts than to recordings, early music has become much more familiar. It has its own musical institutions, its own specialist performers, and its own devotees.

CHAPTER **6**

The Middle Ages

"T he Middle Ages" is a term that embraces nearly a thousand years of European history, extending from the collapse of the Roman Empire in the fifth century of the Christian era to the introduction of new learning, technology, and political organization in the fourteenth and fifteenth centuries. Even though life and culture changed slowly in those days, this is obviously too broad a span of time to mean much as a "period."

Nowhere is this clearer than in music. Music changed radically from the beginning to the end of the medieval era, more than in any other historical period. Two of the central principles of later Western music, *tune* and *polyphony*, originated around the middle of this long period. It is hard for most people in modern times even to conceive of music without tunes, or music without different notes sounding simultaneously, so as to make polyphony and harmony.

Medieval musicians: the boy is tuning his vihuela—a Spanish plucked string instrument—to the pitch being played by the older man (his teacher?).

1 Music and the Church: Plainchant

The early history of Western music was determined by the Christian Church to an extent that is not easy for us to grasp today. The Church cultivated, supported, and directed music as it did art, architecture, poetry, and all learning. All composers were in holy orders, and all musicians got their training as church choirboys.

Exception must be made for popular musicians—called minstrels and jongleurs—but unfortunately we know next to nothing about their lives or their music. The only people who wrote music down were in religious orders, and they cared nothing about the preservation of popular music.

The life of the Church centered around its services; and music's role was to embellish the services and make them more impressive and solemn. Musicians did for the services what the architects of the great cathedrals did for the places of worship, and what the illuminators of manuscripts did for the books preserving the Scriptures.

The worship that music embellished was the worship conducted in monasteries and cathedrals: private devotions for the higher ranks of Christendom, for monks, nuns, and cathedral clergy. Monks and nuns spent an amazing amount of their time in prayer. Besides the Mass—a lengthy ceremony that might take place more than once a day—there were eight other daily services, known collectively as the Divine Office. Large portions of these services were sung. Furthermore, though each service had its standard form, many details in the texts changed from day to day according to the Church calendar (Christmas, Easter, various saints' days, and so on). As a result, there were literally thousands of religious texts specified for the Mass and the Office throughout the year.

All these texts required music, but composing such music was less a matter of free invention than of small additions and adjustments to a hallowed tradition. And listening to it was not so much listening as worshiping, while allowing the music to expand the devotional experience. Hearing traditional chant or later medieval music today, one feels less like a "listener" in the modern sense than like a privileged eavesdropper, someone who has been allowed to attend a select occasion that is partly musical but mainly spiritual. The experience is an intimate and tranquil one, cool and (to some listeners) especially satisfying.

A psalm is the work of the Angels, the incense of the Spirit. Oh, how wise was that Teacher who found a way for us to sing psalms and at the same time learn worthwhile things, so that in some mysterious way doctrine is more deeply impressed upon the mind!

St. Basil, fourth century A.D.

Plainchant

The official music of the Church in the Middle Ages, and far beyond the Middle Ages, was a great collection of melodies designated for the many religious texts to be sung at services throughout the year. This is the repertory of **plainchant** (or plainsong), widely known as Gregorian chant.

It is called "plain" because it is unaccompanied, monophonic (one-line) music, without fixed rhythm or meter. The early Church condemned sensuality, and with it anything that suggested dancing, such as meter or even musical instruments. And the chant is called "Gregorian" after the famous pope and Church father Gregory I (c. 540–604), although this term can be misleading. Gregory assembled and standardized all the chants required for the Church services of his time, but many medieval plainchants were composed later and so cannot strictly speaking be called Gregorian.

Monks singing plainchant from a large choirbook— shown in an illustrated letter O from exactly such a book, dating from the later medieval period. An extra imaginative touch is added by the two trumpeting angels.

Plainchant Genres

The many genres of plainchant, which differ widely in melodic style, fall into three general categories. Some plainchants consist of simple recitation on a monotone, with only slight deviations from a single pitch. Others are intricate songs with hundreds of notes ranging well over an octave, reminiscent of the ecstatic singing still heard in the Middle East today. Still others are among the first real tunes that are known in Western Music.

What determined the genre (and hence the style) of a chant was not the words and certainly not the wish or whim of the composer. The determining factor was its role in a service. At high points of a major service—for example, between the two Scripture readings at Mass—the melodic style was at its most intricate and sumptuous. The daily Office, on the other hand, centered on the recitation of psalms on a near monotone. In monasteries, the entire set of 150 psalms had to be chanted in this fashion every week.

Chant isn't Musak for the elevators of Melrose Place or feel-good ear-mush for Zen Rollerbladers. And despite the way it's been marketed, it has nothing to do with New Age music. . . . It's prayer . . . the yearning of the immortal soul made manifest.

Review of the 1993 international megahit album, *Chant*

Characteristics of Plainchant

In whatever style or genre, all plainchants share two characteristic features. First, they are *nonmetrical;* they have no clearly established meter, and therefore the rhythm is free. Not only is a distinctive beat lacking in this music, but rhythms may change from one performance (rather, one service) to the next.

Second, plainchant is construed not in the later major/minor system but according to one of the **medieval modes.** As discussed in Unit I, the original scale of Western music was the diatonic scale—the "white-note" scale on the piano—and this is still the basic scale today. We use this scale oriented around the pitches C or A as "home" or tonic (see page 32). Oriented around C, the music is said to be in the major mode; oriented around A, in the minor mode. Different keys allow for different placements of the two modes.

Musicians of the Middle Ages organized the scale around other pitches—around D, E, F, or G. The result was music in other modes, different from the modern major or minor. These modes were identified by numbers or by Greek names (for medieval scholars traced them back to the modes of ancient Greek music). The medieval modes are these:

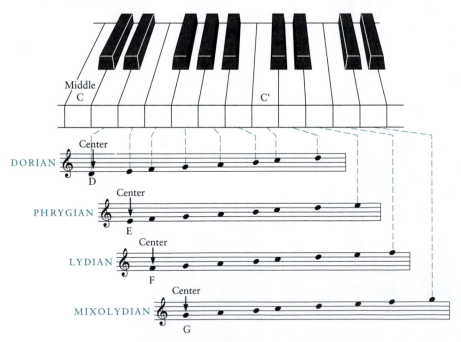

Multicultural medieval music: at a time when half of Spain was in Arab (Moorish) hands, a Moor and a Spaniard are shown playing large vihuelas together. This and other miniatures in this chapter are from *Songs of the Virgin Mary,* written (or perhaps compiled) by King Alphonso X of Spain, "The Wise" (1252–1284), renowned for his support of learning and the arts.

The essential difference between the major and minor modes comes in the different arrangement of half steps and whole steps in their scales. The medieval modes provide four other arrangements. (Compare the preceding diagram with the one on page 32.) In this respect, then, medieval plainchant is actually richer than later music in the major/minor system. The artistic effect of plainchant—music without harmony or definite rhythm—is concentrated in melody, melody built on this rich and subtle modal system.

ANONYMOUS
Gregorian antiphon, "In paradisum"

This antiphon—one of the simpler plainchant genres—is part of the liturgy of the dead. It is in the Mixolydian (G) Mode; "modal" cadences are heard in lines 4 and 5, "Chorus An*ge*lorum" and "quondam pau*pere.*"

To experience "In paradisum," place track 7 (or 3) on repeat and imagine yourself a medieval monk or nun who has lost a brother or sister. Candles have all been extinguished in the church after the Requiem Mass (so called because you have prayed for the soul's eternal rest—in Latin, *requiem aeternam:* see line 6). As the coffin is lifted up, the priest begins "In paradisum," and then the entire religious community joins in. You sing this antiphon again and again, for as long as it takes the slow procession to reach the graveyard.

The melodic highpoint of "In paradisum" comes in line 5. This haunting descending figure was etched in the memory of the Middle Ages as the commemoration of an endless succession of last rites.

In pa-ra-di-sum de-du-cant

te An-ge - li

et cum La - za - ro

quon-dam _ pau-pe - re

Modal cadence

1   1   1A   1A
7   7   3   3

LISTEN	Antiphon, "In Paradisum"

	In paradisum deducant te Angeli:	May the Angels lead you to paradise,
	in tuo adventu suscipient Martyres,	and the Martyrs, when you arrive,
	et perducant te in civitatem Jerusalem.	escort you to the city Jerusalem.
0:40	Chorus Angelorum te suscipiat,	The angel choir sustain you,
	et cum Lazaro quondam paupere	and with Lazarus, who was once poor,
	aeternam habeas requiem.	may you be granted eternal rest.

HILDEGARD OF BINGEN (1098–1179)
Plainchant sequence, "Columba aspexit"

Abbess Hildegard of the little convent of Bingen, in western Germany, was one of the most remarkable figures of the Middle Ages. Most famous for her book relating her religious visions, she also wrote on natural history and medicine; she gained such renown that popes and emperors sought her counsel.

Five hundred years after Gregory I, the first compiler of Gregorian chants, Hildegard composed plainchants in her own highly individual style to go with poems that she wrote for special services. "Columba aspexit" honored one of the many minor saints venerated in those days, Saint Maximinus. It belongs to a late medieval plainchant category called the **sequence.**

Plainsong sequences consist of a series of tunes sung twice, with some variation (and an extra unit at the end: A A' B B' C C' . . . N). A soloist sings A, the choir A', and so on. "Modal" cadences—Mixolydian, once again—at the beginning of the melody ("fenestrae," "eius") give it a deceptively humble quality that contrasts with its ecstatic soaring later.

A miniature illustration of Hildegard, in one of her manuscripts, shows the miracle by which fire came down from heaven to engulf and inspire her.

Our recording includes an instrumental *drone*—a single two-note chord running continuously. Though never written out in medieval manuscripts, there is some evidence that such drones were sometimes used to accompany the singing of plainchant. This drone, the mystical words of Hildegard's poem, and the free, surging rhythm of her music work together to produce a feeling of serene yet intense spirituality.

| LISTEN | Hildegard of Bingen, "Columba aspexit" |

8   4

	A	Columba aspexit	The dove entered
		Per cancellos fenestrae	Through the lattices of the window,
		Ubi ante faciem eius	Where, before its face,
		Sudando sudavit balsamum	Balm emanated
		De lucido Maximino.	From incandescent Maximinus.
0:28	A'	Calor solis exarsit	The heat of the sun burned
		Et in tenebras resplenduit;	And dazzled into the gloom,
		Unde gemma surrexit	Whence a jewel sprang forth
		In edificatione templi	In the building of the temple
		Purissimi cordis benevoli.	Of the most pure loving heart.
0:56	B	Iste turis . . .	He is the high tower of Lebanon . . .
1:28	B'	Ipse velox . . .	The swift hart sped to the fountain . . .
2:02	C	O pigmentarii . . .	O you makers of incense . . .
2:37	C'	Inter vos	This builder shines among you . . .
3:14	D	O maximine . . .	O Maximinus . . .

(two more stanzas)

How Did Early Music Sound?

There is a special problem about old music, a problem that is less troublesome with music of more recent times: although we have the scores of early music, often we do not have a clear idea of how it actually sounded.

One reason for this is that musical instruments have changed enormously over the centuries. Obsolete instruments have survived in an imperfect condition, and one can try to reconstruct them; but figuring out how they were actually played is much more speculative. As for singing, who can guess what a cathedral choir sounded like in the late Middle Ages, to take just one example? Language itself has changed so much since that time that it is hard enough to read a fourteenth-century poet such as Geoffrey Chaucer, let alone imagine how the words that he wrote were pronounced—or sung.

What is more, composers of early music never indicated the tempo and seldom specified the instrumental or vocal forces that they anticipated for their music. With vocal pieces, they did not specify whether a single singer or a whole choir was to sing. It has taken generations of patient research and experiment to "reconstruct," as it were, the probable sounds of early music.

The recordings of early music accompanying this book have been chosen to represent the most modern and sensitive research in this area, but in terms of performance sound, these recordings are all educated guesses. Beware, in any case, of exaggerated claims of "authenticity" in historical performance. Some guesses are more educated (and more artistic) than others, but there is much we can never know about the sound of early music.

2 Music at Court

Over the long span of the Middle Ages, the kings and barons gained political power at the expense of the Church. They also assumed leadership in artistic matters as well. The princely courts joined the monasteries and cathedrals as major supporters of music in the later Middle Ages.

Troubadour and Trouvère Songs

Large groups of court songs have been preserved from the twelfth and thirteenth centuries, the Age of Chivalry. The noble poet-composers of these songs—who, we are told, also performed the songs themselves—were called **troubadours** in the south of France, **trouvères** in the north, and **Minnesingers** in Germany (*Minne* means ideal or chivalric love). Among them were knights and princes, even kings—such as the most famous of all chivalric heroes, Richard I of England, "the Lion-Hearted." Troubadour society (but not trouvère society) also allowed for women troubadours, such as Countess Beatriz of Dia, Maria di Ventadorn, and others.

Perhaps some of these noble songwriters penned the words only, leaving the music to be composed by *jongleurs*, the popular musicians of the time. The music is relatively simple—just a tune, in most cases, with no indication of any accompaniment. We hear of jongleurs playing instruments while the trouvères sang; perhaps they improvised some kind of accompaniment, or played a drone, such as we heard in "Columba aspexit."

There are some very beautiful troubadour poems—crusaders' songs, laments for dead princes, and especially songs in praise of the poets' ladies, or complaints of their ladies' coldness. One interesting poetic type was the *alba*, the "dawn song" of a knight's loyal companion who has kept watch all night and now warns him to leave his lady's bed before the castle awakes. Another was the *pastourelle,* a (typically unsuccessful) seduction dialogue between a knight on horseback and a country maid.

My love and I keep state
In bower,
In flower,
Till the watchman on the
        tower
Cry:
   "Up! Thou rascal, Rise,
I see the white
        Light
        And the night
            Flies."

—Troubadour alba

From an unusual series of medieval portraits—24 portraits of Minnesingers: Heinrich Frauenlob (Henry Praiselady), with his impressive band of jongleurs, and Walther von der Vogelweide (Walter of the Aviary—note his heraldic device), greatest of the Minnesinger poets.

BERNART DE VENTADORN (c. 1135–1194)
Troubadour song, "La dousa votz"

Bernart was one of the finest troubadour poets and probably the most important musically; other troubadour and trouvère songs were derived from some of his pieces. Originally of humble background, he came to serve the powerful Queen Eleanor of Aquitaine, wife of Henry II of England.

Like hymns and folksongs, troubadour songs set all their stanzas to the same melody, resulting in what is called *strophic* form (**A A A . . .**); often each stanza is in **a a′ b** form. "La dousa votz" is in the G (Mixolydian) mode:

La dousa votz ai au-zi - da   Del rosin ho-let sau - va-tge   Et es m'insel cor salhi - da   Si que tot lo co-si - rer

The performance on the recording stresses "secular" aspects of Bernart's song, including an imaginative reconstruction of a possible instrumental accompaniment to it. It sounds far removed indeed from the spiritual atmosphere of Hildegard of Bingen.

The language the troubadours spoke and wrote was Provençal, now almost obsolete. It combines elements from old French and old Spanish.

LISTEN		Bernart de Ventadorn, "La dousa votz"	

0:06	*St. 1:* La dousa votz ai auzida	I have heard the sweet voice
	Del rosinholet sauvatge	Of the woodland nightingale
	Et es m'insel cor salhida	And my heart springs up
	Si que tot lo cosirer	So that all the cares
	E'ls mals traihz qu'amors me dona,	And the unhappy betrayals love gives me
	M'adousa e m'asazona.	Are softened and sweetened;
	Et auria'm be mester	And I would thus be recompensed,
	L'autrui joi al meu damnatge.	In my ordeal, by the joys of others.
0:48	*St. 2:* Ben es totz om d'avol vida	In truth, every man leads a base life
	C'ab joi non a son estatge . . .	Who does not dwell in the land of joy . . .
1:28	*St. 3:* Una fausa deschauzida	One who is false, deceitful,
	Trairitz de mal linhage	Of low breeding, a traitress
	M'a trait, et es traida . . .	Has betrayed me, and betrayed herself . . .

The Estampie

There also survive a few—a very few—dances from the same court circles that produced the chivalric trouvère repertory. Called **estampies,** they are unassuming one-line pieces in which the same or similar musical phrases are repeated many times in varied forms. (This suggests that these estampies may have been written-down jongleur improvisations.) Estampies are marked by lively and insistent rhythms in triple meter. Modern performers often add a touch of spice with the help of percussion instruments.

This is a modest beginning to the long and important history of European dance music. We shall pick it up again in the next chapter.

3   The Evolution of Polyphony

Polyphony—the simultaneous combination of two or more melodies—must have arisen in early Europe because people took pleasure in the sensuous quality of music, in the rich sounds of intertwining melodic lines with their resulting harmony. Many cultures all over the world have developed some kind of improvised polyphony, polyphony that is made up on the spot by people who cannot read music. If you or someone you know can "sing in thirds" without notes, that is improvised polyphony.

But we only know about early European polyphony from its manifestations within the Church (for, once again, all we know about very early music comes from the writing of monks and other clerics). And within the Church, the sensuous aspect of polyphony had to be rationalized away. Polyphony was seen as a way of embellishing Gregorian chants—that is, as yet another way of enhancing the all-important services.

Organum

The earliest type of polyphony is called **organum**. First described in treatises around A.D. 900, actual "live" organum has survived in musical notation from around 1000. Organum consists of a traditional plainchant melody to which a composer/singer/improviser has added another melody, or counterpoint, sung simultaneously to the same words.

The history of organum between about A.D. 1000 and 1200 provides a fascinating record of growing artistic ambition and technical invention. We can trace a number of steps:

❧   Originally, each note of the chant was accompanied by another single note in the counterpoint, or added melody; the two melodies moved along with the same distance, or interval, between them. The rhythm of this early, so-called "parallel" organum was the free rhythm of Gregorian chant.

❧   Soon the counterpoint was treated more independently—it would sometimes go up when the chant went down, and vice versa.

❧   Next, the counterpoint began to include several notes at the same time as each single chant note. The embellishment process was growing richer. As more and more notes were crowded in, making richer and richer melodies, the single chant notes were slowed down to surprisingly long drones.

❧   The next step was a radical one. Two counterpoints were added to the chant—which required much more skill from the composer, since the second counterpoint had to fit both the chant and also the first counterpoint.

❧   Equally radical was the idea of introducing definite rhythms controlled by meter. First the counterpoints and then the chant itself were set in lively rhythms. Fragments of the chant, too, were sometimes isolated and repeated many times, one after another.

Organum of this highly developed kind flourished at the Cathedral of Notre Dame in Paris, which was built slowly over the period 1163–1235. The names of some composers of the so-called Notre Dame school are recorded: Master Leonin and his follower Perotin (called "the Great"). Perotin astonished thirteenth-century Paris by creating impressive organa for as many as four simultaneous voices.

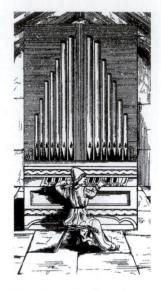

Does the medieval word "organum" imply that early polyphony was accompanied by the organ? We do not know; but churches of the time certainly had organs. The keyboard of this somewhat later organ seems to have heavy levers rather than keys.

Notre Dame Cathedral in Paris. Flying buttresses—the great medieval engineering feat that made such high buildings possible—support the main structure (the apse). With its lofty front towers and its spire, Notre Dame seems to reach up to heaven itself.

PEROTIN (c. 1200)
Organum on the plainchant "Alleluia: Nativitas" (part)

For the birthday of the Virgin Mary—a big day at Notre Dame cathedral—Perotin wrote an organum adding two "free" counterpoints to one of the prescribed Mass plainchants. The chant begins in the usual Gregorian way:

The whole chant lasts much longer, but this "Alleluia" section is the most important part—it comes back twice before the chant is over—and the most beautiful. Notice how the music rouses itself on the syllable *lu* and then springs up still higher, and how this melodic climax is balanced by a tranquil "low climax" in phrase 3. After this (relative) excitement, phrase 4 stays within a calm range of four notes.

Then the organum starts. The higher voices first add a strange, static harmony—which starts to sway, as it were, when the voices intertwine in various rhythms of the kind shown at the right of this page. They are singing no words, just vocalizing the syllables *al—le—lu—ia*. Originally meandering and mysterious, these rhythmicized voices gain strength and clarity; by the end they are sounding jubilant and positively triumphant.

And what is going on underneath these ecstatic, rhythmicized voices? Listen carefully to the lowest of the voices, and you will hear long sustained tones. Notes 1 and 2 of the "Alleluia" chant shown above are each slowed down to amazingly long drones. Then notes 3 to 13 plod along in a slow regular rhythm (with a little break after note 8). Note 14 is another long drone:

But even if one hears these sustained notes or drones, one cannot recognize them as an actual melody, not at that speed—and not with the distractions offered by the counterpoints. The plainchant is an abstract basis for the ecstatic upper-voice melodies, the main focus of interest in this music.

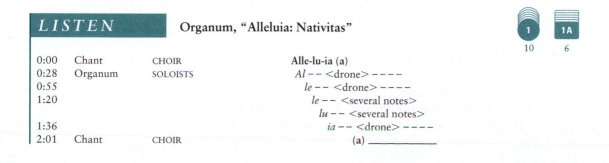

LISTEN		**Organum, "Alleluia: Nativitas"**	
0:00	Chant	CHOIR	Alle-lu-ia (a)
0:28	Organum	SOLOISTS	*Al* – – <drone> – – – –
0:55			*le* – – <drone> – – – –
1:20			*le* – – <several notes>
			lu – – <several notes>
1:36			*ia* – – <drone> – – – –
2:01	Chant	CHOIR	(a)

4 Later Medieval Polyphony

The most significant thing that happened to polyphonic music in the thirteenth century was its gradual distancing from Church services. The "bottom line" was still Gregorian chant, but this was now handled more abstractly. For example, composers would now set only a fragment of chant and repeat it several times in different arbitrary rhythms, as we saw in the "Alleluia: Nativitas" organum.

In another radical development, the upper lines were now given their own words. This sort of polyphony is no longer an organum but a __motet,__ from the French word *mot* ("word"). At first, motets were set to sacred poems in Latin, then to sacred poems in French. Later, when some motets used French love poems for texts, it is clear that a Church genre has been taken over by the courts. Some motets even included bits of actual trouvère songs; but almost all motets were still based on Gregorian chant.

Ars Nova

After 1300 the technical development of polyphony reached new heights of sophistication. Composers and music theorists of the time began to speak of an *ars nova,* a "new art," or "new technique." The organum and motets of the Notre Dame composers were now regarded as "ancient art," *ars antiqua.*

Some historians have compared the fourteenth century with the twentieth, for it was a time of the break-up of traditions—an age of anxiety, corruption, and worse. The Black Death carried away an estimated 75 million people, at a time when the papacy had been thrown out of Rome and two rival popes claimed the allegiance of European Christendom. The motet grew increasingly secular, intricate, and even convoluted, like the painting, architecture, and poetry of the time.

The new intricacy of the motet was mainly in the area of rhythm. The *ars antiqua* composers had introduced rhythm and meter into organum and the motet, as we have seen; the composers of the *ars nova* carried their innovations much further. Rhythm seems to have obsessed them. They superimposed complex rhythmic patterns in the various voices so as to produce extraordinarily complex combinations. We have to go all the way up to 1950 to find anything like the dizzy rhythms of the advanced "new music" of 1400.

The leading composers, Philippe de Vitry (1291–1361) and Guillaume de Machaut (c. 1300–1377), were both churchmen—Vitry ended his life as a bishop—but they were political churchmen in the service of the courts of France and Luxembourg. Machaut was also the greatest French poet of his time, admired (and imitated) by his younger English contemporary, Geoffrey Chaucer.

Of instruments of strings
  in accord
Heard I so play a ravish-
  ing sweetnéss
That God, that Maker is of
  all, and Lord,
Ne heard never better, as
  I guess.

—Geoffrey Chaucer, 1375

GUILLAUME DE MACHAUT (c. 1300–1377)
Motet, "Quant en moy"

Following tradition, Machaut based this motet on a repeated fragment of plainchant, taken from the Eastertide services. On the recording, it is played on a viol, an early bowed stringed instrument.

Above this, he wrote two faster counterpoints set to love poetry (very artificial and elegant poetry, in both form and content: see below). To the

This fascinating spidery manuscript, shaped like a heart because it contains love songs, is a characteristic product of late medieval artifice.

medieval mind, there was nothing sacrilegious about such a combination of sacred and secular elements. Notice the exceedingly complicated rhythm of these upper voices, the nervous, hyperelegant way in which they utter the words, and the spiky harmonies they produce in combination:

Quant en moi vint premièrement Amours, si tres doucette - ment Me vost mon cuer en amourer Que d'un   regart

As the voices stop abruptly, rest, and start up again, they create an intriguing texture—perforated, glittering, asymmetrical. To make things even more intricate, the two singers actually sing two different poems simultaneously.

Each of these poems contains several stanzas with the same syllable counts and rhyme schemes, but Machaut (unlike a troubadour composer such as Bernart) does not repeat the same melodies for each stanza. A more esoteric system of repetition is at work. Successive stanzas are set to entirely different melodies in each voice—but these melodies have basically *the same overall rhythms,* complex patterns of over eighty notes in the soprano, forty notes in the tenor.

This technique of writing successive lengthy passages in identical rhythms but with distinct melodies is called **isorhythm.** Isorhythm represents the height of late medieval ingenuity and artifice, and it is hard to know whether anyone was ever expected to hear such purely rhythmic repetitions.

There are fast echoes between the soprano's two words in line 7 of her poem and the tenor's two words in line 2 of his, thus: "doubter—espoir—celer—d'avoir." This amusing device is called **hocket** (compare our word *hiccup*). Isorhythmic repetitions are easiest to hear at hocket points.

Hocket is a cut-up song, composed for two or more voices. This kind of song is pleasing to the hot-tempered and to young men on account of its fluidity and speed.

From a fourteenth-century treatise on music

LISTEN   Machaut, "Quant en moi"

(The soprano's poem and the tenor's poem start together, and are sung simultaneously, stanza by stanza.)

0:00   STANZA 1: SOPRANO

Quant en moi vint premièrement	When I was first visited by
Amours, si tres doucettement	Love, he so very sweetly
Me vost mon cuer enamourer	Enamored my heart;
Que d'un regart me fist present,	A glance is what he gave me as a gift,
Et tres amoureus sentiment	And along with amorous sentiments
Me donna avuec doulz penser,	He presented me with this delightful idea:

Espoir   D'avoir   To hope   to have

Merci sans refuser.	Grace, and no rejections.
Mais onques en tout mon vivant	But never in my whole life
Hardement ne me vost donner.	Was boldness a gift he meant for me.

TENOR

Amour et biauté parfaite   *Thanks to love and consummate beauty,*

Doubter,   celer   *Fearing,   feigning*

Me font parfaitement.   *Are what consume me entirely.*

0:32   STANZA 2: SOPRANO   TENOR

E si me fait en desirant	*Et vrais desirs, qui m'a fait*
Penser si amoureusement	Qu'amours | *De vous* | secours | *coer doulz,*
Que par force de desirer . . .	*Amer sans finement.*

1:04   STANZA 3: SOPRANO   TENOR

Ne je me weil, qu'en attendant	*Et quant j'aime si finement,*
Sa grace se weil humblement	Je says | *Merci* | de vrai | *vous pris*
Toutes ces dolours endurer . . .	*Car elle me soit faite.*

1:38   STANZA 4: SOPRANO   TENOR

Mais elle attend . . .   *Sans vostre honeur . . .*

CHAPTER 7

The Renaissance

*R*enaissance ("rebirth") is the name given to a complex current of thought that worked deep changes in Europe from the fourteenth to the sixteenth century. By rediscovering and imitating their ancient Greco-Roman civilization, Italians hoped they could bring about the rebirth of their glorious past. It was a somewhat confused dream, which came to nothing in political terms. Instead of becoming a new Roman empire, Italy at the end of the Renaissance consisted of the same pack of warring city-states that had been at each other's throats all through the Middle Ages.

However, the revival of Greek and Roman culture provided a powerful model for new values, which were coming to the fore in Italy and the rest of Europe. In the words of a famous nineteenth-century historian, the Renaissance involved "the discovery of the world and of man." This was the age of Columbus, Leonardo da Vinci, Copernicus, and Shakespeare. Medieval society was stable, conservative, authoritarian, oriented toward God. The Renaissance laid the groundwork for the dynamic world we know today, a world in which human beings and nature, rather than God, have become the measure in philosophy, science, art, and even religion.

Accordingly, Renaissance artists strove to make their work more relevant to people's needs and desires. They began to reinterpret the world around them—the architect's world of space and stone, the painter's world of images, the musician's world of sound—in new ways to meet these ambitions.

Church singers, by the Renaissance sculptor Luca della Robbia (1400–1482). No elderly monks are represented on these panels (compare page 55), but instead handsome boys who seem to be taking the same sensuous pleasure in their singing as Luca did in sculpting them.

1   New Attitudes

A good indication of the Renaissance mindset, in the early fifteenth century, was a new way of treating plainchant in polyphonic compositions. Medieval composers writing organum or isorhythmic motets seem to have felt that so long as they used a traditional plainchant, there was nothing wrong with distorting it. They lengthened its notes enormously to accommodate the added counterpoints. They recast the meterless chant into fixed, arbitrary rhythms.

Renaissance composers no longer felt obliged always to use plainchants; but when they did they tended to treat them as melodies to listen to, not as set foundations for polyphonic structures. They embellished chants with extra notes, set them in graceful rhythms, and smoothed out passages that struck them as awkward or antiquated. This procedure is known as **paraphrase.** The following example shows a fifteenth-century plainchant paraphrase; dashed lines mark the notes taken directly from the chant (shown above the paraphrase):

Music is a thing which delighteth all ages and be-seemeth all states; a thing as seasonable in grief as in joy. The reason hereof is an admirable facility which music hath to express and represent the very standing, rising, and falling, the very steps and inflections every way, the turns and varieties of all passions.

Anglican theologian Richard Hooker, 1593

Gregorian hymn, "Ave maris stella" (see page 69)

Su - mens ____ il - lud A - ve ____ Ga-bri - e - lis o - re ____

The emphasis was on the sonorous, sensuous aspect of the chant rather than on its structural and authoritarian function. (Sonority means either tone color or, more loosely, rich tone color.) A new sensitivity to sonority and melody was perhaps the first sign of Renaissance attitudes toward music.

Having transformed plainchants into "modern" melodies with a more attractive profile, fifteenth-century composers put them not at the bottom of the polyphony but on top, in the soprano, where they could be heard most clearly. And the soprano voice was probably already considered to be the most beautiful.

Early Homophony

The fifteenth century also saw the beginning of composed *homophony*—that is, music in a harmonic texture (see page 29). In the simpler plainchant paraphrases of the time, the melody is often highlighted by an accompaniment that does not really sound polyphonic. Though there are still several polyphonic voices, most of the time their independence vanishes because they move along together and form simple chords.

The result is a plainchant harmonization. Once again the emphasis is on sensuous effect, that of homophony, rather than on the more intellectual process of polyphony.

Guillaume Dufay (c. 1400–1474)

Guillaume Dufay was born and bred in the north of France near Flanders (modern Belgium), a region that supplied the whole of Europe with musicians for many generations. For over twenty-five years he worked in Italy, where he came to know artists and thinkers of the Renaissance and (equally important!) the princely patrons who supported them. His later years were spent in a glow of celebrity at the important French cathedral of Cambrai.

"Ave Maris Stella": the Virgin Mary was the subject of special veneration in the late Middle Ages and the early Renaissance. Countless plainchants, motets, paintings and sculptures were created to honor her. Lost in her own thoughts, this serene, child-like Virgin by the German artist Stefan Lochner (1400–1451) seems oblivious to Jesus, even to God—and no doubt to the music played for her by the baby angels.

GUILLAUME DUFAY
Harmonized hymn, "Ave Maris Stella"

This is a homophonic setting of a Gregorian **hymn,** one of the most tuneful of plainchant genres. A Gregorian hymn consists of a short tune sung through many stanzas, followed by an Amen—much like a modern hymn, in fact. One of the loveliest of these hymns, "Ave maris stella," was also one of the best known, because it was addressed to the Virgin Mary and sung on all of the many special feasts in her honor, and on most Saturdays, too. Note how line 1 contains the words AVE MARI(s stell)A.

"Ave Maris Stella" is in the D (Dorian) mode. You may be able to hear at once that the third note in the tune (the sixth note of the scale) is higher than would be normal in the minor mode. The hymn itself has seven stanzas, but Dufay set only the even-numbered ones to his own music, leaving the others to be sung Gregorian-style in alternation. This makes it fairly easy to hear how he embellished the plainchant.

His music for stanzas 2, 4 and 6 is the same each time—almost entirely homophonic and quite suave. The top voice sings a paraphrased, somewhat longer version of the hymn tune, as shown on page 68. The embellishment consists of a few extra notes and extensions, with the free rhythm of Gregorian chant channeled into a graceful triple meter.

Plainsong hymn, "Ave maris stella"

A - ve _ ma-ris _ stel-la, ____

De - i Ma - ter _ al - ma,

At-que sem-per Vir-go, _____

Fe - lix cae - li por - ta.

LISTEN   Dufay, "Ave Maris Stella"

STANZA 1: Plainchant

Ave maris stella,   Hail, star of the ocean,
Dei Mater alma,   Kind Mother of God,
Atque semper Virgo,   And also still a virgin,
Felix caeli porta.   Our blessed port to heaven.

STANZA 2: Dufay's paraphrase

0:22   Summens illud Ave   May that blessed "Ave"
        Gabrielis ore,   From Gabriel's mouth
        Funda nos in pace,   Grant us peace,
        Mutans Hevae nomen.   Changing the name of "Eva."

STANZA 3: Plainchant

1:13   Solve vincia reis . . .   Solve . . .

STANZA 4: Paraphrase

1:36   Monstra te esse matrem . . .   Monstra . . .

STANZA 5: Plainchant

2:26   Virgo singularis . . .   Virgo . . .

STANZA 6: Paraphrase

2:48   Sit laus Deo Patri,   Praise be to God the Father,
        Summo Christo decus,   To Christ on high,
        Spiritui Sancto,   To the Holy Spirit:
        Tribus honor unus.   Three honored as one.
            Amen.   Amen.

There does not exist a single piece of music, not composed within the last forty years, that is regarded by the learned as worth hearing. Yet at this present time there flourish countless composers who glory in having studied the divine art under John Dunstable, Gilles Binchois, and Guillaume Dufay, recently deceased.

Composer and music theorist Johann Tinctoris, 1477

Dufay and another major composer of the time, Gilles Binchois (c. 1400–1460). Note the portative organ; see page 46.

This counts as a rather simple composition for Dufay, whose fame was and is based on longer, more elaborate pieces; he wrote some of the first polyphonic Masses, for example. Still, plainsong harmonizations make up an appreciable proportion of his output, and they show the new Renaissance attitudes with particular clarity.

The Mass

The new treatment of traditional plainchant, as in the technique of para-phrase, shows Renaissance composers taking a relaxed attitude toward medi-eval authority. The same can be said of their reaction to medieval intricacy, as represented by that most intellectual of musical devices, isorhythm. Fourteenth-century composers such as Machaut had used isorhythm even when writing love songs, but composers now cultivated a much simpler style for their polyphonic songs, or **chansons**: simpler, gentler, and more supple. The modest style of these new chansons was sometimes used for sacred texts, including portions of the Mass.

The rejection of isorhythm did not mean, however, that composers aban-doned the technical development of their craft, which had taken such impres-sive strides from the early days of organum. Rather, such efforts were focused on large-scale musical construction. For the first time, compositions were writ-ten to last—and to make sense—over twenty or thirty minutes.

The problem of large-scale construction that fascinated fifteenth-century composers was how to write music that would in some sense unify the **Mass.** As the largest and most important of all Church services, the Mass included some twenty musical items, originally sung in plainchant. By around 1450, the polyphonic Mass had been standardized into a five-section form. Composers now settled on these five sections for their polyphonic settings:

Kyrie	a simple prayer:	"Lord have mercy, Christ have mercy"
Gloria	a long hymn:	"Glory to God in the highest"
Credo	a recital of the Christian's list of beliefs, beginning	
		"I believe in one God, the Father almighty"
Sanctus	another hymn:	"Holy, holy, holy, Lord God of hosts"
Agnus Dei	another prayer:	"Lamb of God . . . have mercy on us"

The Mass has retained this five-section form down to the present day, in set-tings by Palestrina, Bach, Haydn, Schubert, Stravinsky, and many others.

The five sections of the Mass are very different in the length of their texts, they serve different liturgical functions, and they come at widely separated times in the actual service. Various musical schemes were invented to unify the sections. Similar music could be used to signal the beginning of all five movements, for example. Or all the movements could paraphrase the same Gregorian chant.

So large and complex a structure presented composers with a challenge, and they took this up in a spirit of inventiveness and ambition characteristic of the Renaissance. What the symphony was to nineteenth-century composers and their audiences, the Mass was to their fifteenth-century counterparts: a brilliant, monumental test of artistic prowess.

A Kyrie by Josquin (see page 73), from one of the first books of music to be printed, around 1500. The great Renaissance invention of printing stepped up the dis-tribution of music decisively, just as it did the distribution of books in general.

2 The "High Renaissance" Style

Around 1500 a new style emerged for Masses, motets, and chansons that was to hold sway for much of the sixteenth century. The chief characteristic of this "High Renaissance" musical style was a careful blend of two vocal techniques, *imitative counterpoint* and *homophony* (see pages 29–30).

Imitation

Most polyphony at the beginning of the fifteenth century was nonimitative; most polyphony at the end of the century was imitative. This remarkable change is due partly to the fact that imitative polyphony, or imitation, reflects the ideals of moderation and balance that also characterize the visual arts of the High Renaissance. In the Raphael Madonna on page 48, the calm, dignified repose expressed by the figures and faces is as striking as the beautiful balance among all the pictorial elements.

By its very nature, imitative texture depends on a calm, smooth balance among multiple voice parts. A first voice begins with a motive (see page 26) designed to fit the text being set. Soon other voices enter, one by one, singing the same motive and words, but at different pitch levels; meanwhile the earlier voices continue with new melodies that complement the later voices without swamping them. Each voice has a genuinely melodic quality, and all the melodies are drawn from a single source. None is mere accompaniment or "filler," and none predominates for very long.

We can get an impression of the equilibrium of imitative polyphony from its look on the page, even without reading the music exactly. The following excerpt is from the score of Josquin Desprez's *Pange lingua* Mass:

Homophony

Almost all polyphony involves some chords, as a product of its simultaneously sounding melodies. But in the music of Machaut, for example, the chords are more of a by-product. Late medieval composers concentrated on the "horizontal" aspects of texture at the expense of "vertical" ones, delighting in the separateness of their different voice parts. Chordal sonority was a secondary consideration.

A major achievement of the High Renaissance style was to create a rich chordal quality out of polyphonic lines that still maintain a quiet sense of independence. Composers also used pure homophony—passages of "block chord" writing. They learned to use homophony both as a contrast to imitative texture and as an expressive resource in its own right.

Other Characteristics

In tone color, the ideal at this time becomes *a cappella* performance—that is, performance by voices alone. Tempo and dynamics are relatively constant factors. The rhythm is fluid, without any sharp accents, and shifting unobtrusively all the time, so that the meter is often obscured. The melodies never go very high or very low in any one voice; the ups and downs are carefully balanced. This music rarely settles into the easy swing of a dance rhythm or into the clear patterns of an actual tune.

Music in the High Renaissance style can sometimes strike modern listeners as vague, but if we listen more closely—and always listen to the words as well as the music—its flexibility, sensitivity, and rich expressive potential may come clear. Does it remind us of a wonderfully musical and subtle speaking voice? The sixteenth century would have been pleased to think so.

Josquin Desprez (c. 1440–1521)

Josquin Desprez

The first master of the High Renaissance style was Josquin Desprez. Like Dufay, he was born in the north of France, and like Dufay and many other of his countrymen, in early life he traveled to Italy. The list of Josquin's patrons reads like a Renaissance Who's Who: Pope Alexander VI, the notorious Sforza family of Milan, the Estes of Ferrara, Louis XII of France.

A Kyrie from a dazzling illuminated manuscript book of Mass music. Did singers actually sing from such precious books? The man who commissioned the production of this book is shown here praying with the help of an angel, who also (below) seems to be giving a seal of approval to the family coat of arms.

An amazingly imaginative composer, Josquin brought the fifteenth-century Mass to a brilliant climax and pioneered whole new expressive genres, such as the sixteenth-century chanson and motet. He was famous both for his technical prowess and for his expressive innovations—for the childlike serenity of his motet "Ave Maria," as well as the grief-stricken accents of "Planxit autem David," a setting of King David's lament for his dead son Absalom.

JOSQUIN DESPREZ
Pange lingua Mass (c. 1510)

Josquin wrote eighteen different settings of the Mass—all large pieces in the standard five-section form. The *Pange lingua* Mass, one of his greatest masterpieces, derives its melodic material largely from a hymn called "Pange lingua." This is a Gregorian hymn of the same kind as "Ave Maris Stella," which we have heard in Dufay's harmonized setting. "Pange lingua" (and hence Josquin's Mass) is designed for Corpus Christi, a feast celebrating the Holy Eucharist.

This is a four-part Mass (that is, a Mass for a choir with four separate voice parts). In Josquin's day, boys sang the high parts and men the lower ones; Josquin probably started his musical career as a choirboy. Today women usually substitute for boys in music of this period.

We shall examine the first two sections of Josquin's *Pange lingua* Mass.

Kyrie The men in the choir sing line 1 of the hymn "Pange lingua" before the first section of the *Pange lingua* Mass. This first section, the Kyrie, is an elemental prayer consisting of three subsections:

Kyrie I:	Kyrie eleison.	Lord have mercy.
Christe:	Christe eleison.	Christ have mercy.
Kyrie II:	Kyrie eleison.	Lord have mercy.

For Kyrie I, Josquin wrote a **point of imitation**—a brief passage of imitative polyphony covering one short phrase of a composition's verbal text, and using a single musical motive. Josquin's point of imitation involves seven entries of the following motive, derived from line 1 of the hymn:

Gregorian hymn, "Pange lingua" (see page 75)

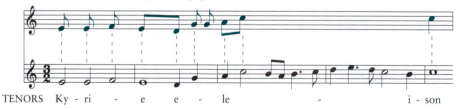

TENORS Ky - ri - e e - le - i - son

(The order of the voice entries is tenor, bass, *wait*, soprano, alto, *wait*, bass, tenor, soprano.) Josquin did not invent this motive—it was derived from the plainchant hymn, as shown above—but his paraphrase is very beautiful, especially at the end.

The Christe has two points of imitation, also derived from the hymn, for the words *Christe* and *eleison;* the motives of these points are rhythmically similar. Kyrie II has a short point of imitation for the words "Kyrie eleison," followed by free (that is, nonhymn) material—a descending sequence and a powerful oscillating passage prior to the drawn-out final cadence.

Throughout the motet ["Planxit autem David," by Josquin] there is preserved what befits the mourner, who at first is inclined to cry out constantly, then murmur to himself, then quiet down or—as passion breaks out anew—raise his voice again in a loud cry. All these things we see most beautifully observed in this composition.

An admirer of Josquin, writing a quarter century after his death

LISTEN	Josquin, *Pange lingua* Mass, Kyrie

0:05	Kyrie eleison	Lord have mercy.
0:44	Christe eleison	Christ have mercy.
2:01	Kyrie eleison	Lord have mercy.

Gloria   In the four remaining sections of the Mass—the Gloria, Credo, Sanctus, and Agnus Dei—countless new points of imitation are heard, but now they are interspersed with occasional text phrases set in homophony.

The second subsection of the Gloria, the "Qui tollis," begins with a passage in which polyphony and homophony are contrasted in a highly expressive way. At the beginning, the effect is like one or two persons timidly invoking Him "who takes away the sins of the world" (polyphony), and then the whole congregation—or the whole of Christendom—urgently responding with a plea for mercy and relief (homophony). This music gives a strong, almost dramatic sense of communal worship.

The "Qui tollis" as a whole includes eight points of imitation and four homophonic or nearly homophonic phrases. (The point for "Tu solus Dominus" is illustrated on page 72.) In the imitative phrases, the vocal lines fit together smoothly into chords, and while the sequence of these chords seems hard to predict, at least for modern ears, it does not seem arbitrary. Indeed, the remarkable mood of Josquin's music—at once sober, quietly energetic, and reverential—owes much to its "unpredictable" Phrygian (E) mode. Like the hymn "Pange lingua," the *Pange lingua* Mass is in this mode.

Plainsong hymn, "Pange lingua"

Pan-ge lin-gua _ glo-ri-o - si

Cor - po-ris mys-te-ri-um, _

San-gui-nis-que pre-ti - o - si,

Quem in mun-di pre-ti-um _

Fruc-tus ven-tris gen-ne-ro-si

Rex ef-fu-dit _ gen - ti-um.

LISTEN	Josquin, *Pange lingua* Mass, from the Gloria

(Capital letters indicate phrases sung in homophony.)

	Qui tollis peccata mundi,	You who take away the sins of the world,
	MISERERE NOBIS.	have mercy upon us.
0:34	Qui tollis peccata mundi,	You who take away the sins of the world,
	SUSCIPE DEPRECATIONEM NOSTRAM.	hear our prayer.
	Qui sedes ad dexteram Patris,	You who sit at the right hand of the Father,
	miserere nobis.	have mercy upon us.
1:18	Quoniam tu solus sanctus,	For you alone are holy,
	tu solus Dominus,	you alone are the Lord,
	tu solus altissimus,	you alone are the most high,
	Jesu Christe,	Jesus Christ,
	cum sancto spiritu,	With the Holy Spirit,
	in gloria Dei Patris.	in the glory of God the Father.
	AMEN.	Amen.

3 Music as Expression

In parts of Josquin's *Pange lingua* Mass, as we have just seen, the music does not merely enhance the service in a general way, but seems to address specific phrases of the Mass text and the sentiments behind them. Music can be said to "illustrate" certain words and to "express" certain feelings. The exploration of music's power to express human feelings was a precious contribution by musicians to the Renaissance "discovery of the world and of man."

Renaissance composers derived inspiration for this exploration from reports of the music of ancient Greece, just as artists, architects, and writers of the time were also looking to ancient Greece and Rome for inspiration. Philosophers such as Plato had testified that music was capable of arousing emotions in a very powerful way. In the Bible, David cures Saul when he is "troubled by an evil spirit" by playing on his harp; there are similar stories in Greek myth and Greek history. How modern music could recapture its ancient powers was much discussed by music theorists and composers after the time of Josquin.

They reasoned somewhat as follows. If poets wish to arouse feelings, they do so by writing about them—by describing, depicting, expressing feelings in words. By doing this poets can arouse similar feelings in their readers. What is the analogy in music? How is it possible for composers to arouse feelings in their listeners?

The Renaissance answer was that this could be done indirectly, by illustrating or otherwise enhancing words. If words can express feelings and music can illustrate words, then music can express feelings and also arouse them, though only in conjunction with a text. Through this new link to the world of human emotions, Renaissance music sought to gain new relevance to humanity.

Devotion to the ideal of musical expression, by way of a text, was one of the main guiding ideas for composers of the later Renaissance. This led them to a new sensitivity to the words they were setting, which manifested itself in two important developments.

🎵 First, composers wanted the words of their compositions to be clearly heard. They strove for accurate **declamation**—that is, they made sure that words were sung to rhythms and melodies that approximate normal speech.

This may seem elementary and obvious, but it is simply not true of most medieval organum and motets (or of many plainchants). The pronunciation of words set to music mattered less than the structure of the music. The Renaissance was the first era in which words were set to music naturally and clearly, vividly and beautifully.

🎵 Second, composers attempted to match their music to the *meaning* of the words that were being set. The term **word painting** is used for this musical illustration of the text. Words such as "fly" and "glitter" were set to rapid notes, "up" and "heaven" to high ones, and so on:

Fly,   Love, a - loft   to heav'n to seek out   for - tune . . .

Sigh was typically set by a motive including a rest, as though the singers have been interrupted by sighing. *Grief, cruel, torment, harsh,* and exclamations such as *alas*—words found all the time in the language of Renaissance love poetry—prompted composers to write dissonant harmony.

Word paintings could become mechanical and silly—for example, when the Italian word for "eyes," *occhi,* was set to two whole notes. But when used sensitively, it could intensify the emotion inherent in words and phrases in a striking way, as Renaissance doctrine demanded. First developed in the sixteenth century, word painting has remained an important expressive resource of all later music. For examples from the Baroque period, when it was especially important, see pages 92, 95, 143, and 147.

oc - chi

4 Late Renaissance Music

As we noted above, the High Renaissance style established by the generation of Josquin Desprez proved to be remarkably stable. Yet it was also flexible enough so that composers were able to do fruitful new things with it until the end of the sixteenth century. While its use was clearest in the Church music of the time, important new secular genres also made use of this style, in a modified form.

The universality of the style is symbolized by the geographical spread of its four most famous masters, Palestrina, Lassus, Victoria, and Byrd. Giovanni Pierluigi da Palestrina (c. 1525–1594) was born just outside Rome and worked in the Holy City all his life. Roland de Lassus (c. 1532–1594), also known as Orlando di Lasso, was a worldly and much-traveled Netherlander who settled at the court of Munich. Tomás Luis de Victoria (c. 1548–1611), a Spanish priest, spent many years in Rome working for the Jesuits but ended his life in Madrid. William Byrd (1543–1623) was organist of England's Chapel Royal under Queen Elizabeth I but also a member of the English dissident Catholic minority, who wrote Masses for illegal and highly dangerous services held in secret in barns and attics.

My Lord, if in our century there is any more excellent music than that of Orlande Lassus, I leave that judgment to masters of that art. I will say only this: that Plato, who liked so much to teach political harmony through musical proportions, would have taken his examples from Orlande had they lived at the same time.

Publisher's dedication (like a jacket blurb) in a Lassus edition, 1575

Singers of the Bavarian Court Chapel in 1565, under Roland de Lassus. Clearly the duke was proud of his choir and of its size; each man and boy is carefully and solemnly depicted, and they make an imposing group. The duke had another such picture painted of his equally large group of instrumentalists.

GIOVANNI PIERLUIGI DA PALESTRINA (c. 1525–1594)
Pope Marcellus Mass (1557)

Palestrina was a singer in, or choirmaster of, many of Rome's most famous churches and chapels, including the Sistine (Papal) Chapel. He lived in the repressive atmosphere of the Counter-Reformation movement, which was launched by the papacy in 1545 to combat the threat of the Reformation. Palestrina wrote secular compositions in his youth, some of which were widely popular, but later he recanted and apologized for them. He wrote over a hundred Masses and published his first examples with a highly symbolic frontispiece, which shows the kneeling composer presenting the pope with a special papal Mass.

Part of the Counter-Reformation program was the reform of supposed abuses in Church music. Palestrina's most famous composition, the *Pope Marcellus* Mass, was supposed to have convinced the Pope and his council that composers of complicated Church music could still set the words with clear enough declamation so that the congregation could hear them. Partly because of this legend, and partly because of the particular calmness and purity of his musical style, Palestrina became the eighteenth and nineteenth centuries' most revered Renaissance composer. His works are still treasured by Catholic choir directors today.

Gloria   A part of the Gloria of the *Pope Marcellus* Mass, the "Qui tollis," shows how the High Renaissance *a cappella* style changed after the time of Josquin. Compared with Josquin's setting of these same words in his *Pange lingua* Mass (see page 75), Palestrina's setting employs much more homophony. Apart from some fuzziness on a few individual words, only the last, climactic line of Palestrina's composition uses polyphony.

Beyond this, we will notice at once that vocal sonority is of major importance in Palestrina's setting. He uses a larger and richer choir than Josquin—six vocal parts, rather than four—and keeps alternating between one choral group, or semichoir, drawn from the total choir, to another. Thus the first phrase, in high voices, is answered by the second, in low voices, and so on. The total choir does not sing all together until the word *suscipe*.

What matters most to Palestrina are the rich, shifting tone colors and harmonies, which he uses to produce a generalized spiritual aura, sometimes ethereal, sometimes ecstatic. And with the ideals of the Counter-Reformation in mind, he is certainly careful to declaim the words very clearly.

The frontispiece of Palestrina's *First Book of Masses*, 1554, announces to all the world that this music has the Pope's blessing. The page is open to the Mass *Ecce Sacerdos magnus* ("Behold the great priest").

LISTEN   Palestrina, *Pope Marcellus* Mass, from the Gloria

1   1A
15   11

(Capital letters indicate phrases sung in homophony.)

	QUI TOLLIS PECCATA MUNDI,	You who take away the sins of the world,
	MISERERE NOBIS.	have mercy upon us.
	QUI TOLLIS PECCATA MUNDI,	You who take away the sins of the world,
	Suscipe DEPRECATIONEM NOSTRAM.	hear our prayer.
1:24	QUI SEDES AD DEXTERAM PATRIS,	You who sit at the right hand of the Father,
	MISERERE NOBIS.	have mercy upon us.
2:02	QUONIAM TU SOLUS SANCTUS,	For you alone are holy,
	TU SOLUS DOMINUS,	you alone are the Lord,
	TU SOLUS ALTISSIMUS,	you alone are the most high,
	JESU CHRISTE,	Jesus Christ,
2:37	CUM SANCTO SPIRITU,	With the Holy Spirit,
	in gloria Dei Patris.	in the glory of God the Father.
	Amen	Amen.

The Motet

The term *motet* has been applied to very different kinds of music over the ages; motets by Palestrina or Byrd have next to nothing in common with motets by Perotin or Machaut. The sixteenth-century **motet** is a relatively short composition to Latin words made up of short sections in the homophony and imitative polyphony that were the staples of the High Renaissance style. The words are nearly always religious, taken from a variety of sources—sometimes directly from the Bible. Thus, as compared with the Mass of the same time, the motet is basically similar in *musical style,* but different in *scope* and, of course, in text.

It was the variety of the text possibilities in the motet, as contrasted to the invariable Mass, that recommended it to sixteenth-century composers. By providing them with new words to express, motets allowed church composers to convey religious messages in their music with more verve and power than ever before.

The Italian Madrigal

It was in the secular field, however, that the Renaissance ideal of music as expression made the greatest inroads. This took place principally in an important new Italian genre, after around 1530, called the **madrigal.**

The madrigal is a short composition set to a one-stanza poem—typically a love poem, with a rapid turnover of ideas and images. Ideally it is sung by one singer per part, in an intimate setting. The music consists of a sometimes equally rapid turnover of sections in imitative polyphony or homophony. Essentially, then, the plan is the same as that in High Renaissance sacred works such as Masses and motets.

But with secular words came a decisive change of emphasis. The points of imitation were shorter, and the imitation itself less strict; there was generally much more homophony; and the words assumed more and more importance. Both declamation and word painting were developed with great subtlety. A line of Italian madrigal composers, or *madrigalists*, pioneered an amazing variety of techniques to make words more vivid and to illustrate and illuminate them by musical means.

> *If therefore you will compose madrigals, you must possess yourself of an amorous humor, so that you must be wavering like the wind, sometimes wanton, sometimes drooping, sometimes grave and staid, otherwise effeminate; and show the very uttermost of your variety, and the more variety you show the better shall you please.*
>
> From a music textbook by madrigal composer Thomas Morley, 1597

The English Madrigal

A genre like the madrigal, tied so closely to its words—Italian words—would seem difficult to transplant. All the same, Italian madrigals became all the rage in Elizabethan England and led to the composition of madrigals in English. This popularity may have reflected the taste and interests of Queen Elizabeth I herself. The Virgin Queen not only maintained a splendid musical establishment, like all other ambitious monarchs and nobles of the time, but she was also an accomplished musician in her own right.

In 1601 twenty-three English composers contributed madrigals to a patriotic anthology in her honor, called *The Triumphs of Oriana*. All the poems end with the same refrain: "Then sang the shepherds and nymphs of Diana: Long live fair Oriana!" Oriana was a mythological name for Elizabeth, and the nymphs and shepherds of Diana—the goddess of virginity—were her subjects. The *Triumphs* was obviously a court-inspired project, and as such it reminds us vividly of one of the main functions of court music of all times—flattery.

Queen Elizabeth I playing the lute. This miniature portrait is reproduced at almost exactly its original size.

THOMAS WEELKES (c. 1575–1623)
Madrigal, "As Vesta Was from Latmos Hill Descending" (1601)

16   12

Thomas Weelkes never rose beyond the position of provincial cathedral organist-choirmaster; in fact, he had trouble keeping even that post in later life, when the cathedral records assert that he became "noted and found for a common drunckard and notorious swearer and blasphemer." Although he is not a major figure, as are the other composers treated in this unit, he is one of the best composers of madrigals in English.

Written in better days, Weelkes's contribution to *The Triumphs of Oriana* is a fine example of a madrigal of the lighter kind. (Weelkes also wrote serious and melancholy madrigals.) After listening to the music of Josquin and Palestrina, our first impression of "Vesta" is of the sheer exuberant brightness of the musical style. Simple rhythms, clear harmonies, crisp melodic motives— all look forward to music of the Baroque era and beyond. This music has a modern feel about it.

The next thing likely to impress the listener is the elegance and liveliness with which the words are declaimed. We have already stressed the importance of declamation in the Renaissance composers' program of attention to verbal texts. Weelkes nearly always has his words sung in rhythms that would seem quite natural if the words were spoken, as shown at the right (where – stands for a long syllable, ◡ for a short one). The declamation is never less than accurate, and it is sometimes expressive: the rhythms make the words seem imposing in the second phrase shown, dainty in the third.

Leav-ing their God-dess all
    a-lone

Then sang the shep-herds
    and nymphs of Di-a-na

To whom Di-a-na's dar-lings

As for the word painting, that can be shown in a tabular form:

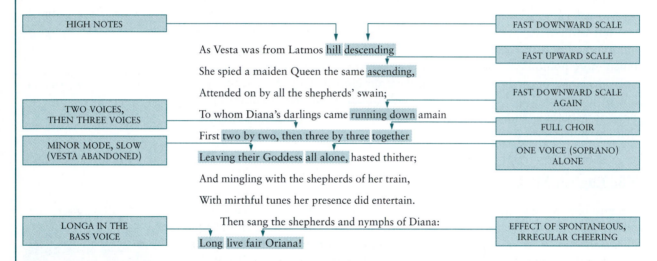

HIGH NOTES		FAST DOWNWARD SCALE
	As Vesta was from Latmos hill descending	FAST UPWARD SCALE
	She spied a maiden Queen the same ascending,	
	Attended on by all the shepherds' swain;	FAST DOWNWARD SCALE AGAIN
TWO VOICES, THEN THREE VOICES	To whom Diana's darlings came running down amain	FULL CHOIR
MINOR MODE, SLOW (VESTA ABANDONED)	First two by two, then three by three together	ONE VOICE (SOPRANO) ALONE
	Leaving their Goddess all alone, hasted thither;	
	And mingling with the shepherds of her train,	
	With mirthful tunes her presence did entertain.	
LONGA IN THE BASS VOICE	Then sang the shepherds and nymphs of Diana:	EFFECT OF SPONTANEOUS, IRREGULAR CHEERING
	Long live fair Oriana!	

(The "maiden Queen" is Elizabeth, and "Diana's darlings" are the Vestal Virgins, priestesses of Vesta, the Roman goddess of hearth and home. The archaic word *amain* means "at full speed.")

This brilliant six-part madrigal uses two sopranos, alto, two tenors, and bass. Weelkes makes particularly good use of this group in his extended imitative setting of the poem's last line. Here we can easily imagine many more than six loyal voices endlessly cheering their Queen in a spontaneous, irregular way, one after another. Shakespeare and his contemporaries, Weelkes among them, were very fond of puns. Weelkes has the word "long" sung by the bass voice on a note four times the duration of a whole note—a note whose Latin name was *longa*.

5 Instrumental Music: Early Developments

The best sixteenth-century composers concentrated almost entirely on vocal genres, on music with words. Except for the English master William Byrd, none of them devoted much attention to music for instruments alone. We have spoken above of the Renaissance preoccupation with expression in music, expression through the association of music with words.

Dance Stylization

"Kemp's Jig" (page 82) can lead us to an important topic that extends past the Renaissance into the music of modern times, up to our own century. An oddity of this particular dance is that in phrase **a**, the cadence—a stopping place (see page 27)—comes in the fourth bar, whereas in phrase **b**, a cadence comes in the fifth. Though the motion does not stop at this point, the tonic is reached in a very solid way in measure 9. Another cadence comes three bars later, in measure 12.

A dancer might be confused, even thrown off by this. A listener, on the other hand, might well enjoy the interesting effect caused by this irregularity in the cadences. "Kemp's Jig" is not as simple as it seems, then. If we like to think that this little dance puts us in touch with true "folk music," we must also suspect that a musician of some sophistication has been tinkering with it.

"Kemp's Jig" illustrates a tendency that will gain more and more importance later: the tendency to make dance music more and more elaborate and "artistic." Composers (and performers making it up on the spot) provided dance music with elements of a more strictly musical, less motor interest—such as irregular cadences, as in "Kemp's Jig," subtle phrase lengths, unusual harmonies, and even counterpoint.

This was the first stage of a process that we can call the *stylization* of dance music. Already well established in the sixteenth century, dance stylization was to attain new heights in the dance suites by Bach and the symphony minuets of Haydn and Mozart. In the twentieth century, fox-trot tunes were (and sometimes still are) "stylized" into jazz numbers. Louis Armstrong and Charlie Parker did not expect that people who came to listen to them were going to dance to such stylized versions.

Nevertheless, instruments and music for instruments developed significantly during this period. The first violins and harpsichords date from the sixteenth century; also perfected were the lute—a guitar-like instrument, originally from the Near East, that was perhaps the most popular of all at the time—and many other instruments. Instrumental music was to become one of the great glories of the Baroque era, and the basis for this was laid in the Renaissance.

Around 1500, hardly any music was written specifically for instruments. Instrumentalists would either play along with singers in vocal music, or else play motets, chansons and other vocal genres by themselves. The principal vocal genre after 1550, however, the madrigal, would not have made much sense performed without its words. By this time, in any case, new genres had been developed for instrumental performance.

Renaissance Dances

The most widespread of Renaissance instrumental genres was the dance, a reflection of the great popularity of dancing at the time.

Many dance types are described in detail in sixteenth-century instruction books—the steps themselves, and also their order or sequence. (In this regard, old dances were closer to square dances than to some modern social dancing, where there is no fixed order for steps or movements.) One of the most popular was the **pavane** (paván), a solemn dance in duple meter, with the participants stepping and stopping formally. The pavane was usually paired with the triple-meter **galliard.** Simpler, less formal Renaissance dance types include the Italian saltarello, the English jig, and the French branle—whose name is related to our word *brawl*.

Conforming to the dance steps, dance music was written in easy-to-follow phrases, almost always four to eight bars long. Ending with especially clear cadences, the phrases were each played twice in succession to produce forms such as **a a b b** or **a a b b c c.**

Not Will Kemp, but another famous comic of Shakespeare's time: Richard Tarleton, with the traditional tools of his trade, the pipe and tabor (a type of simple flute, blown like a recorder, and a snare drum).

ANONYMOUS
Galliard, "Daphne"

The title of this melodious Elizabethan dance suggests that originally it may have been a song. But if so, at some point the song was pressed into galliard form, **a a b b c c,** and this is the only way it has survived.

Played in our recording by an early violin ensemble, "Daphne" is mainly homophonic. The meter is kept very clear, and the distinct quality of the phrases ending **a, b,** and **c** makes it easy for the dancers to remember the place in the dance step sequence. The first violin provides extensive ornamentations at the second playing.

ANONYMOUS
"Kemp's Jig"

Will Kemp was an Elizabethan actor, comedian, and song-and-dance man, immortalized for having created comic roles in Shakespeare, such as Dogberry the Constable in *Much Ado About Nothing*. Kemp specialized in a type of popular dance number, called a jig, that was regularly presented in Elizabethan theaters after the main play.

"Kemp's Jig" is a lively—perhaps "perky" is the right word—and seemingly simple dance tune in **a a b** form. It is played several times on our recording, first by a recorder and then by a viol, an early string instrument in the cello range; ornaments are piled on, first to the repeated phrase **a** and then to all the repetitions. A lute accompanies.

A scene of dancing in the fifteenth century.

CHAPTER 8

The Early Baroque Period

A t the end of the sixteenth century, music was undergoing rapid changes at the sophisticated courts and churches of northern Italy. Composers began to write motets, madrigals, and other pieces more directly for effect—with a new simplicity, in some respects, but also with the use of exciting new resources. A new style, the style of the early Baroque period, took hold rapidly all over Italy and in most of the rest of Europe.

1 From Renaissance to Baroque

As we have seen, the madrigal was the most "advanced" form in late Renaissance music. Toward the end of the sixteenth century, the thirst for expression led madrigal composers to increasingly esoteric kinds of word painting. Extreme dissonances and rhythmic contrasts were explored in order to illustrate emotional texts in a more and more exaggerated fashion.

At the same time, a reaction set in *against* the madrigal. In Florence, an influential group of intellectuals who called themselves the *Camerata*—meaning something like "the Associates"—mounted an attack on the madrigalists' favorite technique, word painting. Word painting was artificial and childish, they said, and the many voices of a madrigal ensemble could not focus feeling or express it strongly. Whatever the madrigalists thought, a choir singing counterpoint could only dilute strong emotions, not concentrate them.

True emotionality could be projected only by a single human agent, an individual, a singer who would learn from great actors and orators how to move an audience to laughter, anger, or tears. A new style of solo singing was developed, *recitative,* that was half music, half recitation. This led inevitably to the stage and, as we shall see, to *opera.* Invented in Florence around 1600, opera became one of the greatest and most characteristic products of the Baroque imagination.

Music in Venice

Meanwhile, equally sensational developments were taking place in Venice, the city of canals. The "Serene Republic," as Venice called itself, cultivated especially brilliant styles in all the arts—matched, it seems, to the city's dazzling

Why cause words to be sung by four or five voices so that they cannot be distinguished, when the ancient Greeks aroused the strongest passions by means of a single voice supported by a lyre? We must renounce counterpoint and the use of different kinds of instruments and return to simplicity.

A Florentine critic, 1581

Venice: the Grand Canal

physical appearance. Wealthy and cosmopolitan, Venice produced architects whose flamboyant, varied buildings were built out of multicolored materials, and painters—the Bellinis, Titian, Tintoretto—who specialized in warm, rich hues. Perhaps, then, it is more than a play on words to describe Venetian music as "colorful."

From the time of Palestrina's *Pope Marcellus* Mass, sixteenth-century composers had often subdivided their choirs into low and high "semichoirs" of three or four voice parts each. The semichoirs would alternate and answer or echo each other. Expanding this technique, Venetian composers would now alternate two, three, or more whole choirs. Homophony crowded out polyphony as full choirs answered one another stereophonically, and seemed to compete throughout entire motets and Masses, coming together for climactic sections of glorious massed sound.

The resources of sonority were exploited even further when sometimes the "choirs" were designated for singers on some parts and instruments on others. Or else whole choirs would be made up of instruments. As the sonorous combinations of Venetian music grew more and more colorful, the stately decorum of the High Renaissance style was forgotten (or left to musical conservatives). Magnificence and extravagance became the new ideals, well suited to the pomp and ceremony for which Venice was famous.

Extravagance and Control

Wherever they looked, knowledgeable travelers to Italy around 1600 would have seen music bursting out of its traditional forms, styles, and genres. Freedom was the order of the day. But they might have been puzzled to notice an opposite tendency as well. Musical form was becoming more rigorously controlled and systematic. As composers sought to make music more untrammeled in one respect, they found they had to organize it more strictly in another, so that listeners would not lose track of what was happening.

The control composers exercised over Baroque form, in other words, was an appropriate response to Baroque extravagance, exaggeration, and emotionality. We shall see rather similar forces and counterforces at other points in musical history later in this book.

GIOVANNI GABRIELI (c. 1555–1612)
Motet, "O magnum mysterium" (published 1615)

The most important composers in Venice were two Gabrielis, Andrea (c. 1510–1586) and his nephew Giovanni. As organists of St. Mark's Cathedral, both of them exploited the special acoustics of that extraordinary building, which still amaze tourists today. By placing choirs of singers and instrumentalists in different choir lofts, they obtained brilliant echo effects that even modern audio equipment cannot recapture.

Giovanni's "O magnum mysterium," the second part of a longer motet, was written for the Christmas season. The text marvels that lowly animals— the ox and the ass—were the first to see the newborn Jesus.

And the music marvels along with the text. Quite in the manner of a madrigal, the exclamation, "O" is repeated like a gasp of astonishment. Then lush chord progressions positively make the head spin, as the words *O magnum mysterium* are repeated to the same music, but pitched higher (that is to say, in sequence: see page 27). A momentary change in the meter—which slips from 2/2 into 3/2—provides a new feeling of majesty, as much as astonishment:

As to the texture, what we are aware of at the start of the motet is a sumptuous blend of brass instruments and voices. In fact, Gabrieli is using two large "choirs," each with three voice parts and four instrumental parts, plus organ, but we do not grasp this at first. We do hear solo voices emerge at *sacramentum*. First solo tenors, then boy sopranos echo one another during the line *iacentem in presipio,* where a new rapid figure bounces back and forth from tenors to sopranos to trumpets.

But it is only with the choral *alleluia* section that Gabrieli really unleashes his musical resources. The music moves in quick triple meter, matching the jubilation of repeated *alleluias,* and the two choirs echo back and forth across the sound space in a veritable stereophonic display:

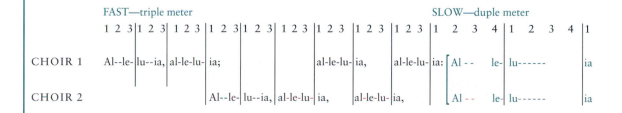

To make a grand conclusion, the choirs come together again. There is another wash of voice-and-brass sonority as the tempo changes to a slow duple meter for a climactic *alleluia*. For yet another *alleluia*, the music adds a solemn extra beat (the meter changes once again):

And for still more emphasis, Gabrieli repeats the entire *alleluia* section, comprising the fast triple-time alternations and the massive slow ending.

Notice the parallel between the beginning and the end of "O magnum mysterium." Similarities include the tempo and meter (slow, changing), the texture (massed choirs), and the musical technique used (sequence). In other words, Gabrieli has imposed organization and control behind the flamboyant chords and solo rhapsodies. Here is a simple example of the combination of extravagance and control in early Baroque music that we discussed above.

LISTEN   Giovanni Gabrieli, "O magnum mysterium"

1   1B

19   1

	O magnum mysterium,	O, what a great mystery,
0:32	et admirable sacramentum	and what a wonderful sacrament—
0:52	ut animalia viderunt Dominum natum	that animals should see the Lord new-born
1:18	iacentem in presepio:	lying in the manger.
1:51	Alleluia, alleluia.	Hallelujah, hallelujah.

---

2 Style Features of Early Baroque Music

Music from the period of approximately 1600 to 1750 is usually referred to as "baroque," a term originally applied to large pearls of irregular shape. A number of broad stylistic features unify the music of this long period.

Rhythm and Meter

Rhythms become more definite and regular in Baroque music; a single rhythm or similar rhythms can be heard throughout a piece or a major segment of a piece. Compare the subtle, floating rhythms of Renaissance music, changing section by section as the motives change. (Renaissance dance music is an exception, and in the area of dance music there is a direct line from the Renaissance to the Baroque.)

Related to this new regularity of rhythm is a new acceptance of meter. One technical feature tells the story: bar lines begin to be used for the first time in music history. This means that music's meter is systematically in evidence, rather than being downplayed as it was in the Renaissance. The strong beats are emphasized by certain instruments, playing in a clear, decisive way. All this is conspicuous enough in Gabrieli's motet "O magnum mysterium."

Texture: Basso Continuo

Some early Baroque music is homophonic and some is polyphonic, but both textures are enriched by a feature unique to the period, the **basso continuo.**

As in a Renaissance score, in a Baroque score the bass line is performed by bass voices or low instruments such as cellos or bassoons. But the bass part in Baroque music is also played by an organ, harpsichord, or other chord instrument. This instrument not only reinforces the bass line, it also adds chords continuously (hence the term *continuo*) to go with it. The basso continuo—or just "continuo"—has the double effect of clarifying the harmony and of making the texture bind or jell.

One can see how this device responds to the growing reliance of Baroque music on harmony (already clear from Gabrieli's motet). In the early days, the continuo was simply the bass line of the polyphony reinforced by chords; but later the continuo with its chords was mapped out first, and the polyphony adjusted to it. Baroque polyphony, in other words, has systematic harmonic underpinnings.

This fact is dramatized by a characteristic Baroque form, the **ground bass.** This is music constructed literally from the bottom up. In ground bass form, the bass instruments play a single short figure many times, generating the same set of repeated harmonies (played by the continuo chord instruments). Above this ground bass, upper instruments or voices play (or improvise) different melodies or virtuoso passages, all adjusted to the harmonies determined by the bass.

Baroque ground bass compositions discussed in this book are "Dido's Lament" from the opera *Dido and Aeneas* by Henry Purcell (page 94) and Vivaldi's *Stravaganza* Concerto in G, Op. 4 No. 12 (page 120).

A ground bass
(the Pachelbel Canon)

= repeated
many times

Functional Harmony

In view of these new techniques, it is not surprising that the art of harmony evolved rapidly at this time. Whereas Renaissance music had still used the medieval modes, although with important modifications, Baroque musicians developed the modern major/minor system. Chords became standardized, and the sense of tonality—the feeling of centrality around a tonic or "home" pitch—grew much stronger.

Composers also developed a new way of handling the chords so that their interrelation was felt to be more logical, or at least more coherent. Each chord now assumed a special role, or function, in relation to the tonic chord (the chord on the "home" pitch). Thus when one chord follows another in Baroque music, it does so in a newly satisfactory, predictable, and purposeful way. "Functional" harmony, in this sense, could also be used as a way of organizing large-scale pieces of music, as we shall see later.

In a Baroque composition, as compared with one from the Renaissance, the chords seem to be going where we expect them to—and we feel they are determining the sense or the direction of the piece as a whole. Harmonies no longer seem to wander, detour, hestitate, or evaporate. With the introduction of the important resource of functional harmony, Baroque music brings us firmly to the familiar, to the threshold of modern music.

Music is a roaring-meg against melancholy, to rear and revive the languishing soul; affecting not only the ears, but the very arteries, the vital and animal spirits, it erects the mind and makes it nimble.

Robert Burton, 1621

A torchlight concert in a German town square. The harpsichord continuo is at the center of the action. Notice the big music stands or racks, and the two timpani sunk in a panel, like a double sink.

3 Opera

Opera—drama presented in music, with the characters singing instead of speaking—is often called the most characteristic art form of the Baroque period. For Baroque opera combined many different arts: not only music, drama, and poetry, but also dancing and highly elaborate scene design. Set designers developed incredibly ingenious machines to portray gods descending to earth, shipwrecks, volcanos, and all kinds of natural and supernatural phenomena. Designers often received top billing, ahead of the composers.

The early Florentine operas were court entertainments put on to celebrate royal weddings and the like. But an important step was taken in 1637 with the opening of the first public opera theater. First in Venice and then in the whole of Italy, opera soon became the leading form of entertainment. By the end of the century, seven opera houses in Venice fulfilled much the same function as movie theaters in a comparable modern city (around 145,000 people).

Opera was a perfect answer to the general desire in the early Baroque era for individual emotionalism. For opera provided a stage on which the single individual could step forward to express his or her feelings in the most direct and powerful fashion. Indeed, composers felt a need to relieve the constant emotional pressure exerted on their characters by the ever-changing dramatic action. They had to contrive moments of relaxation, and this led to a standard dualism that has been with opera ever since: *recitative* and *aria*. This dualism between tension and repose reflects that other Baroque dualism, between freedom and strictness, extravagance and control.

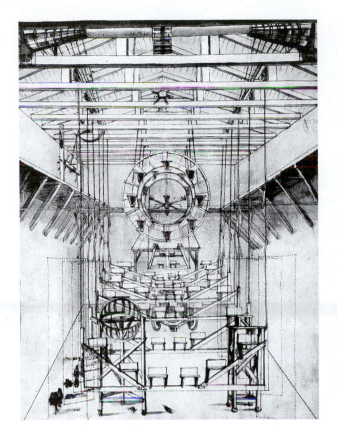

Stage designers of Baroque opera specialized in moving sets for their most dazzling effects. Shown here is the machinery for one such set and a drawing of the intended realization.

Recitative

Recitative (re-sih-ta-téev), from the Italian word for "recitation," is the technique of declaiming words musically in a heightened, theatrical manner. The singing voice closely follows the free rhythm of highly emotional speech; it mirrors and exaggerates the natural ups and downs that occur as an actor raises his or her voice at a question, lowers it in an "aside," or cries out in distress. The accompaniment is usually kept to a minimum, so that the singer-actor can interpret the dialogue or the action as spontaneously as possible, and so that all the words can be heard clearly.

Recitative—the "free" side of the operatic dualism—is used for plot action, dialogue, and other situations in the drama where it is particularly important for the words to be brought out. On the other hand, where spoken drama would call for soliloquies or meditations, opera uses arias.

Aria

An **aria** is an extended piece for solo singer that has much more musical elaboration and coherence than a passage of recitative. The vocal part is more melodic, and typically the accompaniment includes the entire orchestra. Here the singer-actor mulls over his or her feelings at some leisure, instead of reacting moment by moment, as in recitative. Emotion is controlled and "frozen" into a tableau. Paradoxically, when the music gets more elaborate, the emotion stands still.

Recitative required great singing actors, and arias required artists who could convert the notes of a score into these tableaus of brilliant, furious, sensuous, or tragic expression. Opera houses in the seventeenth century became showcases of vocal virtuosity—as they still are today. Ever since the Baroque era, musical drama and vocal display have vied with one another as the driving force of opera.

Claudio Monteverdi (1567–1643)

One figure stood out above all others in music around 1600, just as Josquin Desprez had around 1500. Claudio Monteverdi, an enormously imaginative and innovative composer, also has the dubious distinction of being the first great composer whose music was attacked publicly for being too radical. Radical it was. Monteverdi has aptly been called "the last great madrigalist and the first great opera composer"; and indeed, while his earlier madrigals are close enough in style to those of Thomas Weelkes, some of his later ones are more like small opera scenes.

Monteverdi first worked at the music-loving court of Mantua, in northern Italy. There he wrote his first stage work, *Orfeo* (1607), famous in music history as the first masterpiece of opera. He was then appointed choirmaster of St. Mark's Cathedral in Venice, the most prestigious musical position in Europe. At the end of his life, in the 1640s, he helped inaugurate public opera, Venice's greatest contribution to the history of music.

Title-page of a commemorative edition of Monteverdi's music, published in Venice ("In VENETIA") just after his death. The design includes a portrait and a fine collection of old instruments, including four lutes, shown in front and back views.

Singing Italian

The *Coronation of Poppea* is the first of many Italian texts printed in this book. To follow the recordings, it will help to know a few simple rules about Italian pronunciation and singing conventions.

First: *c* and *g* are soft when followed by *e* or *i* (cello = chello; cio = cho; gelata = jelata), hard when followed by other letters, including *h* (che = kay; coda; spaghetti).

Second: in poems, when an Italian word *ending* with a vowel is followed by another word *beginning* with a vowel, the two vowels are run together as one.

Third: in Italian (and German) *z* is pronounced *dz* or *tz*: pizza, Mozart. Lines from our selection from *The Coronation of Poppea* are sung as indicated below:

3	Pur **teco** io sto	= Pur tec'yo sto
18	**tu a** me verrai	= tw'a me verrai
26	Il **core accarezando	= Il cor'accaretzando
28	E mi **circondi** intanto	= E mi chircond'intanto
33	Per me **guerreggia** Amor	= Per me gwerrej'Amor

CLAUDIO MONTEVERDI
The Coronation of Poppea (1642)

After his first opera, *Orfeo,* none of Monteverdi's operas was printed, and some have been completely lost—a grievous loss indeed. All we have left of his *Arianna* is the heroine's big lament, one of the greatest hits of the day, which Monteverdi published by itself in several different arrangements. Fortunately, two late masterpieces have survived: *The Return of Ulysses* and *The Coronation of Poppea.* After slumbering for three hundred years, *Poppea* has recently proved to be a "sleeper" in opera houses around the world.

Background   Even today, the story of *The Coronation of Poppea* can shock by its startling and cynical dramatic realism. Poppea, mistress of the notorious Roman Emperor Nero, schemes to get his wife, Ottavia, deposed and his eminent adviser, Seneca, put to death. In a counterplot, Ottavia blackmails Ottone, Poppea's rejected lover, into an attempt on Poppea's life. He tries but fails. The counterplotters are all exiled. As an added cynical touch, Poppea's ruthless maneuvering to be crowned empress of Rome is shown to be aided by the God of Love and the Goddess of Fortune.

After a prologue sung by the mythological characters, Act I begins with Ottone arriving at Poppea's house at daybreak, and retreating in dismay after he sees Nero's guards outside it. In an ironic alba (see page 59), the guards curse military life and exchange scurrilous gossip about Poppea's scheming. This is a vivid prelude to the first of the opera's several steamy love scenes.

Recitative   Enter Nero and Poppea, who tries to wheedle Nero into staying with her. Delaying his departure as long as possible, she makes him promise to return. Accompanied by a lute as continuo instrument—a voluptuous sound, in this context—she repeats the question *"Tornerai?"* ("Won't you return?") in increasingly seductive accents until Nero stops evading the issue and agrees: *"Tornerò"* ("Yes, I will return"). Notice how the vocal line does not form itself into real melodies, but goes up or down or speeds or slows, following the words in speechlike fragments.

Nero's most extended evasion is a short aria-like fragment, called an **arioso.** Then the recitative resumes. On the final *addios*—some of them melting, others breathless—the singers improvise delicate vocal ornaments.

Many men's roles in early opera were written for male soprano singers. On our recording, Nero is sung by a female mezzo-soprano, Della Jones, whose lower, more "focused" voice contrasts with that of the soprano singing Poppea.

Aria   As soon as Nero leaves, Poppea shows her true colors in a jubilant aria. It is accompanied by a small orchestra, and contains three short sections. The first is a little dance of triumph, an orchestral tune (strings and recorder) to which Poppea sings her first text couplet:

After a moment of uncertainty ("a mantle that is . . . illusory"), marked by a momentary lapse into recitative, her mood becomes harder and more determined in the aria's second section. Finally, in section 3, she sings lighthearted, fast military fanfares—this is word painting in the madrigal tradition—as she rejoices in the fact that the gods are fighting on her behalf.

Mercurial, manipulative, fearless, dangerously sensual: Poppea has been characterized unforgettably by Monteverdi's music in this scene.

LISTEN   Monteverdi, *The Coronation of Poppea*, from Act I

1   1B
20-21   2

(Italics indicate repeated words and lines.)

RECITATIVE

0:00	**Poppea:**	Tornerai?	Won't you return?
	Nero:	Se ben io vò,	Though I am leaving you,
		Pur teco io stò, *pur teco stò* . . .	I am still really staying . . .
	Poppea:	Tornerai?	Won't you return?
	Nero:	Il cor dalle tue stelle	My heart can never, never be torn away
		Mai mai non si divelle . . .	from your fair eyes . . .
	Poppea:	Tornerai?	Won't you return?

ARIOSO

0:23	**Nero:**	Io non posso da te, *non posso da te,*	I cannot live apart from you
		da te viver disgiunto	
		Se non si smembra l' unita del punto . . .	Unless unity itself can be divided . . .

RECITATIVE

0:56	**Poppea:**	Tornerai?	Won't you return?
	Nero:	Tornerò.	I will return . . .
	Poppea:	Quando?	When?
	Nero:	Ben tosto.	Soon . . .
	Poppea:	Ben tosto, me'l prometti?	Very soon—you promise?
	Nero:	Te'l giuro.	I swear it!
	Poppea:	*E me l'osserverai?*	And will you keep your promise?
	Nero:	*E s'a te non verrò, tu a me verrai!*	If I do not come, you'll come to me!
1:20	**Poppea:**	Addio . . .	
	Nero:	Addio . . .	
	Poppea:	. . . Nerone, Nerone, addio . . .	
	Nero:	. . . Poppea, Poppea, addio . . .	
	Poppea:	Addio, Nerone, addio!	Farewell, Nero, farewell!
	Nero:	Addio, Poppea, ben mio.	Farewell, Poppea, my love. *(exit)*

ARIA

(Section 1)

21	2:25	**Poppea:**	Speranza, tu mi vai	O hope, you
			Il core accarezzando;	Caress my heart;
			Speranza, tu mi vai il genio lusingando;	O hope, you entice my mind;
			E mi circondi intanto	And meanwhile you cloak me
			Di regio si, ma immaginario manto.	In a mantle that is royal, yet illusory.

	(Section 2)	
3:10	No no, *non temo, no*,	No, no! I fear no adversity:
	no no, non temo, no di noia alcuna:	
	(Section 3)	
3:26	*Per me guerreggia, guerreggia,*	I have fighting for me . . .
	Per me guerreggia Amor, *guerreggia*	I have fighting for me Love
	Amor e la Fortuna, *e la Fortuna.*	and Fortune!

Henry Purcell (c. 1659–1695)

Italy was the undisputed leader in music throughout the seventeenth century. However, music also flourished in France, Germany (or what is now Germany), and other countries, always under Italian influence.

The greatest English composer of the Baroque era, Henry Purcell, was the organist at Westminster Abbey and a member of the Chapel Royal, like several other members of his family. In his short lifetime he wrote sacred, instrumental, and theater music, as well as twenty-nine "Welcome Songs" for his royal masters. Purcell combined a respect for native traditions, represented by the music of William Byrd, Thomas Weelkes, and others, with a lively interest in the more adventurous French and Italian music of his own time. His first publication, in 1683, consisted of the first English sonatas.

Henry Purcell

HENRY PURCELL
Dido and Aeneas (1689)

Though Purcell wrote a good deal of music for the London theater, his one true opera, *Dido and Aeneas,* was composed for amateurs. Commissioned for a girls' school, the whole thing lasts little more than a hour, and contains no virtuoso singing roles at all. *Dido and Aeneas* is an exceptional work, then, and a miniature, but it is also a work of rare beauty and dramatic power. Rarer still, it is a great opera in English, perhaps the only great opera in English prior to the twentieth century.

Background   Purcell's source was the *Aeneid,* the noblest of all Latin epic poems, written by Virgil to celebrate the glory of Rome and the Roman Empire. It tells the story of the city's foundation by the Trojan prince Aeneas, who escapes from Troy when the Greeks capture it with their wooden horse. After many adventures and travels, Aeneas finally reaches Italy, guided by the firm hand of Jove, king of the gods.

In one of the *Aeneid's* most famous episodes, Aeneas and the widowed Queen Dido of Carthage fall deeply in love. But Jove tells the prince to stop dallying and get on with his important journey. Regretfully he leaves, and Dido kills herself out of grief.

In Acts I and II of the opera, Dido expresses apprehension about her feelings for Aeneas, even though her courtiers keep encouraging the match in chorus after chorus. Next we see the plotting of some witches, who for malicious reasons of their own make Aeneas believe that Jove is ordering his departure. The witches are a highly un-Virgilian touch, but ever since Shakespeare's *Macbeth,* witches had been popular with English theatergoers, perhaps especially with school-age ones.

In Act III, Aeneas tries feebly to excuse himself; Dido spurns him in a furious recitative. As he leaves, deserting her, she prepares for her suicide.

Our Songs and our Musick
Let's still dedicate
To *Purcell,* to *Purcell,*
The Son of *Apollo,*
'Till another, another,
Another as Great
In the Heav'nly Science
Of Musick shall follow.
—Poet Thomas d'Urfey,
seventeenth century

Recitative   Dido addresses this regal, somber recitative to her confidante, Belinda. Notice the imperious tone as she tells Belinda to take her hand, and the ominous setting of the word *darkness*. Purcell even contrives to suggest a kind of tragic irony in the turn of Dido's melodic line on the word *welcome* in "Death is now a welcome guest."

Aria   The opera's final aria, usually known as "Dido's Lament," is built over a slow ground bass (see page 87), a repeated descending bass line with chromatic semitones. The bass line sounds mournful even without accompaniment, as in measures 1–4. This line is imitated by the upper string parts of the orchestra while Dido is singing, and especially after she has stopped.

As often happens in arias, the words are repeated a number of times; Dido has little to say but much to feel, and the music needs time to convey the emotional message. We experience an extended emotional tableau. Whereas recitative makes little sense unless the listener understands the exact words, with arias a general impression of them may be enough. Indeed, even that is unnecessary when the melody is as poignant as Purcell's is here.

The most heartbreaking place comes (twice) on the exclamation "ah," where the bass note D, harmonized with a major-mode chord during the first six appearances of the ground bass, is shadowed by a new minor chord:

Dec. 6, 1665. *Here the best company for musique I ever was in, in my life, and I wish I could live and die in it, both for the musique and the face of Mrs. Pierce, and my wife, and Mrs. Knipp, who is pretty enough and sings the noblest that ever I heard in my life.*

Civil servant Samuel Pepys, from his diary (first published in 1825)

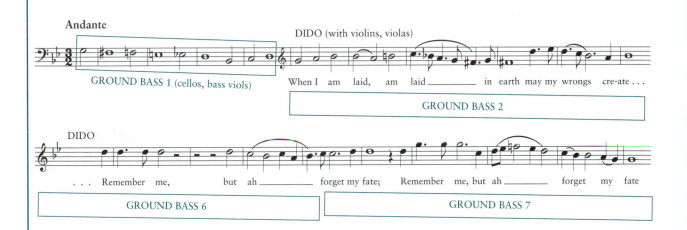

Chorus   The last notes of this great aria run into a wonderful final chorus. We are to imagine a slow dance, as groups of sorrowful cupids (first graders, perhaps) file past the bier. Now Dido's intense personal grief is transmuted into a communal sense of mourning. In the context of the whole opera, this chorus seems even more meaningful, because the courtiers who sing it have matured so much since the time when they thoughtlessly and cheerfully urged Dido to give in to her love.

The general style of the music is that of the madrigal—imitative polyphony and homophony, with some word painting. (The first three lines are mostly imitative, the last one homophonic.) But Purcell's style clearly shows the inroads of functional harmony and of the definite, unified rhythms that had been developing in the seventeenth century. There is no mistaking this touching chorus for an actual Renaissance madrigal.

The chorus is sung through twice—another emotional tableau, and this time the emotion spills over to the opera audience. As the courtiers grieve for Dido, we join them in responding to Dido's tragedy.

LISTEN   Purcell, *Dido and Aeneas*, Act III, final scene

(Italics indicate repeated words and lines.)

RECITATIVE

0:00 **Dido:**   Thy hand, Belinda! Darkness shades me;
                 On thy bosom let me rest.
                 More I would—but death invades me:
                 Death is now a welcome guest.

ARIA

0:55 **Dido:**   When I am laid, *am laid* in earth
                 May my wrongs create
                 No trouble, *no trouble* in thy breast; *(repeated)*
                 Remember me . . . *remember me,* but ah, forget my
                     fate;
2:17   *Remember me, but ah, forget my fate.*
                     (stabs herself)

CHORUS

23   4:05 **Courtiers:**   With drooping wings, ye cupids come
                         (words repeated)
                         And scatter roses, *scatter, scatter roses* on her tomb.
                         Soft, soft and gentle as her heart.
5:28   Keep here, *here* your watch;
                         Keep here, here, keep here your watch,
                             and never, *never, never,* part.

Colored type indicates words treated with word painting.

4 The Rise of Instrumental Music

The development of instrumental music—music that does not depend on words—counts as one of the most far-reaching contributions of composers in the early Baroque period. Broadly speaking, we can trace instrumental music to three main sources.

❧   *Dance,* the first of these sources, is one we have already discussed. In the Baroque period dance received a special impetus from opera, the genre that most fascinated people at the time. The reason is that opera was firmly linked to ballet (as we have seen in *Dido and Aeneas*). Musicians would put together sets of dances selected from operas or ballets; these dance **suites,** as they were called—groups of dances—could then be played by an orchestra and enjoyed apart from an actual stage performance.

French composers also specialized in writing dances and suites for harpsichord. These are "stylized" dances (see page 81), pieces written in the style or the form of dance music but intended for listening rather than dancing, for mental rather than physical pleasure.

❧   *Virtuosity* was the second source from which composers of instrumental music drew. As long as instruments have existed there have surely been virtuoso players ready to show them off—and audiences ready to applaud the show. But the art of early virtuosos was improvised and scarcely ever written down; only in the sixteenth and seventeenth centuries was some of their art incorporated systematically into written-out compositions. And even then, not all the virtuosity on which the compositions depended for their effect was notated. Much was left to be improvised, and so modern performers often have to play a good deal more than what appears in the old scores.

Even that vulgar and tavern music, which makes one man merry, another mad, strikes in me a deep fit of devotion, and a profound contemplation of the first Composer; there is something in it of divinity more than the ear discovers.

Physician–author Sir Thomas Browne, 1642

⁊ *Vocal music* was the third source for instrumental music. More specifically, the principal technique of vocal music, imitative polyphony (imitation), was transferred to the instrumental medium. In fact, this happened already in the Renaissance, which developed several instrumental genres by modeling on vocal music in this way. Each genre consists of a series of points of imitation (see page 74) built on different motives, like a motet or a madrigal.

From these genres developed the characteristic polyphonic genre of the Baroque era, the **fugue**. A typical fugue uses only one theme throughout, like a single gigantic point of imitation, and often treats that theme with a considerable display of contrapuntal ingenuity and learning. The art of improvising and writing fugues was practiced especially by keyboard players: organists and harpsichordists. We will discuss fugue more fully in Chapter 10.

Arcangelo Corelli

Arcangelo Corelli (1653–1713)

The three basic tendencies in instrumental music were merged authoritatively by the Roman violinist-composer Arcangelo Corelli. In an important series of publications, Corelli established models for violin sonatas and concertos that were immediately recognized as classics. These works incorporate emphatic elements of instrumental virtuosity, and yet balance this with a new clarity of form. Corelli experimented with many kinds of dance stylizations, and also wrote fugues (or fuguelike compositions) of a not too complicated kind.

ARCANGELO CORELLI
Sonata da Chiesa (Trio Sonata) in F, Op. 3 No. 1 (1685)*

1   1B
24-27   4

The word **sonata** simply means "sounded," so it can be and has been applied to a great many different types of instrumental music over the centuries. One type that Corelli helped to establish is the **trio sonata,** composed for two high instruments and a bass—usually two violins and a cello. With a keyboard player added for the continuo, a trio sonata takes four players, not three.

There were two categories of trio sonata: the **sonata da chiesa** (keyéhsa) and the **sonata da camera**—"church" and "chamber" sonatas, though both kinds were played in palace rooms and halls. (Concert halls did not exist yet: see page 155). However, the sonata da camera was a lighter genre, consisting mainly of dances, like a suite. The sonata da chiesa always included some meditative slow music and a good deal of imitative counterpoint. And given the instrumental forces involved, the typical "trio" texture features the two violins tumbling over one another, competing for the same musical material.

Sonatas are made up of a series of short **movements,** self-contained segments that are usually complete in themselves, and followed by a pause.

First Movement (Grave)   A church sonata typically (and fittingly) begins with a slow movement, solemn and meditative. About a half of our movement highlights the cello moving in steady slow notes (a so-called *walking bass*), while the violins play slow notes in the high register. On the recording, the continuo keyboard player is an organist, who stays very much in the background.

At the cadences, the violinists improvise swift little ornaments.

Just as Corelli was in the midst of his performance, some in the audience began to discourse together a little unseasonably; Corelli gently lays down his instrument. Being asked if there was anything the matter with him? Nothing, he replied, he was only afraid that he interrupted conversation.

From an eighteenth-century biography

---

*Opus (abbreviated Op.) is Latin for "work." Opus numbers are assigned to compositions when they are published, as a means of identifying them. Twelve trio sonatas were published together as Corelli's Opus 3; our sonata is the first of them.

Second Movement (Allegro)   After the meditation comes a lively, busy movement in imitative or fugal style. A theme is played by the first violin, then by the second violin as the first continues playing, and finally by the cello:

The three entries of the theme are followed by some different contrapuntal material which is less distinctive, though just as vigorous. Alternating with this "free" material, the theme enters four more times in the middle of the piece and once at the very end (in the bass; abbreviated).

The movement, short as it is, breaks into four clear sections of about the same length, with the cello and continuo pausing for a while at the end of each. (The second section is the longest.) The pauses come after strong cadences (stopping places: see page 27), and you may be able to hear that these all come on different scale degrees, except the last. This is an example of how functional harmony—here, the variety and balance of the four cadences—can control musical form.

Third Movement (Vivace)   For variety, there is now a change to triple meter and music with a dance-like swing. Indeed, this is an early *minuet* (the more familiar later minuet goes more slowly), composed in **A A B B** form.

The piece moves in clear four-bar phrases until a striking syncopation ends the **A** section, though not before Corelli makes his point again with a quiet echo. The **B** section also ends with an echo.

There are many places in this sonata where the two violins work the same material in a sort of contest, each one seeming eager to top the other. Best of all, perhaps, is the following passage in the **B** section. Our notation underlines the planned confusion of this highly characteristic "trio" texture:

Fourth Movement (Allegro)   The fourth movement is another imitative or fugal movement, like the second and just as lively.

Indeed, Corelli seems to have designed these two little movements to be parallel, perhaps with the idea of unifying the sonata as a whole. You may find it interesting to detect the various ways in which he made them match. Begin with the fact that both movements feature abrupt flashes of instrumental virtuosity—fast scale passages in the violins, spilling over to the cello on one occasion. A number of Corelli's trio sonatas feature more virtuosity than this, as is true more generally of his solo sonatas and concertos.

The instrumental music of the later Baroque era can all be said to derive from Corelli. We go on to discuss this in Unit III, after an introductory chapter dealing with aspects of the history and culture of the time.

LISTEN

Corelli, Sonata in F

Allegro
0:00 **section 1**
0:16 **section 2**
0:39 **section 3**
0:52 **section 4**

Vivace
0:00 **A**
0:37 **A**
1:15 **B**

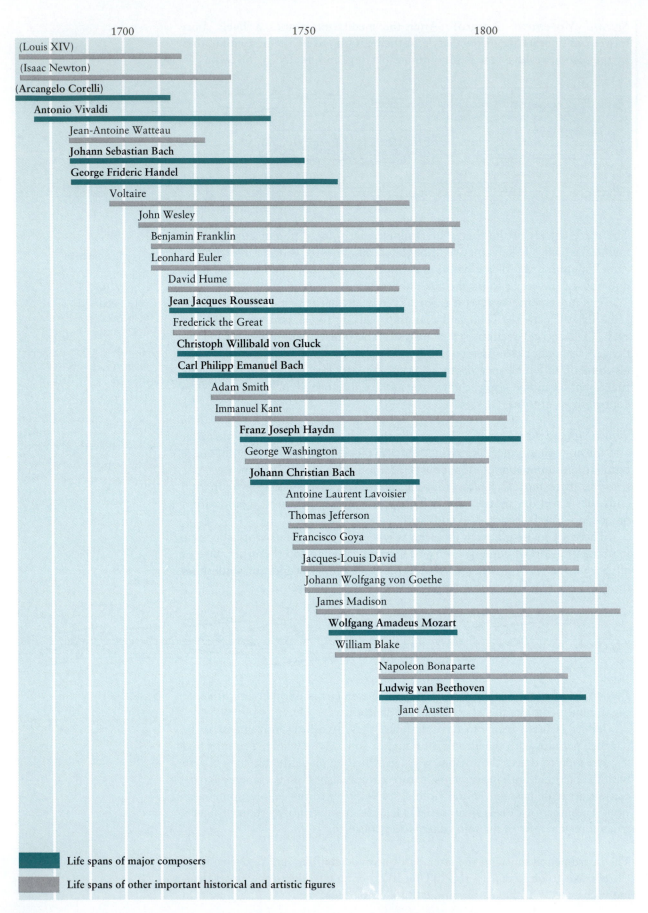

1700   1750   1800

(Louis XIV)

(Isaac Newton)

(Arcangelo Corelli)

Antonio Vivaldi

Jean-Antoine Watteau

Johann Sebastian Bach

George Frideric Handel

Voltaire

John Wesley

Benjamin Franklin

Leonhard Euler

David Hume

Jean Jacques Rousseau

Frederick the Great

Christoph Willibald von Gluck

Carl Philipp Emanuel Bach

Adam Smith

Immanuel Kant

Franz Joseph Haydn

George Washington

Johann Christian Bach

Antoine Laurent Lavoisier

Thomas Jefferson

Francisco Goya

Jacques-Louis David

Johann Wolfgang von Goethe

James Madison

Wolfgang Amadeus Mozart

William Blake

Napoleon Bonaparte

Ludwig van Beethoven

Jane Austen

████ Life spans of major composers

████ Life spans of other important historical and artistic figures

98

UNIT III

The Eighteenth Century

The first body of music that this book takes up in some detail is the music of the eighteenth century, the earliest music that we hear regularly in concerts and on the radio. The eighteenth century in music covers two very different style periods: the late Baroque era and the era of Viennese Classicism. In the following pages we shall spend a good deal of time clarifying the differences between these periods and their music.

In spite of this, the music of the eighteenth century can be thought of as a unit. The reason is not a matter of musical style, at least not directly, important as style may be. Rather, it has to do with a certain quality of musical expression, a certain objectivity in the feelings that this music seems to express or depict. Even when it is powerful and moving, it keeps its distance from the listener. Music of the nineteenth century is more demonstrative, more personal, more obviously intense; this music is called "romantic." In drawing the broadest distinctions, then, it is fair to put Baroque and Classical music on one side, Romantic music on the other. Romantic music often seems to want to share— even impose—feelings. Eighteenth-century music seems rather to demonstrate feelings.

Fair, and also functional, it seems. In one large American metropolitan area (where the authors of this textbook live), two radio stations broadcast what they call "good music" around the clock; and most of the time, eighteenth-century music is played on one of the stations, nineteenth-century music on the other. On some basic level, there must be a distinction between the music of these two centuries; these stations, their advertisers, and their audiences are responding to it. Some listeners are temperamentally attuned to one kind of music, some to the other. Probably still other listeners punch buttons on the car radio depending on their mood of the moment.

Behind this broad distinction in expressive quality are the social and economic conditions under which the music was originally produced. In Chapter 9, and again in Chapter 12, we shall look at the cultural background and the social setting of eighteenth-century music, and suggest how these factors influenced musical style and expression. The other chapters in this unit are devoted to specific works by the leading Baroque composers Bach, Handel, and Vivaldi, and the Classical composers Haydn and Mozart.

Prelude
The Late Baroque Period

M usic from the period of approximately 1600 to 1750 is usually referred to as "baroque," a term adopted early in this century from art history. Art historians borrowed the term from seventeenth-century jewelers, who applied it to large pearls of irregular shape. At one time, then, Baroque art was considered imperfect, bizarre, or at best erratic. With changing taste over the centuries, however, what was originally a negative implication has been turned into a positive one.

And over the last fifty years, with the help of recordings, Baroque music has grown more and more popular. Instruments of the period have been revived to play it, among them the harpsichord, the recorder, and the high Baroque trumpet. (Some of these instruments were discussed on pages 44–46.) Most of the Baroque music heard today dates from the eighteenth century—from around 1700 to 1750, a subperiod sometimes classified as the "late Baroque." Johann Sebastian Bach and George Frideric Handel were the greatest composers of this period, and among their most important contemporaries were Alessandro Scarlatti and Antonio Vivaldi in Italy, François Couperin and Jean Philippe Rameau in France, Domenico Scarlatti (the son of Alessandro) in Spain, and Georg Philipp Telemann in Germany.

1 Absolutism and the Age of Science

"Baroque" is a period term used by art historians and musicologists; it is not frequently met with in historical or literary studies. Political historians are more likely to speak of the period from 1600 to 1750 as the Age of Absolutism, a time when the doctrine of the "divine right of kings" ensured the absolute rule of "God-chosen" monarchs. This was the time when Louis XIV of France because the most powerful and praised monarch in all of European history, and also one of the most ruthless. The pomp and splendor of his court were emulated by a host of lesser kings and nobles.

Students of the history of ideas, on the other hand, speak of this as the Age of Science. In this era, the telescope and the microscope revealed their first secrets; Newton and Leibniz invented calculus; Newton developed the theory of gravity. These discoveries stimulated both technology and philosophy—not only the formal philosophy of the great empiricist thinkers Descartes, Locke,

Louis XIV's palace of Versailles, with a procession of carriages arriving in the great courtyard. Note the formal gardens and canal.

and Hume, but also philosophy in a more informal sense. People began to think about ordinary matters in a new way, affected by the newly acquired habits of scientific experimentation and proof. The mental climate stimulated by science had a significant effect on the art and the music we call Baroque.

Absolutism and science were just two of a number of vital currents that defined life in the seventeenth and early eighteenth centuries. The result was an interesting dualism that can be traced throughout Baroque art: dualism of pomp and extravagance on the one hand, system and calculation on the other. The same dualism can be traced in Baroque music.

Art and Absolutism

Though there had always been royalty in Europe who practiced the arts of peace as well as the arts of war, sponsorship of the arts rose to new heights in the Baroque era. The artistic glories of the Renaissance had also been supported by powerful merchant-princes, such as the Medici family in Florence, who were determined to add luster to the city-states they ruled. But never before the seventeenth century did one state loom so large in Europe as did France under Louis XIV (1638–1715), the so-called Sun King.

All of French life orbited around the royal court, like planets, comets, and cosmic dust in the solar system. Pomp and ceremony were carried to extreme lengths: the king's *levée*—his getting-up-in-the-morning rite—involved dozens of functionaries and routines lasting two hours. Artists, architects, and musicians were supported lavishly, so long as their work symbolized the majesty of the state (and the state, in Louis's famous remark, "is me"—"l'état, c'est moi").

Louis XIV, by the great Italian Baroque sculptor and architect Gianlorenzo Bernini (1598–1680).

Baroque ceiling painting by Giovanni Battista Tiepolo (1696–1770). The oval measures 30 feet by 60 feet.

The influence of this monarch and his image extended far beyond France, for other European rulers envied his absolute rule and did everything they could to match it. If they could not match his actual power, at least they could imitate his style. Especially in Germany—which was not a unified country, like France, but a patchwork of several hundred political units—dukes and princes vied with one another in supporting artists who were to build, paint, and sing their glory. Artistic life in Europe was kept alive for many generations by the patronage of these nobles.

The splendor of much Baroque art derived from this sociological function. Art was to impress, even to stupefy. Thus Louis XIV built the most enormous palace in history, Versailles, outside of Paris. Versailles has over thirteen hundred rooms, including the eighty-yard-long Hall of Mirrors, and great formal gardens extending for miles. Many nobles and prelates built little imitation-Versailles palaces, among them the Archbishop of Würzburg, whose splendid residence was built during Bach's lifetime. The palace was decorated by the Venetian artist Giovanni Battista Tiepolo (1696–1770), a master of Baroque ceiling painting.

Looking up at the ceiling shown on this page, and trying to imagine its true dimensions, we are dazzled by figures in excited motion, caught up in great gusts of wind that whirl them out of the architectural space. Ceiling painting provides a vivid example of the extravagant side of the Baroque dualism.

The Music of Absolutism

Just as painting and architecture could glorify rulers through color and designs extending through space, music could glorify by sound extending through time. The nobility demanded horn players for their ceremonial hunts, trumpeters for their battles, and orchestras for balls and entertainments. They required smaller groups of musicians for *Tafelmusik* ("table music"), background music for their lengthy banquets. And one musical genre was taken over as the specialty of Baroque absolutism: opera.

Opera today is an expensive entertainment in which a drama is presented with music and elaborate stage spectacle. So it was in the Baroque era. The stage set shown below was created by a member of the Bibiena family, foremost set designers of the time, for a German court opera. It conveys the majestic heights and distances of an ideal Baroque palace by means of perspective, though it was actually quite shallow. The figures gesture grandly, but they are dwarfed by pasteboard architecture that seems to whirl as dizzily as does the painted architecture on Tiepolo's ceiling.

One aspect of Baroque opera is unlike opera today: often the dramatic subjects were allegorical tributes to the glory and supposed virtue of those who paid for them. In one favorite Baroque opera story, for example, the Roman Emperor Titus survives a complicated plot on his life and then magnanimously forgives the plotters. This story was set to music by dozens of different court composers. It told courtiers that if they opposed their king, he might well excuse them out of the godlike goodness of his heart (for he claimed to rule by divine right). But it also reminded them that he was an absolute ruler—a modern Roman tyrant—who could do exactly the reverse if he pleased. Operas flattered princes while at the same time stressing their power and, not incidentally, their wealth.

Art and Theatricality

Opera was invented in Italy around the year 1600. Indeed, opera counts as Italy's great contribution to the seventeenth century's golden age of the theater. This century saw Shakespeare and his followers in England, Corneille and Racine in France, and Lope de Vega and Calderón in Spain.

Design for a opera stage set by G. G. Bibiena. This astonishing scene was intended for an opera at the Dresden court.

Madonna of the Pilgrims, by Michelangelo Merìsi da Caravaggio (c. 1565–1609), one of the earliest and most influential of Baroque painters.

The very term *theatrical* suggests some of the extravagance and exaggeration we associate with the Baroque. But the theater is first and foremost a place where strong emotion is on display, and it was this more than anything else that fueled the Baroque fascination with the theater. The emotionality that we generally sense in Baroque art has a theatrical quality; this is true even of much Baroque painting. Compare Raphael's calm Renaissance Madonna on page 48 with the early Baroque Madonna by Caravaggio. The pilgrim at the front is almost falling forward; the Virgin, deeply moved, cranes her neck in response to him. The whole dramatic scene is highlighted by sharply focused stagey illumination.

Science and the Arts

All this may seem some distance away from the observatories of Galileo and Kepler, and the laboratories where Harvey discovered the circulation of the blood and Leeuwenhoek first viewed microorganisms through a microscope. And indeed, the scientific spirit of the time had its most obvious effect on artists who were outside the realm of absolutism. The Dutch were citizens of free cities, not subjects of despotic kings. In Jan Vermeer's painting of his own city, Delft, the incredibly precise depiction of detail reflects the new interest in scientific observation. The painter's analysis of light is worthy of Huygens and Newton, fathers of the science of optics. There is something scientific, too, in the serene objectivity of this scene.

View of Delft, by Jan
Vermeer (1632–1675)

Man's control over nature is also symbolized by Baroque formal gardens.
Today, landscape architecture is not usually regarded as one of the major arts,
but it was very important in the age of the Baroque palace. Baroque gardens
regulate nature strictly according to geometrical plans. Bushes are clipped,
lawns tailored, and streams channeled, all under the watchful eye of big
statues of Venus, Apollo, Hercules, and the rest, lined up in rows. Such gardens spell out the new vision of nature brought to heel by human reason and
calculation.

Below the surface, furthermore, science is at work in even the most
grandiose and dazzling of Baroque artistic efforts. The extraordinary perspective of Tiepolo's ceiling painting or Bibiena's stage set depends on the use of
very sophisticated geometry. This dual influence of extravagance and scien-
tism, of the splendid and the schematic, can also be traced in Baroque music.

Formal gardens in front of
the Nymphenburg Palace,
outside Munich—one of the
many Baroque palaces in-
spired by Versailles.

The Age of Absolutism and
the Age of Science converge:

Louis XIV founding the
Academy of Sciences.

Science and Music

Various aspects of Baroque music reflect the new scientific attitudes that developed in the seventeenth century. Scales were tuned, or "tempered," more precisely than ever before, so that for the first time all possible keys were available to composers. Their interest in exploring this resource is evident from collections of pieces in all the twenty-four major and minor keys, such as Bach's *The Well-Tempered Clavier.* Harmony was systematized so that chords followed one another in a more logical and functional way.

Regularity became the ideal in rhythm, and in musical form—the distribution of sections of music in time—we find a tendency toward clearly ordered, even schematic plans. Whether consciously or not, composers seem to have viewed musical time in a quasi-scientific way. They divided it up and filled it systematically, almost in the spirit of the landscape architects who devised Baroque formal gardens.

In the important matter of musical expression, too, science was a powerful influence. Starting with the philosopher-mathematician René Descartes, thinkers applied the new rational methods to the analysis and classification of human emotions. It had always been felt that music has a special power to express and arouse emotions. Now it seemed that there was a basis for systematizing—and hence maximizing—this power.

Thus scientifically inclined music theorists compiled checklists of musical devices and techniques corresponding to each of the emotions. Grief, for example, was projected with a specific kind of melodic motive and a specific kind of rhythm—even with a specific key. By working steadily with these devices and saturating their pieces with them, composers believed they could achieve the maximum musical expressivity.

The emotions of Hope and Fear, as represented in a Baroque scientific treatise. Like composers of the time, the artist felt that feelings could be isolated and depicted in the abstract.

2 Musical Life in the Early Eighteenth Century

The eighteenth century was a great age for the crafts—the age of Chippendale in furniture making, Wedgwood in pottery, the Silbermanns in organ building, to name just a few. Though attitudes were changing, composing music was also regarded as a craft. The Romantic idea of the composer—the lonely genius working over each masterpiece as a long labor of love expressing an individual personality—was still far in the future. Baroque composers were more likely to think of themselves as servants with masters to satisfy. They were artisans with jobs, rather than artists with a calling, and they produced music on demand to fill a particular requirement.

This is why many Baroque pieces seem relatively anonymous, as it were. They are not so much unique masterpieces as satisfactory examples of their style and genre, of which there are many other equally satisfactory examples.

There were three main institutions where composers could make a living by practicing their craft. In order of increasing glamour, these were the church, the court, and the opera house.

¶ *The church*. In the larger town churches, monasteries, and cathedrals of the Baroque era, the general assumption was that the organists or choirmasters would compose their own music, as well as play and conduct. Organists had to improvise or write out music to accompany solemn places in the ritual, and play long pieces to see the congregation out at the end of the service.

At large institutions, important occasions called for elaborate music scored for chorus, soloists, and instruments: a Catholic Mass for the installation of an archbishop, or a Lutheran church cantata for the anniversary of the Reformation. Church musicians were also responsible for training the boys who sang in their choirs, often in special choir schools.

¶ *The court*. Under the patronage of kings or members of the lesser nobility, a musician was employed on the same terms as a court painter, a master of the hunt, or a head chef. Though musicians had to work entirely at the whim of their masters, they could nevertheless count on a fairly secure existence, a steady demand for their services, and a pension.

Naturally, conditions varied from court to court, depending on the ruler's taste. For some, music was a good deal less interesting than hunting or banqueting. Others could not have enough of it. Frederick the Great of Prussia was an enthusiastic amateur flutist, so at his court concertos and sonatas for flute were composed at an especially healthy rate.

Court musicians kept in better touch with musical developments than church musicians, since they were required to travel with their employer. There were extended trips, sometimes, to major cities where diplomacy was eased along by the music they composed for the occasion.

¶ *The opera house*. Although many opera houses were attached to courts, others were maintained by entrepreneurs in major cities. (As a regular institution, the public opera house existed before the public concert hall, which in the Baroque era was still a thing of the future.) Audiences were alert to the most exciting new singers, and it was part of the composer's job to keep the singers well supplied with music that showed off their talents. Composers traditionally conducted their own operas, sitting at the harpsichord.

A Baroque opera performance (Turin, 1740). The stage set represents a great palace hall; the characters are striking various extravagant attitudes. Clearly visible are the orchestra, a boy selling oranges, and a security guard.

The revival of an older opera—usually because a favorite singer liked his or her part in it—was nearly always the occasion for massive recomposition, because another singer might want *her* part redone too. If the opera's original composer had moved to the next town, other musicians would have no hesitation about rewriting (or replacing) the music. It was an exciting, unpredictable life, promising great rewards as well as humiliating reverses.

The life stories of the two greatest composers of the late Baroque period show a good deal about the interaction between musicians, the patrons who supported them, and the institutions that required music. Johann Sebastian Bach labored as a church organist, a court musician, and then a major composer-administrator for the Lutheran Church. George Frideric Handel, who also had a court position, became a leading opera composer and opera promoter. Their biographies are given on pages 123 and 141.

3   Style Features of Late Baroque Music

If any one characteristic can be singled out as central to the music of the late Baroque period, it would be its thorough, methodical quality. After listening to a short Baroque piece, or to one section of a longer piece, we may be surprised to realize, first, how soon all the basic material is set forth, and second, how much of the music after that consists of inspired repetition and variation. It is as though the composers had set out with some enthusiasm to draw their material out to the maximum extent and wring it dry.

Indeed, the shorter pieces we will be examining in Chapters 10 and 11—pieces like the Fugue in C Sharp from Bach's *The Well-Tempered Clavier,* Book I, and the aria "Tirannia" from Handel's opera *Rodelinda*—contain little if any serious contrast in rhythm, dynamics, melody, texture, or tone color (see pages 128 and 139). Baroque composers preferred thoroughness and homogeneity.

With longer pieces, Baroque composers tended to break them up into blocks of music which contrast with one another in obvious ways, but are still homogeneous in themselves. This is the case with Bach's Fifth *Brandenburg* Concerto, for example, where the orchestral and solo sections contrast with one another sharply, indeed bluntly. Within each orchestral or solo section, however, things are usually quite regular (page 122).

Rhythm

Baroque music is brimming with energy, and this energy is channeled into a highly regular, determined sort of motion. Like jazz and other popular music, Baroque music gets its rhythmic vitality by playing off distinctive rhythms against a very steady beat. The meter nearly always stands out, emphasized by certain instruments playing in a clear, incisive way. Most characteristic of these "marking-time" instruments is the busy, crisp harpsichord.

Another common feature that hammers home the beat is the so-called **walking bass,** a bass part that moves in absolutely even notes, usually eighths or quarters. In the Air from Bach's Suite No. 3 in D (see page 133), the bass shown to the right keeps going for 138 "walking" eighth notes, plus 8 sixteenth notes and one half note (at the final cadence, of course). Rhythmic variety in the upper instruments is heard against absolute regularity below.

Attentive listening will also reveal another aspect of regularity in the steady *harmonic rhythm*—that is, a Baroque piece tends to change chords at every measure, every beat, or at some other set interval. (This must not be taken absolutely literally, but it is the tendency, and it is often the case.)

Dynamics

Another steady feature of Baroque music is dynamics. Composers rarely used loud and soft indications (*f* and *p*) in their scores, and once a dynamic was chosen or set, it remained at about the same level for the whole section—sometimes even for the whole composition.

Neither in the Baroque period nor in any other, however, have performers played or sung music at an absolutely dead level of dynamics. Instrumentalists made expressive changes in dynamics to bring out rhythmic accents, and singers certainly sang high notes louder than low ones. But composers did not go much beyond natural variations of these kinds. Gradual buildups from soft to loud, and the like, were not used.

Abrupt dynamic contrasts were preferred—again, between fairly large sections of a longer piece, or whole movements. A clear *forte/piano* contrast is built in to the concerto genre, with its alternating blocks of music for the full orchestra and for one or more quieter solo instruments. When, exceptionally, a Baroque composer changed dynamics in the middle of a section or a phrase of music, he could count on the great surprise—even the amazement—of his listeners. A famous sudden *forte* in Handel's "Hallelujah" Chorus has been known to electrify the audience, to bring them to their feet (page 145).

We spoke above of a characteristic dualism between extravagance and order that can be detected in various aspects of Baroque culture (page 101). The methodical, regular quality of Baroque musical style that we are tracing here clearly reflects the orderly, quasi-scientific side of this dualism. But we also need to know that Baroque music can also be highly dramatic, bizarre, or stupendous—a reflection of the other side of the dualism. Indeed, the magnificent momentary effects that occur occasionally in Handel (and Bach) are all the stronger because of the regular music around them.

In a typical Baroque texture, singers and violins in the upper register are supported by the *continuo*, played by three musicians in this performance. A cello plays the bass, and the middle range is filled in by two chord-playing instruments (harpsichord and lute).

Tone Color

Tone color in Baroque music presents something of a contradiction. The early part of the period evinced a new interest in sonority, and the end of it echoed with some very sophisticated sounds: Handel's imaginative orchestration in his operas, Bach's notably sensitive writing for the flute, and the refined harpsichord textures developed by several generations of composers in France. There are distinctive and attractive "Baroque sounds" that we do not hear in other periods: the harpsichord, the bright Baroque organ, the virtuoso recorder, and the "festive" Baroque orchestra featuring high trumpets and drums.

On the other hand, a significant amount of music was written to allow for multiple or alternative performing forces. Thus it was a regular practice to designate music for harpsichord *or* organ, for violin *or* oboe *or* flute. Bach wrote a sonata for two flutes and continuo and rewrote it as a sonata for viola da gamba (a cello-like instrument) and harpsichord. Handel took solo arias and duets and rewrote them as choruses for his oratorio *Messiah*. In the last analysis, then, it seems the original tone color was often not critical.

The Baroque Orchestra

The core of the Baroque orchestra was a group of instruments of the violin family. The orchestra maintained by Louis XIV in the late seventeenth century was called "The Twenty-Four Violins of the King"; it consisted of six violins, twelve violas, and six cellos. A great deal of Baroque music in Louis's time and later was written for such an orchestra or a similar one—what would today be called a "string orchestra": violins, violas, cellos, and one or two bass viols.

To this was added a keyboard instrument—generally the harpsichord in secular music and the organ in church music.

Woodwinds and brass instruments were sometimes added to the string orchestra, too, but there was no fixed complement, as was to be the case later. For special occasions of a festive nature—Christmas music ordered by a great cathedral, for example, or a piece celebrating a military victory—composers would augment the "basic Baroque orchestra" with trumpets or French horns, timpani, bassoons, and oboes and/or flutes. This "festive" Baroque orchestra has a particularly grand, open, and brilliant sound.

THE BASIC BAROQUE ORCHESTRA
as in Vivaldi's Concerto in G (page 117)

STRINGS	KEYBOARD
Violins (divided into two groups, called violins 1 and violins 2) Violas Cellos Bass viol (playing the same music as the cellos, an octave lower)	Harpsichord or organ

THE FESTIVE BAROQUE ORCHESTRA
as in Bach's Orchestral Suite in D (page 132)

STRINGS	WOODWINDS	BRASS	PERCUSSION	KEYBOARD
Violins 1 Violins 2 Violas Cellos Bass viol	2 Oboes 1 Bassoon	3 Trumpets	2 Timpani (kettledrums)	Harpsichord or organ

Melody

Baroque melody tends toward complexity. Composers liked to push melodies to the very limits of ornateness and luxuriance. As a rule, the range of Baroque melodies is extended; they use many different rhythmic note values; they twist and turn intricately and elegantly as they reach high and low. It can be maintained that the art of melody reached a high point in the late Baroque era, a point that has never been equaled since.

These long, intricate melodies, with their wealth of "decorations" added to the main direction of the line, are not easy to sing, however. They hardly ever fall into any simple pattern resembling a tune. Even their appearance on the page seems to tell the story:

Not all melodies of the time are as ornate as this one, and some, such as the simpler Baroque dances, are exceptions to the rule. On the other hand, the most highly prized art of the elite musicians of the era, the opera singers, was improvising melodic decorations in the arias they sang night after night in the theater.

An easily recognized feature of Baroque melodies is their frequent use of sequence (see page 27; a sequence is shaded on the melody above). Baroque melodies repeatedly catch hold of a motive or some longer section of music and repeat it at several pitch levels. Sequences provide Baroque music with one of its most effective means of forward motion.

Texture

The standard texture of Baroque music is polyphonic (or contrapuntal). Baroque polyphony is at its most impressive in large-scale pieces, which spin a web of contrapuntal lines filling every nook and cranny of musical spacetime. While cellos, bass viols, bassoons, and organ pedals play the lowest line, the other string instruments stake out their places in the middle, with oboes and flutes above them and the trumpets piercing their way up into the very highest reaches of the sound universe. The density achieved in this way is doubly impressive because the sounds feel alive—alive because they are all in motion, because they are all parts of moving contrapuntal lines.

Again, some exceptions should be noted to the standard polyphonic texture of Baroque music. Such are the homophonic orchestra sections (called *ritornellos*) in the concerto, and Bach's wonderfully expressive harmonizations of old German hymns. But it is no accident that these textures appear *within pieces that feature polyphony elsewhere.* The ritornello in Bach's *Brandenburg Concerto No. 5* alternates with polyphony played by the solo flute, violin, and harpsichord (see pages 122, 124). The harmonized hymn in his *Cantata No. 4* comes at the very end of the piece, where it has the effect of calming or settling the complex polyphony of the preceding music (see page 148).

The Continuo

Yet all this polyphony is supported by a solid scaffold of harmony. The central importance of harmony in Baroque music appears in the universal practice of the *basso continuo,* or just **continuo.**

The continuo is a bass part (the lowest part in polyphonic music) that is always linked to a series of chords. These chords are played by a harpsichord, organ, or lute as support for the important melodies in the other instruments. Support, or accompaniment; indeed, we might say "mere accompaniment," for composers did not bother to write the chords out in detail, but only notated them in an abstract way by a numerical shorthand below the bass part.

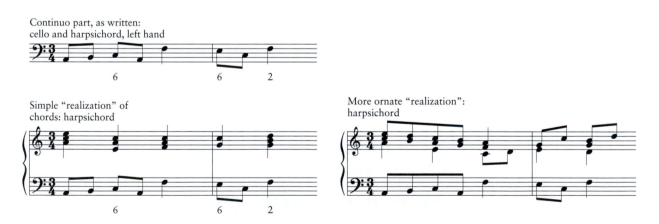

Continuo part, as written:
cello and harpsichord, left hand

Simple "realization" of chords: harpsichord

More ornate "realization": harpsichord

This left continuo players with a good deal to do, even though their role was considered subsidiary. By reading the basso continuo part, the harpsichordist or organist would play along with the cellos or bassoons; so much for the left hand, which "doubles" the base line. But the right-hand chords could be played in many ways—high or low, widely or closely spaced, smoothly connected or not. A certain amount of quick, on-the-spot improvisation was (and still is) required to "realize" a continuo, that is, to derive actual chords from abstract numbers. Another name for continuo, **figured bass**, derives from this numerical shorthand.

Continuo chords provide the basic harmonic framework against which the contrapuntal lines of Baroque music trace their airy patterns. Under the influence of the continuo, Baroque texture may be described as "polarized"—a "polarity of voices" between a strong bass and a clear, high (soprano) range, the domain of the melody. Less clearly defined is a middle space containing the improvised chords. In Baroque works on the largest scale, this space is also filled in by polyphonic lines drawn from the median range of the orchestra and chorus, such as violas, tenors, and altos. In more modest works a characteristic texture is a hollow one: one or two high instruments (violins, flutes) or voices, a bass instrument, and subsidiary chord improvisation in the middle.

Baroque music is usually easily identified by the presence of the continuo —by the continuous but discreet sound of the harpsichord or organ playing continuo chords in the background. Indeed, the Baroque era in music was once called the "basso continuo" era, not a bad name for it.

Eighteenth-century instruments

Musical Form

Musical forms are clearer and more regular in the Baroque period than in most other historical periods. Two factors that appear to have contributed to this, one of them social, the other intellectual, were mentioned earlier.

The social factor is the patronage system, whereby the court and the church demanded a large amount of music and expected it to be produced in a hurry, almost as soon as it was ordered. Therefore composers needed to rely on formulas that could be applied quickly and efficiently. What is amazing about the church cantatas that Bach wrote at Leipzig, one a week, is how imaginatively he varied the standard forms for the various components of a cantata. But it was very helpful—in fact, it was absolutely necessary—for him to have those standard forms there as a point of departure.

The other factor is the scientific spirit of the age, which affected composers only indirectly, but affected them nonetheless. One can detect the composer's ambition to "map" the whole range of a piece of music, and to fill it in systematically, in an orderly, logical, quasi-scientific way. This ambition seems to have been based on the conviction that musical time could be encompassed and controlled at man's will, an attitude similar to that of scientists, philosophers, and craftsmen of the time.

The music of Bach, in particular, shows this tendency on various levels. Look, for example, at the symmetrical arrangement of the seven sections of his Cantata No. 4, diagramed on page 147. The last fugue that Bach conceived (and died before finishing) is another, more famous example. An ordinary fugue, as we shall see, is a polyphonic composition that deals exclusively with a single theme. This fugue deals with *four* themes, one after another, in four sections; then in the last section all four themes combine in four-part counterpoint. Theme No. 4 spells "Bach" in a musical code (!). A simpler Bach fugue may still have a ground-plan that is highly symmetrical (see page 128).

4 The Emotional World of Baroque Music

All music, it seems safe to say, is deeply involved with emotion. But in the music of different cultures, and also in the music of different historical eras within a single culture, the nature of that involvement can be very different. The emotional effect of Baroque music strikes the modern listener as very powerful and yet, in a curious way, also impersonal. Baroque composers believed firmly that music could and should mirror a wide range of human feelings, or "affects," such as had been analyzed and classified by the scientifically oriented psychology of the day. Composers did not believe, however, that it was their task to mirror feelings of their own. Rather, they tried to isolate and analyze emotions in general and then depict them consistently.

The exhaustiveness of their musical technique made for a similar exhaustiveness of emotional effect. A single movement or aria was usually restricted to depicting one specific emotion, feeling, or mood. As the rhythms and themes are repeated, the music intensifies and magnifies a single strong feeling. Sadness in Baroque music is presented as the deepest gloom, calmness as profound quiet, brightness as pomp and splendor, happiness as jubilation.

These are extreme sentiments; the people who can be imagined to experience them would have to be almost larger than life. All this fits perfectly into place with the Baroque fascination with the theater. The Baroque theater concentrated on grand gestures and high passion, on ideal emotions expressed by ideal human beings. Kings and queens were shown performing noble actions or vile ones, experiencing intense feelings, delivering thunderous speeches, and taking part in lavish stage displays. How these personages looked and postured can be seen in the picture on page 108.

Theatrical emotion has the virtues of intensity, clarity, and focus; it has to have, if it is to reach its audience. Actors analyze the emotion they are required to depict, shape it and probably exaggerate it, and then methodically project it by means of their acting technique and craft. It is not their personal emotion, though for the moment they *make* it their own. We may come to feel that Baroque composers worked in much the same manner, not only in their operas—actual stage works set to music—but also in their oratorios and church cantatas, and even in their instrumental concertos and sonatas.

An eighteenth-century opera rehearsal: note, once again, the continuo instruments. The large man in charge may be Handel.

CHAPTER **10**

Baroque Instrumental Music

I n most cultures, music with words is the norm; strictly instrumental music is frequently less common or less important. So it is with popular music today, and so it was with the early music of Europe. Gregorian chant was sung by monks and nuns to liturgical texts, and later some of these same texts were set to new polyphonic music for cathedral choirs and royal chapels. In the Middle Ages, the troubadours set their love poems as solo songs; in the Renaissance, love poetry was set to music as madrigals, intricate part-music for a few solo singers. Vocal music was still very important in the late Baroque era, as we shall see in Chapter 11.

But part of the importance of the Baroque era was that for the first time, listeners and musicians began to take instrumental music much more seriously. A momentous change was set in motion, and the reasons for it are not entirely clear. It can hardly be a coincidence, however, that the rise of instrumental music took place at the same time as a similar development in the technology of instrument making. The name of Antonio Stradivarius (1644–1737) is known to many because of auctions where prices can go past the million mark for one of his violins, unmatched after three hundred years. (They rarely come on the market.) Instruments by other master-builders of the era, less well known, can still sound glorious: the organs of Gottfried Silbermann, the harpsichords of François Etienne Blanchet, the viols of Barak Norman (a viol da gamba is pictured on page 120).

In any case, the rise of instrumental music meant that there had to be a basic understanding between composers and audiences about instrumental forms and genres. To pose the most basic question: when the music starts, how long should the composer keep going, and what should the listener expect? With vocal music, the answer was (roughly speaking): until the words end—when the sense of the sentence, paragraph, or total text is completed with a punctuation mark, a summing-up, or a concluding passage. For instrumental music, there was no such "sense." Conventional forms and genres had to supply it.

In this chapter we shall look at the most important instrumental forms and genres established, developed, and refined in the Baroque era. Baroque vocal music will be treated in Chapter 11.

A Baroque instrument that is now obsolete, the viol da gamba is similar to a cello, with a quieter but also a rather husky sound. The beautiful viols by the English maker Barak Norman have elaborately carved pegboards.

1 Concerto and Concerto Grosso

The concerto and the concerto grosso (plural: concerti grossi) are the most important orchestral genres of the Baroque era. The basic idea underlying these genres is contrast between an orchestra and a soloist (in the concerto) or a small group of soloists (in the concerto grosso). Indeed, the word *concerto* comes from the Latin word *concertare,* to contend—an origin that accurately indicates a sort of contest between solo and orchestra.

This contest pits the brilliance of the soloist or soloists, often involving or suggesting improvisation, against the relative power and stability of the orchestra. Contrast comes to these genres naturally, then; a good deal of Baroque music is more uniform, as we shall see (pages 128, 149). But people soon tire of music that stays more or less the same; composers who wanted to develop large-scale forms had to find ways of bringing contrast into their music. They wanted large-scale forms because audiences, then as now, were more impressed by extensive compositions than by short ones.

Movements

One way to extend a composition was and is to lay it out in several movements (or, to put it another way, join together several movements as a single composite work). A **movement** is a self-contained section of music that is part of a larger work; movements can be compared to chapters in a book. Movements in a multimovement work will always show some variety in tempo, meter, key, mood, and musical form.

The typical late Baroque concerto has three movements. The *first* movement is a bright, extroverted piece in a fast tempo. After this, the *second* movement strikes an obvious contrast: it is quieter, slower, and more emotional. The *third* movement is fast again—if anything, faster than the first. In the first concerto we study, Vivaldi's Concerto in G, the first and last movements are in ritornello form, the second movement in ground bass form.

Ritornello Form

Many concerto movements are in *ritornello form,* from **ritornello,** the name for the orchestral music that typically starts the movement off. Contrast is basic to the concerto, and ritornello form focuses contrast on two musical ideas, or groups of ideas—one belonging to the orchestra and the other to the soloist. The orchestral material (the ritornello) tends to be solid and forceful, the solo material faster and more brilliant.

Ritorno, the Italian word for "return," tells us that the function of the ritornello in ritornello form is to return many times as a stable element of the form. Usually it returns only in part, and usually it is played in different keys as the movement proceeds. As for the "musical ideas" referred to above, sometimes these are virtuoso passages, sometimes themes, sometimes larger sections including themes and other material. To end the movement, the ritornello returns in the tonic key and, often, at full length.

Ritornello form can be diagrammed as shown at the top of page 117, where RIT stands for the entire ritornello, [RIT] for any part of the ritornello, and Solo 1, 2, 3, . . . for the solo sections:

If the first movement [of a concerto] takes five minutes, the Adagio five to six, and the last movement three to four, the whole is of the proper length. And it is in general better if listeners find a piece too short rather than too long.

J. J. Quantz (1697–1773), court composer to Frederick the Great, 1752

RIT		[RIT]		[RIT]		[RIT]		RIT
	Solo 1		Solo 2		Solo 3		Solo 4	

Tonic key ——————————————— Other keys ——————————————— Tonic key

We need not worry too much about the exact number of ritornello fragments, the keys, and other details shown in such form diagrams. More important is the general impression that the form gives: the sense of a sturdy, reliable support in the orchestra for rapid and sometimes fantastic flights by the solo or solo group. As a condition for the quasi-improvisational freedom of the solo instruments, the ritornello is always there, ready to bring them back down to earth, and remind us of the original point of departure.

ANTONIO VIVALDI (1678–1741)
Concerto in G, "La stravaganza," Op. 4 No. 12 (1712–13)

The undisputed champion of the concerto was the Venetian composer Antonio Vivaldi. Vivaldi wrote hundreds of concertos but published only a few of them, in sets of six or twelve; each set was given a work number (*opus* is Latin for "work"). To some opuses he gave titles which evoke the "extravagant" side of the Baroque dualism (see page 101), such as "Harmonic Whims" (*L'estro armonico,* opus 3) and "Extravagance" (*La stravaganza,* opus 4). This Concerto in G is the last and one of the best of his opus 4.

It is a concerto for solo violin and the standard Baroque orchestra of strings and continuo (see page 112); on our recording the continuo chords are played by a large lute (an *archlute*). The orchestra is quite small. In the age of Antonio Stradivarius, violin-maker supreme, a great deal of music was composed at least partly to show off this favorite instrument. The violin's brilliance was especially prized, as was its ability to play expressively.

The Concerto in G begins and ends with movements in ritornello form.

Archlute

First movement: Spiritoso e non presto   "Spirited, not too fast," writes Vivaldi at the start of this triple-meter movement. The first and second violins of the orchestra echo one another brightly. The opening ritornello—with its typical loud, extroverted sound—consists of three parts: the first beginning with a couple of loud chords to catch the audience's attention and set the tempo (**a**), then a central section with sequences (**b**), and then a cadential section featuring loud/soft echoes (**c**):

LISTENING CHART 2

Vivaldi, Concerto in G, first movement

Ritornello form. 2 min., 46 sec.

0:00	Ritornello	a
0:11		b
0:18		c
0:26	Solo 1	Contrasting solo violin music
0:41	Ritornello 2	c
0:49	Solo 2	Virtuoso solo violin music; several different sections
		The continuo drops out for a short time
1:18	Ritornello 3	Part of this is derived from **b** and **c**; the rest is free
		CADENCE Cadence in a minor key
1:33	Solo 3	More expressive
1:51	Ritornello 4	Even freer than Ritornello 3
2:10	Solo 4	Very fast
2:24	Ritornello 5	b c

Once the ritornello ends with a very solid cadence (another typical feature of Baroque ritornellos), the solo violin enters, first with music moving at about the same speed as the ritornello, but soon speeding up. Virtuosity for the Baroque violinist meant jumping from the high strings to the low, executing fast scales, in fact any and all kinds of fast playing.

Ritornello 2 is an exact repetition of **c**. The second solo has several subsections, in one of which the continuo drops out. Ritornello 3 begins with derivatives of **b** and **c** but then wanders off freely; ending in a minor key, it provides a springboard for some expressive playing in the next solo. Ritornello 4 is freer still; it takes just enough from the original ritornello (part **b**) so that it seems to fit in with it and, indeed, to grow out of it spontaneously.

Vivaldi seems to have wanted his first four ritornellos to feel freer and freer, before he finally pulls the piece back in line. After the last solo (following Ritornello 4) cuts in very energetically, he ends the movement with a literal statement of **b** and **c**. (Absent is **a**, perhaps because its "wake-up" function is no longer needed). Compare the "inner form" of this movement with the standard "outer form," diagramed on page 117:

Antonio Vivaldi (1678–1741)

The son of a Venetian violinist, Antonio Vivaldi was destined to follow in his father's footsteps. He entered the priesthood—where his bright red hair earned him the nickname of the "Red Priest"—and in 1703 became a music teacher at the Seminario Musicale dell'Ospedale della Pietà, a Venetian orphanage for girls. The Ospedale was one of several such institutions in Venice that were famous for the attention they paid to the musical training of their students. A large proportion of Vivaldi's works were composed for the school.

The Ospedale allowed him frequent leaves of absence, so Vivaldi toured a good deal, but it was specified in the composer's contract that he should write two concertos a month for the pupils. If he happened to be in town at the time, he would also rehearse those pieces. Near the end of his life, Vivaldi left Venice permanently to settle in Vienna.

Internationally renowned as a virtuoso violinist, Vivaldi is remembered today chiefly for his brilliant concertos. He wrote more than four hundred of these, including concertos for harp, mandolin, bassoon, and various instrumental combinations; we know of more than 250 solo violin concertos, including the Concerto in G of our record set. Critics of the day complained that Vivaldi's music was thin and flashy, and that the com-

poser was always playing for cheap effects. But the young Bach, before writing his *Brandenburg* Concertos, carefully copied out many pages of Vivaldi, as a way of learning how to write concertos himself.

Vivaldi's most famous work—it has been recorded well over a hundred times—is also one of his most unusual: *The Four Seasons,* a set of four concertos which illustrate, in some way, spring (birds singing, gentle breezes, and so on), summer (a nap in the sun), fall (a tipsy peasant dance at a harvest festival), and winter ("the horrible wind," to quote from the score). Baroque composers were fond of musical illustration, especially with the words of vocal music, as we shall see; but they seldom pursued it this far.

Chief Works: Solo concertos for many different instruments ▪ Concerti grossi (i.e., concertos for several solo instruments) for various instruments, including the very famous *Four Seasons* ▪ 21 extant operas; oratorios; cantatas

Baroque Variation Form: The Ground Bass

Variation forms are among the simplest and most characteristic of Baroque forms. Although they are not as common as other forms, they project the Baroque desire for systematic, thorough structures in a very direct way. For **variation form** entails the successive, uninterrupted repetition of one clearly defined melodic unit, with changes that enlist the listener's interest without ever losing touch with the original unit, or theme.

That theme may be a complete melody in the soprano range or a shorter melodic phrase in the bass. Given the emphasis in the Baroque era on the basso continuo, it is not surprising that Baroque variations tend to occur above stable bass patterns; the variations differ mainly by having different polyphonic lines written (or improvised) above the bass. Sometimes the bass itself is slightly varied—though never in such a way as to hide its distinctive quality. Dynamics, tone color, and some harmonies are often changed in variations. Tempo, key, and mode are changed less often.

There are a number of names for compositions in variation form, which seem to have grown up independently all over Europe, first as improvisations

As this child appears to be finding out, music lessons can often serve as a cover for lessons in something else—a fact which helps explain the popularity of "music lesson" pictures.

and then as written-out compositions. Beside the French *chaconne* and the Italian *passacaglia* (passa-cáhlia), there was the old English term *ground* (the repeating bass figure being called the **ground bass**). One seventeenth-century Italian composer left a passacaglia for organ with exactly a hundred variations. More compact examples of variation form sometimes appear as one movement in a larger Baroque genre, such as a concerto.*

ANTONIO VIVALDI (1678–1741)
Concerto in G, "La stravaganza," Op. 4 No. 12 (1712–13)

Second movement (Largo)   As is typical, Vivaldi's Concerto in G has three contrasting movements—the first vigorous and brilliant, the second gentle and slow. This slow movement is in variation (ground bass) form.

Our first impression of this music is probably of its texture—the gentle throbbing, the ingenious weaving in and out of the orchestral violins and the solo violin, and the delicate, subsidiary continuo sounds. There is, however, not much melody to listen to in the violin's music. There is less and less, in fact, as the movement goes along and the texture changes.

Sooner or later we notice that the only real melody is in the bass, where a solemn, quiet theme (the ground bass) is heard repeatedly in the cellos and bass viol. The theme sinks down and down, ending with a strong cadence:

Theme, Variations 1–4, 7

Variations 5–6

*We examine an earlier example of variation (ground bass) form on page 94: Dido's Lament, from the opera *Dido and Aeneas* by Henry Purcell (1659–95).

LISTENING CHART 3

Vivaldi, Concerto in G, Op. 4 No. 12, second movement

Variation (ground bass) form. 2 min., 59 sec.

0:00	Theme	Orchestra and Solo: descending bass
0:21	Var 1	Solo: Flowing material
0:41	Var 2	Faster flowing material
1:02	Var 3	Even faster music, though now in spurts
1:22	Var 4	Faster yet: rapid figuration
		CADENCE Brief stop at the cadence ending Variation 4
1:44	Var 5	Thin texture (organ and lute drop out), with expressive violin material over a varied bass: in the minor mode
2:04	Var 6	Like Variation 5, but the violin is a little faster and more expressive
2:26	Theme	Orchestra and Solo: as at the beginning. (i.e., back to the major mode, and the continuo returns)

We develop a sort of "double listening" for music like this, listening simultaneously to the unchanging theme and to the changing material presented above that theme. (This is no harder to do than taking in a distant view while also watching someone in the foreground). After the theme's initial statement, four more statements with violin variations follow, during which the solo violin plays faster and faster material above the impassive ground bass. In its quiet way, this movement is showing off the violinist's ability to play music that is fast and sleek.

After Variation 4, however, there is a marked stop, and Variation 5 makes a grand contrast of the kind relished by Baroque composers and audiences (especially in music designed to be "extravagant," as this concerto was). The continuo stops, and since the texture is now thin and ethereal, the bass (played by the orchestral violins) can be heard more clearly—and what we hear is that the theme itself has been varied. It is now in the minor mode.

The mood becomes muted and melancholy; the violin is now showing off not its speed, but its expressive capabilities. The mood deepens in Variation 6. Rather abruptly, after this, the original theme returns in the full orchestra and continuo, played just as it was at the beginning.

The construction of this movement, as a set of variations over a ground bass, exemplifies the thorough, methodical quality of so much Baroque music. The effect of the contrast that Vivaldi has added with Variations 5 and 6 is not diminished by the steadily repeating, even obsessive bass. On the contrary, "double listening" can make the contrast seem richer and more interesting.

Third movement (Allegro)   Like the first movement, the third movement of the Concerto in G is a fast one in ritornello form. This time ritornello form is treated much more freely—or, as Vivaldi might have said, "extravagantly."

He begins with a long solo passage for the violin—and when the orchestra finally breaks in, all it can offer by way of a ritornello is a sort of hasty fanfare, interrupted by a short solo. The second ritornello is a much longer, very spirited passage of new music. "Extravagant" features of this movement would include the eviction of the orchestra from its customary place at the beginning;

LISTEN

Vivaldi, Concerto in G, last movement

0:00	**Introduction** solo
0:16	**Ritornello 1** interrupted by solo
0:31	**Solo**
1:15	**Ritornello 2**
2:10	**Ritornello 3**
2:52	**Ritornello 4**
3:46	**Ritornello 5**

the fact that the lively second ritornello has nothing whatsoever to do with the "official" ritornello, namely the fanfare; and the way the solo violin keeps darting around and changing the kind of virtuoso material it plays throughout the movement.

However, order is asserted when the third ritornello takes the original fanfare as its point of departure (in the minor mode), and when the final ritornello returns to its origins almost literally, as in the first movement.

JOHANN SEBASTIAN BACH
Brandenburg Concerto No. 5, for Flute, Violin, Harpsichord, and Orchestra (before 1721)

A concerto grosso is a concerto for a group of several solo instruments (rather than just a single one) and orchestra. In 1721 Johann Sebastian Bach sent a beautiful manuscript containing six of these works to the Margrave of Brandenburg, a minor nobleman with a paper title; the Duchy of Brandenburg had recently been merged into the kingdom of Prussia, Europe's fastest-growing state. We do not know why this music was sent—if Bach was job-hunting, he was unsuccessful—nor if it was ever performed in Brandenburg.

To impress the Margrave, presumably, Bach sent pieces with six different combinations of instruments, combinations that in some cases were never used before or after. Taken as a group, the *Brandenburg* Concertos present an unsurpassed anthology of dazzling tone colors and imaginative treatments of the Baroque concerto contrast between soloists and orchestra.

Brandenburg Concerto No. 5 features as its solo group a flute, violin, and harpsichord. The orchestra is the "basic" Baroque string orchestra (see page 111). The harpsichordist of the solo group doubles as the player of the orchestra's continuo chords, and the solo violin leads the orchestra during the ritornellos.

First Movement (Allegro)   In ritornello form, the first movement of *Brandenburg* No. 5 opens with a loud, bright, solid-sounding orchestral ritornello that is basically homophonic in texture. The melody is attractive and easily recognized but, like so many Baroque melodies, becomes more complicated as it proceeds:

(For simplicity's sake, the music example above omits the note-repetitions on the eighth notes.) You could probably learn to sing phrase **a** easily enough, but **b** and **c** are much harder. There is no clear stop between them, and the melody begins to wind around itself in an intricate way. Yet is is undoubtedly just these features that give the ritornello its strength and its flair and keep it fresh when fragments of it return later in the movement.

1. I shall set the boys a shining example of an honest, retiring manner of life, serve the School industriously, and instruct the boys conscientiously
2. Bring the music in both the principal Churches of this town [Leipzig] into a good state, to the best of my ability
3. Show to the Honorable and Most Wise Town Council all proper respect and obedience . . .

Bach's contract at Leipzig, 1723—the first three of fourteen paragraphs

Johann Sebastian Bach (1685–1750)

During the Baroque era, crafts were handed down in family clans, and in music the Bach clan was one of the most extensive, providing the region of Thuringia in central Germany with musicians for many generations. Most of the Bachs were lowly town musicians or Lutheran Church organists; only a few of them gained court positions. Johann Sebastian, who was himself taught by several of his relatives, trained four sons who became leading composers of the next generation.

Before he was twenty, Bach took his first position as a church organist in a little town called Arnstadt, then moved to a bigger town called Mühlhausen. Then he worked his way up to a court position with the Duke of Weimar. As a church organist, Bach had to compose organ music and sacred choral pieces, and at Weimar he was still required to write church music for the ducal chapel, as well as sonatas and concertos for performance in the palace.

The way his Weimar position terminated tells us something about the working conditions of court musicians. When Bach tried to leave Weimar for another court, Cöthen, the duke balked and threw him in jail for several weeks. At Cöthen the prince happened to be a keen amateur musician who was not in favor of elaborate church music, so Bach concentrated on instrumental music.

In 1723 Bach was appointed Cantor of St. Thomas's Church in Leipzig, an important city in eastern Germany. He not only had to compose and perform, but also organize music for all four churches in town. Teaching in the choir school was another of his responsibilities. Almost every week, in his first years at Leipzig, Bach composed, had copied, rehearsed, and performed a new cantata—a religious work for soloists, choir, and orchestra containing several movements and lasting from fifteen to thirty minutes.

Bach chafed under bureaucratic restrictions and political decisions by town and church authorities. The truth is he was never appreciated in Leipzig. Furthermore, at the end of his life he was regarded as old-fashioned by modern musicians, and one critic pained Bach by saying so in print. Indeed, after his death Bach's music was neglected by the musical public at large, though it was admired by composers such as Mozart and Beethoven.

Bach had twenty children—seven with his first wife, a cousin, and thirteen with his second, a singer, for whom he prepared a little home-music anthology, *The Note-Book of Anna Magdalena Bach.* The children were taught music as a matter of course, and also taught how to copy music; the performance parts of many of the weekly cantatas that Bach composed are written in their hands. From his musical response to the sacred words of these cantatas, and other works, it is clear that Bach thought deeply about religious matters. Works such as his Passions and his Mass in B Minor emanate a spirituality that many listeners find unmatched in any other composer.

Bach seldom traveled, except to consult on organ construction contracts (for which the customary fee was often a cord of wood or a barrel of wine). His last years were spent in blindness, but he continued to compose by dictation. Before this time, he had already begun to assemble his compositions in orderly sets: organ chorale preludes, organ fugues, preludes and fugues for harpsichord. He also clearly set out to produce works that would summarize his final thoughts about Baroque forms and genres; such works are the Mass in B Minor, the thirty-three *Goldberg* Variations for harpsichord, and *The Art of Fugue,* an exemplary collection of fugues all on the same subject, left unfinished at his death.

Bach was writing for himself, for his small devoted circle of students, perhaps for posterity. It is a concept that would have greatly surprised the craftsmen musicians who were his forebears.

Chief Works: More than 200 sacred and secular cantatas; two Passions, according to St. Matthew and St. John; *Christmas Oratorio;* Mass in B Minor; *Magnificat;* motets ■ *The Well-Tempered Clavier,* consisting of 48 preludes and fugues in all major and minor keys for harpsichord or clavichord ■ Three sets of suites (six each) for harpsichord—the French and English Suites and the Partitas; *Goldberg Variations* ■ Organ works: many fugues (including the *St. Anne* Fugue) and chorale preludes ■ *Brandenburg* Concertos; concertos for harpsichord, violin, two violins; orchestral suites; sonatas ■ Late composite works: *A Musical Offering* and *The Art of Fugue* ■ Chorale (hymn) harmonizations

Eighteenth-century Spanish tiles

Once the ritornello ends with a solid cadence, the three solo instruments enter with rapid imitative polyphony. They dominate the rest of the movement; they introduce new motives and new patterns of figuration, take over some motives from the ritornello, and toss all these musical ideas back and forth between them. Every so often, the orchestra breaks in again, always with clear fragments of the ritornello, in various keys. All this has a very, very different effect from that of Vivaldi's Concerto in G, not only because of the sheer length of the movement and its elaborate form, but because of the richness of the counterpoint and the harmony.

During a particularly striking solo section in the minor mode, the soloists abandon their motivic style and play Baroque mood music, with even richer harmonies and intriguing, special textures. After this, you may be able to hear that all the solos are closely related to solos heard before the minor-mode section—all, that is, except the very last. Here the harpsichord gradually outpaces the violin and the flute, until finally it seizes the stage and plays a lengthy virtuoso passage, while the other instruments wait silently.

FLUTE

VIOLIN

etc.

An improvised or improvisatory solo passage of this kind within a larger piece is called a **cadenza.** Cadenzas are a feature of concertos in all eras; the biggest cadenza always comes near the end of the first movement, as in *Brandenburg* Concerto No. 5.

In this cadenza, the harpsichord breaks out of the regular eighth-note rhythms that have dominated this long movement. Its swirling, unexpectedly powerful patterns prepare inexorably for the final entrance of the orchestra, which feels like the releasing of a force that has been pent up for an excruciatingly long time. The whole ritornello is played, exactly as at the beginning; at last we hear it as a complete and solid entity, not in fragments.

This painting is thought to depict Bach and three of his musician sons. The kindly, soberly dressed father is shown holding a cello—a basso continuo instrument—ready to support the treble lines of the boys, who are decked out in the frothy costumes of a later generation.

LISTENING CHART 4

2 1 2A 1A
1-5 11-15 1 7

Bach, *Brandenburg* Concerto No. 5, first movement

Ritornello form, 9 min., 57 sec.

0:00	Ritornello	Complete ritornello is played by the orchestra, **forte:** bright and emphatic
0:22	Solo	Harpsichord, flute, and violin in a contrapuntal texture (often in trio style). Includes faster rhythms; the soloists play new themes and also play some of the motives from the ritornello
0:46	Ritornello (first phrase)	Orchestra, *f*
0:51	Solo	Similar material to that of the first solo
1:11	Ritornello (middle phrase)	Orchestra, *f*
1:18	Solo	Similar solo material
1:39	Ritornello (middle phrase)	Orchestra, *f;* minor mode
1:44	Solo	Similar solo material at first, then fast harpsichord runs are introduced.
2 12 2:26	Ritornello (middle phrase)	Orchestra, *f*
2:33	Solo	This solo leads directly in the central solo.
2:58	Central solo	Quiet flute and violin dialogue (accompanied by the orchestra, *p*) is largely in the minor mode. The music is less motivic, and the harmonies change less rapidly than before.
3:22		Detached notes in cello, flute, and violin; sequence
3:58		Long high notes prepare for the return of the ritornello.
3 13 4:13	Ritornello (first phrase)	Orchestra, *f*
4:17	Solo	
5:03	Ritornello (first and second phrases)	Orchestra, *f;* this ritornello section feels especially solid because it is longer than the others and in the tonic key.
5:14	Solo	
5:42	Ritornello (middle phrase)	Orchestra, *f*
5:50	Solo	Fast harpsichord run leads into the cadenza.
4 14 6:27	Harpsichord cadenza	*Section 1:* a lengthy passage developing motives from the solo sections
8:26		*Section 2:* very fast and brilliant
8:50		*Section 3:* long preparation for the anticipated return of the ritornello
5 15 9:34	Ritornello	Orchestra, *f,* plays the complete ritornello.

Second Movement (Affettuoso)   After the forceful first movement, a change is needed: something quieter, slower, and more emotional (*affettuoso* means just that, emotionally). As often in concertos, this slow movement is in a minor key, contrasting with the first and last, which are in major.

Baroque composers had a simple way of reducing volume: they could omit many or even all of the orchestra instruments. So here Bach employs only the three solo instruments—flute, violin, and harpsichord—plus the orchestra cello playing the continuo bass. The movement has two main motives:

These expressive motives are also played in *inversion*—that is, with all their melodic intervals reversed. Wherever the original motive goes up in pitch, the inversion goes down. Conceived in the abstract, inversion may seem like a merely mathematical device, but here it sounds perfectly elegant and natural.

Third Movement (Allegro)   The full orchestra returns in the last movement, which, however, begins with a lengthy passage for the three soloists. The lively compound meter with its triple component—ONE two three *four* five six— provides a welcome contrast to the duple meter that is so insistent in the two earlier movements.

2 Fugue

Fugue is one of the greatest and most characteristic achievements of Baroque music, indeed of Baroque culture altogether. In broad general terms, fugue can be thought of as systematized imitative polyphony (see page 30). Composers of the Middle Ages first glimpsed imitative polyphony, and Renaissance composers developed it; Baroque composers, living in an age of science, systematized it.

A **fugue** is a polyphonic composition for a fixed number of voices or instruments, built on a single principal theme. This theme, called the **fugue subject,** appears again and again in each of the instruments or voices. The term *fugue* itself comes from the Latin word *fuga,* which means "running away"; imagine the fugue subject being chased from one voice to another.

Exposition

A fugue begins with an **exposition,** in which all the voices present the subject in an orderly, standardized way. (Contrapuntal lines in fugues are referred to as "voices," even when the fugue is instrumental.) At the very start of a fugue, the subject is typically announced in the most prominent fashion possible—by appearing in a single voice without accompaniment. Then the subject appears in a second voice, while the first continues with other musical material, called the **countersubject**—a distinctive contrapuntal line that regularly accompanies the principal subject. Countersubjects stand out from the subject because of their particular rhythmic or melodic profiles.

Then the subject appears in a third voice, and so on. This section of a fugue, the exposition, is over when all the voices have stated the subject.

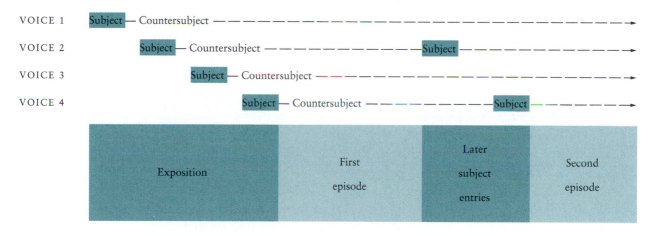

At intervals later in the fugue, the subject enters in one or another of the polyphonic voices. It may come at the top of the texture (the soprano), at the bottom (the bass), or else half hidden away in the middle. It may or may not be accompanied by the countersubject in one of the other voices.

Many of the later **subject entries** come in different keys. Though the modulations to these other keys are not very obvious—less so than in some later music we shall be hearing—without them fugues would seem dull and stodgy.

Episodes

The later subject entries of a fugue are spaced by passages of other music called **episodes**. Episodes provide a contrast to the subject entries, even though their musical material is often derived from the subject or the countersubject.

Even in such cases, however, the episodes sound less distinct and solid than the subject entries, and so stand apart from them. A regular feature of fugal episodes is the use of sequences (see page 27).

After the exposition, the form of a fugue falls into an alternating pattern: episodes alternate with new subject entries in various keys. How long this goes on depends entirely on the skill of the composer:

Exposition (subject enters in each voice)	First episode	Subject entry (or entries)	Second episode	Subject entry (or entries)	Third episode	Etc.

JOHANN SEBASTIAN BACH
Fugue in C Sharp Major, from *The Well-Tempered Clavier,* Book I (1721)

One reason Bach wrote his two famous books of twenty-four preludes and fugues for keyboard in all the keys, *The Well-Tempered Clavier,* was to show that even the rarest keys could be used for real music. Here a formidable key (requiring seven sharps!) accommodates a cheerful, self-assured fugue whose subject has a particularly lively swing. (We grant Bach his point, and write our examples below in a key that is easier to read, C major).

Fugue in C-sharp Major

The countersubject consists mostly of running sixteenth-notes, so the single long note in it makes a welcome rhythmic contrast. This note gives the listener something definite to hear:

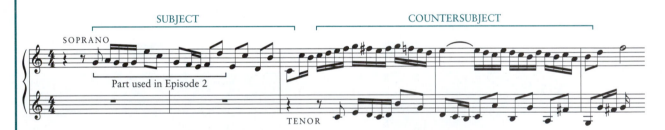

The countersubject appears with the subject every time, sometimes above it, sometimes below, but it is not easy to hear. It is not marked every time on the Listening Chart.

This fugue has three voices, and they enter in order: soprano, tenor (also covering the alto range), and bass. Episode 1 consists of busy three-part counterpoint, derived only vaguely from the subject. It prepares for another entry of the subject in the high register, which leads to a heavy cadence in a minor key.

We now hear two more entries of the subject, spaced out, and sounding a little solemn in the minor mode. They lead to another strong cadence.

At this point Bach invents a quite different kind of episode, thinner in texture and closely derived from the fugue subject. Episode 2 forms a sequence from *just the first part* of the subject (marked on the music example above); this is slightly tricky, because it can sound like two false starts of the actual subject. There is a feeling of satisfaction, then, when full-length subject entries arrive and put the fugue firmly back on track.

LISTENING CHART 5

1	1	2A	1A
31	16	2	8

Bach, Fugue in C♯ Major

Fugue form 2 min., 35 sec.

		subject counter-subject	
0:00	**Exposition**	S ———— ⌇⌇ ········	S = soprano (high range)
		T ———— ⌇⌇	T = tenor (middle range)
		B ————	B = bass (low range)
0:15	**Episode 1**		
0:26	**Subject**	S ————	
		CADENCE Cadence in minor key	
0:36	**Subject entries**	B ————	minor mode
		(delayed) T ————	minor mode
		CADENCE Cadence in another minor key	
1:00	**Episode 2**	Brief sequence on the first half of the subject, leading to the entire subject—	
1:05	**Subject entries**	S ———— ⌇⌇	
		T ————	
1:16	**Episode 3**		
1:32		Longer sequences on the first half of the subject, leading to the entire subject—	
1:52	**Subject entries**	S ———— ⌇⌇ ········ ⎫ same as	
		T ———— ⌇⌇ ⎬ the	
		B ———— ⎭ exposition	
2:09	**Episode 1 (again)**		
2:18	**Final Subject**	S ————	

During the course of another, much longer episode (Episode 3), Bach pulls the same trick again, but with a longer sequence. The melody, slightly varied, moves from the right hand to the left, from the soprano "voice" to the tenor. When the actual subject arrives, after this lengthy tease, it turns out to be the first of three entries which duplicate the opening exposition, countersubject and all. Episode 1 returns, too—a neat preparation for the fugue's final subject entry in the soprano voice.

Fugue and Fugal Devices

There are two further points to be made about fugue.

First, by way of clarification, fugue is a term with several meanings. It is a *genre;* there are pieces identified as "Fugues" because of the way they strictly work out a short theme in polyphony. Fugue is also a *form,* for as we have just seen, fugues fall into a distinct arrangement of subject entries spaced by episodes. But an informal meaning of the term is also important: fugue, as systematized imitative polyphony, is also a *texture* (see page 29) which is used selectively in other Baroque genres—in concerto movements, oratorio choruses, overtures (see page 132), and others.

In these "informal" cases we usually encounter only a fragmentary fugue form, treated freely: perhaps just an exposition, or an exposition plus one episode plus one extra entry. Fugue as a texture outlived the Baroque era, and remained a vital force in music for many years.

Second, fugue developed a reputation for technical (that is, compositional) display. In many fugues—though not all, as we know from the Fugue in C Sharp Major—the subject undergoes various learned operations: it is turned upside down, slowed down, speeded up, even played backwards. A favorite device called **stretto**, has one subject entry overlapping another entry in time, with the second jumping in before the first is over.

Often fugal devices are as academic and dry as they probably sound, but the Baroque masters of fugue drew unexpected expressive dividends from such technical procedures. Bach's encyclopedic *The Well-Tempered Clavier* includes beautiful "learned" fugues, as well as light-hearted ones.

The bearer, Monsieur J. C. Dorn, student of music, has requested the undersigned to give him a testimonial to his knowledge in musicis . . . As his years increase it may well be expected that with his good native talent he will develop into a quite able musician.

JOH. SEB. BACH (a tough grader . . .)

3   The Dance Suite

Dance music was popular in the Baroque era, as has been true in every era, including of course our own. Dance music also inspired the greatest composers of the time to some of their best efforts.

The custom was to group a collection of miscellaneous dances together in a genre called the **suite.** Composers usually wrote "stylized" dances, that is, their music was intended for listening rather than dancing. Compared with music written for the actual dance floor, stylized dances naturally allowed for more musical elaboration and refinement, while still retaining some of the special features of the various dances.

Suites were written for orchestra, for chamber music combinations, or even for solo instruments such as the harpsichord or lute. Which dances occurred in a suite was not subject to any general rule, nor was there any specified order. All the dances in a suite were kept in the same key, and the last of them was always fast—frequently a gigue, a dance in compound meter that may have been derived from the Irish jig. Otherwise there was no standard overall structure to a suite.

Baroque Dances

Many different dances existed in the Baroque era. What distinguished them were features originally associated with the dance steps—a certain meter, a distinctive tempo, and some rhythmic attributes. The dance called the *gavotte,* for example, always begins with a double *upbeat,* two weak beats preceding the first strong beat (the *downbeat*) of a measure.

The following table lists the main Baroque dances and their distinguishing features:

Dance	Usual Meter	Tempo	Some Rhythmic Characteristics
Allemande	4/4	Moderate	Upbeat sixteenth note; flowing motion
Courante	3/2	Moderate	Occasional substitution of 6/4 measures
Sarabande	3/4	Slow	Often a secondary accent on beat 2 (no upbeat)
Minuet	3/4	Moderate	Rather plain in rhythm (upbeat optional)
Gavotte	4/4	Moderate	Long upbeat of two quarter notes
Bourrée	2/2	Rather fast	Short upbeat
Siciliana	12/8	Moderate	Gently moving dotted rhythms; minor mode
Gigue	6/8	Fast	Short upbeat; dotted rhythms; lively movement

Baroque illustration of a stylized country dance ("contredanse") in a ballet. Notice the stage set in the background.

Baroque Dance Form

Although the number, type, and arrangement of dances in a suite varied widely, the *form* of dances was firmly standardized. The same simple form was applied to all types, and it is an easily recognized feature of Baroque dance music.

A Baroque dance has two sections, **a** and **b.** Each ends with a strong cadence coming to a complete stop, after which the section is immediately repeated. Both sections tend to include the same motives, cadences, and other such musical details, and this makes for a sense of symmetry between them, even though **b** is nearly always longer than **a.** In the Baroque era there is usually no full-scale, clear repeat of the whole of **a** after **b,** as we shall see happen in later dances.

Hence Baroque dance form is diagramed

a a b b   *abbreviated as:* |: **a** :||: **b** :|

where the signs |: and :| indicate that everything between them is to be repeated. This form is also called *binary form.*

In addition, the shorter dances (such as the minuet and the gavotte) tended to be grouped in pairs of the same type, with the first coming back again after the second. The result was a large-scale **A B A** form. The **B** dance in such a pair was called the **trio,** because in seventeenth-century orchestral music it had often been scored for only three instruments (and such scoring is sometimes still found in the eighteenth; see page 176).

This made for a simple, agreeable contrast with the full orchestration of the **A** dance. Even when the trio is scored for full orchestra, the idea of contrast between the two dances was always kept; the second is quieter than the first, or it changes mode. (As for the term *trio,* that was still used in the waltzes of Johann Strauss and the marches of John Philip Sousa.)

Thus a Baroque minuet and trio, to choose this dance as an example, consists of one minuet followed by a second, quieter minuet, after which the first is heard again. This time, however, the repeats are normally omitted:

	Minuet	Trio	Minuet
	A	**B**	**A**
	a a b b	c c d d	a b
abbreviated as:	|: a :||: b :|	|: c :||: d :|	a b

The French Overture

A dance suite begins not with the first dance but with a special preparatory number called a **French overture.** *Overture* is of course a general term for any substantial piece of music introducing a play, opera, or ballet. The French overture was a special type developed at the court of Louis XIV and widely used in the early eighteenth century.

The French overture consists of two sharply contrasted sections, a slow **A** section and a faster **B** section. They are arranged in a number of alternative ways, such as |: **A** :| **B** or |: **A** :||: **B** :| or |: **A** :||: **B A′** :|, where **A′** stands for a variant—often an abbreviated variant—of **A.**

The slow **A** section is the one that is distinctively "French." Dotted rhythms (see page 21), sweeping scales, heavy accents, and other such features give it a majestic, pompous gravity that is easily recognized (and was easily imitated). This section was typically labeled with the French word *Grave* (*grahv*), to indicate solemnity and gravity.

The fast **B** section is in imitative polyphony. In some overtures this section amounts to a full-scale fugue.

BACH
Orchestral Suite No. 3 in D (c. 1730)

It is thought that Bach wrote this suite for the Collegium Musicum of the University of Leipzig, a student music organization that seems to have provided a congenial outlet for his later work. The Suite in D is scored for a modified version of the "festive" Baroque orchestra diagramed on page 111: strings, two oboes, three trumpets, two timpani, and harpsichord. Bach carefully varied the style of orchestration from number to number.

This suite, like others written all over Europe, uses French titles as an acknowledgment of French leadership in ballet and the dance.

Ouverture   The French overture that starts the suite is scored for all the instruments, and in fact it is the only movement in which the oboes have (slightly) independent parts that do not always double the violins. What is more, a solo violin emerges unexpectedly to dominate two passages during the **B** part of the overture, which is a full-scale fugue.

The form of this overture is **A B A′.** Shown below is the beginning of the **A** section, the "Grave," with its arresting drum roll and the obligatory "French" dotted rhythms, and part of the fugal exposition in **B:**

The episodes in this fugue are played by the solo violin. Indeed, this **B** part of the movement can be understood in two ways: as a fugue with solo violin episodes, or as a Baroque concerto with a fugal ritornello.

Following the overture come four pieces in dance form. Three of them follow the Baroque pattern |: a :||: b :|. Notice the "full stop" effect after each playing of all the **a**'s and **b**'s. Only the gavotte, the second of the dances, has a trio and so falls into **A B A** form.

Air   "Air" is the French word for aria—and this aria is in dance form, since it has to take its place in a dance suite. It is perhaps Bach's most famous and beloved melody. Only the strings and continuo play, as the quiet melody in the first violins is accompanied by a regular, downward-moving, soothing bass line in the cellos and bass viols (a **walking bass**: see page 109). And there are subsidiary but highly expressive counterpoints in the second violins and violas.

¶   The exquisite fluidity of this melody is a function of its rhythmic variety— variety that is set off by the regularity of the "walking" bass (see page 109). Most of the basic two-beat (half-measure) units in the melody have rhythms not duplicated elsewhere. Consequently, when measures 13–14 do repeat a rhythmic figure several times, they gain a special kind of climactic intensity. This intensity is underpinned by quiet *upward* motion in the bass, which had generally been moving downward, and by a newly prominent second violin part.

¶   Anticipated by some melodic figures in **a**, the figures in **b** keep reaching ever upward, in a wonderfully spontaneous way. This sense of aspiration is balanced by the graceful falling cadences ending **a** and **b**.

¶   To counteract all the rhythmic and melodic variety, Bach puts in several beautiful sequences, whose repetitive quality ensures a sense of organization: see measures 3–4, 13–14, and 15–16.

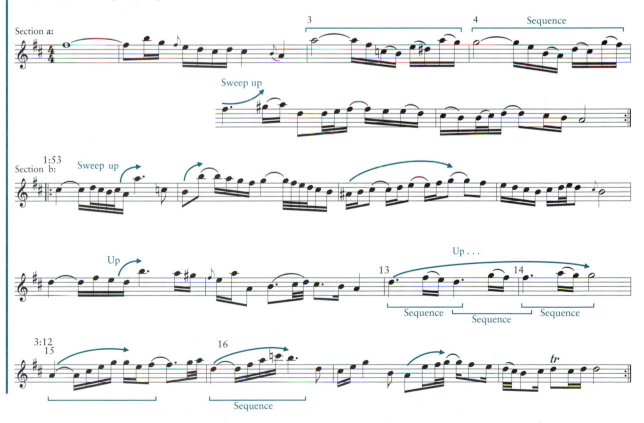

Early concerts were some-
times given in parks, where
music accompanied gossip,
flirting, and food.

Gavotte   The wind instruments and timpani return in this number; the trumpets' military accent fits in well with the strong two-quarter note upbeat of the gavotte (see page 130). Bach inverts the bold opening melody of **a** to obtain the opening of **b**. This inversion may *look* academic—a technical trick to be appreciated by the Collegium Musicum connoisseurs—but it *sounds* fresh and natural, another product of Bach's endlessly fertile melodic imagination:

Section a:

Section b:

Free inversion

LISTEN

2   1   2A   1A
7   17   4   9

Bach, Suite No. 3 in D,
Gavotte

0:00   Gavotte (**A**): **a**
0:16   **a** *repeated*
0:32   **b**
0:56   **b** *repeated*
1:22   Trio (**B**): **c c**
2:11   **d d**
3:01   **A** (**a b**)

The trio, or second gavotte, also fully orchestrated, sounds even more military than the first. Strings and oboes play fanfares to begin both **c** and **d**.

Bourrée   The lightest dance in this suite, a bourrée, is scored for full orchestra; the wind instruments and timpani are used mainly to underscore the sharp, exhilarating rhythms.

Gigue   Another drum roll (as in the French overture) launches this vigorous gigue, the most common dance for the last movement in a suite. The violins, doubled by the oboes, play almost continuous eighth notes in **6/8** time.

CHAPTER 11

Baroque Vocal Music

V ocal music—music for solo voices, choruses, or both—formed a major part of the output of virtually all Baroque composers. We have seen that composers were supported by three main institutions: the church, the opera house, and the court. Each of these demanded vocal music. Indeed, of the three, only the court was a major source of instrumental music—and every court had its chapel, for which the court composers were also required to provide vocal music. Courts had their own opera houses, too.

Words and Music

Theories of musical expression in the Baroque era were touched on in Chapter 9 (page 106). It was believed at the time that emotions could be isolated, categorized, and listed in a fairly simple way, and that music could enhance each emotion by means of certain musical devices applied consistently, even single-mindedly, throughout a piece. Theorists developed checklists of musical devices corresponding to each of the "affects," as they called emotions conceived in this way.

It was particularly in vocal music—where an actual text defines or suggests a specific emotion—that this musical "vocabulary of the emotions" was applied most consistently. If a text refers to "rejoicing," for example, a Baroque composer would almost inevitably match this with fast, lively runs; a mention of "victory" would probably require trumpets and drums to evoke battle music. More literally, when a text speaks of "high" or "low," a setting in high or low voices was likely, and so on.

1 Opera

The principal genre of secular vocal music of the Baroque era was opera. Introduced around the year 1600, opera flourished mightily all over Europe, and soon became the most glamorous and in some ways the most adventurous musical genre of the Baroque era.

In characterizing the emotional world of Baroque art (see page 114), we stressed its theatrical quality. The Baroque was fascinated by the theater, and especially by opera—the ultimate multimedia experience of its day, combining

A German opera house of the Baroque era. Notice that the best seats were actually on the stage.

poetry, drama, music, vocal virtuosity, scenic splendor, dance, and more. Spectacular singing was of the essence in Baroque opera, and so was spectacular stage architecture, featuring amazing transformation scenes and the like. Systems of pulleys and counterweights could rapidly change the set from a palace to a magic garden, with gods and goddesses descending from the heavens in a fiery chariot. Opera offered a wealth of satisfactions, then—most obviously, no doubt, for the vocal connoisseurs of the day, the fans of great singers. They are said to have gossiped and played cards in the boxes while waiting for their favorites to sing their special arias.

But opera's ability to project emotion was the real basis of its appeal. First and foremost, opera erected a stage on which individual singers could step forward to express feelings in the most direct and powerful fashion. The basic convention of opera—having dramatic characters sing instead of speak—must always have seemed artificial, even unnatural; but since the singers *were* dramatic characters, they were repeatedly thrown into situations which made it natural for them to experience (and express) intense emotions. Such emotions were further intensified, of course, by music.

Emotion could be intensified by great vocal virtuosity, too. The most obvious kind of vocal virtuosity is *coloratura* singing—fast brilliant runs, scales, high notes, vocal cadenzas, and so on, stressing technique for its own sake. But the legendary singers of old moved their audiences not only by singing faster than anyone else, but by singing more beautifully, more delicately, and more emotionally.

Italian Opera Seria

The principal type of Italian Baroque opera was **opera seria,** or serious opera. The plots—mostly derived from ancient history, with all kinds of alterations and additions—were designed to stir up powerful emotions, such as passion, rage, grief, and triumph. This gave the singers many opportunities to excel in one kind of expression or another. The most important of these singers were sopranos and altos; tenors and basses took the second place. Opera seria consists almost exclusively of solo singing, with few duets or choruses.

The text of an opera is called the *libretto* ("little book"), and the poet who wrote it is the *librettist*. Librettists were required to build up their total story from texts for *recitatives* and *arias*.

Recitative

Recitative (resita-téev), from the Italian word for "recite," is a technique of declaiming words musically in a heightened, theatrical manner. There is always an instrumental accompaniment. The singing voice closely follows the free rhythm of emotional speech; it mirrors and indeed exaggerates the natural ups and downs that occur as an actor raises his or her voice at a question, lowers it in "asides," or cries out in distress. The composer makes no effort to "organize" these speechlike utterances into real melodies.

Recitative was used for plot action, dialogue, and other places in the drama where it is particularly important for the words to be brought out. Text phrases and individual words are not ordinally repeated, of course, any more than they would be in speech.

Most of the time, recitative accompaniment was kept to a minimum—basso continuo (cello and harpsichord) alone—so that the singer could interpret the dialogue or the action as spontaneously as possible. A name for recitative with continuo accompaniment is **secco recitative,** from the Italian word *secco,* meaning "dry" (think of the sound of the harpsichord).

In every opera, however, one or two of the most excited recitatives were provided with orchestral accompaniment of one kind or another. This type is called **accompanied recitative.**

A much more informal picture of a Baroque opera performance—evidently during a recitative, to judge from the close engagement of the characters on stage and the inattention of the audience. (The painting is perhaps by Antonio Longhi, 1702–1785).

The Castrato

Intimately tied up with Italian opera seria was the castrato singer (plural: *castrati*). The starring male roles in opera were hardly ever sung by tenors or basses, but by men who had submitted to castration as young boys in order to preserve their voices in the soprano or alto range. At its best, the castrato voice was a prized virtuoso instrument, more powerful and brilliant than a woman's soprano.

This whole practice seems an outrage to us today, as it did to everybody outside Italy at the time (and many in Italy itself). It has been pointed out that for an intelligent peasant boy, the classic way to avoid a lifetime of labor in the fields was to enter the priesthood, with its vow of chastity, and that becoming a castrato provided another similar option.

In any case, in Italy and all over Europe—France was a notable exception—castrati were gladly accepted because of their wonderful singing, and given top billing, along with women prima donnas. But the presence of frankly unnatural men in the main opera roles, which were of course usually romantic roles, made it very hard to believe in the ideal of operas as serious drama in music. Often it was closer to "concert in costume." Contributing to the side-show quality, it was common for

Farinelli

male characters to disguise themselves as women (and vice versa). The male soprano voice was used for female impersonation.

The most famous castrati were international stage figures. (While some were pampered stars and objects of ridicule at the same time, others were serious artists. Carlo Broschi, whose stage name was Farinelli, the most famous of all, was also a composer and later in life an influential figure at the court of Spain.) But many more castrati worked out of the limelight, in Italian churches. The last known castrato, a member of the Sistine Choir in Rome, made a recording in 1902; the voice has been described as "penetrating and curiously disembodied."

For a 1995 film about Farinelli, a virtual castrato voice was reinvented by digital wizardry.

Aria

An **aria** is a set piece for solo singer that has much more musical elaboration and coherence than a passage of recitative. The vocal part is more melodic, and typically the accompaniment includes the orchestra, not just the continuo. Here the singer-actor is mulling over his or her emotions at some leisure, "getting his feelings out," instead of reacting moment by moment, as in recitative. Consequently in arias the repetition of poetic phrases or words is common and, in principle, appropriate.

The standard form for the Baroque Italian opera aria is **da capo form**, **A B A** (less usual is free da capo form, **A B A′**). Both the words and music of **A** are repeated after **B**; *da capo* ("from the head") is a direction on scores meaning repeat from the beginning. The composer wrote the music for **A** and **B** only, leaving the performers to do the rest. Indeed, the singer would do more than just repeat **A**. He or she would also ornament the music with improvised runs, cadenzas, and so on, so as to create an exciting enhanced effect the second time around.

For connoisseurs of the day, a great deal depended on the **A** repeats, since it was there that the singers really dazzled their audiences. Many modern singers have relearned the lost improvisational art of the Baroque era, and we can recapture some of the original excitement on records.

If we can neither get [the famous castrato] Senesino, nor Carestini, then Mr. Handel desires to have a man soprano and a woman contralto, and the price (for both) must not exceed 1100 guineas, and that the persons must set out for London the latter end of August, and that no engagement must be made with one without a certainty of getting the other.

Letter from one of Handel's agents, 1730

GEORGE FRIDERIC HANDEL
Rodelinda (1725)

As a young man, Handel wrote a few German operas for the Hamburg opera company (most of the music is lost) and a few Italian operas for theaters in Florence and Venice; in his maturity he wrote as many as forty Italian operas for London. *Rodelinda* is one of a trio of Handel masterpieces written in the years 1724–25, the others being *Tamerlano* and *Giulio Cesare (Julius Caesar)*.

Background   Most opera plots of the late Baroque era deal with subjects from Roman antiquity (like Handel's *Julius Caesar*). The subject of *Rodelinda*, however, is very remotely derived from the history of the medieval Lombards, in north Italy.

Queen Rodelinda of Lombardy mourns her husband, who is presumed dead in battle. Both she and her sister have to fend off a pair of villains called Grimoaldo and Garibaldo (though Grimoaldo, it turns out, has a good side to him). When Grimoaldo seeks Rodelinda's hand and kingdom, she puts him off with elaborate schemes and vague promises. Then it turns out that her husband, Bertarido, had not perished after all. He returns in disguise, and is very upset when he misunderstands his wife's machinations.

After many more turns to this tangled tale, Bertarido saves Grimoaldo from the murderous Garibaldo, and Grimoaldo is grateful enough to obey his better instincts and return the throne to the reunited couple.

The plot is certainly farfetched, but it does have one virtue: it lands the characters in situations that call for strong emotions, which they can then express in some of Handel's finest music. Thus Rodelinda laments her lost husband, and cries out in indignation at Grimoaldo's harshness. Bertarido longs for his wife in one of the opera's greatest hits. Grimoaldo struggles musically with the conflict between his passions and his conscience.

Aria, "Tirannia"   And Garibaldo can express the deepest-dyed villainy. Our short recitative and aria show the type of alternation that is characteristic of opera seria—the recitative accompanied by harpsichord, the aria by orchestra. Unulfo, a minor character, is shocked to hear Garibaldo encouraging Grimoaldo to kill Rodelinda's little son Flavio. But Garibaldo explains: once Grimoaldo has taken the bloody path to power, he says, there can be no stopping now.

When Garibaldo belts out the word *tirannia* on a highly emphatic repeated note, four times in all, we sense that while he may be talking about Grimoaldo's rise to power, "tyranny" is something he craves for himself. Arrogance, power, sheer evil: Handel makes the bass voice project all of these. "Tirannia" is in strict **A B A** form, with the orchestral ritornello before **A** coming back after **A** in an abbreviated form. Since the brief **B** section contains some of the same material as **A**, there is no strong sense of contrast.

People often laugh at the amount of word repetition in Italian operas. The eight words in this aria's **A** section are strung out in four stretches:

Tirannia gli diede il regno, gliel conservi crudeltà, *gliel conservi crudeltà, gliel conservi crudeltà;*

Tirannia gli diede il regno, gliel conservi crudeltà, *gliel conservi crudeltà;*

Tirannia gli diede il regno, gliel conservi crudeltà, *crudeltà, gliel conservi crudeltà;*

Tirannia gli diede il regno, gliel conservi crudeltà.

Samuel Ramey—the Garibaldo on our recording—singing another, equally villainous Handel bass role (Argante, in *Rinaldo*).

Ti - ran - nia . . .

But the most important effect of all these repetitions is to keep bringing Garibaldo back to the word *crudeltà* ("cruelty") with strong—sometimes very strong—cadences. It is as though we are watching an obsessive, sadistic individual gloat about his cruelty. And in the second **A** section, the singer's improvised decorations and his violent, exciting cadenza make Garibaldo sound more malevolent than ever.

LISTEN	Handel, *Rodelinda,* "Tirannia," Recitative and Aria

RECITATIVE (SECCO)

Unulfo:	Massime così indegne consigli così rei tu porgi, o duca, a chi sostien la maestà reale?	Such shameful notions— can you give such evil counsel, O duke, to the upholder of royal majesty?
Garibaldo:	Lascia che chi è tiranno opra da tale.	Let him who is the ruler act like one,
Unulfo:	Vorrai?	You want . . .?
Garibaldo:	Sì, che spergiuro tradisca la sua fè.	Yes, I want that perjurer to betray his word!
Unulfo:	Vorrai?	You want . . .?
Garibaldo:	Che impuro insidi l'onestà.	. . . that villain to subvert her virtue!
Unulfo:	Vorrai?	Can you really want . . .
Garibaldo:	Che crudo con massime spietate, ingiuste ed empie . . .	. . . that oaf, with his instincts for villainy, injustice, and evil . . .
Unulfo:	. . . sparga il sangue reale?	. . . to spill royal blood?
Garibaldo:	Così d'usurpatore il nome adempie.	That's how to earn the name of usurper!

ARIA

0:55	Garibaldo:	A Tirannia gli diede il regno; gliel conservi crudeltà.	Tyranny brought him the kingdom; he will retain it only by cruelty.
2:00		B Del regnar base e sostegno è il rigor, non la pietà.	Power's base and support is severity, not pity!
2:30		A Tirannia . . . *etc.*	Tyranny . . . *etc.*

For a note on Italian pronunciation, see page 91: "Tirannya li dyehd'il rehnyo."

2 Oratorio

Sacred, or religious, vocal music of the Baroque era exhibits considerable diversity in style and form. Most (but not all) of it was written directly for church services, and so its style and form depend first of all on whether those services were of the Roman Catholic, Lutheran, or Anglican rite. Every service has places where music is appropriate, if not actually specified by the liturgy. In principle, each place gives rise to a different musical genre.

There are, however, two general factors that are important for all Baroque sacred-music genres—oratorio and passion, cantata, Mass, and motet. One of these factors is traditional in origin; the other is specific to the Baroque era.

The traditional factor is the participation of the choir. Choral music has had a functional place in the religious music of virtually all rites and of virtually all ages. For when one person utters a religious text, he or she speaks as an individual, but when a choir does so, it speaks as a united community. A church choir, by extension, can be said to speak for the whole church, even for the whole of Christianity.

George Frideric Handel (1685–1759)

Georg Friedrich Händel—he anglicized his name to George Frideric Handel after settling in England—was one of the few composers of early days who did not come from a family of musicians. His father was a barber-surgeon and a valet at a court near Leipzig. He disapproved of music, and the boy is said to have studied music secretly at night, by candlelight. In deference to his father's wishes, Handel studied law for a year at Halle, one of Germany's major universities, before finally joining the orchestra at Hamburg, Germany's leading center of opera.

From then on, it was an exciting, glamorous life. Still in his teens, Handel fought a duel (about who was to get top billing) with another Hamburg musician. In 1706 he journeyed to the homeland of opera and scored successes at Venice, Florence, and Rome. Though he became a court musician for the Elector of Hanover, in northern Germany, he kept requesting (and extending) leaves to pursue his career in London, a city that was then beginning to rival Paris as the world capital.

Here Handel continued to produce Italian operas, again with great success. He also wrote a flattering birthday ode for Queen Anne and some big pieces to celebrate a major peace treaty; for this he was awarded a substantial annuity. In 1717, after the Elector of Hanover had become George I of England, Handel got back into his good graces by composing music to be played on boats in a royal aquatic fete on the River Thames—the famous *Water Music* (two suites for "festive" orchestra).

As an opera composer, Handel had learned to gauge the taste of the public and also how to flatter singers, writing music for them that showed off their voices to the best advantage. He now also became an opera impresario—today we would call him a promoter—recruiting singers and negotiating their contracts, planning whole seasons of opera and all the while composing the main attractions himself: an opera every year, on average, be-

tween 1721 and 1743. He also had to deal with backers—English aristocrats and wealthy merchants who supported his opera companies, and persuaded their friends to take out subscriptions for boxes.

Handel made and lost several fortunes, but he always landed on his feet, even when Italian opera went out of style in Britain, for he never lost a feel for his audience. After opera had failed, he popularized oratorios—retellings of Bible stories (mostly from the Old Testament) in a semioperatic, semichoral form. Opera audiences had always been ready to identify opera's virtuous Roman emperors with local princes. Now they were delighted to identify oratorio's virtuous People of Israel with the British nation.

Handel was a big, vigorous man, hot tempered but quick to forget, humorous and resourceful. When a particularly temperamental prima donna threw a scene, he calmed her down by threatening to throw her out the window. At the end of his life he became blind—the same surgeon operated (unsuccessfully) on both him and on Bach—but he continued to play the organ brilliantly and composed by dictating to a secretary.

Chief Works: 40 Italian operas, including *Giulio Cesare* (Julius Caesar), *Rodelinda,* and *Tamerlano* ▪ Near-operatic works in English: *Semele, Hercules,* and *Acis and Galatea* ▪ Oratorios, including *Messiah, Israel in Egypt, Samson,* and *Saul* ▪ Concerti grossi and organ concertos ▪ *Water Music,* written for an aquatic fete on the River Thames, and *Fireworks Music,* celebrating the end of the War of the Austrian Succession, in 1747 ▪ Sonatas for various instruments; variations ("The Harmonious Blacksmith") for harpsichord

The other important fact about Baroque sacred vocal music is its strong tendency to borrow from secular vocal music—which is to say, from opera. Arias inspired by Italian opera seria appear even in Baroque settings of the Catholic Mass. Solo singers could display their vocal prowess at the same time as they were presenting parts of the divine service.

The most operatic of all religious genres was oratorio, which existed in Catholic and Protestant countries alike. An **oratorio** is basically an opera on a religious subject, such as an Old Testament story or the life of a saint. It has a narrative plot in several acts, real characters, and implied action—even though oratorios were not staged, but presented in concert form, that is, without

Women in Music

Before the twentieth century, women had a single role, that of wife and mother. Occasionally accidents of royal succession placed a woman in a position of great power, and the eighteenth century saw two amazingly long-lasting cases: Queen Catherine the Great of Russia, who ruled from 1762 to 1796, and Maria Theresa, de-facto Empress of the Austrian Empire from 1740 to 1780. But what we now think of as "careers" were simply not open to women, with very few exceptions.

Music provided one of those exceptions. It did so by way of the theater, for an opera singer, like an actress or a ballet dancer, could attain fame and fortune and the opportunity to develop her talents in the same way as men in those same fields. Indeed, opera depended on women singers; without them the genre could never have developed or survived.

The names—though not, alas, the voices—of opera's legendary prima donnas have come down to us, along with those of opera's composers: from Anna Renzi (ca. 1620–ca. 1660), who sang in Monteverdi's *Poppea* (see page 91), to the notorious rival superstars Faustina Bordoni (1700–1781) and Francesca Cuzzoni (1698–1770) in the age of Handel, and beyond. Bordoni received £2000 for her first London visit, equivalent to maybe $100,000 today.

Women of the theater paid a price for their career opportunity, of course. They were displaying themselves—their legs or their voices—for the enjoyment of, mainly, men, who paid for the privilege. There was always a question about the respectability and marriageability of opera singers.

Women opera singers were a fixture in the musical workplace of the Baroque. Women instrumentalists were much rarer, and women composers were simply flukes. We noted on page 123 that Baroque music was largely the product of clans, like the Bachs; but next to none of

Faustina Bordoni

Francesca Cuzzoni

these clans ever thought to make one of their daughters into a composer.

An exception was the Jacquet family, harpsichord makers in Paris for at least four generations. Elizabeth-Claude Jacquet (1667–1729) was a Mozart-style prodigy who was sponsored by Louis XIV himself. Famous as a harpsichordist, she composed harpsichord music, chamber music, cantatas, and an opera that was put on at the forerunner of the Paris Opéra—then as now the grandest venue for opera in Europe.

There was no respectability problem with Jacquet; by the time she was seventeen she was married to an organist, one Marin de la Guerre, whose name is usually hyphenated with hers.

---

scenery, costumes, or gestures. Oratorio takes over such operatic features as recitatives and arias. It also makes much use of the chorus—a major difference from Italian opera of the time.

Unlike most other religious genres, an oratorio was not actually part of a church service. Indeed, in opera-crazed Italy, the oratorio was prized as an entertainment substituting for opera during Lent, a season of abstinence from opera as well as other worldly diversions.

In England, the oratorio was also a substitute for opera, though in a different sense. Thanks largely to Handel, Italian opera became very popular in London for a quarter of a century, but finally audiences tired of it. At that point, Handel, already in his mid-fifties, began composing oratorios, and these turned out to be even more popular yet, the pinnacle of his long career.

On Tuesday the 2nd day of May will be performed, the Sacred Story of Esther, *an Oratorio in English. Formerly composed by Mr. Handel, and now revised by him, with several Additions . . . N.B. There will be no Action on the Stage . . .*

London newspaper announcement, 1731

GEORGE FRIDERIC HANDEL
Messiah (1742)

Handel's oratorio *Messiah,* his most famous work, is also one of the most famous in the whole of Western music. It is perhaps the only composition from the Baroque era that has been performed continuously—and frequently—since its first appearance. Today it is sung at Christmas and Easter in hundreds of churches around the world, as well as at symphony concerts and "*Messiah* sings," where people get together just to sing along with the Hallelujah Chorus and the other well-known choral numbers, and listen to the well-loved arias.

Unlike most oratorios, *Messiah* does not have actual characters acting out a biblical story in recitative and arias, although its text is taken from the Bible. In a more typical Handel oratorio, such as *Samson,* for example, Samson sings an aria about his blindness and argues with Delilah in recitative, while choruses represent the People of Israel and the Philistines. Instead, *Messiah* works with a group of narrators, relating episodes from the life of Jesus in recitative. The narration is interrupted by anonymous commentators who react to each of the episodes by singing recitatives and arias.

All this is similar in many ways to opera in concert form (that is, not staged); but in addition, the chorus has a large and varied role to play. On one occasion, they speak for a group of angels that is actually quoted in the Bible. Sometimes they comment on the story, like the soloists. And often they raise their voices to praise the Lord in Handel's uniquely magnificent manner.

We shall first examine two numbers in *Messiah* covering the favorite Christmas story about the announcement of Christ's birth to the shepherds in the fields. Included are a recitative in four sections and a chorus.

***Recitative** Part 1 (secco)*   Sung by a boy soprano narrator accompanied by continuo (cello and organ), this recitative has the natural, "proselike" flow typical of all recitatives. Words that would be naturally stressed in ordinary speech are brought out by rhythms, higher pitches, and pauses: "*shep*herds," "*field*," "*flock*," and "*night*." No words are repeated.

Part 2 (accompanied)   The slowly pulsing high-string background, a sort of musical halo for the angel, is also a signal for more vigorous declamation—the words *lo, Lord,* and *glory* are brought out with increasing emphasis. The end of this little accompanied recitative is heavily punctuated by a standard cadence formula, played by the continuo. This formula is an easily recognized feature of recitatives.

Part 3 (secco)   Notice that the angel speaks in a more urgent style than the narrator. And in *Part 4 (accompanied),* the excited, faster pulsations in the high strings depict the beating wings, perhaps, of the great crowd of angels. When Handel gets to what they will be "saying," he brings the music to a triumphant high point, once again over the standard recitative cadence.

Chorus, "Glory to God"   "Glory to God! glory to God in the *highest!*" sing the angels—the *high* voices of the choir, in an enthusiastic marchlike rhythm, accompanied by the orchestra, with the trumpets prominent. The *low* voices alone add "and peace on *earth*," much more slowly. Fast string runs following "Glory to God," and slower reiterated chords following "and peace on earth," recall the fast and slow string passages in the two preceding accompanied recitatives.

After these phrases are sung and played again, leading to another key, the full chorus sings the phrase "good will toward men" in a fugal style. The important words are *good will,* and their two-note motive is happily sung (in imitation) again and again by all the voices of the angel choir. To conclude, the "good will" motive is isolated out in an enthusiastic ascending sequence.

good will to-ward men

The whole chorus is quite concise, even dramatic; the angels do not stay long. At the very end, the orchestra gets quieter and quieter—a rare effect in Baroque music, here indicating the disappearance of the shepherds' vision.

good will . . .

| LISTEN | Handel, *Messiah,* Recitative "There were shepherds" and Chorus, "Glory to God" |

2   2A
9   6

(Bold type indicates accented words or syllables. Italics indicate phrases of text that are repeated.)

RECITATIVE PART 1 (secco)

There were **shep**herds abiding in the **field,** keeping **watch** over their **flock** by **night.**

PART 2 (accompanied)

0:13   And *lo!* the angel of the **Lord** came upon them, and the **glo**ry of the Lord shone round about them; and they were sore afraid.   Standard cadence

PART 3 (secco)

0:30   And the angel said unto ***them: Fear*** not, for be**hold,** I bring you good **ti**dings of great **joy,** which shall **be to all peo**ple.   Standard cadence
For unto you is born this **day** in the city of **Da**vid a **Sa**viour, which is **Christ** the **Lord.**   Standard cadence

PART 4 (accompanied)

1:03   And **sud**denly there was with the **an**gel a **mul**titude of the heavenly **host,** praising **God, *and saying:***   Standard cadence

CHORUS

1:19   Glory to God in the highest, and peace on earth,
1:54   goodwill toward men.
2:11   *Glory to God . . .*

An oratorio performance, caught by the satirical pen of Handel's contemporary William Hogarth (1697–1764)

Hallelujah Chorus   This famous chorus brings Act II of *Messiah* to a re-sounding close. Like "Glory to God," "Hallelujah" makes marvelous use of monophony ("King of Kings"), homophony (the opening "Hallelujah"), and polyphony ("And he shall reign for ever and ever": almost a textbook example of musical textures. Compare "And peace on earth," "Glory to God," and "Goodwill toward men" in the earlier chorus.)

Hallelujah,   Hallelujah,   Hallelujah,   Hallelujah, Halle - lujah.

and he shall reign for ever and ev-er

In a passage beloved by chorus singers, Handel sets "The Kingdom of this world is become . . ." on a low descending scale, *piano,* swelling suddenly into a similar scale in a higher register, *forte,* for "the Kingdom of our God, and of his Christ"—a perfect representation of one thing becoming another thing, similar but newly radiant. Later the sopranos (cheered on by the trumpets) solemnly utter the words "King of Kings . . ." on higher and higher long notes as the other voices keep repeating their answer, "for ever, Hallelujah!"

George II of England, attending the first London performance of *Messiah,* was so moved by this chorus that he stood up—in tribute to the King of Kings, perhaps, or to Handel who had praised Him so superbly. The whole audience rose too, of course. It is still customary for audiences to stand for the Hallelujah Chorus.

LISTEN	Handel, *Messiah*, Hallelujah Chorus

2   2A

10   7

(Italics indicate phrases of text that are repeated.)

	Hallelujah, *Hallelujah!* . . .
0:26	For the Lord God omnipotent reigneth. *Hallelujah!* . . .
	For the Lord God . . .
1:16	The Kingdom of this world is become the kingdom
	of our Lord and *of his Christ.*
1:35	And He shall reign for ever and ever, *and he shall reign* . . .
1:50	KING OF KINGS *for ever and ever, Hallelujah!* . . .
	AND LORD OF LORDS *for ever and ever* . . .

3 The Church Cantata

Second in importance to oratorio among Baroque sacred-music genres is the **church cantata.** *Cantata* is a general name for a piece of moderate length for voices and instruments, and in Germany church cantatas were written to be performed during Lutheran church services. Lutheran churches in those days had fixed readings and hymns specified for every Sunday of the year, as well as for special occasions such as Easter and Christmas. The words of cantatas addressed the religious content of the day in question. Sung before the sermon, the cantata was in effect a second, musicalized sermon.

As cantor, or music director, of Leipzig's biggest church (the Thomas-kirche), Bach was required to produce cantatas for the entire year—a stupendous task that kept him very busy indeed for years after he was appointed. Over two hundred cantatas by Bach have survived, each of them with several movements, including some secular cantatas written for court or civic celebrations.

The Lutheran Chorale

The content and structure of the church cantata were quite various. One kind, for example, has singers who represent Hope, Fear, the Soul, and so on, discussing Christian issues in operatic arias and recitatives. This is like a short scene from an oratorio. A special feature of nearly all Lutheran cantatas is their use of traditional congregational hymns. Lutheran hymns are called **chorales** (coráhls), from the German word for hymn (*Choral*).

Martin Luther, the father of the Protestant Reformation, placed special emphasis on hymn singing when he decided on the format of Lutheran services. Two hundred years later, in Bach's time, a large body of chorales served as the foundation for Lutheran worship, both in church services and also at informal pious devotions in the home. Everybody knew the words and music of these chorales, which they had learned in their childhood and sung in church all their lives. Consequently when composers introduced chorale tunes into cantatas (and other sacred-music genres), they were drawing on a rich source of association.

Just how were tunes "introduced"? There were many ways. The last movement of a cantata is usually a single hymn stanza sung straight through, in much the same simple way as the congregation would sing it, but with the orchestra playing.

Longer cantata movements present phrases of the chorale one by one, with gaps in between them, while other music runs on continuously, both during the chorale phrases (that is, in counterpoint with them) and during the gaps. In a **"gapped" chorale**, the gapped melody can be sung, or it can be played by one prominent instrument—an oboe, say, or a trumpet—while the continuous music goes along in the other instrument and/or voices.

I have always been very fond of music. Whoever is proficient in this art is a good man, fit for all other things. Hence it is absolutely necessary to have it taught in the schools. A schoolmaster must know how to sing or I shan't tolerate him.

Martin Luther, 1538

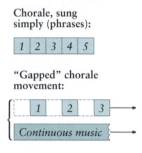

Chorale, sung simply (phrases):

| 1 | 2 | 3 | 4 | 5 |

"Gapped" chorale movement:

| 1 | 2 | 3 |

Continuous music

JOHANN SEBASTIAN BACH (1685–1750)
Cantata No. 4, "Christ lag in Todesbanden" (Christ Lay in Death's Dark Prison) (1707)

In his posts as an organist and cantor, Bach made multiple settings of many hymns, both in cantatas and also as chorale preludes for organ (see page 148). We shall study some (just a few) of his settings of the Easter chorale "Christ lag in Todesbanden" (Christ lay in Death's dark prison).

This rugged old tune had been fitted with even more rugged words by Martin Luther himself, in 1524. The seven stanzas of the chorale, each ending with "Hallelujah!," tell in vivid language of mankind's struggle with Death, and the victory achieved through Christ's sacrifice. The fact that this hymn is in the minor mode throws a tough, sober shadow over all the rejoicing; the mood is unforgettable.

We cannot recapture the associations that Bach's contemporaries would have brought to this tune, but we can begin to learn it by singing the first stanza:

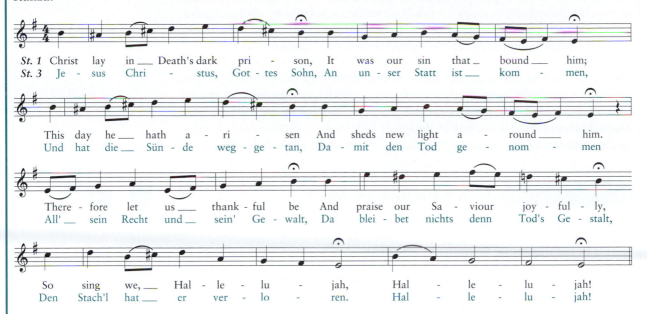

St. 1 Christ lay in __ Death's dark pri - son, It was our sin that __ bound __ him;
St. 3 Je - sus Chri - stus, Got - tes Sohn, An un - ser Statt ist __ kom - men,

This day he __ hath a - ri - sen And sheds new light a - round __ him.
Und hat die __ Sün - de weg - ge - tan, Da - mit den Tod ge - nom - men

There - fore let us __ thank - ful be And praise our Sa - viour joy - ful - ly,
All' __ sein Recht und __ sein' Ge - walt, Da blei - bet nichts denn Tod's Ge - stalt,

So sing we, __ Hal - le - lu - jah, Hal - le - lu - jah!
Den Stach'l hat __ er ver - lo - ren. Hal - le - lu - jah!

The cantata based on "Christ lag in Todesbanden" is one of Bach's earliest. It employs simple forces: voices and a string orchestra, with continuo. (When Bach wrote it he was a young small-town organist, and probably could not count on more than one singer to a part, as on our recording—which compensates, however, by adding reverberation to suggest an echoing church.) The words of the seven movements are the words of the seven stanzas of the famous Easter chorale.

Bach set these seven stanzas with a sharp eye (or ear) for symmetry. The diagram below tallies the voices that sing in the various movements:

SINFONIA	STANZA 1	2	3	4	5	6	7	
Orchestra	Soprano	S		S		S	S	*Color shading indicates which voice sings the chorale melody. (In stanza 6, it is divided between two voices.)*
	Alto		A		A		A	
	Tenor			T	T		T	T
	Bass				B	B		B

After a short orchestral prelude—Bach calls it "sinfonia"—all the stanzas except the last are set as "gapped" chorales of some sort. In the two duets (stanzas 2 and 6) the chorale tune is ornamented, but in the others it is presented plainly, up to the jubilant (sometimes manic) "hallelujah" at the end.

Stanza 3   The tenor sings the "gapped" chorale tune forcefully; follow him along with the music, above. A violin plays an urgent melody at both ends of the piece and in the gaps between the lines. At the word *nichts* ("nothing") the music comes to a wrenching stop and a slow-down, a quite astonishing effect. Then the violin starts up again as though nothing had happened. The sudden absence of music tells us what is left of Death's power: nothing.

Stanza 4   Here it is the alto that sings the gapped chorale tune, more slowly than the tenor of stanza 3. The "continuous" music is assigned to other voices singing faster imitative polyphony to the same words, always using fragments of the chorale melody. Perhaps all this busy imitative polyphony makes a good illustration of the warfare described with such gusto in this stanza. Perhaps, too, the jaunty rhythm at *Spott* can indeed be heard as "mockery."

Stanza 7   No longer gapped, this is a straightforward presentation of the hymn as it might be sung by the congregation. Bach's rich harmonies below the soprano melody are sung by the lower voices, doubled by the instruments. The cantata comes to a restful conclusion at last, as the text turns from battles to the confidence of faith. Even "hallelujah" can now be uttered simply.

| LISTEN | Bach, "Christ lag in Todesbanden" |

2   2A

11-13   8

St. 3: Jesus Christus, Gottes Sohn,
An unser Statt ist kommen,
Und hat die Sünde weggetan,
Damit den Tod genommen
    All sein Recht und sein Gewalt;
Da bleibet *nichts*—denn Tod's Gestalt;
Den Stach'l hat er verloren.
Halleluja!

Jesus Christ, the Son of God,
Has come on our behalf,
And has done away with our sins,
Thereby robbing Death
Of all his power and might;
There remains nothing but Death's image;
His sting is lost.
Hallelujah!

12   St. 4: Es war ein wunderlicher Krieg,
Da Tod und Leben rungen;
Das Leben da behielt das Sieg,
Es hat den Tod verschlungen.
    Die Schrift hat verkündiget das
Wie ein Tod den andern frass;
Ein Spott aus dem Tod ist worden.
Halleluja!

It was a marvelous war
Where Death and Life battled.
Life gained the victory;
It swallowed up Death.
Scripture has proclaimed
How one Death gobbled up the other;
Death became a mockery.
Hallelujah!

13   St. 7: Wir essen und leben wohl
Im rechten Osterfladen.
Der alter Sauerteig nicht soll
Sein bei dem Wort der Gnaden.
    Christus will die Koste sein
Und speisen die Seel' allein,
Der Glaub' will keins andern leben.
Halleluja!

We eat and live fitly
On the true unleavened bread of Passover;
The old yeast shall not
Contaminate the word of grace.
Christ alone will be the food
To feed the soul:
Faith will live on nothing else.
Hallelujah!

4 The Organ Chorale

German churches took special pride in their organs, and organ technology developed prodigiously in the Baroque era. The **chorale prelude** or *organ chorale,* an important genre of keyboard music at the time, is an organ composition incorporating a hymn (chorale) tune.

Like cantatas, organ chorales incorporated hymn tunes in many ways. The "gapped" method (see page 146) was common. Played on the organ, the tune could also be richly ornamented with scales, trills, and so on, for expressive purposes—much the same technique as was applied to opera melodies.

In religious terms, the effect of an organ chorale was probably not very different from a sung one. Lutherans knew their hymns by heart, so the tune on the organ would automatically bring to mind the hymn text and its message or lesson.

A Leipzig church service

BACH
Chorale Prelude, "Christ lag in Todesbanden" (Christ Lay in Death's Dark Prison) (1715)

Motive

ORGAN PEDALS

At some point in a Lutheran service, the organist would play one or more chorale preludes based on seasonal hymns. On Easter Sunday, Bach might well have played this organ prelude on "Christ lag in Todesbanden."

The music is powerful and triumphant—a wordless hallelujah for the miracle of Easter. The chorale tune can be heard on the high organ pipes, played without any gaps, but with a vigorous faster motive accompanying it, a motive that clatters away splendidly in the organ pedals. The rich harmonies are formed by dense counterpoint. Perhaps next in the service the hymn would have been sung by the congregation.

This piece comes from the *Orgelbüchlein*, a "Little Organ Book" of 162 short chorale preludes that Bach planned for services throughout the entire church year. This not-so-little collection bears witness to both sides of Bach's temperament: on the one hand the strictly practical, and on the other the encyclopedic and visionary.

When Bach seated himself at the organ, he used to choose some theme and treat it in all the various forms of organ composition. First, he used this theme for a prelude and fugue, with the full organ. Then he showed his art of using the stops for a trio, quartet, etc., on the same theme. Afterwards followed a chorale, the melody of which was playfully surrounded by the same theme in three or four contrapuntal parts . . .

From the first biography of Bach, 1802

Pipe organ technology developed prodigiously in the Baroque era. Imposing instruments such as this one underpinned the church music of the time.

CHAPTER **12**

Prelude
Music and the Enlightenment

I n the second part of the eighteenth century, a new musical style emerged in Europe. Called the Classical style, it had important pioneers in Italy and northern Germany; one of them was Carl Philipp Emanuel Bach, a son of Johann Sebastian. But the Classical style was developed particularly by several great composers active in Vienna, capital of Austria. Here conditions seem to have been ideal for music. Geographically, Austria stands at the crossroads of four other musical nations—Germany, Bohemia (now the Czech Republic), Hungary, and Italy—and Vienna was also central in political terms. As the capital of the powerful Hapsburg empire, Vienna was plunged into every European conflict of the time and exposed to every new cultural and intellectual current.

Vienna's greatest years were from 1780 to 1790, during the reign of Emperor Joseph II, the most enlightened of the long line of Hapsburg monarchs. Joseph emancipated the peasantry, furthered education, and reduced the power of the clergy; he supported music and literature with his patronage and encouraged a free press. In a city of only 150,000 people, there were three hundred newspapers and journals during Joseph's reign, representing every shade of opinion.

In this liberal atmosphere, Franz Joseph Haydn of nearby Eisenstadt became recognized as the principal composer of Europe; his symphonies were commissioned from far-off Paris and London. The young Wolfgang Amadeus Mozart was drawn to the capital in 1781 from Salzburg, a hundred miles to the west, to spend his brilliant last decade there. And in 1792 a young musician from the other end of Germany, who had composed a long cantata mourning Emperor Joseph's death, decided to come to this great musical center to launch his career. His name was Ludwig van Beethoven.

1 The Enlightenment and Music

To describe Joseph II as an "enlightened" ruler is both to commend him and also to locate him in European intellectual history. Like a number of other rulers of the time, Joseph II derived his principles of governance from an important intellectual movement of the eighteenth century known as the Enlightenment, a movement that also helped to define the music that flourished under his reign.

Emperor Joseph II

150

The Vienna of Haydn, Mozart, and Beethoven; in the center is the Court Theater (Burgtheater), where operas were performed.

Centered in France, the Enlightenment had strong roots in English philosophy and strong offshoots in Germany and Austria. Its original source was the faith in reason that led to the great scientific discoveries of the Baroque period. Now, however, the emphasis veered away from the purely intellectual and scientific toward the social sphere. People were less intent on controlling natural forces by science than on turning these forces to universal benefit. People also began to apply the same intelligence that solved scientific problems to problems of public morality, education, and politics.

Social injustice came under especially strong fire in the eighteenth century. So did established religion; for the first time in European history, religion ceased to be an overriding force in many people's minds. There were currents of agnosticism and even outright atheism—to the outrage of the English poet and mystic William Blake:

> Mock on, mock on, Voltaire, Rousseau:
> Mock on, mock on, 'tis all in vain!
> You throw the sand against the wind,
> And the wind blows it back again.

Voltaire, by Jean-Antoine Houdon (1740–1828), master sculptor of the neo-Roman busts that were much favored at the time. (All the other portrait busts in this chapter are also by Houdon.)

The two French philosophers named by Blake are always mentioned in connection with the Enlightenment: François Marie Arouet, whose pen name was Voltaire (1694–1778), tireless satirist and campaigner for justice and reason, and the younger, more radical, more disturbing Jean Jacques Rousseau (1712–1778). Rousseau is one of the few major figures of European philosophy who had a direct effect on the history of music, as we shall see.

"The Pursuit of Happiness"

The Enlightenment was also the occasion for the first great contribution to Western civilization from America. In colonial days, the austere Puritan spirit was hardly in step with the growing secularization of European society, but the Declaration of Independence and the Federalist Papers proved to be the finest flowers of Enlightenment idealism. The notion that a new state could be founded on rational principles, set down on a piece of paper, and agreed to by men of good will and intelligence—this could only have emerged under the influence of the political and philosophical writings of the eighteenth century.

"Life, liberty, and the pursuit of happiness": the last of these three famous rights, too, was very much of its time. One can imagine the medieval barons who forced King John to accept the Magna Carta insisting on life and liberty, of a sort, but it would never have occurred to them to demand happiness as a self-evident right for all. Voltaire and Rousseau fought passionately for social justice so that people might live good lives according to their own convictions.

The eighteenth century was an age of good living, then, an age that valued intelligence, wit, and sensitivity. The age cultivated elegant conversation, the social arts, and hedonism. One of its inventions was the salon—half party, half seminar: a regular gathering in a fashionable lady's home where notables would discuss books, music, art, and ideas. Another innovation of the time was the coffee house. Another was the public concert.

Thomas Jefferson

Art and Entertainment

Entertainment, for most people, contributes to the good life—though certainly Thomas Jefferson was thinking of more than entertainment when he wrote of "the pursuit of happiness." However, the pursuit of entertainment was not something that the eighteenth century looked down upon at all. The arts were expected to *please* rather than to instruct, impress, or even express, as had been the case in the Baroque era. The result of this attitude is evident in the style of all the arts in the eighteenth century.

For a time at midcentury a light and often frothy style known as *Rococo* was fashionable in painting, decoration, furniture and jewelry design, and so on. Our illustration—a ceramic plaque—catches the spirit of this entertainment art with special charm. Wreathed in leaves that fit in with the border, two well-dressed court gentlemen cavort in an ideal countryside; one plays the flute while the other dances. The subject, the feathery designs on the frame, even the pretty rim itself, are all characteristic of the light art of the Rococo.

A French Rococo ceramic plaque

The youngest son of a famous father, Johann Christian Bach (1735–1782) moved to London, where he sat for this superb portrait by Thomas Gainsborough (1727–1788). The "English Bach" was a highly successful Rococo composer who met the young Mozart and won both his admiration and his affection.

Music at midcentury, just before the formation of the Viennese Classical style, was also very light—charming at best, but often frivolous and empty. A genre that was typical of the time was the **divertimento,** a piece designed to divert, amuse, and entertain. Elaborately decorated music boxes, playing little tunes, were extremely popular.

The Viennese Classical music of Haydn and Mozart is far from this, yet these composers never put pen to paper without every expectation that their audiences were going to be "pleased." Every historical era, of course, has had its entertainment music. But only in the Classical era was great music of the highest quality put forth quite frankly and plainly as entertainment.

Jean Jacques Rousseau and Opera

Rousseau is remembered today as Europe's first "alienated" intellectual. Whatever his subject, he always came around to blasting the social institutions of his day as stifling to the individual. Passionately devoted to nature and to personal feeling, he disseminated the very influential idea of "natural man," who is born good but corrupted by civilization.

To the great French *Encyclopédie* of 1751–1765, which was the bible of Enlightenment thought, Rousseau contributed the articles on two subjects: politics and music. Interestingly, Rousseau was also a self-taught composer, who made his living for years as a professional music copyist.

Both by means of his fiery writings and by actual example, Rousseau launched a devastating attack on the aristocratic opera of the late Baroque era. And to attack opera—the most important, extended, and glamorous musical genre of the time—was to throw Baroque music itself into question. For Rousseau, the complicated plots of Baroque operas were as impossibly artificial as their complicated music. He demanded a kind of opera that would portray real people in actual life. What he and his contemporaries meant by this was simple people, close to nature, singing "natural" music.

Jean Jacques Rousseau

Thus Rousseau acclaimed a famous Italian comic opera of the time, which played in Paris, Giovanni Battista Pergolesi's *La serva padrona* ("The Maid as Mistress," 1733). The music is lively and catchy, with no elaborate coloratura singing, rich harmonies, or exaggerated emotional outpourings, and the story could scarcely be more down-to-earth or uncomplicated: a servant girl uses a simple ruse to trick a rich old bachelor into marriage.

Thanks to Pergolesi and Rousseau—and to Mozart—comic opera became the most progressive operatic form of the later part of the century. It dealt not with Roman emperors and their idealized noble sentiments, but with contemporary middle- and lower-class figures expressing everyday feelings in a relatively vivid and natural way. *Opera buffa*, as Italian comic opera was called, will be discussed on page 195.

Rousseau himself actually composed a very successful opera of the simple kind he recommended. Shown are the shepherdess Colette and her lover Colin and a sheep from *Le Devin du village (The Village Soothsayer)*, 1752

The Novel

In its ideals, this new kind of opera was comparable to the most important new literary genre that grew up at the same time. This was the novel, which—together with the symphony—counts as the Enlightenment's greatest artistic legacy to the nineteenth and twentieth centuries.

Precursors of the novel go back to ancient Rome, but the genre did not really capture the European imagination until around 1750. Among the best-known early novels are Henry Fielding's *Tom Jones,* the tale of a rather ordinary young man and his adventures in town and country, and Samuel Richardson's *Pamela,* a domestic drama that manages to be sexually explicit, sentimental, and moralistic all at the same time. Just before the end of the century, Jane Austen began her subtle explorations of the social forces at work on the hearts of her very sensitive (and sensible) characters in novels such as *Pride and Prejudice.*

Sharp, sympathetic observation of contemporary life, and sensitive depiction of feeling—these are the ideals shared by late eighteenth-century opera and the novel. It is no accident that within a few years of their publication, both *Tom Jones* and *Pamela* were turned into major operas, one French, the other Italian.

In Mozart, opera buffa found a master comparable to Jane Austen in his sensitive response to feeling and action. In his opera *Don Giovanni,* for example, the three women romantically involved with the hero—the coquettish country girl, Zerlina, the steely aristocrat, Donna Anna, and the sentimental Donna Elvira—are depicted in music with the greatest psychological penetration and human sympathy. One can come to feel that the same qualities are reflected in Mozart's symphonies and concertos.

Neoclassicism

It is from the standpoint of "the natural," that great rallying cry of the Enlightenment, that we should understand Neoclassicism, an important movement in the visual arts at this time. The Greek and Roman classics have meant many things to many eras; to the eighteenth century, they meant a return to simple, natural values. They meant a rejection of the complex solemnities of the Baroque on the one hand, and of the pleasant frivolities of the Rococo on the other. The designs of Wedgwood pottery, the impressive portrait busts (modeled on Roman busts) by Jean-Antoine Houdon, and the scenes from ancient history painted by Jacques-Louis David are just a few examples of eighteenth-century Neoclassical art.

A late-eighteenth-century court musician surrounded by the tools of his trade. However, he is depicted not in a palace of the era, but in a sober imitation classical temple—amusing testimony to the Neoclassical enthusiasms and aspirations of the time.

Austere classical subjects were made into powerful operas by Christoph Willibald von Gluck (1714–1787), an important composer active in both Vienna and Paris. His most famous opera is *Orfeo ed Euridice* (1762), based on the Greek myth of Orpheus. When his *Alceste* (derived from a classical Greek drama) was produced in Paris, it was greatly admired by the aging Rousseau.

Apart from the operas of Gluck, however, Neoclassical art has no direct connection with music in what is traditionally called the Classical style. One can perhaps see that a taste inclined toward moderation, simplicity, and balance would also appreciate the order and clarity of late eighteenth-century music, but the traditional label is not a very happy one. It was the nineteenth century that coined the label "Classicism" to distinguish the music of Haydn and Mozart from the "Romanticism" that was then actively being developed.

Christoph Willibald von Gluck

2   The Rise of Concerts

A far-reaching development in the sociology and economics of music was the rise of public concerts. Occasional concerts had been put on before, in taverns, private homes, palaces, and theaters, but it was only in the middle of the eighteenth century that they became a significant force in musical life. Concert series, financed by subscription, were put on by the forerunners of today's promoters. Concerts for the benefit of charity were set up on a regular basis as major society events.

In 1748 Europe's first hall designed especially for concerts was built in a college town, Oxford. Still in use, the Holywell Music Room holds about 150 people.

Music of all kinds was presented at these new public concerts; one major series, the Parisian *Concert spirituel* founded in 1725, originally concentrated on sacred vocal music. But orchestral music was the staple. The importance of

Advertisement from the
Boston Chronicle of 1769.
With only around 15,000
inhabitants, Boston already
had a concert hall and a concert promoter (band master
Josiah Flagg).

concerts lay mainly in the impetus they gave to the composition of orchestral music—symphonies and concertos. For there were, after all, other public forums for church music (churches) and opera (opera houses). Now purely orchestral music, too, moved into the public domain, and its importance and prestige grew rapidly.

Though ultimately the concert hall became the focal point of musical life—the main center of interest for listeners and the main source of support for composers—the late eighteenth century was still a period of transition. Court patronage, the opera house, and the church were still the main sources of a composer's livelihood (see page 107). Concerts were certainly a factor in the lives of both of the great masters of Classical music already mentioned: Haydn's last symphonies, the *London* symphonies, were commissioned for highly successful concerts arranged for the composer's London tours, and most of Mozart's piano concertos—among his greatest works—were written for yearly benefit concerts that he put on in Vienna. All the same, concerts were a resource that Haydn did not draw on in a major way until he was already well established; and they were not an adequate resource, alas, to sustain Mozart.

3 Style Features of Classical Music

In discussing the musical style of the late Baroque period, we started with a single guiding concept. There is a thorough, even rigorous quality in the ways early eighteenth-century composers treated almost all aspects of music, and this quality seems to underpin the expressive gestures of grandeur and overstatement that are characteristic of the Baroque.

Classical music cannot be discussed quite so simply as this. We have to keep two concepts in mind for its understanding, concepts that were constantly on the lips of men and women of the time. One was "natural," and the other was "pleasing variety." In the late eighteenth century, it was taken for granted that these two artistic ideals went hand in hand, and provided mutual support.

Today we can see that sometimes they pulled in opposite directions. For although "variety" was invoked as a guard against boredom, it was also an invitation to complexity, and complexity would seem to run counter to "natural" simplicity and clarity. In any case, in Classical music one or the other—

and sometimes both—of these qualities can be traced in all the elements of musical technique: in rhythm, dynamics, tone color, melody, texture, and form. A new expressive quality developed in this music as a result of its new technique.

Rhythm

Perhaps the most striking change in music between the Baroque and the Classical periods came in rhythm. In this area the artistic ideal of "pleasing variety" reigned supreme. The unvarying rhythms of Baroque music were regarded as dreary, obvious, and boring.

Classical music is highly flexible in rhythm. Throughout a single movement, the tempo and meter remain constant, but the rhythms of the various themes tend to differ in both obvious and subtle ways. In the first movement of Mozart's Symphony in G Minor, for example, the first theme moves almost entirely in eighth notes and quarters, whereas the second theme is marked by longer notes and shorter ones—dotted half notes and sixteenths.

Audiences wanted variety in music; composers responded by refining the rhythmic differences between themes and other musical sections, so that the differences sound like more than differences—they sound like real contrasts. The music may gradually increase or decrease its rhythmic energy, stop suddenly, press forward by fits and starts, or glide by with a carefully calculated smoothness. All this gives the sense that Classical music is moving in a less predictable, more interesting, and often more exciting way than Baroque music does.

Dynamics

Variety and flexibility were also introduced into dynamics. Passages were now conceived more specifically than before as loud, soft, very loud, and so on, and marked *f, p, ff, mf* by composers accordingly. Again, concern for variety went along with a new sensitivity to contrast. By insisting on the contrast between loud and soft, soft and very soft, composers made variety in dynamics clearly perceptible and, we must suppose, "pleasing."

First theme

Second theme

Domestic music making in the eighteenth century: a group portrait by Johann Zoffany (1733–1810), one of many fashionable painters in Britain (and British India). It was not uncommon for members of the gentry—including, here, an earl—to order pictures showing off their musical accomplishments.

Furthermore, instead of using the steady dynamics of the previous period, composers now worked extensively with gradations of volume. The words for growing louder *(crescendo)* and growing softer *(diminuendo)* first came into general use in the Classical period. Orchestras of the mid-eighteenth century were the first to practice long crescendos, which, we are told, caused audiences to rise up from their seats in excitement.

The clearest sign of the new flexibility in dynamics was the rise in popularity of the piano, at the expense of the omnipresent harpsichord of the Baroque era. The older instrument could manage only one sound level, or at best a few sound levels, thanks to its two or three separate sets of strings. The new pianoforte (meaning "soft-loud") could produce a continuous range of dynamics from soft to loud. It attracted composers because they wished their keyboard instruments to have the same flexibility in dynamics that they were teaching to their orchestras.

Tone Color: The Orchestra

The Classical composers also devoted increasing attention to tone color. The clearest sign of this was the emergence of the Classical orchestra. The orchestra standardized in this period formed the basis of the symphony orchestra of later times.

The foundation of the Classical orchestra was still (as in the Baroque orchestra) a group of stringed instruments: violins, divided into two groups, first violins and second violins; violas; and cellos, with a few basses playing the same music as the cellos an octave lower. As we saw on page 111, there was a "basic" Baroque orchestra consisting of just these instruments, plus the continuo, and various other possibilities, including the "festive" Baroque orchestra:

THE BASIC BAROQUE ORCHESTRA

STRINGS	KEYBOARD
Violins (divided into two groups, called violins 1 and violins 2) Violas Cellos Bass viol (playing the same music as the cellos, an octave lower)	Harpsichord or organ

THE FESTIVE BAROQUE ORCHESTRA

STRINGS	WOODWINDS	BRASS	PERCUSSION	KEYBOARD
Violins 1 Violins 2 Violas Cellos Bass viol	2 Oboes 1 Bassoon	3 Trumpets	2 Timpani (kettledrums)	Harpsichord or organ

In the Classical orchestra, however, the woodwind and brass instruments were given clearly defined regular roles. With the strings as a framework, woodwind instruments were added: in the high range, pairs of flutes, oboes, and clarinets; in the low, bassoons. These instruments provided "pleasing variety" by playing certain melodies and other passages; each of the woodwinds contributed its characteristic tone color and participated in carefully calculated combinations of tone colors. They also strengthened the strings in loud sections.

Brass instruments were added in the middle range. The function of French horns and trumpets was mainly to provide solid support for the main harmonies, especially at points such as cadences when the harmonies needed to be made particularly clear. The only regular percussion instruments used were two timpani, which generally played along with the brass.

The great advance in the orchestra from the Baroque to the Classical era was in flexibility—flexibility in tone color and also in rhythm and dynamics.

THE CLASSICAL ORCHESTRA

STRINGS	WOODWINDS	BRASS	PERCUSSION
First violins	2 Flutes	2 French horns	2 Timpani
Second violins	2 Oboes	2 Trumpets*	
Violas	2 Clarinets*		
Cellos	2 Bassoons		
Bass viols		*Optional	

The orchestra now became the most subtle and versatile musical resource that composers could employ, as well as the grandest.

Melody: Tunes

The Enlightenment ideal of "pleasing variety" was a secondary issue with Classical melody. Rather the demand was for simplicity and clarity, for relief from the complex, richly ornamented lines of the Baroque period. When people at the time demanded "natural" melodies, what they meant were tunes: simple, singable melodies with clear phrases (and not too many of them), melodies with easily grasped parallelisms and balances.

Confronted with a Baroque work such as Bach's Suite No. 3 in D (see page 132), a late eighteenth-century audience might have tolerated the fairly straightforward Gavotte, but would have been unmoved by the beautiful Air. Its elegant winding lines and the mere fact of its great length would have struck them as completely "unnatural":

Hence composers of the Classical period moved much closer to folk and popular music than their Baroque predecessors. There is an unmistakable popular lilt in Haydn's music that people have traced to the Croatian folk melodies he may have heard in childhood. Short tunes—or, more often, attractive little phrases that sound as though they might easily grow into tunes—are heard again and again in Classical symphonies, quartets, and other pieces. Tunes are not the only melodic material to be heard in these works, as we shall see in a moment. Nonetheless, by comparison with a Baroque concerto grosso, a Classical symphony leaves listeners with a good deal more to hum or whistle as they leave the concert.

Often entire tunes were worked into larger compositions. For example, variation form (theme and variations) grew popular both for separate pieces improvised by virtuosos and as movements in multimovement genres. Haydn wrote variations on the Austrian national anthem (he also wrote the tune), and Mozart wrote variations on "Twinkle, Twinkle, Little Star" or "Baa Baa Black Sheep," which he knew in its original French version, "Ah vous dirai-je, maman" ("Oh mama, I must tell you"). Occasionally, popular songs were even introduced into symphonies. There is a contemporary opera tune in Mozart's *Jupiter* Symphony, the last he composed.

Texture: Homophony

The predominant texture of Classical music is homophonic. In Classical compositions, melodies are regularly heard with a straightforward harmonic accompaniment in chords, without counterpoint and without even a melodic-sounding bass line. Again, this was thought (not unreasonably) to be a more "natural," clearer way of presenting a melody than polyphony.

All this made, and still makes, for easy listening. The opening of Mozart's famous Symphony No. 40 in G Minor proclaims the new sonorous world of the late eighteenth century:

A single quiet chord regrouped and repeated by the violas; the simplest possible bass support below; and above them all a plaintive melody in the violins—this simple, sharply polarized texture becomes typical.

Homophony or melody with harmony was not, however, merely a negative reaction to what people of the time saw as the heavy, pedantic complexities of Baroque counterpoint. It was also a positive move in the direction of sensitivity. When composers found that they were not always occupied in fitting other contrapuntal parts to their melodies, they also discovered that they could handle other elements of music with more "pleasing variety." In particular, a new sensitivity to harmony was developed for its own sake.

One aspect of this development was a desire to specify harmonies more precisely than in the Baroque era. The first thing to go was the continuo, which had spread its unrelenting and unspecified (because improvised) chord patterns over nearly all Baroque music. Classical composers, newly alert to the sonorous quality of a particular chord, wanted it "spaced" and distributed among various instruments in just one way. They were not prepared to allow a continuo player to obscure the chord with unpredictable extra notes and rhythms.

It may seem paradoxical, then, but the thrust toward simplicity in texture led through the back door to subtlety in other areas, notably in rhythm and in harmony.

Classical Counterpoint

The rise of homophony in the Classical period represents a major turnaround in musical technique. For although Baroque composers did write some homophonic pieces, as we have seen, the predominant texture of music at that time was polyphonic. This turning point was, in fact, one of the most decisive in all of musical history, for polyphony had monopolized music since the Middle Ages.

Yet it is not the way of history to abandon important resources of the past completely, even when the past is discredited. Classical composers rejected Baroque music, but they cautiously retained the basic principle of counterpoint. They were able to do this by refining it into a more delicate, unobtrusive kind of counterpoint than that of the Baroque era. And there was a sharper awareness now of counterpoint's expressive possibilities. In a texture that was mostly "natural" and homophonic, counterpoint attracted special attention; this texture could be used to create the impression of tension, of one line rubbing against another. The more intense, "artificial" texture of polyphony stood out against "natural" homophonic texture.

Hence, as we shall see in the next chapter, the section in Classical sonata form called the development section, whose basic function is to build up tension, typically involves contrapuntal textures. Sonata form was the most important musical form of the time, and so counterpoint was often heard.

Porcelain musicians, c. 1770

4 Form in Classical Music

How can a piece of music be extended through a considerable span of time when listeners expect everything to be "natural," simple, and easily understood? This was the problem of musical form that faced composers of the Viennese Classical era. They arrived at a solution of considerable elegance and power, involving several elements.

Repetitions and Cadences

First, themes in Classical music tend to be *repeated* immediately after their first appearance, so that listeners can easily get to know them. (In earlier music, this happened only in dance music, as a general rule). Later in the piece, those same themes will be repeated again.

Second, themes are *led into* in a very distinctive manner. The music features prominent transitional passages that do not have much melodic profile, only a sense of urgency about arriving someplace—the place where the real theme will be presented (and probably presented twice).

Third, after themes have been played, they are typically *closed off* just as distinctively. Often there are quite long passages consisting of cadences repeated two, three, or more times, as though to make it clear that one musical idea is over and another, presumably, is coming up. Composers would devise little cadential phrases, often with minimal melodic interest, that could be repeated and thus allow for such multiple cadences.

Multiple cadences are a characteristic and easily recognizable feature of Classical music, particularly, of course at the very ends of movements. Two clear examples on our listening set come from the music of Mozart:

✑ *Piano Concerto in G, K. 453:* At the very end of the last movement, the piano and the orchestra play cadences in fast alternation. The piano plays a cadence; the orchestra plays a louder one; the piano repeats its cadence; the orchestra plays one that sounds even more final than before. Dialogue is a prime feature of Mozart's concertos, and here it sounds as though there is a competition on to see who can get in the last word. Whoever wins, this concerto is closed off in a particularly solid way:

⁊ *Aria "Ho capito" from* Don Giovanni: Near the end of this aria, the singer sings much the same cadence over and over again. (A few seconds later, the orchestra has *its* cadence, and the whole piece is over.) The situation is explained on page 198: sputtering with rage at Zerlina, Masetto keeps reiterating his sarcastic taunts until he is finally chased away. This cadence, then, is even more solid than it needed to be—for Mozart, a comical effect:

fac-ciail no-stro ca - va - lie - re ca - va - lie-ra an-co - ra te,   ca - va - lie-ra an-co - ra te,   ca - va - lie-ra an-co - ra te.

Cadence   Cadence   Cadence

Classical Forms

A third feature designed to cope with the problem of musical form in Classical music is perhaps the most far-reaching. Composers and their audiences came to rely on a limited number of "forms," or standard formal patterns, the most important of which are sonata form, minuet form, rondo, and theme and variations form.

There was thus a commonly understood frame of reference for composing music and appreciating it. Broadly speaking, after listening for just a short time to some new piece, an eighteenth-century music lover could always tell what sort of themes and keys it would include, when they would be returned to, and about how long the piece would last. This frame of reference is not so obvious today, so Chapter 13 will devote itself to the four Classical forms just mentioned.

The repetitions, self-conscious transitions, and emphatic cadences that are so characteristic of the Classical style all help clarify the forms. And the forms themselves were a special necessity at a time when composers were filling their compositions with contrasts of all kinds. It is a mark of the aesthetic success of Classical music that the contrasts don't sound too drastic, because the forms control and, as it were, tame them. The seemingly inexhaustible emotional range of Classical music is in direct proportion to the extent of those contrasts, on the one hand, and, on the other, the elegance of their control by musical form.

Houdon's most unclassical portrait bust—of his wife

CHAPTER **13**

The Symphony

T he genres of music that arose in the Classical period, replacing those of the Baroque era, continued to hold their own in the nineteenth century. Indeed, they are still in use today, at least in the sense that their names are still encountered. Not surprisingly, the style, the number of movements, and the forms employed today will bear little relation to norms that were operative two hundred years ago, and more. But it is still true that if you compose a large, impressive concert piece for orchestra, the best way to convey that fact to conductors, musicians, and audiences is to name it a **symphony.**

One reason for the prominence of the symphony in the Classical era is its close association with a crucial development in the sociology of music, discussed in Chapter 12: the growth of public concerts. As concerts became more and more frequent, people felt a need for some genre that would make an effective, substantial focus for these occasions. Symphonies filled the bill—and in turn, required more variety and flexibility of sound than anything orchestras of the early eighteenth century could provide. The symphony spurred a major technical development within music, the evolution of the Classical orchestra (see page 158).

The symphony, then, is rightly viewed as the crowning achievement of Viennese Classical music—but when any musician acknowledges this, he or she wants to add a plea in the same breath: Please don't forget the other genres that grew up alongside the symphony, for these genres accommodate music that you will find just as beautiful, and that has become for me, sometimes, just as irreplaceable. In Chapter 14 we shall study the sonata, the Classical concerto, the string quartet, and—in the field of opera—Italian *opera buffa.*

The Symphony

Opening Movement
    tempo: fast/moderate
    form: sonata form
      sometimes preceded by
      a slow **Introduction**

Slow Movement
    tempo: slow/very slow
    form: no standard form
      (sometimes sonata form,
      variation form, rondo)

Minuet (with Trio)
    tempo: moderate
    form: minuet form

Closing Movement
    tempo: fast/very fast
    form: sonata form or
      rondo form

1 The Movements of the Symphony

As with Baroque genres, works in the Classical period consist of several movements, which contrast in tempo and are composed in different musical forms. The outline on this page gives the particulars for the four movements of a typical symphony. Compare the following brief description with the description given on page 116 for the Baroque concerto:

❧   The *first,* opening movement of a symphony is a substantial piece in fast or moderate tempo, written in the most important new form of the time:

sonata form (which we will study in the next section). Sometimes this fast music is preceded by a short but solemn *introduction* in a slower tempo.

⁊   The *second* movement strikes an obvious contrast with the first by its slow tempo and its quiet mood.

⁊   The *third* movement contrasts in another way, by its persistent dance rhythms: it is always a minuet and trio. A minuet is a moderately paced dance in triple meter: see page 130.

⁊   The *fourth,* closing movement is fast again—if anything, faster than the first. It may also be in sonata form, like the first movement.

If we compare the symphony table shown on the previous page with a parallel table for the Baroque concerto, on the right, we see many differences, but also certain similarities. The forms used for the movements are entirely different, and there is the extra minuet. However, in the broadest terms, the sequence from *fast/complex* to *slow/quiet* to *fast/brilliant* is the same.

A word of caution: the symphony table on page 163 represents the norm, but there are always exceptions. Mozart's *Prague* Symphony lacks a minuet. Haydn's *Farewell* Symphony adds a second slow movement, making five movements in all. (And Bach's First *Brandenburg* Concerto has two dance movements added to the "normal" three.)

The Baroque Concerto

Opening Movement
    tempo: fast/moderate
    form: ritornello form

Slow Movement
    tempo: slow/very slow
    form: no standard form

Closing Movement
    tempo: fast/very fast
    form: ritornello form

2 Sonata Form

A new form developed at this time, called **sonata form,** is closely associated with the symphony—and indeed, with nearly all other music of the time. The opening movement of every symphony is in sonata form, and this movement counts as the intellectual and emotional core of the whole work. Many Classical works have two or as many as three movements in this same form.

The reason for this wide use, perhaps, was that more than any other form, sonata form exploited what was the overriding interest of Classical composers. This was an interest in contrasts of every kind—especially contrast of thematic material and contrast of key, or tonality. In any case, whatever the reason, composers found sonata form particularly rich and flexible in its expressive application. It was something they could use for forceful, brilliant, pathetic, even tragic opening movements, gentle or dreamy slow movements, and lively, often humorous closing movements.

Viewed on the highest level, sonata form is simple enough—a very large-scale example of **A B A′** form, usually with repetitions: |: **A** :||: **B A′** :| or |: **A** :|| **B A′**. What is less simple, and what makes sonata form different from other **A B A** forms, is the nature and the function of the musical material in each letter-section. This is implied by the special terms that are used for them: **A** is called the exposition, **B** the development, and **A′** the recapitulation. We need to look more closely at what each of these terms entails.

Exposition (A)

The **exposition** of a sonata-form movement is a large section of music in which the basic material of the movement is presented (or "exposed"). The material always consists of the following elements:

❡   To begin, a main theme is presented in the first key, the tonic key (see page 32; this key is the key of the piece as a whole—in Mozart's Symphony in G Minor, the tonic is G minor). This **first theme** may be a tune, a group of small phrases that sound as though they are about to grow into a tune, or simply a motive or two (see page 26) with a memorable rhythmic character.

❡   After the first theme is firmly established, often with the help of a repetition, there is a change in key, or *modulation*. The subsection of the exposition that accomplishes this is called the **bridge,** or the *transition*.

❡   The modulation in the bridge is an essential feature (even *the* essential feature) that gives sonata form its sense of dynamic forward movement. With a little experience, it is not hard to hear the contrast of key and sense the dynamism, for the idea is not to make the crucial modulation sound too smooth. There has to be a sense of tension in the way the new themes, now to be introduced, "set" in the new key.

❡   What comes next is a group of themes in the new key, called the **second group.** Composers generally make these new themes contrast with the first theme in melody, rhythm, dynamics, and so on, as well as in key. Usually one new theme stands out by its melodious quality; this is called the **second theme.**

❡   The last theme in the second group, the **cadence theme,** or *closing theme,* is constructed so as to make a solid ending prior to a full stop and the big repeat. The very end of the exposition is marked by a loud series of repeated cadences, as though the composer wanted listeners to know exactly where they are in the form. This **A** (exposition) section was almost always repeated.

Development (B)

The following section, the **development,** heightens the tonal-thematic tension set up by the contrasting themes and keys of the exposition. The themes are "developed" by being broken up, recombined, reorchestrated, extended, and in general shown in unexpected and often exciting new contexts.

Most development sections use counterpoint to create a sense of breakup and turmoil. In tonality, this section moves around restlessly; there are frequent modulations that can easily be heard. The music sounds unstable.

Eighteenth-century American spinet

After considerable tension has been built up in this way, the last modulation of the development section returns to the first key. The passage that accomplishes this, called the **retransition,** has the function of discharging the tension and preparing for the recapitulation to come. Classical composers were amazingly inventive in devising ways to make this crucial juncture of the form seem both fresh and inevitable.

Recapitulation (A′)

With a real sense of relief or resolution, we now hear the first theme again, followed by all the other themes and other elements of the exposition. There may be minor changes, but in principle everything comes back in its original order. Hence the name for this section—the **recapitulation** (meaning a step-by-step review).

But there is an important difference: everything—first theme, bridge, second group—now remains in the same key, the tonic key. Stability of key is especially welcome after the instability of the development section. And what is more, the old material now has a slightly new look. Thus the strong feeling of balance between the exposition and the recapitulation (**A B A′**) is a weighted balance, because **A′** has achieved a new solidity.

The entire **B A′** sequence is sometimes repeated. If even more solidity seems to be needed, another section is added at the end, a post mortem or wrap-up for the main action. This optional section is called the **coda** (coda is a general term for a concluding section in any musical form).

In the following schematic diagram for sonata form, changes of key (tonality) are shown on a continuous band. Notice the tonal stability of the recapitulation, where the steady horizontal band contrasts dramatically with the fluctuations of the exposition and development sections.

I compare a symphony with a novel in which the themes are the characters. We follow their evolution, the unfolding of their psychology. . . . Some of these characters arouse feelings of sympathy, others repel us. They are set off against one another or they join hands; they make love; they marry or they fight.

Swiss composer Artur Honegger, 1951

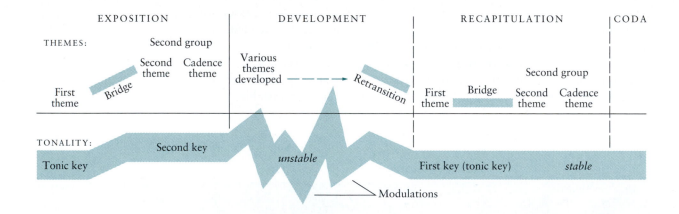

It may not be accidental that the terms used in discussing sonata form resemble those used in discussions of drama. We speak of the "exposition" of a play, where the initial situation is set forth, and of the "development" of the plot. Indeed, sonata form has a "dramatic" quality compared with the more "architectural" quality of Baroque music such as a fugue. In a Classical symphony, the themes seem almost like characters in a play or a novel to whom things are happening. They seem to change, take part in various actions, and react to other themes and musical processes.

WOLFGANG AMADEUS MOZART (1756–1791)
Symphony No. 40 in G Minor, K. 550* (1788)

Mozart's Symphony in G minor is one of the most famous and admired of all his works. The opening movement, with its sharp contrasts and clear demarcations, makes an arresting introduction to sonata form.

Not many Classical compositions convey as dark and uneasy a mood as does this symphony. (Not many Classical symphonies are in the minor mode.) It suggests some kind of muted struggle against inevitable restraints. Mozart's themes alone would not have created this effect; expressive as they are in themselves, they only attain their full pathos in their setting. Mozart needed sonata form to manage these expressive themes—in a sense, to give them something to struggle against.

First movement (Molto allegro) We have already cited this movement's opening texture—melody with a strictly homophonic accompaniment—as characteristic of the Viennese Classical style (see page 160). So also are the delicate dynamic changes toward the end of the theme, and the repeated loud cadences that terminate it. The unique nervous energy of this theme, a blend of refinement and subdued agitation, stamps the first movement unforgettably.

Exposition The first theme is played twice. The second playing already begins the modulation to the exposition's second key, and a forceful bridge passage completes this process, after which the music comes to an abrupt stop. Such stops will come again and again in this movement.

The second theme, in the major mode, is divided up, measure by measure or phrase by phrase, between the strings and the woodwinds:

Then it is repeated with the role of the instruments reversed, the strings taking the notes originally played by the winds, and vice versa. The instrumental alterations contribute something absolutely essential to the character of the theme, and show Mozart's fine ear for tone color.

The second appearance of the second theme does not come to a cadence, but runs into a series of new ideas which make up the rest of the second group. Since all of them are so brief, and leave so little impression on the rest of the movement, it is best not to consider them actual "themes." One of these ideas begins to develop the motive of the first theme—a premature development process, one might think; but once again, it goes by so fast that we do not mistake it for the real development section.

A short cadence theme, *forte,* and a volley of repeated cadences bring the exposition to a very distinct stop. After one dramatic chord, wrenching us back from major to the original minor key, the whole exposition is repeated.

---

*Mozart's works are identified by K numbers, after the chronological catalog of his works compiled by Ludwig von Köchel. The first edition (1862) listed 626 works composed by Mozart in his short lifetime; later editions add many more.

Wolfgang Amadeus Mozart (1756–1791)

Mozart was born in Salzburg, a charming town in central Austria, which today is famous for its music festivals. His father, Leopold, was a court musician and composer who had also written an important book on violin playing. Mozart showed extraordinary talent at a very early age. He and his older sister, Nannerl, were trotted all over Europe as infant prodigies; between the ages of six and seventeen, Wolfgang never spent more than ten successive months at home. His first symphony was played (at a London concert) when he was only eight years old.

But mostly Wolfgang was displayed at courts and salons, and in a somewhat depressing way, this whole period of his career symbolizes the frivolous love of entertainment that reigned at mid-century. The future Queen Marie Antoinette of France was one of those for whose amusement the six-year-old prodigy would guess the keys of compositions played to him, and sight-read music at the piano with a cloth over his hands.

It was much harder for Mozart to make his way as a young adult musician. As usual in those days, he followed in his father's footsteps as a musician at the court of Salzburg, which was ruled by an Archbishop. (Incidentally, one of their colleagues was Joseph Haydn's brother Michael.) But the Archbishop did not much care for music, and cared still less for independent-minded underlings. Mozart hated working for him. In 1781 he extricated himself from his court position, not without a humiliating scene, and set himself up as a free-lance musician in Vienna.

It seems clear that another reason for Mozart's move was to get away from his father, who had masterminded the boy's career and now seemed to grow more and more possessive as the young man sought his independence. Leopold disapproved of Wolfgang's marriage around this time to Constanze Weber, a singer. (Mozart had been in love with her older sister, Aloysia—a more famous singer—but she rejected him.)

Mozart wrote his greatest operas in Vienna, but only the last of them, The Magic Flute, had the success it deserved. Everyone sensed that he was a genius, but his music seemed too difficult—and he was a somewhat "difficult" personality, too. He relied for his living on teaching and on the relatively new institution of concerts. Every year he would set up a concert at which he introduced one of his piano concertos. In addition, the program might contain arias, a solo improvisation, and an overture by somebody else.

But as happens with popular musicians today, Mozart seems (for some unknown reason) to have suddenly dropped out of fashion. After 1787, his life was a struggle, though he did receive a minor court appointment and the promise of a church position, and finally scored a hit with The Magic Flute. When it seemed that financially he was finally getting out of the woods, he died suddenly at the age of thirty-five.

He died under somewhat macabre circumstances. He was composing a Requiem Mass, that is, a Mass for the dead, commissioned by a patron who insisted on remaining anonymous. Mozart became ill and began to think he was writing for his own demise. When he died, the Requiem still unfinished, a rumor started that he had been poisoned by the composer Antonio Salieri.

Unlike Haydn, the other great master of the Viennese Classical style, Mozart allowed a note of disquiet, even passion, to emerge in some of his compositions (such as the Symphony in G minor). The Romantics correctly perceived this as a forecast of their own work. Once we recognize this, it is hard not to sense something enigmatic beneath the intelligence, wit, and sheer beauty of all Mozart's music.

Chief Works: The great comic operas The Marriage of Figaro, Don Giovanni, Così fan tutte (That's What They All Do), and The Magic Flute ▪ Idomeneo, an opera seria ▪ Church music —many masses, and a Requiem (Mass for the Dead) left unfinished at his death ▪ Symphonies, including the Prague, the G minor, and the Jupiter ▪ String quartets and four superb string quintets; a quintet for clarinet and strings; a quartet for oboe and strings ▪ Concertos: seventeen particularly fine concertos for piano; four amusing ones for French horn; also concertos for violin and one for clarinet ▪ Piano sonatas; violin sonatas ▪ Lighter pieces (such as divertimentos, etc.), including the famous Eine kleine Nachtmusik

---

Development   Two more dramatic chords—and then the development section starts quietly, with the first theme accompanied as before. It modulates at once, and seems to be losing itself in grief, until the rest of the orchestra bursts in with a furious and grim contrapuntal treatment of that tender, nervous melody.

This lengthy outburst seems to exhaust itself, and comes to a raging stop. But in the following *piano* passage, the modulations continue, with orchestral echoes based on smaller and smaller portions of the melody, as shown to the right. Breaking up a theme in this way is called *fragmentation*.

LISTENING CHART 6

Mozart, Symphony No. 40 in G Minor, first movement

Sonata form, 8 min., 8 sec.

	EXPOSITION			
	0:02	**Theme 1** (main theme)	Theme 1, *p*, minor key (G minor); repeated cadences *f*	♪ score *p*
	0:26		Theme 1 repeats and begins the modulation to a new key.	
	0:34	**Bridge**	Bridge theme, *f*, confirms the modulation. CADENCE Abrupt stop.	♪ score *f*
		Second Group		
16 19	0:54	**Theme 2**	Theme 2, *p*, in major key; phrases divided between woodwinds and strings	♪ score *p*
0:09	1:05		Theme 2 again, division of phrases is reversed; new ending	
0:27	1:23		Other shorter ideas, *f*, and *p*: echoes of theme 1 motive	
0:52	1:48	**Cadence theme**	Cadence theme, *f*, downward scales followed by repeated cadences. Still in the major mode CADENCE Abrupt stop.	♪ score *f*
1:09	2:05	*Exposition repeated*		
		DEVELOPMENT		
17 20	4:12	**Theme 1 developed**	Theme 1, *p*, with its original accompaniment—modulating	
0:14	4:26	**Contrapuntal passage**	Sudden *f*: contrapuntal treatment by the full orchestra of theme 1	
0:41	4:53	**Fragmentation**	Sudden *p*: beginning of theme 1 echoes between strings and woodwinds; theme fragmented from ♪♪♩ ♩♩ to ♪♪♩ ♩ ♩♩ and finally to ♪♩ ♩	
0:58	5:10		Retransition *f* (full orchestra), *p* (woodwinds), which leads into the recapitulation	
		RECAPITULATION		
18 21	5:24	**Theme 1**	Theme 1, *p*, G minor, as before	
	5:47		Theme 1, again, but modulates differently than before	
0:31	5:55	**Bridge**	Bridge, *f*, considerably longer than before, with more elaborate counterpoint CADENCE Abrupt stop.	
		Second Group		
19 20	6:38	**Theme 2**	Theme 2, *p*, this time in the minor mode (G minor) All the other second-group themes are in the tonic key (minor mode); otherwise much the same as before	
1:00	7:38	**Cadence theme**	Scale part of the cadence theme, *f*	
		CODA		
20 23	7:50		New imitative passage, *p*, strings; based on theme 1 motive	♪ score *p*
	7:59		Repeated cadences, *f*	
			Stop, this time "confirmed" by three solid chords.	

The Mozart family: Nannerl, Wolfgang, and Leopold (with violin; Leopold's book on violin playing was famous). Mozart's mother, who had died when this picture was painted, is represented by a portrait.

Passion breaks out anew in another *forte* passage; but the modulations, we notice, have finally ceased. The fragmentation reaches its final stage, as shown. At last the harmony seems to be waiting or preparing for something, rather than shifting all the time. This passage is the *retransition*.

Recapitulation   After its fragmentation in the development section, the first theme somehow conveys new pathos when it returns in its original form, and in the original tonic key. The bassoon has a beautiful new descending line.

And pathos deepens when the second theme and all the other ideas in the second group—originally heard in a major-mode key—are now recapitulated in the tonic key, which is minor. The result is a great many small but poignant alterations of the exposition material. (Mozart had a special genius for such alterations.) We should have no trouble sensing that the recapitulation is more stable than the exposition, because both the first and second groups are now in the same mode (minor), as well as in the same key. Indeed, the bridge theme, much expanded, also hammers away at the minor mode, in a way that recalls the contrapuntal outburst of the development section.

Coda   In a very short coda, Mozart refers one last time to the first theme. It sounds utterly disheartened, and then battered by the usual repeated cadences.

FRANZ JOSEPH HAYDN (1732–1809)
Symphony No. 88 in G (1787)

During the last twenty years of his active career, from around 1780 to 1800, Joseph Haydn averaged better than one symphony a year, nearly all of them masterpieces. Like most Haydn symphonies, No. 88 is a cheerful piece; concert audiences wanted entertainment—high-level entertainment—and Haydn was always happy to oblige. Listeners of the time also wanted simple, "natural" melodies, and Haydn responded with the melody of the slow second movement, one of the most beautiful he ever composed.

Symphony No. 88 is scored for a relatively small orchestra, without clarinets (compare the Classical orchestra chart, page 159)—and what is more, the trumpets and timpani do not play at all during the forceful opening movement. We shall study all movements of this symphony; compare the outline to the right with the "generic" symphony outline on page 163.

First Movement (Adagio—Allegro)   Haydn treats sonata form differently than Mozart does, for example, in the G-minor Symphony (see page 167). Mozart's themes are clearly separated and sharply differentiated in character. Haydn runs themes and sections into one another, and he treads the fine line between providing just enough contrast to keep the interest up and making the themes similar enough in rhythm to create confusion and fun. The ingenuity Haydn shows in finding new ways of making this rhythm sparkle—there is even a new version of it in the very last measures—seem unlimited. It is qualities of this kind that make people speak of "wit" in Viennese Classical music.

Slow Introduction   This is rather stiff and formal, perhaps as a foil to the light, informal mood that is to follow. There are two parallel phrases, the second ending with a passage of preparation.

Exposition   The first theme is a lively miniature tune with a folk-like swing, played *piano* and repeated *forte*. Two important motives are heard, *x* and *y*:

The second time, the cellos and basses add a new counterpoint introducing motive *y*. And when the second playing of theme 1 runs into a blustery bridge passage, it soon dawns on the listener that Haydn is not going to wait till the official development section to start developing his themes. The rhythm of motive *x* in the theme, is heard repeatedly in this bridge.

The same rhythm also delivers the four heavy accents on the note E (marked *sf*) that end the bridge and drive home the modulation to the second key:

After a cadence (but there is only a very brief stop), the dynamics drop to *piano* for the tiny second theme, which is almost more of a harmonic blur than a melody. After this momentary contrast, more loud music leads to a stronger cadence and to the cadence theme, beginning with the rhythm of motive *x*:

Haydn, Symphony No. 88

Opening Movement
  slow **Introduction**
  tempo: fast/moderate
  form: sonata form

Slow Movement
  tempo: slow
  form: A B A′

Minuet (with Trio)
  tempo: moderate
  form: minuet form

Closing Movement
  tempo: fast
  form: rondo

LISTENING CHART 7

Haydn, Symphony No. 88 in G, first movement (Allegro)

Sonata form, with slow introduction. 6 min., 53 sec.

SLOW INTRODUCTION

| | 0:03 | | First phrase |
| | 0:41 | | Second phrase, preparing for theme 1 |

EXPOSITION

22 2	1:21	**Theme 1** (main theme)	Theme 1, *p*
0:08	1:29		Theme 1 repeated, *f*; extension runs into the bridge
0:26	1:47	**Bridge**	Built out of motive *x*
		CADENCE	

Second Group

23 3	2:04	**Theme 2**	Theme 2
		CADENCE	
0:15	2:19	**Cadence theme**	Cadence theme: woodwinds, then strings
0:40	2:44	***Exposition repeated***	

DEVELOPMENT

24 4	4:09	**Opening passage**	Strings only; tentative modulations using theme 1 with motive *y*, *p*
0:26	4:35	**Main**	Full orchestra; modulations continue
0:42	4:51	**Development**	- momentary appearance of theme 2, *f*
0:49	4:58		- momentary imitation (canon)
1:00	5:09		- music seems to settle in a minor key
			Expectant stop, again using motive *y*

RECAPITULATION

25 5	5:23	**Theme 1**	Theme 1, *p*, with added flute counterpoint
			Theme 1, *f*, with a different, shorter extension
0:25	5:48	**Bridge**	Mostly rewritten
		CADENCE	

Second Group

0:48	6:11	**Theme 2**	Even shorter than before
1:00	6:23	**Cadence theme**	Shortened
		CADENCE	

CODA

| 26 6 | 6:37 | | Theme 1; motive *x* divided between winds and strings |

Haydn's musical handwriting

Franz Joseph Haydn (1732–1809)

Joseph Haydn was born in Austria, the son of a village wheelwright who was a keen amateur musician. Another of his sons, Michael, also became a composer. As a boy Joseph had a beautiful voice, and at the age of eight was sent to Vienna to be a choirboy in St. Stephen's Cathedral. After his voice broke, he spent several difficult years as a free-lance musician in Vienna before obtaining the position of Kapellmeister with Prince Paul Anton Esterházy, one of the most lavish patrons of music at the time.

After this, Haydn's career reflects the changing social situation in the later eighteenth century, when the old system of court patronage coexisted with an early form of the modern concert system. Indeed, there is no finer tribute to the system of court patronage than Haydn's thirty-year career with the Esterházys. The post of Kapellmeister involved managing and writing music not only for the prince's chapel (the *Kapell*), but also for his private opera house, his marionette theater, and for palace chamber music and orchestral performances. Haydn had a good head for administration. Hiring his own musicians, he was able over many years to experiment with the symphony and other genres and develop his style under ideal conditions.

Haydn's output was staggering. He composed 104 symphonies, numerous divertimentos, string quartets, trios, and sonatas, and over twenty operas. He also had to write a great deal of music for baryton—a bizarre archaic instrument fancied by the next Esterházy prince, Nikolaus, which was something like a cello with extra strings that could be plucked, like guitar strings.

The Esterházys had a splendid estate some miles outside of Vienna, but Haydn's duties there did not prevent him from spending a good deal of time in the capital. In the 1770s his string quartets made a particularly strong impression in the metropolis. In the 1780s he befriended Mozart, and the two actually played together in an amateur string quartet.

Meanwhile the spread of Haydn's international fame was accelerated by the growth of public concerts. At first his symphonies were picked up by French concert organizers (who paid Haydn nothing). Then in the 1780s his six *Paris* symphonies were commissioned for concerts in that city, and in the 1790s twelve *London* symphonies were written for two enormously successful tours to Britain.

Toward the end of his life Haydn turned to choral music: six impressive Latin Masses for soloists, chorus, and orchestra, and two German oratorios inspired by Handel, *The Creation* and *The Seasons*, admired by his contemporaries as the apex of an exemplary career in music.

One of the most attractive personalities in the gallery of the great composers, Haydn was shrewd but generous-minded, humorous, always honorable, and though fully aware of his own worth, quite ready to praise his young, "difficult" colleague, Mozart. "Friends often flatter me that I have some genius," he once said—without contradicting them—"but he stood far above me."

Haydn's music combines good-humored simplicity of melody with a very sophisticated delight in the manipulations of musical form and technique. In his reasonableness, his wit, and his conviction that his art should serve humanity (a conviction he both expressed and acted upon), Haydn is the true musical representative of the Enlightenment.

Chief Works: Over 100 symphonies, notable among them the set of twelve composed for London in 1791–1795, including the *Surprise, Clock, Drum Roll,* and *London* symphonies ■ A cello concerto and a delightful trumpet concerto ■ Over 80 string quartets; piano trios and piano sonatas ■ Choral music of his late years, including six Masses and the oratorios *The Creation* (1798) and *The Seasons* (1801)

The loud music following the cadence theme ends with motive *y*. There is an expectant pause, and the exposition is repeated. (Exposition repeats in sonata form do not include the slow introduction.)

Development   The development begins with motive *y*, which we have just heard, but now quietly, in a questioning spirit. Theme 1 is made to modulate, and motive *y* becomes more and more hesitant.

Then, with a really sharp harmonic jolt—another modulation—the full orchestra bursts in for a long, varied, rowdy passage that will lead ultimately to the recapitulation. The main themes and motives get a thorough work-out, with much counterpoint and much modulation. Listen hard and you may be able to hear a snatch of the second theme, played as loudly as everything else.

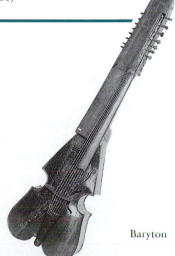

Baryton

Esterháza, where Haydn spent most of his life—a huge palace built by Esterházy princes in imitation of Versailles. It cannot compare with the real item, however: see page 101.

There is no distinct retransition; the loud passage ends with motive *y* and an expectant stop, like the end of the exposition. The parallelism here is a special treatment of sonata form invented by Haydn just for this movement.

Recapitulation   All the tension built up in the development section is relieved when the first theme returns, safe and sound in the original tonic key. But Haydn provides the theme with a charming new feature—a cool counterpoint added high above it by the flute.

The bridge is completely rewritten from its exposition version, though enough of its original gestures remain so that we recognize it. The second group receives this same free treatment, which is a hallmark of Haydn's mature style (and quite unlike Mozart's).

Coda   A short coda, after the cadence theme, provides a final new twist to motive *x*. The wind instruments try to start it twice, and each time they are shouted down by the full orchestra.

Informal pencil drawing of Haydn, which he once singled out as the best likeness he had ever seen: not the choice of a vain man. Compare page 173.

3 Slow Movements

There is no standardized form for the slow movement of a Classical symphony (or of any other Classical instrumental genre). Mozart, in his late symphonies, preferred sonata form, or some derivative of sonata form; Haydn liked his own version of theme and variations. In Symphony No. 88 Haydn employed a unique structure—**A B A′**, but with a difference.

HAYDN
Symphony No. 88 in G, second movement (Largo)

We have stressed the importance of "natural" and pleasing melodies in the formation of the Viennese Classical style. Haydn's genius for simple melody is certainly evident from the slow movement of Symphony No. 88. The following warm, songlike phrases (designated as **a**) are played again and again:

OBOE
a: first phrase
Largo

STRINGS
second phrase

p   *sf*   *sf*   *sf*   *p*   *p*   *sf*   *p*

+ SOLO CELLO (octave lower)

LISTENING CHART 8

27-30   7-10   3   3

Haydn, Symphony No. 88, second movement (Largo)

Irregular ABA form. 5 min., 27 sec.

0:00	**A (major**	**a** (oboe and solo cello)	*a* (first phrase)
0:33	**mode)**	**a** (pizzicato strings added)	
1:06		**b** (strings)	
		a′ (with new string figure) ⟶ *ff*	*p* *sf* ⟶
1:53		New cadences *ff* trumpets and drum	
		Transition: woodwinds	*a* (second phrase)
28 8 2:38	**A**	**a** (violins and flute with held note in the oboe; slightly compressed, and in a new key)	
		b	*p* ⟶ < *sf* ⟶
		a′ (oboe, with faster string figure) ⟶ *ff*	
29 9 3:36	**B (minor**	Begins by overlapping the cadence of **a′**	*b*
	mode)	**Trumpet figure** *ff* recalls the "new cadences"; modulates	
0:19 3:55		**a″** starts in a new key, and then modulates	
		Trumpet figure *ff*	*f* *sf* *sf*
30 10 4:25	**A′ (major**		
	mode)	**a′** (oboe, with new woodwind figure) ⟶ *ff*	
0:36 5:01		New cadences *ff* trumpets and drum (as before)	
0:45 5:10		New ending: woodwinds	

This slow movement is in a very lopsided **A B A′** form, with **A** in the major mode and **B** starting in the minor. The haunting phrases of **a** are part of a tune in |: **a** :| **b a′** form; **b** is unusually short but very expressive (note that its minor-mode harmonies forecast the minor mode of **B**). Haydn actually plays this whole tune twice in the **A** section—with a strange, impressive passage in between, as we shall see. Having given us more than usual in **A,** he then gives us less in **A′,** which consists simply of **a′** and a short coda.

But cutting across the **A B A′** form is an extraordinary eruption in the trumpets and the drums. Entering after the first **a′,** they make just two very loud cadences and then retire, as quiet woodwinds lead to the second playing of the tune. When the trumpets and drums reappear after the second **a′,** they announce a new departure, **B,** the somber contrasting section in the minor mode. These blasts (and there are several more) will greatly surprise and could almost scare listeners to this otherwise mellow movement, for trumpets and drums are totally unexpected. They were absent from the previous movement.

When Haydn repeated this effect a few years later, in the slow movement of one of his last symphonies, people at once nicknamed it "The Surprise" (Symphony No. 94, from the set of twelve *London* Symphonies).

The admirable and matchless HAYDN! *From whose productions I have received more pleasure late in my life, when tired of most Music, than I ever received in the ignorant and rapturous part of my youth.*

English music historian Charles Burney, 1776

4   Minuet Form (Classical Dance Form)

Stylized dances—music of considerable elaboration in the style and form of dances, but intended for listening rather than dancing—reached a state of high development in the Baroque era. In Chapter 9 we saw how various dance types such as the gavotte and the bourrée were assembled into suites. Unlike the Baroque era, which developed a single genre made up of different dances, the Classical era brought a single stylized dance into many different genres.

3
1

1
24

2B
6

1B
6

Minuets for Dancing

It may be interesting to consider a minuet of the time that was written for actual dancing. In 1766 a set of modest pieces by Haydn were published with the title *Menuetti a Ballo*—"Minuets for Dancing." They must have been intended for balls in Vienna or Esterháza, where Haydn was already in charge as Chapel Master.

Note the solemn, stiff melody in the minuet with its heavy triple-meter dance rhythm. Phrases of four and eight measures were standard for minuet dance steps, and Haydn follows this form strictly.

Since this Minuet in D dates from early in Haydn's career, before he had really defined the Viennese Classical style, we should not be surprised to note some old-fashioned features in it. Classical minuet form in the trio (|:c:||:d c′:|) coexists with the older baroque dance form in the minuet (|:a:||:b:|):

Minuet	Trio	Minuet
|: a :||: b :|	|: c :||: d c′ :|	a b
measures: 8 8	8 4 4	8 8

Another antiquated feature is the use of a harpsichord playing the continuo part, a baroque practice that had not entirely died out in the 1760s. Still another is the scoring of the trio—which is in a different key from the minuet—for only three instruments: two flutes and bass (plus the subsidiary continuo instrument).

Attractive, unassuming, and instantly forgettable, this functional dance music stays well below the artistic level that Haydn was developing for minuets in his symphonies even at this early time.

The sole dance type from the Baroque suite to survive in the multimovement genres of the Classical period was the <u>minuet.</u> One reason for this was simply that the dance itself, originally popularized at the court of Louis XIV in the seventeenth century, continued as one of the major fashionable social dances during the eighteenth. Another reason was more technical. As a moderately paced piece in triple meter, the minuet makes an excellent contrast to the quick duple meter that was by far the most common meter in the opening and closing movements of Classical symphonies, quartets, and the like.

Works with four movements—symphonies and string quartets—always included a minuet, usually as a light contrast after the slow movement. Mozart even managed to fit a minuet into some of his piano concertos, though traditionally the concerto, as a three-movement genre, did not leave room for one.

Baroque and Classical Dance Form

A Baroque minuet consists of two sections; each comes to a complete stop and is immediately repeated (|: a :||: b :|). Minuets tend to come in pairs, alternating in an **A B A** pattern. The second dance, **B**, is called the <u>trio,</u> because in early days it was often played by only three instruments.

A Baroque minuet movement can be diagrammed as follows. (Remember that |: :| means repeat, and that in the second **A** the parts are not repeated.)

Minuet	Trio	Minuet
A	**B**	**A**
|: a :||: b :|	|: c :||: d :|	a b

Classical composers extended the internal form of minuets (and trios) by developing internal **a b a** structures according to one of the following schemes:

Minuet	Trio	Minuet		Minuet	Trio	Minuet
A	**B**	**A**	or (more often)	**A**	**B**	**A**
|: a :||: b a :|	|: c :||: d c :|	a b a		|: a :||: b a′ :|	|: c :||: d c′ :|	a b a′

Prime marks (**a′** and **c′**) indicate significant extensions or alterations of the original **a** and **c** sections. It is easy to see why Classical dance form is sometimes called **ternary form.**

And indeed, changes of this kind were a major element in the dance "stylization" of this time. Haydn and Mozart could fashion a microcosm of the art of Classical music out of the simple elements of minuet form, always remaining within earshot of the ballroom with its easy, regular dance beat. We come upon a particularly creative use of minuet form in Haydn's Symphony No. 88.

HAYDN
Symphony No. 88 in G, third movement (Menuetto: Allegretto)

The minuet movement of Haydn's Symphony No. 88 takes a small mental journey from the ballroom to the countryside, and then back again. Perhaps it is not a real countryside but a "stylized" one, such as that pictured on page 152.

Minuet (Menuetto: Allegretto)   The **a** section of the minuet, built mostly from repetitions of a firm-sounding rhythmic motive in various versions (motive *x*), conveys a sense of energy and forthright motion. This robust court dance would seem to have little time for subtleties.

motive *x*

However, when the phrase comes to its strong cadence, it is followed by two more quiet appearances of the motive that are rather strange. While repeated cadences are used regularly in the Classical style to give a feeling of finality, here they seem to leave the music up in the air when the section closes.

And after the repetition of **a** fails to correct this aberration, **b** begins in what one is tempted to call a mood of irritation. Still keeping to the stiff dance rhythm, the music modulates to a new key, then returns to the original key by way of a short, forceful passage in the minor mode. Section **a′** is much like **a**—but whereas the first repeated cadence is quiet, as before, the second is loud and thoroughly final-sounding. As though delighted by this last-minute rescue, the orchestra makes sure we hear it again by repeating **b a′**.

While this description may seem a little imaginative, it does respond to the music's undeniable implication of some kind of action or drama, an implication that Haydn has folded into this otherwise blunt, even clumpy minuet.

Trio   By comparison, the trio feels almost lackadaisical. Quieter than the minuet and moving in faster notes, its melody runs on and on, repeating itself rather aimlessly (this is quite unlike the repetitions of motive *x* in the minuet). In the background, an imitation bagpipe drone allows for just a few changes in harmony. There are places in both the **c** and **d** sections where the rhythm seems to get lost momentarily, returning to normal a beat or two later.

What is more, the melody of **c′**, while certainly very similar to **c**, is just a little off in every measure. That bagpipe drone (or is it a hurdy-gurdy?) sets us thinking: could this be a parody of not-too-competent peasant musicians?

But with these stylized "peasant" pieces by Haydn, one can never be too sure as to who is making fun of whom. Maybe the simple bagpiper doesn't know about **c d c** form, and is improvising in a "primitive," formless way. Or maybe he does, and is deliberately making tricky changes to mix up the sophisticated listener. Can you hear when the original **c** music returns as **c′**?

Be assured, my D. H., that among all your numerous admirers NO ONE *has listened with more* PROFOUND *attention, and no one can have such veneration for your* MOST BRILLIANT TALENTS *as I have. Indeed, my D. H., no tongue* CAN EXPRESS *the gratitude I* FEEL *for the infinite pleasure your Music has given me . . .*

Letter to Haydn from another, more intimate English admirer, 1792

Minuet Form and Sonata Form

The sonata-form movement that opens a symphony is never as simple as the minuet movement, yet for all their differences in scope and material, these two forms are basically similar in plan.

The similarity appears on the largest level: both sonata form and minuet (dance) form entail two main portions which—in principle—come to complete stops and are then marked for repetition. Furthermore, both forms have the same important feature, a free return of opening material.

Of course there are major differences. Whereas the **a**,

b, and **a′** sections of a minuet may be as short as eight-measure phrases, the exposition (**A**), development (**B**), and recapitulation (**A′**) of a sonata-form movement are rich aggregates of contrasting themes, transitional passages, cadence formulas, and so on. More basic yet is the difference in *style*. The guiding force behind the minuet is dance rhythm. The guiding force behind sonata form is contrast.

With these differences clearly in mind, however, it can be helpful to think of sonata form as a transformation and huge expansion of minuet form.

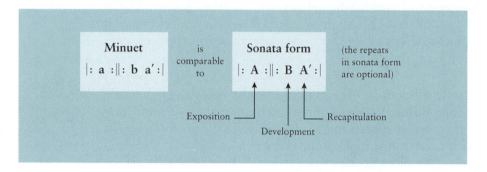

| **Minuet** | is comparable to | **Sonata form** | (the repeats in sonata form are optional) |
| **|: a :||: b a′ :|** | | **|: A :||: B A′ :|** | |

Exposition ─── | └─── Recapitulation
Development

Minuet   The minuet returns unchanged, except that this time there are no repetitions: **a b a′**.

Unlike a recapitulation in a sonata-form movement, the return of **A** after the trio in minuet form does not give the impression of emerging out of previous musical events and completing them. Minuet returns are more formal than organic. We probably listen to them less reflectively than to recapitulations, remembering their origin in the ballroom, where dances are played as many times as the dancers need them, and always gratefully received.

The bagpipe is a peasant instrument with a long history and very wide geographical distribution. Shown here are Spanish medieval bagpipes, a Hungarian peasant instrument, and the familiar Scottish regimental model. Haydn's minuet evokes both the bagpipe's low drone notes, which seem to go on forever, and also the lively tunes of the high "chanter" pipes.

LISTENING CHART 9

| | | 2 | 2 | 2B | 1B |
| | | 31-34 | 11-14 | 4 | 4 |

Haydn, Symphony No. 88 in G, third movement (Menuetto)

Minuet form, 4 min., 34 sec.

MINUET (A)			
	0:00	a	Includes several statements of motive *x*, in various versions
	0:15		Two repeated cadences: both *p*
	0:21	a	*repetition*
32 12	0:42	b	Motive *x*, turning into continuous motion. Modulates to a new key
	1:02		Return passage, momentarily in the minor mode
0:27	1:09	a′	Similar to **a**, but the last cadence is *f*
0:44	1:26	b a′	*repetition*
TRIO (B)			
33 13	2:11	c	
0:14	2:25	c	*repetition*
34 14	2:40	d	Begins like c, higher, in the minor mode
			runs right in, without a stop ⟶
0:13	2:53	c′	Similar (not identical!) to *just the end of* c
0:23	3:03	d c′	*repetition*
MINUET (A) *repetition of a b a′*			

The musical examples show a treble clef passage marked *f* with motive *x* bracketed, and a treble clef passage marked *p*.

5 Rondo Form

The **rondo** is a relatively simple form with popular leanings. In the symphonies and other multimovement genres of the Classical era, it was used mainly for closing movements, which tend to be relatively light.

The basic principle of the rondo is simply repetition, repetition of a full-fledged tune. The main tune (**A**) comes back again and again after *episodes* that serve as spacers between its appearances. If the **A** tune falls into the favorite |:a:||:b a′:| pattern of the time, the repetitions may present only **a b a′** or **a b**, or simply **a**, but there is always enough of the tune for one to recognize.

In the simplest rondos, the episodes are little tunes much like **A**; we shall see such a rondo in Mozart's Piano Sonata in B flat, on page 184. In more elaborate works such as symphonies, the episodes may contain transitions to new themes, cadence formulas, and even sonata-form-style developments. Various schemes are possible; often a coda is added. Whatever the specific structure, the regular return of the main tune **A** is the critical feature of rondo form.*

Rondo schemes:
A B A C A coda
A B A C A B A
A B A C A D A
A B C A coda
—and others

*In some ways, rondo form resembles ritornello form (see page 116), but the differences are worth noting. Ritornello form usually brings back its ritornello in fragments and in different keys; rondo form usually brings back its theme complete and in the same key.

HAYDN
Symphony No. 88 in G, fourth movement (Finale: Allegro con spirito)

Finale (fináhlay) is an Italian term used for the closing movement of a symphony or other instrument genre, and—in opera—for the last number of any one of the acts. Both instrumental and vocal finales sometimes use rondo form.

The theme, **A,** is a cheerful, busy tune in |: **a** :||: **b a′** :| form. The end of **b,** which abruptly changes in dynamics from *f* to *p,* features a "witty" detail, a detail that Haydn will return to later in the rondo. One could almost miss the return (**a′**), since it begins with two upbeat Ds, and the end of **b** runs right into them with two other Ds:

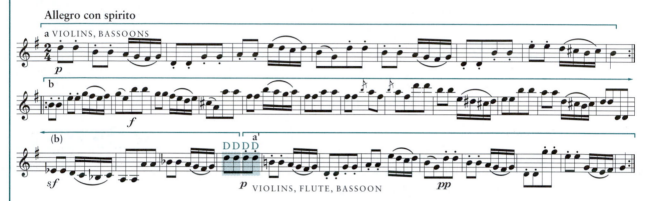

The form outline of this piece is **A B A′ C A Coda.** The rondo episodes **B** and **C** here are not simple tunes, but passages of a more dynamic nature. Section **B** begins *forte* with a vigorous transitional passage, and then continues with a quiet new melodic unit (it is hardly a new theme) derived from the tune's opening motive:

and ends with a forceful cadential passage, running into upward leaps that seem like rough questions concerning the note D.

A mild answer is provided by the rondo tune, with its upbeat Ds:

This first return, **A′,** consists of **a b** only, with some reorchestration and changes of dynamics. Just when the listener is expecting **a′,** Haydn runs off into a modulating contrapuntal passage—the second episode, **C.**

This ends up harping quietly on those same upbeat Ds, in such a way that the listener never quite knows when the theme is going to return:

LISTENING CHART 10

2   2   2B   1B
35-38   15-18   5   5

Haydn, Symphony No. 88 in G, fourth movement

Rondo, 4 min.

	0:00	**A (Tune)**	**a**	The entire tune is presented by the strings with bassoon and
	0:08		**a**	then flute, starting *p*.
	0:16		**b**	
	0:30		**a′**	
	0:38		**ba′**	*repetition*
				Leads into episode 1
36 **16**	1:00	**B (Episode 1)**		Transitional passage, *f*; modulation
	1:19			A new melodic unit, *p*, derived from the tune's first motive; strings. Repeated in the minor mode
0:31	1:31			Cadential passage, *f*
0:45	1:45			Upward leaps—still *f*—emphasizing the note D in preparation for the return of the tune, which starts on D
37 **17**	1:49	**A′ (Tune)**		Part of the tune (**a b**) is presented, starting *p*; French horns accompany **a**. Leads into episode 2
0:22	2:11	**C (Episode 2)**		A developmental episode, *f*; contrapuntal, modulating
0:53	2:42			Another preparation passage, this time p, harping on two Ds. Strings alternate with French horns.
38 **18**	2:58	**A″ (Tune)**		The entire tune is presented, but without repeats (**a b a′**).
	3:27	**Coda**		A brief break in the rhythm, *f*, followed by exuberant runs
0:50	3:48			Final cadence, including echoes of the tune's opening motive. Trumpet fanfares

In the second return, the entire theme is heard (**a b a′**). This goes directly into the coda. There is a sudden (and welcome!) break in the rhythm, and another vigorous running passage brings the rondo to a close—after some more references to the opening motive, accompanied by loud trumpet fanfares.

Thinking back on Haydn's Symphony No. 88, we might ask if there is any aesthetic quality that derives from the combination of the particular four movements we have heard. Is the whole greater than the sum of the parts?

If so, this is not something that musicians or musicologists have been able to elucidate with any consistency. It seems, rather, that Classical composers wrote symphony movements to fit together only in a general way, without thinking very much about connections between them, or any greater whole. This is as true of Mozart's agitated G-minor Symphony as of Haydn's cheerful Symphony No. 88. By concluding his work with two gloomy minor-mode movements, Mozart seems to reinforce the mood of the opening movement without drawing any conclusions from it, as it were.

Indeed, the question only comes up because later, nineteenth-century symphonies often *do* have such connections, and *do* draw such conclusions. The Fifth Symphony by Ludwig van Beethoven seems to trace a psychological process from turmoil to triumph. The *Fantastic* Symphony by Hector Berlioz literally traces the story line of a document written by the composer. See pages 209 and 247.

Haydn's most famous composition is a simple Austrian patriotic song:

It appears with variations in his *Emperor* Quartet, Op. 76 No. 3 (1797). The tune was adopted for the German national anthem, *Deutschland über Alles,* and for the hymn "Glorious Things of Thee are Spoken."

CHAPTER 14

Other Classical Genres

I n Chapter 13 we examined the symphony as exemplified by Haydn's Symphony No. 88 in G and the first movement of Mozart's Symphony No. 40 in G minor. We go on in this chapter to examine the other main genres of music in the Viennese Classical era: the sonata, the Classical concerto, the string quartet, and opera buffa, the name for Italian comic opera of the time.

It would be impractical to spend the same amount of detail on each of these genres as on the symphony, and also somewhat redundant, for many features of the symphony are duplicated in these other genres. Indeed, for Classical instrumental music, the symphony can be used as a sort of prototype. With this use in mind, the symphony outline given on page 163 is reprinted on this page.

In the following pages we select a sonata, a concerto, and a string quartet and then discuss a single one of its movements (using recordings and listening charts, as usual). The discussions will emphasize generic specificity—that is, the specific features that differentiate the music in question from the symphony. In addition, short descriptions of the other movements are added, for those who wish to study any of the complete works as an extra project. With opera buffa, two numbers will serve as samples of the whole.

1 The Sonata

The term **sonata** has multiple meanings. We know its adjectival use in the term "sonata form," the scheme employed in the first movements of Classical overtures, symphonies, quartets, and also (as it happens) sonatas. As a noun, *sonata* refers to a piece for a small number of instruments or a single one. And whereas in the Baroque period there were trio sonatas and solo sonatas—solo plus continuo, usually—in the Classical period the term was restricted to compositions for one or two instruments only.

Sonatas were not designed for concerts, which in any case were still rare at this time, but for private performance, often by amateurs. The symphony is a public genre, the sonata a domestic one. Given their destination in social life, some (not all!) sonatas are easy to play and may be limited in expression.

Piano sonatas were composed for solo piano, the favorite new instrument of the time, and *violin sonatas* were composed for violin and piano. In sonatas

The Symphony

Opening Movement
  tempo: fast/moderate
  form: sonata form
     sometimes preceded by a
     slow **Introduction**

Slow Movement
  tempo: slow/very slow
  form: no standard form
     (sometimes sonata form,
     variation form, rondo)

Minuet (with Trio)
  tempo: moderate
  form: minuet form

Closing Movement
  tempo: fast/very fast
  form: sonata form or
     rondo form

The sonata was said by a German critic to be intended by its earliest writers to show in the first movement what they could do, in the second what they could feel, and in the last how glad they were to have finished.

Philadelphia musician
P. H. Goepp, 1897

with violin or (less frequently) another instrument, the piano is not a mere accompaniment but an equal partner; it can hold its own in such combinations in a way that the earlier harpsichord could not.

Compare the movement plan for the sonata, shown to the right, with the symphony prototype on the previous page. But also note that sonatas are much less uniform than symphonies, concertos, or quartets. With Mozart's sonatas, for example, only 65% follow the plan, leaving many exceptions. None of them has more than three movements, however, and the movements are almost always shorter than those of a symphony.

WOLFGANG AMADEUS MOZART (1756–1791)
Piano Sonata in B Flat, K. 570 (1787)

This sonata finds Mozart in a sunny mood—a more frequent mood for him than the sometimes painful agitation that we recall from Symphony No. 40. The first movement, a lively work in the major mode, is in sonata form. The second is in simple rondo form (see page 179), and the third in an irregular, compressed form similar to a rondo.

First movement (Allegro)   As is usual with Mozart's movements in sonata form, all the formal articulations—bridges, cadences, and the like—are signaled clearly, in fact almost flaunted. There is one novelty, however; after a long bridge that clearly announces the second key, the "second theme" turns out to be the first theme in the left hand with a faster counterpoint in the right:

As always, the recapitulation remains in the tonic key, rather than moving to a new one. Otherwise it stays very close to the exposition (closer than in either of the symphony first movements we have heard). There is no coda.

The Sonata

Opening Movement
  tempo: fast/moderate
  form: sonata form

Slow Movement
  tempo: slow/very slow
  form: no standard form
    (sometimes sonata form,
    variation form, rondo)

Closing Movement
  tempo: fast/very fast
  form: often rondo

From the late eighteenth century on, musical accomplishment—and especially piano playing—was regarded as a highly desirable social asset for young women worldwide: for a French princess (painted by Elizabeth Vigée-Lebrun, a fashionable court painter, 1755–1842) as well as for this unknown American girl (by Mather Brown, 1761–1831).

LISTENING CHART 11

3   3A
2-4   1

Mozart, Piano Sonata in B flat, third movement (Allegro)

A B C A form. 3 min., 43 sec.

0:00	**A**	a			
0:14		b			
0:24		a			
0:39	**B**	c			
0:53	**(Episode 1)**	c	*repetition*		
1:08		d			
1:15		c′			
1:31		d c′	*repetition*		
			Short transition		
3 1:58	**C**	e	In a new key	In our recording, **C** is played with a	
	(Episode 2)	e	*repetition*	muting device (similar to the left pedal	
0:14 2:12		f		on today's piano).	
0:23 2:21		e′			
0:29 2:27		f e′	*repetition*		
			Short transition = end of **b**		
4 2:52	**A**	a	Back in the tonic key		
3:07	**Coda**		Refers to **d** (or **c**), then **f**		
0:41 3:33			CADENCE Trill and strong cadence		
			New cadence motive		

With Mozart's fortepiano, one has the sensation of recreating something that goes to the expressive and dynamic limits of the instrument . . . The tone is very characteristic, sweet and clear . . .

Pianist András Schiff, who plays Mozart's sonata on our recording

Second movement (Adagio)   Mozart is at his most melodious in this lovely slow movement. The first rondo episode, **B**, in the minor mode, offers a whiff of agitation that may recall the G-minor Symphony. The coda makes exquisite free references to **C** and **f**. The form can be diagrammed as follows:

A	**B**	short	**A**	**C**	short	**A**	Coda
|:a:||:b a:|	|:c:||:d c′:|	transition	a′	|:e:||:f:|	transition	a′	

Third movement (Allegretto)   There is sharp edge, almost a bite to this movement; one thing that contributes to this is the set of tart little syncopations (see page 15) within the **a** and **b** phrases of the main tune, **A**. The brittle but highly sensitive tone of the fortepiano (the eighteenth-century piano), used for our recording, seems to bring out the music's playful quality.

Syncopations are also heard in the first episode, **B**, together with a repeated-note figure in the left hand, which Mozart takes over for the beginning of the second episode, **C**. This rather simple-minded repeated-note figure, originally meant for a routine accompaniment function, is soon combined with spiky counterpoints (in phrase **f**).

Mozart's fortepiano. The eighteenth century version of a pianoforte was smaller than today's instrument. It made up in delicacy of tone what it lacked in volume; since the fortepiano did not have an iron frame, the strings could not be strung so tightly.

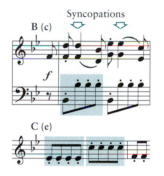

The coda makes witty references to both episodes, and arrives at its cadence with a small flourish and a trill—except that this is not quite the end: Mozart adds a new motive for a doubly emphatic, self-satisfied conclusion.

The form has the feel of a simple rondo because of the structure of the main tune and of the episodes: compare the Adagio. But there is no central **A:**

A	B	short	C	short	A	Coda
a b a	|:c:||:d c′:|	transition	|:e:||:f e′:|	transition	a	

2   The Classical Concerto

On page 116 we discussed the Baroque concerto and concerto grosso at the time of Bach and Vivaldi in terms of the basic concerto idea—the contest between soloist and orchestra. This basic idea was refined and sharpened by the Viennese Classical composers.

Instrumental virtuosity remained a central feature of the Classical concerto. At the same time, the orchestra was growing. With its well-coordinated string, woodwind, and brass groups, the Classical orchestra was much more flexible than the Baroque concerto orchestra could ever be.

So the balance between the two contesting forces presented a real problem, a problem that Mozart worked out in a series of seventeen superb piano concertos written during his years in Vienna, mostly for his own concert use. He pitted the soloist's greater agility, brilliance, and expressive capability against the orchestra's increased power and variety of tone color. The contestants are perfectly matched; neither one can ever emerge definitely as the winner.

Compare the movement plan for the Classical concerto with the symphony prototype on page 182. Concertos have long opening movements—see below—and no minuet movements.

The Classical Concerto

Opening Movement
   tempo: fast/moderate
   form: double-exposition
            sonata form
   cadenza near the end

Slow Movement
   tempo: slow/very slow
   form: no standard form
   (sometimes sonata form,
   variation form, rondo)

Closing Movement
   tempo: fast/very fast
   form: rondo form
   (occasionally variation
   form)

Double-Exposition Form

For the first movements of concertos, Mozart developed a special form to capitalize on the contest that is basic to the genre. Though the diagram for **double-exposition form** may look rather cluttered, it is in fact simply an extended variant of sonata form. Compare the sonata-form diagram, page 166:

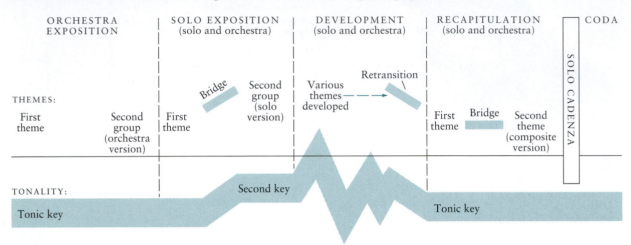

In place of the repeated exposition of sonata form, here each of the competing forces presents the exposition in its own somewhat different version. Note that unlike the exposition in a symphony, in a concerto the **orchestra exposition** does not modulate—an important difference. The point is to save the change of key that counts for so much in all sonata-form compositions until the **solo exposition**. The listener senses that the orchestra can't modulate and the soloist can—evidence of the soloist's superior range and mobility.

The recapitulation in double-exposition form amounts to a composite of the orchestral and solo versions of the exposition. And shortly before the end, there is a big, formal pause for the soloist's **cadenza** (see page 124). The soloist was supposed to improvise at this point—to show his or her skill and flair by working out new thematic developments on the spot, and also by carrying off brilliant feats of virtuosity.

MOZART
Piano Concerto No. 17 in G, K. 453 (1784)

Mozart wrote the Piano Concerto in G for one of his favorite students, Barbara Ployer, then nineteen years old. It is a more delicate, intimate work than most of the concertos he wrote to play himself at his own money-making concerts. The eighteenth century would have called it more "feminine."

Characteristically, the first movement simply overflows with musical material—themes and motives of almost every possible kind. The second movement calls up an indescribable mood, a blend of melancholy and tranquility shaken more than once by displays of deeper emotion. Both movements are in double-exposition form. And the last movement, a theme and variations, exists strictly for fun.

First Movement (Allegro)   The first theme, presented quietly at the start of the *orchestra exposition,* is elegance itself. The more expressive second theme makes a sharp contrast; a jaunty cadence figure carried forward by the bas-

soon and the flute introduces this second theme, and grows more and more important as the work proceeds. The true cadence theme comes later.

In the *solo exposition,* the piano plays the first theme in an ornamented version. Then it adds a new, brighter theme of its own, before taking up—and taking over—the orchestra's expressive second theme. On the other hand, most of the loud music from the orchestra exposition is now subtracted. The solo winds up a brilliant virtuoso passage with a trill and a big cadence. The orchestra plays part of the cadence theme (from the orchestra exposition).

The *development* section consists largely of rapid piano passages, modulating to remote keys; behind them, the wind instruments develop one of the exposition themes. In the *recapitulation,* the dialogue between solo and orchestra becomes closer and more spirited. The composite second group assembles all the material—elegant and bright, loud and soft—from both expositions.

As for the cadenza, Mozart actually wrote out two alternatives as a sort of lesson for Ployer. Most pianists today use one or the other, though Mozart himself would surely have improvised something flashier.

Piano theme

Second Movement (Andante)   Here double-exposition form is used more simply, and for a more profound expressive effect, than in the first movement. Mozart probably never used the form more beautifully.

Orchestra Exposition   The first theme is unusual, consisting of a single quiet phrase leading to a fermata (see page 16), as though raising a question:

An answering theme is played by the woodwinds in transparent imitative counterpoint. This leads to a loud-soft theme, then to a lovely cadence theme featuring minor-mode harmonies:

Solo Exposition   The piano enters and questions with theme 1—and provides its own new answer, an angry, emotional one that modulates to a new key. The solo exposition ends with a piano trill and a cadence.

Development   Now it is the woodwinds' turn to ask the question. The piano answers with new expressive material; in the background, the woodwinds develop a short motive from the cadence theme. Finally—as a retransition—the orchestra wrenches the music back to the original tonic key.

Recapitulation and Coda   The "composite" recapitulation includes all the themes, with the question again answered heatedly by the piano. But after the cadenza comes a very unexpected coda. The woodwinds anxiously press the question one more time, drawing on minor-mode harmonies. The piano's answer this time, unlike all the earlier times, is simple and serene, a quiet reproof to anxiety. At last the uneasy dialogue can come to rest, with an exquisite new piano commentary on the cadence theme.

These piano concertos are a happy medium between too easy and too difficult; they are very brilliant, pleasing to the ear, and natural, without being simpleminded. There are passages here and there which only connoisseurs will be able to appreciate, but less learned listeners will like them too, without knowing why.

Letter from Mozart to his father, 1782

3 Classical Variation Form

Variation form, as we saw on page 119, entails the successive, uninterrupted repetition of a clearly defined melodic unit, the *theme,* with various changes at each repetition. In the Baroque era, the theme was usually a bass pattern (sometimes called a ground bass). The same basic principle is at work in Classical variation form, but now the theme is a tune in the upper register.

We can understand why the Baroque era, which developed the idea of the basso continuo supporting harmonies from below, would have cultivated variations on a bass pattern, whereas the Classical era, with its emphasis on simple melody, preferred variations on short tunes in the upper register.

The point of variations is to create many contrasting moods with the same theme, which is transformed but always somehow discernible under the transformations. Nothing distracts from this process, at least until the end, where composers usually add a coda. There are no contrasting themes, modulations, transitions, cadence sections, or development sections, as there are in sonata form movements (and many rondos).

A Classical **theme and variations** movement begins with a theme in |:a:||:b:| or |:a:||:ba:| or |:a:||:ba′:| form. This miniform "nests" within the larger variation form:

Theme	Variation 1	Variation 2 . . .		Variation n	Coda
|: a :||: b :|	|: a^1 :||: b^1 :|	|: a^2 :||: b^2 :|		a^n a$^{n′}$ b^n b$^{n′}$	(free)

Note the possibility shown under Variation **n:** the exact repetition of a^n may be replaced by a^n plus a variation, a$^{n′}$.

Variations were part of the stock-in-trade of virtuosos of the Classical era. At a musical soirée, someone might suggest a popular opera tune, and the pianist would improvise variations on the spot, for as long as his or her imagination held out. Twelve was a common number for these variations when they were published; virtuosos piled them up for maximum effec

In symphonies and concertos, theme and variation movements are less extended, since they have to fit into a time scale with all the other movements. Our concerto finale has five variations, plus a substantial coda.

Richter, the piano virtuoso, is giving six Saturday concerts . . . The nobility subscribed, but remarked that they really did not care much about going unless I played. So Richter asked me to do so. I promised to play three times and then arranged three concerts for myself, to which they all subscribed.

Letter from Mozart to his father, 1784

MOZART
Piano Concerto in G, K. 453, third movement (Allegretto)

Theme   The orchestra plays the theme, a bouncing little tune in |: a :||: b :| form. Each half of the theme is the same length, and the ends of the sections are clearly demarcated with stops. Yet in spite of its popular tone, this tune includes a contrapuntal detail in the **b** section that is preserved in delightful ways through most of the variations:

In the next example, the theme's **a** section is lined up with the corresponding sections of Mozart's five variations, labeled **a**¹, **a**², **a**³, **a**⁴, and **a**⁵. Color shading shows parallel melody notes, but a glance at this example shows how much else is different—that is, how much has been "varied":

Variation 1   The piano begins, and seems almost to silence the orchestra by showing how to make the theme so much more expressive and personal. Its method is to provide the theme with fluid melodic decorations and some harmonic enrichment. Each half of this variation (**a**¹ and **b**¹) is repeated exactly.

Variation 2   In this variation, where the piano shows off its agility and brilliance, the repeats of each half are varied differently. In **a**² and **b**², the soloist has fast *right-hand* runs while the orchestra plays the theme; in **a**²′ and **b**²′, the soloist has *left-hand* runs.

Variation 3   The next variation is a songlike dialogue between the woodwind instruments—oboe, flute, bassoon in **a**³, then flute, bassoon, oboe in **b**³. After each half, in sections **a**³′ and later **b**³′, the piano makes varied repeats by picking up the woodwinds' material and decorating it flexibly.

Variation 4   Woodwinds are replaced by strings, the mode changes to the minor, and the dynamic drops to a mysterious *pp*. This fascinating variation, with its syncopated melody and its almost ominous-sounding counterpoint, departs farthest from the actual theme, but the original dimensions and cadence structure are easily recognized.

In the repeats (**a**⁴′ and **b**⁴′), the piano works over this mysterious material more quickly and even more expressively.

The variations have gradually been getting more and more profound; only a great composer could have written this fourth variation. But the deepening serious mood of the piece is about to be shattered.

Starling, 34 Kroner

That was neat!

From Mozart's Account Book: the purchase of a bird that actually sang his Concerto in G

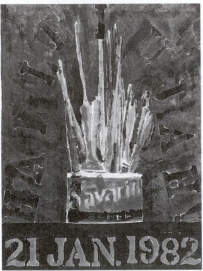

Variations in the visual arts: three monotypes (from a total of seventeen) by the contemporary American artist Jasper Johns. While the variations all differ from the "theme"—an actual coffee can with paint brushes, all bronzed—they never lose it entirely.

Variation 5   Suddenly a rather comical, loud march variation of the theme is presented by the orchestra, which has not been heard in full force since the opening of the movement. The solo cannot match anything as emphatic as this. So instead of a varied repeat, it takes an entirely new tack: it catches fresh interest by reintroducing the long-lost original version of the theme. The theme is certainly welcome back, after all the beautiful mystifications it has endured.

Section **b**⁵′ is extended; there is a slowdown, with a place that Mozart marked for the soloist to improvise a short cadenza (see page 124).

Coda   The riotous conclusion to this movement reminds us that for piano virtuosos of the Classical period, the theme and variations was meant to entertain and to dazzle. This unusual coda almost sounds as though it is starting up a new movement; but in fact most codas are unusual in one way or another— this is an element of the form that follows no rules.

One common feature of theme and variation codas is represented here: the return of the original theme in something very much like (but not exactly like) its original form.

LISTENING CHART 12

3 5-11 | 2 19-25 | 3A 2 | 1B 7

Mozart, Piano Concerto No. 17 in G, third movement

Variation form. 7 min., 48 sec.

Track	Time	Section	Description	Music
		Theme	Orchestra alone. Note the woodwind and horn figure at the cadences of **a** and **b**.	
	0:00	|: **a** :|		
	0:24	|: **b** :|		
6 20		**Variation 1**	Mainly piano, *p*; orchestral part is subsidary.	
	0:48	|: a^1 :|	Piano enters; plays theme with melodic decorations	
0:24	1:12	|: b^1 :|		
7 21		**Variation 2**	Mainly piano, more brilliant; woodwinds	
	1:36	a^2	Fast right-hand runs	
0:11	1:47	$a^{2\prime}$	Fast left-hand runs	
0:23	1:59	b^2	Right-hand runs	
0:35	2:11	$b^{2\prime}$	Left-hand runs	
8 22		**Variation 3**	Woodwinds alternating with piano	
	2:23	a^3	Songlike dialogue in woodwinds	
0:13	2:36	$a^{3\prime}$	Piano answers with its own version of the woodwind dialogue.	
0:25	2:48	b^3	Woodwinds	
0:39	3:02	$b^{3\prime}$	Piano	
9 23		**Variation 4**	Minor mode; strings alternating with piano, *p*	
	3:15	a^4	Strings play mysterious, syncopated counterpoint.	
0:12	3:27	$a^{4\prime}$	Strings answered by piano version; more expressive	
0:26	3:41	b^4	Orchestra	
0:40	3:55	$b^{4\prime}$	Piano	
10 24		**Variation 5**	Major mode; full orchestra alternating with piano, *f*	
	4:09	a^5	Strongly metrical march played by the orchestra	
0:12	4:21	$a^{5\prime}$	Piano counters with original theme, under a trill.	
0:25	4:34	b^5	March continues in orchestra.	
0:38	4:47	$b^{5\prime}$	Piano	
0:50	5:59		Short transition and slowdown	
11 25		**Coda**	Faster; orchestra in free, often rapid dialogue with the piano	
	5:21		Orchestra plays new theme and insistent cadential passage.	
0:19	5:40		Piano and orchestra play the new theme with new continuations.	
1:03	6:24		New version of the original theme (only |: **a″** :| and cadential passages)	
2:12	7:33		Ends with theme fragments echoed	

Mozart composing: a still from the 1984 film *Amadeus*. Mozart is known to have liked billiards; perhaps the cool, smooth, elegant aspects of the game struck some chord in his mind that resonated with his own music.

4 The String Quartet

Developed in the Classical era, the **string quartet** is a genre for four instruments: two violins, a viola, and a cello. ("String quartet" is also the name for a group of four musicians who work together playing quartets.) The plan for a string quartet, with its four movements, is very close to that of the symphony; compare page 182. Indeed, next to the symphony the quartet counts as the most important genre of Classical music.

The quartet may have as many movements as the symphony, but of course it doesn't have as many instruments, and cannot match the symphony's range of volume and tone color. This can disappoint listeners today. For the eighteenth century, however, volume was no issue, because quartets were never intended for concert listening. They were intended primarily for the performers, with small, informal audiences—or none at all.

The String Quartet

Opening Movement
   tempo: fast/moderate
   form: sonata form

Slow Movement
   tempo: slow/very slow
   form: no standard form
      (sometimes sonata form,
      variation form, rondo)

Minuet (with Trio)
   tempo: moderate
   form: minuet form

Closing Movement
   tempo: fast/very fast
   form: sonata form or
      rondo form

String quartets, then and now (below and next page). Nineteenth-century quartets were often led by celebrated violin soloists; shown here is a group led by a virtuosa of the time, Wilma Norman-Néruda (1838–1911). From left to right: two violins, viola (slightly larger), and cello.

The Juilliard Quartet, perhaps the leading American quartet, was formed at the Juilliard School in New York in 1946 and is still active. Two violins, cello, and viola.

As for range of tone color, the quartet compensates for this by its own special qualities: nuance, delicacy, and subtlety. Without any conductor, the quartet players are partners responding to one another as only old, close associates can. As developed by Haydn, the four instruments of the quartet grow more and more similar in their actual musical material, and more and more interdependent. There is a fine interplay as they each react to musical gestures by the others, sometimes supporting them, sometimes countering.

This interplay has been aptly compared to the art of cultivated conversation—witty, sensitive, always ready with a perfectly turned phrase—that was especially prized in eighteenth-century salons (page 152).

The Kronos Quartet, based in San Francisco, plays almost exclusively contemporary music, including jazz arrangements and other "crossover" items. Violinist, violinist, violist, and cellist.

Chamber Music

The string quartet was the main but not the only genre developed at this time for small forces in relatively intimate circumstances. **Chamber music** is a term for music designed to be played in a room (a chamber)—in a palace drawing room, or in a small hall. Chamber music can be taken as encompassing compositions for from two to nine players. Other types are the piano trio (violin, cello, piano) and string quintet (string quartet plus extra viola).

Broadly speaking, what has been said above about the intimate character of the quartet applies to all chamber music, though it is probably obvious that a string octet must be less subtle and more "orchestral" than a string trio.

LUDWIG VAN BEETHOVEN (1770–1827)
String Quartet in A, Op. 18 No. 5: Menuetto (1800)

As we shall see in Chapter 15, when Ludwig van Beethoven was a boy he hoped to study with Mozart, but the older composer—older by only fourteen years—died shortly before Beethoven found his way to Vienna in 1792. He studied instead with Haydn, and the first thing he had to learn was to perfect his command of the Viennese Classical style. His String Quartet in A is actually modeled on a quartet by Mozart in the same key, in which the minuet movement is placed second, rather than third, as usual.

First Movement (Allegro)   The neat, light-hearted opening movement, in sonata form, could easily be taken for a work by Haydn or Mozart. The first of several themes in the second group starts in the minor mode of the new key, changing to major. There is a witty coda that Haydn would have enjoyed.

Second Movement (Menuetto)   The minuet movement is more individual and distinctive, though it too adheres closely to the Classical style. Note the clear cadences, motivic repetitions, form, and general dimensions. One simple thing is novel, however: the quiet beginning, with only two instruments playing. This is a "stylized" dance with a vengeance. Its sound level is as far from the ballroom as is its delicate, distant, somewhat enigmatic mood.

The **b** section is more traditional—up to the point where a cadence in the minor mode turns gruff, even ominous. We are jolted when the music stops dead; but **a'** turns up as though nothing has happened. In **a"** three instruments conduct an ingenious little dialogue on the minuet's opening motive.

As is indicated on the Listening Chart, Beethoven moves his main musical lines elegantly from instrument to instrument (the cello, short-changed in this movement, gets its reward later). Next, with his contrasting trio, Beethoven shows us how the four instruments of the quartet can produce a truly full, rich sound, contrasting with the filigree of the minuet.

Third Movement (Andante cantabile)   For his slow movement, Beethoven wrote a set of variations on a very simple theme in |: **a** :| |: **b a'** :| form. Variations can give the simplest theme fresh interest—harmonic interest in Variation 4, and textural interest in Variation 5, which blows up quite a storm with the four quartet instruments, as though imitating an orchestra.

Fourth Movement (Allegro)   A speedy sonata-form movement concludes the Quartet in A. It is a brilliant demonstration of how well Beethoven had learned to manage the instrumental dialogue of the Classical string quartet.

The young composer thought it best to wait seven years in Vienna before bringing out his first symphony and his first set of string quartets. (We know he did a lot of sketching and revising, too.) To impress the city's connoisseurs, he needed to present them with music that would stand up to Haydn and Mozart, yet at the same time exhibit just the right amount of novelty.

They were in for a major surprise a few years later, when works like Beethoven's Fifth Symphony rocked the Classical style to its foundations. We shall discuss this composition in the next chapter.

LISTENING CHART 13

12-15   3

Beethoven, String Quartet in A, Op. 18 No. 5: Menuetto

Minuet form, 4 min., 55 sec.

MINUET (A)

	0:00	a	Two instruments only: violins 1 and 2
	0:12	a	The violins' music moved to viola and cello
13	0:25	b	For violin 1, with quiet acompaniment
			CADENCE in a minor key; low cello; *cresc.* → *ff*
0:24	0:49	a′	Violins 1 and 2
0:36	1:01	a″	Dialogue: violins 1 and 2 and viola
0:53	1:18	coda	Chordal, homophonic style
1:04	1:29	b a′ a″ coda	*repetition*

p

TRIO (B)

14	2:30	c	Melody in violin 2 and viola
	2:40	c	*repetition*
15	2:50	d	Melody in viola and cello, then violins and cello
	3:00	c′	Melody in violins 1 and 2
0:19	3:09	d c′	*repetition*

p   *sf*

MINUET (A)   *repetition of a a b a′ a″ coda*

---

5 Opera Buffa

In the late eighteenth century, comic opera grew to equal in importance the serious opera that was a hallmark of the Baroque era (see page 103). Roman emperors and their courtly confidants gave way to contemporary peasant girls and soldiers; castratos were edged aside by basses specializing in comical diatribes and exasperated "slow burns," the so-called *buffo* basses (Italian for "buffoon"). Happy endings were the result of pranks, rather than issuing from the decrees of magnanimous princes.

Opera stars had to be funny; they had to act, not just sing. The new flexibility of the Classical style was perfectly suited to the casual, swift, life-like effects that are the essence of comedy. As much as its humor, it was this "natural," lifelike quality of comedy that appealed to audiences of the Enlightenment.

Italian comic opera was the most important, though there were also parallel developments in Germany, France, and England. Serious Italian opera was called *opera seria;* comic Italian opera was called **opera buffa.** Just as Italian opera seria was very popular in London in Handel's time, so Italian opera buffa was in Vienna at the time of Haydn and Mozart. Thus Haydn, whose court duties with the Esterházys included running their opera house, wrote twelve comic operas—all in Italian. Mozart in his mature years wrote six comic operas, three in German (one is a one-acter) and three in Italian.

The Ensemble

Baroque opera seria, as we have seen (page 136), consists of two elements in alternation: recitatives for the dialogue and the action, and numbers that are fully musical—almost exclusively solo arias—for static meditation and "tableaus" of emotional expression. Classical opera buffa works with the same basic scheme, except that the fully musical numbers include *ensembles* as well as arias.

An <u>ensemble</u> is a number sung by two or (often) more people. And given the Classical composers' skill in incorporating contrast into their music, they were able to make their ensembles depict the different sentiments of the participating characters simultaneously. This meant that sentiments could be presented much more swiftly and vividly: swiftly, because we don't have to wait for the characters to sing whole arias to find out what they are feeling, and vividly, because the sentiments stand out in sharp relief one against the other.

The music also depicts these sentiments in flux. For in the course of an ensemble, the action proceeds and the situation changes. This is usually projected by means of new sections with different tempos, keys, and themes. A Classical opera ensemble, then, is a sectional number for several characters in which the later sections represent new plot action and the characters' new reactions to it.

In short, whereas the aria was essentially a static number, the ensemble was a dynamic one. At the end of a Baroque da capo aria (see page 138), the return of the opening music tells us that the dramatic situation is just where it was when the aria started. But at the end of a Classical ensemble, the drama has moved ahead by one notch or more, and the music, too, has moved on to something different. The ensemble transformed opera into a much more dramatic genre than had been possible within the Baroque aesthetic.

In a Haydn opera buffa ensemble, a whole lot of characters register different feelings both visually and musically—by their grimaces, their gestures, and the contrasting melodies they sing.

MOZART
Don Giovanni (1787)

Mozart wrote *Don Giovanni* in 1787 for Prague, the second largest city of the Austrian empire, where his music was enjoying a temporary spurt in popularity. While technically it counts as an opera buffa, *Don Giovanni* is neither a wholly comic drama nor wholly tragic. A somewhat enigmatic mixture of both—what might be called today a "dark comedy"—it seems to convey Mozart's feeling that events have both comical and serious dimensions, and that life's experiences cannot be pigeonholed.

Background   Don Giovanni is the Italian name for Don Juan, the semi-legendary Spanish libertine. The tale of his endless escapades and conquests is meant to stir up incredulous laughter, usually with a bawdy undertone. Certainly a subject of this kind belongs to opera buffa.

But in his compulsive, completely selfish pursuit of women, Don Giovanni ignores the rules of society, morality, and God. Hence the serious undertone of the story. He commits crimes and mortal sins—and not only against the women he seduces. He kills the father of one of his victims, the Commandant, who surprises Giovanni struggling with his daughter.

This action finally brings Don Giovanni down. Once, when he is hiding from his pursuers in a graveyard—and joking blasphemously—he is reproached by the marble statue that has been erected over the Commandant's tomb. He arrogantly invites the statue home for dinner. The statue comes, and when Giovanni refuses to mend his ways drags him off to *his* home, which is hell. The somber music associated with the statue was planted ahead of time by Mozart in the orchestral overture to *Don Giovanni*, before the curtain rises.

Thanks to Mozart's music, our righteous satisfaction at Don Giovanni's end is mixed with a good deal of sympathy for his verve and high spirits, his bravery, and his determination to lead a life of high comedy, ruled only by his own desires. The other characters in the opera too, awaken ambivalent feelings: they amuse us and move us at the same time.

On Monday the 29th the Italian opera company gave the eagerly awaited opera by Maestro Mozard, Don Giovanni, *or* The Stone Guest. *Connoisseurs and musicians say that Prague had never heard the like. Herr Mozard conducted in person; when he entered the orchestra he was received by three-fold cheers, as also happened when he left. The opera is extremely difficult to perform . . .*

Prague newspaper, 1787

"Repent, tell me you will live a new life: this is your last chance!" "No, never, let me alone!" "Repent, villain!" "Never, old fool!"

24th [of August, 1787]
A Piano Sonata with accompanying violin

28th of October
in Prague
The Reprobate Punished, or Don Giovanni: opera buffa in 2 acts.
24 musical numbers. Actors. Ladies: Teresa Saporitti, Bondini,
and Micelli. Gentlemen: Papi, Ponziani, Taglioni and Lolli.

3rd of November
Scena [operatic scene] for Mad.me Dušek. Recitative: "My lovely
flame." Aria: "Stay, dearest." Accompaniment:

		6th	
A Song	—	—	"Little Frederick's Birthday"
		ditto	
A Song	—	—	"The Phantom"

Act I, scene iii   The opera's third scene begins with a chorus of peasants, celebrating the betrothal of Masetto and Zerlina. Don Giovanni enters with his manservant Leporello and immediately takes a fancy to Zerlina. He promises Masetto various favors, and then tells him to leave—and tells Leporello to take him away by force if necessary.

Aria, "Ho capito"   This opera buffa aria, sung by Masetto, shows how vividly (and rapidly!) Mozart could define character in music. Singing almost entirely in very short phrases, Masetto almost insolently tells Don Giovanni that he will leave only because he has to, because great lords can always bully peasants. Then he rails at Zerlina in furious, fast asides; she has always been his ruin (an Italian peasant's honor is shattered when his woman is unfaithful). He sings a very sarcastic little tune when he promises her that Don Giovanni is going to make her into a fine lady:

ORCHESTRA   MASETTO

Fac-cia il nostro ca-va-lie-re Ca-va-lie-ra ancora te, ca-va-liera ancora te!

Toward the end of the aria he forgets all about Don Giovanni and the opening music that he employed to address him, and thinks only of Zerlina, repeating his furious words to her as well as his sarcastic tune. He gets more and more worked up as he sings repeated cadences, so characteristic of the Classical style. A variation of the tune, played by the orchestra, ends this tiny aria in an angry rush.

The total effect is of a simple man (judging from the music he sings) who nonetheless feels deeply and is ready to express his anger. There is also a clear undercurrent of class conflict: Masetto the peasant versus Don Giovanni the aristocrat. Mozart was no political radical, but he had indeed rebelled against court authority; and the previous opera he had written, *The Marriage of Figaro,* was based on a notorious French play that had been banned because of its anti-aristocratic sentiments. Two years after *Don Giovanni* was composed, the French Revolution broke out in Paris.

Mozart kept a little note-book in which he noted every new composition when it was finished. On the right (ruled) page he wrote the first few measures, and on the left the title. The pages shown include *Don Giovanni* (under the title *Il dissoluto punito,* which ultimately became the opera's subtitle).

Mozart met the Czech soprano Josefa Dušek in the 1770s, before moving to Vienna, and may have been involved with her in the 1780s.

Recitative   Next comes an amusing secco recitative, sung with just continuo accompaniment, as in Baroque opera (see page 137). Giovanni invites Zerlina up to his villa, promising to marry her and make her into a fine lady, just as Masetto had ironically predicted.

Duet, "Là ci darem la mano"   Operas depend on memorable tunes, as well as on musical drama. The best opera composers are able to write melodies that are not only beautiful in themselves, but also further the drama at the same time. Such a one is the most famous tune in *Don Giovanni,* the main tune in the following **duet** (an ensemble for two singers) between Don Giovanni and Zerlina.

Section 1 (Andante)   Don Giovanni sings his first stanza to a simple, unforgettable tune that combines seductiveness with a delicate sense of banter. When Zerlina sings the same tune to *her* first stanza, we know she is playing along, even though she hesitates (notice her tiny rhythmic changes, and her reluctance to finish the tune in eight measures—she delays for two more).

Andante

La ci darem la   mano,   La mi di-rai di si;   Ve-di, non e lon - ta - no, Par-tiam, ben mio, da   qui.

In stanza 3, as Don Giovanni presses more and more ardently, yet always gently, Zerlina keeps drawing back. Her reiterated "non son più forte" ("I'm weakening") makes her sound very sorry for herself, but also coy. When the main tune comes back—section 1 of the ensemble falls into a **A A′ B A″ coda** form—Giovanni grows more insistent, Zerlina more coquettish. The words they sing (from stanzas 1–3) are closer together than before, and even simultaneous. Taking a cue from the music, the stage director will place them physically closer together, too.

17 MAY 1788. *To the Opera.* Don Giovanni. *Mozart's music is agreeable and very varied.*

Diary of a Viennese opera buff, Count Zinzendorf

Section 2 (Allegro)   Zerlina falls happily into Don Giovanni's arms, echoing his "andiam" ("let us go"). The "innocent love" they now mean to celebrate is depicted by a little rustic melody (Zerlina is a peasant girl, remember) in a faster tempo. But a not-so-innocent sensuous note is added by the orchestra after the singers' first phrase in this section.

How neatly and charmingly an ensemble can project dramatic action; the whole duet leads us step by step through Don Giovanni's successful "technique." By portraying these people through characteristic action or behavior —Don Giovanni winning another woman, Zerlina playing her own coy game—Mozart exposes their personalities as convincingly as any novelist or playwright.

Don Giovanni and Zerlina, in an early engraving and in a modern production.

LISTEN   Mozart, *Don Giovanni:* from Act I, scene iii

3 3A
16-18 4

ARIA: "Ho capito"

Masetto:	Ho capito, *signor, si!*	I understand you, yes *sir!*
(to Don Giovanni)	Chino il capo, e me ne vò	I touch my cap and off I go;
	Ghiacche piace a voi così	Since that's what you want
	Altre repliche *non fò. . . .*	I have nothing else to say.
	Cavalier voi siete già,	After all, you're a lord,
	Dubitar non posso affè,	And I couldn't suspect you, oh no!
	Me lo dice la bontà,	You've told me of the favors
	Che volete *aver per me.*	You mean to do for me!
0:30 *(aside, to Zerlina)*	(Briconaccia! malandrina!	(You wretch! you witch!
	Fosti ognor la mia ruina!)	You have always been my ruin!)
(to Leporello)	Vengo, vengo!	Yes, I'm coming—
(to Zerlina)	(Resta, resta!	(Stay, why don't you?
	È una cosa molto onesta;	A very innocent affair!
0:44	Faccia il nostro cavaliere	No doubt this fine lord
	cavaliera ancora te.)	Will make you his lady, too!)

(last seven lines repeated)

RECITATIVE (with continuo only)

17	1:31	Giovanni:	Alfin siam liberati,	At last, we're free,
			Zerlinetta gentil, da quel scoccione.	My darling Zerlinetta, of that clown.
			Che ne dite, mio ben, so far pulito?	Tell me, my dear, don't I manage things well?
		Zerlina:	Ma signore, io gli diedi	But sir, I gave him
			Parola di sposarlo.	My word that we would be married.
		Giovanni:	Tal parola	That word
			Non vale un zero! voi non siete fata	Is worth nothing! You were not made
			Per esser paesana. Un'altra sorte	To be a peasant girl. A different fate
			Vi procuran quegli occhi bricconcelli,	Is called for by those roguish eyes,
			Quei labretti sì belli,	Those beautiful little lips,
			Quelle dituccie candide e odorose,	These slender white, perfumed fingers,
			Parmi toccar giuncata, e fiutar rose.	So soft to the touch, scented with roses.
		Zerlina:	Ah, non vorrei—	Ah, I don't want to—
		Giovanni:	Che non voreste?	What don't you want?
		Zerlina:	Alfine	To end up
			Ingannata restar! Io so che raro	Deceived! I know it's not often
			Colle donne voi altri cavalieri	That with women you great gentlemen
			siete onesti e sinceri.	Are honest and sincere.
		Giovanni:	È un' impostura	A slander
			Della gente plebea! La nobiltà	Of the lower classes! The nobility
			Ha dipinta negli occhi l'onestà.	Is honest to the tips of its toes.
			Orsù non perdiam tempo; in quest'istante	Let's lose no time; this very instant
			Io vi voglio sposar.	I wish to marry you.
		Zerlina:	Voi?	You?
		Giovanni:	Certo io.	Certainly, me;
			Quel casinetto è mio, soli saremo;	There's my little place; we'll be alone—
			E là, gioella mio, ci sposeremo.	And there, my precious, we'll be married.

DUET "Là ci darem la mano"

SECTION 1 Andante, **2/4** meter

18	2:58	Giovanni:	A	Là ci darem la mano	There [in the villa] you'll give me your hand,
				Là mi dirai di si!	There you'll tell me yes!
				Vedi, non è lontano;	You see, it isn't far—
				Partiam, ben mio, da qui!	Let's go there, my dear!
		Zerlina:	A′	Vorrei, e non vorrei;	I want to, yet I don't want to;
				Mi tremo un poco il cor.	My heart is trembling a little;
				Felice, è ver, sarei,	It's true, I would be happy,
				Ma può burlarmi ancor.	But he could be joking with me.
	3:39	Giovanni:	B	Vieni, mio bel diletto!	Come, my darling!
		Zerlina:		Mi fa pietà Masetto . . .	I'm sorry for Masetto . . .
		Giovanni:		Io cangierò tua sorte!	I shall change your lot!
		Zerlina:		Presto non son più forte . . .	All of a sudden I'm weakening . . .

(repetition of phrases [both verbal and musical] from stanzas 1–3)

3:59	Giovanni:	A″	Vieni, vieni! Là ci darem la mano	
	Zerlina:		Vorrei, e non vorrei . . .	
	Giovanni:		Là mi dirai di si!	
	Zerlina:		Mi trema un poco il cor.	
	Giovanni:		Partiam, ben mio, da qui!	
	Zerlina:		Ma può burlarmi ancor.	
4:27	Giovanni:	coda	Vieni, mio bel diletto!	
	Zerlina:		Mi fa pietà Masetto . . .	
	Giovanni:		Io cangierò tua sorte!	
	Zerlina:		Presto *non son più forte* . . .	
	Both:		Andiam!	

SECTION 2 Allegro, **6/8** meter

4:65	Both:		Andiam, andiam, mio bene,	Let us go, my dear,
			A ristorar le pene	And relieve the pangs
			D'un innocente amor.	Of an innocent love.

(words and music repeated)

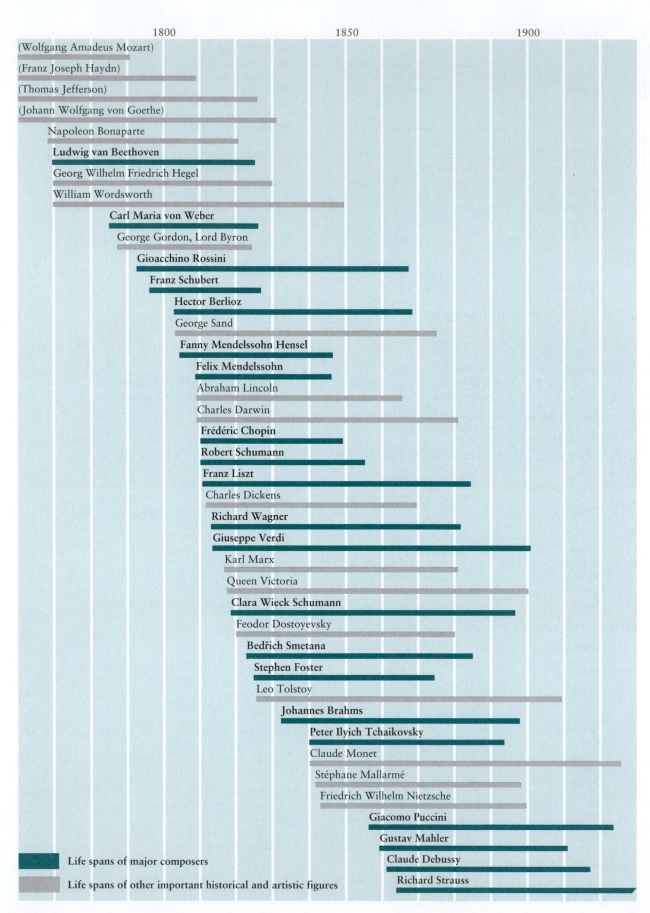

	1800	1850	1900

(Wolfgang Amadeus Mozart)

(Franz Joseph Haydn)

(Thomas Jefferson)

(Johann Wolfgang von Goethe)

Napoleon Bonaparte

Ludwig van Beethoven

Georg Wilhelm Friedrich Hegel

William Wordsworth

Carl Maria von Weber

George Gordon, Lord Byron

Gioacchino Rossini

Franz Schubert

Hector Berlioz

George Sand

Fanny Mendelssohn Hensel

Felix Mendelssohn

Abraham Lincoln

Charles Darwin

Frédéric Chopin

Robert Schumann

Franz Liszt

Charles Dickens

Richard Wagner

Giuseppe Verdi

Karl Marx

Queen Victoria

Clara Wieck Schumann

Feodor Dostoyevsky

Bedřich Smetana

Stephen Foster

Leo Tolstoy

Johannes Brahms

Peter Ilyich Tchaikovsky

Claude Monet

Stéphane Mallarmé

Friedrich Wilhelm Nietzsche

Giacomo Puccini

Gustav Mahler

Claude Debussy

Richard Strauss

▬ Life spans of major composers

▬ Life spans of other important historical and artistic figures

202

The Nineteenth Century

*I*n Unit IV we take up music of the nineteenth century. Starting with the towering figure of Beethoven in the first quarter of the century, famous names now
crowd the history of music: Schubert, Schumann, Chopin, Mendelssohn,
Berlioz, Wagner, Liszt, Verdi, Brahms, Tchaikovsky, Mahler, and others. Nearly
everyone, whether conscious of it or not, knows a fair amount of music by
these masters, or at least some of their timeless tunes. The latter have proved
their resilience by surviving Muzak, Mantovani, and mutilation into pop tunes
and advertising jingles.

Indeed, Romantic music—the music of the nineteenth century—is such a
strong presence in today's musical life that for some time people have been
troubled about musical progress, as if music were some kind of car spinning its
wheels in a rut. We need only observe that the appeal of this music in the symphony hall, the opera house, and the teaching studio today seems to rest on
much the same grounds as those governing its great success a hundred years
ago and more. It is important to realize, first of all, that nineteenth-century
music was a great success story. For the first time in history, music was taken
entirely seriously as an art on the highest level. Composers were accorded a
new, exalted role, to which they responded magnificently, writing music that
sounds important and impressive; and listeners ever since have been thoroughly
impressed.

Music and Individual Emotion

Music's prestige, in the Romantic scheme of things, derived first and foremost
from its unique power to convey individual feeling. Again, composers rose to
the challenge. Nineteenth-century music is more direct and unrestrained in
emotional quality than the music of any earlier time. And for most audiences,
full-blooded emotion in music—even exaggerated emotion—seems never to
lose its powerful attraction.

The individuality of all artists, including composers, was accorded special
value in the nineteenth century. Composers produced music with much more
pronounced personal attributes than in the late Baroque period or the Classical
period (when many pieces by Haydn and Mozart, for example, sounded rather
similar in character). It is therefore a natural tendency to think of the history of
nineteenth-century music in terms of great names, such as those in the list given

above. The prospect of getting to know all these distinct, unusual, and proba-
bly fascinating characters—meeting them, as it were, under the emotional con-
ditions of Romantic music—surely contributes to the appeal of this particular
body of music.

Like eighteenth-century music, music of the nineteenth century is not stylisti-
cally homogeneous, yet it can still be regarded as a larger historical unit. We
shall take up the Romantic style—usually dated from the 1820s—after dis-
cussing the music of Beethoven, who was born in 1770 and who traveled twice
to Vienna, the city of Classicism, in his youth—first to meet Mozart and then to
study with Haydn.

But while in technique Beethoven was clearly a child of the eighteenth
century, in his emotionalism, his artistic ambition, and his insistence on individ-
uality he was a true inhabitant of the nineteenth. Beethoven was, indeed, the
immediate or the remote model for almost every great nineteenth-century
composer who came after him. Understanding Beethoven is the key to an
understanding of Romantic music.

CHAPTER 15

Beethoven

I f any single composer deserves a special chapter in the history of music, that composer is Ludwig van Beethoven (1770–1827). Probably no other figure in the arts meets with such a strong universal response. People may pity Van Gogh, respect Michelangelo and Shakespeare, and admire Leonardo da Vinci, but Beethoven instantly summons up a powerful, positive image: that of the tough, ugly, angry genius delivering himself of one deeply expressive masterpiece after another in the teeth of adversity. Beethoven's music has enjoyed broad-based, uninterrupted popularity from his own day to the present. Today its place is equally secure with unsophisticated listeners and with the most learned musicians.

There is a sense, furthermore, in which music may be said to have come of age with Beethoven. For despite the great music that came before him—that of Bach, Mozart, and many other composers we know—the art of music was never taken so seriously until his symphonies and sonatas struck listeners of his time as a revelation. They were almost equally impressed by the facts of his life, in particular his deafness, the affliction that caused him to retire from a career as a performing musician and become solely a composer.

A new concept of artistic genius was evolving at the time, and Beethoven crystallized this concept powerfully for his own age. He still exemplifies it today. No longer a mere craftsman, the artist suffers and creates; endowed not just with greater talent but with a greater soul than ordinary mortals, the artist suffers and creates for humanity. Music is no longer merely a function of bodily parts like the ear or the fingers. It exists in the highest reaches of the artist's spirit.

There is much to be done on earth, do it soon!

I cannot carry on the everyday life I am living; art demands this sacrifice too. Rest, diversion, amusement—only so that I can function more powerfully in my art.

From Beethoven's journal, 1814

1 Between Classicism and Romanticism

Beethoven is special in another sense, in the unique position he occupies between the eighteenth-century Viennese Classical style and nineteenth-century Romanticism. Beethoven's roots were firmly Classical. He was a student of Haydn when the latter was at the height of his fame—and a very good student, too, as we already know from his early string quartets (see page 194). Indeed, Beethoven remained committed to the principles of the Classical style until the end of his life.

Beethoven was committed to the *principles* of Classicism—but not to every one of its manifestations, and certainly not to the mood behind it. There is almost always a sense of excitement, urgency, and striving in Beethoven's music that makes it instantly distinguishable from that of Haydn and Mozart. These qualities emerged in response to Romantic stirrings of a kind that we shall consider more carefully in the next chapter.

The French Revolution

Romanticism, as we shall see, was originally a literary movement. Though well under way by the beginning of the nineteenth century, it was not yet influential in Vienna; and, in any case, Beethoven did not have a very literary sensibility. At the root of Romanticism, however, there lay one great political event that made a profound impact on the composer's generation. This was the French Revolution. Beethoven was one of many artists who felt compelled to proclaim their sympathy with the ideal of freedom symbolized by that cataclysmic event.

When the Parisian crowd stormed the Bastille in 1789, Beethoven was a highly impressionable eighteen-year-old, already grounded in liberal and humanistic ideals. More than a decade later, Beethoven's admiration for Napoleon Bonaparte as hero of the revolution led him to an extravagant and unprecedented gesture—writing a descriptive symphony called *Bonaparte*. Retitled the *Eroica* (Heroic) Symphony, it was the decisive "breakthrough" work of Beethoven's maturity, the first work to show his full individual freedom as an artist.

Before Beethoven could send the symphony to Paris, Napoleon crowned himself Emperor of France. Liberal Europe saw this as a betrayal of the revolution, and Beethoven scratched out the title in fury. But idealism dies hard. To Beethoven, and to very many of his contemporaries, the French Revolution still stood for an ideal of perfectibility—not so much of human society (as Beethoven himself acknowledged by deleting Napoleon's name) as of human aspiration. That ideal, too, is what Beethoven realized by his own triumph over his deafness. The point was not lost on those of his contemporaries who were swept away by his music.

Storming the Bastille, a contemporary engraving of the most famous event of the French Revolution

And that is what listeners have responded to ever since. Listening to the
Eroica Symphony, we sense that it has less to do with Napoleon than with the
composer's own self-image. The quality of heroic striving and inner triumph is
what emerges so magnificently in Beethoven's most famous compositions.

2   Beethoven and the Symphony

As we have said, what sets Beethoven instantly apart from Haydn or Mozart is
his mood of excitement and urgency. This he achieved by maximizing virtually
all musical elements. Higher and lower registers, sharper syncopations,
stronger accents, harsher dissonances yielding to more profound resolutions—
all of these are found in Beethoven's music. He made new demands on instruments, expanded the orchestra, and stretched Classical forms to their limits.

Given all this, it is not surprising that this composer should be especially
associated with the symphony, the most "public" of Classical genres, with the
greatest range of expression, variety, and sheer volume. In fact, Beethoven
wrote fewer symphonies (nine) than piano sonatas (32) or string quartets
(16)—and no musician would rank these works one whit lower than the symphonies. But at the height of his career, from around 1800 to 1810, even many
of his piano sonatas and string quartets sound like symphonies. The torrents
of sound Beethoven summoned up in these works demanded whole new techniques of piano and string playing.

We can summarize Beethoven's "symphonic ideal" by reference to his Fifth
Symphony, written in 1808. Three main features have impressed generations
of listeners to this famous work: its rhythmic drive, its motivic unity, and the
sense it gives of a definite psychological progression. The first feature is appre-
hended at once, the second by the end of the opening movement, and the third
only after we have experienced all four of the symphony's movements.

*His clothes were very ordi-
nary and not in the least
in the customary style of
those days, especially in
our circles. . . . He was very
proud; I have seen Count-
ess Thun, the mother of
Princess Lichnowsky, on
her knees before him
begging him to play some-
thing—and he would not.
But then, Countess Thun
was a very eccentric
woman.*

An old lady remembers the
young Beethoven (1867)

Ludwig van Beethoven (1770–1827)

It must have been a miserable childhood. Beethoven's father, a minor musician at the court of Bonn in the west of Germany, tried unsuccessfully to promote him as an infant prodigy like Mozart. A trip to Vienna to make contacts (he hoped to study with Mozart) was cut short by the death of his mother. When he was still in his teens, Beethoven had to take charge of his family because of his father's drinking.

Nonetheless, Bonn was an "enlightened" court, ruled by the brother of the liberal Emperor Joseph II of Austria. The talented young musician had an opportunity to mix with aristocrats and intellectuals. The idealism that is so evident in Beethoven's later works—such as his Ninth Symphony, ending with a choral hymn to universal brotherhood—can be traced to this early environment.

Unlike Mozart, Beethoven was a slow developer, but by the age of twenty-two he had made enough of an impression to receive a sort of fellowship to study with Haydn in Vienna, then the musical capital of the world. He was soon acclaimed as a powerful virtuoso pianist, playing his own compositions at the palaces of the music-loving aristocracy of that city. He remained in Vienna until his death.

After the age of thirty, he became progressively deaf—a devastating fate for a musician, which kept him from making a living in the traditional manner, by performing. The crisis that this caused in Beethoven's life is reflected by a strange, moving document (called the "Heiligenstadt Testament," after the town where it was written, in 1802) that is half a proclamation of artistic ideals, half suicide note. But Beethoven overcame his depression and in 1803 wrote the first of his truly powerful and individual symphonies, the Third (Eroica).

Beethoven all but demanded support from members of the nobility in Vienna, who were awed by his extraordinarily forceful and original music as well as by his uncompromising character. An alarmingly brusque and strong-willed person, he suffered deeply and seemed to live for his art alone. His domestic life was chaotic; one anecdote has him standing in the middle of the floor and pouring water over himself to cool off in summer and being asked by his landlord to leave. (He changed lodgings an average of once a year.) At the end of his life he was well known on the streets of Vienna as an eccentric.

Probably the first musician to make a career solely from composing, Beethoven was regarded as a genius even in his lifetime. He had an immense need to receive and to give affection, yet he never married, despite various love affairs. After he died, passionate letters to a woman identified only as his "Immortal Beloved" were found; she has been identified as the wife of one of Beethoven's friends. In his later years Beethoven adopted his own orphan nephew, but his attitude was so overprotective and his love so smothering that the boy could not stand it and actually attempted suicide.

Beethoven had always lived with ill health, and the shock of this new family crisis hastened his death. Twenty thousand attended his funeral; his eulogy was written, and delivered at the funeral, by Vienna's leading poet.

Taste in many matters has changed many times since Beethoven's lifetime, but his music has always reigned supreme with audiences and critics. The originality and expressive power of his work seem never to fade.

Chief Works: Nine symphonies, the most famous being the Third (Eroica), Fifth, Sixth (Pastoral), Seventh, and Ninth (Choral) ■ The opera Fidelio (originally called Leonore), for which he wrote four different overtures; overtures to Egmont and Coriolanus ■ Violin Concerto and five piano concertos, including the Emperor (No. 5) ■ 16 string quartets ■ 32 piano sonatas, including the Pathétique, Waldstein, Appassionata, and the late-period Hammerklavier Sonata ■ Mass in D (Missa solemnis)

❧ *Rhythmic drive.* Immediately apparent is the drive and blunt power of the rhythmic style. Beethoven hammers the meter, piles accent upon accent, and calculates long time spans with special power: a far cry from the elegance and wit of the Classical style.

❧ *Motivic consistency.* During the first movement of the Fifth Symphony, a single motive is heard constantly, in many different forms. They are not random forms; the motive becomes more and more vivid and significant as the work proceeds. People have marveled at the "organic" quality of such music, which seems to them to grow like a plant's leaves out of a basic seed.

¶ Psychological progression. Over the course of the Fifth Symphony's four movements, Beethoven seems to trace a coherent and dramatic psychological progression in several stages. "There Fate knocks at the door!" he is supposed to have said about the first movement—but after two eventful middle stages, Fate is nullified in the last movement, trampled under by a military march.

In Beethoven's hands, the multimovement symphony seems to trace an inspirational life process, one so basic and universal that it leaves few listeners unmoved. This was, perhaps, the greatest of all his forward-looking innovations.

The Scherzo

Another of Beethoven's technical innovations should also be mentioned. On the whole, Beethoven continued to use Classical forms for his symphonies and other multimovement works. As early as his Second Symphony, however, he substituted another kind of movement for the traditional minuet.

This was the **scherzo** (*scaretzo*), which he had already experimented with in sonatas and quartets. The scherzo is a fast, rushing movement in triple meter—inherited from the minuet—and in the basic minuet-and-trio form, **A B A**. With their fast tempo, Beethoven's scherzos sometimes need more repetitions to make their point; **A B A** is sometimes extended to **A B A B A**.

The word *scherzo* means "joke" in Italian. Beethoven's brand of humor is very different from, say, Haydn's: broad, brusque, jocular, even violent. Clearly for Beethoven the mood of the Classical minuet was too closely associated with eighteenth-century formality and elegance. The scherzo became an ideal vehicle for Beethoven's characteristic rhythmic drive.

LUDWIG VAN BEETHOVEN
Symphony No. 5 in C Minor, Op. 67 (1808)

Beethoven composed his Fifth Symphony together with his Sixth *(Pastoral)* for one of the rare concerts in which he showcased his own works. This concert, in December 1808, was a huge success, even though it lasted for five hours and the heating in the hall failed.

Beethoven striding through Vienna: a caricature by one of his contemporaries

First Movement (Allegro con brio)   As we have already said, motivic consistency is a special feature of Beethoven's work. The first movement of the Fifth Symphony is dominated by a single rhythmic motive, ♪♪♪𝅗𝅥 . This motive forms the first theme in the exposition, initiates the bridge, appears as a subdued background to the lyrical, contrasting second theme, and emerges again in the cadence material:

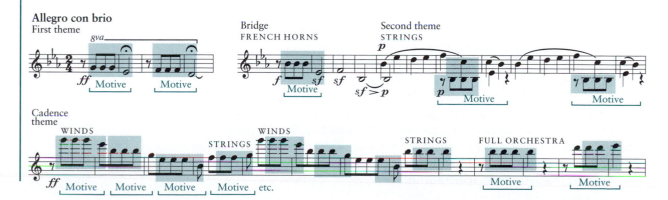

The motive then expands further in the development section and continues growing in the long coda.

How is this different from Classical motivic technique? In such works as Mozart's Symphony No. 40 and Haydn's Symphony No. 88, a single motive is likewise carried through an entire movement with consistency and a sense of growth. But the way Beethoven manages all this gives the Fifth Symphony its particular gripping urgency. The difference is not in basic technique but in the way it is being used—in the expressive intensity it is made to serve. Beethoven is using a Classical device here for non-Classical ends.

Exposition   The movement begins with an arresting presentation of the first theme, in the key of C minor (shown above). The meter is disrupted by two fermatas (see page 16), which give the music an improvisational, primal quality, like a great shout. Even after the theme rushes on and seems to be picking up momentum, it is halted by a new fermata, making three fermatas in all.

The horn-call bridge (see above) performs the usual function of a bridge in an unusually dramatic way. That function is to firmly cement the new key— a major key—and prepare the way for the second theme with power and authority.

The second theme introduces a new gentle mood, despite the main motive rumbling away below it. But this mood soon fades—Beethoven seems to brush it aside impatiently. The main motive bursts out again in a stormy cadence passage, which comes to a satisfying, complete stop. The exposition is repeated.

Development   The development section starts with a new explosion, as the first theme makes an immediate modulation, a modulation back to the minor mode. It sounds like the crack of doom.

For a time the first theme (or rather its continuation) is developed, leading to a climax when the ♪♪♪♩ rhythm multiplies itself furiously, as shown to the right. Next comes the bridge theme, modulating through one key after another. Suddenly the *two middle pitches* of the bridge theme are extracted and echoed between high wind instruments and lower strings. This process is called **fragmentation** (for an example from Mozart, see page 168). Then the two-note echoing figure breaks apart, and echoes start up on just one note:

Beethoven is famous for the tension he builds up in the retransition section of sonata form to prepare for recapitulations. In the Fifth Symphony, the hush at this point becomes almost unbearable. Finally the whole orchestra seems to grab and shake the listener by the lapels, shouting the main motive again and again until the first theme settles out in the original tonic key.

Actually, this is the same technique used by Haydn in preparing humorous thematic returns (see, for example, the rondo of Symphony No. 88, page 180). The opening motive of a theme is played over and over again until it serves as the kickoff for the theme itself. But in place of Haydn's wit, Beethoven gives a sense of tremendous, heroic achievement.

Went to a German charitable concert [the American premiere of Beethoven's Fifth Symphony]. . . . The music was good, very well selected and excellently well performed, as far as I could judge. The crack piece, though, was the last, Beethoven's Sinfonia in C minor. It was generally unintelligible to me, except the Andante.

Diary of a New York music lover, 1841

LISTENING CHART 14

3 1 3B 2A
19-27 25-33 1 1

Beethoven, Symphony No. 5 in C Minor, first movement

Sonata form. 7 min., 8 sec.

EXPOSITION

	0:02	**Theme 1**	Main theme with two fermatas, followed by the *first contin-uation* (based on ♩♩♩♩); another fermata (the third)
	0:20		Main motive (♩♩♩♩), *ff*, is followed by a *second continuation*: timpani, crescendo.
20 26	0:42	**Bridge theme**	French horn, *f*

Second Group

0:03	0:45	**Theme 2**	Major mode, *p*, strings and woodwinds (♩♩♩♩ in background)
21 27	1:13	**Cadence theme**	Based on ♩♩♩♩ motive
	1:21		CADENCE
0:09	1:22	***Exposition repeated***	

DEVELOPMENT

22 28	2:45		First modulation, using ♩♩♩♩ motive; French horns, *ff*; minor mode
	2:50		Development of *first continuation* of theme 1
0:30	3:15		Climactic passage of powerful reiterations: ♩♩♩ | ♩♩♩♩ | ♩♩♩♩ | ♩
0:34	3:19		Development of bridge theme
23 29	3:29		Fragmentation of bridge theme to two notes, alternating between strings and winds
0:09	3:38		Fragmentation of bridge theme to one note, alternating between strings and winds, *p*
0:28	3:57	**Retransition**	Based on ♩♩♩♩ , *ff*, runs directly into the recapitulation.

RECAPITULATION

24 30	4:02	**Theme 1**	Harmonized; two fermatas. *First continuation* of theme; woodwind background
			Slow oboe cadenza in place of the third fermata
0:33	4:35		*Second continuation* of theme 1
0:53	4:55	**Bridge theme**	Bassoons, *f*

Second Group

| 25 31 | 4:58 | **Theme 2** | Strings and winds, *p* (♩♩♩♩ in timpani); major mode |
| | 5:31 | **Cadence theme** | This time it does not stop. |

CODA

26 32	5:38		Another climax of reiterations (as in the development)
	5:52		New expanded version of bridge theme, in counterpoint with new scale figure; minor mode
0:29	6:07		New marchlike theme, brass; winds and strings build up.
27 33	6:39		Theme 1: climactic presentation in brass. Last fermata
	6:47		*First continuation* of theme 1, with a pathetic coloration; oboe and bassoon figures
0:13	6:52		Strong conclusion on ♩♩♩♩

Recapitulation   The exposition version of the main theme was jolted by three striking fermatas. Now, in the recapitulation, the third fermata is filled by a slow expressive cadenza for solo oboe. This extraordinary moment provides a brief rest from the incessant rhythmic drive. Otherwise the recapitulation stays very close to the exposition—a clear testimony to Beethoven's Classical allegiance.

Coda   On the other hand, the action-packed coda that follows is an equally clear testimony to Beethoven's freedom from Classical formulas.

In the exposition, we recall, the stormy cadence passage had been defused by a satisfying "Classical" cadence and a complete stop. At the end of the recapitulation, the parallel passage seems to reject any such easy solution. Instead, after a violent climax reminiscent of the development section, a new contrapuntal idea appears:

STRINGS, FRENCH HORNS

Compare the bottom contrapuntal line of this with the example on page 209. Here the main-theme *pitches* (G E♭ F D) are played in the bridge *rhythm* (♪♪♪ | ♩ ♩ | ♩), so that GGGE♭ FFFD becomes GGGE♭ F D. Then the two middle notes E♭ and F—the common ground between the themes—are emphasized by a long downward sequence.

The sequence evolves into a sort of grim minor-mode march—a moment of respite from the endless thematic evolutions of the main motive. A final appearance of the original theme leads this time to continuations that are unexpectedly poignant. But the very end of the movement consists of affirmative, defiant-sounding cadences, built once again out of the main motive.

The Remaining Movements

The defiant-sounding final cadence of the first movement feels like a standoff at the end of a heroic struggle. Beethoven now builds on this to give the impression of a dramatic psychological progression: another characteristic feature of his symphonic writing.

The later movements of the Fifth Symphony feel like responses to—and, ultimately, a resolution of—all the tension Beethoven had summoned up in the first movement. We are never allowed to forget the first movement and its mood, not until the very end of the symphony. The main reason for this is that a form of the first movement's rhythmic *motive,* ♪♪♪ ♩, is heard in each of the later movements. This motive always stirs uneasy recollections. Furthermore, the later movements all refer to the *key* of the first movement. Whenever this key returns in its original minor mode (C minor), it inevitably recalls the struggle that Beethoven associated with "Fate knocking at the door." When it returns in the major mode (C major), it signifies (or foretells) the ultimate resolution of all that tension—the triumph over Fate.

You need not worry about recognizing C major or distinguishing it from any other major-mode key. Almost any time you hear a very loud, triumphant theme in the later movements, it is in the key of C major. As important as the melody of those themes and their orchestration (often with brass) is the fact that they come in C major, thus negating the first movement's struggle.

A special abbreviated Listening Chart outline for the entire symphony is provided on page 214. All the C-major sections are indicated.

I expected to enjoy that Symphony [Beethoven's Fifth], but I did not suppose it possible that it could be the transcendent affair it is. I've heard it twice before, and how I could have passed by unnoticed so many magnificent points—appreciate the spirit of the composition so feebly and unworthily—I can't imagine.

From the same diary, 1844

A New Year's card from Beethoven to Baroness Ertmann, one of many women with whom his name has been romantically linked

A bizarre nineteenth-century impression of Beethoven's Fifth Symphony. The artist imagined all kinds of fateful (indeed, demonic) fancies behind the bland exterior of the orchestra players.

Second Movement (Andante con moto)   The first hint of Beethoven's master plan comes early in the slow movement, after the cellos have begun with a graceful theme, which is rounded off by repeated cadences. A second placid theme commences, but it soon gets derailed by a grinding modulation—to C major, where it is started again by the trumpets, *ff*.

This enormously solemn fanfare fades almost immediately into a mysterious passage where the ♪♪♪ ♩ rhythm of the first movement sounds quietly. Beethoven is not ready to "resolve" the C-minor turmoil of the first movement just yet. Variations of the first theme follow (one is in the minor mode), but there is something aimless about them. What stays in the memory from this movement are two more of those momentous fanfares in C major.

Third Movement (Allegro)   This movement, in **3/4** time, is one of Beethoven's greatest scherzos (though the composer did not label it as such, probably because its form is so free). There are two features of the smooth, quiet opening theme (**a**) that immediately recall the mood of the first movement—but in a more muted, apprehensive form. One is the key, C minor. The other is the interruption of the meter by fermatas.

Then a forceful second theme (**b**), played by the French horns, recalls in its turn the first movement's rhythmic motive. The two themes alternate and modulate restlessly, until the second makes a final-sounding cadence.

When now a bustling and somewhat humorous fugal section starts in the major mode—in C major—we may recognize a vestige of the old minuet and trio form, **A B A** (though the **A** section, with its two sharply contrasted themes **a** and **b**, has nothing in common with a minuet beyond its triple meter). **B**, the major-mode "trio," is in the traditional |: c :|: d c′ :| form, but with an important modification. The second **d c′** is reorchestrated, becoming quieter and quieter.

After this, the return of the opening minor-mode music, **A′**, is transformed in tone color. Hushed *pizzicato* (plucked) strings for **a** and a brittle-sounding oboe for **b** replace the smooth and forceful sounds heard before. Everything now breathes a quite unexpected mood, approximating mystery, numbness, even terror.

Fourth Movement (Allegro)   The point of this reorchestration appears when the section does not reach a cadence but runs into a marvelous ghostly transition passage, with timpani tapping out the rhythm of **b** over a strange harmony. The music gets louder and louder and clearer and clearer until a forceful military march erupts—in the key, needless to say, of C major.

First movement:

$\frac{2}{4}$ 𝄾 ♪♪♪ ♩ 𝄾 ♪♪♪ ♩

Third movement (b):

$\frac{3}{4}$ ♩ ♩ ♩ ♩. ♩ ♩ ♩ ♩.

LISTENING CHART 15

3   1   3B   2A
19-33   25-39   1-3   1-3

Beethoven, Symphony No. 5 in C Minor (complete work)

31 min., 2 sec.

	FIRST MOVEMENT (Allegro con brio, 2/4; sonata form)		C minor, *ff*	

See Listening Chart 14.

SECOND MOVEMENT (Andante, 3/8; variations)   Ab major, *p*

28 34	0:00	Theme 1	Ends with repeated cadences	
	0:54	Theme 2	Played by clarinets and bassoons	
	1:15		Trumpets enter.	(goes to C MAJOR, *ff*)
	2:01	Theme 1	Variation 1, played by strings	
	2:52	Theme 2	Clarinets and bassoons	
	3:14		Trumpets enter.	(goes to C MAJOR, *ff*)
	3:59	Theme 1	Variations 2–4, ending *f*; then a quiet transition: woodwinds	
	5:56	Theme 2	Trumpets	C MAJOR, *ff*
29 35	6:42	Theme 1	Variations 5 (minor; woodwinds) and 6 (full orchestra); cadences	
	8:11	**Coda**		Ab major

a   CELLOS

b   FRENCH HORNS

THIRD MOVEMENT (Scherzo, 3/4; A B A′)   C minor, *pp*

Scherzo (A)

30 36	0:00	a b		
	0:38	a′ b′		
0:38	1:16	a″ b″	Ends with a loud cadence built from **b**	

Trio (B)   C MAJOR, *ff*

c   DOUBLE BASSES

31 37	1:47	‖: c :‖	Fugal	
	2:17	d c′		
0:57	2:44	d c′	Reorchestrated, *p;* runs into scherzo	(goes to C minor, *pp*)

Scherzo (A′)

1:27	3:14		Scherzo repeated, shorter and reorchestrated, *pp*	
2:39	4:26	**Transition**	Timpani; leads directly in to the fourth movement	

(goes to C MAJOR, *ff*)

with TROMBONES

FOURTH MOVEMENT (Allegro, 2/2; sonata form)

Exposition

32 38	0:00	Theme 1	March theme.
	0:37	Bridge theme	Low horns and bassoons.
1:05	1:05	Theme 2	
1:34	1:34	Cadence theme	

Development

2:06	2:06		Development begins; modulation	
	2:12		Theme 2 developed	
33 39	3:43	**Retransition**	Recall of the scherzo (A′, 3/4 meter)	(recall of C minor, *pp*)

Recapitulation   C MAJOR *ff*

0:35	4:18	Theme 1	
1:11	4:54	Bridge theme	
1:43	5:26	Theme 2	
2:11	5:54	Cadence theme	

Coda

2:42	6:25		Lengthy coda, in several sections, uses elements C MAJOR, *ff*
			of the bridge, cadence theme, and theme 1. Accelerates!

Beethoven's "Third Period"

Beethoven's output is traditionally divided into three style periods. The first period (until around 1802) covers music basically in the style of Haydn and Mozart, such as the Quartet in A, Op. 18 No. 5 (see page 194). The second period contains characteristically "heroic" works like the *Eroica* and Fifth Symphonies.

In the third period (from around 1818 to 1827) Beethoven's music loses much of its earlier tone of heroism. It becomes more abstract, introspective, and serene, and tends to come framed in more intimate genres than the symphony, such as the piano sonata and the string quartet. His control of contrast and musical flow becomes more potent than ever, and a new freedom of form leads to a range of expression that can only be called miraculous, encompassing all the strength of his earlier music together with a new gentleness and spirituality.

To give just an idea of at least the outer aspects of Beethoven's late music, we can mention a few features of his very moving Sonata in A flat, Op. 110, of 1822:

In the *first* movement, one of the key thematic elements is not a melody or a motive, but merely a filmy piano arpeggio, and this returns transformed in later movements. Instead of the usual slow movement, the *second* is a near-frantic scherzo (in **2/4** meter, not the usual **3/4**) which quotes from two comic songs of the day. Meditative music in the style of an opera recitative leads to a sorrowful melody, like an aria; if this is the *third* movement, it has an unusual relationship with the *fourth*, a quiet fugue that seems to offer consolation. For after the fugue the lament returns, and then so does the fugue. We hear the fugue subject with a flood of recognition: it is a variation of the main theme of the first movement.

Through the use of fugue, clearly a throw-back to the Baroque era, Beethoven's music achieves a sort of historical dimension. And indeed, the expressive world of the third-period music was not appreciated in its own historical time. It came into its own as an inspiration for composers—and listeners—only in the twentieth century.

Minor cedes to major, *pp* to *ff,* mystery to clarity; the arrival of this symphony's last movement has the literal effect of triumph over some sort of adversity. This last movement even brings in three trombones, for the first time in the symphony. (They must have really awakened the freezing listeners at that original 1808 concert.)

The march turns out to be the first theme of a sonata-form movement; the second theme includes a speeded-up version of the ♪♪♪♩ rhythm. The end of the development section offers another example of Beethoven's inspired manipulation of musical form. The second theme (b) of the previous movement, the scherzo, returns quietly, a complete surprise in these surroundings (there is even a change from the **4/4** meter of the march back to **3/4**). This theme now sounds neither forceful nor ghostly, as it did in the scherzo, but rather like a dim memory. Perhaps it has come back to remind us that the battle has been won.

All that remains is a great C-major celebration, in the recapitulation and then later in a huge accelerating coda. "There Fate knocks at the door"—but fate and terror alike yield to Beethoven's optimistic major-mode vision.

A modern impression of Beethoven in his later years. The artist has captured both the famous scowl of defiance, and also the chaotic state of Beethoven's household—the broken piano strings, the sheets of musical sketches all over the place, and the useless ear trumpets.

CHAPTER 16

Prelude
Music after Beethoven: Romanticism

B *aroque,* as a designation for a historical style period in music, was adopted by musicologists from the field of art history many years after the period in question. The term *Romantic* was adopted from literature—and it was adopted by the literary Romantics themselves. When the first Romantic composers began their careers in the 1820s, their literary contemporaries were already excitedly talking about "Romantic" music.

This may seem like just one more footnote to history, but it tells us two important things about music after the time of Beethoven. One is that largely thanks to Beethoven, people had become highly aware of music as a major art. Music was treated with a new respect in cultivated circles; it was taken seriously in a way it never had been before.

The other is that it seemed quite natural for observers of the time to link up developments in music with parallel developments in literature. From Homer and Virgil to Shakespeare and Milton, literature had always been considered the most important and most convincing of the arts. The prestige and power of literature were now freely extended to music.

This fact is illustrated in a highly Romantic—not to say romanticized—painting that was popular at midcentury, showing a group of celebrities of the time listening to Franz Liszt at the piano (page 217). Their expressions tell us how profoundly the music moves them; their aesthetic experience is very different, clearly, from the casual enjoyment of eighteenth-century listeners pictured on page 157. For the nineteenth century, Beethoven's symphonies had been a revelation of music's profundity. It is not accident then, that in the Liszt painting a larger-than-life bust of Beethoven rests on the piano, and that Liszt gazes on it so soulfully.

1 Romanticism

Romantic literature and literary theory flourished particularly in and around the first two decades of the nineteenth century. In England, this was the great age of Wordsworth, Coleridge, Shelley, Keats, and Byron. There was also a brilliant outpouring of German Romantic literature at the same period, though the names of its writers are less familiar in the English-speaking world: Tieck, Novalis, Kleist, Hölderlin, and E. T. A. Hoffmann.

The power of Romantic music: Liszt as the inspiration for novelists Alexandre Dumas, Victor Hugo, George Sand, Daniel Stern (on the floor), legendary violinist Niccolò Paganini, and opera composer Gioacchino Rossini.

For us, the word *romantic* refers to love; this usage dates from the nineteenth century and derives from the literary movement. But the glorification of love was only one of the many themes of Romantic literature, themes that were also central to the music of the nineteenth century.

The Cult of Individual Feeling

A forefather of Romanticism was Jean Jacques Rousseau—the same Enlightenment philosopher who had spoken up in the mid-eighteenth century for "natural" human feelings, as opposed to the artificial constraints imposed by society. He also spoke up for simple, "natural" music, particularly in comic opera. Rousseau was hailed as the ideological father of the French Revolution; his music was played at revolutionary ceremonies. His call for individual human fulfillment met an even deeper, more universal response.

Striving for a better, higher, ideal state of being was at the heart of the Romantic movement. Everyday life, to the Romantics, seemed dull and meaningless; it could be transcended only through the free exercise of individual will and passion. The rule of feeling, unconstrained by convention, religion, or social taboo (or anyone else's feelings, often enough)—this became the highest good, and emotional expression became the highest artistic goal. "Bohemians," as they were disparagingly called at the time, proclaimed romantic love, led irregular lives, and wore odd clothes. We have the Romantics to thank for one familiar image of the artist that is still around today.

Romanticism and Revolt

But social convention opposed individual freedom, and so the Romantics were inevitably cast in the role of rebels against the established order. By the end of the eighteenth century, an entire generation of writers and artists was striving actively for freedoms of every kind.

Revolution was the central fact in the politics of the age, beginning with our own American Revolution. The French Revolution of 1789 traumatized Europe as deeply as did the Russian Revolution in our century. It was followed by a whole set of aftershocks up to 1848, a year of major upheavals in France, Germany, Austria, and Italy.

Many composers associated themselves with libertarian politics, starting with Beethoven, who wrote a symphony named *Bonaparte* (which he renamed the *Eroica*). In a later generation, Liszt briefly espoused a strange half-communistic, half-religious movement founded by Father François Lammenais; Giuseppe Verdi's name became an acronym for the Italian liberation movement; and Richard Wagner was thrown out of Germany in 1849 for inflammatory speeches he made from the revolutionary barricades in the town of Dresden.

Along with political revolution went social revolution. The barriers of hereditary nobility were breached, and the lower and middle classes assumed more social mobility. Thus Franz Liszt, who was the son of an estate foreman, could conduct glamorous liaisons—one stormy, the other stable—with a French countess and a Russian princess. The importance of this was not lost on Liszt's contemporaries; the countess is another of the celebrities included in the picture of Liszt at the piano (though the artist tactfully hid her face).

Visible on Paris's most prominent monument, the Arc de Triomphe, is this 1836 representation of *La Marseillaise,* the great rallying song of the French revolution.

Romanticism and the Macabre

The dark side to the cult of individual feeling was also nurtured. In their pursuit of emotional sensation of all kinds, the Romantics did not neglect cruelty and violence, fantasy and nightmare. In *Nightmare,* a weird picture by the early Romantic painter Henry Fuseli, the combination of horror, irrationality, and sexuality is a forecast of many such effusions to come.

The supernatural loomed large in the Romantic firmament. The Grimms' fairy tales—with their frequently ominous undertone—were as characteristic of the era as Johann Wolfgang von Goethe's great dramatic poem about Faust pledging his soul to the Devil for a single moment of transcendent happiness. Mary Shelley wrote *Frankenstein* in 1818. An opera about vampires was composed a little later—*Der Vampyr,* by the German composer Heinrich Marschner. The American writer most admired in nineteenth-century Europe was that specialist in the macabre, Edgar Allan Poe.

Composers cultivated strange harmonies and sinister orchestral sounds as their contribution to this aspect of Romanticism; such sounds can still be heard on some television soundtracks today. A famous scene of devilish conjuration in a deep forest, the Wolf's Glen scene in Carl Maria von Weber's opera *Der Freischütz* ("The Magic Bullet," 1821), was the first impressive monument to Romanticism in music. Verdi wrote spooky music for the witches in his Shakespeare opera *Macbeth,* and Wagner did the same for the ghost ship and its spectral crew in *The Flying Dutchman.* And in the *Fantastic* Symphony, Hector Berlioz wrote a movement called "Dream of a Witches' Sabbath" that bears comparison with Fuseli's *Nightmare.*

Nightmare, by Henry Fuseli, an eighteenth-century pre-Romantic painter, poet, and revolutionary who emigrated from Switzerland to England for political reasons.

Romantic Nostalgia

Romanticism's dissatisfaction with the real world pointed on the one hand to revolution, and on the other to fascination with the past. Indeed, the term *romantic* comes originally from "romance," meaning a type of long medieval narrative poem or story. Both music and the visual arts followed literature in this nostalgia for the mysterious Middle Ages.

In literature, taste in fiction moved away from contemporary subjects, such as *Tom Jones* and *Pride and Prejudice,* to tales of historical adventure,

The Fall of an Avalanche in the Grisons, by J. M. W. Turner (1775–1851)

such as *Ivanhoe* and *The Hunchback of Notre Dame.* Poems were often set in times of yore—Scott's "Lochinvar," Keats's "La Belle Dame sans Merci," and Tennyson's *Idylls of the King,* a lengthy work in "romance" style about King Arthur and the Knights of the Round Table. Longfellow's *Song of Hiawatha* is an American example of the same sort of work as the *Idylls*—a grandiose blend of Romanticism, nostalgia, and national pride.

But the best example of all is Richard Wagner's four-evening opera *The Ring of the Nibelung,* based on the main early medieval Nordic cycle of myths. One of the towering art works of the century, the *Ring* tells how the world ruled by Wotan, king of the gods, is corrupted by gold and then redeemed by the love of Wotan's daugher Brünnhilde and the hero Siegfried. Wagner himself wrote the words, a cloudy but powerful tract with political, ethical, and nationalistic overtones.

Some composers experimented with real or simulated old music to give their work an antique flavor. There was something of a cult at this time for the famous Renaissance composer Giovanni Pierluigi da Palestrina (see page 77). Though Palestrina lived in the sixteenth century, long after the Middle Ages, he was the earliest composer whose music was known in the early nineteenth century. The modal harmony and spiritual style of Palestrina's church music were much admired and imitated.

Artistic Barriers

The Romantics' search for higher experience and more intense expression provoked a reaction against the restraints of artistic form and genre. Artists resisted all rules and regulations, any abstract notions of "beauty" or "decorum" that they felt might hamper their spontaneity.

An American Romantic painting of a newer myth: *Daniel Boone and His Cabin on the Great Osage Lake,* by Thomas Cole (1801–1848)

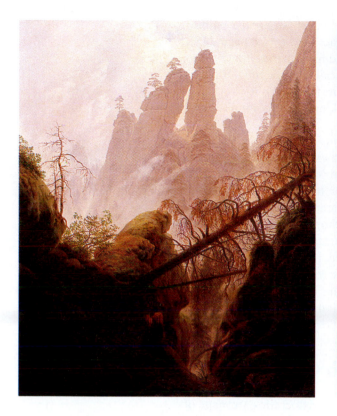

Two Romantic depictions of nature: *Mountainous Landscape* by Caspar David Friedrich (left) and *The Bard* by John Martin (right). The paintings suggest both the menacing and inspirational aspects of nature.

Eighteenth-century drama, for example, was hemmed in by such rules until the Romantics overturned them, citing the works of Shakespeare. Locations change dizzily from scene to scene in Shakespeare's plays, as tragedy clashes with farce, rich poetry with bawdy prose, and noble characters with clowns. The lifelike turbulence and the loose, casual form of these plays made Shakespeare enormously popular in the nineteenth century. The list of composers who wrote music associated with them is practically endless, from Mendelssohn and Berlioz to Tchaikovsky, Wagner, and Verdi.

In music itself, composers worked to break down barriers of harmony and form. All the Romantic composers experimented with chords, or chord progressions, that had previously been forbidden by the textbooks. From the time of Schubert on, their music was enriched by imaginative new harmonies. And sonata form, the hallmark of Classicism, was treated so freely in Robert Schumann's piano sonatas, written in the 1830s, that he finally labeled the last (and greatest) of them "Fantasy"—a proclamation of his spontaneity on the one hand, and insurance against accusations of "breaking the rules" on the other.

Music and the Other Arts

"Shakespearean," open-ended, sometimes fragmentary, and above all contemptuous of formal barriers are the characteristics of Romantic art. Efforts were made to blend the arts together: poetry became more "musical," paintings and musical works were given "poetic" titles, and poetry, drama, music, and stagecraft merged in Wagner's unique and enormously influential "total art work," or *Gesamtkunstwerk*. Within individual arts, blurred effects were cultivated—half-obscure verbal meanings, ambiguous shapes and color blends, and musical sounds that are imprecise but rich and evocative.

No one went further in this respect than the English landscape painter J. M. W. Turner, with his swashes of nearly "abstract" color (see page 219). Whereas Rousseau in the eighteenth century had admired nature for its simplicity, Turner in the nineteenth captured what was called at the time its "sublime" quality: the majesty and mystery of nature, its boundlessness, even its menace. The great Romantic artists stared unblinkingly at the infinite, and tried to set it down in their art.

And it was exactly the boundless quality of music that gave it its enormous prestige and status. Music, people felt, could express inner experience more deeply than the other arts because the musician's imagination is not tied down to the meaning of words (like the poet's) or to the representation of things (like the painter's). The special place of music in the Romantic scheme of things was forcefully expounded by Arthur Schopenhauer, a much-read German philosopher of the time. Wagner's opera *Tristan und Isolde* practically spells out Schopenhauer's philosophy, as we shall see.

"All art aspires to the condition of music," wrote a famous Victorian critic, Walter Pater. All Romantic art tried to capture music's depth and freedom of emotional expression, and its continuous, "infinite" quality.

2 Concert Life in the Nineteenth Century

First introduced in the Baroque era, during the age of aristocratic patronage of the arts, public concerts rapidly grew more important in the days of Haydn, Mozart, and Beethoven. As the nineteenth century progressed, the concert hall came to dominate the presentation of music. Every town of any size had its symphony association, organized by merchants, bankers, government officials, lawyers, and other members of the middle class. The concert halls built to accommodate symphony concerts were also expressions of civic pride. In May of 1891 the New York Symphony, that city's second orchestra (the New York Philharmonic was founded in 1842) proudly presented a five-concert music festival led by Tchaikovsky in brand-new Carnegie Hall.

Ground-breaking ceremony for Carnegie Hall in New York (visible is the famous railroad and steel baron Andrew Carnegie, the donor) and the program of the first music festival there

By the end of the century even intimate, "domestic" musical genres, designed for the drawing room or the studio, were presented on the concert stage. Concerts of *Lieder* (songs) and quartet concerts became established, though they were not as important as orchestral concerts. Concerts made more and more music available to more and more people. Improved transportation brought musicians on tour to remote areas, such as the American west.

However, the institutionalization of concert life also had its negative aspect, in that audiences gradually became more conservative in their musical tastes. The old aristocratic system had actually been more neutral in this respect. While many aristocratic patrons cared less about music than display, and some exercised the most whimsical of tastes, others actually encouraged composers to pursue new paths, or at least left them alone to do so. On the other hand, the concert public tended to conservatism. The mainly middle-class buyers of concert tickets naturally wanted "value," as with anything else they bought. What counted as value was something already established as a "masterpiece," something that they already knew and liked.

The Artist and the Public

For the reasons above, composers with an interest in innovation—and that includes every composer discussed in this unit—felt at one time or another that their work was being neglected by the concert world. A paradoxical situation developed. The composer's dependence on the public was tinged with resentment, and the public's admiration for composers was tinged with distrust, even hostility.

Thus the composer Robert Schumann started an important magazine to campaign for Romantic music, in the face of public indifference to serious art and preference for what he regarded as flashy trivia. Editor Schumann invented a "League of David" to slay the "Goliath" of the concert audience (Goliath was the champion of the Philistines; it was around this time that the adjective "philistine" came to mean "uncultured"). Later, the music of Liszt and Wagner was attacked by hostile critics as formless, dissonant, and overheated. Later still, the symphonies of Gustav Mahler were repeatedly rejected in Vienna, in spite of Mahler's important position as head of the Opera there.

The gap between innovative music and a conservative concert public, which opened up in the nineteenth century, widened in the twentieth, as we shall see. Here as elsewhere, the nineteenth century set the tone for twentieth-century musical life.

3   Style Features of Romantic Music

Since the main artistic value in the Romantic era was the integrity of personal feeling, every genuine artist was expected to have a personal style. Many artists cultivated styles that were highly personal and even eccentric. Furthermore, Romanticism's constant striving after ever-new states of consciousness put a premium on innovation; this could be seen as an exciting breaking down of artistic barriers on the one hand, and as a heroic personal breakthrough on the other. Consequently it is harder to define the Romantic style in general than to spot innovations, novelties, and individual peculiarities.

To be sure, nineteenth-century composers were united by some common interests, which will be discussed below: technical interests concerning melody, harmony, tone color, and perhaps especially musical form. But it is important to remember that one such common interest was to sound different from everybody else.

Rhythm: Rubato

The general Romantic tendency to blur all sharp edges found its musical coun-
terpart in the rhythmic practice of *tempo rubato,* or just **rubato.** Rubato
means that in musical performance the rhythm is handled flexibly; the meter
itself may waver, or else the beat is maintained strictly in the accompaniment
while the melody is played or sung slightly out of phase with it. (Literally
tempo rubato means "robbed time"—that is, some time has been "stolen"
from the beat—but the beat is likely to be slowed and the time "given back" a
moment later.)

Rubato was practiced in the service of greater individual expressivity.
Though seldom indicated in a score—indeed, no one has ever found an accurate way to indicate rubato in musical notation—its practice is documented by
old recordings, made around 1900 by musicians who were close to the
Romantic composers (or even by the composers themselves). Improvisation, in
the sense of adding notes to a score, gradually died out during the nineteenth
century. But performers of the time improvised rhythmically, in that they applied rubato freely to nearly every score they played.

Considered a sign of bad taste in Baroque or Classical music, at least
when applied vehemently, rubato is an essential expressive resource in the
playing, singing, and conducting of Romantic music. A musician's sensitivity
and "feeling" depends to a great extent on his or her artistic use of rubato.

Romantic Melody

The most instantly recognizable feature of Romantic music is its melodic style.
Melody in the Romantic era is more emotional, effusive, and demonstrative
than before. Often the melodic lines range more widely than the orderly, restrained melodies of the Classical era; often, too, they build up to more sustained climaxes. Melodies became more irregular in rhythm and phraseology,
so as to make them sound more spontaneous.

A fine example is the so-called "love" theme of Tchaikovsky's Overture-
Fantasy *Romeo and Juliet* (page 270). It begins with a great outburst—a climax, at the very start—and then sinks down an octave and more, in melodic
curves whose yearning quality grows more and more sensuous. Especially
striking is the second part of the melody, where a rhythmic figure surges up
and up, seven times in all, before exploding into a free return of the first part:

When one thinks of Romantic melody, what comes first to mind is the
grand, exaggerated emotionality of Tchaikovsky, perhaps, or Mahler. Some
Romantic melodies are more intimate, however—and they are no less emotional for sparing the handkerchief, as it were. Each in an individual way,
Romantic composers learned to make their melodies dreamy, sensitive, passionate, ecstatic, or whatever shade of feeling they chose to express.

Romantic Harmony

Harmony was one of the areas in which Romantic music made the greatest technical advances. On the one hand, composers learned to use harmony to underpin melody in such a way as to bring out its emotionality. Romantic melody is, in fact, inseparable from harmony. In the *Romeo and Juliet* love theme, for example, a rich new chord goes hand in glove with the warm upward scoop of the melodic line in measure 5.

On the other hand, harmony was savored for its own sake, and composers experimented freely with new chord forms and new juxtapositions of chords. These, it was found, could contribute potently to those mysterious, sinister, rapturous, ethereal, or sultry moods that Romantic composers sought to evoke. There are even some themes and motives in Romantic music that gain their memorable quality from harmony, rather than from melody and rhythm, as in earlier music (see page 263).

Chromaticism is a term for a style that employs all twelve notes of the chromatic scale (see page 19) liberally. Baroque and Classical style is not "chromatic" in this sense, but all Romantic composers pursued chromaticism to some extent, in order to expand the expressive range of both their melodies and their harmony. If you look at the *Romeo and Juliet* theme, you will find nearly all twelve notes of the chromatic scale included—something that seldom if ever happens in earlier music. Chromaticism was carried furthest in the nineteenth century by Richard Wagner, and further yet by the early twentieth-century modernists.

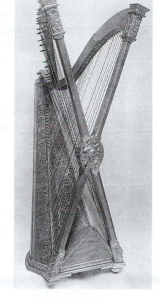

A response to the increased chromaticism of nineteenth-century music, this bizarre harp was really two harps, criss-crossed, to accommodate all the notes of the chromatic scale.

The Expansion of Tone Color

While tone color had been treated with considerable subtlety by the Viennese Classical composers, the Romantics seized on this aspect of music with particular enthusiasm. For the first time in Western music, the sheer sensuous quality of sound assumed major artistic importance on a level with rhythm, melody, and musical form.

All instruments went through major technical developments during the nineteenth century—the piano not least. As orchestral instruments reached their present-day forms, the orchestra was expanded, soon reaching its present standard make-up. The chart below for a typical Romantic orchestra, when compared with the Classical orchestra chart on page 159, shows how the ranks of the brass, woodwind, and percussion sections were filled out:

A TYPICAL ROMANTIC ORCHESTRA

STRINGS	WOODWINDS	BRASS	PERCUSSION
First violins (12–16 players)	2 Flutes	4 French horns	3 Timpani
Second violins (12–16)	1 Piccolo	2 Trumpets	Bass drum
Violas (8–12)	2 Oboes	3 Trombones	Snare drum
Cellos (8–12)	1 English horn	1 Bass tuba	Cymbals
Bass viols (6–10)	2 Clarinets		Triangle
	1 High E♭ clarinet		Tubular bells
	1 Bass clarinet		
Note: Each string section is sometimes divided into two or more subsections, to obtain richer effects.	2 Bassoons		
	1 Contrabassoon		
2 Harps			Piano

What such charts cannot show, however, are the ingenious and fascinating new *combinations* of instruments that were now investigated. Composers learned to mix instrumental colors with something of the same freedom and virtuosity with which painters mix actual colors on a palette. The clear, sharply defined sonorities of the Classical era were replaced by multicolored shades of blended orchestral sound.

Romantic composers and audiences alike were fascinated by the symphony orchestra, and for the first time conductors came to the fore. In earlier times, orchestras had simply followed the first violin or the continuo player, but now the need arose for experts to control and balance out those special blended effects. The orchestra also became increasingly important in nineteenth-century opera; major opera composers, such as Weber, Meyerbeer, and Wagner, specialized in orchestral effects that sometimes even threatened to put the voices in the shade. If today the symphony orchestra comes to mind almost automatically when one thinks of "classical music," that is a holdover from the Romantic nineteenth century.

An early picture of a conductor using a baton—or, rather, a tight scroll of paper. He is the German opera composer Carl Maria von Weber (see page 253).

4 The Problem of Form in Romantic Music

Individual spontaneity was an important goal of the Romantic movement. And if there was any area in which composers wanted to seem particularly free and spontaneous, it was the area of musical form. The music should bubble out moment by moment, irrepressible and untrammeled, like churning emotion itself. The problem that composers faced was how to channel and control that spontaneity, how to provide their music with enough sense of coherence so that listeners could follow it.

In their use of standard forms or form types, nineteenth-century composers broke with Classical norms. To return to the distinction we noted on page 49, the Romantics wanted each work of art to express its own individual "inner form"; "outer forms" they distrusted as dry and conventional. Even when they did use such forms as sonata form and rondo, they tended to follow them so loosely and freely that it becomes a matter of opinion whether they were doing so at all. Themes blend into one another, and there is less of the neat, clear cadencing of Classical music.

Some Romantic compositions deliberately break down the boundary between music and nonmusical silence. Robert Schumann's song "Im wunderschönen Monat Mai" (page 235) begins hesitantly, as though already in the middle a transition; we feel we have just begun hearing music that started long ago. Instead of ending with a decisive cadence, the song comes to a questioning dissonance—then: silence. The vague, atmospheric quality at the start, and the suggestion of "infinity" at the end—again, these are typically Romantic.

Yet the music had to avoid real formlessness if it was to hold the attention of an audience. Once again, for Romantic composers the problem was how to create the impression of spontaneity while at the same time providing enough formal structure to give the listener some means of following the music. They developed a number of interesting and characteristic solutions.

"Miniature" Compositions

While many nineteenth-century compositions are about the same length as works from the eighteenth century, special classes of music arose with quite different dimensions.

The man has put down his violin to sit with the woman at the piano; we can imagine the four-hand music they are playing, perhaps, but we cannot see their faces. This picture catches both the intimacy and privacy of the Romantic "miniature" and also its characteristic milieu, the middle-class living room.

First of all, composers cultivated what we will call **miniatures**, pieces lasting only a few minutes. Mostly songs and short piano pieces, these were designed to convey a particularly pointed emotion, momentary and undeveloped. In this way the composer could commune with the listener intensely but intimately, as though giving him or her a single short, meaningful glance.

Though short pieces were also written in earlier times (the minuet movements in Classical symphonies, for example), usually they were elements within larger units where their effect was balanced by other, longer movements. In the Romantic era, miniatures came singly, standing out as individuals in their own right. Piano miniatures were sometimes given general titles, such as Chopin's Preludes, Schubert's Impromptus (Improvisations), and Brahms's Capriccios (Whims), and sometimes they masqueraded as dances, like Chopin's Mazurkas (a Polish dance). Often they were given more poetic titles: the *Songs Without Words* by Mendelssohn, *Years of Pilgrimage* by Liszt, and *Woodland Sketches* by Edward MacDowell, America's leading late Romantic composer. Schumann was particularly imaginative with the names of his miniatures: "The Poet Speaks," "Confession," "The Bird as Prophet," and "Why?"

As for the "problem of musical form," in such pieces this was not so much solved as bypassed. They are over before the listener begins to wonder where the music is going, what the next effect will be, and why.

"Grandiose" Compositions

Another Romantic tendency was diametrically opposed to the miniatures. Many composers wrote "grandiose" compositions—larger and larger symphonies, cantatas, and other works, with more movements, a greater number of performers, and a longer total time span. For example, Hector Berlioz, in his hour-and-a-half-long "dramatic symphony" *Romeo and Juliet* (1839), starts with the augmented symphony orchestra, adds voices to some movements and a narrator in between the movements, and then throws in an offstage chorus for still other movements. In the field of opera, we have already mentioned Wagner's *The Ring of the Nibelung,* an opera lasting for four long evenings with a huge orchestra including specially invented instruments, a cast of thirty, and fifteen separate stage sets.

The nineteenth century produced many conservative-minded, if amusing, sketches making fun of the "grandiose" compositions of the time.

Again, these grandiose compositions dealt with the problem of musical form in their own way, for as the above examples suggest, such works provided more than just music. These are the works in which the Romantic urge to transcend the boundaries of the individual arts finds expression. With literature joined to music, the total effect was laced with poetry, philosophical or religious ideas, a loose story line, and perhaps dramatic action.

Listeners were impressed, even stupefied, by a combination of opulent sounds, great thoughts, powerful emotions, and sheer length. And composers could draw on extramusical factors as elements of artistic form. While music could add emotional conviction to the story, in return the story could supply a rationale for the sequence of the musical events, that is, for the musical form.

Program Music

Indeed, even without words, in strictly instrumental music, Romantic composers sometimes derived musical form from nonmusical sources. **Program music** is the term for nonvocal music that is associated with a poem, a story, or some other literary source; the literary text itself is the "program." Certain passages in the music would then be explainable in terms of the source; in fact, these passages might illustrate or express that source.

Although we are discussing program music in the context of the problem of musical form, problem solving was doubtless not the main impetus for its development. Program music answered the general Romantic demand for transcending the boundaries of the separate arts. Music could be made even more expressive, it was felt, by linking it to poetry and ideas. The help this provided in the matter of musical form was a sort of fringe benefit for the composer (and the listener).

Program music sparked a great debate in the nineteenth century, a debate that still goes on. Does the music *really* illustrate the program? Suppose the music is played without listeners knowing about the program: could they tell it from the music? Shouldn't the music make complete sense on its own terms, even if we grant that the program provides it with an added dimension?

But the point is that the Romantics did not *want* to be without the program. They did not necessarily *want* the music to make sense "on its own terms." Nor were they bothered, it seems, by the apparent inconsistency between their view of purely instrumental music as the highest form of art on the one hand, and their enthusiastic adoption of program music on the other.

The Principle of Thematic Unity

An important general principle developed in nineteenth-century music was that of thematic unity. Romantic composers increasingly tended to maintain some of the same thematic material throughout whole works, even (or especially) when these works were in many movements.

Several different "levels" of thematic unity can be distinguished in nineteenth-century symphonies and other such works:

❧   Most obviously, themes from one movement may be cited literally and quite clearly in other movements. We have already seen this happen with the third-movement scherzo theme of Beethoven's Fifth Symphony, which is heard again in the last movement.

❧   In other compositions, new *versions* of a single theme are used at important new points in the music, either later in the same movement or in the course of later movements. Although the new versions can be regarded as free variations of the original theme, this procedure differs fundamentally from Classical theme-and-variations form (see page 188). In Classical variation form, the "theme" is an entire tune, and the variations follow one another directly. In the Romantic procedure, the theme is more fragmentary than a tune, and the new versions of the theme appear at irregular intervals.

The term **thematic transformation** is used to describe this variationlike procedure in Romantic music, in which short themes are freely varied at relatively wide intervals of time. A precedent for it can be traced to works such as Beethoven's Fifth Symphony, where the ♩♩♩ ♩ motive of the first movement is evoked freely in each of the later ones.

❧   In still other nineteenth-century pieces, we hear themes with even looser relationships among them. Clearly different, they nonetheless seem to exhibit mysterious inner similarities—similarities that seem to help unify the music, though they are too shadowy to count as "transformations" in the Romantic definition, let alone as "variations" in the Classical. Wagner's operas are famous for such themes; in the Prelude to *Tristan und Isolde,* for example, the family resemblance between some of the motives can't be missed—yet it can scarcely be pinned down, either (see page 264).

Of all the levels of thematic unity employed by nineteenth-century composers, this last is the most typical of all. Vague similarity rather than clear likeness, suggestion rather than outright statement, atmosphere rather than discourse, feeling rather than form: all these go to the heart of Romanticism. We cannot appreciate Romantic music fully if we approach it in too literal a frame of mind. In much of this music, the "inner form"—the special spontaneous form of the individual piece, as distinct from standard "outer forms" such as sonata form and rondo—is tied to the principle of thematic unity. Listening to Romantic music requires ears that are not only attentive but also imaginative, exploratory, and more than a little fanciful.

CHAPTER **17**

The Early Romantics

P erhaps the most brilliant generation of composers in the entire history of music was that of the early Romantics. Franz Schubert was born in Vienna in 1797; then the ten-year period between 1803 and 1813 saw the birth of Robert Schumann, Frédéric Chopin, Felix Mendelssohn, Franz Liszt, Hector Berlioz, Richard Wagner, and Giuseppe Verdi. It was a brilliant generation, but not a long-lived one. Only the last four of these composers survived to continue their major work into the second half of the century.

Two general points are worth making about this early Romantic galaxy. First, Beethoven's music had a profound effect on them, though this was naturally felt more strongly by German composers than by non-Germans. Schubert, who lived in Vienna under Beethoven's shadow, was influenced by the older master much more directly than Chopin, a Pole who lived in Paris.

The second important point is that these composers were deeply influenced by literary Romanticism, which had flourished some decades before their time. Schubert wrote many songs to texts by Romantic poets such as Goethe, Novalis, and Friedrich Schlegel, and Schumann's enthusiasm for the German Romantic novelist Jean Paul Richter was reflected in his music, as well as in his own prose writings. We have mentioned that Shakespeare was particularly admired by the Romantics; nearly all the composers mentioned here wrote music associated with Shakespeare's plays.

1 The Lied

The ordinary German word for song is *Lied* (plural, *Lieder*—pronounced "leader"). The word also has a special application: the <u>lied</u> is a particular type of German song that evolved in the late eighteenth century and flourished in the nineteenth. As such, the lied is one of the most important miniature genres of Romanticism.

Though one cannot generalize about the melodies of these songs—some consist of little more than a tune, others are melodically much more complex—they share certain other characteristic features.

 Accompaniment. A lied is nearly always accompanied by piano, and the accompaniment contributes significantly to the artistic effect. Indeed, the pianist becomes more of a discreet partner to the singer than a mere accompanist.

Beethoven: a late Romantic view. The awesome, ideal figure—nude, and carved in marble, like a Greek statue—sits on a superb throne. He seems to be both reigning over and deploring the music that was written after his own time.

❦ *Poetry.* The text of a lied is usually a Romantic poem of some merit (at least in the composer's estimation). Hence, although we need to understand the words of almost any vocal music, with the lied we should also try to appreciate how the poem's words and meanings fit together as poetry. The art of the lied depends on the sensitivity of the composer's response to the poetic imagery and feeling.

❦ *Mood.* A third characteristic, harder to explain, is the intimacy of expression that is captured by these pieces. The singer and the pianist seem to be sharing an emotional insight just with you, rather than with an entire audience; words and music are uttered softly, inwardly. Lieder are best heard in the intimacy of a living room, not in a formal concert hall.

Is not music the mysterious language of a distant realm of spirits, whose lovely sounds re-echo in our soul and awaken a higher, more intensive life? All the passions, arrayed in shining armor, vie with each other, and ultimately merge in an indescribable longing that fills our breast.

Arch-Romantic novelist, critic, and composer
E. T. A. Hoffmann, 1816

FRANZ SCHUBERT
"Der Jüngling an der Quelle" ("The Youth at the Spring") (c. 1817)

The earliest and (for most musicians) the greatest master of the lied is Franz Schubert. There are many unsuspected treasures among the more than six hundred songs he wrote; let us begin with a very short, lesser-known one. The speaker of the song's rather faint poem has been communing with nature in an effort to forget his unkind beloved, but he hears her name echoing in the trees and the rippling water of a spring.

The piano begins with a delicate, tinkling evocation of the spring. The water is just barely flowing, it seems; the lovesick boy himself is half asleep, and can hardly rouse himself to sing a full-fledged melody. The harmonies are extremely simple—up to the repetition of the word *seufzen* (sigh), the poem's most emotive word. This word is underpinned by one rich, quiet, romantic harmony, like the fleeting memory of an amorous encounter. The trickling, tinkling spring lulls the boy back into a delicious dream.

The song lasts for less than two minutes. A perfect Romantic miniature, it conveys an unforgetable whiff of intimate emotion. With Schubert and the best lieder composers who followed him, a quiet Romantic song with piano accompaniment can be as moving as a great symphony or an opera.

| LISTEN | Schubert, "Der Jüngling an der Quelle" |

Leise, rieselnder Quell,	Gentle, rippling spring
Ihr wallenden, flispernden Pappeln:	With your tossing, whispering poplars:
Euer Schlummergeräusch	Your lullaby stirrings
Wecket die Liebe nur auf.	Speak of nothing but love.
Linderung sucht ich bei euch	Comfort I sought with you,
Und sie zu vergessen, die Spröde;	And to forget her, that coy one;
Ach, und Blätter und Bach	Ah, both the leaves and the brook
Seufzen, Luise, dir nach.	Are sighing, Louise, for you.

SCHUBERT
"Erlkönig" ("The Elfking") (1815)

"The Elfking," probably Schubert's best-known lied, is a musical setting of a poem by Johann Wolfgang von Goethe. The greatest literary figure of the day, Goethe was by turns a Romantic and a Neoclassical poet, playwright, novelist, scientist, philosopher, and inspiration for several generations of lieder composers. Cast in the old ballad form, which enjoyed a vogue in the Romantic era, and dealing with death and the supernatural, the poem is famous in its own right.

Though the poem consists of eight parallel stanzas, Schubert did not set them to the same music. He wrote different or modified music for the later stanzas; such a song is said to be **through-composed** (in contrast to a **strophic** song, which uses the same music for each stanza: see page 60). In mood, Goethe's poem changes so dramatically as it proceeds that it almost demands this kind of musical setting. It tells of a father riding furiously through the night with a feverish child who thinks he sees and hears the demon Elfking beckoning him. The Elfking first invites the child to join him, then cajoles him, then threatens and assaults him. The father, uncomprehending, tries to quiet his child, but by the time they reach home the boy is dead.

The piano introduction sets the mood of dark, tense excitement. The right hand hammers away at repeated notes (triplets), suggesting the horse's hooves, while the left hand has an agitated motive:

Schubert wrote different music for each of the poem's three characters (and also for the narrator). Each "voice" characterizes the speaker and differentiates him from the others. The father is low, stiff, and gruff; the Elfking sings ominously graceful tunes; and the boy sounds frantic.

Two things help hold this long song together as an artistic unity. First, there are some dramatic musical repetitions: the agitated bass motive associated with the riding (stanzas 1 and 8), and the frantic melodic phrase sung higher and higher by the boy (stanzas 4, 6, and 7). Second, the piano's repeated notes continue ceaselessly, until just before the end, when the ride is over. During the Elfking's first and second speeches, when the child is hearing him in a feverish half-sleep, the horse's hooves are muted (*p*). But during the third speech they pound away distinctly; as Schubert saw it, when the Elfking claims the child, he is wide awake in terror.

The triplet accompaniment keeps the whole song alive and gives it more unity, as it were; yet one could wish that Herr Schubert had occasionally transferred it to the left hand; for the ceaseless striking of one and the same note in triplets tires the hand, if the piece is to be played at the rapid pace demanded by Herr Schubert.

Review of *Erlkönig*, 1821

Franz Schubert (1797–1828)

Schubert was the son of a lower-middle-class Viennese schoolmaster. There was always music in the home, and the boy received a solid musical education in the training school for Viennese court singers. His talent amazed his teachers and also a number of his schoolmates, who remained devoted to him throughout his career. Schubert began by following in his father's footsteps as a schoolteacher, without much enthusiasm, but soon gave up teaching to devote all his time to music.

Schubert was an endearing but shy and unspectacular individual who led an unspectacular life. However, it was the sort of life that would have been impossible before the Romantic era. Schubert never married and never held a regular job; he was sustained by odd fees for teaching and publications and by contributions from a circle of friends who called themselves the Schubertians—young musicians, artists, writers, and music lovers. They recognized him as a genius, promoted his songs, and helped pay his bills. One of the Schubertians, Moritz von Schwind, who later was to become an important painter, has left us many charming pictures of the group at parties, on trips to the country, and so on.

It was an atmosphere especially conducive to an intimate musical genre such as the lied. Schubert wrote more than six hundred lieder and many choral songs. For a time he roomed with a poet, Johann Mayrhofer, who provided him with gloomy texts for about fifty of them.

It is unfortunate that Schubert's wonderful songs have tended to overshadow his symphonies, sonatas, and chamber music (even, alas, in this book). Starting out with Classical genres, Schubert in his very short lifetime transformed them under the influence of Romanticism. He never introduced himself to Beethoven, even though they lived in the same city; perhaps he instinctively felt he needed to keep his distance from the overpowering older master. It speaks much for Schubert that he was able to write such original and powerful works as the *Unfinished* Symphony, the so-called *Great* Symphony in C, the String Quintet in C, and others, right under Beethoven's shadow.

A few of Schubert's instrumental works include melodies taken from his own songs: the popular *Trout* Quintet, the String Quartet in D Minor (*Death and the Maiden*), and the *Wanderer* Fantasy for piano.

Schubert died in a typhoid fever epidemic when he was only thirty-one. He never heard a performance of his late symphonies, and much of his music came to light only after his death.

Chief Works: Many lieder, including the song cycles *Die schöne Müllerin, Winterreise,* and *Schwanengesang;* "The Elfking," "Gretchen at the Spinning Wheel," "Hedgerose," "Death and the Maiden," "The Trout," and hundreds of others ▪ "Character" pieces for piano; waltzes ▪ Eight symphonies, including the *Unfinished*—Schubert completed only two movements and sketches for a scherzo—and the *Great* Symphony in C ▪ Many piano sonatas—five (plus a wonderful "Unfinished Sonata") in his mature years; Wanderer Fantasy for piano ▪ Four mature string quartets; a string quintet; the genial *Trout* Quintet for piano and strings (including double bass)

Title page of the first edition of "The Elfking" (1821)— Schubert's opus 1

LISTEN   Schubert, "Erlkönig"

35   26   6   4

Wer reitet so spät, durch Nacht und Wind?	Who rides so late through the night and wind?
Es ist der Vater mit seinem Kind;	It is the father with his child.
Er hat den Knaben wohl in dem Arm,	He holds the youngster tight in his arm,
Er fasst ihn sicher, er hält ihn warm.	Grasps him securely, keeps him warm.

0:55
"Mein sohn, was birgst du so bang dein Gesicht?"	"Son, what makes you afraid to look?"
"Siehst, Vater, du den Erlkönig nicht?	"Don't you see, father, the Elfking there?
Den Erlenkönig mit Kron' und Schweif?"	The King of the elves with his crown and train?
"Mein Sohn, est ist ein Nebelstreif."	"Son, it's only a streak of mist."

1:30
"Du liebes Kind, komm, geh mit mir!	*"Darling child, come away with me!*
Gar schöne Spiele spiel' ich mit dir;	*I will play the finest of games with you;*
Manche' bunte Blumen sind an dem Strand;	*Many bright flowers grow by the shore;*
Meine Mutter hat manch' gülden Gewand."	*My mother has many golden robes."*

"Mein Vater, mein Vater, und hörest du nicht	"Father, father, do you not hear
Was Erlenkönig mir leise verspricht?"	What the Elfking is softly promising me?"
"Sei ruhig, bleibe ruhig, mein Kind:	"Calm yourself, be calm, my son:
In dürren Blättern säuselt der Wind."	The dry leaves are rustling in the wind."

2:17
"Willst, feiner Knabe, du mit mir gehn?	*"Well, you fine boy, won't you come with me?*
Meine Töchter sollen dich warten schön;	*My daughters will wait upon you.*
Meine Töchter führen den nächtlichen Reihn	*My daughters lead the nightly round,*
Und wiegen und tanzen und singen dich ein.	*They will rock you, dance for you, sing you to sleep!"*

"Mein Vater, mein Vater, und siehst du nich dort	"Father, father, do you not see
Erlkönigs Töchter am düstern Ort?"	The Elfking's daughters there in the dark?"
"Mein Sohn, mein sohn, ich seh es genau:	"Son, my son, I see only too well:
Es scheinen die alten Weiden so grau."	It is the gray gleam in the old willow trees."

3:04
"Ich liebe dich, mich reizt deine schöne Gestalt,	*"I love you, your beauty allures me,*
Und bist du nicht willig, so brauch' ich Gewalt."	*And if you're not willing, then I shall use force."*
"Mein Vater, mein Vater, jetzt fasst er mich an!	"Father, father, now he is seizing me!
Erlkönig hat mit ein Leids getan!"	The Elfking is hurting me!"

3:31
Dem Vater grauset's, er reitet geschwind,	Fear grips the father, he rides like the wind,
Er hält in Armen das ächzende Kind,	He holds in his arms the moaning child;
Erreicht den Hof mit Müh and Not;	With effort and toil he reaches the house;
In seinen Armen das Kind war tot.	The child in his arms was dead.

The Song Cycle

A **song cycle** is a group of songs with a common poetic theme or an actual story connecting all the poems. Composers would either find whole coherent groups of poems to set, or else make their own selections from a larger collection of a poet's work. Schubert, who wrote two great song cycles relatively late in his career, was able to use ready-made groups of poems published by a minor Romantic poet named Wilhelm Müller: *Die schöne Müllerin* ("The Fair Maid of the Mill") and *Winterreise* ("Winter Journey").

The advantage of the song cycle was that it extended the rather fragile expression of the lied into a larger, more comprehensive, and hence more impressive unit. It was, in a sense, an effort to get beyond "miniaturism." The "unity" of such larger units, however, is always loose, even when the songs are related by melodic or rhythmic means, as occasionally happens. The individual songs can often be sung separately, as well as in sequence with the rest of the cycle.

ROBERT SCHUMANN (1810–1856)
Dichterliebe ("A Poet's Love") (1840)

"Schubert died. Cried all night," wrote the sixteen-year-old Robert Schumann in his diary under a date in 1828. Yet living in Zwickau, Germany, far from Schubert's Vienna, Schumann did not know many of the older composer's best-known works, his lieder. He loved Schubert's piano music, and indeed, for the first ten years of his own career as a composer, Schumann wrote only piano music.

Then in 1840, the year of his marriage, he suddenly started pouring out lieder. Given this history, it is not surprising that in Schumann's songs the piano is given a more complex role than in Schubert's. This is particularly true of his most famous song cycle, *Dichterliebe,* the first and last songs of which (nos. 1 and 16) we shall examine here. *Dichterliebe* has no real story; its series of love poems traces a psychological progression from cautious optimism to disillusionment and despair. They are the work of another great German poet, Heinrich Heine, a man who reacted with bitter irony against Romanticism, while acknowledging his own hopeless commitment to its ideals.

To cast light into the depths of the human heart—the artist's mission!

Robert Schumann

"Im wunderschönen Monat Mai" ("In the wonderfully lovely month of May")   The song begins with a piano introduction, halting and ruminative in quality—which seems at first to be a curious response to the "wonderfully lovely" month of May. The piano part winds its way in and out of the vocal line, ebbing and flowing rhythmically and sometimes dwelling on quiet but piercing dissonant harmonies.

What Schumann noticed was the hint of unrequited longing in Heine's very last line, and he ended the song with the piano part hanging in midair, without a true cadence, as though in a state of reaching or yearning: a truly Romantic effect. Technically, the last sound is a dissonance that requires resolution into a consonance but does not get it (until the next song).

In this song, both stanzas of the poem are set to identical music. As mentioned earlier, such a song is called *strophic;* strophic setting is of course familiar from folk songs, hymns, popular songs, and many other kinds of music. For Schumann, this kind of setting had the advantage of underlining the similarity in the text of the song's two stanzas, both in meaning and in actual words. Certainly his music deepens the tentative, sensitive, hope-against-hope quality of Heine's understated confession of love.

The qualities of intimacy and spontaneity that are so important to Romantic miniatures can be inhibited by studio recording. Our recording of Schumann's song was made at a concert (you will hear applause as the artists enter).

LISTEN   Schumann, "Im wunderschönen Monat Mai"

3   2   3A   2A
36   27   7   5

Im wunderschönen Monat Mai,	In the wonderfully lovely month of May,
Als alle Knospen sprangen,	When all the buds were bursting,
Da ist in meinem Herzen	Then it was that in my heart
Die Liebe aufgegangen.	Love broke through.
Im wunderschönen Monat Mai	In the wonderfully lovely month of May,
Als alle Vögel sangen,	When all the birds were singing,
Da hab' ich ihr gestanden	Then it was I confessed to her
Mein Sehnen und Verlangen.	My longing and desire.

"Die alten, bösen Lieder" ("The hateful songs of times past")   After many heart-wrenching episodes, the final song in the *Dichterliebe* cycle begins strongly. The very insistent rhythm in the piano part sounds a little hectic and forced, like the black humor of Heine's poem. Although basically this is a through-composed song, there are musical parallels between many of the stanzas, and the music of stanza 1 comes back even more forcefully in stanza 5.

Stanza 1

The hateful songs of times past,   The hateful, brutal dreams

Stanza 5

It's   they that must haul the   cof - ffn

But there is a sudden reversal of mood in stanza 6, as the poet suddenly offers to tell us what this morbid action is about. In the music, first the accompaniment disintegrates and then the rhythm. All the poet's self-dramatization vanishes when he speaks of his grief in recitativelike accents; the end of the song would be a whimper if Schumann at the piano did not take over quietly and firmly. In a lovely meditative piano solo, the composer comments on and comforts the frantic poet.

Not only does the composer interpret the poet's words with great art, both in the hectic early stanzas and the self-pitying final one, but he adds something entirely his own. The sixteen vignettes by Heine and Schumann in *A Poet's Love* add up to a memorable anthology of the various fervid states of love celebrated by the Romantics.

During the night of October 17, 1833, I suddenly had the most frightful thought a human being can possibly have: "What if you were no longer able to think?" Clara, anyone who has been crushed like that knows no worse suffering, or despair.

Letter from Robert Schumann, 1838

LISTEN   **Schumann, "Die alten, bösen Lieder"**

3   3A

37   8

	Die alten, bösen Lieder,	The hateful songs of times past,
	Die Träume bös' und arg,	The hateful, brutal dreams,
	Die lasst uns jetzt begraben:	Let's now have them buried;
	Holt einen grossen Sarg.	Fetch up a great coffin.
	Hinein leg' ich gar Manches,	I've a lot to put in it—
	Doch sag' ich noch nicht, was.	Just what, I won't yet say;
	Der Sarg muss sein noch grösser	The coffin must be even bigger
	Wie's Heidelberger Fass.	Than the Great Cask of Heidelberg.
0:46	Und holt eine Todtenbahre	And fetch a bier,
	Und Bretter fest und dick,	Boards that are strong and thick;
	Auch muss sie sein noch länger	They too must be longer
	Als wie zu Mainz die Brück'.	Then the river bridge at Mainz.
	Und holt mir auch zwölf Riesen,	And fetch me, too, twelve giants
	Die mussen noch stärker sein	Who must be stronger
	Als wie der starke Christoph	Than St. Christopher, the great statue
	Im Dom zu Köln am Rhein.	At the Cathedral of Cologne on the Rhine.
1:23	Die sollen den Sarg forttragen	It's they that must haul the coffin
	Und senken in's Meer hinab,	And sink it in the sea,
	Denn solchem grossen Sarge	For a great coffin like that
	Gebührt ein grosses Grab.	Deserves a great grave.
1:54	Wisst ihr, warum der Sarg wohl	Do you know why the coffin, then,
	So gross und schwer mag sein?	Has to be so huge and heavy?
	Ich senkt' auch meine Liebe	I sank my love, yes,
	Und meinen Schmerz hinein.	And my grief in it.

Robert Schumann (1810–1856)

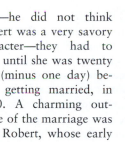

Robert Schumann's father, a bookseller and writer, encouraged the boy's musical talent and started him studying the piano at the age of six. When his father died, his mother wanted him to go into law; he attended the University of Leipzig, but finally persuaded her to let him pursue the career of a piano virtuoso. He had to give this up, however, after an injury sustained when he tried to strengthen his fingers with a mechanical device.

Besides his musical talent, Schumann had a great flair for literature, no doubt inherited from his father. When he was twenty-three, Schumann founded a magazine to campaign for a higher level of music, *Die Neue Zeitschrift für Musik* ("The New Music Journal"—it is still being published). For several years he wrote regular music criticism, often couched in a fanciful romantic prose style. For example, he signed some of his reviews with the names "Florestan" or "Eusebius," representing the opposite (but both thoroughly romantic) sides of his character—the impetuous side and the tender, dreamy side. He encouraged fledgling composers such as Chopin and (later) Brahms.

Schumann's piano works—among his most important music—are mostly "character pieces," often with imaginative titles, and occasionally signed "Eu." or "Fl." at the end. They are arranged in loosely organized sets, with titles such as *Butterflies, Kreisleriana* (after a character in a Romantic novel), *Scenes from Childhood,* and *Carnaval* (see page 240).

Schumann fell in love with Clara Wieck, the daughter of his piano teacher; at the age of fifteen she was already a famous pianist. Thanks to her father's fanatical opposition—he did not think Robert was a very savory character—they had to wait until she was twenty one (minus one day) before getting married, in 1840. A charming outcome of the marriage was that Robert, whose early compositions were almost entirely for the piano, suddenly started to write love songs for Clara. Nearly 150 songs were composed in this "song year."

A little later, he also turned to the composition of larger works: concertos, symphonies, chamber music, choral music, and one opera. Thereafter he assumed some important musical positions, but his withdrawn personality made him less than successful. Schumann suffered from mood swings, and had experienced breakdowns in his youth, and now he began to show tragic signs of insanity. In 1854, tormented by voices, hallucinations, and loss of memory, he tried to drown himself in the River Rhine and was committed to an asylum. He died two years later.

Chief Works: Sets of "miniatures" for piano, among them *Scenes of Childhood, Album for the Young, Arabesque, Papillons* ("Butterflies"), and *Carnaval* ▪ Songs and song cycles: *Woman's Life and Love, A Poet's Love* ▪ Piano Fantasy (a sort of free sonata); Piano Concerto; four symphonies ▪ Chamber music: a quintet and a quartet for piano and strings ▪ An opera, *Genoveva;* incidental music to Byron's *Manfred* and Goethe's *Faust;* choral works

CLARA SCHUMANN
"Der Mond kommt still gegangen" ("The moon has risen softly") (1843)

This lied is another perfect Romantic miniature, in spite of the cliché-filled poem, with its quiet moonlight, its dreams of love, and its unaccountably melancholy lover. Both the melody and the piano accompaniment are very plain, but the slightly unusual chords chosen by Schumann create a unique pensive mood. The form, too, is simple: modified strophic form, **A A A'**. Some modification, however slight, had to occur in stanza 3, where the poem's speaker, catching sight of the lit-up windows in the house, registers his excitement by crowding his poetic lines with extra syllables—which require extra notes.

There is an obvious, banal way of setting such crowded lines: see page 239. But instead Schumann very skillfully pulls them out of phase with the musical phrases, achieving beautiful rhythmic matches for some of the extra words: slower for *drunten* (down), a bit livelier for *funkeln* (alight—literally, sparkle), and very slow for *still:*

Clara Wieck (Clara Schumann) (1819–1896)

Clara Wieck was the eldest child (there were two younger brothers) of a highly ambitious music teacher named Friedrich Wieck (pronounced *Veek*). Wieck had his own piano method, and he determined to make Clara a leading pianist. By the age of fifteen she was widely known as a prodigy. Like most virtuosos of the time, she also composed music to play at her own concerts: variations on popular opera arias, waltzes, a piano concerto.

Robert and Clara Schumann figure in what must be music's greatest love story. Still, there seems to have been just a little friction between them because she was so much better a pianist; she, on her part, felt diffident about composing under his shadow, though he did encourage her to some extent, and they published one song cycle jointly, containing music by both of them. Clara often wrote songs to give Robert on his birthdays. The last of these is dated 1853, the year before his hospitalization.

Even before that, Robert's depression and instability made life difficult for Clara. She continued her career as best she could, but more and more, she had to take care of the family. During the 1848 revolution in Leipzig, for example, it was up to her to get the five Schumann children out of town (three were born later).

Things were difficult in another way when Robert died. At the age of thirty-seven, after losing the husband whom she loved and revered, Clara found herself more than half in love with his twenty-two-year old prodigy Johannes Brahms (see page 277). It is not known which of them withdrew from the relationship. They remained

close friends; Brahms was a lifelong bachelor, and she did not remarry.

Today we tend to regret that Schumann decided to give up composing, for she left enough good pieces to make us wish there were more of them. But she knew it would have been an uphill battle, given the common nineteenth-century view that great music couldn't be written by a woman. With so many children to support, she can hardly be blamed for concentrating instead on activities that had already earned her admiration and respect—and a good living: playing and teaching.

Clara Schumann went on to further establish herself as one of Europe's leading pianists and a much-sought-after pedagogue. She concertized and toured widely. Brahms (who always asked her to critique his new compositions) was just one in the eminent circle of her friends and associates. Outliving Robert by forty years, Clara became a major force in late nineteenth-century music.

Chief Works: Miniatures for piano, with names such as *Romances* and *Soirées musicales* ("Musical Evenings"); songs ■ A piano concerto and a trio for piano, violin, and cello ■ *Piano Variations on a Theme by Robert Schumann* (Brahms wrote a set of variations on the same theme)

St. 1: ¹The moon has ri-sen soft-ly ²With gleaming rays of gold ³Be-neath its shin-ing splendor ⁴The wea-ry earth's at rest.
St. 2: ¹And on the drifting breez-es ²From man-y faith-ful minds ³Endearing thoughts by the thousand ⁴Waft down on those who sleep.

St. 3: ¹Und drun-ten im Ta-le, die funkeln ²Die Fenster von Lieb-chens Haus; ³Ich a-ber blikke im Dunkeln Still . . .
¹And down in the val-ley, the window's ²A-light in my loved one's house ³But I keep staring in darkness silently

Three things help make the climactic word *Liebchens* (loved one) radiant: the new long high note, the new harmony, and the expansive phrase (5 bars in place of 4). Schumann's piano postlude adds a wistful minor-mode aftertaste. As with many great lieder, music here far transcends the words.

LISTEN   Clara Schumann, "Der Mond kommt still gegangen"

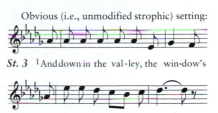

0:00	*St. 1:* ¹Der Mond kommt still gegangen	The moon has risen softly
	²Mit seinen goldn'en Schein,	With gleaming rays of gold,
	³Da Schläft in holdem Prangen	Beneath its shining splendor
	⁴Die müde Erde ein.	The weary earth's at rest.
0:34	*St. 2:* ¹Und auf den Lüften schwanken	And on the drifting breezes
	²Aus manchem treuen Sinn	From many faithful minds
	³Viel tausend Liebesgedanken	Endearing thoughts by the thousand
	⁴Über die Schläfer hin.	Waft down on those who sleep.
1:05	*St. 3:* ¹Und drunten im Tale, da funkeln	And down in the valley, the window's
	²Die Fenster von Liebchens Haus;	Alight in my loved one's house;
	³Ich aber blikke im Dunkeln	But I keep staring, in darkness,
	⁴Still in die Welt hinaus.	Silently out to the world.

Obvious (i.e., unmodified strophic) setting:

St. 3 ¹And down in the val-ley, the win-dow's

²A-light in my loved one's house; _

An amazing nineteenth-century score of Schumann lieder. The poems are given in ornate calligraphy and illustrated in the richest, most opulent Romantic style. The picture might well be for Clara's "The Moon Has Risen Softly" (actually, it is for Robert's similar song "Moonlit Night").

2 The "Character Piece" for Piano

Besides the lied, the other chief type of Romantic miniature composition was the short piano piece. Such pieces were written in great profusion in the nineteenth century, and they appeared under many names. Frédéric Chopin preferred simple genre titles such as Nocturne, Waltz, Scherzo, or Etude (study). Robert Schumann preferred descriptive titles. Piano miniatures were composed at all levels of difficulty, ranging from virtuoso tours de force, which hardly anyone but their composers could negotiate, to unassuming pieces playable (and enjoyable) by beginning students.

A good general name for these short Romantic piano pieces (one sometimes used by the Romantics themselves) is **character pieces,** for the essential point about them is that each portrays some definite mood or character. In principle, at least, this is as true of the brilliant virtuoso works as of the simple ones. Each conveys an intense, distinct emotion—an emotion often hinted at by an imaginative title supplied by the composer.

This explains why the Romantic character piece can be thought of as analogous to the Romantic song, or lied, though without its poem. Indeed, six books of such piano pieces by Felix Mendelssohn—pieces that enjoyed a great vogue in Victorian times—are entitled *Songs without Words*. Some of them have subtitles that stress still further their similarity to lieder: "Spinning Song," "Venetian Boat Song," and the famous "Spring Song."

ROBERT SCHUMANN
Carnaval (1833–35)

3   2   3A   2A
39-40   28   10-11   6

Schumann's style of piano writing has a warmth and privacy that set it somewhat apart from the elegance and glitter of other pianist-composers of his day, such as Chopin and Liszt. A favorite marking on his scores is the German word *innig,* meaning "inward," "intimate," or "heartfelt." Schumann typically assembled his piano pieces into collections with some general title and, often, some interesting musical means of connection among them. If the Romantic character piece for the piano is analogous to the Romantic lied, these collections are analogous to song cycles.

Such a collection is *Carnaval,* a set of twenty very short character pieces that really *are* characters—musical portraits of masked guests at a Mardi Gras ball. After the band strikes up in an introduction, the sad clown Pierrot arrives, followed by the pantomime figures Harlequin and Columbine, Schumann himself, two of his girlfriends masquerading under the names Estrella and Chiarina, a Coquette, the composers Paganini and Chopin, and many others. This diverse gallery provided Schumann with an outlet for his whimsy and humor, as well as all his Romantic melancholy and passion.

"Eusebius"   "Eusebius" was Schumann's pen name for his tender, dreamy self, and this little piece presents him at his most introspective. In the passage below, the yearning effect of the high notes (shaded) is compounded by the vague, languorous rhythm. The right-hand triplets and quintuplets blur with the left-hand eighth notes, especially when played with Romantic rubato. The unusual form is **aa ba b′a′ ba,** in which **b′a′** stands out although it differs from **ba** only in its much thicker chords and its use of the pedal:

Eusebius: "In sculpture, the actor's art becomes fixed. The actor transforms the sculptor's forms into living art. The painter turns a poem into a painting. The musician sets a picture to music." Florestan: "The aesthetic principle is the same in every art; only the material differs."

Robert Schumann, 1833

"Florestan"   After "Eusebius" ends very tentatively, Schumann's impetuous other self makes his entrance. "Florestan" is built out of a single explosive motive; the piece moves in fits and starts. The end gets faster and faster, almost madly, ending completely up in the air. This non-cadence is resolved only in the next number.

"Chiarina"   As we are probably meant to guess from the letters in the name, this is a musical portrait of then-sixteen-year-old Clara Wieck. The heading is "Passionato," and by the end of the little **a a′ | :b a′: |** form the dynamic has risen to *fortissimo*. Robert did not see his future wife as a shrinking violet.

FRÉDÉRIC CHOPIN
Etude in C Minor, Op. 10, No.12 ("Revolutionary" Etude) (?1830)

More than any other composer, Chopin transformed the piano into an ideal medium for Romanticism, instead of the rather matter-of-fact instrument it had been in earlier times. He created entire new sound worlds of pianistic melancholy, languor, and delicacy; technically, he developed a range of power and brilliance that far outshone the efforts of the barnstorming virtuoso pianists of his day. Besides his sensitivity to piano tone color, Chopin had a fantastic ear for harmony and a great instinct for rhythm. There is always a rhythmic sparkle to his music, in addition to the exquisitie piano sound.

   Chopin's **etudes** ("studies"), which are still unequaled for perfecting keyboard technique, have as distinct a "character" as any other Romantic miniature. The Etude in C Minor begins in the middle of things (like many Romantic works), with a sort of furious summons answered by a rush of left-hand scales. After this, the etude consists of two playings of a melody (**A**) that catches the Romantic spirit at its most hectic and magnificent. The melody is much intensified the second time (**A′**). Finally the piece settles down into an ominous hush—only to explode into a spectacular *fortissimo* conclusion.

LISTEN

Chopin, Etude in C minor

0:15   **A**
1:33   **A′**
2:35   hush; explosion

   Nicknamed (*not* by Chopin) the "Revolutionary" Etude, this piece was said to express his anguish after the Russian capture of Warsaw in 1831. It is performed on our record set by the Russian-American pianist Vladimir Horowitz (1903–1989), perhaps the greatest piano virtuoso of this century.

Frédéric Chopin (1810–1849)

Chopin was born near Warsaw, where his father, a Frenchman who had emigrated to Poland and married a Polish lady, ran a private school for young gentlemen. In this atmosphere Fryderyk—later he adopted the French form Frédéric—acquired his lifelong taste for life in high society. Provided with the best teachers available, he became an extraordinary pianist. There are many reports of the exquisite delicacy of his playing, and his miraculous ability, as it seemed at the time, to draw romantic sounds out of the piano.

Furthermore, his variations on Mozart's "Là ci darem la mano" (see page 199), written when he was seventeen, was already an impressive enough composition to earn a rave review from Robert Schumann.

Chopin settled in Paris, where he found ready acceptance from society people and from other artists and intellectuals, such as the novelist Honoré de Balzac and the painter Eugène Delacroix, who produced a famous portrait of the composer. Chopin made his way as a highly fashionable piano teacher and by selling his music to publishers. The facts that he was Polish, and that Poland was being overrun by Russia at that time, seem to have made him even more glamorous to the French. Among Chopin's piano miniatures are over fifty Mazurkas and sixteen Polonaises, which are stylized Polish dances.

Chopin was a frail and fastidious personality. Though he sometimes played in public, he truly disliked the hurly-burly of concert life and preferred to perform for select audiences in great houses. More than any other of the great composers, he restricted his work to music for *his* instrument, the piano. Even his works for piano and orchestra—two concertos and a few other works—were all from his pre-Paris days.

The major event of his personal life was his ten-year romance with Madame Aurore Dudevant, an early feminist and a famous novelist under the pen name George Sand. (They were introduced by Liszt, who wrote an admiring book about Chopin after his death.) The relationship was a rocky one; Sand sketched some unkind scenes from their life together in one of her novels. After the affair broke up in 1847, Chopin's health declined with his spirits. He toured England and Scotland unhappily in 1848 and died the next year, at the age of thirty-nine, of tuberculosis, a major killer in the nineteenth century.

Chief Works: Character pieces for piano: Preludes (including the "Raindrop" prelude), Nocturnes, Etudes, Ballades, Waltzes (including the "Minute" waltz) and Polish Mazurkas and Polonaises ■ Three piano sonatas, including one with a famous funeral march as the slow movement ■ Two piano concertos ■ A cello sonata; a few Polish songs

Vladimir Horowitz

FRÉDÉRIC CHOPIN
Nocturne in F-sharp, Op. 15 No. 2 (1831)

Chopin's twenty-one **nocturnes**, meaning "night pieces," written throughout his career, are as different as twenty-one different nights. But each features a particularly striking tune—a languid serenade, for example, or a dark secret lament. Something else is usually heard or overheard in the night, too, such as a distant procession, a passionate encounter, or even a fragment of a dance or a folk song.

The opening tune in Chopin's Nocturne in F-sharp has an elegance unique to the composer—an elegance that stems partly from the wonderfully graceful rhythm, partly from the Romantic turns of harmony, and partly from the pianistic decorations of the melodic line. We have seen decorated melodies before, but Chopin's have an almost liquid quality, caused partly by chromaticism—by the free use of all the notes of the chromatic scale, as in this fragment:

LISTEN

Chopin, Nocturne in F-sharp

0:00 **a**
0:31 **a′** ornamented
1:06 **b**
1:36 **c**
2:23 **a′**
3:07 **coda**

Romantic form contributes to the Romantic effect. Chopin avoids sharp demarcations and literal returns; the music seems to grow spontaneously, in an almost improvisational way. The main tune, **A** (**a, a′b**), does not really end; it is interrupted by plaintive sounds emerging out of nowhere, which surge up to a moment of real passion. Then the return of the tune (**a′**) is fragmentary, though in a way more intense, and the whole is capped by an unexpected little coda: delicious right-hand arpeggios over a bolero rhythm in the left. Free rhythm in the performance (rubato) mirrors the freedom of form.

"That's not your own fingering, is it?" he asked, in his melodious little voice. "No, Liszt," I said. "Ah, that one has ideas, I tell you!" And Chopin began to try this fingering. "But one could go down the whole keyboard this way like a crayfish scuttling back to his stream. It is perfect, your fingering! I shall use it!"

Reminiscence by a student of Chopin, 1859

Was this striking painting, by a minor late nineteenth-century artist, done with Chopin's nocturnes in mind? Called *Notturno*, its cool elegance, faint sensuality, and vaguely apprehensive quality might suggest so.

Franz Liszt (1811–1886)

Liszt learned music on the estate of the princes Esterházy near Vienna, where Haydn had once served, and where Liszt's father worked as an estate manager. By the time he was eleven, the young Hungarian was giving his first concert in Vienna. He was introduced to Beethoven, and published his first music, in 1823.

His dashing looks and personality, his radical opinions, and his liaisons with noblewomen dazzled Europe as much as his incredible piano technique. He attracted crowds like a modern rock star, and cultivated the flamboyant manner, on stage and off, that seems necessary to sustain such fame. Among his most popular concert numbers were brilliant piano transcriptions of Schubert songs and of opera highlights from Mozart, Wagner, and Verdi.

In 1833, when he was twenty-two, he met the Countess Marie d'Agoult, who wrote novels under the name Daniel Stern. She left her husband and bore Liszt three children, one of whom, Cosima, abandoned *her* husband (some twenty years later) for Richard Wagner. Liszt's relationship with Marie had a strong intellectual component; she had an influence on many piano compositions he wrote in those years. After this relationship came to a stormy end, Liszt spent a few years touring Europe, giving triumphant concerts from Portugal to Turkey and Russia.

Finally, Liszt tired of concert life and settled at Weimar, in Germany, where there was still a court that supported the arts in the eighteenth-century manner. But far from retiring, he now completely retooled himself as a musician. He became a conductor and the director of the theater there. In his composing, he pioneered a highly influential new Romantic musical genre, the symphonic poem. From this period also date his two program symphonies, entitled *Dante* and *Faust*.

At Weimar he took up with another formidable woman, Princess Carolyne Sayn-Wittgenstein. Under the princess's influence, Liszt turned to religion and became an *abbé,* an unordained priest. He spent most of his last years in Rome, and composed a number of "grandiose" Masses and other compositions for the Catholic Church.

Like so many other Romantic composers, Liszt was a writer as well as a musician, though some of what he published may have been ghost-written by d'Agoult or Sayn-Wittgenstein. A powerful advocate of Wagner's music, he gave the premiere of the latter's opera *Lohengrin* at a time when the composer was exiled from Germany. The two men learned a good deal from each other's music. Friend and foe alike linked Liszt's symphonic poems with Wagner's "music dramas" as "Music of the Future" (see page 259).

As a personality, however, Liszt was as genial and magnanimous as his son-in-law was self-centered and devious. The grand old man died at Bayreuth, where Wagner had built a theater for his operas, during the 1886 Wagner Festival.

Chief Works: *Les Préludes* and twelve other symphonic poems; *Faust* and *Dante* symphonies (program symphonies, both with chorus) ▪ Two piano concertos and the *Totentanz* ("Dance of Death"), a sort of program concerto; the popular "Rákóczy March" and Hungarian Rhapsodies ▪ For piano solo: Sonata in B Minor; Transcendental Etudes; other miniatures, including the famous *Liebestraum* ("Dream of Love") ▪ Piano versions of Schubert songs and opera medleys ▪ Songs (a neglected portion of his enormous output) ▪ Masses and oratorios

---

FRANZ LISZT
Transcendental Etude No. 10 in F Minor (1851)

LISTEN

Liszt, Transcendental Etude in F minor

0:27 **A** theme
1:13   cadence theme
1:24   transition
2:02 **A′** theme 1
3:36   cadence theme

Liszt was, in his younger days, the greatest of the nineteenth-century piano virtuosos. The very title of his celebrated *Etudes of Transcendental Execution* defied any mere earthbound pianist to play them. In its dazzling cascade of piano sounds, Etude No. 10 catches both the intense agitation and the supercharged melodic style that thrilled Liszt's devotees.

The etude is in a loose, Romantic form—an expansion of Chopin's plan in the "Revolutionary" Etude: **A A′** with hints of sonata form. For example, we experience only one real theme, but we also hear a solemn left-hand figure that sounds very much like a cadence theme. Opening fast piano figuration leads to the main melody, which gradually works its way around from agitation to high passion:

Sometimes Liszt actually did break, if not pianos, piano strings. This helped to ruin one prominent Viennese piano maker (Graf).

The melody is cut off by abrupt, brilliant cadences, after which the cadence theme is heard. After a short development-like passage—really not much more than a transition—the opening figure and the melody return. This time the melody develops much more intensely, in one of those spontaneous transports of emotion so treasured by the Romantics. The cadence theme is followed by more brilliant piano action, as a coda.

The world persisted to the end in calling Liszt the greatest pianist in order to avoid the trouble of considering his claims as one of the most remarkable composers.

Fellow composer Camille Saint-Saëns, 1885

3 Early Romantic Program Music

The lied and the character piece for piano—the two main forms of early Romantic miniature compositions—were intimately tied up with nonmusical, usually poetic, ideas. Furthermore, in a work such as Schumann's *Carnaval*, the various piano portraits are juxtaposed in such a way as to hint at their interaction—hint, that is, at some kind of shadowy story line. Poems, stories, and nonmusical ideas in general were also associated with large-scale instrumental pieces.

Program music is a term used for instrumental compositions associated with poems, stories, and the like. Program music grew up naturally in opera overtures, for even in the eighteenth century it was seen that an overture might gain special interest if it referred to moods or ideas in the opera to come by citing (or, rather, forecasting) some of its themes.

This happens in Mozart's *Don Giovanni*, in which the next-to-last scene has Don Giovanni carried off to hell by the Statue of the murdered Commandant (see page 197). The somber music associated with the Statue is first heard in the opera's overture, even before the curtain has gone up. Lively, effervescent music follows; but the half-serious, half-comical mood of Mozart's opera is already manifest in the overture.

Felix Mendelssohn: though his best music (the concert overtures, and more) was deeply imbued by Romanticism, he remained a classicist at heart. Works such as the oratorios *St. Paul* and *Elijah*, modeled on Bach and Handel, were among the most popular choral works of his day.

Fanny Mendelssohn (1805–1847), Felix's older sister and also a composer, could not engage in music professionally because this was deemed improper for an upper-class lady (the Mendelssohns were a banking family). Her many compositions remained unknown until quite recently.

The Concert Overture: Felix Mendelssohn

A further step, conceptually, was the <u>concert overture</u>, never intended to be followed by a stage play or an opera—never intended, indeed, for the theater. To speak only of the composers we have met so far, Robert Schumann wrote an overture to *Hermann und Dorothea,* which is not a play but an epic poem (by Goethe).

Probably the best-known and best-loved concert overtures are by Felix Mendelssohn (1809–1847), a composer who deserves brief mention here even though we will not be examining any of his music. Mendelssohn is a prime example of an all-round musician: composer, pianist, organist, conductor, important educator, even a sort of musicologist—he organized a famous revival of Bach's *Passion According to St. Matthew,* exactly a hundred years after its first performance in 1729. As a boy Mendelssohn was an extraordinary talent, fully comparable to Mozart or Schubert. His concert overture to *A Midsummer Night's Dream* was written at the age of seventeen, with no theatrical occasion in mind, though years later it was indeed used in productions of the Shakespeare play.

A work in sonata form, following classical models quite clearly, this overture nonetheless includes some representational features. Music illustrates the delicate, fluttering fairies in the service of King Oberon and Queen Titania, the sleep induced by Puck's magic flower, and even the braying of Bottom the Weaver when he is turned into a donkey.

Another fine example by Mendelssohn is the *Hebrides* Overture, an evocative, moody depiction of lonely Scottish islands rich in romantic associations. This is evidently program music, but what makes it an overture? Nothing more than the fact that it follows the standard scheme for overtures at the time—namely, a single movement in sonata form.

Hector Berlioz (1803–1869)

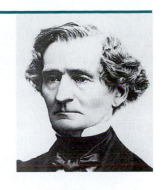

If the deaf Beethoven was the first great composer who made his living actually as a composer, rather than a performer or conductor, Berlioz was the first great composer who played no standard instrument at all. His father, a country doctor, sent him to medical school in Paris. But, as Berlioz told it, he was so horrified when he entered the dissecting room, where the rats were nibbling at the scraps, that he leaped out the window and went to the Paris Conservatory of Music instead.

The anecdote is typical of his emotional and utterly Romantic personality. More than any other composer of his generation, except Wagner, Berlioz "thought the unthinkable" in music; his "grandiose" program symphonies had simply no precedent and were not matched in ambition until the time of Gustav Mahler. The only instrument he played well was the guitar, but his imagination for orchestral tone color was extraordinary. Like almost all the Romantic composers, he was inspired by literary models, including especially Shakespeare—his bizarre *Lélio* is a meditation on *Hamlet,* and his opera *Béatrice et Bénédict* is taken from *Much Ado about Nothing*—and Virgil. *The Trojans* (1858), his long two-part opera derived from Virgil's *Aeneid,* was seldom performed until modern times, but it is now regarded as his masterpiece.

Berlioz had two unhappy marriages, the first to the Irish Shakespearean actress Harriet Smithson, who is immortalized as the *idée fixe* in the *Fantastic* Symphony. In spite of suffering from constant gibes on the one hand, and wretched health on the other, it was a triumph of his impetuous personality that Berlioz ultimately managed to get most of his enormous compositions performed and to gain a good measure of recognition in musically conservative Paris.

He was obliged throughout his life to support himself with musical journalism, at which he was a master; his *Memoirs* is one of the most delightful books ever written about music. He also wrote important treatises on orchestration and conducting. One of the first great conductors, Berlioz toured extensively as a conductor of his own music, especially in Germany, where he was welcomed in modernist circles.

His last years were spent in physical pain and depression. After 1862 he listened to little music and composed none. Berlioz died in Paris in 1869.

Chief Works: Program symphonies: *Fantastic* Symphony, *Harold in Italy, Romeo and Juliet* ▪ Concert overtures, among them the *Roman Carnival* Overture ▪ Operas: *Benvenuto Cellini, The Trojans* (after Virgil's *Aeneid*) ▪ Oratorios: *The Damnation of Faust, The Childhood of Christ* ▪ a Requiem Mass for orchestra, chorus, and four brass bands, and a *Te Deum*

The Program Symphony: Hector Berlioz

PROGRAM OF THE SYMPHONY: A young musician of unhealthy sensibility and passionate imagination poisons himself with opium in a fit of lovesick despair. Too weak to kill him, the dose of the drug plunges him into a heavy sleep attended by the strangest visions, during which his sensations, emotions, and memories are transformed in his diseased mind into musical thoughts and images. Even the woman he loves becomes a melody to him, an *idée fixe* [a fixation], as it were, that he finds and hears everywhere.

So begins a long pamphlet that the French Romantic composer Hector Berlioz distributed at performances of his first symphony—a symphony which he could justifiably call *Fantastic,* and which to this day remains his most famous work. It certainly represents a more radical approach to program music than that of the concert overture. Berlioz, too, had written a concert overture, to Sir Walter Scott's novel *Waverly,* but he now felt the need for a broader canvas. In his **program symphonies**—entire symphonies with programs, spelled out movement by movement, in this case—Berlioz set the tone for the "grandiose" compositions that were to become as characteristic of Romanticism as its musical miniatures.

HECTOR BERLIOZ
Fantastic Symphony: Episodes in the Life of an Artist (1830)

Clearly Berlioz had a gift for public relations, for the program of his *Fantastic* Symphony was not a familiar play or novel, but an autobiographical fantasy of the most lurid sort. Here was music that encouraged listeners to think it had been written under the influence of opium, the drug of choice among the Romantics, which shocked society at large. What is more, half of Paris knew that Berlioz was madly in love (from afar) with an Irish actress, Harriet Smithson, who had taken the city by storm with her Shakespearean roles.

Audiences have never been quite sure how seriously to take it all, but they continue to be bowled over by Berlioz's effects of tone color. He demanded an orchestra of unprecedented size, which he used in incredibly original and imaginative ways. Also highly original was the notion of having a single theme recur in all the movements as a representation of the musician's beloved—his **idée fixe.** Here is the *idée fixe* theme as it first appears:

This tune shows many typical features of Romantic melody. The whole of line 2 seems like a passionate struggle to inch higher and higher up the scale. Measure 19, just before the final cadence, provides a positive shudder of emotion. Notice, too, the profusion of dynamic, rubato, and other marks added by the composer to ensure just the right expressive quality.*

To illustrate his drastic mood swings, Berlioz subjects the *idée fixe* to thematic transformation (see page 229) for all its other appearances in the opium dream. The last movement, for example, has a grotesque parody of the theme; its new jerky rhythm and squeaky orchestration (using the small E-flat clarinet) thoroughly undermine the original Romantic mood.

First Movement: Reveries, Passions (Largo—Allegro agitato e appassionato assai)

We first hear a short, quiet run-in—a typically Romantic touch suggesting that the music has grown up imperceptibly out of silence. Then the "soul-sickness" mentioned in the program is depicted by a halting, passionate melody. A faster section begins with the *idée fixe,* and the music picks up energy (the "volcanic love" of the program).

---

*The music example has been simplified to facilitate reading. *Canto espressivo* = expressive song; *dolce* = sweetly; *poco* = somewhat; *poco a poco* = bit by bit; *animato* = animated; *ritenuto* = slowed down (ritardando); *a tempo* = back to the original tempo.

THE PROGRAM CONTINUES: First he recalls the soul-sickness, the aimless passions, the baseless depressions and elations that he felt before first seeing his loved one; then the volcanic love that she instantly inspired in him; his jealous furies; his return to tenderness; his religious consolations.

This fast section follows sonata form, but only very loosely indeed. The *idée fixe* is the main theme, and a second theme which appears in the exposition's unusually short second group is simply a derivative of the first theme. There is no clear stop after the "exposition."

Some of the finest strokes in this movement run counter to Classical principles—for example, the arresting up-and-down harmonized chromatic scale that crops up in the development section without any logical connection to anything else. The recapitulation, too, is extended in a very un-Classical fashion; it actually includes a whole new melody for the oboe.

Near the end, beginning an outsized coda, the *idée fixe* returns noisily at a faster tempo—the first of its many transformations. At the very end, slower music depicts the program's "religious consolations."

Second Movement: A Ball (Allegro non troppo)

A symphony needs the simplicity and easy swing of a dance movement, and this ballroom episode of the opium dream conveniently provided one. The dance in question is not a minuet or a scherzo, but a waltz, the most popular ballroom dance of the nineteenth century. The *idée fixe,* transformed into a lilting triple meter, first appears in the position of the trio (**B** in the **A B A** form) and then returns hauntingly in a coda.

Third Movement: Scene in the Country (Adagio)

Invoking nature to reflect human emotions was a favorite Romantic procedure. The "pastoral duet" is played by an English horn (evidently the boy shepherd) and an offstage oboe (the girl). At the end, the English horn returns to the accompaniment of distant thunder sounds, played on four differently tuned timpani. Significantly, the oboe is no longer to be heard.

In between these evocative pipings, the movement is built on another rich melody. The *idée fixe* returns in a new, strangely agitated transformation. It is interrupted by angry sounds swelling to a forceful climax, indicative of the anxieties chronicled in the program.

Fourth Movement: March to the Scaffold (Allegretto non troppo)

The final fall of the axe is illustrated vividly by the sound of a guillotine chop and a snare-drum roll, right after measures 1–2 of the *idée fixe.*

This movement has two main themes: a simple theme consisting of a long downward scale ("gloomy and wild") and a blaring, ominous military march ("brilliant and grand"). Later the scale theme appears divided up in its orchestration between plucked and bowed strings, woodwinds, brass, and percussion—a memorable instance of Berlioz's novel imagination for tone color. Finally the scale theme appears in a truly shattering inverted form (that is, moving upward).

Fifth Movement: Dream of a Witches' Sabbath (Larghetto—Allegro)

Now the element of parody is added to the astonishing orchestral effects pioneered earlier in the symphony. First we hear the unearthly sounds of the nighttime locale of the witches' orgy. Their swishing broomsticks are heard, and some kind of distant horn calls that are summoning them. Mutes are used in the brass instruments—perhaps their first "poetic" use ever.

As Berlioz remarks, the "noble and timid" *idée fixe* sounds thoroughly vulgar in its last transformation, played in a fast jig rhythm by the shrill E-flat clarinet. The treatment of the *idée fixe* here is strictly "programmatic": when the theme first arrives, only two phrases are played before the orchestra breaks in, with a "roar of joy" welcoming Harriet Smithson to the orgy.

WOODWINDS STRINGS

dolce < < *ff*

. . . He encounters his beloved at a ball, in the midst of a noisy, brilliant party.

. . . On a summer evening in the country, he hears two shepherds piping in dialogue. The pastoral duet, the location, the light rustling of trees stirred gently by the wind, some newly conceived grounds for hope—all this gives him a feeling of unaccustomed calm. But *she* appears again, his heart misses a beat—what if she is deceiving him?

. . . He dreams he has killed his beloved, that he is condemned to death and led to execution. A march accompanies the procession, now gloomy and wild, now brilliant and grand. Finally the *idée fixe* appears for a moment, to be cut off by the fall of the axe.

. . . He finds himself at a Witches' Sabbath. . . . Unearthly sounds, groans, shrieks of laughter, distant cries echoed by other cries. The beloved's melody is heard, but it has lost its character of nobility and timidity. It is *she* who comes to the Sabbath! At her arrival, a roar of joy. She joins in the devilish orgies. A funeral knell; burlesque of the *Dies irae.*

As the merriment is brought to an end by a dramatic funeral bell, Berlioz prepares his most sensational stroke of all—a burlesque of one of the most solemn and famous of Gregorian chants, the *Dies irae* (Day of Wrath). This chant is the centerpiece of Masses for the dead, or Requiem Masses; in Catholic France, any audience would have recognized the *Dies irae* instantly. Its distorted rhythms and grotesque orchestral sounds paint a blasphemous, shocking picture of the witches' black mass:

Original Gregorian chant:

Di - es   i - rae   di - es   il - la   Sol - vet ___ sae - clum ___ in   fa - vil - - la . . .
Day of wrath, that dreadful day,   *When heaven and earth shall pass away*

Verson 1: TUBAS and BASSOONS

Version 2: FRENCH HORNS and TROMBONES

Version 3: WOODWINDS and PIZZICATO STRINGS

The final section of the movement is a "Witches' Round Dance." Berlioz wrote a free fugue—a traditional form in a nontraditional context; he uses counterpoint to give a feeling of tumult. The subject is an excited one:

The climax of the fugue (and of the symphony) comes when the Round Dance theme is heard together with the *Dies irae,* played by the trumpets. Berlioz wanted to drive home the point that it is the witches, represented by the theme of their round dance, who are parodying the church melody. The *idée fixe* seems at last to be forgotten. But in real life Berlioz did not forget; he married Smithson and both of them lived to regret it.

Witches' Sabbath, by
Francisco Goya (1746–1828)

LISTENING CHART 16

Berlioz, *Fantastic* Symphony, fifth movement

9 min., 45 sec.

INTRODUCTION

	0:00		Mysterious orchestral effects
	0:28	*Fanfare*	Like a distant trumpet or horn summons; woodwinds. Echoed by muted French horn
	1:08	*Fanfare*	Again

IDÉE FIXE

	1:21		Prefatory statement: two phrases (only) of the *idée fixe*; riotous orchestral response, *ff*
2/2	1:40	*Idée fixe*	Entire tune presented in a grotesque transformation, in 6/8 meter, played by "squeaky" E-flat clarinets
0:29	2:09	*Crescendo*	
0:50	2:30	**Upward motive**	A short, expectant motive (later this motive initiates the fugue subject of the "Round Dance")
0:53	2:33	*Transition*	Quiet descending passage
1:16	2:56	**Funeral bells**	Three sets of three bells (the third set is muted); the upward motive also appears

DIES IRAE

3/3	3:26	**Phrase 1**	Phrase 1 of the plainchant is played in three versions:
			(1) tubas and bassoons—slow
0:22	3:48		(2) horns and trombones—faster
0:32	3:58		(3) woodwinds—faster still (the rhythm here recalls that of the *idée fixe*)
0:37	4:03	**Phrase 2**	Phrase 2 of the plainchant, in the same three versions
1:01	4:27	**Phrase 3**	Phrase 3 of the plainchant, in the same three versions
			(Meanwhile the funeral bells and the upward motive are occasionally heard)
1:36	5:02	*Transition*	The upward motive is developed; crescendo

WITCHES' ROUND DANCE (free fugue)

4/4	5:16	**Exposition**	Four entries of the fugue subject
	5:46	*Episode 1*	
0:47	6:03	**Subject entries**	*Three more entries, in stretto*
5/5	6:19	*Episode 2*	A passage starting with a loud rhythmic motive, derived from the subject, comes four times.
0:24	6:43		The music dies down.
0:39	6:58		Fragments of the *Dies irae*
0:56	7:15		Long transition; big crescendo over a drum roll
1:35	7:54	**Subject entry**	The original subject returns.
6/6	8:01	**Subject plus** *Dies irae*	The two themes together in a polyphonic combination. This is a climax; trumpets play the *Dies irae* for the first time.
0:30	8:31	**Subject entry**	Final appearance of subject: over strings *col legno* (played with the wood, that is, the back of the bow). Some notes are lengthened.
7/7	9:06	*Dies irae*	Phrase 1 hastily recollected in the same three versions as at its first appearance; big drum strokes
0:09	9:15	**Conclusion**	Final passage of cadences: very loud. The last note is sustained.

CHAPTER 18

Romantic Opera

A n important theme of Romanticism was the transcendence of artistic barriers. The idea of combining music with poetry and other forms of literature, and even with philosophy, made perfect sense to Romantic composers and their audiences. The age that produced the lied—a German song with an important poetic dimension—was also fascinated by the union of music and drama. The nineteenth century was a golden age of opera, which flourished all over Europe from Germany, France, and Italy to Bohemia and Russia.

Opera in the nineteenth century was affected by another important Romantic theme: the celebration of music as the most profound of all the arts. Opera composers and librettists began thinking seriously about the meaning and "message" of their work; they came to view opera as a type of serious drama in music, not just a vehicle for song, spectacle, and entertainment, as had often been the case before. Richard Wagner is famous for embracing, publicizing, and even co-opting this notion. Indeed, he pursued it much further than anyone else in his "music dramas"—works that fascinated the nineteenth century. Nonetheless, Wagner was building on new attitudes toward opera that were developing all over Europe even when he was still an unknown provincial conductor.

Carve this into your head, in letters of brass: an opera must draw tears, cause horror, bring death, by means of song.

Opera composer Vincenzo Bellini, 1834

The Wolf's Glen Scene from Weber's *Der Freischütz,* most famous of early German Romantic operas (see opposite)

Early Romantic Opera

Romantic opera made its serious start in the 1820s, after the end of the Viennese Classical period. It did not, however, start or flourish in the heartland of Classical music, which was Vienna. In that city, both Beethoven and Schubert felt threatened by the popular rage for the operas of Gioacchino Rossini, a young Italian whose meteoric career left a mark on the whole of Europe.

Gioacchino Rossini (1792–1868)

Rossini is most famous today for crisp, elegant opera buffas in a style that is not all that far from Mozart—the immortal *Barber of Seville* among them. The overtures of these operas, which are popular as concert pieces, are even written in sonata form, the true trademark of Classicism in music.

But in his own day Rossini was admired equally for his serious operas, which established the style and form of Italian Romantic opera. This is called *bel canto* opera because of its glorification of beautiful singing (*bel canto* means just that—"beautiful song"). Rossini's operas provided models of Romantic emotional melodic expression, such as Desdemona's "Willow Song" from his Shakespeare opera *Otello*. The same operas are also well stocked with coloratura arias, showcases for the legendary virtuoso singers of that era.

Gaetano Donizetti (1797–1848)

Donizetti, who dominated Italian *bel canto* opera after Rossini's sudden retirement in 1830, moved decisively in the direction of simple, sentimental arias and blood-and-thunder "action" music. Enormously prolific, he wrote more than sixty operas in his relatively short lifetime.

The most famous are *Lucia di Lammermoor,* based on the historical novel by Scott mentioned on page 254, and *Don Pasquale,* a very late example of opera buffa. In the 1970s, the American soprano Beverly Sills starred in a Donizetti trilogy featuring famous queens of English history: *Anna Bolena* (Anne Boleyn, the ill-fated second wife of Henry VIII), *Maria Stuarda* (Mary Stuart—Mary, Queen of Scots), and *Roberto Devereux* (about Queen Elizabeth I and Robert Devereux, Earl of Essex).

Vincenzo Bellini (1801–1835)

Vincenzo Bellini strikes listeners today as the most refined among the three early *bel canto* composers. He wrote many fewer operas than the others, and his most beautiful arias have a unique Romantic sheen. The title role in *Norma,* his finest work, is the final testing ground for sopranos, for it demands highly expressive singing, coloratura fireworks, and great acting, all in unusual quantities.

Verdi often expressed his admiration for the supremely melodious Bellini. All the same, he learned more from the more robust and dramatic Donizetti.

Carl Maria von Weber (1786–1826)

Weber was the founder of German Romantic opera. His most important work, *Der Freischütz* (The Magic Bullet), has the quality of a German folk tale or ballad put to music. Max, a somewhat driven young huntsman, sells his soul to the devil for seven magic bullets, but is redeemed by the sacrifice of his pure, blond fiancée, Agatha.

Two spiritual arias sung by Agatha in this opera represent Romantic melody at its best; there are also German choruses in a folk-song style. A famous scene of devilish conjuration in the Wolf's Glen depends for its effect on sensational orchestral writing of a kind previously unknown to opera.

The supernatural subject matter, with its strongly moral overtone—very different from the historical subjects chosen by Donizetti, for example—and the emphasis on the orchestra became characteristic of German Romantic opera. These features can still be clearly discerned in the mature "music dramas" of Richard Wagner, who started his career in the 1830s as an opera composer in Weber's mold. Otherwise, however, Wagner's music dramas leave early Romantic opera far behind.

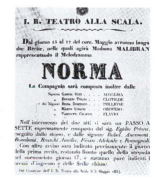

Legendary singers of the *bel canto* era: Pauline Viardot (1821–1910), Maria Malibran (1808–1836), and Giulia Grisi (1811–1869), along with a playbill for one of their favorite showcases, the opera *Norma* by Vincenzo Bellini

Thus many operas took their subjects from highly regarded Romantic novels, such as *Ivanhoe*, *The Lady of the Lake*, and *The Bride of Lammermoor*, by Sir Walter Scott. Since poets and playwrights were turning with new enthusiasm to Shakespeare's plays, opera composers, too, drew on them widely. Giuseppe Verdi set versions of Shakespeare's tragedies *Macbeth* and *Othello* as well as the comedy *The Merry Wives of Windsor*. Over his long career, Verdi developed his own form of musical drama, which bears comparison with that of Wagner or anyone else for seriousness and power.

1   Verdi and Italian Opera

Giuseppe Verdi, the greatest of Italian opera composers, was the dominant figure in nineteenth-century opera houses. For while Wagner's "music dramas" and his theories of opera attracted much excited attention, Verdi's operas got many more performances. Then as now, people were inevitably drawn to compare and contrast these two masters.

The heart of the contrast lies in Verdi's unswerving commitment to the human voice. In this, he was a faithful follower of the *bel canto* principles of Rossini, Donizetti, and Bellini. Verdi never allowed the voice to be overshadowed by the orchestra, and over the course of his long career he learned to write more and more beautiful melodies. Opera was a singing art to Verdi, and generations of Italians before, during, and after his lifetime have enthusiastically agreed with him.

But while audiences have always loved Verdi's melodies, what he himself cared most about was the dramatic quality of his operas. First and foremost, Verdi was interested in people, people placed in situations in which strong exciting actions bring out equally strong emotions. He sought out dramatic subjects full of stirring action, and he had a genius for finding just the right vocal melody to enhance a dramatic situation.

Recitative and Aria: The Orchestra

As an opera composer, Verdi never wavered in his commitment to the human voice. Once this basic point has been made, however, it must also be said that the orchestra plays a much richer role in Verdi's operas than in those of any of his Italian predecessors. This was all but inevitable in the orchestra-intoxicated nineteenth century.

The role of the orchestra was especially expanded in passages of recitative or near-recitative—the relic or descendant of the recitatives of Baroque opera seria and Classical opera buffa. Italian opera still held roughly to the old division of declamation (recitative) for the "action" and dialogue portions of an opera and melody (arias) for reflective, emotional expression. (Ensembles encompassed both.) But plot action and dialogue were now always accompanied by the full orchestra. The orchestra is usually not restricted to the simple chords that were usual in earlier recitative styles; it plays more active, motivic, and excited music that points up the words and urges the singers on.

"Recitative" is no longer a satisfactory name—though no other name exists—for this "action" music in Verdi's operas. Highly melodramatic, it is always on the point of merging into a full-fledged melodic style. What distinguishes this music from actual arias is that arias are formally complete and distinct. Unlike passages of Verdian "recitative," Verdian arias can be (and often are) extracted and sung separately, as concert numbers.

Giuseppe Verdi (1813–1901)

The son of a storekeeper in a tiny village in northern Italy, Verdi had a spotty education. He played church organ and conducted the band of the neighboring little town. A local merchant, Antonio Barezzi, who became a patron and almost a second father to the young man, sent him to Milan to study music.

In those days, the center of musical life in Italy was Milan's famous opera house, La Scala. After several discouraging years in that city, Verdi scored a huge success with his biblical opera *Nabucco* (Nebuchadnezzar) when he was twenty-nine years old. For the next ten years—Verdi called them his *anni di galera*, his years as a galley slave—he composed operas at a furious rate for opera houses in Italy, Paris, and London. He finally scored with three great hits in the early 1850s, and they are still his most popular works: *Rigoletto,* which chronicles cynical and deadly court intrigues (the original play was banned), *Il trovatore,* a grisly tale in the age of chivalry, and— entirely up to date—*La traviata,* about a "good" courtesan. After this Verdi took more time with his operas, and his later works became richer and more subtle.

Verdi was an ardent supporter of the Risorgimento, or Italian liberation movement, and many of his early operas had patriotic themes. The most beloved number in *Nabucco* was a nostalgic hymn of the Hebrew slaves in Babylon—a clear reference to the Italians under the heel of the Austrian Empire. In the year of revolution, 1848, Verdi wrote the rousing *Battle of Legnano.* "Verdi" actually became a patriotic acronym for the popular choice for king—*Vittorio Emmanuele, Re d'Italia*—and after independence was achieved, the composer was made an honorary deputy in the first Italian parliament.

Verdi was devoted to Italian traditions in opera, naturally enough, and suspicious of any others. Rossini was his idol. He kept his peace about Wagner's music dramas, but he reacted very bitterly when his own later works were criticized as Wagnerian (mainly because of their increasingly rich and sophisticated orchestral style).

A dour character and a tough businessman, Verdi drove hard bargains with opera impresarios, bullied his librettists, and insisted on supervising the production of his new operas. When he had accumulated enough money, he retired to a fine country estate near his birthplace and spent his later years hunting and raising livestock. After fifteen years of this life, he was coaxed out of retirement by his canny publisher and by an eminent librettist, Arrigo Boito. In his seventies, Verdi wrote his two greatest operas with Boito on Shakespearean subjects: the tragedy *Otello* and the comedy *Falstaff.*

Verdi's first marriage, to the daughter of his early patron Barezzi, ended in tragedy when his young wife and two babies died within two years. The composer bore the emotional scars of this all his life, and it may be that the many moving scenes between fathers and daughters in Verdi's operas served to channel his feelings about fatherhood. He later married a remarkable woman, Giuseppina Strepponi, a singer who had assisted him in his early career and starred in his first success, *Nabucco.* She had been Verdi's mistress for many years.

By the time he died, at the age of eighty-eight, Verdi was a national institution, and he was mourned throughout Italy. Schools closed. Eulogies were delivered in a special session of the senate in Rome. Nearly 300,000 people saw the old man to his grave. His operas remain the most popular of all in the international repertory.

Chief Works: Twenty-four operas, including *Nabucco, Macbeth, Rigoletto, Il trovatore, La traviata, Don Carlo, The Force of Destiny, Aida* ■ Two great Shakespeare operas composed after his retirement, *Otello* and *Falstaff* ■ A Requiem Mass, and a few other choral works; a string quartet

A popular graffito of the Italian revolution: "Viva VERDI" (meaning "Long live Victor Emmanuel, King of Italy")

In arias and duets, the orchestra's role is smaller; here, however, Verdi makes use of another Romantic resource, that of rich harmonies underpinning melodic high points and climaxes. Many—though by no means all—of Verdi's arias might be described as simple strophic songs in his own exuberant style of Romantic melody. Some of his most famous music consists of timeless tunes such as the tenor aria "La donna è mobile" from *Rigoletto,* the choral hymn "Va pensiero" from *Nabucco,* and the duet "O terra, addio" from *Aida,* which we will examine next.

GIUSEPPE VERDI
Aida (1871)

Aida is one of the most frequently performed of all operas. It includes gorgeous arias—including a tenor favorite, "Celeste Aida"—and grandiose stage display, including elephants. Africa is the locale; this work was written to celebrate a milestone in the history of nineteenth-century imperialism, the opening of the Suez Canal in Egypt in 1869. In view of his commission, Verdi chose an Egyptian subject and wrote some exotic Egyptian-sounding music.

In other hands, perhaps, all this might have been merely pretentious. But Verdi's arias, display, and exoticism are coupled with an absorbing drama, a drama of credible human beings destroyed by powerful political forces and equally powerful emotions.

Amneris

Background   The plot of *Aida* is thoroughly romantic (in the sense of amorous). A tragic love triangle is projected against a war between ancient Egypt, controlled by a sinister priesthood, and Ethiopia.

Acts I and II introduce a young Egyptian general, Radames, and a captive Ethiopian slave girl, Aida, who are secretly in love. (The Egyptians don't know that Aida is the daughter of Amonasro, King of Ethiopia.) Unfortunately, Radames has also attracted Amneris, a passionate and jealous Egyptian princess.

In Act III, by a turn of the plot that we need not follow here, Radames is tricked into revealing his country's battle plans to Aida. Amneris has eavesdropped on their tryst, and she turns Radames over to the all-powerful priests for judgment as a traitor. Aida escapes in the confusion.

In Act IV Amneris offers to save Radames if he will return her love. To her dismay, he says he would rather die than live without Aida; Amneris realizes too late that she has assured the doom of the man she loves. His trial by the priests, in Act IV, scene i, which she witnesses, is one of the most dramatic in the entire opera. Radames makes no defense and is condemned to be buried alive in a tomb under the temple, sealed up by a huge stone.

Aida

Tomb Scene (Act IV, scene ii)   Radames has just been entombed. Verdi called for a very striking stage set, divided horizontally: below, a cramped cell containing Radames; above, the Temple of Vulcan, complete with altar, colossal statue of Osiris, and other grandiose Egyptian paraphernalia. Although the

The final scene of *Aida,* from a contemporary illustrated newspaper

impact of Verdi's music seldom fails, outside of the theater a special effort is required to envisage the stage and the action, so as to appreciate the full range of Verdi's dramatic art.

Recitative   The scene opens with quiet, ominous music in the strings—already, in its understated way, a forecast of doom. The first singing consists of three short passages of recitative. Each follows the same general plan. In each recitative passage, simple declamatory singing (with very light orchestral accompaniment) leads to an intense moment of genuine melody, with rich harmonic and orchestral support.

Thus Radames begins singing on a lengthy monotone, but works up some emotion when he thinks of Aida and hopes she will be spared knowledge of his fate. Then his more excited second speech is still fragmentary, up to the point when he discovers that Aida has hidden in his tomb to see him once again and die with him. He cries out "You, in this tomb!" on a high note, picking up from an anguished downward scale in the orchestra.

The third recitative passage, Aida's reply, begins simply, over a knell-like orchestral accompaniment. It melts into a beautiful and sensuously harmonized melodic phrase when she tells him she wants to die in his arms.

Ariosos   There follow two concise tunelike sections, or *ariosos* (see page 91). In the first of them, sung by Radames, notice the subdued, subservient role of the orchestra. The next arioso is more tuneful yet, with Aida's phrases falling into an almost Classical **a a′ b a′ c** pattern. The harmony is fully Romantic, however, especially in phrase **b**.

Duet (with Chorus)   Then Verdi mounts his impressive final scene. At the top level of the stage, priests and priestesses move slowly as they sing a funeral hymn with an exotic, Near Eastern flavor. They are invoking the great god Ptah. At the bottom level, Aida and Radames begin their final duet, a farewell to the sorrows of earth and a welcome to eternity. It is a famous instance of Verdi's simple and yet highly expansive melodic style:

I would like something sweet, ethereal, a very brief duet, a farewell to life. Aida should sink gently into Radames's arms. Meanwhile, Amneris, kneeling on the stone above the underground chamber, should sing "Requiescant in pace" [May they rest in peace].

Letter from Verdi to his librettist, during the planning stages of *Aida*

Amonasro

There is an exquisite Romantic harmony at the climax of the melody, in **c** of the **a a′ b a′ c** form—and that climax, on just about the highest note in the tenor's range, has to be sung very softly. This gives the melody a uniquely ethereal effect, as befits a couple who are about to die from lack of oxygen.

Other features reinforce this effect: the melodic line that focuses on just a few notes (high and low G♭ and D♭), and the high accompanying haze of string instruments that later swell up ecstatically. We sense that Aida and Radames are already far out of this world, perfectly attuned to each other (they sing the same tune in octaves) in a love that transcends death itself.

LISTEN	Verdi, *Aida*, Tomb Scene, Act IV, scene ii	4	4A
		8-11	2

RECITATIVE: Radames alone, then Aida

Part 1: Radames reflects *Quiet orchestral introduction (strings) sets the mournful mood. Radames sings his first three lines on a monotone. Accompaniment: slow and halting.*

0:24	**Radames:**	La fatal pietra sovra me si chiuse;	The fatal stone closes over me;
		Ecco la tomba mia.	This is my tomb.
		Del dì la luce più non vedro . . .	The light of day I'll never see again.
		Non rivedrò più Aida.	I'll never see Aida.
		Aida, ove sei tu? possa tu almeno	Aida, where are you?
1:27		Viver felice, e la mia sorte orrenda	Live happily, and never know
		Sempre ignorar!	Of my terrible death.

Part 2: Radames hears a sound *Accompaniment: the rhythm picks up*

1:40	**Radames:**	Qual gemito—una larva—un vision . . .	What sound was that? a ghost? a vision?
		No! forma umana è questa . . . Ciel, Aida!	No, a human form . . . Aida!
	Aida:	Son io . . .	Yes . . .
	Radames:	Tu, in questa tomba!	You, in this tomb!

Part 3: Aida explains *Accompaniment: mournful low notes*

2:12	**Aida:**	Presago il core della tua condanna,	A presentiment of my heart foretold your sentence;
		In questa tomba che per te s'appriva	This tomb awaited you—
		Io penetrai furtiva,	I hid secretly in it,
		E qui lontana da ogni umano sguardo	And here, far from any human gaze,
		Nelle tue bracia desiai morire.	I wanted to die in your arms.

ARIOSO I

9 **Radames reacts in despair** *"Con passione"—passionately*

2:56	**Radames:**	Morir! si pura e bella!	Dying, so innocent and beautiful,
		Morir per me d'amore,	Dying, for love of me!
		Degli anni tuoi nel fiore,	So young,
		degli anni tuoi nel fiore fuggir la vita!	so young to give up life!
		T'avea in cielo per l'amor creata,	You were made in heaven for love
		Ed io t'uccido per averti amata!	And I have killed you by loving you!
		No, non morrai, troppo t'amai, troppo	You cannot die! You are too beautiful, I
		sei bella!	love you too much!

ARIOSO II

Aida, "almost in a trance" *Ethereal high strings*

10	4:06	**Aida:**	Vedi? di morte l'angelo	See, the angel of death
			Radiante a noi s'appressa,	Approaches us in radiance,
			Ne adduce a eterni gaudii	Leading to eternal joys
			Sovra i suoi vanni d'or.	On his golden wings.
			Già veggo il ciel dischiudersi;	I see the heavens open;
			Ivi ogni affano cessa,	Here pain ceases,
	4:41		Ivi *commincia l'estasi*	Here begins the ecstasy
			D'un immortal amor.	Of immortal love.

CHORUS (on the upper stage) with interjections by Radames and Aida *Modal harmonies, harp, and flute*

5:03	**Aida:**	Triste canto!	Mournful chant!	**Chorus:**	Immenso Ftha,
	Radames:	Il tripudio dei sacerdoti . . .	The priestly rites . . .		del mondo spirito animator,
	Aida:	Il nostro inno di morte.	Our funeral hymn.		noi t'invocchiamo.
	Radames:	Nè le mie forti braccia	All of my strength cannot		
		Smuovere ti potranno, o fatal pietra!	Move that fatal stone!		Great Ptah,
	Aida:	Invan—tutto e finito	In vain—all is finished		the world's Creative spirit,
		Sulla terra per noi.	For us on earth.		we invoke thee.
	Radames:	È vero, è vero!	True, it is true.		

DUET: First Aida, then Radames with Aida *With quiet high strings*

11	5:59	**Aida and Radames:**

O terra, addio, addio, valle di pianti,	Farewell to earth, vale of tears,
Sogno di gaudio che in dolor svanì,	Dream of happiness which vanishes in grief;
A noi *si schiude* il ciel,	The heavens open,
si schiude il ciel e l'alme erranti	And our fleeing souls
Volano al raggio dell'eterno dì.	Escape to the rays of eternal day.

CHORUS (on the upper stage) singing with Aida and Radames

DUET continues: Aida and Radames together (same music) with Amneris and the Chorus

8:21	**Aida and Radames:**				

O terra addio, addio valle di pianti,		7:50 **Chorus:**	Immenso Ftha,
Sogno di gaudio che in dolor svanì,			del mondo spirito animator,
A noi *si schiude* il ciel,			noi t'invocchiamo.
si schiude il ciel e l'alme erranti			
Volano al raggio dell'eterno dì.			Great Ptah,
			the world's Creative spirit,
8:31 **Amneris:** Pace t'imploro, salma adorata,	I beg you for peace, beloved spirit;		we invoke thee.
Isi placata, *Isi placata* ti schiuda il ciel,	May Isis, placated, welcome you to		
9:45 *pace t'imploro, pace . . .*	heaven . . . peace, peace . . .		

Ends with violins playing the "O terra" tune, Amneris singing "Pace, pace," and the Chorus repeating "Immenso Ftha!"

Conclusion   Before the final curtain, a figure in mourning enters the temple above the tomb to pray. Drained of all the emotion that she poured out in earlier scenes, Amneris can only whisper on a monotone, "Peace, I pray for peace" *(Pace t'imploro)*. The different psychic states of the characters are made more vivid by simultaneous contrast, a principle we saw at work in Mozart's opera buffa ensembles (see page 196). Amneris's grief is set directly against the ecstatic, otherworldly togetherness of Radames and Aida.

High violins take over the duet melody; one can almost visualize the souls of Aida and Radames ascending to "eternal day." And by giving the last words to the priests—the judges of Radames and the proponents of Egypt's wars—Verdi hands them the ultimate responsibility for the threefold tragedy.

CHORUS OF PRIESTS AND PRIESTESSES (with harp accompaniment)

Im - - menso, immenso Ftha, del mon - - do _ spirito ani - ma - tor ____
Great Ptah, the world's creative spirit

2 Wagner and "Music Drama"

Richard Wagner was, after Beethoven, the most influential of all nineteenth-century composers. His strictly musical innovations, in harmony and orchestration, revolutionized instrumental music as well as opera. In terms of opera, Wagner is famous for his novel concept of the "complete work of art" (*Gesamtkunstwerk,* see below) and his development of a special operatic technique, that of the "guiding motive" (leitmotiv).

Unlike earlier innovative composers, it seems Wagner could not just compose; he had to develop elaborate theories announcing what art, music, and opera ought to be like. (Indeed, he also theorized about politics and philosophy, with unfortunate results.) Wagner's extreme self-consciousness as an artist was prophetic of attitudes toward art of a much later period.

Richard Wagner (1813–1883)

Wagner was born in Leipzig during the turmoil of the Napoleonic wars; his father died soon afterward. His stepfather was a fascinating actor and writer, and the boy turned into a decided intellectual. Wagner's early interests, literature and music (his idols were Shakespeare and Beethoven), later expanded to include philosophy, mythology, and religion.

As a young man he worked as an opera conductor, and he spent an unhappy year in Paris trying to get one of his works produced at the influential Opéra there. Wagner's strong anti-French sentiments stemmed from this experience. Back in Germany, he produced the first of his impressive operas, *The Flying Dutchman* and *Tannhäuser,* and wrote *Lohengrin;* the last two of these soon became very popular. Though all three works basically adhere to the early Romantic opera style of Carl Maria von Weber, they already hint at the revolutionary ideal for opera that Wagner was pondering.

This he finally formulated after being exiled from Germany (and from a job) as a result of his part in the revolution of 1848–1849. He wrote endless articles and books expounding his ideas—ideas that were better known than his later operas, for these were extremely difficult to stage. His chief book, *Opera and Drama,* set up the principles for his first "music drama," *The Rhinegold,* the first number of the extraordinary four-evening opera *The Ring of the Nibelung.* He also published a mean essay attacking Mendelssohn, who had just died, and other Jews in music; fifty years after Wagner's death, his anti-Semitic writings (and his operas) were taken up by the Nazis.

Wagner's exile lasted thirteen years. His fortunes changed dramatically when he gained the support of the young, unstable, and finally mad King Ludwig II of Bavaria. Thanks to Ludwig, Wagner's mature music dramas were at last produced (*The Rhinegold,* completed in 1854, was not produced until 1869). Wagner then promoted the building of a special opera house in Bayreuth, Germany, solely for his music dramas—grandiose, slow-moving works based on myths, and characterized by high-flown poetry of his own, a powerful orchestral style, and the use of *leitmotivs* (guiding or leading motives). To this day the opera house in Bayreuth performs only Wagner. For many years his last music drama, *Parsifal* (1882), was allowed to be produced only at Bayreuth, which became in effect a Wagnerian shrine.

A hypnotic personality, Wagner was able to spirit money out of many pockets and command the loyalty and affection of many distinguished men and women. His first marriage, to a singer, ended in divorce; his great operatic hymn to love, *Tristan und Isolde,* was created partly in response to his love affair with the wife of one of his patrons. His second wife, Cosima, daughter of Franz Liszt, had been married to an important conductor, Hans von Bülow, who nonetheless remained one of Wagner's strongest supporters. Cosima's diaries tell us a great deal about Wagner's moods, dreams, thoughts, and musical decisions, all of which he shared with her. After the death of "the Master," Cosima ruled Bayreuth with an iron hand.

Half con man and half visionary, bad poet and very good musician, Wagner created a storm of controversy in his lifetime which has not died down to this day. He was a major figure in the intellectual life of his time, a thinker whose ideas were highly influential not only in music but also in other arts. In this sense, at least, Wagner was the most important of the Romantic composers.

Chief Works: Early operas, including *The Flying Dutchman, Tannhäuser* and *Lohengrin* ▪ Mature "music dramas": *Tristan und Isolde, The Mastersingers of Nuremberg, Parsifal,* and *The Ring of the Nibelung,* a four-opera cycle consisting of *The Rhinegold, The Valkyrie, Siegfried,* and *The Twilight of the Gods* ▪ *Siegfried Idyll,* for small orchestra (based on themes from *Siegfried;* a surprise birthday present for Cosima)

Wagner, Cosima, and their son Siegfried. Named after the hero of *The Ring of the Nibelung,* Siegfried eventually succeeded Cosima as director of the Bayreuth festivals of his father's operas.

His theory of opera had its positive and negative sides. First, Wagner wanted to do away with nearly all the conventions of earlier opera, especially the French and Italian varieties. Opera, he complained, had degenerated from its original form as serious drama in music—Wagner was thinking of ancient Greek drama, which he knew had been sung or at least chanted—into a mere "concert in costume." He particularly condemned arias, which were certainly at the heart of Italian opera, as hopelessly artificial. Why should the dramatic action keep stopping to allow for stretches of pretty but undramatic singing?

The "Total Work of Art"

The positive side of Wagner's program was the development of a new kind of opera in the 1850s, which he called **music drama**. Music, in these works, shares the honors with poetry, drama, and philosophy—all furnished by Wagner himself—as well as the stage design and acting. Wagner coined the word **Gesamtkunstwerk**, meaning "total work of art," for this powerful concept.

Since words and ideas are so important in the *Gesamtkunstwerk,* the music is very closely matched to the words. Yet it is also unrelievedly emotional and intense, as Romantic doctrine required. The dramas themselves deal with weighty philosophical issues, or so at least Wagner and his admirers believed, and they do so under the symbolic cover of medieval German myths and legends.

This was another Romantic feature, one that strikingly anticipated Freud, with his emphasis on myths (for example, the myth of Oedipus) as embodiments of the deepest unconscious truths. Thus Wagner employed the old romance of Tristan and Iseult, the saga of the Nordic god Wotan, and the Arthurian tale of Sir Perceval to present his views on love, political power, and religion, respectively.

Wagner was one of the first great conductors, and a superb orchestrator. He raised the orchestra to new importance in opera, giving it a new role modeled on Beethoven's symphonies with their motivic development. Leitmotivs (see below) were among the motives he used for this "symphonic" continuity. The orchestra was no longer used essentially as a support for the singers (which was still the situation, really, even in Verdi); it was now the orchestra that carried the opera along. Instead of the alternation of recitatives, arias, and ensembles in traditional opera, "music drama" consisted of one long orchestral web, cunningly woven in with the singing.

Leitmotivs

A **leitmotiv** (guiding, or leading, motive) is a musical motive associated with some person, thing, idea, or symbol in the drama. By presenting and developing leitmotivs, the orchestra in a Wagner music drama guides the listener through the story.

Leitmotivs were easy to ridicule when they were used mechanically—when, for example, the orchestra obligingly sounded the Sword motive every time the hero spoke about his weapon. On the other hand, leitmotivs could suggest with considerable subtlety what the hero was thinking or feeling even when he was saying something else. Wagner also became very skillful in thematic transformation—the characteristic variationlike technique of the Romantic composers (see page 229). By transforming the appropriate motives, he could show a person or an idea developing and changing under the impact of dramatic action.

Music never expresses outer phenomena, but only mankind's inner nature, the "in-itself" of all phenomena: the Will itself.

Philosopher Arthur Schopenhauer, 1818

And since, for the Romantics, music was the undisputed language of emotion, leitmotivs—being music—could state or suggest ideas in *emotional* terms, over and above the intellectual terms provided by mere words. This was Wagner's theory, a logical outcome of Romantic doctrine about music. Furthermore, the complex web of leitmotivs provided his long music dramas with the thematic "unity" that Romantic composers sought. On both counts, psychological and technical, leitmotivs were guaranteed to impress the nineteenth century.

RICHARD WAGNER (1813–1883)
Tristan und Isolde (1859)

Two major life experiences helped inspire Wagner's first completed music drama, *Tristan und Isolde*. One was his discovery of the Romantic philosophy of Arthur Schopenhauer, and the other was his love affair with Mathilde Wesendonck, the wife of one of his wealthy patrons.

Schopenhauer had made his own philosophical formulation of the Romantic insight into the central importance of music in emotional life. All human experience, said Schopenhauer, consists either of emotions and drives—which he called "the Will"—or of ideas, morals, and reason, which he downgraded by the term "Appearance." He insisted that the Will always dominates Appearance, and that our only direct, unencumbered sense of it comes through music.

For the philosopher, the inevitable domination of the Will was a source of profound pessimism. But a composer could read another message in Schopenhauer's work. It reinforced Wagner's conviction that music was specially privileged for emotional representation, that the deepest truths—those to do with the Will—could indeed be plumbed by music, in a music drama. And what would exemplify the Will better than the most exciting human drive that is known, sexual love? As usual, the story itself would be taken from a medieval legend.

Tristan und Isolde is not just a great love story, then, but something more. It is a drama that presents love as the dominant force in life, one that transcends every other aspect of worldly Appearance. Many love stories hint at such transcendence, perhaps, but Wagner's story makes it explicit, on the basis of an actual philosophy that the composer espoused.

Background   Written by Wagner himself, though derived from a medieval legend, the story of *Tristan und Isolde* shows step by step the growing power of love. In Act I, when Tristan and Isolde fall in love by accidentally drinking a love potion, the Will overpowers Isolde's fierce pride, which had previously made her scorn Tristan as her blood enemy. It also dissolves Tristan's heretofore perfect chivalry, the machismo of the medieval knight, which had demanded that he escort her safely to her marriage to King Mark of Cornwall, his uncle and liege lord.

In Act II, love overcomes the marriage itself when the two meet adulterously (in the longest unconsummated love scene in all of opera). The lovers' tryst is discovered, and Tristan is mortally wounded—but love seems to negate the wound. In Act III he simply cannot or will not die until Isolde comes to him. Then, after Isolde comes and he dies in her arms, she herself sinks down in rapture and expires also. For both of them, death is not a defeat but an ecstatic expression of love.

Mathilde Wesendonck

Never in my life having enjoyed the true happiness of love, I shall build a monument to this most beautiful of dreams, in which love will for once find utter, complete fulfillment, from first to last. I have devised in my mind a Tristan und Isolde . . .

Letter from Wagner to Liszt, 1854

At this point (if not earlier) the plot passes the bounds of reality—which was exactly Wagner's point. Tristan and Isolde, representing Schopenhauer's Will, move in a realm where conventional attitudes, the rules of society, and even life and death have lost their powers. Transcendence was a recurring theme of Romanticism; here love becomes the ultimate transcendent experience, beyond reality. Indeed, the opera's transcendental quality brings it close to mystical experience.

Incidentally, Wagner and Mathilde did not live up to their operatic ideals. After a while, Wesendonck—the King Mark in this triangle—put his foot down and the affair came to an end.

Prelude   Given Wagner's emphasis on the orchestra in his music dramas, it is not surprising that the strictly orchestral Prelude (or Overture) to *Tristan und Isolde* is already a magnificent depiction of romantic love. Or at least one aspect of romantic love: not the joys of love, but love's yearning.

The Prelude opens with a very slow, fragmentary motive whose harmonies create a remarkably sultry, sensual, yearning feeling. The motive is actually made up of two fragments in counterpoint, easily heard because *x* is played by the cellos and *y* by an oboe. Fragment *x* consists of four (later five) rising notes of the chromatic scale:

Langsam und schmachten (*"Slowly and languishing"*)

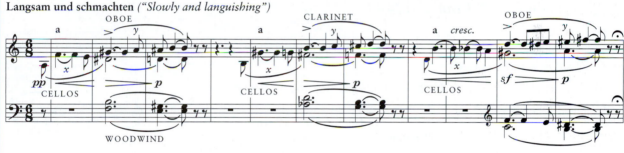

Often treated (as here) in a threefold sequence (see page 27), motive **a** turns out to be the opera's chief leitmotiv. It becomes associated with a rich compound of meaning, including passion, yearning, and release in death. At the risk of oversimplification, we can label it the Love–Death motive.

This Love–Death motive is an example of a Romantic theme that derives its essential character from harmony, rather than from melody or rhythm. The harmony is dissonant: it does not feel at rest, and we expect it to proceed to some other harmony. After the slow opening sequence, the music stretches up and up—still very slowly!—but when the dissonance finally resolves, it resolves in the "wrong" place and still sounds decidedly uneasy.

In other words, the cadence has been undercut; instead of the chord we expect (because it has been clearly prepared by the upward motion), we hear a different chord. This is called a *deceptive cadence*. Deceptive cadences were not new with Wagner, of course; we have heard many of them in works studied in this book. But Wagner used them continuously in order to keep his music surging ahead. When the music stops, it stops "deceptively" at an unexpected place. Those places sound unstable, and so they motivate further surging.

Here, near the beginning of the Prelude, a flowing melodic theme follows, played by the cellos:

As new themes emerge—yet are they new, or are they subtle transformations of earlier themes?—we realize that Wagner is never going to let the music rest. A marvelous dark churning of emotion is produced by the incessant sequences, by Wagner's marvelous orchestration, and by his very characteristic trick of avoiding true cadences in favor of deceptive cadences. The music constantly shifts in key (modulates); every time it seems ready to stop, it starts moving forward restlessly.

In form, the total Prelude amounts to a gradual, irregular crescendo, reaching a climax with a return of the original threefold sequence on the Love–Death motive. Then there is a hush. The motive is heard again in brooding new versions, growing quieter and quieter, so that when the curtain goes up the orchestra has fallen entirely silent, without ever having come to a cadence.

It is not easy to make a Listening Chart for music that sets out to create the sense of formless waves of emotion, as this Prelude does. In addition to motive **a** and the surging cello theme **B**, we are using the symbol **d/c** to refer to specially prominent deceptive cadences.

LISTENING CHART 17

4   4A
12-16   3

Wagner, Prelude to *Tristan und Isolde*

10 min., 9 sec.

---

*(Note: **d/c** stands for deceptive cadence.)*

MAIN THEMATIC GROUP (a d/c B): dynamics *pp*, surge to *f*, back to *p*

0:00	**a** in 3-fold sequence		With fermatas (long gaps)
1:38	**d/c**		Deceptive cadence, *f*: French horn
1:42	**B**		B followed by extension: cellos
2:26		**d/c**	(different deceptive cadence)
2:28		**C**	Descending sequence
2:49			Momentary low trombone motive

OBOE

a   y

x

CELLOS

13 **B WITH NEW EXTENSIONS**

B CELLOS

0:00	3:12	**B**		B followed by extension
0:21	3:34			Quieter material; strings answered by strings and woodwinds
1:03	4:16		**d/c**	(different deceptive cadence)
1:10	4:22		**C**	Descending sequence
1:26	4:39			Trombone motive
2:00	5:11	**B**		Big surge begins
2:15	5:28		**B** again, overlapping	

C VIOLAS

14 **RETRANSITION PASSAGE**   (bass is more static)

0:00	5:50		New, excited string music
0:15	6:05	*y* in 3-fold sequence	*y* is first heard in the oboe
0:46	6:36	**d/c** - **B** overlaps	Louder and louder: *ff*
15	7:05	*x*, **a** ⟶	Climactic horn calls: preparation for:

ENTIRE THEMATIC GROUP dynamics *ff* down to *p* and *pp*

0:09	7:12	**a** in 3-fold sequence	Varied, and with the gaps filled in
1:18	8:20	**d/c**	Deceptive cadence, as at first, but *p*
1:21	8:24	**B** fragments	Varied; minor-mode coloration drum roll
	9:04	**a**, 2-fold sequence	Varied (English horn) ⟶ curtain goes up

"Philter" Scene from Act I   A short segment of the action from Act I of *Tristan und Isolde* will show how Wagnerian music drama works, and how it makes dramatic use of previously introduced leitmotivs—in this case, the Love–Death motive and its threefold sequence, featured in the opera's Prelude.

In Act I, a bleak shipboard scene, Isolde is being escorted by Tristan to Cornwall, the kingdom of King Mark. To her maid and confidante, Brangaene, she furiously denounces Tristan, bewails her coming marriage to King Mark, and mutters something about a loveless marriage. "Loveless?" answers Brangaene. "But anyone would love you; and if he doesn't, we have our magic potions."

First, we hear a short solo passage that is as close as Wagner got to writing a clear-cut aria. The music is seductive and sweet, but though Brangaene certainly sings rich melodic phrases, they do not fall together into a tune. Her melody follows the words closely, without word repetitions. Such repetition, which was taken for granted in all Baroque and Classical arias and ensembles, Wagner would have called an "artificial" feature. The orchestra develops its own seductive motive more freely and more consistently than does the singer.

Lowering her voice, and glancing meaningfully at Isolde, Brangaene asks her if she has not forgotten her mother's magic love potion. (Isolde's mother was a famous sorceress.) Here her singing line is like heightened recitative. In the orchestra the Love–Death leitmotiv sounds its sultry way, three times, in a sequence, as in the Prelude. Through the orchestra, Brangaene is hinting about the love potion.

Isolde answers her by imitating or parodying her recitative: no, she has not forgotten her mother's magic; and the Love–Death motive sounds again. But whatever Brangaene was hinting about, Isolde in her despair is thinking instead of the "death philter," a poison. She recalls a special philter that she marked for just such an occasion as this. At the thought (not even the mention!) of death, a sinister new motive emerges in the trombones. And when Isolde actually *mentions* the death philter and Brangaene realizes that she means to kill herself, the orchestra practically explodes. A harsh, intense passage paints Brangaene's horror.

Wagner's time-scale is often enormously slow, as we recall from the Prelude. He can, however, move fast enough when he chooses. Before Brangaene can fully absorb the enormity of the situation, she is cut off by a vigorous sailors' sea chantey announcing that land is in sight—the Cornwall so hated and feared by Isolde. The women's moody talk is dramatically interrupted. Tristan's squire, Kurvenal, enters and tells them roughly to get ready for landing.

Again, this passage for Kurvenal is not really a song or an aria. Exactly the same points can be made about it as about Brangaene's speech. Though Kurvenal's song is melodious enough, the main musical idea is an orchestral motive, not the singer's melody; no one will leave the theater humming Kurvenal's music. Yet its bluff accents characterize the man sharply, especially by comparison with the more sensitive, more impassioned women.

(Isolde's suicide never takes place, of course. Brangaene switches the philters, and Isolde and Tristan drink the aphrodisiac, setting the opera's slow, inexorable action into motion.)

Sept. 27 1878 R. had a restless night, he dreamed of a clarinet that played by itself. . . . Toward the end of the evening, he sits down at the piano and plays Tristan; he does this so beautifully, in a way so far transcending the ordinary bounds of beauty, that I feel the sounds I am hearing will bless me when I die.

Cosima Wagner's diary

LISTEN   Wagner, *Tristan und Isolde*, "Philter" Scene, from Act I

17–19   4

(Note: The English translation attempts to reproduce the "antique" quality of Wagner's poetry.)

BRANGAENE'S SONG

Brangaene: Wo lebte der Mann,
Der dich nicht liebte? Der Isolden säh'
Und Isolden selig nicht ganz verging'?
Doch, der dich erkoren, wär' er so kalt,
Zög ihn von dir ein Zauber ab,
Den Bösen wüsst' ich bald zu binden
Ihn bannte der Minne Macht.

Where lives a man
Who does not love you? Who sees you
And sinks not into bondage blest?
And, if any bound to you were cold,
If any magic drew him from thee,
I could soon draw the villain back
And bind him in links of love.

ORCHESTRA

(Secretly and confidentially)

1:23   Kennst du der Mutter Künste nicht?
Wähnst du, die alles klug erwägt,
Ohne Rath in fremdes Land
Hätt' sie mit dir mich entsandt?

Mind'st thou not thy mother's arts?
Do you think that she the all-wise
Helpless in distant lands
Would she have sent me with you?

Love–Death motive, three
times:

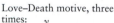

18   2:04 Isolde: Der Mutter Rath gemahnt mich recht;
Willkommen preis' ich ihre Kunst;
Rache für den Verrath,
Ruh' in der Noth dem Herzen!
Den Schrein dort bring' mir her!

My mother's counsel I mind aright;
And highly her magic arts I hold:
Vengeance for treachery,
Rest for the broken heart!
Yon casket hither bear!

Love–Death motive, three
times:

2:59 **Brangaene:**   Er birgt was heil dir frommt,

It holds a balm for thee:

*(Brings out a golden medicine
chest)*

So reihte sie die Mutter,
Die mächt'gen Zaubertränke:
Für Weh' und Wunden Balsam hier,
Für böse Gifte Gegengift;
Den hehrsten Trank, ich halt' ihn hier.

Your mother filled it with
The most potent magic philters;
For pain and wounds there's salve,
For poisons, antidotes;
The noblest draught is this one—

(Takes out a phial)

4:14 **Isolde:**   Du irrst, ich kenn' ihn besser;
Ein starkes Zeichen schnitt ich ihm ein.
Der Trank ist's, der mir taugt!

Not so, you err: I know a better;
I made a mark to know it again:
Here's the drink that will serve me!

New, ominous motive–
Death motive

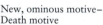

(Seizes another flask)

4:51 **Brangaene:**   Der Todestrank!

The death philter!

**19   4:58 Sailors
(offstage):**   *Ho, he, am Untermast!
Die Segel ein! Ho, he!*

*Ho, heave ho! Watch the lower mast!
The mainsail in! Heave ho!*

Ho!   he!   ho!   he!

Isolde: Das deute schnelle Fahrt.
Weh' mir, Nahe das Land!

That tells of a swift journey;
Woe's me! Near to the land!

*(Kurvenal enters, boisterous and
insolent)*

KURVENAL'S SONG

5:14 **Kurvenal:**   Auf, auf, ihr Frauen!
Frisch und froh! Rasch gerüstet!
Fertig nun, hurtig und flink!
Und Frau Isolden, sollt' ich sagen
Von Held Tristan, meinem Herrn:
Vom Mast der Freude Flagge
Sie wehe lustig ins Land;
In Marke's Königschlosse
Mach' sie ihr Nahen bekannt.
Drum Frau Isolde bät' er eilen,
Für's Land sich zu bereiten
Dass er sie könnt' geleiten.

Up, up, ye ladies!
Look lively, now! Bestir you!
Be ready, and quick, prepare!
Dame Isolde, I'm told to tell you,
By Tristan our hero, my master:
The mast is flying the joyful flag;
It waveth landwards aloft;
From King Mark's royal castle
May our approach be seen.
So, Dame Isolde, he bids you hasten
For land to prepare you,
So that he may there conduct you.

Left: The Philter Scene, pictured in a medieval manuscript of the original Tristan story. *Right:* Brangaene and Isolde, from a Metropolitan Opera production.

Opera at the end of the nineteenth century could boast of two masterful composers as successors to both Verdi and Wagner. The operas of Giacomo Puccini (1858–1924) are as widely loved as those of Verdi himself, thanks to Puccini's special gift for short, intense melodic phrases and his very canny sense of the stage. Three operas that he wrote around 1900 are special favorites: *La Bohème,* which depicts both humorous and tragic episodes in the life of carefree young artists; the sanguinary melodrama *Tosca;* and the tearful *Madama Butterfly,* about an innocent Japanese geisha who is deserted by her cynical American husband.

The most impressive German opera composer after Wagner was Richard Strauss (1864–1949), who was dubbed "Richard II" on account of his frank adoption of Wagnerian methods. With Strauss opera entered the era of modernism, the vital new current in the arts of the twentieth century. We return to Strauss in Chapter 22.

Madama Butterfly: the publisher's handsome cover for the original edition

CHAPTER 19

The Late Romantics

T he year 1848 in Europe was a year of failed revolutions in France, Italy, and in various of the German states. Political freedom, which for the Romantics went hand in hand with freedom of personal expression in life and art, seemed further away than ever. While not all the early Romantics lived in free societies, at least by today's standards, freedom was an ideal they could take seriously as a hope for the future. We recall Beethoven's enthusiasm for Napoleon as a revolutionary hero, reflected in the *Eroica* Symphony of 1803, one of the landmarks of nineteenth-century music. And in the 1820s, the Romantics thrilled to Byron's personal role in the struggle for Greek independence, then lamented his death near the field of battle.

But the failure of the revolutions of 1848 symbolized the failure of Romantic aspirations. In truth, those aspirations had had little to nourish them since the days of Napoleon. Romanticism lived on, but it lived on as nostalgia.

The year 1848 is also a convenient one to demarcate the history of nineteenth-century music. Some of the greatest early Romantic composers—Mendelssohn, Chopin, and Schumann—died between the years 1847 and 1856. By a remarkable coincidence of history, too, the 1848 revolution transformed the career of Richard Wagner; he was exiled from Germany for revolutionary activity, so that he had no opera house to compose for. Instead of composing, he turned inward and—after a long period of philosophical and musical reflection—worked out his revolutionary musical ideas. Wagner's music dramas, written from the 1850s on, came to dominate the imagination of musicians in the second part of the century, much as Beethoven's symphonies had in the first part.

Romanticism and Realism

It is interesting that European literature and art from the 1850s on was marked not by continuing Romanticism, but by realism. The novel, the principal literary form of the time, grew more realistic from Dickens to Trollope and George Eliot in Britain, and from Balzac to Flaubert and Zola in France. In French painting, there was an important realistic school led by Gustave Courbet. Thomas Eakins was a realist painter in America; William Dean Howells was our leading realist novelist. Even more important as regards realism in the visual arts, no doubt, was that powerful new invention, the camera.

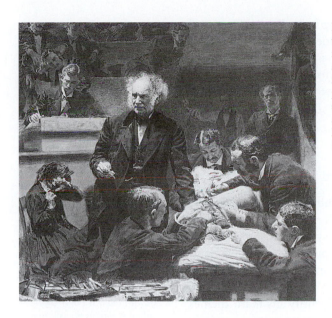

Realists in the arts tended toward glum or grim subject matter. The Philadelphia artist Thomas Eakins was so fascinated by surgery that he painted himself in among the students attending a class by a famous medical professor, Dr. S. D. Gross *(Gross Clinic,* 1875)

There was a move toward realism in opera at the end of the nineteenth century, in France as well as in Italy. On the other hand, the myth-drenched music dramas of Wagner were as unrealistic as could be. And what would "realism" in orchestral music be like? Given music's nature, it was perhaps inevitable that late nineteenth-century music assumed a sort of inspirational and emotional escape function—an escape from political, economic, and social situations that were not romantic in the least.

Perhaps, too, music serves a similar function for many listeners of the late twentieth century. Significantly, concert life as we know it today, with its emphasis on great masterpieces of the past, was formed for the first time in the late nineteenth century.

1 Late Romantic Program Music

Late Romantic program music took its impetus from an important series of works called "symphonic poems," composed in the 1850s by Franz Liszt. A **symphonic poem** is a one-movement orchestral composition with a program, in a free musical form. By using the word "poem," Liszt insisted on the music's programmatic nature.

It is not often that a great virtuoso pianist such as Liszt, who started out composing etudes and other miniatures of the kind cultivated by Chopin and Schumann, turns himself into a major composer of large-scale orchestral works. Liszt's formula was simply to write a long one-movement piece for orchestra associated in one way or another with a famous poem, play, or narrative poem. Though obviously inspired by the earlier genres of program music (see page 245), Liszt departed from them in musical form, as well as in style. Unlike a Berlioz program symphony, a symphonic poem was in one movement. Unlike a Mendelssohn concert overture, it was not written in sonata form or some clear derivation of sonata form. Although the term failed to gain universal acceptance, symphonic poems under that or some other name became very popular in the later nineteenth century.

Among Liszt's symphonic poems are *Hamlet, Orpheus, Prometheus,* and *Les Préludes,* the latter loosely connected with a poem by the French Romantic poet Alphonse de Lamartine. But except for *Les Préludes,* these works are heard less often today than other symphonic poems written by composers influenced by Liszt's example. The most popular of later symphonic poems are those by Peter Ilyich Tchaikovsky and Richard Strauss (see page 326).

PETER ILYICH TCHAIKOVSKY
Romeo and Juliet (Overture-Fantasy) (1869, revised 1880)

Tchaikovsky wrote several symphonic poems, including one on a subject already used by Liszt (and Berlioz), Shakespeare's *Hamlet*. Rather than "symphonic poem," he preferred the descriptions "symphonic fantasia" or "overture-fantasy" for these works. They are lengthy pieces in one movement, with free forms adopting some features from sonata form, rondo, and so on.

In his *Romeo and Juliet,* Tchaikovsky followed the outlines of the original play only in a very general way, but one can easily identify his main themes with elements in Shakespeare's drama. The surging, romantic string melody clearly stands for the love of Romeo and Juliet. The angry, agitated theme suggests the vendetta between their families, the Capulets and the Montagues—and, more generally, the fate that dooms the two "star-cross'd lovers," as Shakespeare calls them. The hymnlike theme heard at the very beginning of the piece (later it sounds more marchlike) seems to denote the kindly Friar Laurence, who devises a plan to help the lovers that goes fatally wrong.

Slow Introduction   The slow introduction of *Romeo and Juliet* is already heavy with drama. As low clarinets and bassoons play the sober Hymn theme, the strings answer with an anguished-sounding passage forecasting an unhappy outcome. The wind instruments utter a series of solemn announcements, interspersed by strumming on the harp, as though someone (Friar Laurence?) was preparing to narrate a serious, tragic tale. This sequence of events is repeated, with some variation, and then both the woodwind and string themes are briefly worked up to a climax over a dramatic drum roll.

Allegro   The tempo changes to allegro, and we hear the Vendetta or Fate theme. It is made up of a number of short, vigorous rhythmic motives, which Tchaikovsky at once begins to develop. Then the Vendetta theme returns in a climax punctuated by sensational cymbal claps.

The highly romantic love theme (illustrated on page 224) is first played only in part, by the English horn and violas—a mellow sound. It is halted by a curious but affecting passage built out of a little sighing figure:

The Love theme, now played at full length by the French horn, is made doubly emotional by a new two-note accompaniment derived from the sighing motive (marked with a bracket above).

The kernel of a new work usually appears suddenly, in the most unexpected fashion . . . All the rest takes care of itself. I could never put into words the joy that seizes me when the main idea has come and when it begins to assume definite shape. You forget everything, you become a madman for all practical purposes, your insides quiver . . .

Tchaikovsky writes to Mme. Von Meck about his composing, 1878

Peter Ilyich Tchaikovsky (1840–1893)

Tchaikovsky was born in the Russian countryside, the son of a mining inspector, but the family moved to St. Petersburg when he was eight. In nineteenth-century Russia, a serious musical education and a musical career were not accorded the social approval they received in Germany, France, or Italy. Many of the famous Russian composers began in other careers and only turned to music in their mature years, when driven by inner necessity.

Tchaikovsky was fortunate in this respect, for after working as a government clerk for only a few years, he was able to enter the brand-new St. Petersburg Conservatory, founded by another Russian composer, Anton Rubinstein. At the age of twenty-six he was made a professor at the Moscow Conservatory. Once Tchaikovsky got started, after abandoning the civil service, he composed prolifically—six symphonies, eleven operas, symphonic poems, chamber music, songs, and some of the most famous of all ballet scores: *Swan Lake, Sleeping Beauty,* and *The Nutcracker.*

Though his pieces may sometimes sound "Russian" to us, he was not a devoted nationalist like some other major Russian composers of the time (see page 275). Of all the nineteenth-century Russian composers, indeed, Tchaikovsky had the greatest success in concert halls around the world. His famous Piano Concerto No. 1 was premiered in 1875 in Boston, and he toured America as a conductor in 1891.

Tchaikovsky was a depressive personality who more than once attempted suicide. He had been an extremely delicate and hypersensitive child, and as an adult he worried that his dominant homosexual bent would be discovered and exposed. In an attempt to raise himself above suspicion, he married a highly unstable young musician who was in love with him. The marriage was a fiasco; in a matter of weeks, Tchaikovsky fled and never saw his wife again. She died in an asylum.

For many years Tchaikovsky was subsidized by a remarkable woman, Nadezhda von Meck, a wealthy widow and a recluse. She not only commissioned compositions from him but actually granted him an annuity. By mutual agreement, they never met; nevertheless, they wrote intimate letters every day over the thirteen years of their friendship. This strange arrangement was terminated, without explanation, by Madame von Meck.

By this time Tchaikovsky's position was assured, and his music widely admired. By a tragic mishap, he died after drinking unboiled water during a cholera epidemic.

Chief Works: Symphonies No. 4, 5, and 6 *(Pathétique);* violin concerto; piano concertos ▪ Operas: *The Queen of Spades* and *Eugene Onegin,* based on works by the Russian Romantic poet Alexander Pushkin ▪ Symphonic poems: *Romeo and Juliet, Hamlet, Francesca da Rimini, Overture 1812* (about Napoleon's retreat from Russia in that year) ▪ Ballet scores: *Swan Lake, Sleeping Beauty, The Nutcracker*

After the Love theme dies down at some length, a lively development section begins (a feature suggesting sonata form). Confronted by various motives from the Vendetta theme, the Hymn theme takes on a marchlike character. We may get the impression of a battle between the forces of good and evil.

The Vendetta theme returns in its original form (suggesting a sonata-form recapitulation). The sighing motive and the lengthy Love theme also return, but the end of the latter is now broken up and interrupted by angry sounds—a clear reference to the tragic outcome of the drama. At one last appearance, the Vendetta theme is joined more explicitly than before with the Hymn theme.

Coda (slow)   A fragment of the Love theme appears in a broken version over funeral drum taps in the timpani. This seems to depict Romeo's pathetic final speeches, where he refers to his love before taking poison. A new, slow theme in the woodwinds is really a transformation of the sighing motive heard earlier.

A famous Juliet of Tchaikov-sky's time: Mrs. Patrick Campbell in an 1895 London production of Shakespeare's play

But the mood is not entirely gloomy; as the harp strumming is resumed, the storyteller seems to derive solace and inspiration from his tale. Parts of the Love theme return for the last time in a beautiful new cadential version, surging enthusiastically upward in a way that is very typical of Tchaikovsky. Doesn't this ecstatic surge suggest that even though Romeo and Juliet are dead, their love is timeless—that their love transcends death? The influence of Wagner's *Tristan und Isolde* was felt here as everywhere in the later nineteenth century.

2 Nationalism

One legacy of Romanticism's passion for freedom played itself out all through the nineteenth century: the struggle for national independence. The Greeks struggled against the Turks, the Poles rose up against Russia, the Czechs revolted against Austria, and Norway broke free of Sweden. All over Europe, people were becoming more conscious of their history and destiny, their national character, and their artistic heritage.

This gave rise to a musical movement, **nationalism** in music. The characteristic feature of this movement is the incorporation of national folk music into concert pieces, songs, and operas. Symphonic poems or operas were based on programs or librettos that took up on national themes—a hero of history such as Russia's Prince Igor; a national literary treasure such as the Finnish Lemminkaïnnen legends; or a beloved river such as the Vltava (Moldau) in Bohemia. Such national themes were reinforced by actual musical themes taken from folk song. The result was music that stirred strong emotions at home, and often made an effective ambassador abroad.

Though in the nineteenth century political nationalism was certainly a major factor all over Europe, composers in Germany, Italy, and France are not categorized with the musical nationalists. For musical nationalism also strove to make local music independent of Europe's traditional cultural leaders.

The art of music is above all other arts the expression of the soul of a nation. The composer must love the tunes of his country and they must become an integral part of him.

Nationalist composer Ralph Vaughan Williams

LISTENING CHART 18

20-31   30-41   1   3

Tchaikovsky, Overture-Fantasy, *Romeo and Juliet*

18 min., 43 sec.

INTRODUCTION (Andante)

	0:00	Hymn theme	In the low woodwinds, *pp*
	0:49	String motives	Anguished quality; contrapuntal
	1:28	Strumming harp	With "announcements" in the high woodwinds
21 31	2:10	Hymn theme	High woodwinds with pizzicato strings. Followed by the string motives and harp; the "announcements" are now in the strings.
22 32	4:00	Buildup	Ends with drum roll, *f*
	4:34	Preparation	Prepares for the main section; *p*, then *crescendo*

MAIN SECTION (Allegro)

23 33	5:04	Vendetta theme	Full orchestra, *f*
	5:26		Development of the Vendetta theme; contrapuntal
0:46	5:50		Reaches a climax: cymbals
0:57	6:01	Vendetta theme	Full orchestra, *ff*
1:17	6:21		Relaxes, in a long slowdown
1:57	7:01		Prefatory statement of Love theme (English horn): phrase **a**

| 24 34 | 7:16 | | "Sighing" theme; muted strings, *pp* |
| 25 35 | 7:55 | Love theme | Form is **a b a**, in woodwinds, with the sighing motive played by the French horn. |

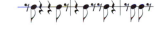

| 0:59 | 8:54 | | Harp. Cadences; the music dies down and nearly stops. |

Development

| 26 36 | 9:55 | Developmental combination | Vendetta theme fragments are combined with the Hymn theme, which now sounds more like a march than a hymn. |
| 27 37 | 11:09 | | This works up to a climax, marked by a cymbal clash. |

CYMBALS

| | 11:33 | Hymn theme | Played by trumpets; syncopated rhythm in the cymbals |

Free Recapitulation (abbreviated)

28 38	12:00	Vendetta theme	Full orchestra, *ff*
	12:24		Sighing theme; woodwinds
1:02	13:02	Love theme	**a b a**; ecstatically in the strings, with the sighing motive again in the French horn; the last **a** is *ff*.
29 39	14:04		Fragments of the Love theme
	14:31	(Love theme)	Sounds like another ecstatic statement, but is interrupted.
0:35	14:39		Interruption by the Vendetta theme: conflict! Cymbals
0:50	14:54	Developmental combination	Vendetta theme fragments combined with the Hymn theme Builds up to *fff*
1:22	15:26		Then dies down, rather unwillingly; ends on drum roll, *f*

Coda (Moderato)

| 30 40 | 16:01 | Love theme | A broken version of the Love theme, with muffled funeral drums. The music seems to be ending. |
| 31 41 | 16:40 | New theme | Woodwinds; ends with a transformation of the sighing motive |

| | 17:46 | Love theme | Section **a** in a slow cadential "transcendent" version. The strumming harp of the slow introduction has returned. |
| | 18:20 | | Final cadences; a drum roll and solemn ending gestures |

Nationalism: Finnish myths inspired both the composer Jan Sibelius and his compatriot the painter Akseli Gallen-Kalela. The wounded hero Lemminkaïnen is tended by his mother, who sends bees to fetch a healing balm from a magic fountain.

Nationalist composers often deliberately broke the traditional rules of harmony, form, and so on. They did this both in a spirit of defiance, and also in an effort to develop new, genuinely local musical styles.

BEDŘICH SMETANA (1824–1884)
The Bartered Bride (1866): Overture

1–5   1–5   1   1

The Bohemian composer Bedřich Smetana had a position as orchestra conductor in Sweden when his country (now the Czech Republic) achieved independence in 1860. He returned home and devoted himself to the establishment of Czech opera. This meant first of all opera sung in the native language, rather than in German or Italian, the usual languages for opera at the time; Smetana also sought out librettos with a national character, and incorporated Czech folktunes and dances into his scores.

His light-hearted opera *The Bartered Bride,* the acknowledged model for Czech national music, was discussed on page 6. It presents a somewhat rose-tinted story of Bohemian peasant life. The work contains many folk dances; we have already heard one, a polka, in the opera's overture (pages 2–7). We can listen to the Overture to *The Bartered Bride* again, and this time see how Smetana has poured his new nationalistic wine into a rather old bottle.

With the help of the outline at the right, Listening Chart 1 on page 7 can be edited to reveal a sonata form—though to be sure, one with many novel features. The "outburst" portion of the first theme is re-used as the cadence theme; although the development section shows one traditional characteristic, modulation, it hardly develops anything; and in fact development (of theme 1) is delayed until *after* the start of the recapitulation. The overture's lengthiest melody and its main "nationalist" element, the polka, is the second theme.

Composers of the later nineteenth century found endless imaginative, free ways of using sonata form. Both Smetana's *The Bartered Bride* Overture and Tchaikovsky's *Romeo and Juliet* bear witness to this, each in its own way.

LISTEN

Smetana, Overture
The Bartered Bride

0:00 **First theme**
1:10 **Second theme**
2:26 **Modulatory section**
3:04 **Recapitulation**
3:10 **Development**
4:00 **Second theme**
4:59 **Coda**

Nationalist Composers

Nationalism enjoyed new life after the turn of the century. Some of the most impressive nationalists were also among the earliest modernists, among them Béla Bartók in Hungary, Charles Ives in America, and Igor Stravinsky, a Russian active in Paris. We shall study these composers in Chapters 21 and 22, restricting ourselves here to a listing of some of the main nineteenth-century nationalists.

⁊ *Russia* The most vociferous and self-conscious of all nationalists were Russians, identified as a group (*kuchka,* in Russian) of five. Today we mainly remember Alexander Borodin (1837–1910), Modest Mussorgsky (1839–1881), and Nikolai Rimsky-Korsakov (1844–1908). Mussorgsky's great opera *Boris Godunov* is a profound exploration of Russian history and the Russian spirit.

⁊ *Bohemia* Smetana was followed by an even more famous composer, Antonin Dvořák (Dvorzháhk) (1841–1904), author of the popular *Slavonic Dances,* as well as important symphonies and other large-scale works. Dvořák actually spurred Nationalist music in America: see page 361.

⁊ *Scandinavia* Edward Grieg (1843–1907) wrote piano miniatures that were very popular all over Europe, with titles such as *Norwegian Folksongs* and *Scenes from Peasant Life.* His well-known *Peer Gynt* Suite was written for the great drama by his countryman Henrik Ibsen.

In a later generation, Jan Sibelius (1865–1957), a distinguished late Romantic symphonist, produced a whole series of symphonic poems on the folklore of his native Finland: *The Swan of Tuonela, Finlandia,* and others.

⁊ *Spain* Spanish nationalist composers include Enrique Granados (1867–1916), Joaquín Turina (1882–1949), and Manuel de Falla (1876–1946), best known for his *Nights in the Gardens of Spain* for piano and orchestra.

⁊ *Great Britain* The major English nationalist in music was Ralph Vaughan Williams (1872–1958). His *Fantasia on a Theme by Thomas Tallis* is a loving meditation on a psalm tune that was written by a major composer from Britain's national heritage, at the time of Queen Elizabeth I.

Furiant   Another Czech folkdance, called a *furiant,* is used for a quite short dance number that helps launch Act II of *The Bartered Bride.* The irregular rhythm here sounds much more earthy than polka rhythm; you can count time to it as a very rapid ONE *two* ONE *two* ONE *two* | ONE *two three* ONE *two three* (at this speed, counting is more practical than to trying to beat time).

In the trio, which changes to a slower waltz-like triple meter, Smetana contrives to modulate in a vague, dreamy way even while keeping an identical rising figure in the cellos and violas (it comes twelve times in all). Then at the end he works a noisy combination of furiant and waltz rhythms. This brings his brilliant orchestral miniature to a rousing close.

LISTEN

6	6	2	2

Smetana, Furiant
The Bartered Bride

0:00 **Furiant:**
          a a b a b a
0:31 **Trio**
1:30 **Furiant**
1:43 **Combination**

3 Responses to Romanticism

At the beginning of this chapter, we remarked that European art and literature after the 1850s were marked not by continuing Romanticism, but by realism, which was in fact a reaction against Romanticism. In music, an art that can hardly be realistic in the usual sense, the anti-Romantic reaction came later—at a time when realism was no longer an ideal in the other arts.

After 1850, music continued to develop along Romantic lines, but it seemed oddly out of phase with a no-nonsense world increasingly devoted to industrialization and commerce. In the world of Victorian morality, people devoted to the work ethic denied themselves and others the heady emotion that the Romantics had insisted on conveying in their art. There is probably some truth to the contention that late nineteenth-century music assumed the function of a sort of never-never land of feeling. Music was an emotional fantasy-world for a society that placed a premium on the suppression of feeling in real life.

The work of the two greatest late nineteenth-century German composers can be viewed in terms of their responses to this situation. Johannes Brahms, a devoted young friend of Robert Schumann, one of the most Romantic of composers, nonetheless turned back to the Classicism of the Viennese masters. Evidently he saw this as a way of tempering the unbridled emotionalism of Romanticism, which he expressed only in a mood of restraint and resignation.

A younger man, Gustav Mahler, reacted differently. Lament was his mode, rather than resignation; his music expresses an intense, bittersweet nostalgia for a Romanticism that seems to have lost its innocence, even its credibility. The lament for this loss is almost clamorous in Mahler's songs and symphonies.

The Renewal of Classicism: Brahms

Born in the dour industrial port city of Hamburg, Johannes Brahms gravitated to Vienna, the city of Haydn, Mozart, and Beethoven. The move seems symbolic. For Brahms rejected many of the innovations of the early Romantics and went back to Classical genres, forms, and, to some extent, even Classical style.

Brahms devoted his major effort to traditional genres such as string quartets and other chamber music works, symphonies, and concertos. In these works, he employed and indeed found new life in the Classical forms—sonata form, theme and variations, and rondo. The only typical Romantic genre he cultivated was the "miniature"—the lied and the characteristic piano piece; he never contemplated "grandiose" works such as philosophical program symphonies, mythological operas, and the like. Almost alone among the important composers of his time, he made no special effort to pioneer new harmonies or tone colors.

Brahms, without giving up on beauty and emotion, proved to be a progressive in a field that had not been cultivated in half a century [i.e., the classical tradition]. He would have been a pioneer if he had simply returned to Mozart. But he did not live on inherited wealth; he made a fortune of his own.

Modernist composer
Arnold Schoenberg, 1947

Violinist Joseph Joachim, for whom Brahms wrote his Violin Concerto, playing with another Brahms friend, Clara Schumann

Johannes Brahms (1833–1897)

The son of an orchestral musician in Hamburg, Brahms was given piano lessons at an early age. By the time he was seven, he was studying with one of Hamburg's finest music teachers. A little later he was playing the piano at dockside taverns and writing popular tunes.

A turning point in Brahms's life came at the age of twenty when he met Robert and Clara Schumann. These two eminent musicians befriended and encouraged the young man and took him into their household. Robert wrote an enthusiastic article praising his music. But soon afterward, Schumann was committed to an insane asylum—a time during which Brahms and Clara (who was fourteen years his senior) became very close. In later life Brahms always sent Clara his compositions to get her comments.

With another musician friend, Joseph Joachim, who was to become one of the great violinists of his time, the young Brahms signed a foolish manifesto condemning the advanced music of Liszt and Wagner. Thereafter he passed an uneventful bachelor existence, steadily turning out music—chamber music, songs, and piano pieces, but no program music or operas. Indeed, he was forty-three before his first symphony appeared, many years after its beginnings at his desk; it seemed that he was hesitating to invoke comparison with Beethoven, whose symphonies constituted a standard for the genre. In fact, this symphony's last movement contains a near-quotation from Beethoven's Ninth Symphony that is more like a challenge. When people pointed out the similarity, Brahms snarled, "Any fool can see that," implying that it was the differences between the two works that mattered, not their superficial similarities.

Brahms would eventually write four symphonies, all harking back to forms used by Beethoven and even Bach, but thoroughly Romantic in their expressive effect.

For a time Brahms conducted a chorus, and he wrote much choral music, including *A German Requiem*, a setting of sober texts from the Bible. As a conductor, he indulged his traditionalism by reviving music of Bach and even earlier composers, but he also enjoyed the popular music of his day. He wrote waltzes (Johann Strauss, the "Waltz King," was a valued friend), folk song arrangements, and the well-known *Hungarian Dances*.

Chief Works: Four symphonies, *Academic Festival* Overture, *Tragic* Overture, *Variations on a Theme by Haydn* (for piano, four hands, arranged for orchestra) ▪ Violin concerto and two piano concertos ▪ Much chamber music, including a beautiful quintet for clarinet and strings, a trio for French horn, violin, and piano, as well as string quartets, quintets, and sextets ▪ Piano music and many songs ▪ Choral music, including *A German Requiem* and *Alto Rhapsody* ▪ Waltzes, *Hungarian Dances*

What impels a great composer—and Brahms *was* a great composer, not a timid traditionalist—to turn back the clock in this way? One can only speculate that he could not find it in himself to copy or continue the enthusiastic, open-ended striving of the early Romantics. In the late nineteenth century, this type of response no longer rang true, and Brahms recognized it.

On the other hand, the timeless nobility and power of Beethoven inspired him with a lifelong model. Seen in this way, Brahms's effort was a heroic one: to temper the new richness and variety of Romantic emotion with the traditional strength and poise of Classicism.

JOHANNES BRAHMS
Violin Concerto in D, Op. 77 (1878)

Concertos are always written to show off great virtuosos—who are often the composers themselves, as with Mozart, Chopin, and Liszt. Brahms wrote his one violin concerto for a close friend, Joseph Joachim, a leading violinist of the time and also an excellent composer. Even this late in life—Brahms was then forty-five—he accepted advice about certain details of the composition from Joachim; and Joachim wrote the soloist's cadenza for the first movement.

Brahms was a serious man; this is one of the few pictures of him smiling. He is sketched with some bachelor friends at his favorite Vienna tavern, the Red Hedgehog.

We can appreciate Brahms's traditionalism as far as the Classical forms are concerned by referring to the standard movement plan for the Classical concerto, on page 186. Like Mozart, Brahms wrote his first movement in double-exposition sonata form; this must have seemed extremely stuffy to the many writers of Romantic concertos who had developed new and freer forms. Brahms's last movement, too, is a rondo—the most common Classical way to end a concerto. If it is a relatively simple movement, by Brahms's standards, that is because the last movements of Classical concertos were typically the lightest and least demanding on the listener.

Third Movement (Allegro giocoso, ma non troppo vivace)   "Giocoso" means "jolly"; the first theme in this rondo, **A,** has a lilt recalling the spirited gypsy fiddling that was popular in nineteenth-century Vienna. The solo violin plays the theme (and much else in the movement) in *double stops,* that is, in chords produced by bowing two violin strings simultaneously. Hard to do well, this makes a brilliant effect when done by a virtuoso.

The theme falls into a traditional **a a b a′** form; in Brahms's hands, however, this becomes something quite subtle. Since the second **a** is identical to the first, except in instrumentation, the last **a** (**a′**) might be dull unless it were varied in an interesting way. Brahms extends it and yet also makes it compressed and exciting by free diminutions of the basic rhythmic figure:

Such "cross-rhythms"—**3/8** fitted in for a moment within **2/4**—are a characteristic fingerprint of Brahms's style. There are other examples in this movement.

32-37   42-47   2   4

LISTENING CHART 19

Brahms, Violin Concerto, third movement

Rondo, 7 min., 48 sec.

	0:00	**A (Tune)**	The entire tune is presented.	
	0:00	**a**	Solo violin, with double stops	
	0:12	**a**	Orchestra	
	0:23	**b**	Solo violin	
	0:36	**a′**	Orchestra	
	0:47		The solo violin begins the cadences ending the tune, which lead into a transition.	
	1:06		Fast scales prepare for **B** (solo, pizzicato accompaniment).	
33 **43**	1:14	**B (Episode 1)**	Melody (emphatic upward scale) in the violin, with inverted motive below it, in the orchestra	
0:22	1:36		Melody in the orchestra, with inverted motive above it, in the violin	
0:37	1:51		Cadential passage (orchestra), *f*	
34 **44**	2:02	**A′ (Tune)**	Phrase **a** (solo) Phrase **a″** (orchestra)	
0:20	2:22		Transition (orchestra and solo, *p*	
35 **45**	2:40	**C (Episode 2)**	Lyrical tune (solo and orchestra), *p*	
	3:13		Expressive climactic section, solo	
0:44	3:24		Orchestra interrupts, *f*.	
0:50	3:30		Scales prepare for **B** (solo, pizzicato accompaniment).	
0:58	3:38	**B**	Scale melody in the solo violin, as before	
1:19	3:59		Scale melody in the orchestra, as before	
1:35	4:15		Cadential passage in the orchestra, *f*	
36 **46**	4:25	**A″ (Tune)**	Starts with **b** (solo)	
	4:46	**a′**	In orchestra, extended; the real feeling of "return" comes only at this point.	
0:47	5:12	**Short cadenza**	Solo, double stops again; orchestra soon enters.	
1:03	5:28		Solo trills and scales; motive 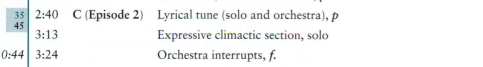	
1:32	5:57		Passage of preparation: motive 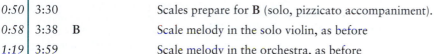 in low French horns	
37 **47**	6:13	**Short cadenza**		
	6:24	**Coda**	Mostly in **6/8** time. Starts with a marchlike transformation of phrase **a** (solo), over a drum beat	
0:35	6:48		**B** briefly interrupts.	
0:57	7:10	**B**		
1:08	7:21		Final-sounding cadences	
1:20	7:33		The music dies down and ends with three loud chords.	

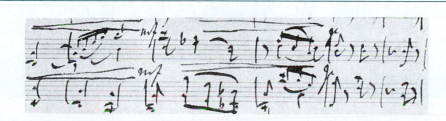

From Brahms's score of his Violin Concerto

The first rondo episode, **B,** a theme with a fine Romantic sweep about it, begins with an emphatic upward scale played by the solo violin (high double stops in octaves). This is answered by a *downward* scale in the orchestra in lower range. When the orchestra has its turn to play **B,** timpani are added; the upward scale is transferred down to the low register, and the downward scale up to the high register.

The second rondo episode, **C,** involves another rhythmic change; this charming melody—which, however, soon evaporates—is in **3/4** time:

The coda presents a version of the **a** phrase of the main theme in **6/8** time, in a swinging march tempo. Again the timpani are prominent. Most of the transitions in this movement are rapid virtuoso scale passages by the soloist, who is also given two short cadenzas prior to the coda.

Romantic Nostalgia: Mahler

If, like Brahms, Gustav Mahler felt ambivalent about the Romantic tradition, he expressed this ambivalence very differently. He eagerly embraced all the excesses of Romanticism that Brahms had shrunk from, writing huge program symphonies (though he vacillated on the question of distributing the programs to his audiences) and symphonies with solo and choral singing. Mahler once said that a symphony is "an entire world." Again and again his works encode seemingly profound metaphysical or religious messages.

Mahler's Symphony No. 8, called "Symphony of a Thousand," represents a peak in the nineteenth-century tradition of "grandiose" compositions (see page 227). Understandably, it is rarely heard live; a New York performance in 1995 required 697 players and singers.

Gustav Mahler (1860–1911)

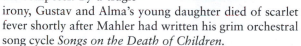

Mahler's early life was not a happy one. Born in Bohemia to an abusive father, five of his brothers and sisters died of diphtheria, and others ended their lives in suicide or mental illness. The family lived near a military barracks, and the many marches incorporated into Mahler's music —often distorted marches—have been traced to his child-hood recollections of parade music.

After studying for a time at the Vienna Conservatory, Mahler began a rising career as a conductor. His uncom-promising standards and his authoritarian attitude to-ward the orchestra musicians led to frequent disputes with the authorities. What is more, Mahler was Jewish, and Vienna at that time was rife with anti-Semitism. Nonetheless, he was acknowledged as one of the great conductors of his day and also as a very effective musical administrator. After positions at Prague, Budapest, Ham-burg, and elsewhere, he came to head such organizations as the Vienna Opera and the New York Philharmonic.

It was only in the summers that Mahler had time to compose, so it is not surprising that he produced fewer pieces (though they are very long pieces) than any other important composer. Ten symphonies, the last of them unfinished, and six song cycles for voice and orchestra are almost all he wrote. The song cycle *The Song of the Earth* of 1910, based on translated Chinese poems, is often called Mahler's greatest masterpiece.

He married a famous Viennese beauty, Alma Schindler, who after his death went on to marry the great architect Walter Gropius and later the novelist Franz Werfel and then wrote fascinating memoirs of her life with the composer. By a tragic irony, Gustav and Alma's young daughter died of scarlet fever shortly after Mahler had written his grim orchestral song cycle *Songs on the Death of Children*.

Despite his eminence, Mahler's life was clouded by psychological turmoil, and he once consulted his famous Viennese contemporary, Sigmund Freud. It has been said that his disputes with the New York Philharmonic direc-tors, which discouraged him profoundly, may have con-tributed to his early death.

Chief Works: Ten lengthy symphonies, several with chorus, of which the best known are the Fourth and Fifth ■ Orchestral song cycles: *The Song of the Earth, Songs of a Wayfarer, The Youth's Magic Horn* (for piano or orchestra), *Songs on the Death of Children*

Yet it would appear that Mahler felt unable to enter freely into this Ro-mantic fantasy world. There is an uneasy quality to his music that sets it apart from other late Romantic music. For while we may feel that the emotion ex-pressed in Tchaikovsky's music, for example, is exaggerated, we do not feel that Tchaikovsky himself thought so. Mahler's exaggeration, on the other hand, seems deliberate and self-conscious.

Exaggeration spills over into another characteristic feature, distortion. Mahler tends to make more or less slight distortions of melody, motive, and harmony. Sometimes these distortions put a uniquely bittersweet touch on the musical material; sometimes they amount to all-out parody. The parody does not seem harsh, however, but affectionate, nostalgic, and ultimately melan-choly. Distortion for Mahler was a way of acknowledging his inability—and the inability of his generation—to recapture the lost freshness of Romantic music.

To give an example: the slow movement of his Symphony No. 1 quotes the cheerful children's round, "Frère Jacques," strangely distorted so as to sound like a funeral march. Mahler explained that this march was inspired by a well-known children's painting of the time, *The Huntsman's Funeral Pro-cession,* showing forest animals shedding crocodile tears around the hearse of

A symphony must be like the world, it must embrace everything.

Famous dictum of Gustav Mahler

The Huntsman's Funeral Procession, inspiration for the slow movement of Mahler's Symphony No. 1

a hunter. But an innocent children's song was not distorted in this way in order to mock childhood or childish things. If anything, Mahler used it to lament his own lost innocence, and that of his time.

GUSTAV MAHLER
Symphony No. 1 (1888)

Mahler's first symphony started out as a symphonic poem in one movement, grew to a five-movement symphony, and was finally revised into four movements. As is also true of many of the later symphonies, Symphony No. 1 includes fragments from a number of earlier songs by Mahler, songs about lost love. Indeed, the program that Mahler once published for the symphony, and then withdrew, concerns the disillusion, self-pity, and anguish of disappointed love, ending with the hero pulling himself together again.

An important general feature of Mahler's style is a special kind of counterpoint closely tied up with his very individual style of orchestration. He picks instruments out of the orchestra to play momentary solos, which are heard in counterpoint with other lines played by other "solo" instruments. The changing combinations can create a fascinating kaleidoscopic effect, for the various bright strands are not made to blend, as in most Romantic orchestration, but rather to stand out in sharp contrast to one another.

Third Movement (Moderate tempo; solemn, not too slow)   This ironic funeral march is also a personal lament, for its trio is taken from an earlier song by Mahler about lost love. (Though the musical form of the movement is quite original, it is based on march and trio form, analogous to the Classical minuet and trio.)

Section 1   Mahler had the extraordinary idea of making his parody funeral march out of the familiar French round "Frère Jacques," as we have said. He distorts the "Frère Jacques," tune by playing it in the minor mode at a slow tempo (only a few of the notes are changed):

Mahler and his daughter:
an informal photo

The mournful drumbeat that continuously accompanies the march is derived from the ending of the tune. The tune itself is played first by a single muted double bass playing in its high register—a bizarre, deliberately clumsy sonority. An additional figure, played by the oboe, that Mahler appends to his version of "Frère Jacques" fits so naturally that we almost accept it as part of the traditional tune. The music dies out on the drumbeat figure (played by the harp), then on a single repeated note.

Section 2   This section is a study in frustration, as fragmentary dance-music phrases that sound distorted, parodistic, and even vulgar, give way to equally fragmentary recollections of the funeral march. One dance starts up in band instruments, with a faster beat provided by pizzicato strings; notice the exaggerated way in which its opening upbeat is slowed down. It is cut short by a new dance phrase—louder, more vulgar yet, scored with bass drum and cymbals. "With Parody," Mahler wrote on the score at this point:

This phrase, too, is cut short, and a varied repetition of the material introduced so far does not proceed much further. Instead, a long, grieving cadential passage is heard over the funeral-march drumbeat. Other fragments of "Frère Jacques" are recalled. Mourning gives way to utter exhaustion.

Section 3   A note of consolation is sounded by this contrasting "trio," beginning with warm major-mode sounds and a triplet accompaniment on the harp. (The funeral-march beat dissolves into a faster but gentler throb.) The melody introduced is the one that belonged originally to a nostalgic song about lost love. Played first by muted strings, then the oboe and solo violins, the tender song melody soon turns bittersweet.

LISTENING CHART 20

38-45   48-55   3   1

Mahler, Symphony No. 1, third movement, Funeral March

10 min., 54 sec.

SECTION 1

	0:00	**Funeral March**	Drum beat, then four main entries of the round "Frère Jacques" (minor mode), which is the march theme.
	0:10		Entry 1: Double bass, muted (drum beat continues)
	0:35		Entry 2: Bassoon (a subsidiary entry follows: cellos)
	1:00		Entry 3: Tuba
	1:16		("Additional" fragment: oboe)
	1:32		Entry 4: Flute in low register
	1:56		("Additional" fragment). The march gradually dies away; the drum beat finally stops.

OBOE

p

SECTION 2

39 49	2:37	**Dance-Band Phrases**	**a** Oboes, *p*, repeated (trumpets in counterpoint); pizzicato string beat
0:29	3:06		**b** Faster, *mf;* high (E-flat) clarinets, bass drum, and cymbals
40 50	3:24		**a** Strings, with varied repeat (trumpets in counterpoint)
	3:55		**b′** With new continuation
0:54	4:18	**Conclusion**	Descending cadential passage, a little slower, based on **a**
1:26	4:50	**Return to Funeral-March Motives**	The funeral-march drumbeat, which entered during the previous passage, continues in the background. The march dies away; the drumbeat almost stops.

rit.   a tempo

< p

SECTION 3

2:14	5:38	**Trio (Song)**	The rhythm gradually picks up: a gentle triplet accompaniment with a throbbing background
41 51	5:52		A songlike melody starts in muted strings, then moves to the flute, two solo violins, clarinet, and oboe.
0:02	5:54		The trio dies away (violins).
42 52	7:19		Gong strokes
	7:26		Flutes play two new phrases, as though waiting.

pp

SECTION 4

43 53	7:41	**March**	Drumbeat, faster, in a new key: march ("Frère Jacques")
	8:00		("Additional" fragment: E-flat clarinet, strings, flute)
44 54	8:22		March theme with new, parodistic counterpoint: trumpets
	8:48		Dance-band phrase **b**: clarinets, cymbals, drums
45 55	9:10		March theme with new trumpet counterpoint; new sudden speedup: clarinets, *ff*
0:21	9:31	**Conclusion**	Descending cadential passage, based on **a**, with drumbeat as in section 2
1:06	10:16		("Additional" fragment, in low range: bassoon)
1:20	10:30		The music dies down; gong strokes

The rhythm is halted by quiet but dramatic gong strokes. Flutes play a few strangely momentous new phrases, also taken from the song.

Section 4   The final section combines elements from sections 1 and 2. Soon after the "Frère Jacques" round commences, in a strange key, a new counterpoint joins it in the trumpets—another parodistic, almost whining sound:

One of the dance phrases from section 2 interrupts, suddenly picking up the tempo; and when "Frère Jacques" and the trumpet tune return, the tempo picks up even more for a wild moment of near chaos. But the mourning passage that ended section 2 returns, with its constant somber drumbeat. The movement ends after another series of gong strokes.

From the score Mahler was working on at his death—the unfinished Symphony No. 10

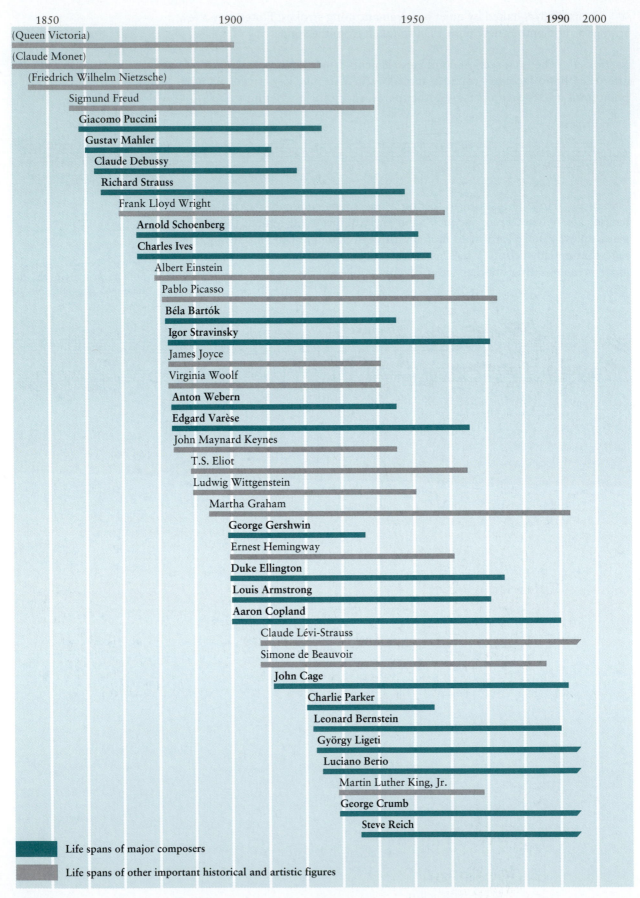

1850   1900   1950   1990 2000

(Queen Victoria)

(Claude Monet)

(Friedrich Wilhelm Nietzsche)

Sigmund Freud

Giacomo Puccini

Gustav Mahler

Claude Debussy

Richard Strauss

Frank Lloyd Wright

Arnold Schoenberg

Charles Ives

Albert Einstein

Pablo Picasso

Béla Bartók

Igor Stravinsky

James Joyce

Virginia Woolf

Anton Webern

Edgard Varèse

John Maynard Keynes

T.S. Eliot

Ludwig Wittgenstein

Martha Graham

George Gershwin

Ernest Hemingway

Duke Ellington

Louis Armstrong

Aaron Copland

Claude Lévi-Strauss

Simone de Beauvoir

John Cage

Charlie Parker

Leonard Bernstein

György Ligeti

Luciano Berio

Martin Luther King, Jr.

George Crumb

Steve Reich

▬ Life spans of major composers

▬ Life spans of other important historical and artistic figures

UNIT V

The Twentieth Century

*T*his unit, which deals with music from around 1900 on, brings our survey of Western music up to the present. Looking back to the year 1900, we can recognize today's culture in an early form. Large cities, industrialization, inoculation against disease, advertising, processed food, even the first automobiles, telephones, movies, and phonographs—all were present by the beginning of the twentieth century.

Hence many of the phenomena treated in this unit will strike us as fairly familiar, compared to those of earlier centuries. For one thing, the widespread availability of art to mass audiences—not just to the various select groups, as in the past—is something we take for granted. The new mass audience emerged because of sociological factors, as distinctions among the classes of society gradually broke down, in tandem with technological factors—the amazing development of the phonograph, radio, television, and more. We also take for granted the split that has occurred between "art" (or so-called classical) music and popular music. A rift that had opened up in the nineteenth century widened in the twentieth.

We are also aware of the force of American popular music—music whose characteristic features emerged around the year 1900, once again. With the evolution of ragtime and early jazz, a vital rhythmic spring derived from African-American sources was brought into the general American consciousness. This led to a long series of developments: swing, bebop, rhythm and blues, rock, rap. After World War II, when the United States began to play a commanding political role in the world at large, our popular music became a world language.

Modernism and Traditionalism

What was "art" music like in this same period? Art music itself experienced a split. On the one hand there was music that we shall call "modernist," on the other hand, music of a more traditional nature.

The term modernist requires a word of explanation. It is not the same as contemporary or modern, *terms that refer to anything at all that happens to take place in the present; the -ist at the end of the word* modern *gives it an extra twist. The modernists of 1900 were artists and intellectuals who insisted on their modernity—that is, their anti-traditionalism—and who formed a specific cultural movement marked by radical experimentation. Though its roots go back earlier, this movement peaked during the years 1890 to 1918— a period of astonishing breakthrough works by such novelists, poets, and painters as Marcel Proust and James Joyce, Ezra Pound and T. S. Eliot, Pablo Picasso and Henri Matisse.*

The chief composers associated with the modernist movement were Claude Debussy, Arnold Schoenberg, and Igor Stravinsky. Sometimes they are referred to as members of the "avant-garde"; **avant-garde**—*"vanguard"—is a military or at least a militant term that has long been embraced by radical artists and intellectuals to denote the forefront of their activity.*

At the same time, some twentieth-century artists and composers resisted modernism, and some artists turned back from it. They found they could comfortably continue in the general spirit of late Romanticism, or even look back to earlier styles. Though the avant-gardists often claimed that the old principles of art had been "used up," there was still plenty of potential left in more traditional methods.

In this unit we shall study the music of modernism and also the reaction against modernism. Our final chapter deals with America's characteristic music, jazz, and some of its consequences.

CHAPTER 20

Prelude
Music and Modernism

M odernism in art, literature, and music flourished especially from around 1890 to 1918, the end of World War I. It was an unusually brilliant movement. A sharp reaction to late nineteenth-century culture, especially to the accepted rules of art within that culture, modernism found amazing resources within the materials of the arts themselves. It is probably the case that never before have all the arts gone through such revolutionary developments together.

1 Industrialization and Progress

Industrialization is the overriding historical fact of the nineteenth century. Ever since the first so-called age of science in the seventeenth century, technological discoveries had come faster and faster, and industry was transformed. The harnessing of steam power in the eighteenth century was matched by the discovery of electricity in the nineteenth. Europe and America were crisscrossed with railroads, built for the benefit of industry and commerce. In the early twentieth century, automobile and air travel were in their early stages of development, as were telephones, movies, and sound recordings.

Music (as we have seen in this book) is a popular subject for artists; but few have been so fascinated by music as Raoul Dufy (1877–1953).

What had been essentially rural societies, controlled by stable aristocracies, turned into urban societies run by self-made entrepreneurs. These changes occurred at breakneck speed, as people saw at the time. Yet no one could have forecast how the stresses caused by such social changes would lead on the one hand to the disturbing artistic-intellectual movement known as modernism, and on the other to the catastrophe of World War I.

On the contrary, "official" nineteenth-century culture was permeated by a sense of confidence in progress. Progress in science and technology, it was thought, would be matched in due time by progress in human affairs. And although there was ample evidence to the contrary—for example, in the terrible conditions of the new industrial poor, as exposed by the novels of Charles Dickens—this evidence was easy to ignore, especially by the rich and powerful who were profiting from technology's advances.

Science and Uncertainty

But another side of progress became evident in the ominous development of weaponry. The deadly novelty of the American Civil War was the rifle, effective over five times the range of previous shoulder weapons. In World War I, tanks, submarines, and poison gas showed technology's terrible potential for destruction: an estimated 40 million military and civilian dead from war, famine, and epidemic, and 20 million wounded. With World War I, nineteenth-century confidence in progress—a response to the successes of technology—was thrown into question by technology itself.

By this time, however, the groundwork for such loss in confidence had already been laid by science in other areas. Men and women were shaken in their most basic assumptions about life by puzzling advances in physics, biology, and psychology.

❦ The impact of Einstein's theory of relativity (which later in the century made its own contributions to the technology of weaponry) was at first more philosophical than practical in nature. The idea that things depend on the standpoint of the observer, and cannot be counted on according to the "objective" rules of Newtonian physics, rocked people's sense of certainty.

❦ For many, this uncertainty simply deepened a crisis in religion that the Victorians had already experienced as a result of scientific theories of evolution. Here the key figure was Charles Darwin. Were human beings created by God in God's image, as the Bible teaches, or were they descended by an impersonal process from animals? The disturbance that this caused in people's sense of stability is still reflected in today's disputes about creationism.

❦ Meanwhile the psychological theories of Sigmund Freud suggested that in spite of what people thought they were doing or feeling, they were in fact controlled by unconscious drives. The idea of men and women in the grip of irrational forces of their own (or their parents') making was a troubling one. At the same time, the prospect of working out one's "problems" through psychoanalysis gave the new century its paradigm for personality change.

2 The Response of Modernism

If the traditional laws of physics, biblical authority, and psychological certainty could no longer be accepted, it seemed a small enough step to question the rules, assumptions, and prohibitions surrounding the arts.

Cubism was one of the earliest forms of abstract or near-abstract art; this painting is by the leading cubist, Georges Braque. One can discern the score of *Socrate*, by a leading modernist composer, Erik Satie.

One such assumption was that visual art had to represent something. Once this idea was questioned, and then abandoned, the materials of painting and the other arts could be used for themselves—and a whole world of abstract (or nonrepresentational) painting opened up. This general category includes cubism, abstract expressionism, op art, and other such subcategories.

In literature, the basic assumptions were those of ordinary sentence structure, syntax, and grammar. Freedom from these conditions allowed novelists and poets to move into a whole new sphere of suggestion. Using the so-called stream of consciousness method, James Joyce ended his novel *Ulysses* of 1922 with a famous long section—forty pages, without punctuation or paragraphs—tracking the miscellaneous but not-so-idle thoughts of a character who hadn't even spoken until then, Molly Bloom, as she lies in bed.

In music, the basic assumptions were melody and its close associates harmony and tonality. These assumptions, too, were thrown into doubt. Arnold Schoenberg's famous—indeed, notorious—song cycle *Pierrot lunaire* ("Moonstruck Pierrot") of 1912 employs a kind of half-speaking, half-singing style that the composer called *Sprechstimme* (speech-song). Ranging from a throaty whisper to a near-hysterical shriek, *Sprechstimme* was an explicit denial of melody—and the entire song cycle of twenty-one songs is written in this style (see page 313).

New Languages for Art

Avant-garde artists developed whole new languages for art—for example, the "languages" of cubism and serialism (discussed on page 300) for communication in painting and music, respectively. If we use the word *language* literally, the most dramatic case is that of James Joyce. At the end of his life, the great Irish novelist wrote *Finnegan's Wake* in a language that is part English, part other languages, and part a construction of words he invented.

Schoenberg, once again, provides a striking analogue in music. His twelve-tone method, or **serialism,** developed in the 1920s, replaced the old "language" for music based on harmony and tonality. By arranging the twelve notes of the chromatic scale into fixed patterns, and manipulating those patterns by means of mathematical operations, Schoenberg arrived at a radical new way of composing music—and hearing it, too. His experiments were continued with great energy after World War II, as we shall see in Chapter 22.

New York City, by Piet
Mondrian, 1940–41

Art and Objectivity

The "new languages" for art were unquestionably (and unapologetically) difficult. To this day, few people understand *Finnegan's Wake* or follow Schoenberg's serial compositions. A good deal of avant-garde art became detached
from music's ordinary public, and hence abstracted from a base in society.

At the same time, the modernists' concentration on artistic materials led
to abstraction of another kind, the abstraction of technique from expression.
By some, this emphasis on technique was welcomed as a relief from the overheated emotionality of late Romantic music, of Tchaikovsky, Mahler and the
like. Especially in the 1920s, "objectivity" was an ideal espoused by many
artists. And their works sometimes struck the public as "abstract" in a cold,
dry sense.

Characteristic of this phase of the avant-garde were various experiments
with schematic, even mathematical devices in the arts. The Dutch painter
Piet Mondrian made striking pictures out of straight lines at right angles to
one another, and juxtaposed planes of bright color. Among composers, Igor
Stravinsky was known for his provocative statements extolling objectivity and
attacking Romantic music—and certainly the brisk, almost mechanistic
rhythms that characterize Stravinsky's style are diametrically opposed to rubato, the rhythmic "stretching" that contributes so much to nineteenth-
century music's emotionality.

Several lesser composers, fascinated by "machine" rhythms, even tried to
evoke machinery in their works: the American George Antheil *(Ballet mécani-
que),* the Russian A. V. Mosolov *(The Iron Foundry),* and the Swiss Arthur
Honegger *(Pacific 231—a locomotive).*

3 Literature and Art before World War I

A significant social development of the avant-garde was the tendency for
artists of various kinds to gravitate together in formal or informal groups,
both for mutual encouragement and for the exchange of ideas.

Thus Claude Debussy was friends with several symbolist poets. Schoenberg, himself a painter, associated with a group of artists who set forth their ideas in *The Blue Rider*, a magazine named after a picture by the pioneer non-representational painter Wassily Kandinsky (see page 296). Stravinsky and Maurice Ravel belonged to a group of artists and intellectuals in Paris who called themselves the Apaches. With all this interchange, it is not surprising that one can sometimes detect similar tendencies in music and the other arts.

Cover for *The Blue Rider*, a magazine that promulgated expressionist art and music

Impressionists and Symbolists

As we have already remarked, modernism got its start in the late nineteenth century and then peaked in the twentieth. The best-known modernist movement, **impressionism,** dates from the 1870s, when people were astonished by the flickering network of color patches by which impressionist painters rendered simple scenes from everyday life (as in Edouard Manet's *In the Boat*). Yet the impressionists claimed that to catch the actual, perceived quality of light on a river, they had to use such a technique. They proudly called themselves "realists," in reaction to the idealized and overemotional art of Romanticism.

Roughly contemporary with impressionism was **symbolism,** a consciously *un*realistic movement. Symbolist poets revolted against the "realism" of words being used for reference—for the purpose of exact definition. They wanted words to perform their symbolizing or signifying function as freely as possible, without having to fit into phrases or sentences. The meaning of a cluster of words might be vague and ambiguous, even esoteric—but also rich, "musical," and endlessly suggestive.

"Musical" was exactly what the symbolists called it. They were fascinated by the music dramas of Richard Wagner, where again musical symbols—Wagner's leitmotivs—refer to elements in his dramas in a complex, ambivalent,

In the Boat, an impressionist painting by Edouard Manet (1832–1883)

multilayered fashion. All poets use "musical" devices such as rhythm and rhyme, but only the symbolists were prepared to go as far as to break down grammar, syntax, and conventional thought sequence to approach the elusive nonreferential quality of music.

Claude Debussy is often called an impressionist in music, because his fragmentary motives and little flashes of tone color recall the impressionists' painting technique. Debussy can also be called a symbolist, since suggestion, rather than outright statement, is at the heart of his aesthetic. Famous symbolist texts inspired two famous Debussy works: the orchestral *Prelude to "The Afternoon of a Faun"* (a poem by Stéphane Mallarmé), and the opera *Pelléas et Mélisande* (a play by Maurice Maeterlinck), where Debussy's elusive musical symbols and Maeterlinck's elusive verbal ones combine to produce an unforgettable effect of mysterious suggestion.

There was also a symbolist movement in painting. In his picture entitled *Music,* the Viennese painter Gustav Klimt (1862–1918) used the girl's bowed head, her mysterious instrument, the sculpted lion, and the mask to suggest much more in the way of a mood than they actually represent (see page 295). Symbolism is also the force behind the powerful images in the work of Vincent van Gogh (1853–1890). In his *Les Chaumes à Cordeville* (page 296), the distorted rooftop and the almost liquid tree are not there to represent reality, but to symbolize the artist's disturbing vision of the universe.

Expressionists and Fauves

Even in Van Gogh's most extreme works, however, the trees are still recognizably trees. At Paris and Vienna—artistic centers which were also centers of avant-garde music—two émigré artists pursued separate but parallel paths toward completely abstract painting.

This mysterious, suggestive image of Music, with her even more mysterious symbolic attributes, haunted the Viennese painter Gustav Klimt; she appears in several of his works.

Does nature imitate art? This snapshot of Debussy (second from the left) and some friends is startlingly similar in mood to the impressionist painting by Manet shown on page 294.

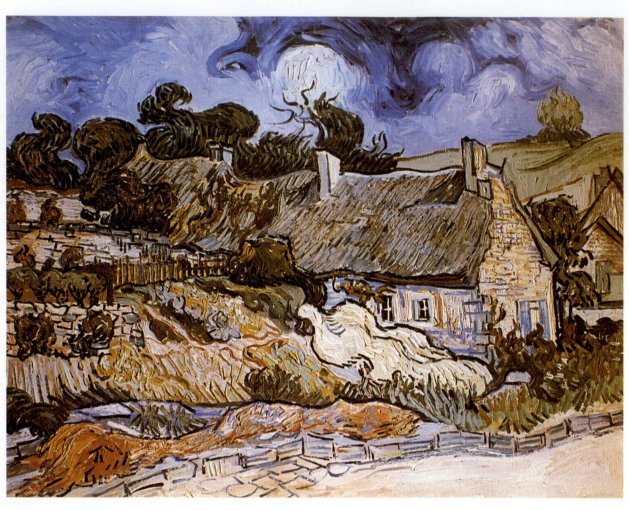

Les Chaumes à Cordeville,
by Vincent van Gogh, 1890

Our horse-and-rider pictures on page 297 by the Russian-born Wassily Kandinsky (1866–1944) show step by step how the process was accomplished. Kandinsky belonged to a German movement in the arts called **expressionism,** which sought to express the most extreme of human feelings by divorcing art from everyday literalness. Anguish, even hysteria, could be conveyed by the harsh clashing of strong colors, irregular shapes, and jagged lines. What seems to be conveyed is the artist's inner turbulence—almost entirely abstracted, by the time of Kandinsky's *Romantic Landscape,* from the outer world.

Parallel to the expressionists was a short-lived group in Paris who were dubbed *Les fauves,* "the wild beasts." The *fauves* experimented with distorted images bordering on the grotesque; they also employed motifs from primitive art as though in defiance of what they saw as a decadent European culture. In Pablo Picasso's famous *fauve* painting *Les Démoiselles d'Avignon* of 1907 (Avignon is a street in the red-light district of Barcelona), the quality of abstraction is evident in the angular bodies and the African-mask–like heads—a complete break with the conventional rules of human portrayal (see page 298). Picasso took a further step toward abstraction a little later when he turned to cubism (see page 291).

There is violence in both Kandinsky's and Picasso's work of this period. Such, at least, was the shocked perception of a generation used to the non-threatening art of the impressionists—painters of flickering summer landscapes, soft-edged nudes, and diaphanous action pictures of the ballet.

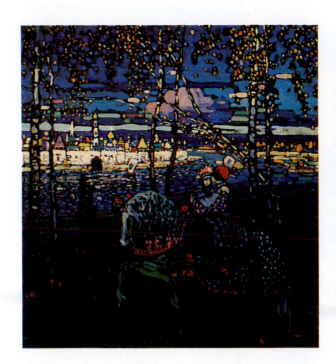

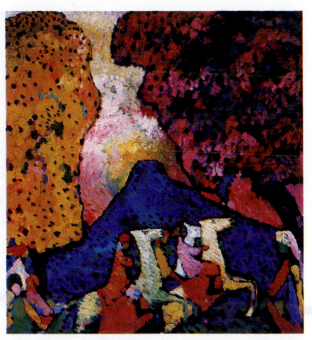

Horses and riders, as depicted by Wassily Kandinsky over a four-year period, show his path toward non-representational painting. In the first picture, the figures are quite clear; in the last, they could be missed entirely. Top left: *Couple on Horseback* (1907); top right: *Blue Mountain* (1909); bottom: *Romantic Landscape* (1911)

Picasso's famous *fauve* shocker *Les Démoiselles d'Avignon* (1907)

Composers, too, courted violence in their music; they sent similar shock waves through the devotees of Wagner, Verdi, Brahms, and Tchaikovsky. The Hungarian composer Béla Bartók wrote a "barbarous" piano piece entitled *Allegro barbaro*. Stravinsky, in his ballet *The Rite of Spring*, depicted ritual rape and murder in the fertility ceremonies of primitive Slavic tribes.

4 Music before World War I

Music never enjoyed (or suffered) a link to the tangible world that was comparable to representation in painting, or to reference in poetry, but it did have its own stable, universally accepted set of principles, its own traditional "internal logic." This rested upon elements that we have discussed many times in this book: tune, motive, harmony, tonality, tone color, and rhythm.

The music of Bach, Beethoven, and Brahms was based on this "logic," and so was the entire stream of Western European folk songs, popular songs, dances, military marches, and the rest. Avant-garde music moved away from this norm. Like abstract, nonrepresentational painting, music worked out new principles based on the materials of the art itself.

With music before World War I, we can lay our main emphasis on developments in melody, harmony, and tonality, for on the whole, these features were the main preoccupations of avant-garde composers in that period. Developments in tone color and rhythm—or, more broadly, musical sonority and musical time—dominated music after World War II.

Experiment and Transformation: Melody

Melody, harmony, and tonality all work closely together. In historical terms, harmony arose as a way of supporting and adorning melody, and tonality first arose as a means of clarifying harmony; then tonality functioned as a more general way of organizing music. Each of these functions was transformed in the early twentieth century.

We have seen the Viennese Classical composers bring tunes to the fore in their music, and the Romantics capitalize on tunes as the most emphatic means of conveying powerful emotion. Yet Wagner, despite the melodic quality of many of his leitmotivs, was criticized for the confusing quality of his singing lines, and Mahler's audiences were puzzled and irritated by the bittersweet distortions that he applied to folklike melodies. In his later works, such as his unfinished Tenth Symphony of 1911, Mahler wrote increasingly intricate and difficult melodic lines. The long melodies surge, swoop, and yearn in a strange, painful manner.

And by that time another Viennese composer, Arnold Schoenberg, was writing even more complex melodies that simply made no sense to contemporary listeners. The intense rhythms and the anguished intervals of Romanticism were there, but the actual notes did not appear to fit together at all.

The disintegration of traditional melody was accomplished in other ways by French composers. In many (not all) of his works, Claude Debussy used only the most shadowy motives—a constant suggestion of melody without clear tunes. A little later Igor Stravinsky, writing in Paris, seized upon Russian folk songs but whittled them down (or abstracted them) into brief, utterly simple and impassive fragments.

New Scales

The traditional diatonic scale had been used for so long that it was almost regarded as a fact of nature. But composers around 1900 cast a speculative eye over the basic sound materials of music; for the first time in centuries, new scales were experimented with seriously. Thus Debussy and others used the **pentatonic scale**, a five-note scale playable on the black notes of the keyboard. Imported from folk song and Asian music, this scale was tried in all kinds of music, not only (as before) in nationalist or other folk-derived compositions.

Two further scales are abstract constructions, significantly enough, which anyone can figure out by systematically analyzing the total chromatic scale. The **whole-tone scale** divides the octave into six equal parts—all of its intervals are whole steps; again, Debussy made much use of this resource. The **octatonic scale**—a specialty with Stravinsky—fits eight pitches into the octave by alternating whole and half steps.

Less used, the **quarter-tone scale** employs all the pitches of the chromatic scale plus the pitches that come halfway between each pair of them.

More important as a means of composition than the use of any of these scales was serialism, the "new language" for music invented in the 1920s by Arnold Schoenberg. As is explained in the box on the following pages, serialism in effect creates a special scale for every serial composition.

Pentatonic scale

Debussy, "Clouds"

Whole-tone scale

Octatonic scale

Quarter-tone scale

Schoenberg and Serialism

Of all early twentieth-century composers, Arnold Schoenberg (1874–1951) was the most keenly aware of the problem caused by ever-broadening dissonance and atonality. The problem, to put it simply, was the clear and present danger of chaos. In the early 1920s Schoenberg found a way to impose a kind of order or control over the newly "emancipated" elements of music.

This resulted in the **twelve-tone system**, defined by Schoenberg as a "method of composing with the twelve tones solely in relation to one another"—that is, *not* in relation to central pitch, or tonic, which is no longer the means of organizing music. This method was later known as **serialism**. Serialism can be regarded as a systematization of chromaticism, as developed by Romantic composers, especially Richard Wagner (see pages 225, 302).

Schoenberg's "Twelve-tone System"

Schoenberg developed a way of composing with the twelve pitches of the chromatic scale held to a *fixed ordering*. An ordered sequence of the twelve pitches is called a **twelve-tone row** or **series**: hence the term *serialism*. For any composition, he would determine a series ahead of time and maintain it (the next piece would have another series).

What does "maintain" mean in this context? It means that Schoenberg composed by writing notes only in the order of the work's series, *or of certain carefully prescribed modifications and extensions of the series* (see below). As a general rule, he always went through the entire series without any repetitions or backtracking before starting over again. The pitches can, however, appear in any octave, high or low. They can assume any rhythm.

Shown on page 301 is a twelve-tone series, and certain of those carefully prescribed modifications of it, resulting in *retrograde, inverted,* and *transposed* forms of the series, as well as combined forms. The wistful tune derived from this series opens Schoenberg's Piano Concerto, Op. 42, of 1942. Listen to just the beginning of this concerto, while following the music on page 301. The tune is played by the piano soloist, with the orchestra in the background.

The tune includes just a few notes that do not follow the order of the series (marked with asterisks) and some note repetitions. Note that the rhythm has nothing to do with the series. Some of the series notes are rhythmically very prominent—they are the long notes on the strong beat of a measure. Other series notes go by almost without being noticed.

Serialism and Unity

Part of the point of twelve-tone composition is that each piece has its own special "sound world" determined by its series, and that this permeates the whole piece. The next composition has a new series and a new sound world.

Indeed, serialism can be regarded as the end result of an important tendency in nineteenth-century music, the tendency to seek strong means of unity within individual compositions. We have traced the "principle of thematic unity" in music by Hector Berlioz, Richard Wagner, and others, and mentioned the different "levels" on which it operated—actual recurring themes, thematic transformations, and subtler similarities between motives (see page 229). A serial composition is, in a sense, totally unified, since every measure of it shares the same unique sound world. Thus, on its own special level, Schoenberg's serialism seemed to realize the Romantic composers' ideal of unity.

"The Emancipation of Dissonance"

As melody grew more complex, more fragmentary, or more vague, harmony grew more and more dissonant. The concepts of consonance and dissonance, as we noted on page 28, rest on the fact that certain chords (consonant chords) sound stable and at rest, whereas others (dissonant chords) sound

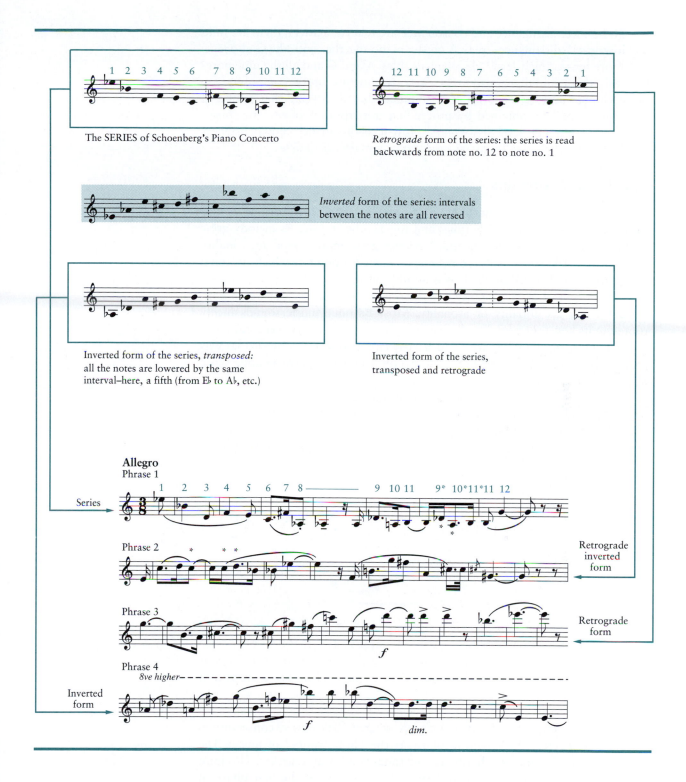

The SERIES of Schoenberg's Piano Concerto

Retrograde form of the series: the series is read backwards from note no. 12 to note no. 1

Inverted form of the series: intervals between the notes are all reversed

Inverted form of the series, *transposed:* all the notes are lowered by the same interval–here, a fifth (from E♭ to A♭, etc.)

Inverted form of the series, transposed and retrograde

Allegro
Phrase 1

Series

Retrograde inverted form

Phrase 2

Phrase 3

Retrograde form

Phrase 4

Inverted form

tense and need to resolve to consonant ones. In a famous phrase, Schoenberg spoke of "the emancipation of dissonance," meaning emancipation from that need to resolve. Dissonance was to be free from the "rule" that says it must always be followed by the appropriate consonance.

To be sure, dissonance and consonance are relative matters; there are mild or "low-level" dissonances (play A on the piano together with the G above it) and more tense, "high-level" dissonances (play A and G and all the nine notes between them simultaneously). As early twentieth-century composers explored higher and higher levels of dissonance, they discovered that a kind of resolution could be obtained by proceeding not from dissonance to consonance, but from high-level dissonance to low-level dissonance. Slowly listeners began hearing this, too. Today we accept it as a matter of course.

Tonality and Atonality

Tonality is the feeling of centrality, focus, or "homing" toward a particular pitch that we get from simple tunes and much other music. As melody grew more complex or fragmented, and harmony grew more dissonant, tonality grew more indistinct. Finally, some music reached a point at which no tonal center could be detected at all. This is **atonal** music.

However, just as consonance and dissonance are not open-and-shut concepts, neither are tonality or atonality. Most Baroque music sounds firmly rooted in its key, for example, whereas certain Romantic music seems rather to hover around a general key area. Much early twentieth-century music that was criticized as "atonal" can be heard on careful listening to have a subtle sense of tonality after all.

Wagner, as we recall, went further than other Romantic composers in the direction of *chromaticism,* the free use of all twelve pitches of the chromatic scale. For example, there are as many as ten different chromatic notes in the phrase shown here from his opera *Tristan und Isolde* (see page 263), a phrase which is as compact as it is emotional.

Chromatic scale

Since tonality depends on one pitch standing out from the others in the ordinary diatonic scale (for example, C in the C-major scale C D E F G A B), when all twelve chromatic pitches are used freely, the centrality of any single one is automatically diluted. Wagner's technique of chromaticism was a significant forecast of the coming trend toward atonality.

Melody, harmony, tonality: all are closely related. Beleaguered conservatives around 1900 referred to them jocularly as the "holy trinity" of music. The "emancipation" of melody, harmony, and tonality all went together. This joint emancipation counts as the central style characteristic of the first phase of twentieth-century avant-garde music.

CHAPTER 21

The Early Twentieth Century

T he first major phase of avant-garde music began in Paris and Vienna and flourished from around 1890 to 1914. Claude Debussy, Igor Stravinsky (a young Russian working in Paris), and Arnold Schoenberg were the leading figures in this brilliant era. And there were strong echoes of it in Russia itself, Hungary, and the United States.

It was a period of rapid development in all the arts, as we have seen, in which the basic tenets of nineteenth-century art were everywhere challenged. In particular, nineteenth-century ideas of melody, harmony, and tonality came under attack. Developments in tone color and rhythm—or, more broadly, musical sonority and musical time—dominated the second phase of modernism, which followed after World War II.

To be sure, musical elements such as melody, harmony, rhythm, and sonority affect each other intimately, and composers hardly ever think of them in isolation. Debussy, Stravinsky, and Schoenberg were all noted for their novel treatment of tone color and rhythm. In terms of historical impact, however, Stravinsky's rhythm, though widely imitated, really worked for him alone, and Debussy's concept of tone color was not fully absorbed until the post–World War II period. It was the revolution in tonality—which went along with a radical reconsideration of melody and harmony—that caught the imagination of the early twentieth century.

1 Debussy and Impressionism

Claude Debussy occupies the border area between the late nineteenth- and early twentieth-century styles. His investigation of sensuous new tone colors for orchestra and for piano, his development of new rich harmonies, and his search for ways to express emotion in music—all this reminds us of the Romantics. Yet while in some ways his work seems tied to Romanticism, in others it represents a direct reaction against it.

Thus Debussy's tone colors avoid the heavy sonorities that were usual in late Romantic music, merging instead into subtle, mysterious shades of sound. His harmonies sound strangely vague, and the tonality of his music is often clouded. Debussy's themes and motives are usually fragmentary and tentative, and often draw on the vague-sounding new scales mentioned in Chapter 20.

(. . . Sounds and perfumes sway in the evening air)

Title of a Debussy "miniature" for piano; the parentheses and dots are his

Claude Debussy (1862–1918)

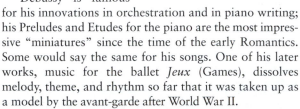

Claude Debussy studied long and patiently at the famous Paris Conservatory of Music, which he entered at the age of ten. He did not do well in the piano exams, or at least not well enough, but won medals and various awards in theory and composition. He was finally awarded the coveted Grand Prix (Top Prize)—a three-year fellowship to study in Rome.

Before this, Debussy took a job with Madame von Meck, the eccentric patron of Tchaikovsky, playing in a trio at her house in Moscow. Russian music (music of the *kuchka*: see page 275) was one of several vivid influences on the young composer; another was the gamelan, the Indonesian orchestra composed mostly of bronze instruments struck by mallets. Debussy encountered the fascinating tuned-percussion sonorities of the gamelan, and its strange scales, at a World Exhibition in Paris in 1889.

Visits to Bayreuth, the shrine of Wagner's music dramas, afforded another strong influence. But Debussy soon turned against Wagner and German music in general, which he felt was a stifling influence on modern music in France.

Debussy settled into Parisian café life, becoming a familiar bearded figure in his broad-brimmed hat and flowing cape. In his early thirties he seems to have rather suddenly crystallized his musical style, reflecting the influences of the French symbolist poets and impressionist painters. One remarkable work after another was given its premiere, greeted with a flurry of controversy, and then generally accepted by the critics and the public. His one opera, *Pelléas et Mélisande* (1902), written directly to the words of a play by Maurice Maeterlinck, aroused the opposition of the author, who was a prominent symbolist. But today Maeterlinck's play is remembered mainly on account of Debussy's opera.

Debussy is famous for his innovations in orchestration and in piano writing; his Preludes and Etudes for the piano are the most impressive "miniatures" since the time of the early Romantics. Some would say the same for his songs. One of his later works, music for the ballet *Jeux* (Games), dissolves melody, theme, and rhythm so far that it was taken up as a model by the avant-garde after World War II.

For a short time Debussy wrote music criticism, in which he expressed in pungent prose the anti-German attitudes that were already manifest in his music. Debussy died of cancer in Paris during World War I, actually during a bombardment of his city by the Germans he hated.

Chief Works: For orchestra, *Prelude to "The Afternoon of a Faun"* (a famous poem by the French symbolist poet Mallarmé), Three Nocturnes, *La Mer* (The Sea), *Iberia*, *Jeux* (Games) ▪ One opera (though he began several others): *Pelléas et Mélisande* ▪ For piano: Preludes and Etudes, *Children's Corner* Suite, and *Suite bergamasque*, including "Clair de lune" ▪ Songs to poems by Baudelaire, Verlaine, and Mallarmé ▪ A string quartet and other chamber music ▪ *Syrinx* for solo flute

Debussy's orchestral sound differs sharply from that of his contemporary, Gustav Mahler, another great innovator in orchestration. Mahler treated the orchestra more and more contrapuntally; each instrument tends to stand out from the others like a Romantic hero striving for his own say in the world. Debussy's orchestra is more often a single, delicately pulsing totality to which individual instruments contribute momentary gleams of color. One thinks of an impressionist picture, in which small, separate areas of color, visible close up, merge into indescribable color fields as the viewer stands back and takes the painting in as a whole.

CLAUDE DEBUSSY
Three Nocturnes (1897–1899)

Debussy's Three Nocturnes, like most of his works for orchestra, might be described as impressionist symphonic poems, though they have no narrative programs. They evoke various scenes without attempting to illustrate them literally.

The title "nocturne" evokes a nighttime scene, the great examples before Debussy being the piano nocturnes of Chopin (see page 243). The first nocturne, *Clouds,* is a pure nature picture. The second, *Festivals,* depicts mysterious nighttime fairs and parades. The title of the third, *Sirens,* refers to the legendary sea maidens who tempt lonely sailors and pull them into the deep.

Clouds   We first hear a quiet series of chords, played by clarinets and bassoons, which circle back on themselves repeatedly. They seem to suggest great cumulus clouds, moving slowly, silently, and inexorably across the sky.

As a "theme," however, these chords do not function conventionally; they make no strong declarations and lead nowhere definitive. This is also true of the next motive that is introduced—a haunting motive that occurs many times in *Clouds,* with hardly any change. (It is built on an octatonic scale: see page 299.) Yet even this muted gesture by the English horn, with its vague rhythm and its fading conclusion, seems sufficient to exhaust the composition and bring it to a near halt, over a barely audible drum roll:

After this near stop, the "cloud" theme begins again, leading this time to a downward passage of remarkably gentle, murmuring chords in the strings—chords all of the same structure (major ninth chords):

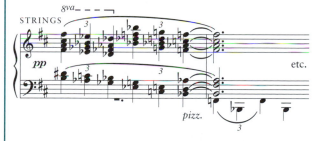

These rich chords slip by without establishing a clear sense of tonality; gorgeous in themselves, they are not "functionally" significant. This use of parallel chords is one of Debussy's most famous inventions.

Clouds might be said to fall into an **A B A′** form—but only in a very general way. Debussy shrinks from clear formal outlines; the musical form here is much more fluid than that of **A B A** structures observed in earlier music. This fluidity is something to bear in mind when following *Clouds* and other avant-garde music with Listening Charts. By design, avant-garde composers break down the sharp and (to them) oversimple divisions of older musical styles. If they avail themselves of form types such as rondo, sonata form, and so on, they do so in very free, imaginative ways.

In the **A** section of *Clouds,* the return of the "cloud" theme after a more active, restless passage suggests an internal **a b a′** pattern as well. The next idea, **B** (illustrated on page 299), sounds at first like a meditative epilogue to

The title "Nocturnes" should be taken here in a more general and especially in a more decorative sense. . . . Clouds: the unchanging aspect of the sky, the slow, melancholy motion of the clouds, fading away into agonized grey tones, gently tinged with white.

Claude Debussy

LISTENING CHART 21

Debussy, *Clouds*

7 min., 3 sec.

	0:00	**A** **a**	Cloud theme: clarinets and bassoons	
	0:20		English-horn motive	
	0:27		Quiet timpani roll—music almost stops	
	0:45		Cloud theme: high strings	
2 / 9	0:58		Downward chord passage	
	1:12		Further development: strings	
0:33	1:31		English-horn motive, with a new echo in the French horn	
1:04	2:02		Downward chord passage	
3 / 10	2:20	**b**	Rising section, more restless: woodwinds added	
	3:00		Brief climax	
0:44	3:04		English-horn motive (with new even-note rhythm accompaniment) is repeated several times, until it dies away.	
4 / 11	3:56	**a′**	Cloud theme, with new solo viola counterpoint	
	4:12		Downward chord passage	
5 / 12	4:28	**B**	A new tune enters tentatively, but then repeats itself; flute and harp	
	4:51		Tune in strings and solo violin	
0:38	5:06		Tune in flute and harp	
		(A′)	*Not a real "return" of* **A,** *only of selected elements standing in for* **A**	
6 / 13	5:25		English-horn motive, with its echo	
	5:58		Quiet timpani and low strings—prominent until the end	
			Recollection of thematic fragments:	
0:58	6:23		Cloud theme: bassoons, then cellos	
1:17	6:42		**B** tune	
1:22	6:47		French-horn echo to the English-horn motive	

ENGLISH HORN

FLUTE

A; but when the little tune is repeated several times, it begins to feel like a substantial section of contrast. The "return," **A′**, is really just a reference to some of **A**'s material, notably the English-horn figure. Then at the end the bassoons play a dim, disturbed fragment of the cloud theme, the flute hovers for a moment on the **B** tune, and the drum roll is extended—so as to suggest distant thunder, perhaps.

2 Stravinsky: The Primacy of Rhythm

Stravinsky's earliest work followed from that of his teacher, the Nationalist composer Rimsky-Korsakov. But in three famous ballet scores written for the Ballets Russes in Paris, Stravinsky rapidly developed his own powerful, hard-edged avant-garde style, a style that can be compared to the contemporary

Igor Stravinsky (1882–1971)

The son of an important opera singer, Igor Stravinsky studied law and did not turn seriously to music until he was nineteen. He was fortunate to be able to study with Nikolai Rimsky-Korsakov, a survivor of the Nationalist *kuchka* (see page 275) who was still composing actively.

Rimsky's brand of nationalism served young Stravinsky well in the famous (and still outstandingly popular) ballet scores *The Firebird, Petrushka,* and *The Rite of Spring*, which he wrote for the Ballets Russes, a Russian company centered in Paris. This enormously dynamic organization, run by a brilliant producer and man-about-the-arts named Serge Diaghilev, astonished the blasé Parisian public with its exotic spectacles combining the newest and the most sensational in dance, music, scenery, and costume design. Among Diaghilev's dancers were Vaslav Nijinsky and George Balanchine; among his designers were Pablo Picasso and Henri Matisse.

After World War I Stravinsky composed more ballets for Diaghilev, as well as other works in a dazzling variety of styles, forms, and genres. One of the first composers, along with Debussy, to be interested in jazz, Stravinsky wrote *Piano Ragtime* in 1917 (and, much later, *Ebony Concerto* for clarinettist Woody Herman's jazz band). He became an outspoken advocate of "objectivity" in music, which meant in particular the rejection of Romantic emotionality. For many years he modeled his music on pre-Romantic composers such as Bach, Handel, and Mozart, transforming the music by his own unique rhythmic and harmonic style.

His final work in this vein, called *Neoclassicism*, was an opera, *The Rake's Progress*, which is a modern transformation of Mozart's *Don Giovanni*. This was written in America (to English words), where Stravinsky moved in 1939. After World War II his music grew more abstract

and formal in style. During the last twenty years of his life, Stravinsky had as his protégé the young American conductor and critic Robert Craft, who helped to manage his affairs, conducted and promoted his music, and introduced him to the music of Schoenberg and Webern. Craft published fascinating books of conversations, in which Stravinsky spoke with extraordinary gusto and dry humor about his long career.

For a quarter of a century people had regarded Stravinsky (and he regarded himself) as the leading Neoclassical composer in the French orbit, at the opposite pole from Schoenberg and the Viennese serialists. So he created yet another sensation when, in his seventies, he produced a remarkable group of late compositions employing serial technique.

After some scarifying stays in American hospitals, on which the composer's comments were particuarly sardonic, Stravinsky died at his home in New York in 1971. He is buried in Venice, near the grave of Diaghilev.

Chief Works: Ballet scores, including *The Firebird, Petrushka, The Rite of Spring, The Wedding, Orpheus, Agon* ▪ *The Solider's Tale,* and unusual chamber-music piece with narrator ▪ An "opera-oratorio," *Oedipus the King; The Rake's Progress,* an opera in English (words by the poet W. H. Auden) ▪ Two symphonies; concertos; *Symphony of Psalms* for orchestra and chorus ▪ Other religious works: a Mass, *Requiem Canticles, Threni* (settings from the Lamentations of Jeremiah)

---

fauve style in French painting. These ballets reveal a fascinating progression toward more and more abstraction of folk material. Compare the development of abstraction in art by Kandinsky and Picasso, which we spoke of earlier.

The first ballet, *The Firebird* (1910), spins a romantic fairy tale about the magical Firebird, the ogre Kastchei, and Prince Ivan Tsarevitch, son of the tsar. Its rich, half-Asian setting is matched by beautifully colored folk music and orchestral sound worthy of Debussy himself. But in the next ballet, Stravinsky moved from the steppes to the urban marketplace, to the pre-Lenten fair at St. Petersburg. *Petrushka* (1911), the story of a carnival barker and his puppet, encouraged him to put a hard, satirical edge on his folk material. Then in *The Rite of Spring* (1913), Stravinsky boldly and brutally depicted the fertility cults of prehistoric Slavic tribes. Here Russian folk music, simplified and abstracted, is treated as the source of primitive rhythmic and sexual energy, rather than picture-postcard charm.

The musical style that Stravinsky brought to a head in the *Rite* has many features that struck listeners of the time as "barbaric," apart from its use of deliberately crude folk-tune fragments. The music was "abstract" in the sense that it sounded utterly unemotional, by Romantic standards. It was grindingly dissonant. It emphasized meter in a very heavy, exciting way, and the rhythms themselves were dazzling and unpredictable. Finally, the score is enormously loud: it demands a colossal orchestra, as though the composer wanted to show how he could control—and transform—the chief powerhouse of musical Romanticism. A symbol of prewar opulence in musical terms, the *Rite* orchestra was twice as large as anything Stravinsky ever chose to use later.

Stravinsky, drawn by Picasso during the period when they were associated at the Ballets Russes

IGOR STRAVINSKY
The Rite of Spring (1913): Part I, "The Adoration of the Earth"

The first performance of *The Rite of Spring* caused a riot; the audience was shocked and infuriated by the violent, dissonant sounds in the pit and the provocative choreography on the stage, suggesting rape and ritual murder.

The ballet has no real story, and Stravinsky even said that he preferred to think of the music as a concert piece. However, inscriptions on the score specify a series of primitive fertility rites of various kinds, culminating in the ceremonial choice of a virgin for sacrifice. After this she is evidently danced to death in the ballet's second part, entitled "The Sacrifice."

Almost the entire Rite of Spring *was written in an eight-feet-by-eight room, whose only furniture was a small upright piano which I kept muted (I always work at a muted piano), a table and two chairs. . . . My idea was that the Prelude should represent the awakening of nature, the scratching, gnawing, wiggling of birds and beasts.*

Igor Stravinsky, reminiscing in 1960

Introduction   The halting opening theme is played by a bassoon at the very top of its normal register. Avant-garde composers strained all the elements of music, including the ordinary capabilities of instruments. The bleating bassoon is joined by odd hootings on other woodwinds, gradually building up an extraordinary texture that is highly dissonant. The instrumental parts sound rather like a static series of preliminary fanfares—or perhaps like the calls of strange prehistoric wildlife.

"Omens of Spring"—"Dance of the Adolescents"   After a brief introduction, in which the dancers presumably "register" an awareness of spring's awakening, the "Dance of the Adolescents" commences with a famous instance of Stravinskian rhythmic irregularity. (Probably this was where the original audience started their catcalls.) A single very dissonant chord is repeated thirty-two times in even eighth notes—but with heavy accents reinforced by short, fat chords played by eight (!) French horns on the most unexpected beats:

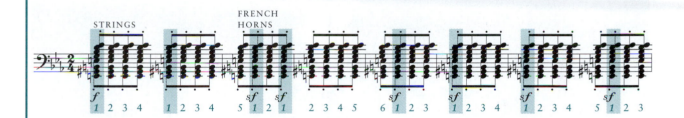

This completely upsets ordinary meter. Instead of eight standard measures of four eighth notes— *1* 2 3 4, *1* 2 3 4, etc.—Stravinsky makes us hear *1* 2 3 4, *1* 2 3 4 5, *1* 2, *1* 2 3 4 5 6, *1* 2 3, *1* 2 3 4, *1* 2 3 4 5, *1* 2 3. (Try beating time to this passage for a truly bewildering experience.) Yet these irregular rhythms are also exhilarating, and they certainly drive the music forward in a unique way. One really wants to join the dance.

The repeating chords are now overlaid with new motives, derived from Russian folk song. The motives are repeated with slightly different rhythms and at slightly different lengths. This distinctive repetition technique, or *ostinato*, is indicated by brackets on the example below. Like Debussy, Stravinsky tends to concentrate on small melodic fragments, but whereas Debussy soon abandons his fragments, Stravinsky keeps repeating his in this irregular, almost obsessive way.

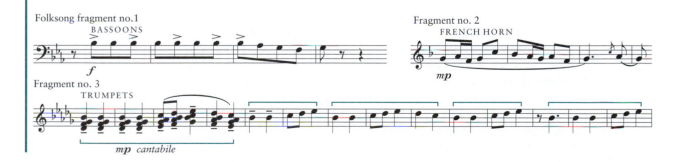

"The Game of Abduction"   New violence is introduced with this section, a whirlwind of brilliant rhythms, with much frantic pounding on the timpani.

"Round Dances of Spring"   After a moment of respite, a short, quiet introduction conveys a remarkably desolate, empty feeling (partly as a result of its novel orchestration: a high (E♭) clarinet and low (alto) flute playing two octaves apart). Then a slow dragging dance emerges, built out of the third folk-tune fragment from the "Dance of the Adolescents."

The very strong downbeat makes the meter hypnotic—but one or two added or skipped beats have a powerful animating effect. The dance reaches a relentless climax with glissando (sliding) trombones, gong, cymbals, and big drum. After a sudden fast coda, the bleak introduction returns to conclude the section.

The climax of *The Rite of Spring*

Four more sections follow our selection in Act I of *The Rite of Spring*. The dynamic "Games of the Rival Tribes" introduces two more folktune fragments. A huge masked figure is borne aloft by the male dancers in a very impressive slower section, the "Procession of the Sage"; the Sage then performs a brief ceremony, "Adoration of the Earth." The concluding orgiastic "Dance of the Earth" is built on a fast and furious ostinato.

What is conspicuously absent from any of this is emotionality. Tough, precise, and barbaric, it is as far from old-line Romantic sentiment as it is from the delicate, shadowy vision of Debussy. In Stravinsky's later works the barbarism was tamed, but the dry, precise quality remained, and so did the exhilarating irregular rhythms. Throughout his long career they provided him with a powerful strategy for movement, unlike that of any other composer. It was the primacy of rhythm that produced Stravinsky's "new language" for music.

LISTENING CHART 22

5	3	5A	3A
2-8	14-20	1	3

Stravinsky, *The Rite of Spring*, from Part 1

Ballet score, 11 min., 50 sec.

	0:02	**Introduction**	Bassoon "fanfare," *p,* twice interrupted by English horn	
	1:14		Fanfares in oboe, high (E♭) clarinet, bass clarinet	
	1:55		Buildup	
3 / 15	2:23		New motive in the oboe and E♭ clarinet	
	3:00		Stop; return of the bassoon fanfare, *p*	
0:46	3:09	**Omens of Spring**	Faster; transition to the Dance of the Adolescents	
1:05	3:28		Tempo is established; trill, ♩♩♩♩ rhythm introduced	
4 / 16	3:34	**Dance of the Adolescents**	Loud rhythmic passage with irregular accents (French horns); various motives are introduced	
0:38	4:12		Rhythmic passage again	
5 / 17	4:21		Folk song fragment no. 1—bassoons and contrabassoon, etc.	
	4:59		Return of the introductory "Omens" music	
0:54	5:15		Folk song fragment no. 2—French horn, flutes	
1:28	5:49		Folk song fragment no. 3—trumpets (triangle)	
1:53	6:14		Folk song fragment no. 2—flutes; buildup	
6 / 18	6:49	**The Game of Abduction**	Faster; frantic rhythms. Brass is prominent, sliding horn calls	
0:55	7:44		Ending passage: alternation between scurrying figures in the strings and heavy booms in the drums	
7 / 19	8:09	**Round Dances of Spring**	Slower; introduction: flute trills, clarinet melody	
0:27	8:36		The main slow dance rhythm is introduced; woodwind motive	
8 / 20	9:15		Folk song fragment no. 3 (slower than before)—violas, *mf*	
	10:15		Folk song fragment no. 3, *ff,* with cymbals	
1:26	10:41		Climactic passage—brass	
1:49	11:04		Short coda: faster, with violent rhythmic interjections	
2:07	11:22		Brief return of the slow introduction, *p*	

Musical sketches for
The Rite of Spring

3 Expressionism

In Paris during the first decades of the twentieth century, Debussy's shifting musical shadows and Stravinsky's extroverted gestures were on display nightly at the Ballets Russes. Some analogies can be drawn between these composers in stylistic terms, but primarily what they had in common was their rejection, in their different ways, of the steamy emotionalism of late Romanticism.

In Austria and Germany, however, and especially in Vienna, composers pressed forward with music that was increasingly emotional and complex. As though intent on taking Romantic fervor to its ultimate conclusion, they found themselves exploiting extreme states, extending all the way to hysteria, nightmare, even insanity. This movement, *Expressionism,* shares its name with important parallel movements in art and literature (see page 296).

These years also saw the publication of Freud's first works, with their bold new analysis of the power of unconscious drives, the significance of dreams, and the central role of sexuality. Psychoanalytical theory had a clear impact on German expressionsim; a vivid example is *Erwartung* (Anticipation), a monologue for soprano and orchestra written by Arnold Schoenberg in 1909. A woman comes to meet her lover in a dark wood and spills out all her terrors, shrieking as she stumbles upon a dead body she believes to be his. One cannot tell whether *Erwartung* represents an actual scene of hysteria, an allegory, or a Freudian dream fantasy.

Schoenberg was the leading Expressionist in music. He pioneered in the "emancipation of dissonance" and the breakdown of tonality, and shortly after World War I he developed the revolutionary technique of serialism (see pages 300–301). Even before the war, Schoenberg attracted two brilliant Viennese students who were only about ten years his junior, and who shared almost equally in his path-breaking innovations. Schoenberg, Anton Webern, and Alban Berg are often referred to as the Second Viennese School, by analogy with the earlier Viennese triumvirate of Haydn, Mozart, and Beethoven.

Nightmarish images recur in expressionist art. This disturbing yet beautiful (disturbingly beautiful?) painting is by the Norwegian artist Edvard Munch (1863–1944).

Arnold Schoenberg (1874–1951)

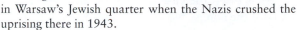

The most conscious and self-conscious member of music's avant-garde was Arnold Schoenberg, who grew up in Europe's most intense musical environment, the Vienna of Johannes Brahms and Gustav Mahler. He was largely self-taught in music, though he found a mentor in the conductor and composer Alexander von Zemlinsky, whose sister became Schoenberg's first wife. His second wife, Gertrud Kolisch, was the sister of the leader of an important string quartet—a quartet that featured Schoenberg's music. A man of unusual versatility, Schoenberg produced important books on music theory, painted (and gave exhibitions of) pictures in expressionist style, and wrote the literary texts for many of his compositions.

His early music—notably *Transfigured Night* of 1899, still his best-known work—followed from the late Romantic tradition of Brahms and Mahler. But Schoenberg soon came to feel that he was destined to carry this tradition through to its "logical" modern development, by way of increasing chromaticism and atonality. Listeners felt otherwise, and Schoenberg's revolutionary compositions of the 1900s probably met with more hostility than any in the entire history of music. At the same time, they attracted the sympathetic interest of Mahler and Richard Strauss, and drew a coterie of brilliant young students to Schoenberg.

Schoenberg's music grew progressively more and more atonal, but he was nearly fifty before he developed the twelve-tone (or serial) system. Of all the "new languages" for music attempted by the early avant-garde composers, serialism was the most radical and also the most fruitful. After World War II, even though some leading radicals rejected Schoenberg's music, they still made use of his fundamental idea of a serial language for music.

As a Jew, Schoenberg was forced to leave Germany when the Nazis came to power, and he spent the rest of his life in Los Angeles, becoming a U.S. citizen in 1941.

His remarkable unfinished opera *Moses and Aaron* of 1933 is both a Judaic epic and also an allegory of the problem of modernist communication with the public. *A Survivor from Warsaw* was written in memory of the slaughter that occurred in Warsaw's Jewish quarter when the Nazis crushed the uprising there in 1943.

Schoenberg was a strange personality: gloomy, uncompromising, inordinately proud, and also highly superstitious. Of all the major composers, he was the first great teacher since Bach; besides his close associates of the Second Viennese School, he strongly influenced many other musicians who sought him out as a teacher. At the end of his life he taught at UCLA. Though only some of his music has won popular approval, Schoenberg is regarded by most musicians as the most significant composer of this century.

The Schoenberg Institute at Los Angeles makes his scores available to students, puts on concerts of his music, and preserves the room he composed in, just as it was, in perpetuity.

Chief Works: An early "symphonic poem" for string sextet, *Transfigured Night*; Five Orchestral Pieces; two chamber symphonies, a piano concerto and a violin concerto ▪ *Erwartung* ("Anticipation"), an expressionist monodrama for one singer and orchestra; the unfinished opera *Moses and Aaron* ▪ Choral works, including *Gurrelieder,* the unfinished oratorio *Jacob's Ladder,* and *A Survivor from Warsaw* ▪ Songs, including *The Book of the Hanging Gardens,* to texts by the German symbolist poet Stefan George; *Pierrot lunaire* ("Moonstruck Pierrot"), a chamber-music piece with *Sprechstimme* singer ▪ Four string quartets and other chamber music

ARNOLD SCHOENBERG
Pierrot lunaire (1912)

40–44   2

This highly influential song cycle sets text by a minor symbolist poet, Albert Giraud. Like many artists of the time—poets as well as composers—Giraud is not easy to figure out at once. Pierrot is the eternal figure of the sad clown, and hence perhaps also the alienated artist; but why is he called "lunar"? In poems that are dotted with Freudian imagery, we hear about his obsession with the moon, his amorous frustrations, his neurotic aspirations, his pranks and adventures.

To match this, Schoenberg wrote music which utterly lacks the tunes that one might expect to find in a set of songs. The soprano does not exactly sing or exactly speak, but performs in an in-between style of Schoenberg's invention called *Sprechstimme* ("speech-song"). **Sprechstimme** is an extreme example of the avant-garde composers' search through the most basic artistic materials—here, sound that is not even fully organized into pitches—for new expressive means. Through *Sprechstimme*, Giraud's strange moonstruck poems are somehow magnified and emphasized, distorted and parodied all at the same time.

Pierrot lunaire calls for five instrumentalists—flute, clarinet, violin, cello, piano—three of whom double on other instruments; that is, the flutist sometimes switches to piccolo, the clarinetist to bass clarinet, and the violinist to viola. Not all the songs involve all the players, so nearly every song has its own unique accompaniment, ranging from a single flute in No. 7 to all eight instruments in No. 21 (the players switching within this one). Schoenberg's dazzling variety of instrumental effects compensates for the inherent sameness of the *Sprechstimme*.

As is often the case in song cycles, there are musical transitions between many of the songs. We will examine the songs from No. 18 to the end.

No. 18: "The Moonfleck" (voice, piano, piccolo, clarinet, violin, cello)   The piano plays a short introduction, or transition from the previous number. Listen to this piano passage several times. Dense, dissonant, atonal, and alarmingly intense in its motivic insistence, the passage gives us Schoenberg's uncompromising version of musical modernism in a nutshell.

41   The song itself is also short, and one of the most fascinating in the cycle from a technical standpoint. Simultaneous fugues and canons are at work, but what the listener perceives is a fantastic lacework of sounds—as if Pierrot were frantically brushing a thousand flickering moonflecks off his tuxedo. Like much later avant-garde music, "The Moonfleck" uses extremely complicated technical means to achieve a unique sonorous effect.

Einen weissen Fleck des hellen Mondes	With a white speck of the bright moon
Auf dem Rücken seines schwartzen Rockes,	On the back of his tuxedo,
So spaziert Pierrot im lauen Abend. . . .	Pierrot saunters off this languid evening. . . .

42   *No. 19: "Serenade"* (voice, cello, piano)   The poem of "Serenade" is a parody of the traditional lover's night song:

1:03	Mit groteskem Riesenbogen	With a grotesque, giant bow
	Kratzt Pierrot auf seiner Bratsche,	Pierrot scratches on his viola
	Wie der Storch auf einem Beine. . . .	Like a one-legged stork. . . .

and Schoenberg's long, expressionistic cello solo is a parody of a romantic serenade melody. It begins with very widely spaced, exaggerated intervals—Pierrot's "giant bow," perhaps—in a rhythm that seems like a distorted version of waltz time.

42   *No. 20: "Journey Home"* (voice, piano, flute, clarinet, viola, cello)   At the end of "Serenade," the other instruments come in to prepare for "Journey Home." The clarinet is prominent in this beautiful song, in which the overall restless, haunting quality suggests Pierrot's rocking boat:

3:31	Der Mondstrahl ist das Ruder,	A moonbeam is the oar,
	Seerose dient als Boot;	A waterlily serves as a boat
	Drauf fährt Pierrot gen Süden. . . .	On which Pierrot journeys southward. . . .

As a teacher I never taught only what I knew, but rather what the student needed. [But if I say] that I tried to invent something for every student to serve his personal necessities, that does not mean that I made it any easier for them.

Arnold Schoenberg, 1948

No. 21: "O Ancient Scent" (voice and all eight instruments)   The final song of the cycle is one of the simpler, quiet ones, set to a relatively simple poem:

5:34 O alter Duft aus Märchenzeit	O ancient scent from days of fairy lore,
Berauschest wieder meine Sinne!	Intoxicate again my senses!
Ein närrisch Heer von Schelmerein	A foolish swarm of idle thoughts
Durchschwirrt die leichte Luft.	Pervades the gentle air.
Ein glückhaft Wünschen macht mich froh	A happy whim makes me aspire
Nach Freuden, die ich lang verachtet:	To joys that I have long not known;
O alter Duft aus Märchenzeit,	O ancient scent from days of fairy lore,
Berauschest wieder mich!	Intoxicate again my senses!
All meinen Unmut gab ich preis;	All my depression is cast off;
Aus meinen sonnumrahmten Fenster	From my sun-encircled window
Beschau ich frei die liebe Welt	I gaze out freely on the lovely world
Und träum hinaus in selge Weiten:	And dream far beyond the fair horizon:
O alter Duft . . . aus Märchenzeit!	O ancient scent . . . from days of fairy lore!

Romantic nostalgia had been made into a specialty by Mahler; Schoenberg seems to strain that sentiment into something almost painfully exquisite. The opening, for voice and piano alone, is bittersweet with dissonance: by measure 2, the piano has touched on all twelve pitches of the chromatic scale, a good example of the growing chromaticism of avant-garde music.

When the other instruments enter, most of the time they utter sorrowful little comments when the singer-speaker pauses.

In "O Ancient Scent" the same music comes back at the verbal refrains within the poem, making an **a b a′ c a″** form. At lines 7–8 of the poem, the piano music of line 1 is repeated an octave higher. Then at line 13, the first few notes of line 1 are played in a slight variation by the cello and viola:

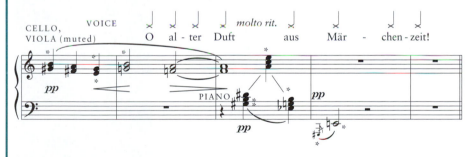

Some kind of cadence—however unconventional—was required for the conclusion of a large composition, so Schoenberg emphasized the three notes of the tonic chord (E, G♯, and B: marked with asterisks) in a very deliberate way. One can hear these notes gingerly pick the key of E major out of the wispy pianissimo instrumental sounds and the singer's final sigh.

Tonality, as we noted earlier, is a relative concept, and this passage would certainly sound atonal by Mozart's standards. But by the standards of the rest of *Pierrot lunaire*, it sounds tonal. Compare the feeling of centrality or finality here with the piano transition introducing song No. 18.

Half troubled and half parodistic, Schoenberg's song cycle about Pierrot and his neuroses ends at a relatively solid resting place—as solid, perhaps, as the twentieth century knows.

I only know that on the two occasions I heard Pierrot lunaire *I was conscious of the most profound impression I have ever experienced from a work of art, and that the enigmatic power of these pieces has left permanent traces on my innermost being. But when I look at the score it still remains completely mysterious. . . .*

Letter to Schoenberg from student Alban Berg, 1914

The Second Viennese School

This is a term often applied to Schoenberg and his two closest associates. Both studied with him in Vienna before World War I, and both followed him in adopting serialism in the 1920s. They were very different in musical personality, and serialism did not really draw them together; rather it seems to have accentuated the unique qualities of each composer.

Anton von Webern (1883–1945), who later dropped the aristocratic *von*, was an unspectacular individual whose life revolved around his strangely fragile artistic accomplishment. Despite his aristocratic background, he became a devoted conductor of the Vienna Workers' Chorus, as well as holding other rather low-profile conducting positions.

From the start, Webern reacted against the grandiose side of Romanticism, as represented by the works of Richard Strauss and Gustav Mahler. He turned his music about face, toward abstraction, atomization, and quiet: so quiet, that listening to his music, one listens to the rests almost as much as to the notes themselves. His compositions are all extremely brief and concentrated (we will discuss one of them briefly on page 341). Webern's entire musical output can be fitted on three CDs.

But both Webern's remarkable vision of musical abstraction and his brilliant use of serialism made him a vital link between the first phase of modernism, around World War I, and the second. Though he died in 1945, shot in error by a member of the American occupying forces in Austria, his forward-looking compositions caught the imagination of an entire generation of composers after World War II.

Alban Berg (1885–1935), on the other hand, looked back; more than Schoenberg and certainly more than Webern, he kept lines of communication open to the romantic tradition, by way of Mahler. Berg's first opera, *Wozzeck,* was an immediate success on a scale never enjoyed by the other "Second Viennese" composers. His second opera *Lulu* (1935) is now also a classic, though it made its way slowly—Berg had only partly orchestrated Act III when he died, and both operas were banned by the Nazis.

Berg died at the age of 50 as a result of an infected insect bite. After his death, it came out that he had been secretly in love with a married woman, and had employed a musical code to refer to her and even to address her in his compositions—among them a very moving Violin Concerto (1935).

ALBAN BERG (1885–1935)
Wozzeck (1923)

After Schoenberg, the most powerful exponent of expressionism in music was his student Alban Berg. Berg's opera *Wozzeck,* first conceived of during World War I, was completed in 1923. In general plan, this opera can be described as Wagnerian: it depends on musical continuity carried by the orchestra, makes extensive use of leitmotives, and contains no arias. Its musical style owes much to Schoenberg's *Pierrot lunaire.*

Background   Berg set a remarkable fragmentary play by the German dramatist Georg Büchner, a half-legible draft that was discovered after his death in 1837. In a series of brief, savage scenes spoken in the plainest vernacular, Büchner presents an almost paranoid vision of the helpless poor oppressed by society. Berg's music for the play's dialogue is all highly intense, and he kept the tension up by writing continuous orchestral interludes during the blackouts between all the scenes.

Franz Wozzeck is an inarticulate and impoverished soldier, the lowest cog in the military machine. He is troubled by visions and tormented for no apparent reason by his captain and by the regimental doctor, who pays him a pittance for serving as a human guinea pig in bizarre experiments. Wozzeck's mistress, Marie, sleeps with a drum major, who beats Wozzeck up when he makes some objection. Finally Wozzeck murders Marie, goes mad, and drowns himself.

Alban Berg

Act III; Interlude after Scene ii   Scene ii is the murder scene. When Wozzeck stabs Marie, she screams, and all the leitmotives associated with her blare away in the orchestra. It is said that all the events of our lifetime flash before our eyes at the moment of dying.

Blackout: and the stark interlude between the scenes consists of a single note played by the orchestra in two gut-bursting crescendos. Don't turn the sound down if this passage hurts your ears—it is supposed to. (The interlude is also pretty hard on the stagehands, who have less than half a minute for the scene change.)

Scene iii   The lights snap on again. In a sordid tavern, Wozzeck gulps a drink and seeks consolation with Marie's friend Margret. Berg's idea of a ragtime piano opens the scene—one of many signs that European music of the 1920s had woken up to American influences. But it is a distorted, utterly dissonant ragtime, heard through the ears of someone on the verge of a breakdown.

The music is disjointed, confused, shocking. When Margret gets up on the piano and sings a song, her song is distorted, too:

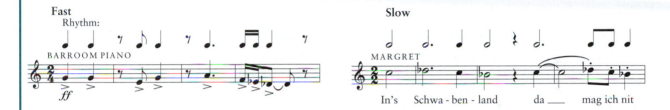

Suddenly she notices blood on Wozzeck's hand. It smells like human blood, she says. In a dreadful climax to the scene, the apprentices and street girls in the inn come out of the shadows and close in on Wozzeck. He manages to escape during another blackout, as a new orchestral interlude surges frantically and furiously.

The whole of scene iii is built on a single short rhythm, repeated over and over again with only slight modifications—*but presented in many different tempos*. This twitching "master rhythm" is marked above the two previous examples, first at a fast tempo, then at a slow one; we first heard it in the timpani in the interlude between scenes ii and iii. Another obvious instance comes when Margret first notices the blood:

Even though this master rhythm may elude the listener in a good many of its appearances, the hypnotic effect of this unusual kind of rhythmic ostinato (see page 309) contributes powerfully to the sense of nightmare and fixation.

LISTEN   Berg, *Wozzeck,* Act III, scenes iii and iv

5   5A

9-13   3

SCENE iii: A tavern

0:25   **Wozzeck:**   Tanzt Alle; tanzt nur zu, springt,   Dance, everyone! Go on, dance, sweat
schwitzt und stinkt, es holt Euch   and stink,
doch noch einmal der Teufel!   the devil will get you in the end.
(Gulps down a glass of wine)
(Shouts above the pianist:)

Es ritten drei Reiter wohl an den Rhein,   *Three horsemen rode along the Rhine,*
Bei einer Frau Wirtin da kehrten sie ein.   *They came to an inn and they asked for wine.*
Mein Wein ist gut, mein Bier ist klar,   *The wine was fine, the beer was clear,*
Mein Töchterlein liegt auf der . . .   *The innkeeper's daughter . . .*

Verdammt! Komm, Margret!   Hell! Come on, Margret!
(Dances with her)

Komm, setzt dich her, Margret!   Come and sit down, Margret!
Margret, Du bist so heiss. . . . Wart' nur,   Margret, you're hot!
wirst auch kalt werden!   Wait, you too will be cold! Can't you sing?
Kannst nicht singen?

(She sings:)

1:42   **Margret:**   *In's Schwabenland, da mag ich nit,*   *Swabia will never be*
Und lange Kleider trag ich nit.   *The land that I shall want to choose,*
Denn lange Kleider, spitze Schuh,   *For silken dresses, spike-heeled shoes,*
Die kommen keiner Dienstmagd zu.   *Are not for servant girls like me.*

Wozzeck: Nein! keine Schuh, man kann auch   No shoes! You can go to hell just as well
blossfüssig in die Höll' geh'n! Ich   barefoot! I'm feeling like a fight today!
möcht heut raufen, raufen. . . .

10   2:29   **Margret:**   Aber was hast Du an der Hand?   But what's that on your hand?

Wozzeck: Ich? Ich?   Me? my hand?

Margret: Rot! Blut!   Red! Blood!

Wozzeck: Blut? Blut?   Blood? blood?
(People gather around)

Margret: Freilich . . . Blut!   Yes, it is blood!

Wozzeck: Ich glaub', ich hab' mich geschnit-   I think I cut myself, on my hand. . . .
ten, da an der rechten Hand. . . .

Margret: Wie kommt's denn zum Ellenbogen?   How'd it get right up to the elbow, then?

Wozzeck: Ich hab's daran abgewischt.   I wiped it off there. . . .

Apprentices: Mit der rechten Hand am rechten Arm?   Your right hand on your right arm?

Wozzeck: Was wollt Ihr? Was geht's Euch an?   What do you want? What's it to you?

Margret: Puh! Puh! Da stinkt's nach   Gross! It stinks like human blood! *(curtain)*
Menschenblut!

Confusion. The people in the Inn crowd around Wozzeck, accusing him. Wozzeck shouts back at them and escapes.

SCENE iv: A pond in a wood

11   3:30   **Wozzeck:**   Das Messer? Wo ist das Messer?   The knife! where is the knife? I left it
Ich hab's dagelassen . . . Näher,   there, around here somewhere. I'm
noch näher. Mir graut's! Da regt   scared! Something's moving.
sich was. Still! Alles still und tod   Silence. Everything silent and dead
. . . Mörder! Mörder! Ha! Da   Murderer! Murderer! Ah, someone
ruft's! Nein, ich selbst.   called! No, it was just me. . . .

Marie! Marie! Was hast Du für eine   Marie, Marie! What's that red cord
rote Schnur um den Hals? Hast   around your neck? A red necklace,
Dir das rote Halsband verdient,   payment for your sins, like the
wie die Ohrringlein, mit Deiner   earrings? Why is your dark hair so wild?
Sünde? Was hangen Dir die schwart-
zen Haare so wild?

4:43		Mörder! Mörder! Sie werden nach mir suchen . . . Das Messer verrät mich! Da, da ist's!	Murderer! Murderer! They will come look for me. . . . The knife will betray me! Here, here it is.
		So! da hinunter! Es taucht ins dunkle Wasser wie ein Stein. Aber der Mond verrät mich . . . der Mond ist blutig. Will denn die ganze Welt es ausplaudern?!— Das Messer, es liegt zu weit vorn, sie finden's beim Baden oder wenn sie nach Muscheln tauchen.	There! Sink to the bottom! It plunges into the dark water like a stone. But the moon will betray me. . . . The moon is bloody. Is the whole world going to incriminate me? The knife is too near the edge— they'll find it when they're swimming or gathering mussels.
		Ich find's nicht . . . Aber ich muss mich waschen. Ich bin blutig. Da ein Fleck . . . und noch einer.	I can't find it. But I must wash myself. There's blood on me. A spot . . . another. . . .
		Weh! Weh! Ich wasche mich mit Blut! Das Wasser ist Blut . . . Blut. . . .	Oh, woe! I am washing myself in blood! The water is blood . . . blood. . . . *(drowns)*
12 6:18	Captain:	Halt!	Wait!
	Doctor:	Hören Sie? Dort!	Can you hear? There!
	Captain:	Jesus! Das war ein Ton!	Jesus! What a sound!
	Doctor:	Ja, dort.	Yes, there.
	Captain:	Es ist das Wasser im Teich. Das Wasser ruft. Es ist schon lange Niemand entrunken. Kommen Sie, Doktor! Es ist nicht gut zu hören.	It's the water in the pond, the water is calling. It's been a long time since anyone drowned. Come away, Doctor! This is not good to hear.
	Doctor:	Das stöhnt . . . als stürbe ein Mensch. Da ertrinkt Jemand!	There's a groan, as though someone were dying. Somebody's drowning!
	Captain:	Unheimlich! Der Mond rot und die Nebel grau. Hören Sie? . . . Jetzt wieder das Achzen.	It's weird! the red moon, the gray mist . . . Do you hear? That moaning again.
	Doctor:	Stiller, . . . jetzt ganz still.	It's getting quieter—now it's stopped.
	Captain:	Kommen Sie! Kommen Sie schnell!	Let's get away! Come quickly! *(curtain)*
13 8:04	ORCHESTRAL MUSIC (LAMENT)		

Scene iv   Fatefully, Wozzeck returns to the pond where he murdered Marie. The orchestra engages in some nature illustration, making strange macabre sounds (so different from the nature illustration in Debussy's *Clouds*!). Wozzeck's mind has quite cracked. He shrieks for the knife (in powerful *Sprechstimme:* see page 313), discovers the corpse, and sees the blood-red moon and the pond, too, seemingly filled with blood. He walks into the water, saying that he has to wash himself.

At this point, his principal tormenters walk by. The Captain and the Doctor hear the vivid orchestral gurgles and understand that someone is drowning, but like people watching a mugging on a crowded city street, they make no move to help. "Let's get away! Come quickly!" says the terrified Doctor—in plain, naturalistic, prosaic speech, rather than the *Sprechstimme* used by Wozzeck.

In the blackout after this scene, emotional music wells up in the orchestra, mourning for Wozzeck, Marie, and humanity at large. Here Berg adopts and even surpasses the late Romantic style of Gustav Mahler. Our recording fades after a few minutes of this great lament.

Scene v   Berg (following Büchner) has yet another turn of the knife waiting for us in the opera's final scene. Some children who are playing with Wozzeck's little son run off to view his mother's newly discovered corpse. Uncomprehending, he follows them. The icy sweetness of the music here is as stunning as the violent music of the tavern scene and the weird pond music. In turning Büchner's visionary play fragment into an expressionist opera, Berg created one of the great modernist theater pieces of the twentieth century.

4   Modernism in America: Ives

As we have seen, Paris and Vienna, centers of intense activity in all the arts, were also the first centers of modernist music. Echoes of modernism, some loud, some soft, were heard elsewhere in Europe: in Italy, where there was a short-lived movement called Futurism, and in Germany, Russia, Hungary, and England. We will discuss the case of two important modernist composers, Béla Bartók and Richard Strauss, in Chapter 22.

It is still amazing, however, that a major modernist composer should have emerged in the United States as early as around 1900; for at that time America had no rich musical tradition, and what we did have was resolutely conservative. "Emerged" is not quite the word, for what also amazes is that Charles Ives worked in isolation, composing in his spare time, and his music was scarcely performed until the 1950s.

Many of Ives's compositions have American subjects, such as *Central Park in the Dark* and *Some Southpaw Pitching.* His *Holidays* Symphony includes movements titled "The Fourth of July," "Thanksgiving," and so on. These pieces regularly employ or quote American music: folk songs, popular songs by Stephen Foster, gospel hymns, ragtime—sometimes in great profusion. The hymns Ives remembered from his youth are especially favored.

Ives was our first important nationalist composer, then. But he was also more than that: a true American "original," a man with amazingly radical ideas about music, and an insatiable experimenter with musical materials. Ives

Charles Ives (1874–1954)

Charles Ives was the son of a Civil War military bandmaster and music teacher of Danbury, Connecticut, near New York City. Ives senior was an extraordinary character, who enjoyed musical games such as playing two tunes simultaneously in different keys. His father's unconventionality—and his association with popular music—left a lasting impression on Charles.

Ives was a church organist as a teenager, and then went on to Yale, where he was a popular undergraduate (with a D+ average; he was a top athlete, too). He absorbed everything that his professor, the eminent composer Horatio Parker, had to teach him. But the American musical climate in the 1890s was basically hostile to modern trends; Parker wrote in a dull, traditional style. For Ives, this was not only dull but somehow also unmasculine. His vision was of a much more vigorous, rough grained, enthusiastic, experimental kind of music.

So when he got his B.A. he hedged his bets and took a job in insurance as well as another church organist position. After a few years he relegated music entirely to his spare time, while pursuing a very successful and innovative business career during the day. He seldom mixed with musicians and for years made little effort to get his works performed or published. (There is an interesting parallel here with Wallace Stevens, a major twentieth-century American poet, who also made a good living in insurance.)

All the while Ives was developing his unique mystical notions about music, notions that have been linked to nineteenth-century New England transcendentalism. To Ives, the actual sound of music seems to have counted less than the idea of music making as a basic human activity. All kinds of music were equally valid, then, whether popular or sophisticated, whether simple or wildly dissonant, whether played in or out of tune. What mattered was people's communal joy in music making. Believing also that all musical experiments have equal validity, Ives launched into visionary projects that no other composer of the time would have considered.

Ives's late years were clouded by pathos, for after 1920 he gave up music almost entirely due to discouragement and bad health. He also sometimes tinkered with his old music to make it appear even more revolutionary than it was—though the music as he originally wrote it still amazes music historians. For his last thirty years Ives lived in quiet affluence with his wife, Harmony, the sister of a college friend (he had taken her to his junior prom); Harmony seems to have had a strong influence on her husband's ideas about music and life. They lived long enough to see his music admired first by a growing number of American musicians and then by the public at large.

Chief Works: for orchestra, 4 symphonies and the *Holidays* Symphony, several "Orchestral Sets," *Central Park in the Dark* and *The Unanswered Question* ■ *Three Quarter-Tone Pieces for Two Pianos, Concord* Sonata for piano (movements entitled "Emerson," "Hawthorne," "The Alcotts," "Thoreau") ■ *Variations on "America"* for organ (written at age 17; best known in its arrangement for orchestra) ■ Chamber music—many of the movements having programmatic titles ■ Church music, choral music, and important solo songs, among them "General William Booth enters into Heaven"

anticipated many of the most talked-about musical innovations of the early part of the twentieth century—and of the later part, too.

Writing highly dissonant music was the least of it. He also wrote music for pianos tuned to quarter tones, and several works in which certain elements can be played, or not played, or played differently, depending on the performer's choice. For the whole length of his *Psalm 90,* for chorus, organ, and bells, low C sounds continuously in the organ pedals—for nearly eleven minutes. In one of his major works, the *Concord* Sonata, the pianist has to use his elbow and a special wooden block that holds sixteen notes down at a time.

To get an idea of the extraordinary range of Ives's work, we should examine two works—one of them little known, the other very famous.

LISTENING CHART 23

Ives, The Rockstrewn Hills

4 min., 44 sec.

0:00	Introductory
0:16	Dance fragment, strings; interrupted
0:29	Dance fragment, woodwinds; interrupted
0:48	Ragtime fragment, piano
	Kaleidoscopic array of fragmentary ideas; build-up
1:25	Brass becomes prominent.
1:58	Cakewalk fragment
2:08	Climax: homophony
2:34	Slowdown and pause (solo string instruments)
2:43	March fragment, trombones
3:00	The hymn is prefigured.
3:13	Hymn fragment—collapse
3:26	Hymn, clearer
3:57	At last the hymn emerges clearly: "I am coming, Lord!"
4:08	Fades: a fragmentary whole-tone scale in the piano

Second Orchestral Set, second movement: "The Rockstrewn Hills Join in the People's Outdoor Meeting" (1909)

This orchestral piece is the second of three that make up Ives's Second Orchestral Set. Ives wrote four symphonies; if his orchestral sets are thought of as (very) informal examples of the same genre, this movement would count as the scherzo. For all its obscurity, the title has a true Ivesian ring: the grandeur of nature joins a human festivity, apparently some sort of revival meeting.

The piece begins with several false starts, as though any effort to formulate a melody is bound to be defeated by other sounds, rhythms, and bits of tunes coming from this way and that. A dance fragment, first in the strings, then in the woodwinds, is interrupted by snatches of brass march music and piano ragtime. The hubbub gets more and more dissonant and atonal.

Gradually the kaleidoscopic array of "sound bites" builds up to a passage of forceful irregular rhythms. We catch an exuberant fragment of a cakewalk, a ragtime dance of the 1890s. At the climax the confused superimposition of various ideas gives way momentarily to homophony; the irregular pounding rhythms here remind us of Stravinsky's *The Rite of Spring*—a work written four years after Ives wrote this one. There is a slowdown and a quiet pause.

A new section begins with a fragmentary march in the trombones. Then at last a phrase of a hymn tune crystallizes out, as it were, in four tries: only at the fourth try does the melody become clear. "I am coming Lord!," the rousing chorus from one of Ives's favorite hymns, is orchestrated like a march:

I remember, when I was a boy—at the outdoor Camp Meeting services in Redding (Conn.), all the farmers, their families and field hands, for miles around, would come afoot or in their farm wagons. I remember how the great waves of sound used to come through the trees . . . There was power and exaltation in those great conclaves of sound from humanity.

Charles Ives

Hymn, "I Hear Thy Welcome Voice"

I am coming, Lord!   Com-ing now to Thee!   Wash me, cleanse me, in the blood That flowed on Calva - ry.

Ives
Slow, swinging tempo

rit. 4

(tune fades)

After this collapses, the piano can be heard playing four-note segments of the whole-tone scale (a hallmark of Debussy—but Ives probably learned it from his inquisitive father, not from the French composer). The outdoor meeting ends on an intense but quiet dissonance that is strangely serious, even spiritual—a characteristic Ivesian feature.

Whole-tone scale

A revival meeting and a gospel hymn book of the time, open at the hymn used in Ives's Second Orchestral Set

The Unanswered Question (1906)

This famous work—utterly quiet, serene, and solemn—is as different as could be from the cheerful clatter of *The Rockstrewn Hills*. It requires two conductors. We cannot describe it better than Ives did himself:

> The strings play *ppp* throughout, with no change in tempo. They represent "The Silences of the Druids" who know, see, and hear nothing. The trumpet intones "The Unanswered Question of Existence" and states it in the same tone of voice each time. But the hunt for "The Invisible Answer" undertaken by the flutes and other human beings [Ives is personalizing the other woodwind instruments] gradually becomes more active and louder. The "Fighting Answerers" seem to realize a futility, and begin to mock "The Question"—the strife is over. . . . After they disappear, "The Question" is asked for the last time, and the "Silences" are heard beyond in "Undisturbed Solitude."

LISTENING CHART 24

5   5A

16-17   5

Ives, The Unanswered Question

5 min., 14 sec.

TRUMPET

	0:00	Strings, **ppp**: The Silences of the Druids
	1:17	Trumpet *(always the same, up to the last note):* The Unanswered Question of Existence
	1:41	Woodwinds: *hunting for* The Invisible Answer
	1:58	Trumpet
	2:15	Woodwinds
	2:39	Trumpet
17 2:54		Woodwinds: *somewhat denser*
0:21	3:15	Trumpet
0:33	3:27	Woodwinds: *more intense rhythm*
0:52	3:46	Trumpet
1:07	4:01	Woodwinds: *followed by low hum*
1:20	4:14	Trumpet
1:32	4:26	Woodwinds mock The Question *(by picking up the trumpet motive); longer*
2:04	4:59	Trumpet: The Question asked for the last time
2:14	5:08	Strings: Undisturbed Solitude

What is so novel here is the concept of three distinct, independent levels of music: the smooth string choir, playing consonant harmonies; the dissonant woodwinds, a sort of frustrated modernist challenge to the strings; and the single trumpet, sounding like a voice, with its haunting Question.

TRUMPET

These simultaneous levels do not fit together in the least, in terms of traditional polyphony; Ives even wanted them all sitting at different places on the stage (or backstage). They lack any kind of rhythmic or contrapuntal relationship. Yet this unusual non-dialogue between "Silences," "Questioner," and "Answerers" proves to be both coherent and poignant: a foretaste, perhaps, of our own age, an age marked by the quiet desperation of non-communication.

CHAPTER 22

Alternatives to Modernism

I n music, as in all the arts, modernism was the main source of creative energy in the period from before World War I until after World War II. The vision of new languages to express the new conditions of modern life was a powerful one, even if the public at large often had difficulty understanding those languages. The success of many avant-garde works of art—for example, Alban Berg's opera *Wozzeck*—shows that they met with a deep response from minds and hearts battered by the events and attitudes of the early twentieth century.

Not everyone was as successful as Berg, however; much modernist music played to a small, esoteric audience. A figure like Schoenberg, convinced that music's progress depended on his leadership, could accept this and hold uncompromisingly to modernist principles. Many others, too, never blinked—to speak only of Americans after Ives, this country could boast of such impressive modernist composers as Carl Ruggles (1876–1971), Roger Sessions (1896–1985), and Edgard Varèse (1883–1965; Varèse came here from France).

Twentieth-Century Traditionalism

But other equally impressive composers, both here and abroad, developed a more ambivalent attitude toward modernism. No one could escape its influence, and not many wanted to; but not everyone wanted to accept it fully. The force of Romantic tradition was still strong. Some famous twentieth-century names never joined the avant garde at all, and kept on mining the reliable quarries of Romanticism for their own private seams of (they hoped) musical gold.

Other composers worked selectively with the ideas of Schoenberg or Stravinsky, adopting and adapting no more than they needed to fulfill their own creative needs. Still others started out wholeheartedly on the avant garde, only to turn back to stylistic amalgams of one kind or another between the modern and the more traditional. As to the reasons for this ambivalence, no doubt many composers reacted against the difficulty of modernist music and its ready rejection by the musical public. Some simply developed other agendas besides that of pursuing music's development and supposed "progress."

It is impossible to generalize. However, there is no question that some of the best—and most popular—music of the early twentieth century was written either by composers who never called themselves modernists, or by composers who could not be called modernists at the time they wrote that music. We shall examine music by three such figures in this chapter.

1 Richard Strauss (1864–1949)

Perhaps the most interesting case of all was that of the German composer Richard Strauss. (He was not related to the Viennese Strauss family of waltz composers.) In the 1890s—when Schoenberg and Stravinsky were still youngsters—Strauss was *the* modernist discussed by everyone, feared by some, and attacked by many. He first attracted this attention through some sensational symphonic poems, but the climax of his early career was a pair of operas that are still in the repertory, *Salome* and *Elektra*.

They are real shockers, both because of their librettos and this music. *Salome* (1905) enlarges on the story of the Biblical Princess Salome, who is rejected by St. John the Baptist. In return for sexual favors for her incest-prone father Herod, she demands John's head. The music matches the extremity of the libretto; notorious at the time was a chord that Strauss invented including seven different pitches.

Once Kaiser Wilhelm II said to his General Manager, "I'm sorry Strauss composed this Salome; I'm quite fond of him otherwise, but this is going to do him a lot of damage." Thanks to this damage, I was able to afford my villa at Garmisch!

From the reminiscences of Richard Strauss, 1949

There was no missing this loud and spectacularly dissonant chord: it comes at the final curtain when Salome kisses John's dead head on the lips and is crushed under the shields of Herod's soldiers. And *Elektra* (1909) revisits the most dreadful of Greek myths to show Clytemnestra, murderer of her husband Agamemnon, slain in turn by her son Orestes, who is spurred on by the almost maniacally vengeful Electra, her daughter. The music is often violent and distorted. It verges on and sometimes slips into atonality.

But after 1909, to the astonishment of the musical world, Strauss pulled sharply back from such extremes. His later operas are either frankly Romantic or Neoclassical, and he ended his career in 1948 with some of the loveliest songs ever written in a Romantic style. So great is the pull-back in *Der Rosenkavalier* (The Knight of the Rose), his next opera after *Elektra*, that it is hard not to feel that the composer was bluntly criticizing modernism.

RICHARD STRAUSS
Presentation of the Rose, from *Der Rosenkavalier*, Act II (1911)

Der Rosenkavalier is a brilliant comedy—half sentimental, half cynical—about life in eighteenth-century Vienna. It opens before breakfast in the boudoir of an aging (i.e., thirty-something) field marshal's wife, who is entertaining her very young lover, the handsome Count Octavian. Strauss has him sung by a mezzo-soprano dressed as a man; the idea seems to be that he is so young his voice hasn't changed yet. They chatter about love and transcendence in a very amusing parody of Wagner's *Tristan und Isolde*.

Richard Strauss

Act II introduces Sophie, the innocent young daughter of a wealthy merchant. She is in a state of almost hysterical excitement at the prospect of marriage to an older nobleman. Now, the custom in Vienna—a custom invented by Strauss's librettist—was that the bridegroom in an arranged marriage would not meet his bride-to-be until a relative had come on his behalf and made a formal presentation of a silver rose. The "knight of the rose" *(Rosenkavalier)* in this case is none other than Octavian. When he and Sophie set eyes on each other they fall instantly, giddily in love.

Strauss catches this feeling with music that seems almost suspended in time, as an oboe winds slowly around gorgeous yet restrained melodic phrases. The music is purely tonal. Yet the oboe shares space with the celesta, flutes, and high strings playing a series of quiet chords which, while not dissonant in themselves, clash dissonantly with the surrounding harmony. Instead of distortion or violence, dissonance here makes for a kind of magical tinkling, as though Sophie and Octavian were literally seeing stars. This effect could only have been obtained by a master of the techniques of musical modernism.

Notice how the singing starts in a declamatory, recitative-like style, when the two exchange formal remarks, and gradually gets more aria-like as they sink into their own thoughts. At the end, their thoughts and feelings merge in a duet. The words, too, grow less "realistic" and more poetic as feelings take over from ceremony.

LISTEN	Strauss, *Der Rosenkavalier*, Act II, Presentation of the Rose

5   5A
18-20   6

(Enter Octavian, bareheaded, dressed all in white and silver, carrying the Silver Rose in his hand. Behind him his servants in his colors, white and pale green. Octavian, taking the rose in his right hand, advances with high-born grace toward Sophie, but his youthful features bear traces of embarrassment, and he blushes. Sophie turns pale with excitement at his splendid appearance. They stand opposite each other, each disconcerted by the confusion and beauty of the other.)

	Octavian:	Mir ist die Ehre widerfahren, dass ich der hoch- und wohlgeborenen Jungfer Braut, in meines Herrn Vetters Namen, dessen zu Lerchenau Namen, die Rose seiner Liebe überreichen darf.	The honor has fallen to me, most noble and high-born [*very formal*] lady and bride, on my kinsman's behalf, by name the Baron von Lerchenau, to present to you the rose of his love.
1:17	Sophie:	Ich bin Euer Liebden sehr verbunden . . . ich bin Euer Liebden in aller Ewigkeit verbunden . . .	I am deeply indebted to your highness . . . I am forever eternally indebted to your highness . . . [*embarrassed*]
		Hat einen starken Geruch wie Rosen, wie lebendige!	Oh, it has a powerful fragrance, just like a real rose!
2:06	Octavian:	Ja, ist ein Tropfen persischen Rosenöls darein getan . . .	[*Tries to make conversation*] Yes, a drop of Persian attar has been put on it . . .
2:40	Sophie:	Wie himmlische, nicht irdische, wie Rosen vom hochheiligen Paradies. Ist ihm nicht auch?	It's like a heavenly rose, not an earthly one—like the roses of paradise. Do you think so too?
3:26		Ist wie ein Gruss von Himmel . . . ist bereits zu stark als dass man's ertragen kann! Zieht einen nach, als lägen Stricke um das Herz . . .	It's like a message from heaven . . . it's so strong, I can scarcely bear it! It's like something pulling at my heart . . .
4:24	Sophie (with Octavian):	(Wo war ich schon einmal und war so selig? Dahin muss ich zurück, dahin, und müsst' ich völlig sterben auf dem Weg. Allein ich sterb ja nicht. Das ist ja weit! Ist Zeit und Ewigkeit in einem sel'gen Augenblick, den will ich nie vergessen bis an meinen Tod.)	[*To herself*] (Have I ever been here before? Was I ever so blissful? If I could recapture this moment, I'd be ready to die—but I'm not dying, not yet! All time and eternity are in this moment, which I'll remember till the day I die.)
	Octavian (with Sophie):	(Wo war ich schon einmal und war so selig? Ich war ein Bub, da hab ich die, die noch nicht gekannt. Wer bin denn ich? Wie komm' denn ich zu ihr? Wie kommt denn sie zu mir? Wär' ich kein Mann, die Sinne möchten mir vergehn; das ist ein sel'ger Augenblick, den will ich nie vergessen bis an meinen Tod.)	[*To himself*] (Have I ever been here before? Was I ever so blissful? Up to now I've been just a child, before I saw her. Who am I? What fate has brought me to her, brought her to me? If I weren't a grown man, I'd go mad. This moment I'll remember till the day I die.)

19 (at 2:40)
20 (at 4:24)

2 Béla Bartók (1881–1945)

Growing up in Hungary in the 1890s, the young composer Béla Bartók was first swept away by the international avant-garde leaders Debussy and especially Richard Strauss. Later in his career he was also influenced by his close contemporary Stravinsky. Bartók was, however, a man of multiple careers—pianist, educator, and ethnomusicologist as well as composer. His deep commitment to folk music, and his professional involvement with it, had a decisive impact on his music. It is often said that Bartók was more successful in integrating folk music into classical music than any other composer.

Stravinsky too, as we have seen, started out in the tradition of nationalism, with his ballets on Russian themes such as *The Rite of Spring* (page 307). But for Stravinsky nationalism turned out to be no more than a passing phase. For Bartók, folk music was an inspiration from first to last.

Folk music assured that Bartók's music would never (or seldom) become as abstract as much modernist music was. There is always an earthy feel to it. Even at its most dissonant, there will be an infectious folkdance swing or a touch of peasant melody. This is true even in works he wrote in his most modernist period, around 1925–1935, when he wrote his First and Second Piano

The right type of peasant music is most perfect and varied in its forms. Its expressive power is amazing, and at the same time it is devoid of all sentimentality and superfluous ornaments. It is simple, sometimes primitive, but never silly. . . . A composer in search of new ways cannot be led by a better master.

Béla Bartók

Béla Bartók (1881–1945)

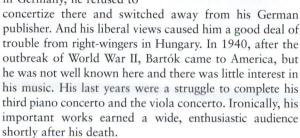

Béla Bartók showed unusual talent as a pianist and composer at an early age. Music was the avocation of his father, who was principal of an agricultural school in Hungary; after his death Bartók's mother worked as a piano teacher, tirelessly promoting her son's career.

Few musicians have ever had as varied a career as Bartók. He was a prolific composer and a fine pianist, as was his second wife; they appeared as a two-piano team. (Both of his wives had been his students.) In conjunction with another important Hungarian composer, Zoltán Kodály, he directed the Budapest Academy of Music, where the two men tried out new ideas in music teaching. An outcome of this side of Bartók's career is his *Mikrokosmos,* a series of 153 graded piano pieces starting with the very easiest. Well known to most piano students today, the *Mikrokosmos* has probably done more than any other work to introduce modernism to large numbers of musicians in their impressionable years.

Also with Kodály, Bartók undertook a large-scale investigation of Hungarian (and other) folk music, writing several standard books in the field of ethnomusicology, which is the scientific study of folk music and the music of non-Western cultures. He published many folksong and folkdance arrangements, and his other compositions are saturated with folk elements such as rhythms, modes, and melodic turns. The outstanding nationalist composer

of the twentieth century, Bartók left a body of work that equals or surpasses that of any nineteenth-century nationalist.

Bartók was strongly opposed to the Nazis. After they came to power in Germany, he refused to concertize there and switched away from his German publisher. And his liberal views caused him a good deal of trouble from right-wingers in Hungary. In 1940, after the outbreak of World War II, Bartók came to America, but he was not well known here and there was little interest in his music. His last years were a struggle to complete his third piano concerto and the viola concerto. Ironically, his important works earned a wide, enthusiastic audience shortly after his death.

Chief Works: Concerto for Orchestra, Violin Concerto No. 2, Piano Concerto No. 3, *Music for Strings, Percussion, and Celesta* (for small orchestra) ▪ Six string quartets; a fascinating Sonata for Two Pianos and Percussion ▪ An opera, *Bluebeard's Castle,* and a ballet, *The Miraculous Mandarin* ▪ *Cantata profana,* for chorus, soloists, and orchestra ▪ *Mikrokosmos* and other works for piano ▪ Many folk song arrangements for various ensembles, including Six Roumanian Dances

Concertos and several string quartets. The austere Quartet No. 4 of 1928 is often regarded as Bartók's masterpiece.

After that time Bartók's music gradually became more accessible, and the references to folksongs became more mellow and, often, more poignant. He often used established forms such as sonata form and rondo; this meant that his music was easier to follow by listeners who were already accustomed to

Bartók was one of the first folksong collectors to use recording equipment. Around 1906, these rural Hungarians seem less amazed by the primitive phonograph than by the camera.

these forms from eighteenth- and nineteenth-century music. And many of his last works include passages reminiscent of Romanticism: Violin Concerto No. 2, the Concerto for Orchestra, and Quartet No. 6 of 1939—another good candidate for Bartók's greatest composition.

BÉLA BARTÓK
Music for Strings, Percussion, and Celesta (1936)

Written for a specially constituted small orchestra, this interesting composition consists of four movements that are closely—and richly—interrelated. One of the watershed works of music history, as we recall, proposed a new relationship between the four movements of a symphony. That work was Beethoven's Fifth Symphony, with its sense of triumphal progress from the first movement to the last. A tough question faced every composer after Beethoven: why must *this* movement follow *that* movement, in a multi-movement work that you want us to listen to at a single sitting?

Bartók's Music for Strings, Percussion, and Celesta lets us see the sort of answer provided by a twentieth-century composer closely in touch with modernism. A concise Listening Chart for the total work is given on page 334.

First movement (Andante tranquillo)   Bartók's first movement is a fugue. We spoke above (page 228) of Neoclassicism in music after World War I. Here is a vivid example: fugue, the most Baroque of Baroque forms, revived as strictly and conspicuously as could be—yet all in the aid of a modern vision.

The fugue subject is a corkscrew of chromatic notes and shifting rhythms. Depressingly aimless as this melody may seem at first, it is actually shaped carefully, in four phrases, each crawling upward: a′ expands on a, b is slightly higher, and b′—retracing b a half-step lower—returns the melody to its beginning. Simple graphics added above the notation may make it easier to grasp Bartók's tormented melody:

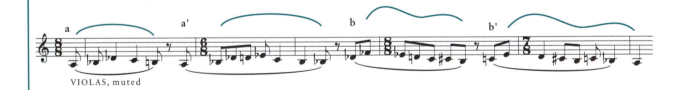

VIOLAS, muted

In the exposition, the subject is accompanied by a countersubject (see page 126), but this is not carried through with Bach-like consistency.

More than half of the movement consists of a long, gradual, relentless crescendo for strings alone, starting with the exposition. As the contrapuntal lines grate against one another, the dissonant harmony grows more and more austere and expressive. After a short episode comes a pair of subject entries in stretto (see page 130); the cello enters on the heels of the first violin. Tension builds further in a second, longer episode, built on fragments of the subject.

At the climax, the fugal texture breaks—first into a harmonic texture, with percussion, then into a single urgent high note. As this note scoops down abruptly, low instruments play fragments of the fugue subject inverted, that is, with its intervals reversed: an enormously dramatic gesture.

We've rehearsed a lot . . . the conductor and orchestra have all worked with me showing the greatest affection and devotion; they claim to be very enthusiastic about the work (I am too!). A couple of spots sound more beautiful and startling than I had imagined. There are some very unusual sounds in it!

Bartók writes to his wife about rehearsals for the premiere of Music for Strings, Percussion, and Celesta

a inverted

a′ inverted

The rest of the movement is a long diminuendo. We hear further fragments of the inverted fugue subject, inverted entries in stretto, and a passage in which the inversion appears simultaneously with and above the regular version of the subject, as the celesta makes its first entrance. The music ends with increasingly isolated subject and inversion fragments. Two violins make an exquisite cadence, almost unbelievably restful after all the dissonance.

Second movement (Allegro) As though in reaction to the intense, monolithic first movement, Bartók wrote a second movement bubbling over with variety, an exhilarating rush of little melodic tags, rhythms, folkdance fragments, and novel percussion sounds. It is all held together by sonata form.

The orchestra now divides into two groups that echo and answer one another, each consisting of a full string complement and certain of the percussion instruments. The first theme—preceded by a "preface" in *pizzicato* (plucked) strings—is divided between the two groups:

Motive **a** energizes the preface, theme 1, and also the bridge passage. It works especially well in the timpani, which have a powerful role in this movement.

There is a full stop after the bridge, so self-conscious that one wonders if Bartók is making fun of sonata form conventions. The second group contains at least three additional very short themes, themes 2, 3, and 4. Theme 3 has a folkdance lilt about it:

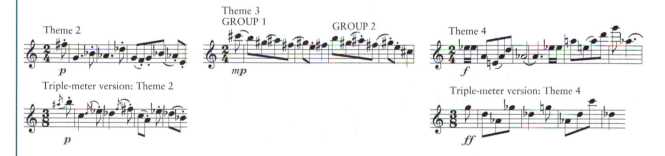

Suddenly the piano enters with a theme containing odd note-repetitions. Since the pianist has hardly played at all up to this point, this new theme feels more like a beginning than like a conclusion. Still, it functions as a cadence theme; very soon the exposition ends with another exaggerated cadence.

The timpani introduce the *development section.* Motive **b,** played *pizzicato,* comes in for an extensive work-out. After a moment the strings drop down into an accompaniment for an amazing passage for piano, snare drum, and xylophone, punching out syncopated notes. This must have been inspired by the Dance of the Adolescents in Stravinsky's *Rite of Spring* (see page 309).

Next, *pizzicato* string scales in imitative polyphony weave endless new knots and tangles. The scales blend into another folklike tune, similar to theme 3, which is repeated very freely (sometimes in inversion)—and then become

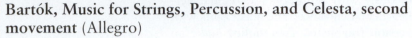

5   3   5B   3B
25–31   23–29   3   1

LISTENING CHART 25

Bartók, Music for Strings, Percussion, and Celesta, second movement (Allegro)

Sonata form. 7 min., 2 sec.

EXPOSITION

	0:00	**Theme 1**	With pizzicato "preface"
	0:23		Held note, drum
	0:26	**Bridge**	
			CADENCE Big stop, after drum beat

Second group

26 24	0:55	**Theme 2**	
	1:10	**Theme 3**	Folklike tune, strong beat
			Developmental
0:38	1:33	**Theme 4**	Over a string trill
1:09	2:04	**Cadence theme**	Piano
			CADENCE Exaggerated cadence; drum beat

DEVELOPMENT

27 25	2:29	**Section 1**	Irregular rhythms: piano and percussion
		Section 2	Pizzicato scales, from the "preface"
28 26	3:31		New folklike tune
			Drum prepares:
0:30	4:01	**Section 3**	Crescendo
1:23	4:54	**(retransition)**	Drum grows insistent; slowdown ⟶

RECAPITULATION

29 27	5:09	**Theme 1**	With timpani; meter changed
	5:29	**Bridge**	

Second group

30 28	5:39	**Theme 2**	Transformation: triple meter
			New continuations
0:25	6:04	**Theme 4**	Transformation: triple meter
0:46	6:25	**Cadence theme**	Piano, as before

CODA

31 29	6:32		New dialogue on theme 1

un-blended again. Again introduced by the timpani, a fugue starts up in the lowest register, preparing for the recapitulation. The subject is derived from theme 1, with the meter askew.

And when the *recapitulation* comes, after much signalling from the timpani, and a slow-down, the meter is changed throughout. Theme 1 vacillates between duple and triple meter, and the second group tips the balance: themes 2 and 4 each return in swinging triple meter (as shown in the examples on page 331). Theme 3 returns more freely. The entire exposition has been "transformed" in Liszt's manner (see page 229). It takes the piano's odd "cadence theme" to bring us back to the solid duple meter of the start, and to a final forceful dialogue on theme 1 by the two orchestral groups.

Duple meter   Triple

Third movement (Adagio)   The second slow movement, a tour de force of delicate tone colors, makes use of one of Bartók's favorite forms, **A B C B′ A′**, sometimes called *arch form*. Section **A** features the xylophone and pedal timpani (see page 41); one can obtain a sort of ghostly echo by working the tuning device while actually playing the timpani. In **B**, multiple string trills provide the background for an eerie, rambling melody played by the celesta. **C** opens with ethereal special-effect swishing sounds in the harp and the piano.

These unusual and quite fascinating instrumental sounds give the movement a mood of mystery and, somehow, precariousness. Even the loud, faster conclusion of section **C**—blank, hammered repetitions of a single five-note figure, sometimes in inversion—has an unsettling effect. And perhaps the mystery is only deepened by veiled references to the fugal first movement. Each of the letter sections is introduced—cued, we might say—by a very quiet playing of one phrase from the first movement's fugue subject; and the rambling tune in section **B** resembles that subject both in rhythm and in phrase structure.

The movement ends (**A′**) with the slightly sinister coalition of moaning strings and mechanically clicking xylophone—in the reverse order from that which we heard originally, in **A**.

Fourth movement (Allegro molto)   The last movement is a riotous rondo in an extended form, **A B A C A′ D A″ E . . .**, with some surprises down the line. It would repay close study, but two points must suffice here. First, the main rondo theme is very close to a folk dance. It is in a characteristic Bulgarian rhythm of 3 + 3 + 2 eighth-notes, accompanied by *pizzicato* strings strumming the same rhythm two beats earlier (strong beats are marked with an x):

After its second appearance, this theme is always radically transformed—even, the last time, into a romantic outburst.

Second, this movement is saturated with backward references. Most obvious and impressive, thanks to a slowdown, is the prolonged return of the first-movement fugue subject completely transformed, along with its inversions and strettos (after **B′**). There are shorter references to themes and effects in the second and third movements, too, some of them obvious, others less so. How many do you hear? (Start with the *pizzicato* "preface.")

If we listen to Music for Strings, Percussion, and Celesta movement by movement, each movement makes a perfectly fine effect by itself—up to the fourth movement. There is much that is exhilarating here even if we don't know any of the earlier music. But the impressive slowdown near the end makes no sense unless we know the first-movement fugue. The return of this fugue is a revelation, for the tormented melody is now at peace with itself, surging and soaring confidently in a rich chordal style. Most of its chromatic intervals are smoothed out, made diatonic, and therefore "resolved." Add to this the strange hints of the fugue subject in the third movement, and the other backward references in the fourth, and the total experience of the four movements becomes vastly greater than the sum of the parts.

What I like about music is its ability to be convincing, to carry an argument through to the finish, though the terms of the argument remain unknown quantities.

Poet John Ashberry, 1976

21-40   2-5

LISTENING CHART 26

Bartók, Music for Strings, Percussion, and Celesta, complete work

27 min., 17 sec.

FIRST MOVEMENT (Andante tranquillo: fugue) *starts pp, with mutes on all the string instruments*

	0:00	**Fugal exposition**	Viola ——— ∿∿ *Countersubject*
	0:21		Vn 2 ——— ∿∿
	0:40		Cello ——— ∿∿
	1:01		Vn 1 ——— ∿∿
	1:22		Bass ———
	1:44	**Episode 1**	Short slow **crescendo**
22	2:09	**Stretto**	Vn 1 ———
	2:11		Cello ——— slow **crescendo**
0:35	2:44	**Episode 2**	Using fragments of the subject; *mutes off;* **cresc.** to *f*
0:52	4:01	**(Textural**	First climax, *ff*: percussion enter
23	4:17	**break)**	Second climax, *fff*: single high note, downward scoops
	4:21		Fragments of *inverted subject* announced, *fff*, then *mf, p*: *mutes on again*
0:52	5:09	**Stretto**	*Inverted subject:* violin 2 (muted), then viola, then violin 1 + cello
24	5:53	**Combination**	Celesta enters: subject (above) + *inverted subject (below)*
	6:16		Fragments of subject and inverted subject; "converging" cadence

pp

fff

SECOND MOVEMENT (Allegro: sonata form: see page 332)

25	0:00	**Exposition**
	2:29	**Development**
	5:09	**Recapitulation**
	6:25	**Coda**

THIRD MOVEMENT (Adagio: arch form)

32	0:00	**A**	Introductory: xylophone and pedal timpani, viola and violin ruminations
33	1:57		**(Background cue: fugue subject: a)** *low strings*
	2:26	**B**	More oscillations: celesta and solo violins. Background trills, *pp*
34	3:19		**(Background cue: fugue subject: a′)** *strings* (after a brief recollection of **A**)
		C	Further slow oscillations. Background glissandos. **Crescendo** ——→ *f*
0:59	4:18		Piano: new motive in 5/4 meter, *f*—faster, climactic
35	4:55		**(Background cue: fugue subject: b)** *strings*
	5:05	**B**	B melody now in canon
36	5:55		**(Background cue: fugue subject: b′)** *celesta and piano*
	6:04	**A**	Terminal: violin and viola ruminations, xylophone, pedal timpani

---

FOURTH MOVEMENT (Allegro molto: rondo form)

37	0:00	**A**	With a *pizzicato* "preface"
	0:26	**B**	Timpani launch a repetitive theme: piano and *pizzicato* strings
	0:43	**A**	
	0:52	**C**	
38	1:14	**A′**	Piano; theme is transformed
	1:25	**D**	Timpani launches another folklike theme
	1:58	**A″**	Piano; extension of **A′**
39	2:22	**E**	
	2:35	**B**	Piano
0:40	3:02		Transition
40	3:26	**Original**	Transformed; slower tempo ⎫ strings
	4:42	**fugue subject**	Fragments in inversion ⎬ alone
1:45	5:11	**F**	Cello solo—reference to the third movement (the string solos in **A**)
2:01	5:27	**A‴**	In various transformations

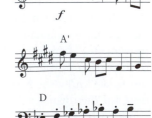

A

f

A′

D

3 Aaron Copland

America's leading composer of the generation after Charles Ives was Aaron Copland. (Born in 1874, Ives was active from around 1895 to 1920; Copland, born in 1900, wrote his main works from 1925 to 1950.) Aspiring young composers coming of age after World War I found many more options open to them than Ives had when he graduated from college in 1898. The musical climate was much more favorable to new ideas, partly beause the United States had been growing more aware of all things European, including European new music. Like important American writers who lived abroad—Gertrude Stein, T. S. Eliot, Edith Wharton, Ernest Hemingway—composers now associated themselves with European modernism in a way that their predecessors never did.

The chief modernist influence on Copland was Stravinsky, and one of his most impressive works is a strenuous set of twenty Variations for Piano (1930) which reflects Stravinsky's dry rhythmic style and his "objective" aesthetic. But after this Copland's music grew more traditional. Like Strauss, Bartók, and most other composers of the time, he held back from the most extreme manifestations of modernism, and forged his own style using such elements of modernism as he needed.

Music for Americans

Again like Bartók, Copland adopted a nationalist agenda. From the start he felt that as an American, he should write music that would speak to his fellow Americans. Unlike Bartók, however, and unlike Ives, he did not focus on the music of his own immediate tradition—in the one case, Hungarian folksong and dance, and in the other, hymns and popular songs known in New England. Copland reached out for American music of all kinds, regions, and ages: jazz in orchestral pieces called *Music for the Theater* and *El salón México,* cowboy songs in the ballets *Rodeo* and *Billy the Kid,* an old Shaker melody in *Appalachian Spring,* and square dancing in *The Tender Land,* an opera about growing up in the corn belt. In this eclectic attitude we can perhaps again trace

It bothers me not at all to realize that my range as a composer includes both accessible and problematic works. To have confined myself to a single compositional approach would have enhanced my reputation for consistency, no doubt, but would have afforded me less pleasure as a creator.

Aaron Copland, 1941

A worker, a farmer, and a boss are shown "harmonizing": a political allegory by New York painter Ben Shahn (1898–1969), a friend of Copland

Aaron Copland (1900–1990)

Copland was the son of Russian-Jewish immigrants living in Brooklyn. He received a solid musical education, and at the age of twenty he went abroad to study in Paris. Like many other overseas students, Copland was fortunate to be able to work with a remarkable musician named Nadia Boulanger. Boulanger became an outstanding teacher and mentor of composers, even though she gave up composition herself in deference to the talent of her sister Lili, also a composer, when Lili died tragically at the age of twenty-four. Boulanger encouraged Copland's interest in Stravinsky, whose avant-garde style influenced him greatly.

Back in America, Copland tirelessly promoted American music in various ways. He organized an important series of concerts (with another composer, Roger Sessions) to showcase new American scores, wrote articles and books, and formed a Composer's Alliance. Like many artists and writers of the 1930s, he was attracted by leftist ideology and its insistence that art should "serve the people." Many works drawing on American folk materials stem from this period of Copland's career, as does his high-school opera *The Second Hurricane*. The much-performed patriotic works *A Lincoln Portrait* and *Fanfare for the Common Man* were composed during World War II.

After 1940 Copland headed up the composition faculty at the important summer school at Tanglewood, Massachusetts in association with the Boston Symphony Orchestra, but his output as a composer decreased. Among his students was Leonard Bernstein. Devoid of the egoism characteristic of so many artists, Copland was one of the most beloved figures of modern American music.

Chief Works: for orchestra: 3 symphonies, *A Lincoln Portrait* (with a speaker), *El salón México* (incorporating South American jazz) ▪ Film scores: *Of Mice and Men* and *The Red Pony* (by John Steinbeck), *Our Town* (Thorton Wilder) ▪ Clarinet Concerto, written for jazzman Benny Goodman ▪ Operas: *The Second Hurricane* and *The Tender Land;* ballet scores *Billy the Kid, Rodeo, Appalachian Spring* ▪ For piano: Variations (Copland's outstanding modernist work: 1930), a sonata, Piano Fantasy (a fine late work: 1957) ▪ A song cycle to poems by Emily Dickinson; *Old American Songs* for soprano and orchestra, including "Simple Gifts" (also arranged for choir and soloists)

the influence of Stravinsky, who over his long career also tapped many musical sources, from Russian folksong to Bach, Tchaikovsky, and Schoenberg.

AARON COPLAND
Appalachian Spring (1945)

6   5B

7-10   6

The ballet *Appalachian Spring* was choreographed and danced by Martha Graham, a towering figure in American modern dance. She conceived of "a pioneer celebration in spring around a newly built farmhouse in the Pennsylvania hills in the early part of the last century." From his ballet music, Copland arranged a concert suite in six continuous sections.

Section 1   The ballet begins with a very still, clear, static passage of a kind that Copland made very much his own. It seems to catch the spirit of a vast silent landscape at dawn, perhaps, or just before dawn. Solo instruments play meditative figures in counterpoint; an occasional solemn pulse is heard in the harp.

Section 2   Here "the bride-to-be and the young farmer husband enact the emotions, joyful and apprehensive, their new domestic partnership invited." The celebration of their new house starts with a lively square dance. Soon a new slower melody—something like a hymn—looms up in counterpoint to the dance figures, first in the wind instruments and then in the strings:

'Tis the gift to be simple,
  'tis the gift to be free,
'Tis the gift to come down
  where you ought to be,
And when we find ourselves
  in the place just right
'Twill be in the valley of
  love and delight. . . .
When true simplicity is
  gained
To bow and to bend we
  shan't be ashamed,
Turn, turn will be our
  delight,
Till by turning, turning
  we come round right.

—"Simple Gifts"

8

Allegro

The music dies down into a prayerful version of the hymn, together with little fragments of the dance.

Sections 3 and 4   The next two sections pick up the tempo: section 4 evokes another whirling square dance and section 5 is a danced sermon by a revivalist and his followers. Both sections include quiet statements of the hymn.

9 ***Section 5***   The next dance is choreographed to a set of variations on a Shaker song, "Simple Gifts." The Shakers, a religious sect adhering to celibacy and common ownership of property, founded scattered communities from New York to Kentucky in the late eighteenth century.

The four variations are little more, really, than playings of the tune or part of the tune by different instruments, in different keys, and in different tempos. Sometimes melodic phrases are heard in imitation.

10 ***Section 6***   Finally, after some music that the program says is "like a prayer," the hymn and the landscape music return once again. The ballet concludes very quietly. Perhaps the housewarming celebrations have gone on all night, and we are now experiencing another clear gray dawn, a reminder of the many lonely dawns the pioneer couple will face together in the years to come.

> **LISTEN**
>
> Copland, *Appalachian Spring*
>
> SECTION 5
>
> 8:11   **Theme**
> 8:47   **Variation 1**
> 9:06   **Variation 2**
> 10:01   **Variation 3**
> 10:41   **Variation 4**

Two great American art forms are jazz and modern dance. One of the legendary group of women who created modern dance in the early twentieth century, Martha Graham (1894–1991), commissioned and choreographed Copland's *Appalachian Spring*.

CHAPTER 23

The Late Twentieth Century

O nly twenty-one years, from 1918 to 1939, separated the two cataclysmic wars of the twentieth century. It was an uneasy period. The terrible devastation of World War I had stunned artists as well as everybody else,
and the sorts of extravagant experimentation that had marked the prewar
period no longer seemed appropriate. There was a new tendency toward abstraction, and also a search for standards and norms. At the time, Schoenberg's serialism and Stravinsky's neoclassicism were seen as two different
efforts to achieve some kind of consolidation, organization, and order.

But these efforts were undercut by a new round of devastating events.
First came the economic depression, worldwide and protracted, that began in
the late 1920s. Then, in the 1930s, the ominous rise of Hitler and the unbe-
lievable (and, by many, disbelieved) tyranny of Stalin led to a second world
war. With the attack on Pearl Harbor, the United States was thrown into this
war to an extent that made our involvement in World War I seem minor. The
occupation of France, the siege of Leningrad, the bombings of London,
Dresden, and Tokyo, the mass murders in the concentration camps, the deto-
nation of atom bombs—these events were virtually impossible for human
beings (including artists) to take in. History seemed to be showing that all
human conceptions or representations of the world were illusory.

In the postwar world, artists in any medium faced greater uncertainties
than ever before. One response to this among composers was the assumption of
a kind of absolute freedom. While some of them continued to write music according to models of the past, a radical generation of avant-garde composers
invented new systems—or entertained the idea of destroying all systems.

1 Modernism in Music: The Second Phase

Modernism was still the driving force in music during the third quarter of the
twentieth century, but it was modernism in a new, more extreme phase. It was
a fascinating phase—and no less fascinating because its two main tendencies
can seem almost contradictory.

First of all, highly intellectual constructive tendencies came to the fore,
inspired by Schoenberg's serialism, but going far beyond it. There were even
efforts to "serialize" rhythm, sonority, and dynamics—that is, to set up pre-

determined series of twelve note durations, or twelve tone colors, and compose with them in a fixed order. Never before had such complex mathematical theories been advanced to compose and explain music.

Second, composers demanded new sound materials. The ordinary orchestra, even as expanded by Debussy, Stravinsky, and others, now struck them as stiff and antiquated. Amazing new sonorities were explored—nonmusical noises, unexpected new sounds squeezed out of old instruments, and an infinite range of musical materials produced not by instruments at all, but by electronics.

It may indeed seem strange to find the same composers both fascinated by sonority and also preoccupied—almost obsessed, sometimes—by musical construction. The first of these propensities is surely sensuous in orientation, the second intellectual. Yet perhaps we can see how they go together. Especially when radical new artistic means become available, artists seem to feel a need to systematize ways of keeping them under control. This was what Schoenberg, too, had done; his development of the twelve-tone method was a response to the atonality that resulted from the "emancipation of dissonance."

Early in this book we made a similar point about the beginnings of Baroque music, around 1600. The extravagance of Baroque music was controlled by a new emphasis on musical form. So the contradictions of modernism can be understood as part of a recurring phenomenon in artistic development.

New Sound Materials

The search for new sonorities began with an attack on the standard sources of music for unexpected new effects. Singers were instructed to lace their singing with hisses, grunts, clicks, and other "nonmusical" noises. Pianists were told to stand up, lean over the piano, and pluck the strings or hit them with mallets. Using a special kind of breath pressure, clarinetists learned to play chords called *multiphonics*—weird-sounding chords, by conventional standards, but fascinating to those attuned to the new sound universe.

Percussion instruments of all kinds began to be used much more widely than before. Indeed, Western orchestras and chamber music groups had always been weak in percussion, as compared to their counterparts in many non-Western cultures, notably the gamelans of Indonesia. Even more to the point, Western art music had been weak in this respect as compared to jazz. Marimbas, xylophones, gongs, bells, and cymbals of many kinds—percussion instruments that had been used only occasionally in the art music of earlier times—became standard in the postwar era.

However, the truly exciting prospect for new sonorities in music emerged out of technology developed during the war: the production of music not by standard instruments, not by standard instruments treated in new ways, and not even by nonstandard instruments, but by electronic means.

Electronic Music

Recording equipment can *reproduce* sounds of any sort—music, speech, and all the sounds and noises of life. Electronic sound generators can *generate* sounds from scratch—in principle, any sounds that can be imagined, or calculated using formulas derived from the science of acoustics.

A technological breakthrough during World War I, the development of magnetic tape, made the storing and handling of sound much easier. It also opened up exciting possibilities for modifying it, by manipulating the tape: making tape loops, changing speed, cutting and splicing, and so on.

An early, room-sized synthesizer

❧ *Musique concrète*   A few composers shortly after World War II began to incorporate the sounds of life into their compositions. This they called "concrete" music because it used actual sound, as contrasted to the "abstract" products of electronic sound generators. Sounds (traffic noise was a favorite) were recorded, painstakingly manipulated in ways such as those mentioned above, and then (usually) put on phonograph discs.

Musique concrète lives on, in a sense, in *sampling,* now that technology has made it easy for anything that is recorded—traffic noise, commercial records, special effects—to be put under keyboard control for easy combination.

❧ *Synthesizers*   In the early postwar period electronic sound-generation was unbelievably clumsy, requiring whole rooms full of radio equipment and complicated machinery to carry out tape manipulations. Only after the advent of transistors (silicon chips were still in the future) could viable equipment be envisaged. In the 1960s various *synthesizers* appeared, apparatus designed specifically for music, with arrays of sound-producing modules connected by "patch cords" to create complex sounds.

At first they worked one note at a time. Still, they allowed many composers to produce taped music, and also to combine music on tape with performed, live music. It was still difficult to produce "customized" sound in real time.

❧ *Computer music*   The amazing evolution of computers has allowed for an equally amazing evolution in music. Today electronic music can be produced on a home computer, using sequencer software to record, edit, and reproduce digital sounds in patterns and sequences at will. Advanced synthesizers now produce their stuff in real time (as the simpler synthesizers of popular music have been doing for years). They can interact via computer with live musicians as they perform, to produce today's cutting-edge interactive computer music.

On the Boundaries of Time

Sonority is one of the two areas in which avant-garde music in its second postwar phase made the greatest breakthroughs. The other area was time and rhythm.

To understand one aspect of this development, let us try to contrast two radically different pieces of music. One is a tiny piece by Schoenberg's student

Affixing real-life objects and papers to paintings, called *collage,* an artistic technique developed by Picasso's generation, recalls musique concrète in music. Scraps of sheet music and envelopes were favorite collage objects for the American painter Robert Motherwell (1915–1991).

and friend Anton Webern, the fourth of his Five Orchestral Pieces of 1913 (see page 316). The whole piece—it is all of six measures long—can be shown on one line of music:

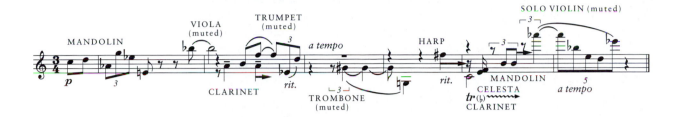

The music feels exceptionally concentrated, because the relationship between the notes is so strained by the "atomized" orchestration and the complex network of pitches and rhythms. Each note somehow becomes a separate little source of tremendous energy. This might be described as a very short time segment of very high intensity.

Contrast this with *In C,* a famous avant-garde work from the 1960s by the American composer Terry Riley. *In C* lasts for about forty-five minutes. During this time the instruments repeat over and over again a set of fifty-three tiny melodic figures that spell out only three harmonies—three harmonies drawn out over the music's total span. The pitches and rhythms are simple, indeed deliberately soothing. This might be described as a very long time segment of very low intensity.

With both Webern and Riley, we measure time (because we have no other way) in the same units: minutes and seconds. Yet the *feeling* of time is very different in the two. It is like the difference between one minute at the end of a tied basketball game and one minute in the middle of an all-night truck run across South Dakota. Such contrasting perceptions of time were now widely explored and exploited by musicians of the avant-garde.

Webern's unique vision of time made him a major influence in the postwar years, even though he died at the end of World War II. Composers were fascinated by his intense, seemingly disconnected note patterns, with their flickering instrumental sounds and their highly complex rhythms. Riley's *In C* and works like it became prophetic of a later development in music which gathered force in the 1970s and 1980s, *minimalism* (see page 355).

Chance Music

A striking new trend in music of the 1950s was **chance music,** also called *aleatoric music,* from *alea,* Latin for "dice." This term covers a great variety of music in which certain elements are not precisely specified by the composer, but left to chance—in a way that usually *is* specified by the composer.

In an extreme case, a chance composer would work out a way of throwing dice so as to determine which instruments, which pitches, and so on were to be used in his or her music. Or else the performer might be instructed to do the dice-throwing him or herself. In a less extreme case, a performer getting to a certain place in a piece would be told to play anything at all, so long as it was (for example) loud and fast. Strictly speaking, what would be heard would be determined by chance, but the composer could count on a type of controlled chaos for a limited span of time, a span situated between two passages of fully written-out music.

Whereas earlier modernists had questioned traditional assumptions about melody and dissonance, chance composers questioned even more basic assumptions about musical time. We tend to think of time as linear and goal-directed; time is conventionally plotted on a graph in the same way distance is—see page 21—and a "timer" tells us when to get things done. Is time always (chance composers would ask: is it *ever*) actually experienced in this way? Their "timeless" musical vision was like the suspended consciousness that we experience in certain kinds of meditation. This radically new consciousness, a passive sense of time that goes against our goal-oriented culture, lies at the root of chance music.

2   The Postwar Avant-Garde

After World War II, exciting composers seemed to appear like magic from almost every corner of the globe. Among the leaders from France, Germany, and Italy were Olivier Messiaen (1908–1994), Pierre Boulez (b. 1925), Karlheinz Stockhausen (b. 1928), and Luciano Berio (b. 1925). They were joined by the Poles Witold Lutosławski (1913–1994) and Krzysztof Penderecki (b. 1933), the Hungarian György Ligeti (b. 1923), the Greek Iannis Xenakis (b. 1922), the Americans Milton Babbitt (b. 1916), John Cage (1912–1992), and Elliott Carter (b. 1908), and the Japanese Tōru Takemitsu (b. 1930).

Many of these composers are still composing actively—and interestingly—forty years later, in the 1990s. But forty years later, it cannot be said that their music has gained a firm place in the musical repertory, or in the hearts of most music listeners (at least, as far as the United States goes). Modernism's first phase—the phase just before World War I—produced works that now count as "classics": Berg's *Wozzeck,* a fixture in the opera house; Bartók's string quartets, played by every professional string quartet; and Stravinsky's *Rite of Spring,* an all-time favorite in the CD catalogue, with more than fifty listings. For acknowledged masterpieces written after World War II, however—such as Boulez's fascinating chamber-music work *Le Marteau sans maître,* or Berio's moving *Sinfonia*—similar acceptance has been slow in coming.

György Ligeti (b. 1923)

György Ligeti studied at the Budapest Academy of Music, and as a young man was appointed professor there. Unable to pursue his unique sound visions under the Communist restrictions prevailing in Hungary, he left for the West in 1956. Ligeti was past thirty before his advanced music became known.

Ligeti typifies both the search for new sonorities that occupied the postwar avant-garde and also their new attitudes toward time. His music often uses no clear pitches, or chords; or, more accurately, while he may start with pitches and chords, he soon adds so many more pitches that all sense of consonance, dissonance, and even the quality of pitch itself is lost. What remain are "sound complexes" that cannot be described (they can only be experienced), sound complexes that slowly change with time.

And in the time dimension, there is no discernible meter or rhythm. Rather there is a sense of gradual, almost glacial surging of the sound complexes, followed by a sense of receding—all the while revealing incredibly diverse new tone colors.

My idea was that instead of tension-resolution, dissonance-consonance, and other such pairs of opposition in traditional tonal music, I would contrast "mistiness" with passages of "clearing up." "Mistiness" usually means a contrapuntal texture, a micropolyphonic cobweb technique . . .

From an interview with Györgi Ligeti, 1978

Violet, Black, Orange,
Yellow on White and Red,
by the American painter
Mark Rothko (1903–1973).
The overwhelming yet placid
patches of color merging
into one another recall the
musical technique in compositions such as Ligeti's *Lux*
aeterna.

GYÖRGY LIGETI
Lux aeterna (1966)

Ligeti's *Lux aeterna* is written for sixteen solo singers and chorus; often they sing chords that include all twelve pitches of the chromatic scale. We need a new vocabulary even to talk about music such as this, and some new diagrams —our pitch-time graph on page 21, which indicated melodies by lines, doesn't work for Ligeti's sound complexes. To represent them and show how they develop over time, we have to use nonmusical figures:

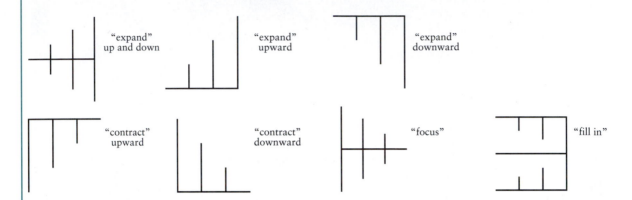

Lux aeterna starts with a single pitch, which Ligeti "expands" both upward and downward by slowly adding a dense mix of pitches above and below it. At other times he starts with a single pitch and expands it upward (adding mainly higher pitches) or downward (adding lower ones). Starting with a full-range sound, Ligeti can "contract" it: either downward (by removing notes till only a single low pitch remains), or upward, or to some pitch in the middle—an effect that can be called "focusing," on the analogy of a camera lens.

The interest of this music, as we have said, is in the astonishing rich sonorities that are revealed by the slow ebbing and flowing of the sound complexes. Once we have accustomed our ears to this, we can appreciate that the musical form of *Lux aeterna* is simplicity itself. Of the four lengthy sound surges that constitute the piece, No. 1 (going up) seems to be "resolved" by No. 4 (going down). Nos. 1 and 4 are parallel, too, in that a high pitch is added halfway through—in this music, a very dramatic effect.

The words of *Lux aeterna* are taken from the Requiem Mass, but Ligeti makes sure that they can scarcely be heard and understood. Ligeti has written other "sound complex" pieces employing other forces, such as *Atmosphères* for full orchestra. *Lux aeterna* is his most famous work, thanks to its use in the 1968 Stanley Kubrick movie *2001: A Space Odyssey*.

György Ligeti

Lux aeterna luceat eis, Domine, cum sanctis tuis in aeternum, quia pius es. . . .

May everlasting radiance shine upon them, O Lord, with thy saints in eternity: for you are merciful. . . .

Luciano Berio (b. 1925)

Luciano Berio was born in a little Italian seaside town and lived there all his early life. Then he studied in Milan. A visit to America was a revelation; he married an American singer Cathy Berberian, and has since lived here for many years. In 1955 he organized the electronic-music studio at Milan's radio station. Berio has endeared himself to musicians by writing a series of virtuoso avant-garde solos for all possible instruments: *Sequenza I* for flute solo, *III* for voice, *V* for trombone, and many more.

6 12-15   6A 2

LISTENING CHART 27

Ligeti, *Lux aeterna*

7 min., 3 sec.

	0:00	**1:** WOMEN'S VOICES Single pitch, high voices *(Lu)*. The sound "expands," *up and down*.	
	1:30	A high pitch is added: SOPRANO	
	1:47	The sound "contracts" *upward*, ending in . . .	
	2:06	a two-note chord, a single pitch.	
13	2:16	**2:** MEN'S VOICES The high pitch stops, replaced by a chord, in the middle voices *(cum sanctis tuis)*. The sound expands *downward*.	
0:42	2:58	More lower voices; higher voices drop out; the sound "focuses" to . . .	
1:26	3:42	a held, dissonant chord.	
14	3:48	**3:** Complex sound, *f* (with a clear high, low, middle). The sound becomes "filled in." The sound "contracts" *downward* to . . . a two-note chord, then one note.	
15	5:25	**4:** Complex sound—low voices *(Domine)*. Sound expands, *up*.	
0:25	5:50	A high note is added: SOPRANO	
0:53	6:18	The high note is dropped; the sound contracts *downward* to . . .	
1:36	7:01	a two-note dissonant chord.	

LUCIANO BERIO
Sinfonia (1969)

6 16   3 30   6A 3   3B 2

Not exactly a symphony, *Sinfonia* is an extended work for a very large orchestra and eight amplified vocal soloists, who sing and speak a bewildering assemblage of literature, anthropology, graffiti, and phonemes—that is, pure vowel and consonant sounds, as analyzed by linguists and psychoacousticians. We can scarcely scratch the surface of the multiple meanings suggested by this composition, some of which are certainly obscure. The second of the five movements, however, conveys a simple message that no one can miss.

Luciano Berio

Second movement   Entitled "O King," this movement was written earlier than the others, in response to the 1968 assassination of the Rev. Martin Luther King, Jr. Only four words are sung, again and again, like a lament: "O Martin Luther King," a phrase that contains all the vowel sounds *(a, e, i, o, u)*. First the soloists sing just the vowels, not the consonants. Then gradually, as the movement proceeds, the consonants are added until the words themselves can be heard.

On paper, this sounds cold and abstract, yet the emotional effect is powerful. The eight voices seem to be reaching out for Martin Luther King repeatedly, until finally they are able to speak his name and, by so doing, commune with him. Punctuated by solemn, irregular bursts of orchestral music, the voices sing their vowel phonemes to a special scale devised by Berio.

The form of "O King" is simple—as simple as the message. During the opening very gradual crescendo, syllables become recognizable. However, full (or nearly full) clarity comes only at a climax near the end of the movement. The music has been growing more agitated: suddenly "King" is sung by the soprano—alone, for just a moment—in the high register, joined by a cascade of other sounds. A slow snare drum tattoo evokes a military funeral, as though King were a general felled in battle. The soprano follows this with little sobs; then the music dies down with quiet—but strikingly new—sounds (the organ is prominent). The movement ends with the men's voices mouthing the one word "Martin": a haunting lullaby effect.

Edgard Varèse (1883–1965)

Edgard Varèse is an older figure who bridged both phases of modernism in twentieth-century music. Though he had started his career in France before World War I, he emigrated to America in 1915, and it was here that he found his voice (late in life, like Haydn).

The music Varèse wrote in the 1920s was probably the most radical in the world at that time. He developed an approach to rhythm and especially to sonority that surpassed anything the other early avant-garde composers had attempted. *Hyperprism* is scored for seven wind instruments and seven percussion, and *Ionisation* is for percussion alone—thirteen percussionists playing forty-five percussion instruments, including a siren. The manipulation of what had been thought of as "noise" into coherent musical patterns was a heady forecast of modernist music of the post–World War II era.

Edgard Varèse

EDGARD VARÈSE
Poème électronique (1958)

4   6A

46   4

Indeed, it was after World War II that this veteran of many a modernist battle really came into his own. Around 1930, Varèse had unsuccessfully tried to persuade the Bell Telephone Company to set up a research center for electrically produced music. Now the introduction of electronic composing equipment was a vindication of his vision. His *Déserts* (1950–54), for instruments and tape, was one of the most ambitious early essays in electronic music. And his entirely electronic *Poème électronique* is recognized as one of the masterpieces of the genre.

Poème électronique (1958) (ending)   As we stroll within earshot of *Poème électronique* (see box), a heavy electronic crash is followed by various seemingly random rustles. Then a brilliant section displays a veritable anthology of electronic effects: low sliding groans, rattles, bell-like noises, and watery sounds. Suddenly something human joins these space-age sounds—a short vocal hum. This tells us that Varèse makes use of **musique concrète** in *Poème*: that is, he uses prerecorded sounds from real life, such as humming, singing, bells, and train noises, as well as material that is generated electronically.

The rhythm has been highly irregular. Now it slows down, and a sustained chord appears quietly, grows almost unbearably loud, and then fades. Varèse introduces isolated pitches that appear to be arbitrary, though in fact they merge into another sustained chord. We hear drum rhythms, too, and a *musique concrète* snare drum (remember Varèse's affection for percussion instruments).

Modernist Music and Architecture

The *Poème électronique* of Edgard Varèse was just one part of an extraordinary multimedia experience. It was written for an exhibit at the 1958 Brussels World Fair by the Philips Radio Corporation, held in a pavilion designed by the famous modernist architect Le Corbusier (1887–1965). Corbu, as he was called, also designed a sequence of colored lights and images to be projected while Varèse's three-track tape was played from 425 speakers.

Here is another example of modernist artists of various kinds working in tandem (see page 292). Le Corbusier himself had been a painter in his youth.

As visitors entered the pavilion and walked around, the music came at them from various angles. Likewise, as they kept turning corners they kept seeing different parts of the superb building and of the light show. All this was very new at that time.

There was obviously an element of chance in the way one got to experience *Poème électronique*—an element that the composer of course encouraged. John Cage would have concurred enthusiastically. So it is quite in Varèse's spirit for us to take a quick tour of the pavilion, as it were, and happen to hear just the last few minutes of this music, rather than the entirety.

Humanity seems to reassert itself in the form of a soprano solo—but this is manipulated electronically so as to shriek its way out of hearing in the high register. Sharp, explosive punctuations decimate the men's voices that follow. A mournful three-note motive (also heard earlier in *Poème*) is played twice with the notes sliding into one another. Then a momentous-sounding siren moves up, falters, and moves up again until it becomes a violent noise, which ceases abruptly and mechanically.

So ends the Varèse *Poème électronique*: for some, on a strange note of unspecified disquiet.

John Cage (1912–1992)

The most consistent radical figure of postwar music was John Cage, the father of chance music (Charles Ives has to count as the grandfather). He studied with Schoenberg, among others—this was when Schoenberg was teaching in California, Cage's home state—and early developed an almost bewildering variety of interests. Cage exhibited specially prepared prints, toured as music director of avant-garde dancer Merce Cunningham's dance company, and was a recognized mycologist (mushroom authority). In the 1950s, his study of Zen led him to a fresh attitude toward music, time, and indeed all experience.

Cage posed questions that challenge all the assumptions on which traditional music rests. Why should music be different from the sounds of life? Why compose with "musical" sounds, rather than noises? Why work out music according to melodies, climaxes, twelve-tone series, or anything else that gives the impression of one thing following another in a purposeful order?

When you get right down to it, a composer is simply someone who tells other people what to do. I find this an unattractive way of getting things done.

John Cage

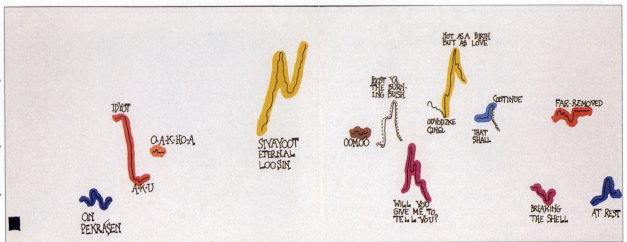

Score for a multilingual solo vocal work by John Cage, *Aria* (1958). Much is left to the singer's imagination!

Why not leave it to chance? The basic message that Cage has conveyed is that we should open our ears to every possible kind of sound and every possible sound conjunction.

JOHN CAGE
4' 33" (1952)

Often, indeed, the actual sounds Cage produced were less crucial than the "statement" he was making about sound by means of his music (as well as through actual, verbal statements—Cage left many writings on music and modernism). This is the case with *4' 33"*, perhaps his most celebrated work (or statement). Any number of players can perform it. They sit silently on the stage for 4 minutes and 33 seconds.

One's first reaction to *4' 33"*—a reaction that some people never get over—is that the whole thing is an exasperating hoax. But what Cage is saying is that silence is an entity, too, as well as sound. When did you last really concentrate on silence? (Try it.) In fact, *4' 33"* consists not of silence but of little bits of random audience noise, sounds from outside the hall, and the thump of the irate listener's heartbeat. And how does the experience of concentrating on near silence for exactly 4 minutes and 33 seconds compare with concentrating for exactly three minutes, or exactly five?

We seldom really analyze our experience freshly; life is unpredictable and full of surprises. Music should be, too. This is the philosophy represented by Cage and his music, and it had a major impact on avant-garde composers all over the world.

John Cage

3   Music at the End of the Century

It is not easy to characterize the confused, multivalent, multicultural music of our own time, on the cusp of the twenty-first century. A date comes to mind, 1971—not because anything as complex as music changes in a year, but because an event in it can symbolize a complex historical process. When Stravinsky died in 1971, at the age of 88, music lost its last great master, and a figure whose role in music history was uniquely comprehensive.

His first, Russian works were wholehearted essays in late nineteenth-century nationalism. Then works for Paris such as *The Rite of Spring* were prime monuments of modernism in its first, early twentieth-century phase. In Los Angeles, Stravinsky remained a major player in modernism in its second phase, the extreme phase following World War II.

Since the 1970s modernism has mellowed; works that we will now study absorb modernist ideas and ideals but also show more concern for communication than did music of the immediate postwar period. Two other bodies of music loom large on the musical scene today. One of them is mainly "made in America"—music in a distinctive new style called *minimalism.* The other stems from Eastern Europe, our former Cold War opponents prior to the break-up of Communism. Less distinctive in style than in mood, this music has impressed Western listeners by its quality of spirituality, even mysticism.

George Crumb (b. 1929)

A later representative of the American postwar avant-garde is George Crumb, who teaches at the University of Pennsylvania. Unlike Ives, he is not a "chance" composer, and unlike Varèse (and many much more recent composers) he does not write electronic or computer music—though he makes powerful use of amplication effects, as we shall see. Instead he has devised new ways of playing an astonishing array of standard and nonstandard instruments. In *Black Angels,* as we shall hear, he asks string quartet players to do things to their instruments that would make a traditional violin teacher turn pale. By such means Crumb obtains a predominantly violent, grotesque quality that could not be achieved in any other way.

In other works (and occasionally in this one), Crumb achieves remarkably delicate effects—quiet, precise, vibrant, a controlled musical kaleidoscope of fascinating elegance. Like many American composers today, he has been much influenced by Asian music; thanks to such composers, Western music has for the first time employed large groups of percussion instruments with something of the subtlety known to the Far East.

I think composers are everything they've ever experienced, everything they've ever read, all the music they've ever heard. All these things come together in odd combinations in their psyche, where they choose and make forms from all their memories and their imaginings.

George Crumb, 1988

GEORGE CRUMB
Black Angels, For Electric String Quartet (1970)

5   6A

41-45   6

Subtitled "Thirteen Images from the Dark Land," *Black Angels* was inspired by the Vietnam War, if not directly, at least by way of the anguished mood that the war instigated. "There were terrifying things in the air," the composer has said recently; "they found their way into *Black Angels.*"

This highly unconventional string quartet consists of thirteen short (often very short) sections arranged in three groups, of which we will hear the first. A sense of doom is conveyed partly by the titles—"Threnody" means a funeral lamentation song—and partly by various quotations of earlier music with lethal associations. But of course it is the music itself that conveys the sense of stress most powerfully.

No. 1 Threnody I: Night of the Electric Insects   The skittery, amplified string playing creates an unforgettable image of menacing insect life, as a deafening clatter alternates with quiet scratching. Against this, the high violins play fast glissandos, or scooping effects. Crumb marks them *piangendo,* "crying."

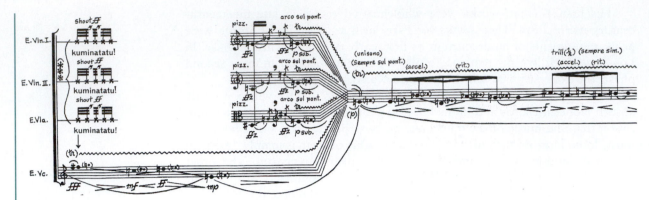

The scores of Nos. 1, 3, and 4 of *Black Angels* are not written with bar-lines, and the music has no discernible meter. In contrast, Nos. 2 and 5 project dance rhythms quite clearly, and in No. 2, at least, one can often beat out a regular meter.

42   ***No. 2 Sounds of Bones and Flutes***   This section evokes Asian music. The players click their tongues and chant "Ka-to-ko to-ko" to illustrate the bones, and imitate a flute by bowing their strings with the back of the bow, that is, with the wood *(col legno).*

43   ***No. 3 Lost Bells***   A duo for violin and cello, which mimic the mournful, bell-like noises characteristic of electronic music. Fragmentary melodies at the end remind us of the "flute" in No. 2.

44   ***No. 4 Devil-music***   An extremely vehement solo for the first violin is accompanied by the other players, one of whom also strikes a gong. The violinist produces what can only be called retching sounds; then the cellist, followed by the other players, rasps or grates by dragging the bow very slowly over the strings while applying maximum pressure. Toward the end there are some alarming siren effects, and the electric insects put in another appearance.

45   ***No. 5 Danse Macabre***   Rhythmic energy picks up again, as the players tap on the wood of their instruments and jiggle maracas. Crumb borrowed the title for this section from a nineteenth-century concert piece by the French Composer Camille Saint-Saëns, and he quotes bits of Saint-Saëns's music as well as *Dies irae,* from the Mass for the dead (see page 250). Isolated phrases of this plainchant appear high in the violin; they are vaguely reminiscent of the "flute" in No. 2 and the ending melodic fragments of No. 3.

The players end up with some mysterious chanting (actually, they count from one to seven in Hungarian).

Tania León (b. 1943)

Tania León came to the United States as a refugee from Cuba in 1967; she traces her ancestry to France, Spain, Africa, Cuba, and China. Her first position was with the Dance Theater of Harlem, the pioneering African-American ballet company founded by Arthur Mitchell (Mitchell was a protégé of Stravinsky's co-worker in the Ballets Russes, George Ballanchine). León teaches composition and conducting at Brooklyn College; in 1994 she was appointed Composer in Residence with the New York Philharmonic Orchestra.

Avant-garde music has made obsolete the old "pitch–time" graph that forms the basis of traditional musical notation (see page 21). Composers often invent their own notations: George Crumb, above, and John Cage, page 348.

George Crumb

LISTENING CHART 28

6	3	6A	3B
17-20	31-34	6	3

León, *Kabiosile*

6 min., 30 sec.

SLOW INTRODUCTION

0:00   Improvisatory: arpeggios up to high held notes

FAST SECTION

18	0:24	Piano picks up the rhythm	
32	1:03	Orchestra interrupts	
	1:17	Held note in the orchestra: F	
	1:22	Piano returns to a meditative mode	
	1:30	Picks up the rhythm again	
	2:02	Held note in the orchestra: F	
	2:17	Crash: piano slows	
	2:26	Orchestra interrupts	
		Held note in the orchestra: G♯	

SLOW SECTION

19		2:41	Improvisatory
33			A series of quiet held notes in the strings: G♯, then A
0:59		3:40	Steady rhythm in piano
1:17		3:58	Orchestra interrupts
1:20		4:01	Steady rhythm continues
1:43		4:24	Improvisatory

FAST SECTION

20		5:00	Piano picks up the rhythm
34		5:43	Held note in the orchestra: C♯
0:45		5:45	Ostinato on a driving, irregular rhythmic pattern
0:56		5:56	Pause, prior to the final drive
1:00		6:00	Cadence: held note in the piano: F

TANIA LEÓN
Kabiosile (1988)

This work for piano and orchestra takes its name from an African god of thunder, lightning, and fire who is also known in Cuba. What is most striking about the music is its enormously dynamic rhythm, which owes something to African and Latin drumming, and also something to modernist masters of rhythm such as Stravinksy and Bartók. León has melded all this into a rhythmic style of her own that is very individual.

Kabiosile (Kabiósilay) starts with strong but meditative gestures by the piano, which plays various figures consisting of fast notes ending with a held note, usually in the high register. Some of the rhythms are indicated at the right; the piano seems to be improvising in a free, imaginative way. Then the piano picks up the beat, the orchestra enters with a bang, and León starts her rhythmic fireworks. Punctuated by the orchestra, these complex piano rhythms are highly energetic, sometimes almost convulsive; at other times they focus into powerful repetitive ostinatos. The seemingly random alternation of high and low notes, at a fast tempo, is a hallmark of much recent modernist music.

After a crash, the piano slows down and—though not without another spasmodic eruption from the orchestra—resumes its meditative improvisa-

This piece [Kabiosile] is an acknowledgment of a part of me and a salute to my ancestors and the power they gave me to do what I do now—which is music.

Tania León

Tania León goes over a difficult place in her *Kabiosile* with pianist Ursula Oppens, who gave the work its U.S. premiere.

tions. In the slower passage that follows, the orchestral violins dwell on a quiet note occasionally, a sort of anchor for the piano. A slower, more regular rhythm ensues, alternating left- and right-hand piano notes. Though at first it seems plodding, this music becomes unexpectedly expressive.

For a second time the piano returns to its original halting improvisations, and then picks up the rhythm in much the same way as at the beginning. The fireworks return, with a vengeance; this time the rhythm focuses into this frenetic division of triple meter:

Piano			
Triple meter	1	2	3
Orchestra			

(The seven septuplet sixteenth notes played by the piano are split between beats 1 and 2; the orchestra is always syncopated, coming in after beat 3.)

This becomes a pounding ostinato, repeated many times at different pitches: an electrifying climax to this vehement piece. It is interrupted just once by another held note in the orchestra; and at the very end the piano acknowledges the orchestra by stopping on a held note of its own. Somehow this gesture of reciprocity gives the work a convincing conclusion, though it is very sudden.

Sofia Gubaidulina (b. 1931)

In our international survey on page 342, no mention was made of Russia. From the Russian Revolution in 1917 to the collapse of Communism in the late 1980s, music in the Soviet Union was treated as an instrument of the totalitarian state. Modernist music and Western popular music were banned, both denounced as products of the decadent West, in favor of pompous symphonies and cantatas celebrating official events, national heroes, and the like. Only a few artists, prepared for a truly heroic struggle, could maintain their individuality and integrity in face of this crushing state control.

Today you play jazz, tomorrow you betray your country.

Russian poster in Stalin's time

When the so-called "Iron Curtain" that separated East and West came down around 1990, several impressive composers who were already in their fifties became visible (or, rather, audible) for the first time in the West. Among them were Henryk Górecki from Poland, whose lengthy Third Symphony enjoyed international success, Arvo Pärt from Finland, and Sofia Gubaidulina from Russia. These three, although their styles are not very similar, have been grouped loosely into a "school" because of qualities of spirituality or mysticism that have been perceived in their music.

Born in Kazan, three hundred miles due east of Moscow, Sofia Gubaidulina (Goobyeduléena) ran into some trouble for her "mistaken path" in composition, but gained the public support of Russia's leading composer, Dmitri Shostakovich (1906–1975)—himself a well-known, indeed tragic victim of Soviet policy. Her early music, virtually unknown in the West, included many film scores. Soviet Russia was famous for its great virtuosos—among them violinist David Oistrakh, pianist Sviatoslav Richter, and cellist Mstislav Rostropovich. Violinist Gidon Kremer has been an important advocate for Gubaidulina's music in the world at large.

Sofia Gubaidulina

SOFIA GUBAIDULINA
Pro et Contra (1989)

Our selection comes from one of Gubaidulina's major creative efforts: a three-movement orchestral piece, *Pro et Contra* (For and Against), paired with a long cantata for voices and orchestra, *Lauda* (Praise; titled *Alleluia* in an earlier version). The alleluia is a plainchant, like a Gregorian chant but for the Russian Orthodox Church; *Pro et Contra* depicts forces working "for" and "against" this chant. The chant melody is suggested but never stated fully.

Third movement   The final movement begins with an ostinato (see page 309) in the violins' low range. Its rigid, somber dotted rhythms (see page 21) will grow claustrophobic before the work is over. After repeating itself several times, the ostinato figure attempts to inch its way up the scale, against a background of seemingly unrelated gestures from various other instruments. It cannot get very far. The music softens into a blend of string, woodwind, and celesta sounds, unexpectedly beautiful after the previous cramped ascent.

The entire movement consists of such attempts or initiatives, some rewarded by melody, some not. The second effort, with the ostinato in the strings, loses its way and returns fretfully to the pitch of the opening, and below.

The next three surging passages seem to be coordinated into a single initiative, twice interrupted, and this time reaching a goal. As low brass instruments enter (French horns and trombones) and the crescendo gets under way, the ostinato rhythms begin to blur. The climax merges into a phrase of melody played by a high trumpet, and echoed by other instruments. This melody hovers around a single pitch, E, that has been emphasized previously. Notice how fresh—and moving—the pattern of nine flowing notes is, as compared to the convulsive rhythms of the ostinato:

LISTENING CHART 29

Sofia Gubaidulina, *Pro et Contra*, III

7 min., 8 sec.

FIRST INITIATIVE

	0:00	Ostinato: violins	Slow climb
		pizzicato strings, winds	
	0:48	interlude	

SECOND INITIATIVE

22	1:05	Ostinato: strings	Vacillation
		interlude: low trill	

THIRD INITIATIVE

23	1:45	Ostinato: brass (slightly different rhythms)	Slow surge
		interlude	
0:25	2:10	Ostinato: strings	
		interlude	
0:50	2:35	Ostinato: brass crescendo	
1:15	3:00	**Melodic phrase (No. 1), trumpet**	
			Subsides

FOURTH INITIATIVE

24	3:32	Timpani, brass ostinato (blurred); crescendo	Build-up
	3:43	First climax: **five outbursts, *ff***	
1:33	4:05	Timpani and low piano	Second build-up
25	5:08	Second climax: **Melodic phrase (No. 2), *f*, full brass section**	
0:14	5:22	Aftershock: timpani, *fff*, with ostinato-related rhythms	Subsides
		Fades: *pp pizzicato* strings "liquidate" the ostinato rhythms	
		(silence)	
26	6:10	**Melodic phrase (No. 3): Alleluia chant,**	
		muted trumpet, centered on note E	
0:18	6:28	Final cadence: E alternates with F, E trill, E	

The next two surges can also be considered as one coordinated attempt to reach a goal. The timpani are added to the brass, leading to five frantic *fortissimo* outbursts, unmelodic and inarticulate. The music has to try again—the ostinato rhythms have by now disappeared—with the timpani joined by the piano playing in the low register. And this final surge leads to another isolated phrase of new music, blared out by the orchestra's full brass section:

This disturbing climax produces a sort of aftershock in the timpani, playing a final transformation of the ostinato rhythms very loudly—and perhaps desperately, for the ostinato is doomed, decimated by bleak *pizzicato* strings.

Just when the music feels completely drained, we hear something entirely unexpected: a muted trumpet sounding from back stage. We can barely catch its melody (the third of the three short, isolated melodic phrases that stand out in this movement). Its free, chantlike rhythm, and the way it dwells on the pitch E, identify it as the long-sought-after "alleluia":

pp

Quiet instruments return to the note E and meditate on and around it for a few more seconds, to make an exquisite final cadence.

It is easy to view *Pro et Contra* as a parable about the futility of striving, and the solace conferred by the unexpected and miraculous. Much *too* easy, Gubaidulina might say; composers tend to resist attempts to pin down their music to facts, figures, or philosophies. We need not insist on this particular interpretation to sense the component of spirituality in Gubaidulina's art.

STEVE REICH (b. 1936)
Tehillim (1981)

One of the most interesting new musical styles to develop in the last twenty years is called **minimalism**. A sharp reaction to the complexities of modernist composition, minimalist music uses very simple melodies, motives, and harmonies repeated many, many times. Terry Riley's *In C*, mentioned on page 341, is an ancestor of minimalism (some say, the first great example of it). This style has worked wonders for American opera, which has become the success story of modern music since *Einstein on the Beach* (1976) by leading minimalist composer Philip Glass (born 1937). *Einstein, Satyagraha,* and *Akhnaten* by Glass and *Nixon in China* and *The Death of Klinghoffer* by John Adams (born 1947) have been performed again and again in this country and abroad, all of them in spectacular productions.

Steve Reich

Steve Reich, a philosophy major at Cornell, studied music subsequently and is perhaps the most subtle exponent of minimalist style. A keyboardist, he performs his work with his own special group—a procedure that is followed by a number of other contemporary composers, including notably Philip Glass.

Tehillim (tehéelim) is the Hebrew word for "psalms." Reich has written a long composition in four sections, in which verses from the biblical psalms are sung by a women's choir accompanied by orchestra. The first two sections are fast-moving, the third is slow, and the climactic last section is fast again, almost as though the composer were writing a "symphony of psalms."

Minimalism has proved to be an unusually successful style for American opera: a scene from *Nixon in China* (1987) by John Adams (b. 1947).

LISTENING CHART 30

Steve Reich, *Tehillim*, Part 4

6 min. 43 sec.

	0:00	A regular drum beat has accelerated from the previous slow movement.
	0:14	Theme: two sopranos sing the entire text of three psalm verses—**a b c c'**
		Voices in harmony, percussion. Quiet sustained chords in the orchestra below, shifting at irregular intervals
28	0:42	Variation 1: two-part canon **a b c c'**
0:29	1:11	Maracas enter
		Variation 2: four-part canon; each psalm verse is repeated many times
1:11	1:53	**b**—starts with a very brief punctuation (instruments stop).
1:36	2:18	**c**—starts with another brief punctuation (instruments stop).
		Each voice sings **c** five times (**c'** is absent).
29	2:55	Variation 3: two voices with clarinets (drums enter a little later)
		Some new high notes for soprano
0:45	3:40	Instrumental interlude. Intense, irregular accents by the strings and electric organ
30	4:17	Variation 4: Voices return; from now to the end, they are more intense.
		New melody. High notes for the soprano
0:55	5:12	Climactic note—higher still—for the soprano
31	5:27	Coda: "Halleluyah" repeated again and again. Electric organs, bells enter.
		Intensity increases.
0:21	5:48	After a punctuation, more "Halleluyahs"; bells prominent
1:08	6:35	. . . plus one more climactic fast "Halleluyah"
1:13	6:40	Abrupt stop (a cessation, not a cadence)

The text for the last "movement" comes from the very last psalm, Psalm 150. And the last *word* in this Psalm, "hallelujah," has echoed down the ages in never-ending praise of God. The word is the same in Hebrew, English, Latin, and Greek (see pages 85, 145, and 353).

Fourth Movement ("Haleluhu")   To begin, the full text of "Haleluhu" is sung by two sopranos in harmony, backed by a steady beat on tambourines.

1 Haleluhu batof umachol,	a Praise the Lord with tambourines and dancing,
Haleluhu baminim va-ugav;	praise him with flute and strings;
2 Haleluhu batzil-tzilay shamah,	b praise him with the clash of cymbals,
Haleluhu batzil-tzilay taruah;	praise him with triumphant cymbals;
3 Kol hanshamah tahalail Yah, Haleluyah.	c let everything that has breath praise the Lord! Hallelujah.
Kol hanshamah tahalail Yah, Haleluyah.	c' *Let everything that has breath praise the Lord! Hallelujah.*

(This text, with its reiterations of "haleluhu" and "haleluyah," seems perfectly suited to Reich's repetitious musical technique.) Each syllable of the words gets a single note, and these notes are arranged in lively irregular rhythms; note the changing time signatures. The melody falls into an **a a b c c'** form (**c'** differs slightly from **c**), with verse 3 of the text repeated for **c'**.

Kol han-sha-mah ta – ha-lail Yah, Ha – le-lu-yah.   Kol han-sha-ma ta – ha-lail Yah, Ha – le-lu-yah.

Internally, the melody is repetitive in its own special way: for instance, both "haleluyahs" and both "Kol hanshamahs" use the same four notes but in different orders. The many repetitions of this kind *within* the melody, combined with the many repetitions *of* the melody, gives this music its feeling of incantation, both static and ecstatic, always changing yet always the same.

Back of the singing, a few chords are played by the orchestral strings and then sustained for long periods—a solemn counterpoint to the sprightly soprano melody. These strange, irregularly placed chords continue through nearly all the movement, including the orchestral interlude.

Now Reich writes variations on this melody. In *Variation 1,* two sopranos sing the melody as a canon—that is, one of them starts several beats after the other. The constant melodic intertwining adds new energy and charm. *Variation 2,* the longest and most complicated variation, is a four-part canon on the original melody. (What is more, each verse is sung several times before the next is heard, so that **c,** for example, comes twenty times. Of course Reich does not expect the listener to hear or discriminate each of these fragments. What we apprehend is a sort of controlled and yet ecstatic babble that promises to go on forever.)

In *Variation 3* the melody itself is varied, so as to include several exhilarating high notes for the soprano. The rhythm is somewhat different, too.

After an orchestral interlude, the strings grow more intense. *Variation 4* follows; something like the original "Hallelujah" melody is heard again at the end of **c,** with the highest soprano note yet.

In an enthusiastic *coda,* extra instruments pile in—two organs, a vibraphone playing along with the tambourines, and bells. United in their joyous ritual, the voices cry out "Hallelujah" again and again, until a final quick, loud "Hallelujah" brings the music to an abrupt close.

So [in Baroque music] you have the fixed beat, relatively straightforward dynamic situations, and working over a ground bass or a series of harmonies. I never met a jazz musician who didn't love Bach.

Steve Reich, 1987

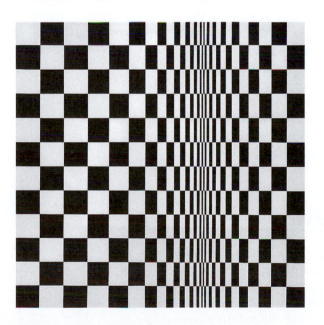

Movement in Space by Bridget Riley (b. 1931). Perhaps this picture recalls those compositions by Steve Reich where he has tape-recorded a simple repetitive pattern, copied the tape, and then played the tape and the copy simultaneously at slightly different speeds, so that the music goes slowly in and out of phase.

CHAPTER 24

Music in America: Jazz

A s we have observed a number of times in this book, in the nineteenth century a rift opened up between popular music and the music we now call "classical." Nowhere has this rift been more apparent than in the United States of America, the most populist of all nations. And nowhere have such strenuous efforts been made to close the rift. We can see this if we think back to the various American composers discussed in the last few chapters, from the unlikely modernist Charles Ives to the minimalist Steve Reich, American pioneer in a world-wide movement. It is not accidental that we have seen more than one of these composers working with popular as well as "classical" music sources—and that in this chapter we shall see more.

"Popular" and "classical" are fuzzy terms; think of the popularity of the Three Tenors, the Spanish monks, and other purveyors of so-called classical music. For music in America, the terms "cultivated" and "vernacular" have proven to be more illuminating. To "cultivate" means to nurture, as microorganisms are cultivated on a petri dish in a laboratory, or as orchids are cultivated in a greenhouse. "Vernacular," on the other hand, refers to one's native language, as opposed to some other that may be in use, such as Latin in the Church, universities, and law courts of the Middle Ages. **Cultivated music,** then, is music that has been brought to this country and consciously developed, fostered at concerts and taught in conservatories. **Vernacular music** is music we sing and hear as naturally as we speak our native argot.

There is a special twist to this terminology as applied to American music. The word *vernacular* comes from the Latin word *vernaculus,* which is itself derived from *verna:* and "verna" means a family slave. The heritage of African-American music was and is central to the story of American music.

Philadelphia music in the 1890s: *The Concert Singer,* by Thomas Eakins

1 Early American Music: An Overview

Before coming to this matter, however, we should briefly sketch the history of American music in its early years, starting with the pilgrims. It is not a very rich history. The Puritans disapproved of music; they thought it was frivolous, except for its supporting role in religion. In Puritan services, metrical versions of the psalms were sung like hymns, but when the words of the psalms were printed in the *Bay Psalm Book* of 1640—the first book ever printed in North

America—the music was not included, because just a few tunes, known to everyone, were used for all one hundred and fifty psalms. In succeeding years, much of the energy of early American musicians was devoted to the composition of new psalm and hymn tunes, and to the teaching and improvement of church singing.

William Billings (1746–1800) of Boston is often mentioned as our first composer. He wrote hymns and **fuguing tunes,** which are simple anthems based on hymns, with a little counterpoint. (An anthem is a choral piece in the vernacular for use in Protestant services—originally, in Anglican services.) When sung with spirit, fuguing tunes sound enthusiastic, rough, and gutsy.

Billing's more secular-minded contemporaries enjoyed the Classical music of the era. Benjamin Franklin, who tried his hand at most everything, also tried his hand at composing. But without well-established musical institutions, there was not much support for native composers outside the church. The problem in those years is hardly that of distinguishing between cultivated and vernacular music. The problem is finding music to listen to and talk about at all.

The "Cultivated" Tradition

After the United States won its independence, things changed. As cities grew, first on the East coast and then progressively to the West, more and more concerts appeared, and with them inveterate concertgoers. One such was a New York lawyer and civic leader named George Templeton Strong, who left a four-and-a-half-million-word diary discussing (among other things) all the symphonies, oratorios, and organ music he heard in unending enthusiastic detail. By the mid-1800s, all our major cities had their concert and opera organizations and amateur choral societies. The 1860s saw the foundation of our first conservatories of music, in Boston, Baltimore, Cincinnati, and Oberlin, Ohio.

Americans eagerly bought tickets to hear traveling celebrities from Europe, and good native composers and performers began to appear. The first American musicians to gain worldwide reputations were the immigrant German composer Anthony Philip Heinrich (1781–1861), a quirky early romantic, and the Louisiana piano virtuoso Louis Moreau Gottschalk (1829–1869).

Louis Moreau Gottschalk

A Wagner opera performed in Cincinnati's 3600-seat Music Hall, built in 1878

On the whole, however, Americans were content to look to Germany for their music. That the cultivated tradition in American music was essentially German in orientation is not surprising. Ever since the time of Mozart and Beethoven, German music had achieved wonders and had earned enormous prestige throughout the world. The mid-nineteenth-century immigration from Germany brought us many musicians who labored long and hard for the cause of music in this country. We can hardly blame them for their German bias.

There were significant native composers at the end of the century: John Knowles Paine, Arthur Foote, and Henry Chadwick of the "Boston School," and Edward MacDowell of New York. They wrote symphonies, piano "miniatures," and so on, in a competent but conservative German romantic style. Time has not been kind to their work, though efforts are now under way to revive it.

The music of Amy Beach (1867–1944), in particular, has stirred interest in recent years. Active as both a composer and a pianist—she made her debut with the Boston Symphony Orchestra at the age of seventeen—"Mrs. H. H. A. Beach" (as she always signed her works) contributed to many traditional genres, such as the piano concerto, the piano quintet, and the symphony. Her *Gaelic* Symphony of 1896 was the first symphonic work ever composed by an American woman.

The emergence of Charles Ives in the midst of this conservative tradition seems like a miracle of music history (see page 320). Yet Ives profited more than he sometimes cared to admit from the grounding in traditional music that he received from his German-trained professor, Horatio Parker.

Music in the Vernacular

We might well count the psalms and hymns mentioned above as "vernacular" music, for in colonial days everybody who could carry a tune sang them at church and in the home, and later they were widely sung at revival meetings and the like. Nineteenth-century America was also rich in secular popular music. Our most famous composers wrote timeless tunes and ever-popular marches, respectively: Stephen Collins Foster (1826–1864) and John Philip Sousa (1854–1932).

Foster, it is sad to say, led a dispiriting life. Even in those days, song writing was closely tied to the music business; Foster was dependent on Christie's Minstrels, the leading traveling theater troupe of the time. They had exclusive rights to his songs and helped popularize them—very successfully; some of them soon achieved the status of folk songs. But even so, Foster had a hard time making ends meet. His marriage broke up; he turned to drink, and died at the age of thirty-eight.

John Philip Sousa, son of Spanish and German immigrant parents, was a Marine Corps bandmaster who later formed a wildly successful touring band of his own. Every American knows his masterpiece *The Stars and Stripes Forever* (even if they don't all know its name). Leonard Bernstein once said that his greatest regret as a musician was that he hadn't composed that march.

African-American Music

Many of Stephen Foster's best-known songs have to do with the black slaves of his time. There are sentimental "plantation songs" such as "Swanee River" ("The Old Folks at Home") and "Old Black Joe," and comic minstrel songs such as "Oh, Susanna!" and "Camptown Races." The **minstrel show**, per-

[Music] takes us out of the actual and whispers to us dim secrets that startle our wonder as to who we are, and for what, whence and whereto.

Ralph Waldo Emerson, 1838

Title page of *Foster's Melodies,* a collection of songs by Stephen Foster (1854)

Hymn singing at home, in an engraving by Paul Revere (Psalm 23, "The Lord is my shepherd")

formed by white actors in blackface, was very popular at mid-century; it consisted of comedy routines, "Ethiopian" songs, dances, and solos on the banjo (an instrument with African roots). Though today this kind of entertainment strikes us as an ugly parody of black speech and character, it was also an acknowledgment of the vitality of the slaves' music. From at least the time of Foster, African-American music has had a profound effect on the music of America at large.

What was the slaves' music like? This is hard to say, for no one ever thought of writing it down (and recordings were far in the future). Nonetheless, by studying somewhat later black American music, and comparing it with today's African music, scholars have been able to show how much the slaves preserved of their native musical cultures.

For example, a musical procedure known as *call and response* is common in West Africa. Phrases sung by a leader—a soloist—are answered or echoed again and again by a chorus. This procedure is preserved in black American church music, when the congregation answers the preacher's "call," as well as in spirituals, work songs, and "field hollers," by which the slaves tried to lighten their labors. It is also an important feature in blues and in jazz, as we shall see.

Spiritual is a term for a religious folk song that came into being outside an established church (white or black). Moving "Negro spirituals," such as "Nobody Knows the Trouble I've Seen," "Go Down, Moses," and others, were the first body of black American music to gain the admiration of the white world. After Emancipation, black colleges formed choirs to tour with them. To be sure, spirituals in their concert versions were considerably removed from folk music.

The music of African Americans got a powerful boost from the first major European composer to spend time in America, Antonin Dvořák (Dvórzhahk). This highly respected Bohemian musician, head of New York's National Con-

The singing was accompanied by a certain ecstasy of motion, clapping of hands, tossing of heads, which would continue without cessation for about half an hour. One would lead off in a kind of recitative style, others joining in the chorus.

A former slave recalls call and response singing, 1881

The Fisk Jubilee Singers, a group of former slaves who were the first to popularize Negro spirituals. In 1871 they toured to raise funds for Fisk, one of the earliest African-American colleges.

servatory of Music (ancestor of the Juilliard School) in the 1890s, announced his special admiration for spirituals, advised his American colleagues to make use of them in their concert music, and showed the way himself. He incorporated the essence of spirituals so skillfully in his ever-popular *New World* Symphony that one of the tunes was actually adapted to made-up "folk-song" words, "Goin' Home."

Go-in' home, . . .

But if Dvořák and his contemporaries could have been whisked for a moment into the late twentieth century, they would have been astonished to see and hear what actually happened. With no help from the cultivated tradition, a strictly vernacular type of music emerged called—at first contemptuously— jazz. From the most modest beginnings, this music developed prodigiously. It produced a whole series of new musical styles, performers of the greatest artistry, and composers of genius.

Jazz developed into America's most distinctive—many would say greatest —contribution to the arts worldwide. And if our time-travellers were to find it hard to believe their ears, there would be something else to amaze them. All this music was actually preserved, preserved on acetate discs by means of a revolutionary new technique: sound recording.

2 Jazz: The First Half Century

Jazz is a performance style that grew up among black musicians around 1910 and that has gone through a series of extraordinary developments since.

The key features of jazz are, first, *improvisation*. When jazz musicians play a song, they do not play it the way they hear it or see it on paper; they always improvise *around* a song. They add embellishments and sometimes also short interludes, called **breaks**; in effect, they are always playing variations on whatever tunes they are working with. With its own African-American accent, jazz employs a musical form—variation form—we have seen many times in European music.

The second key feature of jazz is a special rhythmic style involving highly developed *syncopation* (see below). Notice that jazz is not so much a kind of

Ragtime: Scott Joplin (1868–1917)

Scott Joplin

Ragtime, a precursor of jazz, was a style of piano playing developed by black musicians playing in bars, dives, and brothels. The music resembled march music, but while the left hand played strictly on the beat, the right hand syncopated the rhythm in a crisp, cheerful way. "To rag" meant to play in a syncopated style; "ragging" evolved into jazz syncopation.

In the early 1900s, when phonographs were still new and most music in the home was played on the piano, ragtime became enormously popular throughout America by means of sheet music and piano rolls for mechanical ("player") pianos. The term ragtime could also be applied to non-piano music: witness the famous song *Alexander's Ragtime Band* of 1911 by Irving Berlin.

Scott Joplin was the leading rag composer. Frustratingly little is known about his early life. The son of an ex-slave, he grew up in Texarkana and worked as a pianist and band musician in many midwestern towns. *Maple Leaf Rag*, named after the Maple Leaf Club in Sedalia, Mis-

souri, where Joplin played, was published in 1899 and soon sold a million copies.

Joplin followed *Maple Leaf* with *The Entertainer* and many other rags. They stand out for an elegance that might not have been expected in this simple and commercial genre. But after he moved to New York in 1907, Joplin's ambition to break into the "cultivated" world of opera was not realized. The second of his two operas, *Treemonisha,* was Joplin's idea of what a European opera had to be like. It received a single unstaged, unsuccessful performance in 1915.

There was a strong new surge of interest in ragtime in the 1960s. At last, in 1972, *Treemonisha* was fully staged and recorded.

music—the music it is based on usually consists of popular songs, blues, or abstract harmonic patterns called "changes"—but a special, highly charged way of performing that music.

Jazz Syncopation

Syncopation occurs when some of the accents in music are moved away from the main beats, the beats that are normally accented. For example, in **2/2** meter, instead of the normal ONE *two* ONE *two,* the accent can be displaced from beat 1 to beat 2—*one* TWO *one* TWO (see page 15). This is called a "back beat" in jazz parlance.

Some syncopation occurs in all Western music. In jazz, there is much more of it. Syncopation becomes a regular principle, so much so that we can speak of at least two rhythmic "levels" in a jazz piece. One rhythmic level is a simple one—the **rhythm section** of percussion (drums, cymbals), piano, string bass, and sometimes other instruments, emphasizes the meter forcefully, and continuously. A second, more complex rhythmic level is produced by the melody instruments—trumpet, clarinet, trombone, piano, and the saxophones that were so brilliantly developed in jazz. They play a constantly syncopating music that always cuts across the rhythm section.

In addition, jazz developed syncopation of a more subtle kind, sometimes called **beat syncopation.** Derived from African drumming, this technique can also be traced in earlier black American music. In beat syncopation, accents are moved *just a fraction of a beat* ahead of the metrical points. When this happens in just the right way, the music is said to "swing."

Syncopation was the first and is still the main feature of jazz adopted in other popular music, from 1920s show tunes to modern rock. (It is fair enough to call such music jazzy, but technically it is not correct to call it jazz.)

The Blues

The **blues** is a special category of black folk song whose subject is loneliness, trouble, and depression of every shade. Indeed, the blues is more than song, more than music: it is an essential expression of the African-American psyche. Though gloom and dejection are at the heart of the blues, not infrequently blues lyrics also convey humor, banter, hope, and resilience.

Emerging around 1900, the blues was a major influence on early jazz—and has remained a major force in American music ever since.

A blues melody consists typically of three four-measure phrases ("twelve-bar blues"), repeated again and again as the blues singer develops a thought by improvising more and more stanzas. The stanzas are just two lines long, with the first line repeated and with the ends of the lines rhyming. Here are stanzas 1 and 4 of "If You Ever Been Down" Blues:

a If you ever been down, you know just how I feel,
a *If you ever been down, you know just how I feel,*
b Like a tramp on the railroad ain't got a decent meal.

a Yes, one thing, papa, I've decided to do,
a *Oh pretty daddy, I've decided to do,*
b I'm going to find another papa, then I can't use you.

Composed blues—for example, W. C. Handy's famous *St. Louis Blues*—can be more complicated than this, but the *aab* poetic scheme is basic for the blues.

Blues melodies (and especially the bass lines under blues melodies) provided jazz musicians with powerfully emotional patterns for improvisation. But more than that, blues also provided jazz with a sonorous model. Jazz instrumental playing has an astonishing vocal quality, as though in imitation of the blues. The trumpet and saxophone, in particular, sound infinitely more expressive and "human" when played in jazz style as compared to their earlier usage in military bands. Jazz instruments seem to have absorbed the vibrant accents of black singing.

I'd like to think that when I sing a song, I can let you know all about the heartbreak, struggle, lies and kicks in the ass I've gotten over the years for being black and everything else, without actually saying a word about it.

Blues, gospel, and soul singer Ray Charles, 1970

SIPPIE WALLACE
"If You Ever Been Down" Blues (1927) (Composed by G. W. Thomas)

Sippie Wallace with Louis Armstrong, trumpet, and Artie Starks, clarinet

Here is an example of unvarnished blues singing, by one of the legendary woman blues singers who dominated the earliest recordings. Sippie Wallace is not as renowned as Mamie Smith, Ma Rainey, or the great Bessie Smith, but she poured her heart out with the best of them in response to the eternal themes of the blues:

I'm a real good woman but my man don't treat me right,
He takes all my money and stays out all night.   (Stanza 2)

and

I'm down today but I won't be down always,
'Cause the sun's going to shine in my back door some day.   (Stanza 3)

Wallace accompanied herself on the piano, and although for purposes of the recording two jazz musicians accompany her, she would have sung just about the same way if she had been performing alone. One of the musicians is the outstanding genius of early jazz, Louis Armstrong.

6   3   6B   3B
32   35   1   4

LISTEN

Blues

0:09 **Stanza 1**
0:44 **Stanza 2**
1:18 **Trumpet**
1:50 **Stanza 3**
2:24 **Stanza 4**

Louis Armstrong (ca. 1898–1971)

Louis Armstrong was born into abject poverty in New Orleans; his birth date is unknown. He learned to play the cornet in the Colored Waifs' Home, where he had been placed for a juvenile infraction of the law. Determined to become a musician, Armstrong played in seedy clubs and on riverboats, which were floating dance halls that travelled from town to town on the Mississippi every summer, and became a cradle of early jazz.

Soon Armstrong was playing in the pioneering jazz bands led by King Oliver and Fletcher Henderson, where he rapidly emerged as a more exciting artist than any of his colleagues. His sophisticated, flowing rhythms, his imaginative "breaks" and variations, and the sheer beauty of his trumpet tone—all these were unique at the time. A famous series of records he made in the 1920s, playing with small New Orleans-style bands, drew jazz to the serious attention of musicians all over the world.

In the 1930s, the ensuing popularity of jazz led to a great deal of commercialization, and to the cheapening and stereotyping that always seems to result from this process. Armstrong went right along, though often contributing moments of breathtaking beauty to records that are "listenable virtually only when Louis is playing," in the words of one jazz critic. Armstrong became a nationally loved star, familiar from his appearances in nearly twenty movies. The State Department sponsored him on so many international tours that people called him "Ambassador Satch" ("Satchmo," his nickname, was derived from "satchel-mouth").

However, the more successful Armstrong became in the world of popular music, the more he drifted away from true jazz, to the distress of jazz enthusiasts. His last hit record was *Hello, Dolly!,* the name song of a 1964 Broadway musical.

After a brief instrumental introduction, Wallace sings two blues stanzas from the piano bench. The instruments play short breaks in between her lines —the trumpet in stanza 1, the clarinet in stanza 2. Sympathetic respondents to her "call," they deepen the melancholy of her song and nuance it:

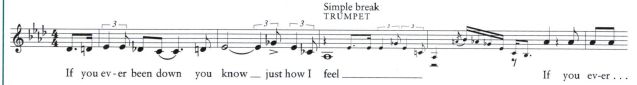

Simple break
TRUMPET

If you ev-er been down you know __ just how I feel _____   If you ev-er . . .

Then Armstrong gets to play a solo section—an entire 12-bar blues stanza —for himself. He does not play the blues melody note by note, but improvises around the melody and its bass. Armstrong has a wonderful way of speeding up the dragging blues rhythm, and his rich, almost vocal tone quality echoes and complements the singer's bleak sound. The clarinet joins him; this is a simple example of improvised jazz polyphony.

Wallace, too, joins in quietly during this instrumental chorus; she too, no doubt, was singing on impulse. She then sings two more stanzas, with instrumental breaks as before. Records at the time were just three minutes long, or these blues performers would have spun out the number by many more stanzas.

Perhaps the essential sound of jazz is Louis Armstrong improvising the breaks in the blues sung by [famous blues-singer] Bessie Smith. . . . In the break we have the origin of the instrument imitating the voice, the very soil in which jazz grows.

Composer Leonard Bernstein, 1955

It's necessary to listen to this recording in a different spirit from that in which we approach the other recordings accompanying this book. The scratchy sound on these old "race" discs cannot be helped by digital remastering, and the music itself is not "composed," of course. It lies somewhere in between true folk music and jazz, a fascinating juxtaposition of the direct, powerful simplicity of Sippie Wallace and the artistry of Armstrong. With a little imagination, one can virtually hear history happening in this recording: jazz evolving from the blues.

Louis Armstrong in his first important band, Joe ("King") Oliver's Creole Jazz Band. The pianist, Lil Hardin—also a band leader and song writer—later married Armstrong and is credited with directing his early career.

Sippie Wallace (1898–1986)—her nickname is said to derive from a childhood lisp—was equally known for gospel music and for the blues. And indeed *gospel* music—ecstatic choral singing associated with black American church services—grew up at the same time as ragtime and the blues. Wallace was also a pianist and songwriter, who usually sang her own compositions, and published a good many of them. Her long performing career began at little churches in Houston, and ended with a concert at Lincoln Center, the sprawling New York music facility that houses the New York Philharmonic Orchestra and the Metropolitan Opera.

New Orleans (Dixieland) Jazz

Early jazz was local entertainment for black audiences, an informal, low-budget, and essentially unassuming art. Small bands, usually of six to eight players, would typically feature three melody instruments to do the "swinging"— trumpet, clarinet, and trombone. The rhythm section could include piano, banjo, string bass, or even tuba, along with drums and other percussion.

   Early jazz players developed the art of collective improvisation, or "jamming." They learned to improvise simultaneously, each developing the special resources of his instrument—bright melodic spurts for the trumpet, fast running passages in the high register for the clarinet, forceful slides for the trombone. They also acquired a sort of second sense for fitting in with the other improvisers. The nonimitative polyphony produced in this way is the hallmark of early jazz.

The first important center of jazz was New Orleans, home of the greatest early jazzman, Louis Armstrong, who played cornet and trumpet. Armstrong and his colleagues developed wonderfully imaginative and individual performance styles; aficionados can recognize any player after hearing just a few measures of a jazz record. With players of this quality, it is not surprising that solo sections soon became a regular feature in early jazz, along with collective improvisation.

Recording technology was (and is) crucial in the dissemination of jazz. As popular records in those days were all just three minutes long, the jazz that has survived from that era is all slimmed down into three-minute segments. Originally issued on labels that appealed to black audiences—coldly categorized as "race records" by the music business—Louis Armstrong's discs of the late 1920s and thirties not only attracted white listeners, but also excited the admiration of a new breed of jazz musicologists and critics.

Swing

Around 1930, jazz gained significantly in popularity, thanks in part to Armstrong's recordings. With popularity came changes, not all of them to the good. Jazz now had to reach bigger audiences in ballrooms and roadhouses. This meant **big bands,** with ten to twenty players, and carefully written out arrangements of the songs played. Improvisation, which was really the rationale behind jazz, was necessarily limited under these conditions.

Benny Goodman, most famous of all clarinetists

However, big-band jazz—called **swing**—compensated for some of its lost spontaneity by variety of tone color and instrumental effects. A novel style of band orchestration was developed, based on the contrast between brass (trumpets and trombones) and "reed" (mainly saxophone) groups. Soloists cut in and out of the full-band sounds. Jazz "arrangers," who "arranged" current songs for the bands, treated this style with the greatest technical ingenuity and verve; they deserve the name of composers. Sometimes they contrived to allow for some improvisation within their arrangements.

With popularity, too, came white musicians and managers, who moved in on what had previously been a relatively small black operation. Not only were black jazzmen marginalized in the mass market, but their art was watered down to suit the growing audience. The big swing bands that were commercial successes were white, and their leaders—Benny Goodman, Glenn Miller, Artie Shaw—were household names in the 1930s and 1940s. But the best of the big bands were black: those led by Count Basie (1904–1984), Jimmie Lunceford (1902–1947), and Duke Ellington.

DUKE ELLINGTON (1899–1974)
Conga Brava (1940)

33   36   2   5

The tune used in *Conga Brava* was written by Ellington together with his Puerto Rican sideman Juan Tizol. (A conga is a dance of Afro-Cuban origin, named after the *conga* drum.) In it, the characteristic beat of Latin American music is appropriated by jazz—a mild tit-for-tat on behalf of a musical genre that had given up much more to the non-black world.

Only the beginning of this unusual tune—the **a a** section of the **a a b** form—has a Latin beat. Played by trombonist Tizol, the first **a** is presented with minimum accompaniment; but after this ends with a fancy clarinet break, the second **a** includes brilliant interpolations from the muted brass (an Ellington specialty). From now on things change rapidly. The brass choir plays **b**, with a speedy low clarinet cutting in. The rhythm section switches from a Latin beat to a typical jazz back-beat duple meter. The music begins to swing hard.

My band is my instrument.

Duke Ellington

Duke Ellington and His Famous Orchestra (which on this occasion included violins)

Duke Ellington (1899–1974)

Edward Kennedy Ellington was born in Washington, D.C., son of a butler who occasionally worked at the White House. The young Ellington considered a career as an artist, but he started playing the piano in jazz bands—ragtime was a major influence—and soon organized his own. He learned arranging too, and became an almost unique phenomenon: a major bandleader who was also its composer and its arranger.

He was called "Duke" because of a certain aristocratic bearing—and he was fastidious about his music, too. Ellington held fast to his own high standards of innovation and stylishness. And although his band never "went commercial," it did as well as any black band could in the 1930s and 1940s. "Duke Ellington and his Famous Orchestra" were renowned as the backup to sumptuous revues put on at the Cotton Club, an up-scale Harlem night spot that catered to white audiences. Their recordings from around 1930 to 1940 constitute Ellington's major legacy.

After World War II, Ellington went his own imperturbable way, keeping his big band at a time when such organizations were regarded as jazz dinosaurs. He had experimented with long, symphonic-style jazz compositions as a young man, and now wrote more of these, as well as movie scores, a ballet, and an opera. The Ellington band, which had toured Europe twice in the 1930s, now toured all over the world, including the Soviet Union.

Ellington was finally recognized for what he was, just about America's most eminent composer, and he received the Presidental Medal of Freedom and other tributes. His last creative phase found him writing lengthy religious pieces, called *Sacred Concerts,* for the Ellington band with a Swedish soprano, Alice Babs, who was not really a jazz singer at all.

Ellington's *Sacred Concerts* would have been impossible without Babs—but the same is true of his earlier, better-known music and the musicians of his early bands. These individual soloists, or *sidemen,* in jazz parlance—among them Barney Bigard (clarinet), Cootie Williams (trumpet), Johnny Hodges (alto saxophone), and Juan Tizol, who is featured on valve trombone in *Conga Brava* (page 368)—were vital to Ellington's art in a way singers or instrumentalists very rarely are in classical music. He molded his music so closely to their sometimes eccentric styles of playing that we cannot conceive of his music without them.

Ellington's sidemen can be regarded as co-composers of his music—or, better, as its *material,* like the songs and the blues that were transformed by Ellington's magic.

Chief Works: very many songs—one estimate is 2,000—and jazz arrangements. Some titles: *East St. Louis Toodle-oo* (pronounced "toad-lo"), *Mood Indigo, Koko, Cotton Tail, Sophisticated Lady, Harlem Airshaft, Don't Get Around Much Anymore, Satin Doll* ■ Large-scale jazz compositions, including *Creole Fantasy* and *Black, Brown, and Beige* ■ Musical comedies, ballets, an incomplete opera *(Boola)* and other stage music ■ Five film scores; *Sacred Concerts*

The second appearance of the tune is a dazzling free improvisation by tenor sax player Ben Webster. He sounds genuinely spontaneous; he probably never again improvised around this melody in just this way. After he has gone through **a** and **a,** the muted brass come in again with a lively variation of **b.**

Webster has strayed far from the tune, so it is good to hear the third appearance of the tune in its original form (more or less), now on the reed choir (saxophones). This time the brilliant interpolations are by sideman Rex Stewart on trumpet. And this time, after a single **a,** there comes an extraordinary brass-choir version of **b,** with wildly irregular rhythms. The coordination of the brass instruments is breathtaking, and the sheer verve of their variation makes this the high point of the composition.

At the piano, Duke gives a quiet signal for this brass episode before it starts; he also plays a single, hardly audible note in the middle of the episode, as though to remind us who is in charge. The piece ends as it started, with the tune played by Tizol, but it fades halfway through.

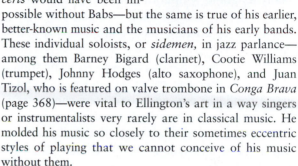

LISTEN

Ellington, *Conga Brava*

0:02	**a a**	Trombone
0:44	**b**	Brass
0:58	**a a**	Sax
1:39	**b**	Muted brass
1:46	**a**	Reed Choir
2:06	**b′**	Brass Choir
2:31	**a**	Trombone

How strange to be back to the rather mournful and uneventful conga melody, with its Latin beat! The listener to *Conga Brava* can end up feeling a bit mystified. All that exhilarating jazz activity that blew up so suddenly and has now been cut off—was it some kind of dream? Only a master of musical form like Ellington could make you think of such questions, make you feel that way about a piece of music.

3 "Symphonic Jazz"

How was jazz first received in this country's "cultivated" musical circles? Many longtime symphony and opera subscribers certainly hated it. They considered its saxes and muted trumpets vulgar, its rhythm dangerously sexual and likely to corrupt their children. This reaction was strongly tinged by racism.

The basic difference between classical music and jazz is that in the former the music is always greater than the performance—whereas the way jazz is performed is always more important than what is being played.

André Previn, who plays Gershwin's Concerto in F on our recording.

On the other hand, jazz was an inspiration as well as a delight for less hidebound musicians, for music students, and for young composers. The 1920s was a confident era, and composers coming of age at that time promised a bright new day for American music. A vital, fresh musical idiom had emerged—the decade from 1920 to 1930 called itself the Jazz Age—and the idea of working jazz into symphonic music was both natural and exciting.

Only one person really carried it off: a Broadway song writer and pianist named George Gershwin. Harboring an ambition for the world of cultivated music, Gershwin electrified musical America with his *Rhapsody in Blue* of 1924. Billed as "An Experiment in Modern Music," this short work for piano and orchestra was first performed by Paul Whiteman's Orchestra, a sleek forerunner of the 1930s big bands. Note that this music is not true jazz, but Gershwin's own translation of jazz features into his own individual idiom.

After this Gershwin wrote *An American in Paris,* a symphonic poem for orchestra; a piano concerto; and a jazz opera, *Porgy and Bess,* works that have been widely popular ever since they were written, known and loved by millions of Americans. Gershwin had thrown a bridge across the canyon between vernacular and cultivated music. Of course, the existence of bridges doesn't mean that the rift has gone away.

GEORGE GERSHWIN (1898–1937)
Piano Concerto in F (1925)

Born in New York, Gershwin received a sketchy musical education. He quit school at sixteen to work as a song plugger or music publisher's agent, hawking new sheet music to singers and band leaders. Soon he was writing his own songs, and he went on to compose some of the finest tunes of the 1920s. His many successful revues and musicals include *Lady, Be Good; Oh, Kay!; Strike Up the Band;* and *Of Thee I Sing.* Gershwin was more attuned to jazz than either of his main competitors, Jerome Kern or Richard Rodgers (see page 274); he was an accomplished and original jazz pianist.

The Piano Concerto in F was Gershwin's most ambitious essay in symphonic jazz, and also the one that caused him the most labor. He always regretted his lack of composing technique, and as an adult took lessons on and off

Constantin Alajálov, who left unforgettable pictures of the Jazz Age, sketched himself painting George Gershwin in 1932.

with a long list of teachers. (Eventually he even sought out the archmodernist Arnold Schoenberg in Los Angeles, and the two men struck up a somewhat unlikely friendship.) Commissioned by an important American conductor of the time, Walter Damrosch, the Concerto in F was first played by a very nervous Gershwin in 1925.

The concerto's strong, extroverted opening movement is followed by a bluesy second movement and a third in rondo form, the traditional form for concerto finales (see pages 185, 278).

Third Movement   The main rondo theme, **A,** is an open-ended one, built up out of repetitions of a fast, brassy motive with a lively syncopated ending:

The jazzy accents are intensified when the piano takes the theme over from the orchestra. A transition, in which the **A** motive is developed by the piano, leads to the bluesy **B** theme, which is *all* syncopated—a tribute to jazz syncopation that goes beyond the call of duty:

LISTENING CHART 31

6 3 6B 3B
34-39 37-42 3 6

Gershwin, Piano Concerto in F, last movement

Rondo form, 6 min., 26 sec.

	0:00	**Rondo Theme** **A**	A fast theme built out of a syncopated motive is played first by the orchestra, next by the piano (in a new key).
			A modulation is carried out by the piano.
35 38	0:56	B	Syncopated, bluesy theme (piano and strings; in a new key)
	1:22	A	Sudden return to **A** in the piano
36 39	1:41	C	Jaunty muted-trumpet phrase—slowdown—trumpet again
	2:14	A	An expanded, developmental version of **A,** blended with the **C** motive
0:45	2:26		**A** in the xylophone
1:05	2:46		**A** in the piano, very briefly
37 40	2:49	D	A sentimental new tune in the strings; the piano answers with **C.**
0:32	3:21		Brass instruments play a loud contrapuntal treatment of **C.**
0:46	3:35	A	Another sudden appearance of **A** in the piano and xylophone
38 41	3:57	E	A new, playful tune in the strings (with piano runs); the piano answers with **C,** once again.
0:15	4:12		Brief piano solo
0:36	4:33	A	The climactic *orchestral* presentation of **A;** big slowdown
39 42	4:52	B	A gong stroke introduces a loud, slow, swinging, version of **B** in the orchestra (the piano plays chords). This dies down for a moment.
0:54	5:46	A	The climactic *piano* presentation of **A,** back in the original tempo; orchestral crescendo
1:10	6:02	**Coda**	Nine powerful timpani strokes quote the first-movement theme. The piano winds the piece up.

In section **C,** a jaunty new tune is played by a muted trumpet (considered *the* characteristic sound of the jazz bands of Gershwin's time). **C** becomes important in the form, for the next, expanded **A** section is ingeniously blended with the **C** motive. **C** is also the motive with which the piano answers the orchestra in the next two rondo sections, **D** and **E.**

When played by the piano, the **C** motive sounds light and whimsical, as though the sophisticated soloist were a bit amused by the orchestra's melodies (which sound like typical Broadway show tunes—sentimental in **D,** more playful in **E**). It is by such means that Gershwin obtained the sense of spirited dialogue that is at the heart of the concerto style.

After **E,** the orchestra returns to **A** once again, this time slowing down into a solo gong stroke—a garish sound. Then the orchestra plays **B** again loudly, at a slow, dragging tempo. After this climax subsides, the piano has its last chance with **A.** The loud drum motive heard just before the end is a quotation from the beginning of the concerto's first movement.

4 The American Musical

Throughout the ages and throughout the world, the theater has always provided fertile soil for the growth of popular music. America, once the Puritan spirit had subsided somewhat, proved no exception. One of the main sources of modern American popular music can be located in the thriving New York theatrical scene in the decades around 1900. Then, as now, the New York City theater district was centered around Broadway.

Operetta

Operetta is a name for nineteenth-century light opera, a European genre that swept Broadway also. Operettas employ spoken dialogue (rather than recitative) between the musical numbers—light, attractive tunes and plenty of dances. Their plots are amusing, farfetched, and frothy. Typically they are set in some mythical eastern European country, where amorous, fun-loving aristocrats rub shoulders with merry, contented peasants.

Among the best European composers of operettas were Johann Strauss, Jr., the "Waltz King" (*Die Fledermaus*— "The Bat"), and Arthur Sullivan (*The Mikado, HMS Pinafore,* and others. These are called "Gilbert and Sullivan" operettas as a tribute to the very witty librettist, W. S. Gilbert.) The most important American composer in this tradition was Victor Herbert (1859–1924). Born in Ireland and educated in Germany, Herbert produced more than forty operettas from the 1890s on.

Musical Comedy and Popular Song

It was around 1910 that the American popular theater picked up its characteristic accent. It was a musical accent, and this came from jazz. Although Broadway did not employ actual jazz, it swiftly appropriated and assimilated jazz syncopation and swing. As projected by white theater bands and carried over into popular songs, this jazz accent contributed more than anything else to the appeal of a new kind of musical show.

Theatergoers had also begun to demand stories that were American and up to date, and so the writers of the song lyrics learned to make up smart, catchy verses full of American locutions. To distinguish them from operettas—with their Old World ambience, their waltzes, and their students' drinking songs—these new shows were called **musical comedies**, or **musicals**.

A typical operetta, 1910: Victor Herbert's *Naughty Marietta*. An American captain pursuing a New-Orleans-based pirate falls in love with a run-away French countess. Famous songs: "I'm Falling in Love with Someone," "Ah, Sweet Mystery of Life," "Tramp, Tramp, Tramp."

The Southern Four, a vaudeville team of the 1890s

The rise of the musical in the 1920s and thirties was closely tied to the great outpouring of popular songs in this era. It was truly a golden age for song. Not all of them were written for musicals, of course (Ellington, for example, wrote many songs that had no link to the theater). But the theater provided songwriters with an extra fee and gave songs invaluable exposure, magnified after 1926 by "talking pictures." Theater songs were popularized by the very successful movie musicals of the 1930s, as well as by radio and 78-rpm recordings.

The two principal composers of early American musical comedy were also composers of many tunes we love: Jerome Kern (1885–1945) and George

Irving just loves hits. He has no sophistication about it—he just loves hits.

Said of Irving Berlin (1888–1990), author of *"Alexander's Ragtime Band," "Always," "Easter Parade,"* and *"White Christmas,"* among other hits

A musical of the 1920s: George Gershwin's *Lady Be Good*. Two bright young people who are out of money break into high society. Famous songs: "Oh Lady be Good," "Fascinating Rhythm."

Gershwin (1898–1937). Kern's masterpiece, *Show Boat* (1927), has returned to the stage again and again—most recently on Broadway in 1994—and Gershwin's *Porgy and Bess* (1935), which is more like a jazz opera than a musical, occupies a solid place in the operatic repertory.

Gershwin's actual musicals are seldom heard because most of the plots now seem so silly—but there are exceptions: *Of Thee I Sing* (1931), a hilarious spoof of the presidential election process, is available on a commercial recording, as are some of his other musicals. We have already met Gershwin as the pioneer of symphonic jazz (page 370).

The Musical after 1940

Show Boat and *Of Thee I Sing* both look forward to the new sophistication of the musical in the postwar era. From the 1940s on, the plots of musicals were worked out with more care. Instead of the plot being a mere pretext for songs and dances, the musical numbers now seemed to grow logically out of a plot that had interest in its own right. Novel and topical subjects were treated—psychoanalysis, trade unionism, teenage gang warfare.

The music, too, was often more sophisticated. As was true in jazz of the time (see page 380), some "classical" techniques were imported to good effect. Composers found that richer, more elegant treatment of rhythm, harmony, and the rest did not scare people away but piqued their interest. One of the most successful musicals of the 1950s was *West Side Story,* with music by the classically trained composer and symphony conductor Leonard Bernstein.

The next development acknowledged the rock revolution: *Hair* (1967), a one-shot hit by composer Galt MacDermott, has been described as a "plotless American tribal love-rock musical." But apart from some British follow-ups (best known is *Tommy*), the rock musical has not flourished extensively. For some years, indeed, Broadway has been dominated by foreign musicals, most of them by the English composer Andrew Lloyd Webber: *Cats* (1981), *The Phantom of the Opera* (1986) and others.

Oh sweet and lovely
Lady be good,
Oh lady be good
   To me.
I'm just a lonely
Babe in the wood,
Oh lady be good
   To me . . .
—*Gershwin song lyric*

A musical of the 1950s: *My Fair Lady* by Frederick Loewe. A cockney flower girl takes voice lessons from an exasperated professor. Famous songs: "I Could Have Danced All Night," "Show Me," "Get Me to the Church on Time." Based on a play by George Bernard Shaw.

Leonard Bernstein (1918–1990)

Born in Lawrence, Massachusetts, Leonard Bernstein was playing in a jazz band at 13, entered Harvard at 17, and studied conducting at the Curtis Institute in Philadelphia. Appointed assistant conductor of the New York Philharmonic in 1943—an unheard-of achievement for a twenty-five-year old—he got his big break just six weeks later. He made a sensation on national radio when he substituted at short notice for an ailing older conductor, and from then on his path was assured.

This dramatic career launching was typical of Bernstein. His podium manner was dramatic, too: gesticulations, gyrations, crouches, and sometimes the famous "Lenny leap." Orchestra musicians paid no heed to this, but audiences loved it, and it obviously helped Bernstein convey his sense of the music. Recognized early on as America's finest conductor, by the end of his life he was probably the most sought-after conductor in the entire world.

As a composer, Bernstein was greatly influenced by Aaron Copland (see page 336), and resolved to go even further than his mentor in bridging classical and popular music styles. In his twenties and thirties, he wrote serious symphonies and chamber music; he also wrote ballets for Broadway, and five musicals, of which *West Side Story* was the best. By turns funny, smart, enormously dynamic, and tender, *West Side Story* gave us song classics such as "Maria" and "Tonight."

A man of multiple talents, Bernstein also composed movie music, wrote books on music, and ran stunning TV programs on music in the early days of television. He won Grammys, Emmys, and a Tony. It is not clear why he gave up writing musicals, but in fact as his conducting career flourished, he composed less music of any kind. Many of his compositions have religious associations. Old Testament themes inspired his *Jeremiah* and *Kaddish* Symphonies (the Kaddish is a Hebrew prayer for the dead); his *Chichester Psalms* were written for the Anglican cathedral at Chichester, England; and he wrote a rock Mass/theater piece for the inauguration of the Kennedy Center in Washington, D.C.

Leonard Bernstein ran his life as recklessly as he conducted—always in the fast lane, and often in the gossip columns. "The great thing about conducting," he once said, "is that you don't smoke and you breathe in great gobs of oxygen." When Bernstein died in 1990, he was mourned as the most brilliant, expansive, and versatile American musician of his generation or, indeed, of any other.

Chief Works: For orchestra, three symphonies, some with voices, entitled *Jeremiah, The Age of Anxiety,* and *Kaddish; Chichester Psalms* for chorus and orchestra ▪ Ballet *Fancy Free* ▪ Musicals: *On the Town, Wonderful Town, Candide* (from the novel by Voltaire), *West Side Story* ▪ Score for the Marlon Brando movie *On the Waterfront* ▪ *Mass* (a theater piece: 1971), and an opera, *A Quiet Place*—his last major work (1983) ▪ Songs, including an early song cycle called *I Hate Music*

LEONARD BERNSTEIN
West Side Story (1957)

6   3   6B   3B
40   43   4   7

Often called Leonard Bernstein's best work, the Broadway musical *West Side Story* is acknowledged as a landmark in the genre. It boasts three exceptional features—its moving story, its sophisticated score, and its superb dances, created by the great American choreographer Jerome Robbins. Our recording of *West Side Story* is from the soundtrack to the 1961 movie version of the show, which is well known from its continued success on videotape.

Background   Shakespeare's play *Romeo and Juliet* tells of young lovers thwarted and driven to their deaths by an implacable, meaningless feud between their families, the Montagues and the Capulets of Verona. *West Side Story* transplants this plot to a turf war between teenage gangs on the West Side of Manhattan. In Shakespeare, the feud is a legacy from the older generation, but in *West Side Story* the bitter enmity is the kids' own, though it has ethnic overtones. The Jets are whites, the Sharks Puerto Ricans.

West Side Story: trouble at
the gym

Thus Bernardo, leader of the Sharks, is livid when he learns that his sister
Maria is in love with Jet Tony. As in Shakespeare, one Jet (Capulet) and one
Shark (Montague) die tragically on stage, in a street fight. Tony is shot in re-
venge, and Maria is left distraught.

Some of the transpositions into the modern world are ingenious. For example, Shakespeare's famous soliloquy "Romeo, Romeo, wherefore art thou
Romeo?" shows the love-struck Juliet fondly repeating her lover's name; Tony
babbles "Maria" over and over again in his famous song of that title. (An aria
in an opera or a song in a musical is, in fact, equivalent to a soliloquy in a play.)
And whereas Shakespeare's young lovers fall in love at a Capulet masked ball,
which Romeo has crashed, Bernstein's are smitten at a gym dance organized by
a fat-headed teacher who hopes to make peace between the gangs.

Cha-cha   This is the music danced to by the Puerto Rican girls—the Sharks'
girlfriends—at the gym where Tony and Maria first meet. The cha-cha, a
Cuban dance, was new to the United States when *West Side Story* was written.

The charm of the fragile cha-cha melody owes a good deal to Bernstein's
skillful accompaniment. Melody and accompaniment seem nervously aware of
each other, but they keep slipping out of synchronization:

Meeting Scene   Quite soon Tony and Maria catch sight of one another: the
cha-cha may be continuing, but they don't hear it, so neither do we. Or at
most they hear fragments of the cha-cha slowed down and made unexpectedly
tender, as background for their "voice-over."

And a little later, when Tony gets to sing the opera's big romantic number,
"Maria," the music is yet another transformation of the cha-cha melody, now
sounding rich and enthusiastic. Thematic transformation technique, which
Bernstein knew from Liszt and other Romantic composers, allowed him to
show Tony's love emerging and blossoming out of that one tense, shy, heart-
stopping moment in the gym.

Ma-ri-a! _ I've just met a

girl named Ma-ri-a! _

"Cool"   A little later in the action, the Jet leader, Riff, tries to persuade his "troops" to stay calm in the face of Shark provocations. The main production number of Act I, this consists of an introduction, again with voice-over; a short song by Riff; a dazzling dance; and then Riff's song again.

The song's introduction uses the basic motive of the cha-cha melody—the same motive that turns into "Maria"—in a highly charged, rhythmic form:

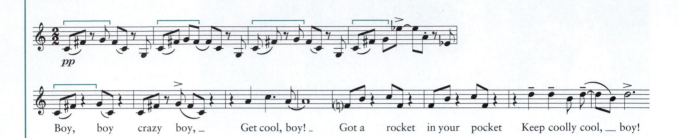

After the introduction, Riff sings two stanzas of his song, in 1950s "hip" street language. There is a steady jazz percussion accompaniment.

The dance that follows, subtitled "Fugue," is accompanied throughout by the soft jazz drum beat. First played by muted trumpet, the fugue subject consists of four slow notes, with an ominous snap at the end of the last of them. Soon another theme—the fugue countersubject (see page 126)—comes in, played by flute and vibraphone in the style of a lively jazz improvisation. The two themes combine in counterpoint, along with fragments of the introduction, getting louder and more intricate as the dance proceeds. Bernstein must have thought that fugue, about the most "controlled" of musical forms, would depict perfectly the Jets' effort to stay cool.

But things appear to get out of hand toward the end, where the music stomps angrily and breaks into electrifying improvised drum solos. The Jets yell various words taken from the song, and the song's melody returns, orchestrated in the exuberant, brash style of a big swing band. While the brasses blare away on the tune, "breaks" are played by the reeds at the end of each line.

To conclude, the Jets sing parts of "Cool" quietly, prior to an atmospheric conclusion. The vibraphone recollects the fugue countersubject.

Swing was becoming outdated but was still familiar in the 1950s, so Bernstein evokes it in the "big band" version of Riff's song. But the vibraphone and cymbal at the end pay tribute to the more innovative "cool jazz" of the time. Meanwhile, for classical music connoisseurs, Bernstein's fugue subject recalls the famous "Great Fugue" of Ludwig van Beethoven.

Boy, boy, crazy boy,
Get cool, boy!
Got a rocket
In your pocket,
Keep coolly cool, boy!
Don't get hot
'Cause, man, you got
Some high times ahead.
Take it slow,
And, Daddy-o,
You can live it up
    and die in bed!

LISTEN

Bernstein, *Cool*

0:14 **Riff: "Cool"**
1:11 **Fugue** begins . . .
2:40 . . . **breaks down**
3:10 **Band version of "Cool"**
3:39 **Jets: "Cool"**
4:09 **Countersubject**

MUTED BRASS

5 Later Jazz

After World War II the popularity of the big bands collapsed suddenly. They were too expensive to run; furthermore, styles in entertainment had changed, and the smooth, high-powered band sound struck people as cold and slick. The mass market turned to rock and roll, itself the outcome of a vital new form of African-American music, rhythm and blues. Even during the war, this collapse had been forecast by a revolutionary new movement within jazz called *bebop.*

Bebop

Discontented young black musicians found it hard to find work compared to white big-band players, whom they viewed—rightly, on the whole—as having co-opted a style that had emerged from the black experience. And when they did find work, the big-band setup discouraged free improvisation, the life and soul of jazz, as black players knew. They got together in small groups after work for jam sessions at small clubs in Harlem. In the new **bebop** style they developed, the typical combo (jazz parlance for a small instrumental group, or "combination") was just trumpet and saxophone, with a rhythm section, including piano.

Bebop was a determined return to improvisation, then—but improvisation of a new technical virtuosity. "That horn ain't supposed to sound that fast," an elder musician is said to have complained to bebop saxophonist Charlie Parker. In addition to unprecedented velocity, Parker cultivated hard, percussive sax sounds and sharp, snap rhythms (one derivation of the term "bebop").

Equally radical was the treatment of harmony in bebop. New Orleans jazz used simple, in fact naïve, harmonies. The swing arrangers used much more sophisticated ones. Bebop musicians took these complex harmonies and improvised around them in a more and more "far out" fashion. In long stretches of their playing, even the tonality of the music was obscured. Bebop melodies grew truly fantastic; the chord "changes" became harder and harder to follow.

Playing bop is like playing Scrabble with all the vowels missing.

Duke Ellington, 1954

CHARLIE PARKER (1920–1955) and MILES DAVIS (1926–1991)
Out of Nowhere (1948)

6	3	6 B	3 B
42	45	6	9

The life of Charlie ("Bird") Parker, bebop's greatest genius, reads like a modern-day version of a persistent Romantic myth—the myth of the artist who is driven by the demon of his creativity, finding fulfillment only in his art. Parker was on drugs from the age of fifteen, and in later years could not control his immoderate drinking and eating. A legend in his own lifetime, Parker died at the age of thirty-four after a suicide attempt and a period of hospitalization in a California mental institution.

Out of Nowhere is one of the many popular songs of the 1930s that were used as the basis for jazz, swing, and bebop singles. Our version of the number was recorded live in a New York nightclub, so it can give us an exact idea of what an improvised bebop number actually sounded like. Notice the informal opening—no arranged introduction as in Ellington's *Congo Brava*, or even in the Wallace-Armstrong blues number. Parker plays the attractive song fairly "straight" to begin with, but he inserts a sudden skittering passage just before the **A′** section (the song is in **A A′** form). This is a preview of things to come.

The trumpet solo by Miles Davis has the characteristic tense, bright bebop sound, some very rapid passage work, and one or two piercing high notes. Then Parker's improvisation shows his impressive powers of melodic development. He works mainly with the opening motive of three eighth notes in the original song:

LISTEN

Parker, *Out of Nowhere*

0:00 **Tune**
0:50 **Trumpet**
1:36 **Sax**
2:25 **Piano**
2:47 **Tune**

In a recording studio, Charlie Parker listens to a playback as the other musicians wait for his reaction. Will he approve this "take" of the number they are recording, or will they have to do another?

He had already expanded these three notes to many more, much shorter and faster ones, in his original presentation of the tune. Now he builds a whole series of phrases of different lengths, all starting with fast, increasingly elaborate runs derived from this basic rhythmic idea. The irregular, almost discontinuous-sounding rests between Parker's phrases have their own special fascination. You may recognize an Irish jig, named "The Kerry Dancers," which seems to have popped into Parker's head right in the middle of the solo, as the outgrowth of a short melody figure he had come to. He plays the jig at a dizzying rate for just a moment, before inventing something else; fantastically, it fits right in.

At the end of his solo the nightclub audience applauds, and the pianist plays an interlude. The number ends with the **A′** section of *Out of Nowhere* played once again quite simply, except for new trumpet breaks and a new comical ending.

Jazz after Bebop

Melody, harmony, and tonality—these were the very elements in music that had been "emancipated" by Schoenberg, Stravinsky, and other avant gardists in the early 1900s. With the bebop movement, the avant-garde finally came to jazz.

Many new jazz styles followed after the bebop emancipation, from the 1950s to the present day. Jazz aficionados distinguish between cool jazz, free jazz, Afro-Cuban jazz, electric jazz, and even avant-garde jazz. Among the leaders in this diverse, exciting music were pianist Thelonious Monk (1917–1982), trumpeter Miles Davis (1926–1991), keyboardist Sun Ra (1928–1994), and saxophonists John Coltrane (1926–1967) and Ornette Coleman (b. 1930). They were the first to improvise really freely—that is, without a song or blues or any pre-existing chord "changes" as a basis.

The synthesizer has changed everything, whether purist musicians like it or not. It's here to stay and you can either be in it or out of it. I choose to be in it because the world has always been about change.

From Miles Davis's autobiography, 1989

43   46   7   10

MILES DAVIS (1926–1991)
Bitches Brew (1969)

Trumpeter Miles Davis was one of the most innovative, various, and controversial figures in the whole history of jazz. As we have just heard, he started out playing with Charlie Parker and other bebop musicians, but soon realized that his own aptitude (or at least one of his main aptitudes) was for a more relaxed and tuneful kind of melody. Davis's style went through many stages as he worked in various groups with a veritable who's-who of modern jazz artists.

Bitches Brew, one of his biggest hits, was also one of his most original. A conscious attempt to combine jazz with rock, the album used a rhythm section with electric guitar, bass, and two electric keyboards in addition to regular jazz drums and augmented percussion. Instead of the traditional chord changes of jazz, this group produced repetitive, rock-like rhythms of extraordinary variety, and often of extraordinary delicacy. This backdrop provides an unlikely, but also an unforgettable setting for Davis's haunting improvisations.

Most of the tracks on *Bitches Brew* are 10–20 minutes long; our selection covers Davis's second main solo in the title track. Before Davis begins, the electric piano and guitar pick out rhythmic patterns against a quiet jazz drum background; mostly the electric guitar has isolated single notes and the electric piano has syncopated chords. This dies down and new fascinating rhythms are heard in the bass.

LISTEN

Davis, *Bitches Brew* (part)

0:00 **Backdrop**
0:42 **Dies down**
1:05 **Trumpet solo**
2:42 **Snaps**
2:56 **Ostinato**
3:39 **Climax**

Thelonious Monk and his quartet

Miles Davis

Popular Music Since the 1950s

There are a number of reasons why this book makes no effort to cover rock and other forms of later American popular music. Among them is the authors' confidence that their readers are already adequately (and in many cases awesomely) informed about today's pop music and its precursors.

We therefore offer only an outline or abstract of popular music since 1950 to at least check off some main points in our broad historical survey of American music. The importance of <u>rock</u> in that history is hard to overestimate. More than jazz or swing had ever done, rock affirmed American dominance in the world music scene.

Perhaps this is because rock is the true music of modern technology. The *electric guitar* and electronic *keyboards, synthesizers* and computer software, long-playing records and CDs, and high-tech marketing are all essential to rock. Yet its origins conformed to an age-old pattern in American music, one we have seen in the minstrel show and 1930s swing. Rock began as *rock 'n roll,* a white version of an African-American genre that had grown up among urban blacks, **rhythm and blues,** mixed with elements from *hillbilly* or *country* (also known as *country-western*) *music.*

Country, the most stable of American popular genres, is closely associated with "traditional" values—as has been true from time immemorial of "the country," as opposed to "the city." Rock, on the other hand, became strongly identified with youth culture. Rock lyrics have registered teenage rebellion, anti–Vietnam War sentiment, and a broad urge for freedom. Rock greats from Elvis to the erstwhile Prince have stood for (and mimed) uninhibited sex. Rock and drugs share a long history.

To words and music, modern technology added sights: first in spectacular *megaconcerts* held in stadiums, exhibition halls, and (famously) even in huge fields, then in **music videos.** In fact, it was probably only in combination with music that video technology came of age as an art.

The latest major innovation in popular music came in the early 1980s. **Rap** marked a return to words and also a return to African-American improvisation, though the improvisation is not primarily musical but verbal. **Sampling**—the piecing together of background tracks from preexisting sound sources—can be an art of its own, even if older musicians will never believe it. But what counts for the most in rap is obviously the blunt poetry. If the most memorable rock lyrics express rebellion, the most memorable raps express hostility. And the on-going, flowing form of rap verse, reminiscent of the blues but more relentless, allows messages to be made explicit in a way that is rarely possible in the short lyrics of rock.

As compared to earlier genres such as jazz or country music, rock laid less emphasis on melody, and rap de-emphasized it further. What remains is rhythm: a simple (very simple) meter enhanced by an extraordinary variety of rhythmic nuance. Today, at the end of a century in which American popular music conquered the world, its one irreducible essence is clearer than ever: this rhythmic enhancement, in its endlessly inventive, exhilarating manifestations.

The trumpet solo starts with short patterns of relatively long notes, a Davis signature. The mood is meditative, almost melancholy: an evocation of the blues. A rock-like ostinato is heard in the bass. Soon Davis is employing more elaborate patterns—a string of repeated notes, scale-like passages up and down—but the effect is, in its own way, as repetitive as the backdrop. Suddenly he explodes into a series of little snaps: a recollection of bebop. As the backdrop drives harder and harder, we realize that Davis has now arrived at a wild, free ostinato in the high register. The solo sinks down again after a climactic high trumpet squeal, another Davis hallmark.

With jazz-rock or *fusion,* Davis and others reached out for vernacular roots in American music. Still, jazz in its modern stage is usually complex and often difficult to follow. Formerly America's dominant form of truly popular music, today this music can really only be described as "popular" with loyal fans who crowd to jazz festivals from Newport, Rhode Island, to Monterey, California. These fans view with mixed emotions recent efforts by Washington's Smithsonian Institution and New York's Lincoln Center to cultivate jazz in a classical-concert format. The life and soul of jazz is its spontaneity. Will spontaneity survive institutionalization?

Jazz continues to flower cumulatively, taking on and transforming the new without ever abandoning the old. It is a fugue with a life of its own, endlessly recapitulating.

Time magazine, 1976

6 Conclusion

Just a few words in conclusion: not so much to this chapter on American music and jazz, but rather to our total endeavor in this book as a whole.

We might recall what was said at the end of the introductory unit, on page 51. Our basic goal has been to learn how to listen better, in order to understand and appreciate music—music of the European art tradition, mostly, but also other kinds of music. Some musical terminology has been introduced that should help clarify listening, and a rapid trip has been conducted through the history of Western music from Hildegard of Bingen to Steve Reich, by way of Bach, Mozart, Beethoven, Wagner, Stravinsky, and Ellington. The most important thing we've done, by far, is *listen:* listen with some care to numerous individual pieces of music, pieces that have been found rewarding by many people over a period, in most cases, of many generations.

Rewarding is a pale, neutral term that will cover beautiful, fascinating, profound, exciting, blissful, comforting, and any other adjective that may correspond to something deep down in your personal experience. Feelings of this kind about music tend to last for a long time. If you have come to appreciate and love some of the pieces this book has introduced you to, it may be forever. Consider yourself ahead.

Glossary of Musical Terms

The italicized words refer to other definitions in the glossary, which you can look up if necessary. The page numbers refer to fuller explanations in the text.

A cappella (ah kah-pél-la): Choral music for voices alone, without instruments *(73)*

Accelerando (a-chel-er-áhn-do): Getting faster *(16)*

Accent: The stressing of a note—for example, by playing it somewhat louder than the surrounding notes *(13)*

Accidentals: In musical notation, signs indicating that a note is to be played *sharp, flat,* or *natural*

Accompanied recitative: See *recitative (137)*

Adagio: Slow tempo *(16)*

Alba: *Troubadour* song about a knight leaving his lady at dawn *(59)*

Allegro, allegretto: Fast; moderately fast *(16)*

Allemande: A Baroque dance in moderately slow duple meter *(130)*

Alto, contralto: The low female voice

Andante: A fairly slow tempo, but not too slow *(16)*

Andantino: A little faster than *andante (16)*

Aria: A vocal number for solo singer and orchestra, generally in an opera, cantata, or oratorio *(89, 138)*

Arioso: A singing style between recitative and aria *(91)*

Ars antiqua, ars nova: Contemporary terms for the "old technique" of the 13th-century *organum* and the new *polyphonic* music of the 14th century *(64)*

A tempo: At the original tempo *(16)*

Atonality: The absence of any feeling of *tonality (302)*

Avant-garde: In the most advanced style *(288)*

Bar: Same as *measure (13)*

Bar line: In musical notation, a vertical line through the staffs to mark the measure *(13)*

Baritone: A type of adult male voice similar to the *bass,* but a little higher

Bass: (not spelled "BASE") (1) The low adult male voice; (2) the lowest vocal or instrumental line in a piece of music

Basso continuo: See *continuo (87)*

Basso ostinato: An *ostinato* in the bass *(87)*

Beam: In musical notation, the heavy stroke connecting eighth notes (two beams connect sixteenth notes, etc.) *(21)*

Beat: The regular pulse underlying most music; the lowest unit of *meter (12)*

Beat syncopation: In jazz, the fractional shifting of accents away from the beats *(363)*

Bebop: A modern jazz style of the 1940s *(379)*

Bel canto: A style of singing that brings out the sensuous beauty of the voice *(253)*

Bel canto opera: Term for early Romantic opera, which featured *bel canto* singing *(253)*

Big bands: The big jazz bands (10 to 20 players) of the 1930s and 1940s *(367)*

Binary form: A musical form having two different sections; **AB** form *(131)*

Blue note: A note deliberately sung or played slightly off pitch, as in the *blues (20)*

Blues: A type of African-American folk music, used in jazz, rhythm and blues, and other forms of popular music *(364)*

Bourrée: A Baroque dance in fast duple meter *(130)*

Break: In jazz, a brief solo improvisation between song phrases *(362)*

Bridge: In sonata form, the section of music that comes between the first theme and the second group, and which makes the modulation; also called "transition" *(165)*

Cadence: The notes or chords (or the whole short passage) ending a section of music with a feeling of conclusiveness. The term *cadence* can be applied to phrases, sections of works, or complete works or movements *(27)*

Cadence theme: In sonata form, the final conclusive theme in the exposition *(165)*

Cadenza: An improvised passage for the soloist in a concerto, or sometimes in other works. Concerto cadenzas usually come near the end of the first movements *(124, 186)*

Canon: Strict *imitative polyphony,* with the identical melody appearing in each voice, but at staggered intervals

Cantata: A composition in several movements for solo voice(s), instruments, and perhaps also chorus. Depending on the text, cantatas are categorized as secular or *church cantatas (145)*

Chaconne (cha-kón): Similar to *passacaglia (120)*

Chamber music: Music played by small groups, such as a string quartet or a piano trio *(194)*

Chance music: A type of contemporary music in which certain elements, such as the order of the notes or their pitches, are not specified by the composer but are left to chance *(341)*

Chanson (shahn-sohn): French for song; a genre of French secular vocal music *(71)*

Chant: A way of reciting words to music, generally in *monophony* and generally for liturgical purposes, as in *Gregorian chant (55)*

Character piece: A short Romantic piano piece that portrays a particular mood *(240)*

Choir: (1) A group of singers singing together, with more than one person singing each voice part; (2) a section of the orchestra comprising instruments of a certain type, such as the string, woodwind, or brass choir

Chorale (co-ráhl): German for hymn; also used for a four-part *harmonization* of a Lutheran hymn, such as Bach composed in his Christmas Oratorio and other works *(146)*

Chorale prelude: An organ composition based on a *chorale* tune *(148)*

Chord: A grouping of pitches played and heard simultaneously *(28)*

Chromaticism: A musical style employing all or many of the twelve notes of the *chromatic scale* much of the time *(225)*

Chromatic scale: The set of twelve pitches represented by all the white and black notes on the piano, within one octave *(19)*

Church cantata: A *cantata* with religious words *(145)*

Clef: In musical notation, a sign at the beginning of the *staff* indicting the pitches of the lines and spaces. The main clefs are the *treble clef* (𝄞) and the *bass clef* (𝄢) *(22)*

Climax: The high point of a melody or of a section of music *(27)*

Closing theme: Same as *cadence theme (165)*

Coda: The concluding section of a piece or a movement, after the main elements of the form have been presented. Codas are common in sonata form *(166)*

Coloratura: An ornate style of singing, with many notes for each syllable of the text *(136)*

Compound meter: A meter in which the main beats are subdivided into three, e.g., $\frac{6}{8}$ *(one two three four five six)* $\frac{6}{4}$, $\frac{9}{8}$, and $\frac{12}{8}$ *(13)*

Con brio: Brilliantly, with spirit

Concerto, solo concerto: A large composition for orchestra and solo instrument *(116)*

Concerto grosso: The main Baroque type of concerto, for a group of solo instruments and a small orchestra *(116)*

Concert overture: An early nineteenth-century genre resembling an opera overture—but without any following opera *(246)*

Con moto: Moving, with motion

Consonance: Intervals or chords that sound relatively stable and free of tension; as opposed to *dissonance (28)*

Continuo (basso continuo): (1) A set of chords continuously underlying the melody in a piece of Baroque music; (2) the instrument(s) playing the continuo, usually cello plus harpsichord or organ *(87, 112)*

Contralto, alto: The low female voice

Counterpoint, contrapuntal: (1) *polyphony;* strictly speaking, the technique of writing *polyphonic* music; (2) the term *a counterpoint* is used for a melodic line that forms polyphony when played along with other lines; (3) *in counterpoint* means " forming polyphony" *(30)*

Countersubject: In a fugue, a subsidiary melodic line that appears regularly in counterpoint with the *subject (126)*

Courante (koor-ahnt): A Baroque dance in moderately slow triple meter *(130)*

Crescendo (kreh-shén-doe): Getting louder *(10)*

Cultivated music: In America, genres and styles of music that were brought from Europe and subsequently nurtured here through formal training and education *(358)*

Da capo: Literally, "from the beginning"; a direction to the performer to repeat music from the beginning of the piece up to a later point *(138)*

Da capo aria: An aria in **ABA** form, i.e., one in which the **A** section is sung *da capo* at the end *(138)*

Dance suite: See *suite (95, 130)*

Declamation: The way words are set to music, in terms of rhythm, accent, etc. *(76)*

Decrescendo: Getting softer *(10)*

Development: (1) The process of expanding themes and motives into larger sections of music; (2) the second section of a sonata-form movement, which features the development process *(165)*

Diatonic scale: The set of seven pitches represented by the white notes of the piano, within one octave *(18)*

Dies irae: "Day of wrath": a section of the *Requiem Mass (250)*

Diminuendo: Getting softer *(10)*

Dissonance: Intervals or chords that sound relatively tense and unstable; in opposition to *consonance (28)*

Divertimento: An 18th-century genre of light instrumental music, designed for entertainment *(153)*

Divine Office: The eight daily services, other than the Mass, specified by the Roman Catholic Church *(55)*

Dotted note: In musical notation, a note followed by a dot has its normal duration increased by a half *(21)*

Dotted rhythm: A rhythm of long, dotted notes alternating with short ones *(21)*

Double-exposition form: A type of *sonata form* developed for use in concertos *(186)*

Downbeat: A strong or accented *beat*

Duet, duo: A composition for two singers or instrumentalists *(199)*

Duple meter: A meter consisting of one accented beat alternating with one unaccented beat: *one* two *one* two *(14)*

Duration: The length of time that a sound is heard *(11)*

Dynamics: The volume of sound, the loudness or softness of a musical passage *(9)*

Eighth note: A note one-eighth the length of a whole note *(21)*

Electronic music: Music in which some or all of the sounds are produced by electronic generators or other apparatus *(339)*

Ensemble: A musical number in an opera, cantata, or oratorio that is sung by two or more people *(196)*

Episode: In a fugue, a passage that does not contain any complete appearances of the fugue subject *(127)*

Espressivo: Expressively

Estampie (ess-tom-pee): An instrumental dance of the Middle Ages *(61)*

Étude (áy-tewd): A piece of music designed to aid technical study of a particular instrument *(241)*

Exposition: (1) The first section of a *fugue (126);* (2) the first section of a sonata-form movement *(164)*

Expressionism: An early 20th-century movement in art, music, and literature in Germany and Austria *(296)*

Fermata: A hold of indefinite length on a note; the sign for such a hold in musical notation *(16)*

Figured bass: A system of notating the *continuo* chords in Baroque music, by means of figures; sometimes also used to mean continuo *(113)*

Finale (fih-náh-lay): The last movement of a work, or the ensemble that concludes an act of an opera buffa or other opera

First theme: In sonata form, a motive or tune (or a series of them) in the tonic key that opens the exposition section *(165)*

Flag: In musical notation, a "pennant" attached to a note indicating that the length is halved (two flags indicate that it is quartered, etc.) *(21)*

Flat: In musical notation, a sign (♭) indicating that the note to which it is attached is to be played a semitone lower. A double flat (♭♭) is sometimes used to indicate that a note is played two semitones lower *(19)*

Form: The "shape" of a piece of music *(47)*

Forte (fór-teh); **fortissimo:** Loud; very loud *(f; ff) (9)*

Fragmentation: The technique of reducing a theme to fragmentary motives *(210)*

French overture: A Baroque type of overture to an opera, oratorio, or suite *(132)*

Fugue (fewg): A composition written systematically in *imitative polyphony,* usually with a single main theme, the fugue *subject (96, 126)*

Fuguing tune: A simple anthem based on a hymn, with a little counterpoint *(359)*

Functional harmony, functional tonality: From the Baroque period on, the system whereby all chords have a specific interrelation and function for the total sense of centrality *(tonality) (87)*

Galliard: A Renaissance court dance in *triple meter (81)*

Gapped chorale: A setting of a chorale melody in which the tune is presented in phrases with "gaps" between them, during which other music continues in other voices or instruments *(146)*

Gavotte: A Baroque dance in duple meter *(130)*

Genre (jáhn-ruh): A general category of music determined partly by the number and kind of instruments or voices involved, and partly by its form, style, or purpose. "Opera," "symphonic poem," and "sonata" are examples of genres *(50)*

Gesamtkunstwerk (geh-záhmt-kuhnst-vairk): "Total work of art"—Wagner's term for his music dramas *(261)*

Gigue (zheeg), jig: A Baroque dance in a lively compound meter *(130)*

Glissando: Sliding from one note to another on an instrument such as a trombone or violin *(310)*

Gospel, gospel music: Genre of African-American choral church music, associated with the *blues (366)*

Grave (grahv): Slow; the characteristic tempo of the first section of a *French overture (16)*

Gregorian chant: The type of *chant* used in the early Roman Catholic Church *(55)*

Ground bass: A short motive, phrase, or theme in the bass repeated again and again as the basis for a composition *(87, 120)*

Half note: A note half the length of a whole note *(21)*

Half step: The *interval* between any two successive notes of the chromatic scale; also called a *semitone (19)*

Harmonize: To provide each note of a melody with a chord *(28)*

Harmony, harmonic: Having to do with chords, or the "vertical" aspect of musical texture *(28)*. The term *harmonic* is sometimes used to mean *homophonic*

Hocket: The alternation of very short melodic phrases, or single notes, between two voices, used in late medieval *polyphony (65)*

Homophony, homophonic: A musical texture that involves only one melody of real interest, combined with chords or other subsidiary sounds *(29)*

Hymn: A simple religious song in several stanzas, for congregational singing in church *(69)*

Idée fixe: (ee-day feex): A fixed idea, an obsession; the term used by Berlioz for a recurring theme used in all the movements of one of his program symphonies *(248)*

Imitation, imitative polyphony, imitative counterpoint: A polyphonic musical texture in which the various melodic lines use approximately the same themes; as opposed to *nonimitative counterpoint (30)*. See also *point of imitation*

Impressionism: A French artistic movement of the late 19th and early 20th centuries *(293)*

Interval: The difference or distance between two pitches, measured by the number of *diatonic scale* notes between them *(17)*

Introduction: An introductory passage: the "slow introduction" before the exposition in a symphony, etc.; in an opera, the first number after the overture

Inversion: Reading or playing a melody or a *twelve-tone series* upside down, i.e., playing all its upward intervals downward and vice versa *(300)*

Isorhythm: In 14th-century music, the technique of repeating the identical rhythm for each section of a composition, while the pitches are altered *(65)*

Jazz: A major African-American performance style that has influenced all 20th-century popular music *(362)*

Jongleur: (jawn-gler): A medieval secular musician *(59)*

K numbers: The numbers assigned to works by Mozart in the Köchel Catalogue; used instead of opus numbers to catalogue Mozart's works *(167)*

Key: One of the various positions for the major- and minor-mode scales made possible by using all the notes of the chromatic scale *(33)*

Key signature: Sharps or flats placed at the beginning of the staffs to indicate the *key,* and applied throughout an entire piece, in every measure and in every octave *(23)*

Largo; larghetto: Very slow; somewhat less slow than largo *(16)*

Ledger lines: Short lines above or below the staff to accommodate pitches that go higher or lower *(22)*

Legato: (leh-gáh-toe): Playing in a smooth, connected manner; as opposed to *staccato* *(22)*

Leitmotiv: (líte-moh-teef): "Leading motive" in Wagner's operas *(261)*

Lento: Very slow *(16)*

Libretto: The complete book of words for an opera, oratorio, cantata, etc. *(137)*

Lied: (pl. *Lieder*): German for song; also a special genre of Romantic songs with piano *(230)*

Line: Used as a term to mean a melody, or melodic line *(25)*

Madrigal: The main secular vocal form of the Renaissance *(79)*

Major mode: One of the modes of the *diatonic scale,* oriented around C as the *tonic;* characterized by the interval between the first and third notes containing four semitones; as opposed to *minor mode* *(32)*

Mass: The main Roman Catholic service; or the music written for it. The musical Mass consists of five large sections: Kyrie, Gloria, Credo, Sanctus, and Agnus Dei *(71)*

Mazurka: A Polish dance in lively triple meter *(242)*

Measure (bar): In music, the unit of *meter,* consisting of a principal strong beat and one or more weaker ones *(13)*

Medieval modes: See *mode* *(56)*

Melody: The aspect of music having to do with the succession of pitches; also applied ("a melody") to any particular succession of pitches *(25)*

Meter: A background of stressed and unstressed beats in a simple, regular, repeating pattern *(13)*

Metronome mark: A notation of tempo, indicating the number of beats per minute as ticked out by a metronome; from *metronome,* the mechanical or electrical device that ticks out beats at all practicable tempos *(16)*

Mezzo: (mét-so): Medium (as in *mezzo forte* or *mezzo piano—mf, mp*) *(9)*

Mezzo-soprano: "Halfway to soprano": a type of female voice between *contralto* and *soprano*

"Miniature": A term for a short, evocative composition for piano or for piano and voice, composed in the Romantic period *(227)*

Minimalism: A late-twentieth century style involving many repetitions of simple musical fragments *(355)*

Minnesingers: Poet-composers of the Middle Ages in Germany *(59)*

Minor mode: One of the modes of the *diatonic scale,* oriented around A as the *tonic;* characterized by the interval between the first and third notes containing three semitones; as opposed to *major* *(32)*

Minstrel show: A type of variety show popular in 19th-century America, performed in blackface *(360)*

Minuet: A popular 17th- and 18th-century dance in moderate triple meter *(130)*; also a movement in a sonata, symphony, etc., based on this dance *(176)*

Mode, modality: In music since the Renaissance, one of the two types of tonality: major mode or minor mode; also, in earlier times, one of several "orientations" of the *diatonic scale* with D, E, F, and G as tonics *(32)*

Moderato: Moderate tempo *(16)*

Modulation: Changing key within a piece *(33)*

Molto allegro: Faster than allegro *(16)*

Monophony: A musical texture involving a single melodic line and nothing else, as in Gregorian chant; as opposed to *polyphony* *(29)*

Motet: (Usually) a sacred vocal composition *(64, 78)*. Early motets were based on fragments of Gregorian chant.

Motive: A short fragment of melody or rhythm used in construction a long section of music *(26)*

Movement: A self-contained section of a larger piece, such as a symphony or concerto grosso *(96, 116)*

Music drama: Wagner's name for his distinctive type of opera *(261)*

Music video: Video "dramatization" of a popular song, rock number, or rap number *(382)*

Musical comedy, musical: American development of *operetta,* involving American subjects and music influenced by jazz or rock *(373)*

Musicology: The scholarly study of music history and literature

Musique concrète: (mew-zeek kohn-krét): Music composed with natural sounds recorded electronically *(340)*

Mute: A device put on or in an instrument to muffle the tone *(249)*

Nationalism: A nineteenth-century movement promoting music built on national folksongs and dances, or associated with national subjects *(272)*

Natural: In musical notation, a sign (♮) indicating that a sharp or flat previously attached to a note is to be removed *(23)*

Neoclassicism: (1) An 18th-century movement in the arts returning to Greek and Roman models *(154)*; (2) a 20th-century movement involving a return to the style and form of older music, particularly 18th-century music *(307)*

Nocturne: "Night piece": title for Romantic "miniature" compositions for piano, etc. *(243)*

Nonimitative polyphony, counterpoint: A *polyphonic* musical texture in which the melodic lines are essentially different from one another; as opposed to *imitation (30)*

Non troppo: Not too much (as in *allegro non troppo,* not too fast)

Note: (1) A sound of a certain definite pitch and duration; (2) the written sign for such a sound in musical notation; (3) a key pressed with the finger on a piano or organ.

Octatonic scale: An eight-note scale (used by Stravinsky and others) consisting of half and whole steps in alternation *(299)*

Octave: The interval between a pair of "duplicating" notes, eight notes apart in the *diatonic scale (17)*

Opera: Drama presented in music, with the characters singing instead of speaking *(88, 135)*

Opera buffa (bóo-fa): Italian comic opera *(195)*

Opera seria: A term for the serious, heroic opera of the Baroque period in Italy *(136, 195)*

Operetta: A 19th-century type of light (often comic) opera, employing spoken dialogue in between musical numbers *(373)*

Opus: "Work"; opus numbers provide a means of cataloguing a composer's compositions *(117)*

Oratorio: Long semidramatic piece on a religious subject for soloists, chorus, and orchestra *(141)*

Orchestra exposition: In Classical concerto form, the first of two expositions, played by the orchestra without the soloist *(186)*

Orchestration: The technique of writing for various instruments to produce an effective total orchestral sound

Organ chorale: See *chorale prelude (148)*

Organum: The earliest genre of medieval *polyphonic* music *(62)*

Ostinato: A motive, phrase, or theme repeated over and over again at the same pitch level *(6, 309)*

Overtone: In acoustics, a secondary vibration in a sound-producing body, which contributes to the tone color; also called "partial" *(10)*

Overture: An orchestral piece at the start of an opera, oratorio, etc. (but see *concert overture) (132)*

Paraphrase: The modification and decoration of *plainchant* melodies in early Renaissance music *(68)*

Part: Used as a term for (1) a section of a piece; (2) one of the *voices* in contrapuntal music; (3) the written music for a single player in an orchestra, band, etc. (as opposed to the *score)*

Passacaglia: (pas-sa-cáh-li-a): A set of variations on a short theme in the bass *(120)*

Passion: A long, oratorio-like composition telling the story of Jesus' last days, according to one of the New Testament gospels

Pavane (pa-ván): A slow 16th-century court dance in duple meter *(81)*

Pedal board: That keyboard of an organ which is played with the feet *(41)*

Pentatonic scale: A five-note scale (familiar from folk music) playable on the black notes of a keyboard *(299)*

Phrase: A section of a melody or a tune *(27)*

Piano; pianissimo: Soft; very soft *(p; pp) (9)*

Piano trio: An instrumental group usually consisting of violin, cello, and piano; or a piece composed for this group; or the three players themselves

Pitch: The quality of "highness" or "lowness" of sound; also applied ("a pitch") to any particular pitch level, such as middle C *(9)*

Più: More (as in *più forte,* louder) *(10)*

Pizzicato (pit-tzih-cáh-toe): Playing a stringed instrument that is normally bowed by plucking the strings with the finger *(36)*

Plainchant, plainsong: Unaccompanied, monophonic (one-line) music, without fixed rhythm or meter, such as *Gregorian chant (55)*

Poco: Somewhat (as in *poco adagio* or *poco forte,* somewhat slow, somewhat loud)

Point of imitation: A short passage of *imitative polyphony* based on a single theme, or on two used together *(74)*

Polyphony, polyphonic: Musical texture in which two or more melodic lines are played or sung simultaneously; as opposed to *homophony* or *monophony (29)*

Prelude: An introductory piece, leading to another, such as a fugue or an opera (however, Chopin's Preludes were not intended to lead to anything else)

Première: The first performance ever of a piece of music, opera, etc.

Presto; prestissimo: Very fast; very fast indeed *(16)*

Program music: A piece of instrumental music associated with a story or other extramusical idea *(228)*

Program symphony: A symphony with a program, as by Berlioz *(247)*

Quarter note: A note one-quarter the length of a whole note *(21)*

Quarter-tone scale: A 24-note scale, used in the 20th century, consisting of all the semitones of the chromatic scale and all quarter tones in between the semitones *(299)*

Quartet: A piece for four singers or players; often used to mean *string quartet*

Quintet: A piece for five singers or players

Ragtime: A genre of American popular music around 1900, usually for piano, which led to *jazz (363)*

Range: Used in music to mean "pitch range," i.e., the total span from the lowest to the highest pitch in a piece, a part, or a passage

Rap: Genre of African-American popular music of the 1980s and nineties, featuring rapid, continuous recitation in rhyme *(382)*

Recapitulation: The third section of a sonata-form movement *(166)*

Recitative (reh-sih-ta-téev): A half-singing, half-reciting style of presenting words in opera, cantata, oratorio, etc, following speech accents and speech rhythms closely. Secco recitative is accompanied only by *continuo;* accompanied recitative is accompanied by orchestra *(89, 137)*

Reed: In certain wind instruments (oboe, clarinet), a small vibrating element made of cane or metal *(38)*

Registration: In organ music, the choice of stops with which to play a passage

Requiem Mass, Requiem: The special *Mass* celebrated when someone dies

Resolve: To proceed from *dissonant* harmony to *consonance (28)*

Rest: A momentary silence in music; in musical notation a sign indicating momentary silence *(21)*

Retransition: In sonata form, the passage leading from the end of the development section into the beginning of the recapitulation *(166)*

Retrograde: Reading or playing a melody or twelve-tone series backward *(300)*

Rhythm: The aspect of music having to do with the duration of the notes in time; also applied ("a rhythm") to any particular durational pattern *(11, 12)*

Rhythm and blues: Genre of African-American music of the early 1950s, forerunner of *rock (382)*

Rhythm section: In jazz, the instrumental group used mainly to emphasize the meter (drums, bass, and piano) *(363)*

Ritardando: Slowing down the tempo *(16)*

Ritenuto: Held back in tempo

Ritornello: The orchestral material at the beginning of a concerto grosso, etc., which always returns later in the piece *(116)*

Ritornello form: A Baroque musical form based on recurrences of a *ritornello (116)*

Rock: The dominant popular-music genre of the late twentieth century *(382)*

Rondo: A musical form consisting of one main theme or tune alternating with other themes or sections (**ABACA, ABACABA,** etc.) *(179)*

Round: A simple type of sung *canon,* with all voices entering on the same note after the same time interval *(30)*

Row: Same as *series (300)*

Rubato: "Robbed" time; the free treatment of meter in performance *(224)*

Sampling: The recording of instruments, voices, or other sounds that are then subjected to further electronic manipulation *(340)*

Sarabande: A Baroque dance in slow triple meter, often with a secondary accent on the second beat *(130)*

Scale: A selection of ordered pitches that provides the pitch material for music *(17)*

Scherzo (scáre-tzo): A form developed by Beethoven from the *minuet* to use for movements in larger compositions; later sometimes used alone, as by Chopin *(209)*

Score: The full musical notation for a piece involving several or many performers *(23)*

Secco recitative: See *recitative (137)*

Second group: In sonata form, the group of themes following the *bridge,* in the second key *(165)*

Second theme: In sonata form, one theme that is the most prominent among the second group of themes in the *exposition (165)*

Semitone: Same as *half step (19)*

Sequence: (1) In a melody, a series of fragments identical except for their placement at successively higher or lower pitch levels *(27);* (2) in the Middle Ages, a type of plainchant in which successive phrases of text receive nearly identical melodic treatment *(58)*

Serialism, serial: The technique of composing with a *series,* generally a twelve-tone series (but see also *rhythmic series) (291, 300)*

Series: A fixed arrangement of pitches (or rhythms) held to throughout a serial composition *(300)*

Sforzando: An especially strong accent; the mark indicating this in musical notation (*sf* or >) *(13)*

Sharp: In musical notation, a sign (♯) indicating that the note it precedes is to be played a semitone higher. A double sharp (×) is occasionally used to indicate that a note is played two semitones higher *(19)*

Siciliana: A Baroque dance type in *compound meter (130)*

Simple meter: A meter in which the main beats are subdivided into two, e.g., **2/4, 3/4** *(13)*

Sixteenth note: A note one-sixteenth the length of a whole note *(21)*

Slur: In musical notation, a curved line over several notes, indicating that they are to be played smoothly, or *legato (22)*

Solo exposition: In Classical concerto form, the second of two expositions, played by the soloist and the orchestra *(186)*

Sonata: A chamber-music piece in several movements, typically for three main instruments plus *continuo* in the Baroque period, and for only one or two instruments in all periods since then *(96, 182)*

Sonata da camera, sonata da chiesa: Categories of Baroque trio and solo sonatas *(96)*

Sonata form (sonata-allegro form): A form developed by the Classical composers and used in almost all the first movements of their symphonies, sonatas, etc. *(164)*

Song cycle: A group of songs connected by a general idea or story, and sometimes also by musical unifying devices *(234)*

Sonority: A general term for sound quality, either of a momentary chord, or of a whole piece or style *(68)*

Soprano: The high female (or boy's) voice

Spiritual: Religious folksong, usually among African-Americans (called "Negro spiritual" in the 19th century) *(361)*

Sprechstimme: A vocal style developed by Schoenberg, in between singing and speaking *(313)*

Staccato: Played in a detached manner; as opposed to *legato (22)*

Staff (or stave): In musical notation, the group of five horizontal lines on which music is written *(22)*

Stanza: In songs or ballads, one of several similar poetic units, which are usually sung to the same tune; also called *verse*

Stop: An organ stop is a single set of pipes, covering the entire pitch range in a particular tone color *(44)*

Stretto: In a fugue, overlapping entrances of the fugue subject in several voices simultaneously *(130)*

String quartet: An instrumental group consisting of two violins, viola, and cello; or a piece composed for this group; or the four players themselves *(192)*

Strophic form, strophic song: A song in several *stanzas,* with the same music sung for each stanza; as opposed to *through-composed song (232)*

Structure: A term often used to mean *form*

Style: The combination of qualities that make a period of art, a composer, or an individual work of art distinctive *(50)*

Subito: Suddenly (as in *subito forte* or *subito piano,* suddenly loud, suddenly soft) *(10)*

Subject: The term for the principal theme of a fugue *(126)*

Subject entries: In a fugue, appearances of the entire fugue *subject* after the opening exposition *(127)*

Suite: A piece consisting of a series of dances *(95, 130)*

Symbolism: A late 19th-century movement in the arts that emphasized suggestion rather than precise reference *(293)*

Swing: A type of big-band jazz of the late 1930s and 1940s *(368)*

Symphonic poem: A piece of orchestral program music in one long movement *(269)*

Symphony: A large orchestral piece in several movements *(163)*

Syncopation: The accenting of certain beats of the meter that are ordinarily unaccented *(15)*

Synthesizer: An electronic apparatus that generates sounds for electronic music *(45)*

Tempo: The speed of music, i.e., the rate at which the accented and unaccented beats of the meter follow one another *(16)*

Tenor: The high adult male voice

Ternary form: A three-part musical form in which the last section repeats the first: **ABA** form *(177)*

Texture: The blend of the various sounds and melodic lines occurring simultaneously in a piece of music *(29)*

Thematic transformation: A variationlike procedure applied to short themes in the various sections of Romantic symphonic poems and other works *(229)*

Theme: The basic subject matter of a piece of music. A theme can be a phrase, a short motive, a full tune, etc. *(26)*

Theme and variations: A form consisting of a tune (the theme) plus a number of *variations* on it *(119, 188)*

Through-composed (*durchkomponiert*) song: A song with new music for each stanza of the poem; as opposed to *strophic song* *(232)*

Tie: In musical notation, a curved line joining two notes of the same pitch into a continuous sound *(21)*

Timbre (tám-bruh): Another term for *tone color (10)*

Time signature: In musical notation, the numbers on the staff at the beginning of a piece that indicate the meter *(22)*

Toccata: A piece in free form designed partly to show off the instrument and the technique of the player (usually an organist or harpsichordist)

Tonality, tonal: The feeling of centrality of one note (and its chord) to a passage of music; as opposed to *atonality (32)*

Tone: A sound of a certain definite pitch and duration; same as *note*

Tone color: The sonorous quality of a particular instrument, voice, or combination of instruments or voices *(10)*

Tone poem: Same as *symphonic poem*

Tonic (noun): In *tonal* music, the central-sounding note *(32)*

Transition: A passage whose function is to connect one section of a piece with another; see *bridge.*

Transpose: To move a whole piece, or a section of a piece, or a twelve-tone series, from one pitch level to another *(300)*

Trill: Two adjacent notes played very rapidly in alternation

Trio: (1) A piece for three instruments or singers; (2) the second or B section of a minuet movement, scherzo, etc. *(131, 176)*

Trio sonata: A Baroque sonata for three main instruments plus the *continuo* chord instrument *(96)*

Triple meter: Meter consisting of one accented beat alternating with two unaccented beats: *one* two three *one* two three *(14)*

Triplet: A group of three notes performed in the time normally taken by two *(22)*

Troubadours, trouvères: Aristocratic poet-musicians of the Middle Ages *(59)*

Tune: A simple, easily singable melody that is coherent and complete *(25)*

Twelve-tone series (or *row*): An ordering of all twelve notes of the *chromatic scale,* used in composing serial music *(300)*

Twelve-tone system: Method of composition devised by Arnold Schoenberg in which the twelve pitches of the octave are ordered and strictly manipulated *(300)*

Upbeat: A weak or unaccented beat leading to a *downbeat*

Variation form: A Baroque form in which a single melodic unit is repeated with harmonic, rhythmic, dynamic, or timbral changes *(119)*

Vernacular music: Music that was developed in America outside of the European concert music tradition *(358)*

Vivace, vivo: Lively *(16)*

Voice: (1) Throat sound; (2) a contrapuntal line—whether sung or played by instruments—in a polyphonic piece such as a fugue

Walking bass: a bass line consisting of equal note values, usually eighths or quarters *(109)*

Waltz: A nineteenth-century dance in triple meter

Whole note: The longest note in normal use, and the basis of the duration of shorter notes (half notes, quarter notes, etc.) *(21)*

Whole step, whole tone: The interval equal to two half steps (semitones) *(20)*

Whole-tone scale: A scale, used sometimes by Debussy, comprising only six notes to the octave, all at the interval of the whole tone (i.e., two semitones) *(299)*

Word painting: Musical illustration of the meaning of a word or a short verbal phrase *(76)*

Music and Literary Credits

Illustration Credits

96 Lauros-Giraudon/Art Resource, NY

101 *top:* Pierre Patel, *Carriages Arriving at Versailles*, 1688. Photo: Giraudon/Art Resource, NY; *bottom:* Scala/Art Resource, NY

102 Giovanni Battista Tiepolo, painted ceiling, Residenz, Wurzburg. Photo: Scala/Art Resource, NY

103 G. G. Bibiena, stage set for *Didone Abbandonata*. Photo: Blauel/Artothek

104 Scala/Art Resource, NY

105 *top:* Scala/Art Resource, NY; *bottom:* Canaletto, *Nymphenburg Palace* (detail). Photo: Blauel/Artothek

106 *top:* Giraudon/Art Resource, NY; *bottom:* from Le Brun's *Conférence sur l'Expression*, 1698

108 Oliviero, *Performance at Turin Theater*. Photo: Scala/Art Resource, NY

110 Steve J. Sherman

113 Munari, *Still Life with Instruments* (detail). Photo: Scala/Art Resource, NY

114 Marco Ricci, *Rehearsal of an Opera*, c. 1709, Yale Center for British Art, Paul Mellon Collection

115 *both:* Boltin Picture Library

117 The Bettmann Archive

119 Culver Pictures

120 Gaspar Netscher, *The Viola da Gamba Lesson*. Photo: Giraudon/ArtResource, NY

123 *top:* The Bettmann Archive; *bottom:* Patrimonio Nacional, Madrid/MAS

124 Private Collection

127 Lancret, *The Concert*. Photo: Blauel, Gramm/Artothek

131 The Bettmann Archive

134 Thomas Rowlandson, *Old Vauxhall Gardens*. Victoria & Albert Museum, London

136 Kupferstich-Kabinett, Staatliche Kunstsammlung Dresden. Photo: Deutsche Fotothek

137 School of Longhi, *L'Opera Seria*. Photo: Scala/Art Resource, NY

138 The Bettmann Archive

139 Metropolitan Opera Press Office. Photo: Winnie Klotz

141 The Bettmann Archive

142 *both:* Mary Evans Picture Library

148 AKG London/Photo Researchers, Inc.

149 Archiv/Photo Researchers, Inc.

150 The Bettmann Archive

151 *top:* Österreichische Nationalbibliothek, Vienna; *bottom:* Jean-Antoine Houdon, statue of Voltaire (detail). Photo: H.H. Arnason, by permission of the Comédie Française

152 *top:* Jean-Antoine Houdon, bust of Thomas Jefferson (detail), 1789, marble, Museum of Fine Arts, Boston, George Nixon Black Fund; *bottom:* faïence plaque, *The Magic Flute*, Museum of Fine Arts, Lille. Photo: Giraudon/Art Resource, NY

153 *top:* Thomas Gainsborough, *Johann Christian Bach*. Photo: Giraudon/Art Resource, NY; *bottom:* Jean-Antoine Houdon, bust of Rousseau (detail). Photo: H. H. Arnason, collection of Edmond Courty

154 The Bettmann Archive

155 *top:* Peter Jacob Horemans, *Court Musician with Stringed Instruments*. Photo: Blauel/Artothek; *bottom:* Jean-Antoine Houdon, statue of Gluck (detail), National Forschungs-und Gedenkstätten der Klassischen Deutschen Literatur in Weimar

156 The Bettmann Archive

157 Zoffany, *George 3rd Earl Cowper, with the Family of Charles Gore*, Yale Center for British Art, Paul Mellon Collection

161 Scala/Art Resource, NY

162 Jean-Antoine Houdon, bust of Mme. Houdon (detail), Louvre. Photo: Giraudon/Art Resource, NY

165 The Metropolitan Museum of Art, Purchase, Anonymous Gift, Friends of the American Wing Fund, Sansbury-Mills, Dodge and Pfeiffer Funds, and Funds from various donors, 1976

168 The Bettmann Archive

170 The Bettmann Archive

172 University of California at Berkeley Music Library

173 *top:* John Hoppner, *Franz Joseph Haydn*, 1791, Royal Collection, copyright reserved to Her Majesty Queen Elizabeth; *bottom:* The Metropolitan Museum of Art, The Crosby Brown Collection of Musical Instruments, 1889

174 *top:* Pesci, *Esterháza Castle*, Orszagos Müemleki Felügveloség. Photo: Gabor Barca; *bottom:* The Bettmann Archive

176 The Bettmann Archive

178 *left:* Patrimonio Nacional, Madrid/MAS; center: MTI/Eastfoto; *right:* D. & J. Heaton/Stock, Boston

183 *left:* Marie-Louise-Elizabeth Vigée-Lebrun, *Princesse de Polignac*, 1783. The Courtauld Institute of Art, London; *right:* Mather Brown, *Portrait of a Young Girl*, The Metropolitan Museum of Art, gift of Mrs. Theodore Newhouse, 1965

185 Mozart's pianoforte by Anton Walter (1752-1826), c.1780. Internationale Stiftung Mozarteum, Salzburg

190 *top left:* Jasper Johns, *Painted Bronze*, 1960; *top right, bottom left and bottom right:* Monotypes #7, #16, and #4 from Judith Goldman, Jasper Johns. Reproduced courtesy of Universal Limited Art Editions, Inc.

192 *top:* MOMA Film Stills Library

193 *top:* Catherine Ursillo/Photo Researchers, Inc.; *bottom:* Courtesy Elektra/Nonesuch

196 Holland Festival Press Office

197 Culver Pictures

198 University of California at Berkeley Music Library

199 University of California at Berkeley Music Library

200 *left:* The Bettmann Archive; *right:* Metropolitan Opera Press Office. Photo: Winnie Klotz

206 The Bettmann Archive

207 Jacques-Louis David, *The Coronation of Napoleon I* (detail), The Louvre, Paris. Photo: Alinari/Art Resource, NY

208 Library of Congress

209 The Bettmann Archive

212 Beethoven Archiv, Bonn, H.C. Bodmer Collection

213 Staatgeschichtliches Museum, Leipzig

215 *Beethoven Nearing the End* by Batt (Plate 18, The Oxford Companion to Music, copyright Mrs. W.A. Barrett) is reproduced by kind permission of the copyright owner

217 The Bettmann Archive

218 Rude, *Le Départ des Voluntaires.* Photo: Giraudon/Art Resource, NY

219 *top:* Henry Fuseli, *The Nightmare,* 1771, The Detroit Institute of Arts, gift of Mr. and Mrs. Bert L. Smokler and Mr. and Mrs. Lawrence A. Fleischman; *bottom:* Turner, *The Fall of an Avalanche in the Grisons.* Photo: Tate Gallery/Art Resource, NY

220 Thomas Cole, *Daniel Boone and his Cabin at Great Osage Lake,* 1826, oil on canvas, 38 × 42½", Mead Art Museum, Amherst College, Amherst, MA

221 *left:* Caspar David Friedrich, *Mountainous Landscape,* c. 1812, Kunsthistorisches Museum, Vienna. Photo: Saskia/Art Resource, NY; *right:* John Martin, *The Bard,* c. 1817, oil on canvas 50 × 40", Yale Center for British Art, Paul Mellon Collection

222 *left:* Courtesy Carnegie Hall Archives; *right:* G.D. Hackett/Archive Photos

225 The Metropolitan Museum of Art, the Crosby Brown Collection of Musical Instruments, 1889

226 The Bettmann Archive

227 Wilhelm von Lindenschmit the Younger, *The Music Makers,* 1856, Neue Pinakotek, Munich. Photo: Blauel/Artothek

228 The Bettmann Archive

231 Max Klinger, *Beethoven,* bronze, marble, ivory, etc., Museum der Bildenen Künste, Leipzig

233 *top:* The Bettmann Archive; *bottom:* Private Collection

237 The Bettmann Archive

238 The Bettmann Archive

239 Archiv/Photo Researchers, Inc.

242 *top:* The Bettmann Archive; *bottom:* Steve J. Sherman

243 Ludwig von Hofmann, *Notturno,* Neue Pinakotek, Munich. Photo: Blauel/Artothek

244 Mary Evans Picture Library

245 Mary Evans Picture Library

246 *both:* The Bettmann Archive

247 The Bettmann Archive

250 Francisco Goya, *Witches' Sabbath.* Photo: Scala/Art Resource, NY

252 Deutsches Theatermuseum, Munich. Photo: Klaus Broszat

253 *left, right and center:* Culver Pictures; *far right:* The Bettmann Archive

255 *top:* Courtesy of La Scala, Milan; *bottom:* The Bettmann Archive

256 *top and center:* The New York Public Library Picture Collection; *bottom:* The Bettmann Archive

257 The New York Public Library Picture Collection

260 *both:* Richard Wagner Museum, Bayreuth

262 The Bettmann Archive

267 *left:* Musée Condé, Chantilly. Photo: Giraudon/Art Resource, NY; *right:* Metropolitan Opera Press Office. Photo: Winnie Klotz; *bottom:* The Bettmann Archive

269 Thomas Eakins, *The Gross Clinic* (detail), 1875. The Metropolitan Museum of Art, Rogers Fund, 1923 (23.94)

271 The Bettmann Archive

272 Mary Evans Picture Library

274 Akseli Gallen-Kallela, *Lemminkäinen's Mother,* 1897. The Fine Arts Academy of Finland

276 The Bettmann Archive

277 Scala/Art Resource, NY

278 Snark/Art Resource, NY

279 University of California at Berkeley Music Library

280 Jack Vartoogian

281 *both:* The Bettmann Archive

282 New York Public Library, Astor, Lenox and Tilden Foundations

283 Österreichische Nationalbibliothek, Vienna

285 University of California at Berkeley Music Library

289 Raoul Dufy, *Le Concerto de Mozart.* Photo: Giraudon/Art Resource, NY

291 Georges Braque, *Still Life with Score by Satie,* Museum of Modern Art, Paris. Photo: Scala/Art Resource, NY

292 Piet Mondrian, *New York City,* 1940–41, Private Collection. Photo: Giraudon/Art Resource, NY

293 Wassily Kandinsky, design for cover of *The Blue Rider Almanac,* Städtische Galerie im Lenbachhaus, Munich. Photo: Blauel/Artothek

294 Edouard Manet, *In the Boat,* Neue Pinakotek, Munich. Photo: Scala/Art Resource, NY

295 *top:* Gustav Klimt, *Music,* 1895, Neue Pinakotek, Munich. Photo: Blauel/Artothek; *bottom: Debussy, Chausson, Bonheur and Mme. Chausson on the banks of the Marne,* Bibliothèque Nationale, Paris

296 Vincent Van Gogh, *Les Chaumes á Cordeville,* 1890, Jeu de Paume, Paris. Photo: Scala/Art Resource, NY

297 *top left:* Wassily Kandinsky, *Couple on Horseback,* 1907, Städtische Galerie im Lehnbachhaus, Munich. Photo: Blauel/Artothek; *top right:* Wassily Kandinsky, *Blue Mountain,* 1908–9, oil on canvas, 41¾ × 38". The Solomon R. Guggenheim Museum. Photo: David Heald, The Solomon R. Guggenheim Foundation; *bottom:* Wassily Kandinsky, *Romantic Landscape,* 1911, Städtische Galerie im Lehnbachhaus, Munich. Photo: Blauel/Artothek

300 The Bettmann Archive

304 Giraudon/Art Resource, NY

307 Sanford A. Roth/Photo Researchers, Inc.

308 Pablo Picasso, *Stravinsky*, 1920. Photo: Giraudon/Art Resource, NY

310 G. D. Hackett/Archive Photos

311 University of California at Berkeley Music Library

312 Edvard Munch, *Angst*, 1894, Oslo Kommunes Kunstsamlinger; Munch-Museet

313 *top:* Man Ray, *Arnold Schoenberg*, 1926, gelatin-silver plate, 11⅜ × 8¾", Collection of The Museum of Modern Art, New York. Gift of James Thrall Soby. Copyright Juliet Man Ray, 1987; *bottom:* Rouault, *The Clown*, Stedelijk Museum

316 Culver Pictures

319 Beth Bergman

321 The Bettmann Archive

323 *left:* The Bettmann Archive

326 Österreichische Nationalbibliothek, Vienna

327 Beth Bergman

329 *top:* The Bettmann Archive; *bottom:* G.D. Hackett/Archive Photo

335 Ben Shahn, *Trio*. © 1995 Estate of Ben Shahn/Licensed by VAGA, New York, N.Y. Photo: Scala/Art Resource, NY

336 Marcos Blahove, *Portrait of Aaron Copland*, 1972 (detail). National Portrait Gallery, Smithsonian Institution, Washington D.C. Photo: Art Resource, NY

337 Barbara Morgan, *Martha Graham in "Deep Song"*

340 *top:* Bill Stanton/International Stock; *bottom:* Robert Motherwell, *In Yellow Ochre with Pink*, 1974. Acrylic and collage on canvasboard, 72 × 24". Private Collection © Dedalus Foundation. 1995/Licensed by VAGA, New York, N.Y. Photo: Courtesy Knoedler & Company, NY

343 Mark Rothko, *Violet, Black Orange, Yellow on White and Red*, Gift of Elaine and Werner Dannheisser and the Dannheisser Foundation. Photo: David Heald/The Solomon R. Guggenheim Foundation

344 University of Louisville, Courtesy Mrs. Doris Keyes. Photo: Anderson/Schott Archive

345 NYT Pictures

346 The Bettmann Archive

347 Lucien Hervé, Paris

348 *top:* John Cage, *Aria* © 1960 by Henmar Press, Inc., N.Y. Reprinted with permission of the publisher; *bottom:* James Klosty.

350 G. D. Hackett/Archive Photos

352 Marbeth, 1986

353 Dr. Detlef Gojowy

355 *top:* Jack Vartoogian; *bottom:* Martha Swope © Time Inc.

357 Bridget Riley, *Movement in Space*, 1961, collection of Arts Council of England

358 Thomas Eakins, *The Concert Singer*, 1892 (detail), The Philadelphia Museum of Art. Given by Mrs. Thomas Eakins and Miss Mary Adeline Williams

359 *top:* The Bettmann Archive; *bottom:* From the Collections of Henry Ford Museum and Greenfield Village

360 The Bettmann Archive

361 The Bettmann Archive

362 Culver Pictures

363 The Bettmann Archive

365 Archive Photos

366 Culver Pictures

367 Culver Pictures

368 Rex USA

369 Institute of Jazz Studies, Rutgers

371 Illustration by Constantin Alajálov, private collection

373 Carol Rosegg

374 *both:* Culver Pictures

375 Culver Pictures

376 Barton Silverman/NYT Pictures

377 Martha Swope © Time Inc.

380 Herman Leonard

381 *left:* The Bettmann Archive; *right:* Peter Carrette/LGI

396

Index